TAYLOR SWIFT

SWIFT

CHRONICLES

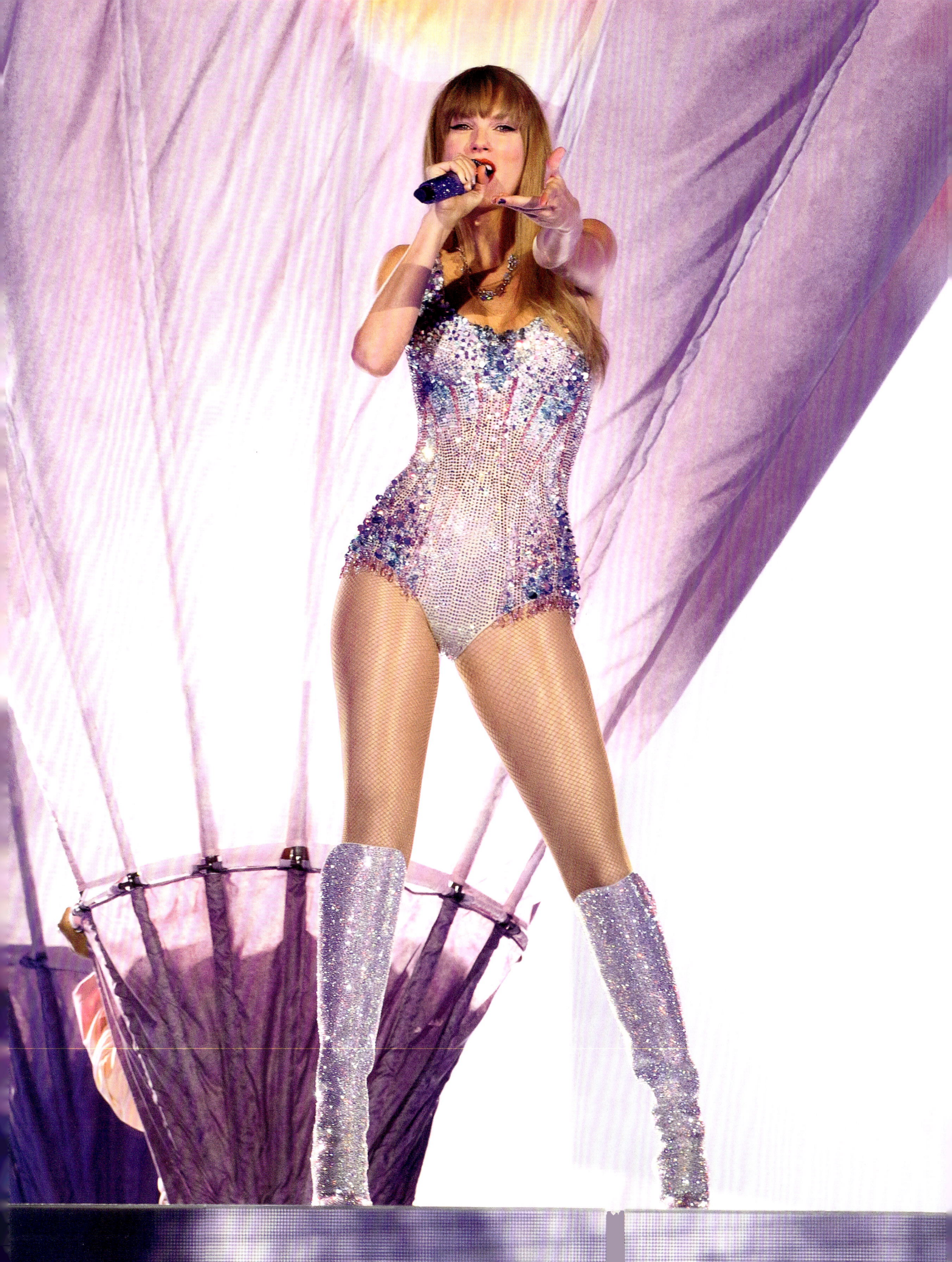

TAYLOR SWIFT
CHRONICLES

LINDSEY SMITH

Artwork by Laurie-Anne Poquet

weldon**owen**

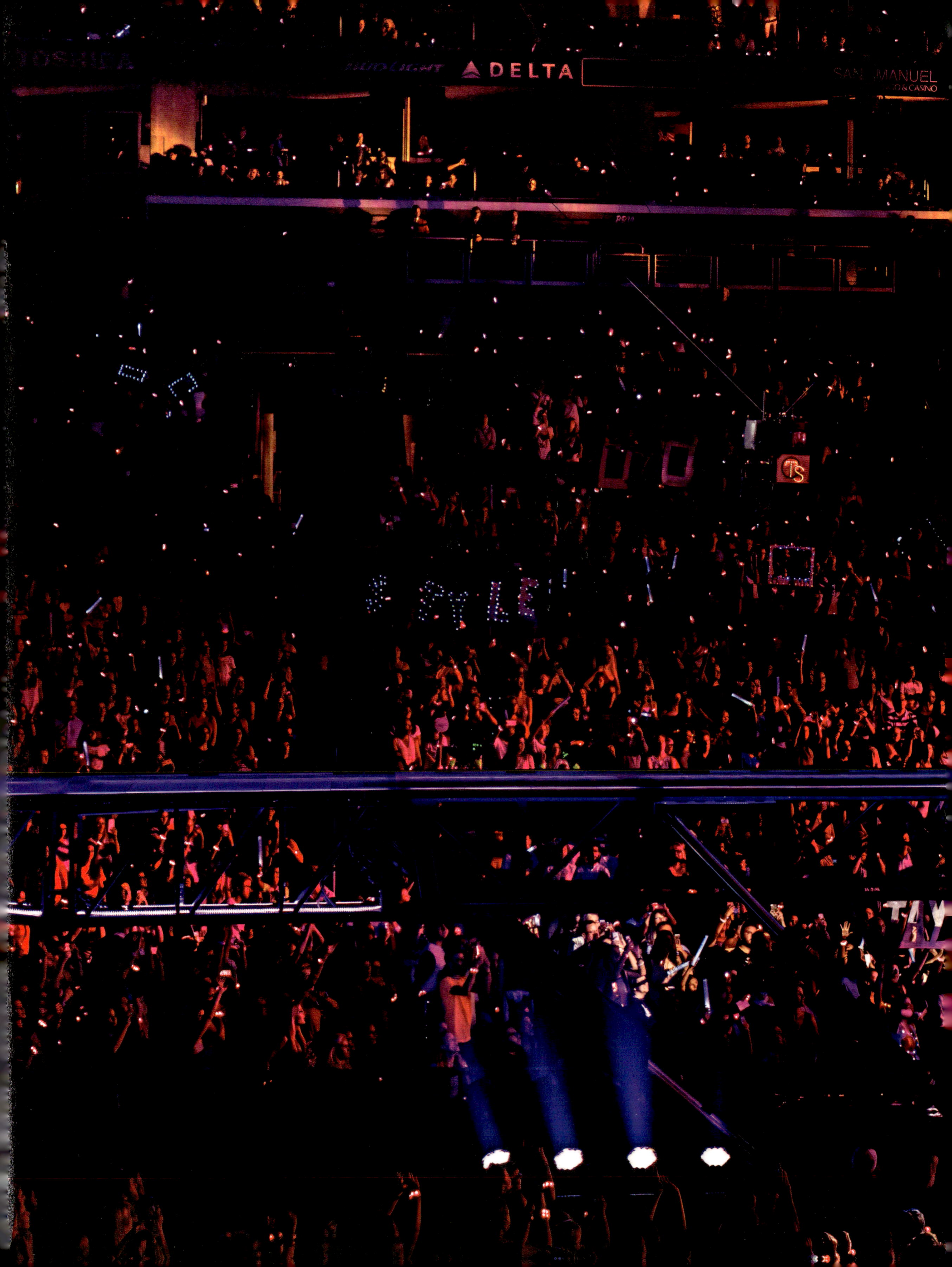
DELTA

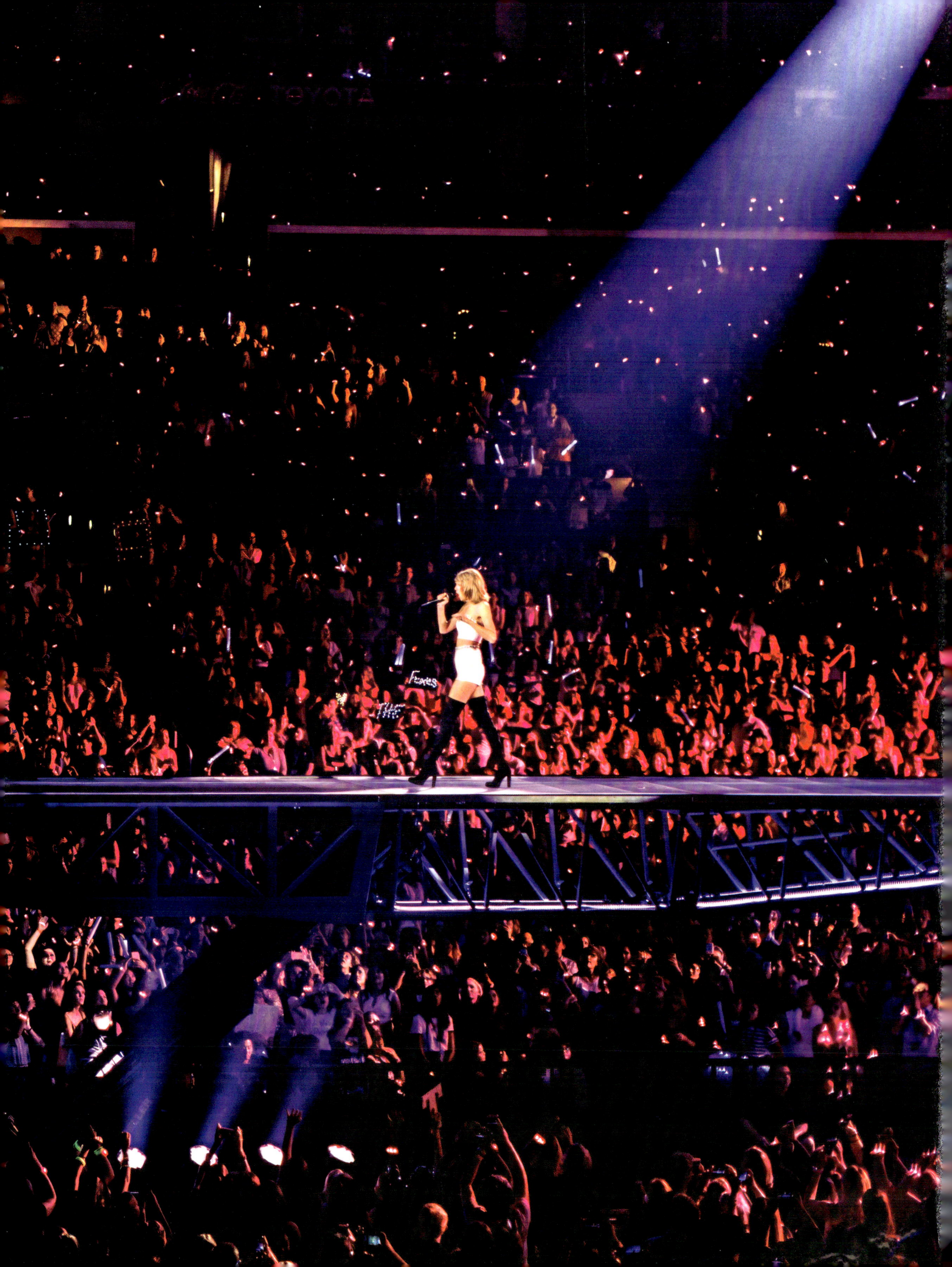

CONTENTS

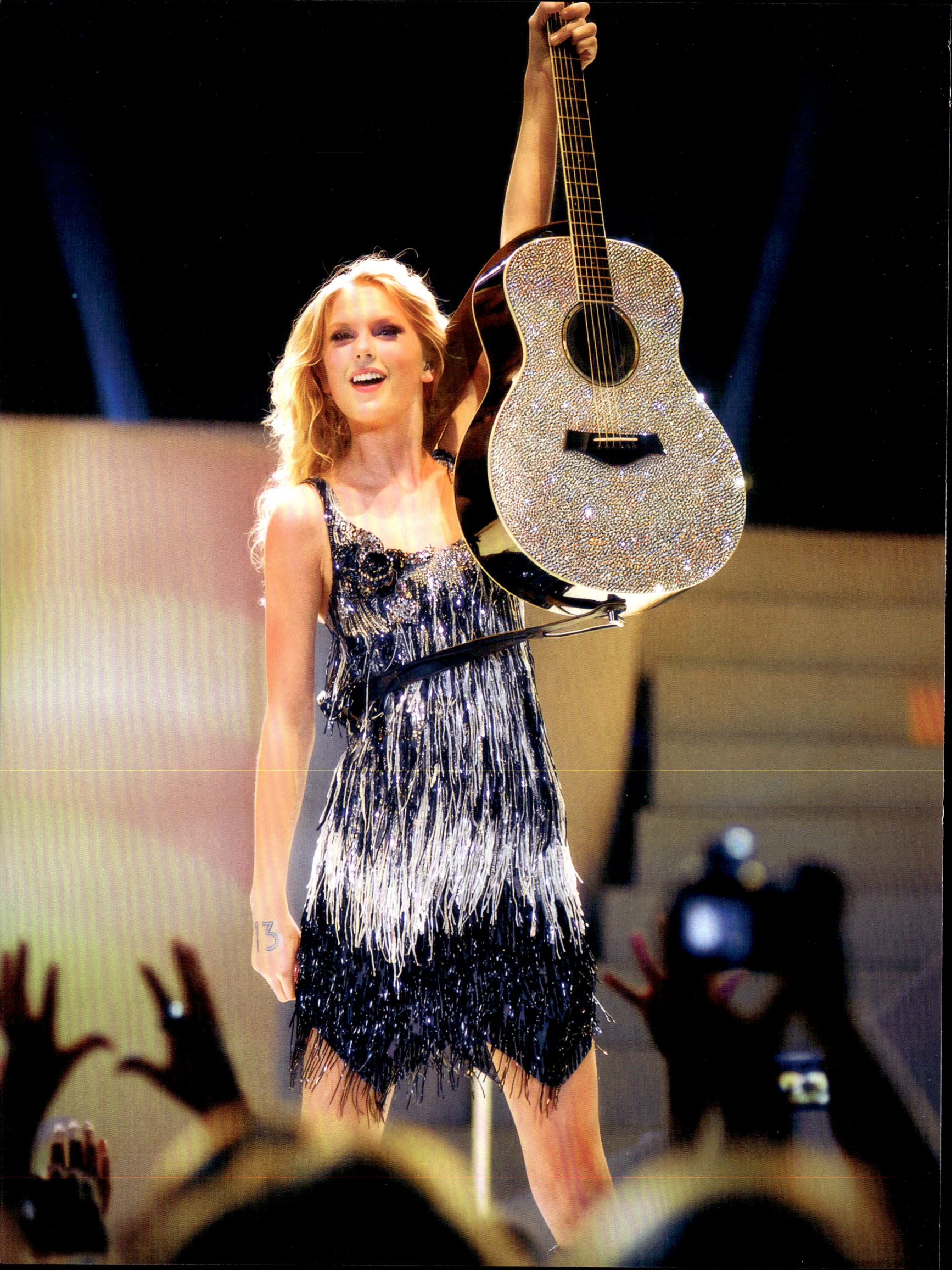

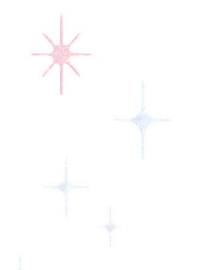
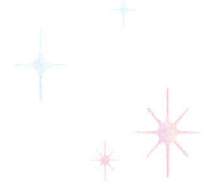
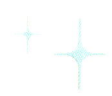

INTRODUCTION

Big Reputation

I was ridin' shotgun with my hair undone when "Tim McGraw" first came on the car radio. It was the summer of my senior year, and while I was not necessarily a country-music fan, there was something about a song that named another musician that piqued my interest.

Who was this fresh new voice, naming names? None other than Taylor Swift.

I was curious about this young new artist, especially once I learned that we were around the same age and both grew up in a small, rural Pennsylvania town. I immediately felt some common kinship to her beyond her music alone.

I continued to be on the lookout for her next singles, but it wasn't until "Picture to Burn" that I went from casual listener to full-on Swiftie. (I guess it didn't take too long considering that was only her fourth single ever!)

Growing up, I was an aspiring writer. By the time I was in fourth grade, I had published several of my poems in anthologies and local papers. By the time I was in ninth grade, I wrote my very first tiny book called *Maxin' and Relaxin'*. It was a self-help book intended to teach my peers how to practice mindfulness and stress-reducing techniques. Because of my love of words and stories, I was awestruck at how Taylor could use lyrics to write such vivid stories that played out in my mind like movies. I was hooked and dove headfirst into the rabbit hole of fandom, and honestly, it's been a really good time.

Aside from her songs that may or may not have narcotics in them, I watched Taylor in interviews, in online spaces, at award shows, and during fan interactions. I watched her grow as an artist and performer and got to witness the magic of her live shows. During The Red Tour, I even had the opportunity to work on one of Taylor's activations for her perfume line at the Pittsburgh stop.

The way she has been able to navigate fame, relationships, and her career is especially inspiring to me. In many ways, I felt like we were growing up together and going through similar things at similar times. From breakups to business relationships to owning your own creative work, I always gleaned a lesson from Taylor.

But one thing that gets me a bit teary-eyed every time is how grounded and kind she has remained. From special Easter egg connections and inside jokes with her fans to hospital visits, staff bonuses, and baking pastries for others to enjoy, it's clear that this is not for clout. It is truly who Taylor is.

When I met with the team about writing this book, I said from the very beginning that I want this book to focus on Taylor's biggest reputation of all: her kindness. While these pages certainly chronicle Taylor's career, songs, and professional achievements, during every era, there are glimmers of an invisible string that ties together her incredible life and career.

That invisible string is her kindness.

Some may call it karma, but it's very clear that the kindness that Taylor exudes in everything she does is the reason why she is still standing, while so many others fade.

Whether you are a longtime Swiftie like me or a newly anointed tortured poet, I hope that seeing Taylor in this light inspires you to embrace more kindness in your own life.

lovelovelove

-L-

Performing in Jonesboro, Arkansas, April 24, 2009.

TAYLOR SWIFT

2006

AUTHENTICITY IS KIND

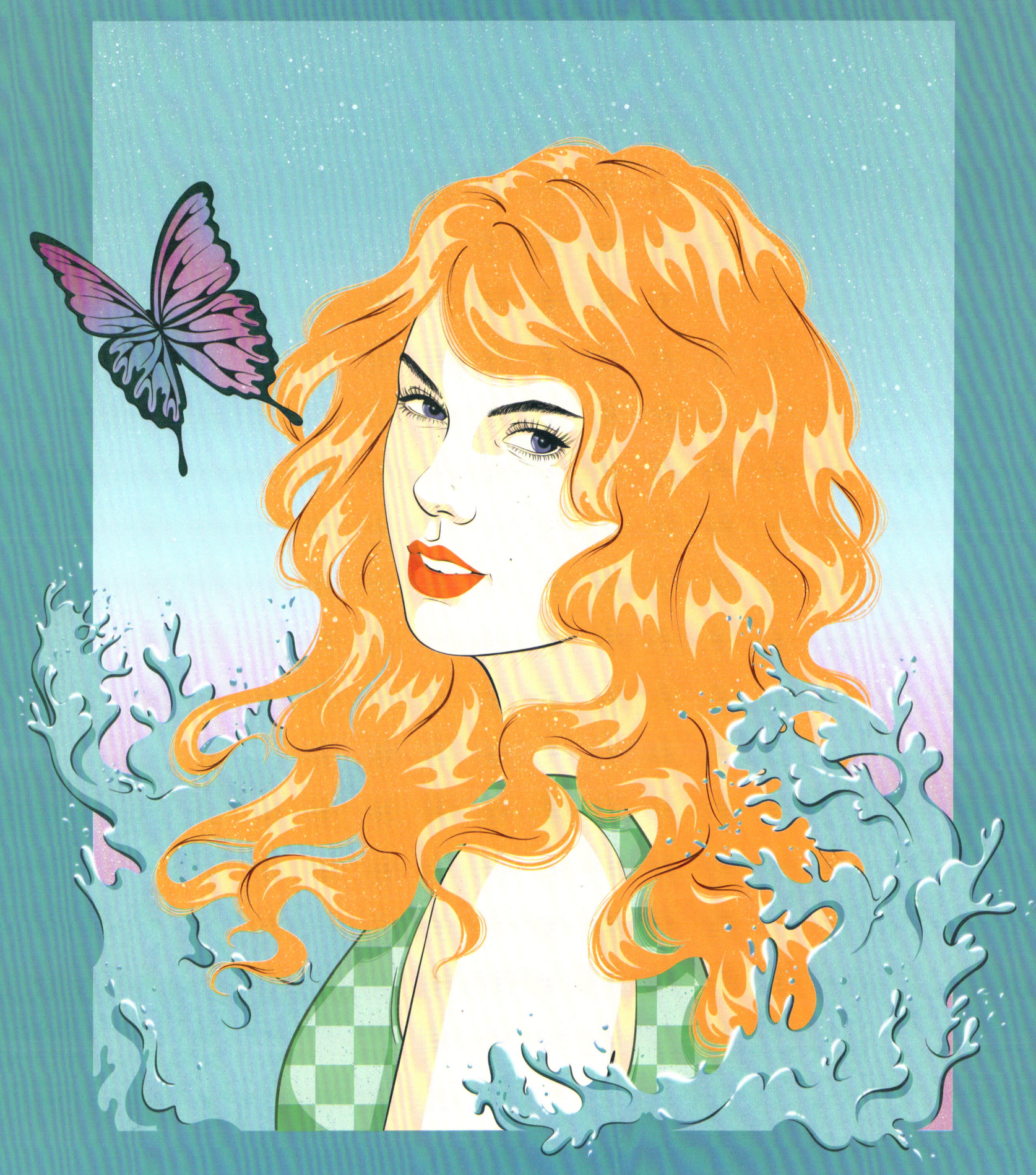

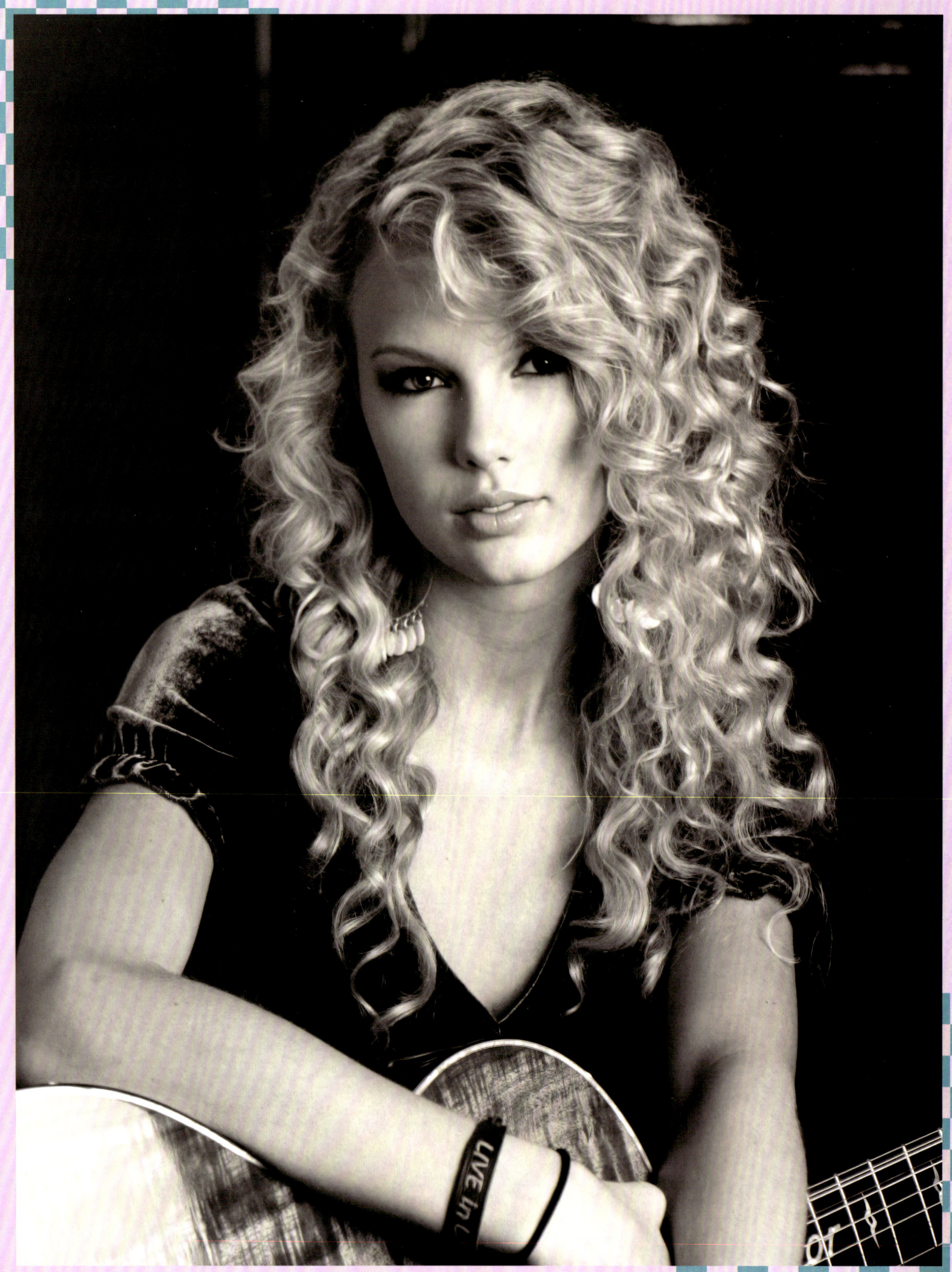

"I'm really weird sometimes, but you are too."

Taylor, 2007

THE ERA THAT STARTED ALL ERAS

At just sixteen years old, Taylor Swift made her splash in the country-music space with her debut single, "Tim McGraw." This bold choice—to name another musician not just in a song but in the title-track listing—caught people's attention early on. Almost as soon as the debut single hit airwaves, it landed a spot on the top 40 Billboard Hot 100 chart for twenty weeks and the Billboard Hot Country Songs chart for thirty-two weeks.

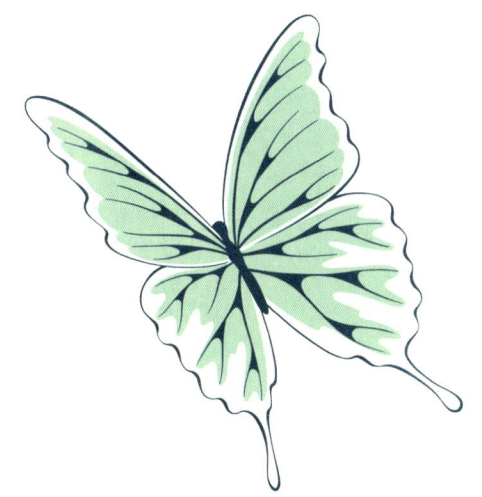

It begged the question of how someone so young could be bold enough to debut their first single with a celebrity name in the song title. But this was, and is, Taylor. From the very start, she wasn't afraid to be different and take bold chances when it aligned with who she is as a person.

Taylor Alison Swift was born on December 13, 1989, and raised near Wyomissing, Pennsylvania, a small town in Bucks County, Pennsylvania, about an hour from Philadelphia. She grew up on a Christmas tree farm with her parents, Andrea and Scott, and her younger brother, Austin.

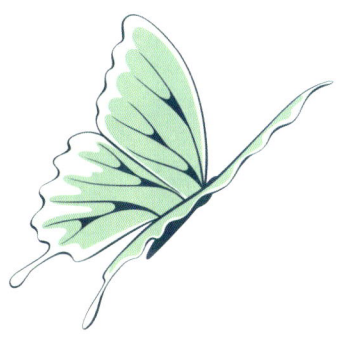

YOUNG SUPERSTAR

Taylor Swift's self-titled debut album made waves in the country-music scene, and selling forty thousand records in the first week was just the beginning. Taylor and her mom, Andrea, traveled around the country in a rental car, with Taylor reaching out to radio shows for interviews and free concert spots, begging people to play her new song. In typical Taylor fashion, she also brought baked goods for the hosts. This hard work paid off, as radio stations continued to play her song and the later singles: "Teardrops on My Guitar" (February 20, 2007), "Our Song" (September 4, 2007), "Picture to Burn" (February 3, 2008), and "Should've Said No" (May 19, 2008).

At the time, country was seen by some as a middle-aged genre, and it was thought that women in that space mainly wanted to hear male country singers. In a 2007 *Entertainment Weekly* interview, Taylor pushed back on this notion, saying, "In addressing the stereotype that middle-aged women want to hear male voices: I think they want to hear female voices too, but they want to hear female voices singing songs that they believe . . ." She went on to discuss her debut single, "Tim McGraw," and said, "I think the reason why 'Tim McGraw' worked out was it was reminiscent, and it was thinking about a relationship that you had and then lost. I think one of the most powerful human emotions is what should have been and wasn't. I think everyone can relate to that."

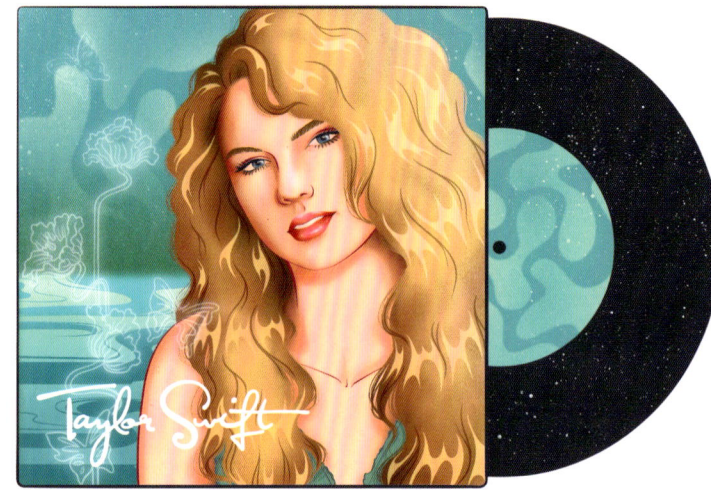

ALBUM
Taylor Swift

DATE LAUNCHED
October 24, 2006

FIRST SINGLE
"Tim McGraw" (June 19, 2006)

OTHER SINGLES
"Teardrops on My Guitar" (February 20, 2007), "Our Song" (September 4, 2007), "Picture to Burn" (February 3, 2008), and "Should've Said No" (May 19, 2008)

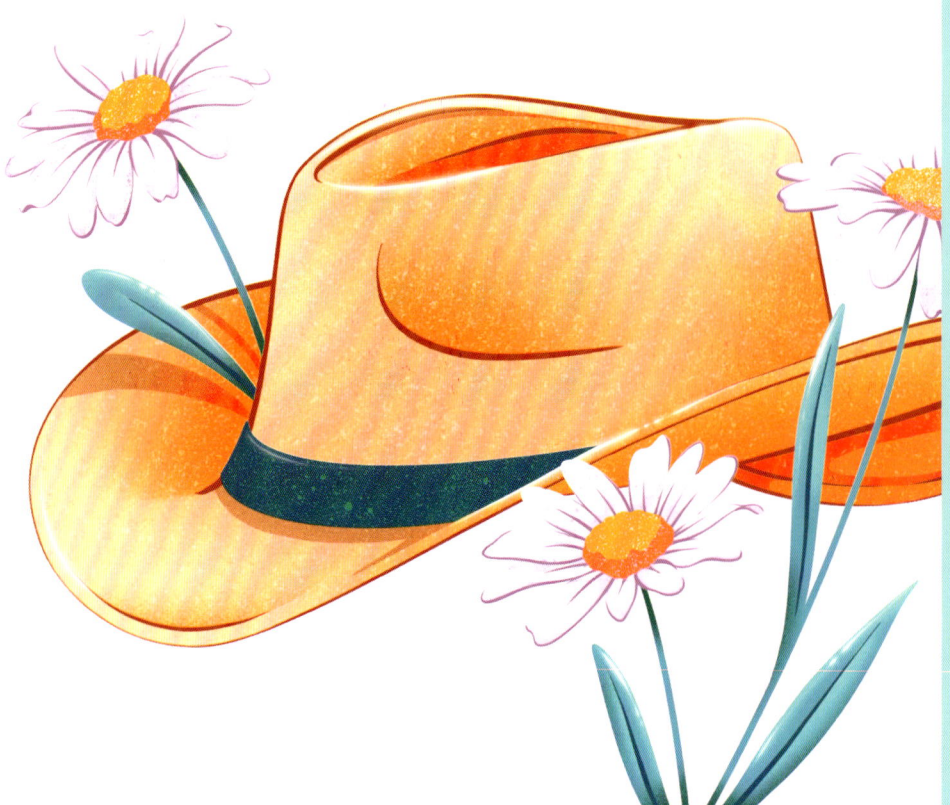

Early on, Taylor had a way of crossing musical genres and creating songs with relatability across generations. She is also credited with bringing a younger age group to the country-music scene, especially as a result of leaning into MySpace. By July 2007, just one month after the release of her debut album, Taylor's MySpace account had more than fourteen million plays of her songs. That, mixed with her radio tour, quickly catapulted her into superstar status.

By the fall of 2007, she had sold more than one million records and become certified platinum. And at only seventeen years old, Taylor was just getting started. Her newfound fans were ready to go on the journey with her.

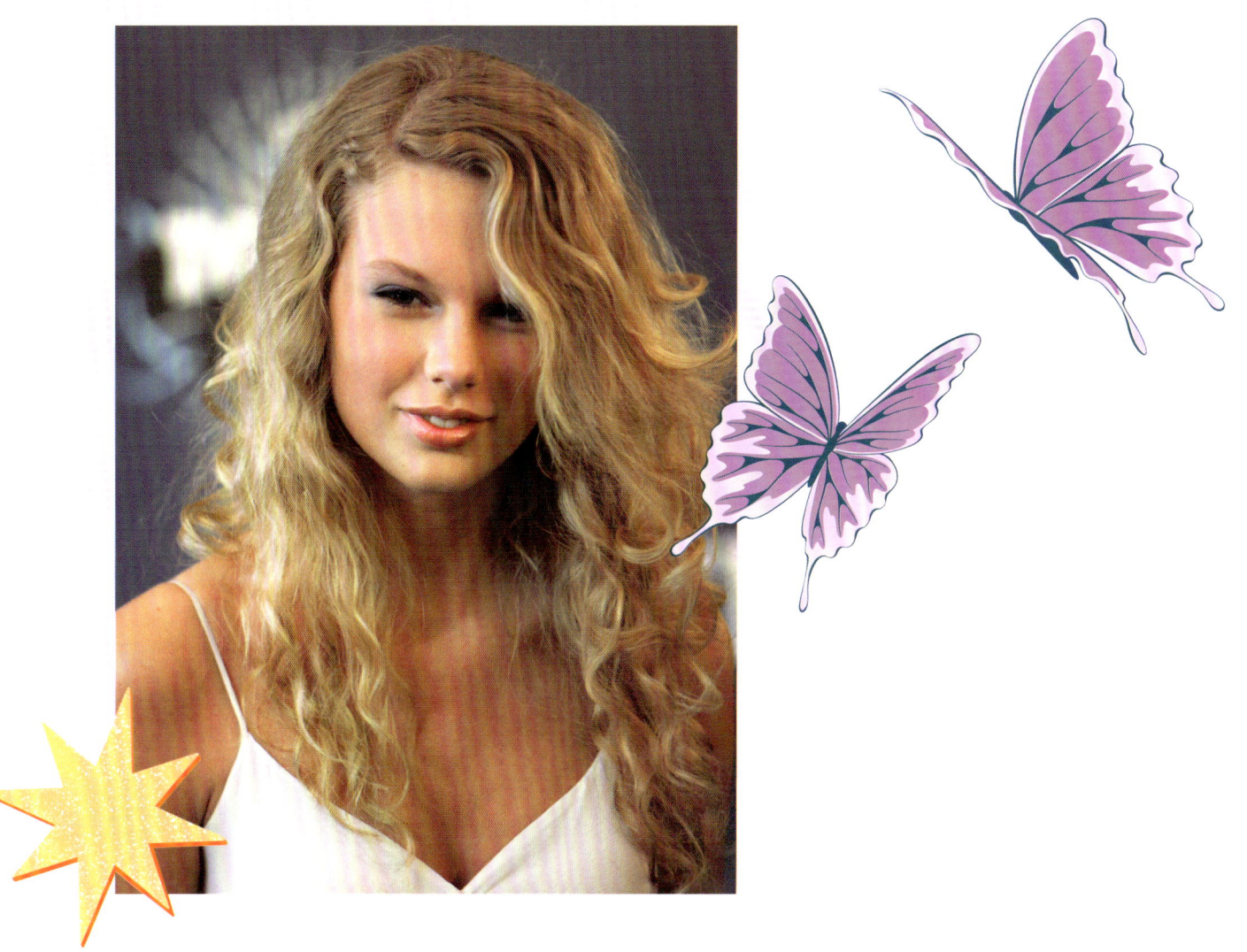

Taylor was always a creative child. Whether it was singing a song from *The Lion King* on the beach to any stranger who would listen or painting in her dining room with her mom, she has always shown a propensity for the creative arts.

Since the age of ten, Taylor knew she wanted to be a singer. She has said in interviews that she feels lucky to have known from a young age what she wanted to do with her life. (Her backup plan was to become a novelist or creative director for advertisements, and while she would have excelled at either, I think it's safe to say we are glad she became a singer.)

As a kid, Taylor was in a children's theater group, winning roles like Sandy in *Grease* and Kim in *Bye Bye Birdie*. While she loved performing, she was even more excited for

the after-party karaoke sessions, where she would perform songs by some of her favorite country artists. At one karaoke after-party, her mother's friend commented that Taylor sounded like a country singer, not a Broadway singer. That ignited something within Taylor and inspired her to lean in to country music. That's the moment she credits with realizing that she wanted to pursue the path to becoming a musician.

Taylor took no time to lose. After that night, she started entering karaoke contests, festivals, talent shows, and fairs, performing cover songs by her favorite country artists. By age eleven, she performed for her biggest crowd yet, singing "The Star-Spangled Banner" at a Philadelphia 76ers basketball game.

PAGE 12: Taylor photographed in Nashville, October 19, 2006.

ABOVE: A sixteen-year-old Taylor attends the 2006 CMT Music Awards in Nashville. Just one year later she would win the Breakthrough Video of the Year award for "Tim McGraw."

Born Writer

While Taylor enjoyed singing in front of crowds, she realized that her first real, true love was writing. She would go on family vacations and spend hours tucked away inside writing fictional novels and creating characters based on people she knew in real life.

A twist of fate occurred when Taylor was about twelve years old. Her home computer was having issues, and a computer tech, Ronnie, came over to fix it. He noticed a guitar in the corner of the room and asked Taylor if she knew how to play, and she said she didn't. He asked her if she wanted to learn a few chords, and she immediately responded, "YES!" Taylor was hooked right away and began to spend every spare second practicing guitar, often until her fingers bled.

Now equipped with a guitar in hand, Taylor went from writing novels to writing songs. She composed her first song on her guitar when she was just twelve years old. Instead of singing other musicians' songs, she performed her own songs any chance she got and spent most days writing new songs in her bedroom after school.

Even at this young age, Taylor knew that to make it as a singer, she needed an edge. This edge had to be authentic to her, not something manufactured. For her, this authentic edge

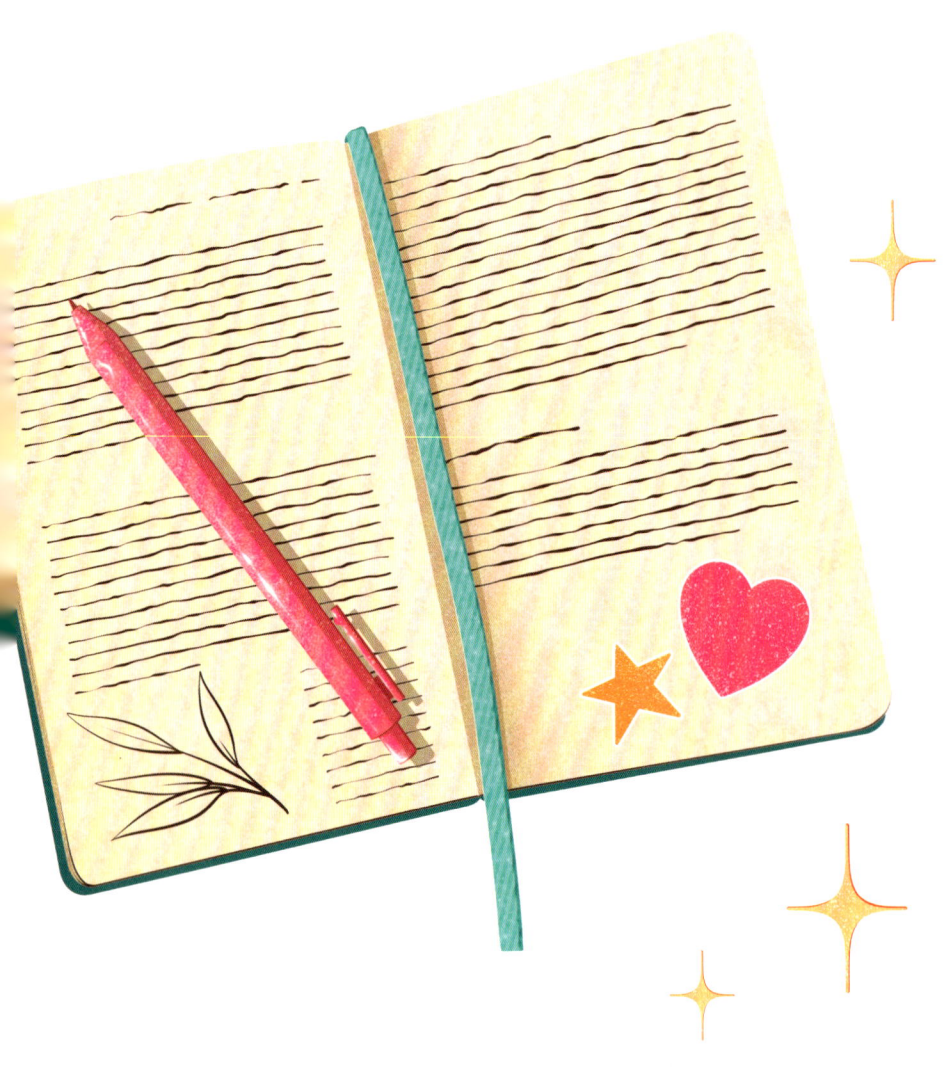

"I wanted there to be something that set me apart. And I knew that had to be my writing."

Taylor, 2007

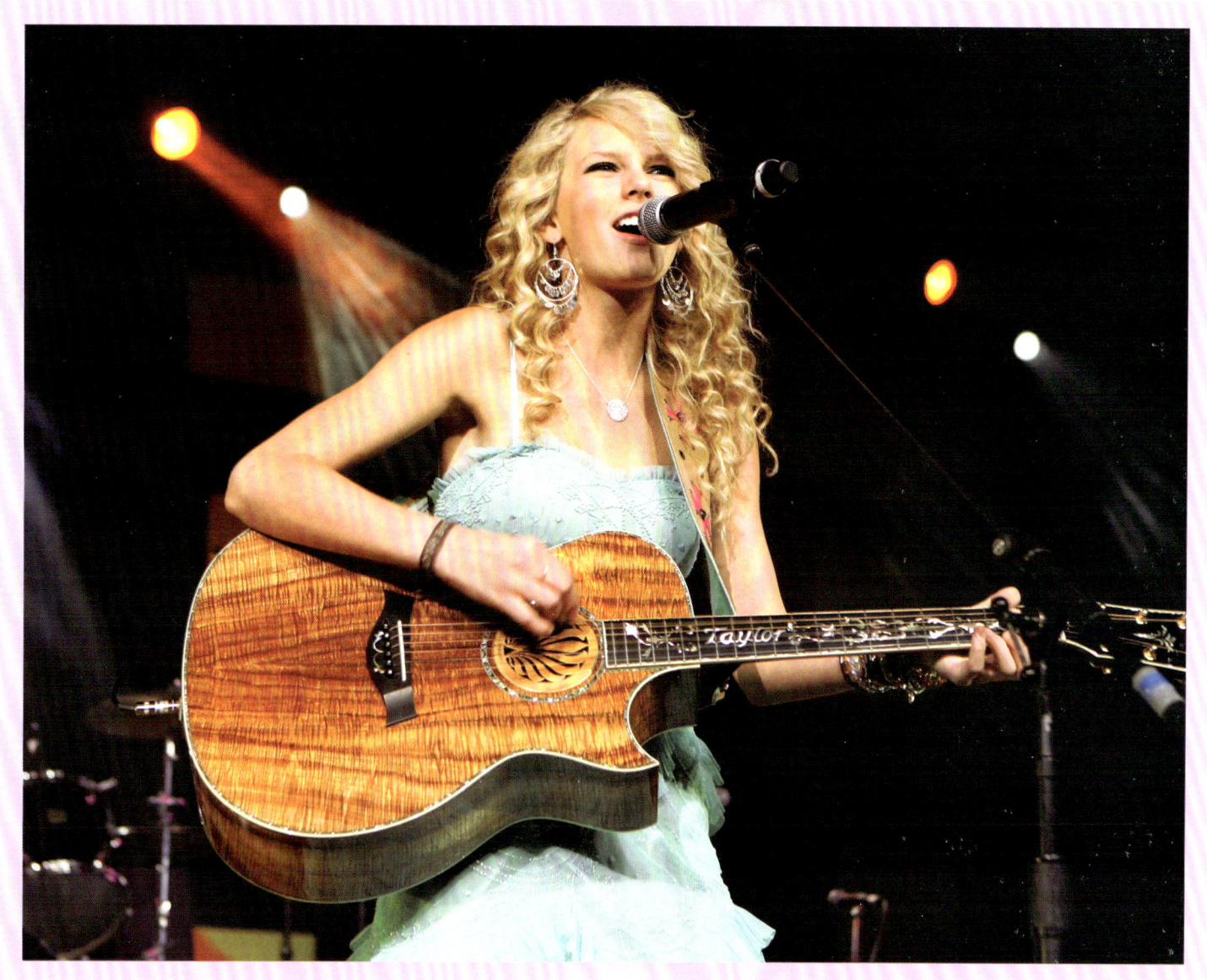

was her songwriting. She loved being able to tell stories through songwriting and knew that writing her own songs would set her apart from other mainstream musicians at the time.

The times that Taylor felt the most comfortable were when she was writing songs on the pages of her journal and performing onstage. When it came to school, she had a harder time. Because of her budding music career and obsession with singing and songwriting, she stood out more than she fit in. She was teased and bullied, often being left out of parties and events, even sitting by herself at the lunch table. Taylor has said that if the local paper did a write-up about one of her performances, she knew the next day at school would not be a good one because it made her susceptible to ridicule from her classmates.

When these situations occurred and this feeling of being an outsider started to surface, Taylor did what she does best. She channeled her feelings and turned them into songs. The first song she ever wrote, "Lucky You," was all about a girl who dared to be different. In fact, many of her earliest songs were about being an outsider or trying to find your place in the world.

ABOVE: Playing for a cause: Taylor performs at the Academy of Country Music New Artists' Show benefiting the ACM Charitable Fund, May 14, 2007, in Las Vegas.

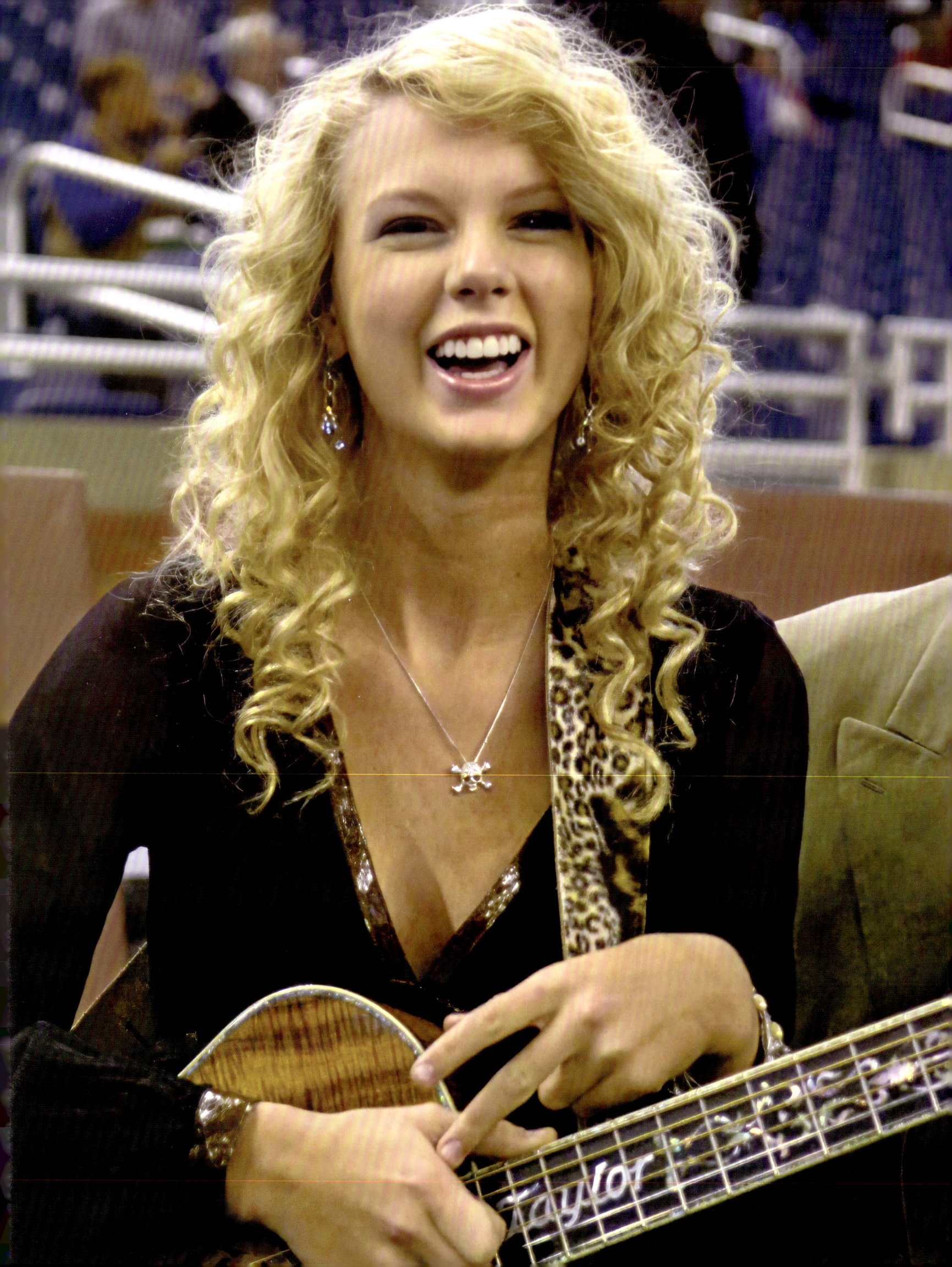

This connection drew in her early fans (and current ones!). It was the first time that many people had heard someone being vulnerable and sharing their feelings as an outsider. It was easy to look at someone like Taylor and think, "Wow! She has it all." But through her lyrics, she was able to paint stories of feeling alone, different, and inadequate, and build a connection and trust with her fans.

Taylor didn't let the bullying stop her. She continued to write songs, practice the guitar, and pursue her dream of becoming a country singer. She studied the industry greats and learned that most of the country singers she admired, such as Faith Hill and Keith Urban, were discovered at The Bluebird Cafe in Nashville, Tennessee. She begged and pleaded with her parents to go to Nashville so she could sing at The Bluebird like the greats before her and try to get discovered. She asked them almost every day for an entire year. Her persistence paid off. At the age of fourteen, Taylor Swift moved with her family from Pennsylvania to Nashville to pursue her career.

In Nashville, Taylor had a bit of an easier time in school and found solace in her best friend, Abigail, with whom she is still friends today. It wasn't long before Taylor's life started to change.

When she arrived in Nashville, Taylor burned her music onto compact discs and carried her demo tape with her at all times. Taylor's mother, Andrea, would drive her up and down Music Row, and Taylor would hop out of the car and give her demo tape to various record labels. She'd say, "Hi, I'm Taylor. I wrote these songs and would love for you to hear them."

This hustle and hard work eventually landed her an opportunity with Sony/ATV Music Publishing. They signed her on for a development deal, which meant that they

SONG SPOTLIGHT

"Tied Together with a Smile"

This is a non-autobiographical song on Taylor's debut album, about a friend who was a beautiful pageant queen but struggled with an eating disorder. Taylor wrote the song the day she found out that a friend was struggling.

ALBUM
Taylor Swift

RELEASED
2006

OPPOSITE: Giving thanks: Taylor gets ready to sing the national anthem at a Detroit Lions game, Thanksgiving Day, 2006.

LIFE IS JUST A CLASSROOM

In 2007 and 2008, as Taylor was promoting her debut album, she didn't just focus on performances and radio appearances. She also found unique ways to connect with her fans and give back to local communities. Taylor partnered with radio stations across the country and held contests and fan-driven campaigns, with the winning schools receiving a visit from Taylor.

More than just meet-and-greets, she also donated music equipment and school supplies for their classrooms. During these visits, it was notable that Taylor didn't just show up and quickly leave. On all her visits, she makes sure to really spend time and be present with everyone involved, asking questions and learning about her fans.

Over the years, Taylor has continued to give back to the arts and education, donating to literacy programs and funding scholarships.

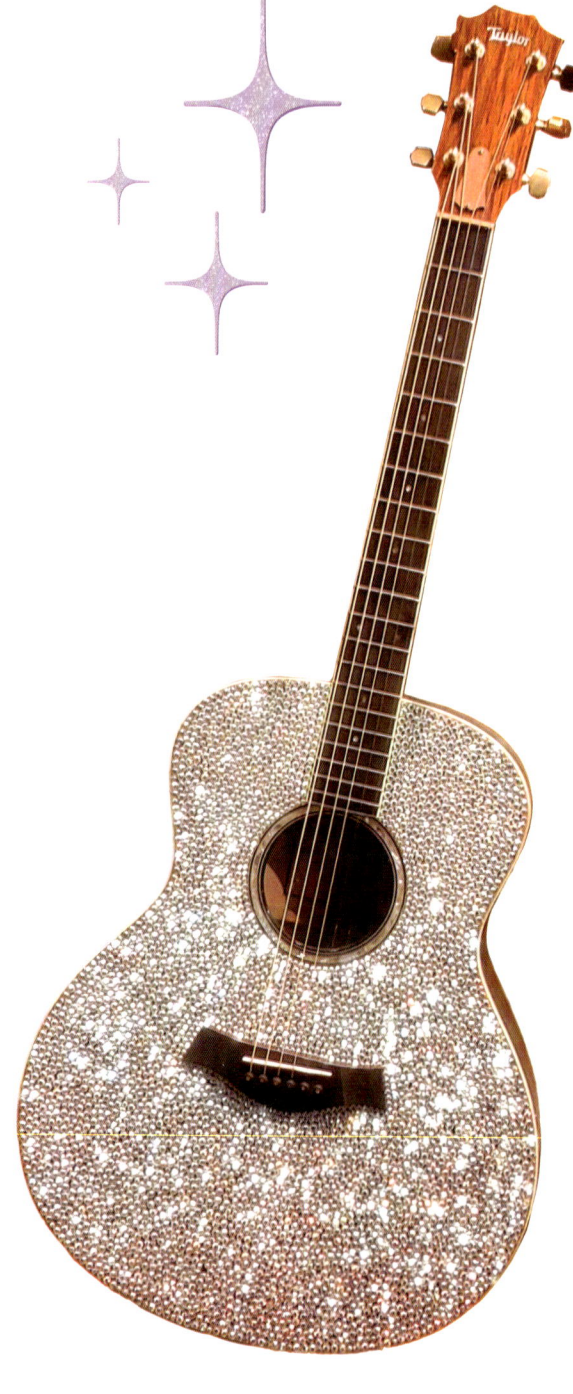

ABOVE: Taylor's go-to guitars are Taylors, many of which are customized for her. One of her most iconic is the Taylor GS6 Grand Symphony guitar covered in Swarovski crystals.

would record an album of songs and at the end of the deal, they could decide whether to pursue publishing the album. After a year, the record label wasn't ready to publish the songs and instead wanted to sign her for another year of development. With no other prospects, Taylor was forced to decide whether to stay with the record label or go back to the drawing board.

While potentially risking ending up with nothing (who walks away from a big record label?!), Taylor knew that she wanted her songs heard by others, not held up in could've, would've, should've. So, at just fourteen years old, she walked away from the development deal and decided to bet on herself—a bold move for a young woman, and a testament to her continued resilience.

Nashville, TN 2004

What started off as frequent trips to Nashville with her family—including a spring break that involved an eleven-year-old Taylor dropping off demo discs to record labels along Music Row—turned into her and her family moving to Nashville by the time she was thirteen so that she could pursue a career in music. While Taylor grew up in Pennsylvania and owns several homes in other cities, she considers Nashville home.

FANNY'S HOUSE OF MUSIC

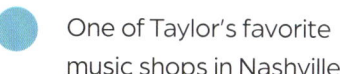

One of Taylor's favorite music shops in Nashville.

PANCAKE PANTRY

A favorite pancake spot, where Taylor's favorite is the sweet-potato pancakes.

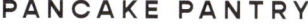

CENTENNIAL PARK

Taylor gave this park a shout-out in her song "invisible string."

COUNTRY MUSIC HALL OF FAME

Home of The Taylor Swift Education Center.

16TH AVENUE - MUSIC ROW

Where eleven-year-old Taylor dropped off her demo CDs to music executives. She even calls out 16th avenue in her song "I Think He Knows."

FIDO CAFE

A favorite coffee spot, where Taylor is known to order a nonfat caramel latte.

VANDERBILT HOSPITAL

Taylor frequently visits children and families to bring them a little joy during a difficult time.

Taylor has paid homage to Nashville through several lyrics and music videos. The music video for "The Story of Us" was filmed in the Central Library in Nashville, and the music video for "Love Story" was filmed at Castle Gwynn—just thirty minutes outside the city proper.

THE BLUEBIRD CAFE

The venue where fourteen-year-old Taylor got her start.

RADNOR LAKE

A favorite spot of Taylor's to walk on a fall day. She has said, "I've had some of my best days walking there with my dad, talking about life."

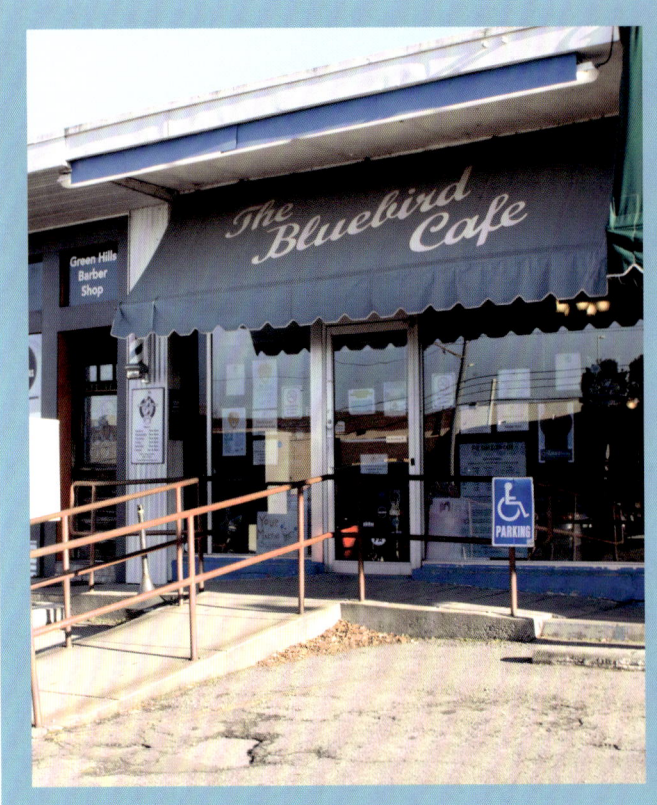

The Bluebird Cafe

ESTABLISHED
June 3, 1982

ICONIC VENUE
Located in Nashville, Tennessee, this café, owned by Amy Kurland, started as a typical café, but quickly transformed into a late-night ninety-seat venue for songwriters to perform their latest work. It became a go-to spot where new talent was discovered and helped singers like Kathy Mattea, Garth Brooks, Keith Urban, and, yes, a fourteen-year-old Taylor Swift, get record deals.

On Her Own

Now, a young, record-label-less Taylor was more determined than ever. Booking as many gigs as she could around Nashville, she finally got her shot to perform at The Bluebird Cafe in 2005. This was the venue she had dreamed of for years. At the end of her set, a man named Scott Borchetta approached her and said that he loved her set and would like to sign her to his record label. When she asked what the record label was, he replied, "It's called Big Machine Records, but I haven't started it yet. You would be one of my first artists."

While this indie record label was unestablished, Taylor loved the idea of being able to get her music out sooner and retain more control over her songwriting and the process. She signed with Big Machine Records in 2005, and her debut album, *Taylor Swift*, released on October 24, 2006.

At fifteen, she started homeschooling to embark on a radio tour for her new album, where her and her mom drove across the country in a rental car, sharing her new songs with radio stations. Her first single track, "Tim McGraw," debuted in June 2006. She released four more singles off that album, including "Teardrops on My Guitar," "Our Song," "Picture to Burn," and "Should've Said No."

Young Taylor opened for country acts like Brad Paisley and Rascal Flatts, taking on every opportunity she could get . . . and people took notice. Through her unapologetic lyrics and vulnerability, she gave so many others the permission to be themselves and find solace that they were not alone. This relatability and that kindness have built and kept her fan base from the very beginning.

ABOVE: The Bluebird Cafe, Nashville.

FOLLOWING PAGES: Taylor performs at Stagecoach, a country-music festival held in Indio, California, May 3, 2008.

BAKER WITH HEART

Early in her career, while promoting her debut album, Taylor embarked on a radio tour across the country. In true Taylor fashion, she didn't just show up with her guitar and demo tape; she arrived with homemade cookies for the station staff as well. These small, thoughtful treats became her signature, leaving a lasting impression on DJs and producers alike.

Baking became one of Taylor's signatures early on. She mentioned it in one of her very first MySpace posts, sharing some of the things she baked for herself and her friends. In 2014, she shared her recipe for her Christmas chai sugar cookies. These have since become a must-bake holiday cookie for Swifties everywhere.

While her roots are in country music, even then, you could see glimpses of her music crossing over into the mainstream. This was especially true for people who'd never considered themselves country fans and now found a connection through Taylor's lyrics and songs. Her songs hit both pop and country charts, forming a fan base that was younger than the typical country-music fan.

Taylor never took any of her opportunities or rising fame for granted, especially when it came to her fans. A great example of this is Holly Armstrong, who is credited with being Taylor Swift's first fan. In 2003, Holly was on vacation in Point Pleasant Beach, New Jersey, when she stumbled upon a concert on the beach. Holly was struck by this young singer's lyrics and connection to the crowd, even though there were only a few people watching.

The young singer? Taylor Swift.

Young Taylor opened for country acts like Brad Paisley and Rascal Flatts.

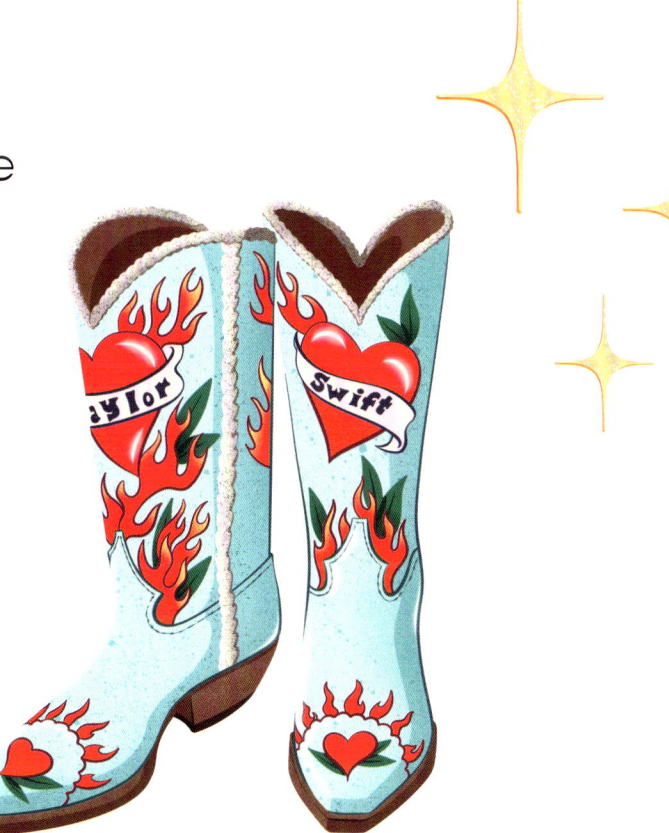

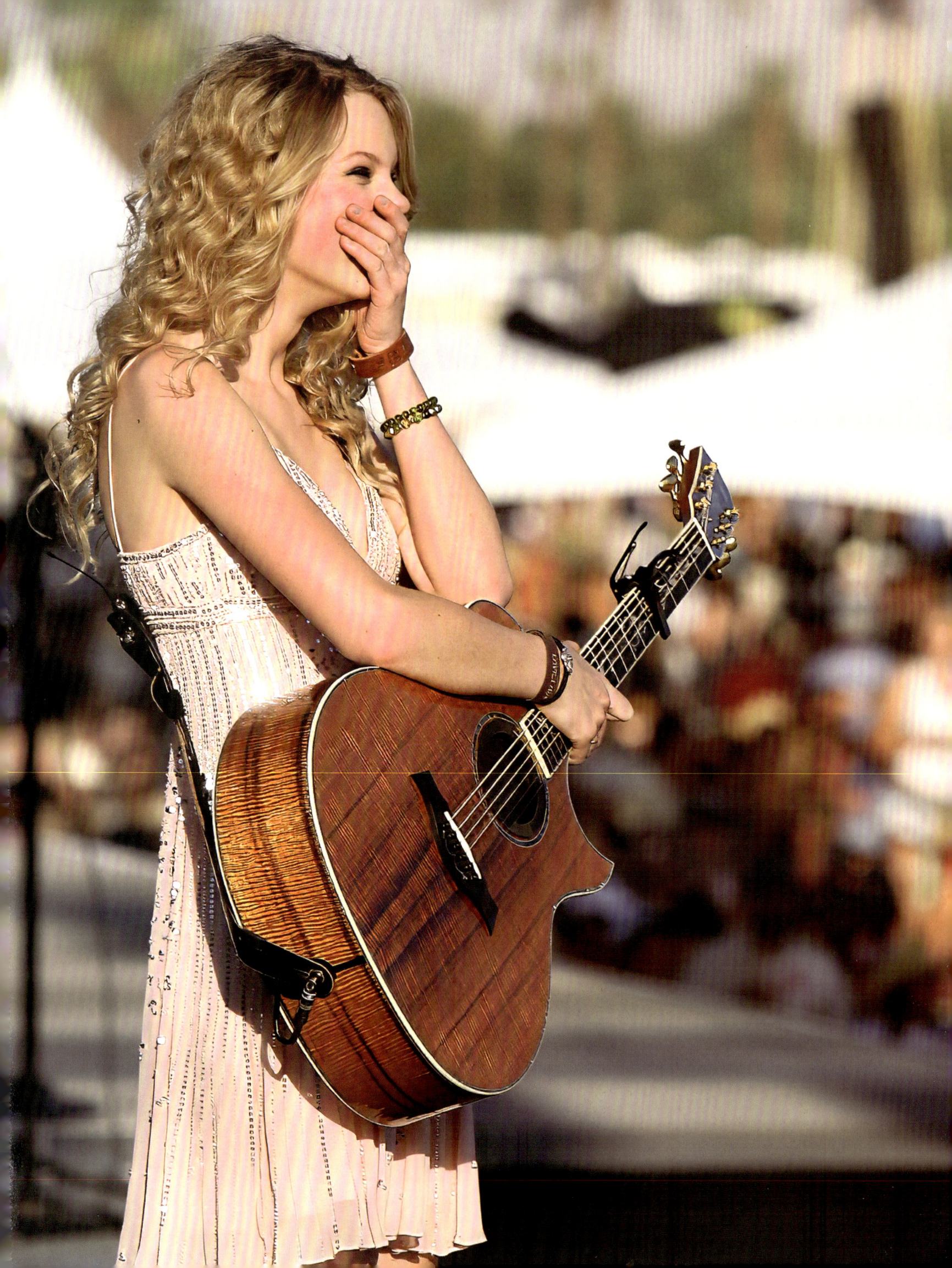

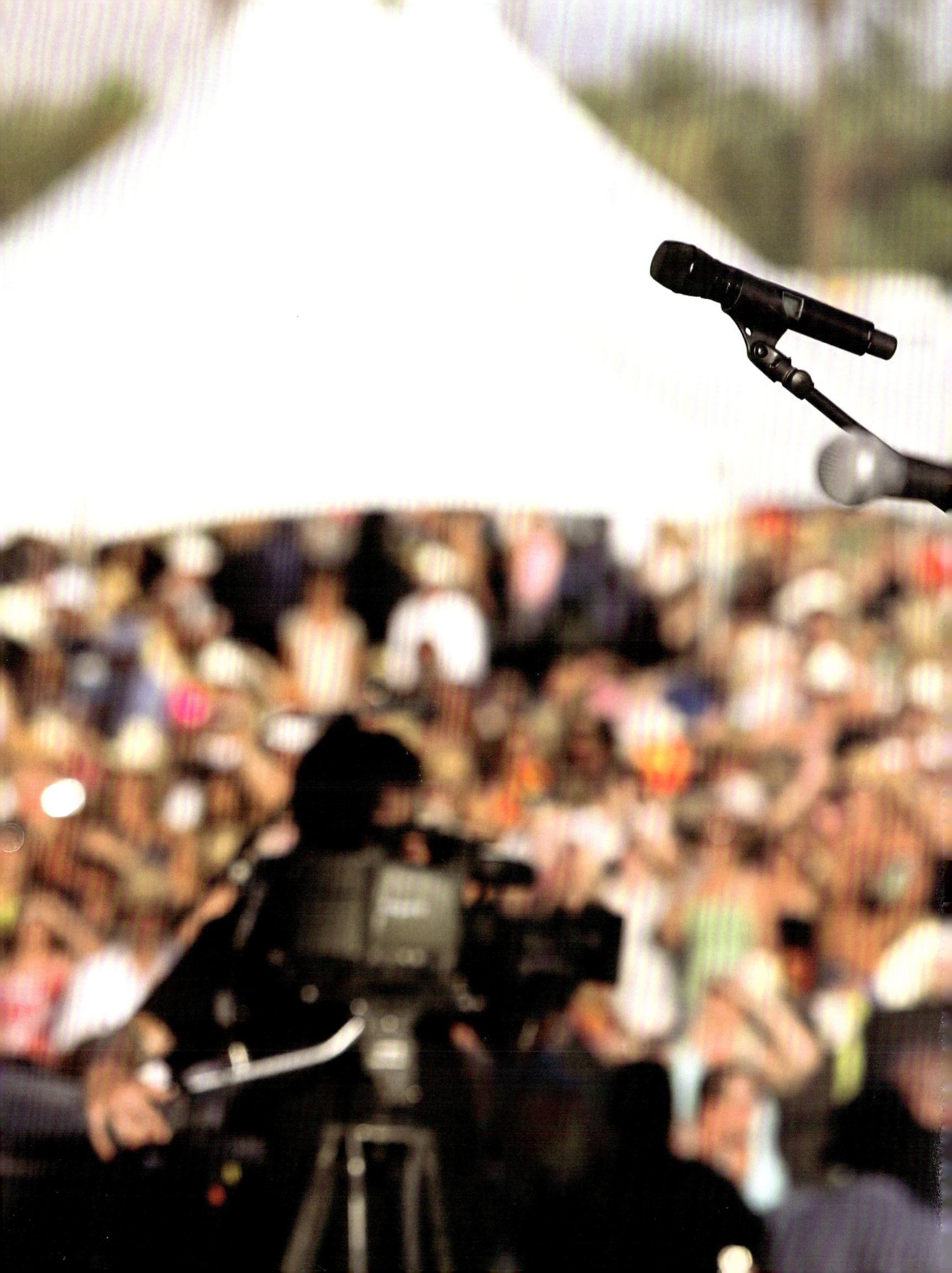

After the performance, Holly spoke with Taylor, who gave her a signed copy of her demo CD. The two snapped a photo together that has since been shared online and serves as proof of Holly being the first official Swiftie. After all, this was three years before Taylor released any official music publicly. Holly has said that she listened to that CD for three straight years and found solace in the lyrics and reliability.

Holly continued to follow Taylor throughout her career. In 2019, the two were reunited at one of the Secret Sessions Taylor held at her home in advance of her *Lover* album. In a TikTok video, Holly described how she hopes that when people see those photos of her with Taylor in 2003 and 2019, it reminds them of the longevity and resilience of Taylor Swift.

Holly went on to say, "There was a manager that she had after we met for the first time that, if I remember correctly, who told her to sell a million records, you have to shake a million hands. And I think intuitively she knew that, but she really took it and ran with it. And with the utmost love, it has been the core of her career forever."

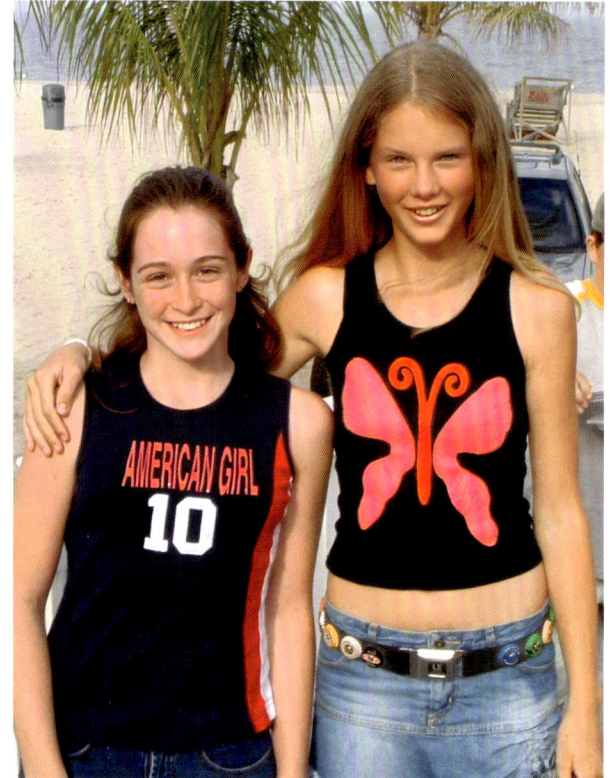

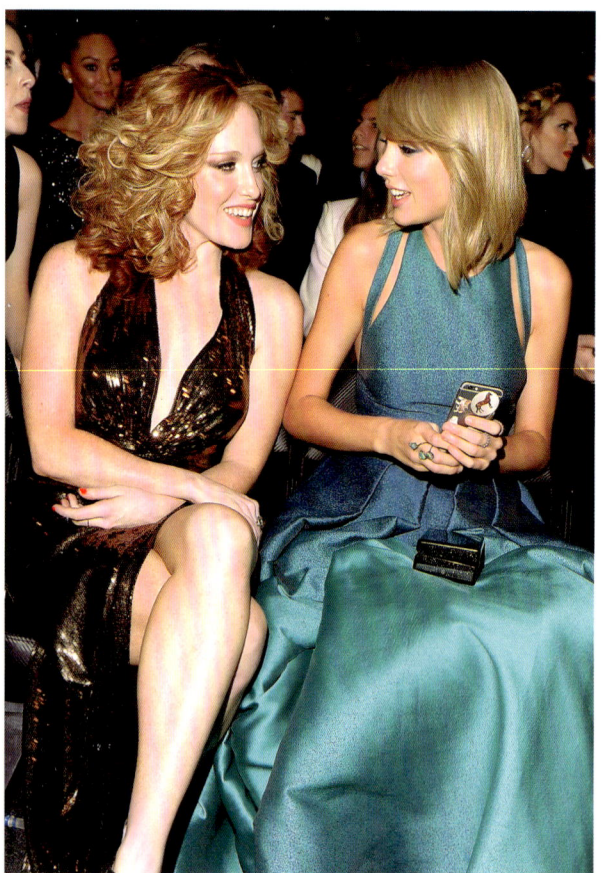

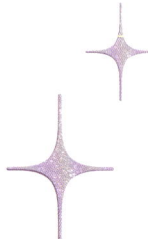

TOP: Taylor with her first fan, Holly Anderson, Point Pleasant, New Jersey, 2003.

BOTTOM: Friends forever: Taylor took her best friend, Abigail Anderson, to the 57th Annual Grammy Awards, February 8, 2015.

FROM MYSPACE TO OUR SPACE

Taylor launched her MySpace account in 2005. Her first profile photo featured her wearing a Garland Elementary School Spelling Bee T-shirt from a contest that she won. (We always knew she loved a dictionary!) As one of the earliest adopters of social media, Taylor used her channels to promote herself and to connect more directly with her fans. She was even credited with bringing a younger fan base to the country-music scene thanks to social media and how younger people could relate to her stories and experiences.

During Taylor's MySpace era, she posted blog updates of life on the road, like opening for the Rascal Flatts' tour, new music she was working on, award shows, and behind-the-scenes content that fans hadn't seen before. It opened a doorway and conversation into her life that was completely new at the time for artists. But Taylor didn't just post about tour updates and fancy awards shows; she also engaged directly with her fans online, commenting on their blogs, asking for updates about their lives, and even offering encouragement to fans who were being bullied or feeling down. She knew their names and their kids' names, and she expressed gratitude to any fan who liked her music.

Multiple times over the years, Taylor has stood up for fans who have been bullied or ridiculed. She knows the feeling all too well, both from being bullied as a child and the scrutiny that comes with fame. She began commenting on this during her MySpace days, and she has continued to do so across every social media platform, including Tumblr, Instagram, Facebook, and TikTok.

In 2014, a young fan, Hannah, was being bullied for the videos she posted online. Taylor consoled the young girl, sharing that she could relate. She responded on the post, "You're going into high school this week and this is your chance to push the reset button on how much value you give the opinion of these kids, most of whom have NO idea who they are. I'm so proud of you and protective of you because you DO. If they don't like you for being yourself, be yourself even more. Every time someone picks on me, I'll think of you in the hopes that every time someone picks on you, you'll think of me . . . and how we have this thread that connects us. Let them keep living in the darkness and we'll keep walking in the sunlight."

Those glimmers of unprompted kindness and connection have kept Taylor's fandom growing.

When she was eighteen, her MySpace intro ended with, "I'm a fan of fans. You are absolutely wonderful to me. I've got your back, just like you've had mine. To anyone who has gone out and bought my CD, or come to a show, or even turned up my song when it came on the radio, all I can say is thank you."

I truly believe that Taylor Swift is a fan of her fans. She remains grateful for, humbled by, and in awe of every award, every show, every album release—and she's been this way since the very start of her career.

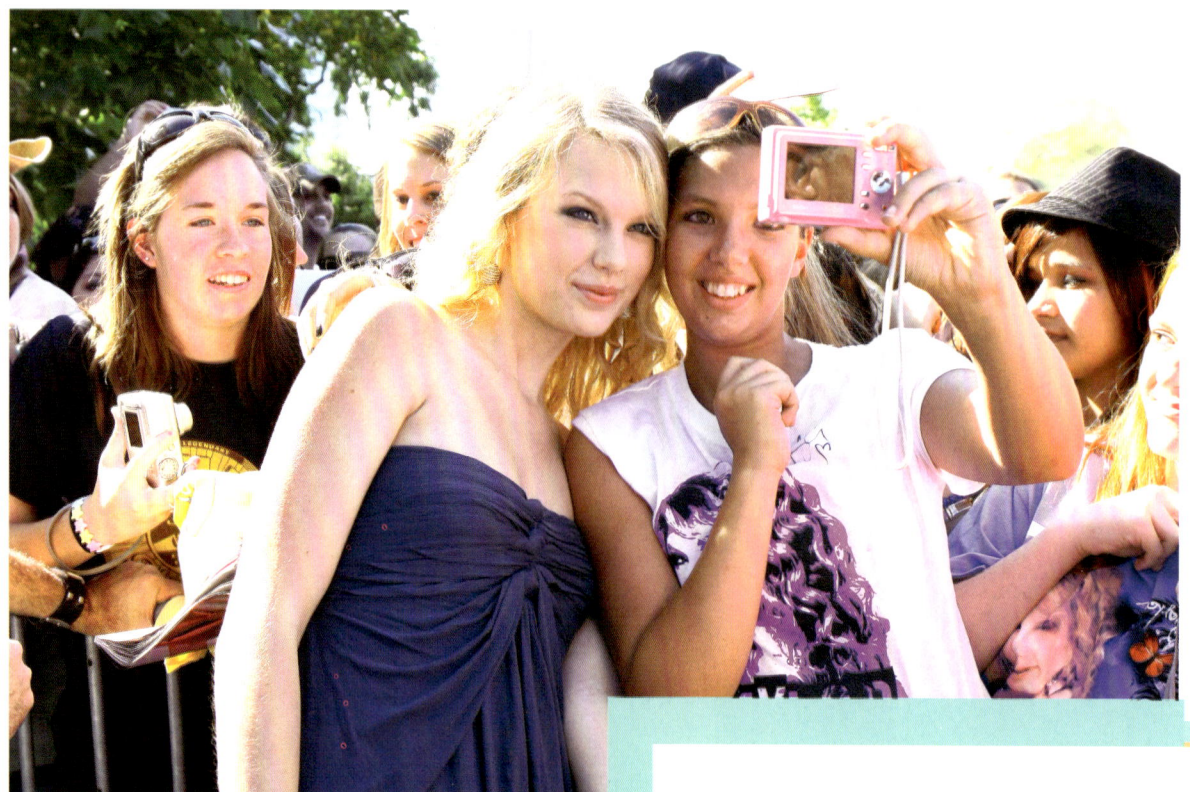

Taylor has always valued staying connected with and being close to her fans—so much so that she would often stay for hours after shows to ensure that she could meet every single fan who wanted to meet her. Taylor never charged for a meet-and-greet, and that remains true to this day.

Why do so many musicians fade, and she's still here? It's because of who Taylor's always been. Taylor has continued to build a connection with her fans through her words and her actions. This isn't contrived or something she's done once; this is at the center of who she is as a person. From playing to a crowd of five to sold-out stadium tours with tens of thousands of concertgoers, she's continued to let her generosity lead and her authenticity connect her to people. She has reiterated that if not for her fans, she would not be in the position she is in, and she takes that relationship very seriously. This level of care and dedication is what turns people from casual listeners into die-hard Swifties.

I guess you can say it's karma.

"Swiftie"

Used to describe a passionate and loyal fan of Taylor Swift.

EST.

Fans called themselves Swifties starting around 2010. Taylor cemented this in an interview in 2012 on Vevo, where she called it "adorable."

TRADEMARK

Taylor filed a trademark for commercial use of the term in March 2017.

OFFICIAL

The term "Swiftie" was officially added to the *Oxford English Dictionary* in 2023.

Keep walking in the sunlight, just as Taylor does.

OPPOSITE: Taylor spends time with her fans before performing at the Chicago Country Music Festival, October 12, 2008.

SMALL BUT MONUMENTAL GESTURES

In 2008, as Taylor Swift's profile started to rise, she sought out new ways to brighten someone's day using the platform she's been given. That year, she made her first visit to Vanderbilt Children's Hospital in Nashville, Tennessee, to visit patients. This was an unpublicized act of kindness with the sole intention of bringing comfort, joy, and maybe even music to children facing difficult health battles. This first visit created a cascade of yearly surprise visits to hospitals across the United States. For Taylor, these visits became a way to stay grounded in who she is as a person while remaining connected to her true core values.

In 2014, Taylor spent more than five hours at Boston Children's Hospital, visiting young patients and singing with them. One mother shared how Taylor sang "We Are Never Ever Getting Back Together" to her six-year-old who had undergone multiple surgeries. Taylor's visits have given many patients a few moments of joy and normalcy, and the ability to get lost in a song and forget about their medical challenges for a bit.

In 2018, days before launching her Reputation Stadium Tour, Taylor invited children in foster care, in group homes, or children who were adopted from foster care and their families to a private "dress rehearsal" concert. She gave out two thousand tickets in total and treated her guests to a pizza party and even included time for a photo opportunity with her after the show.

These gestures demonstrate how even the smallest interactions can feel monumental. Whether it is bringing a present to a patient, singing a song with them, or just comforting their parents in a time of need, those acts of kindness can create hope for people during their darkest hours. So, keep walking in the sunlight, just as Taylor has taught us.

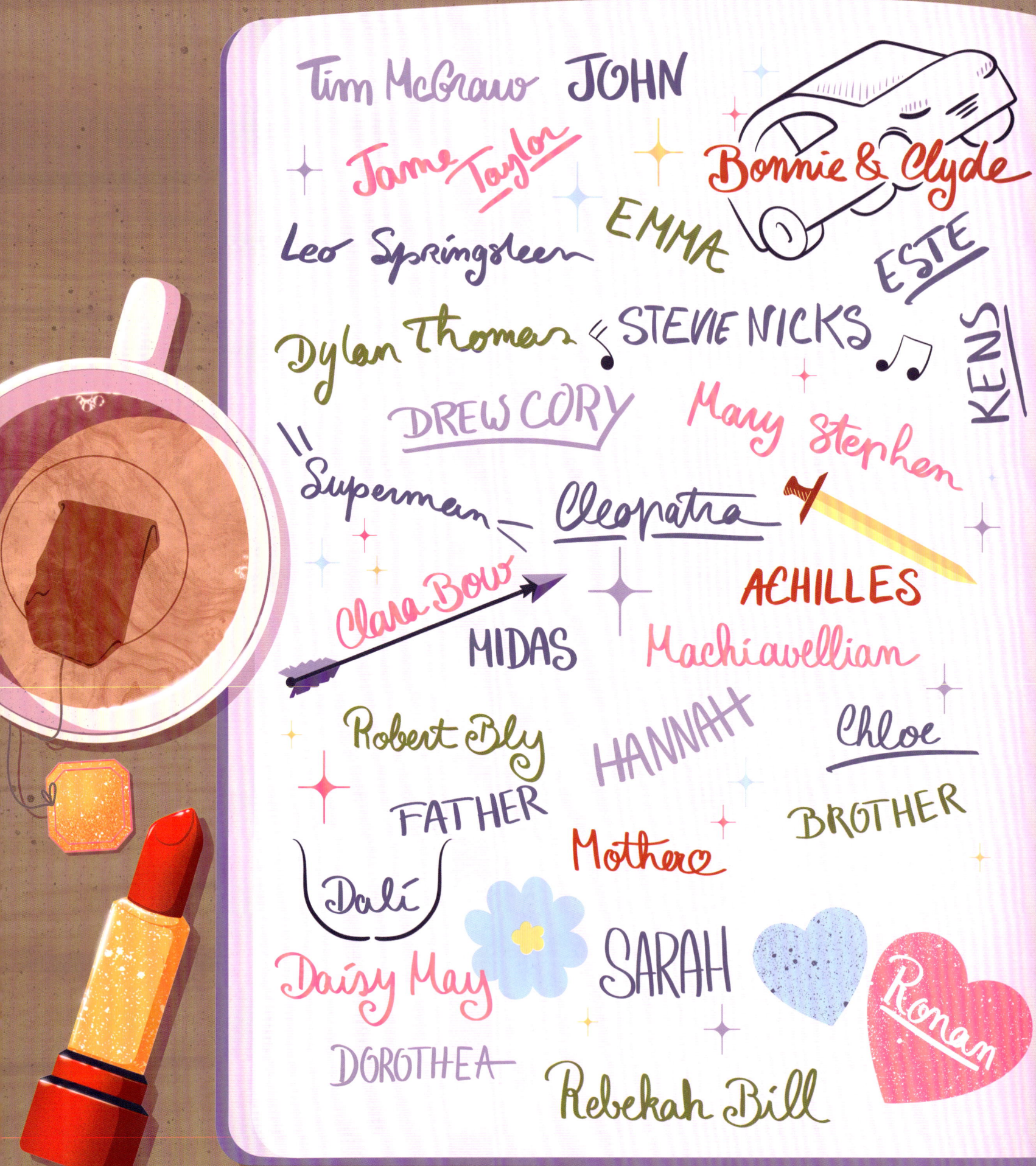

When you hear the name Tim McGraw, do you think of Taylor Swift? With the release of her debut single, "Tim McGraw," Taylor showed that she was not afraid to feature names in her songs. Whether it was the name of a musician she likes, a boy she went to high school with, her best friend, a fictional character she made up, or a character in Greek mythology, her discography contains more than sixty names.

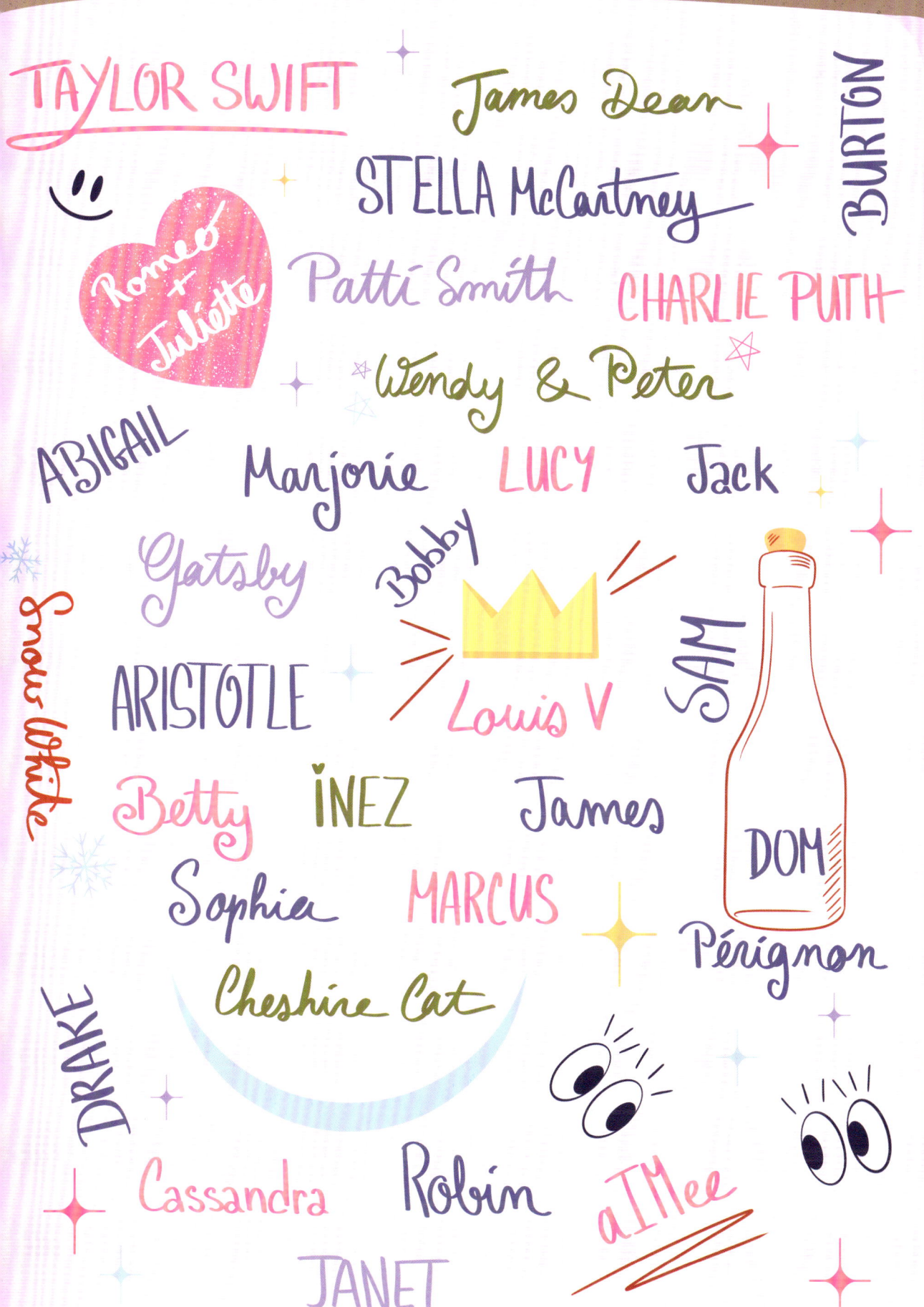

TAYLOR SWIFT

James Dean

BURTON

STELLA McCartney

Romeo + Juliette

Patti Smith

CHARLIE PUTH

Wendy & Peter

ABIGAIL

Marjorie

LUCY

Jack

Gatsby

Bobby

Snow White

ARISTOTLE

Louis V

SAM

Betty

INEZ

James

DOM

Sophia

MARCUS

Pérignon

Cheshire Cat

DRAKE

Cassandra

Robin

aIMee

JANET

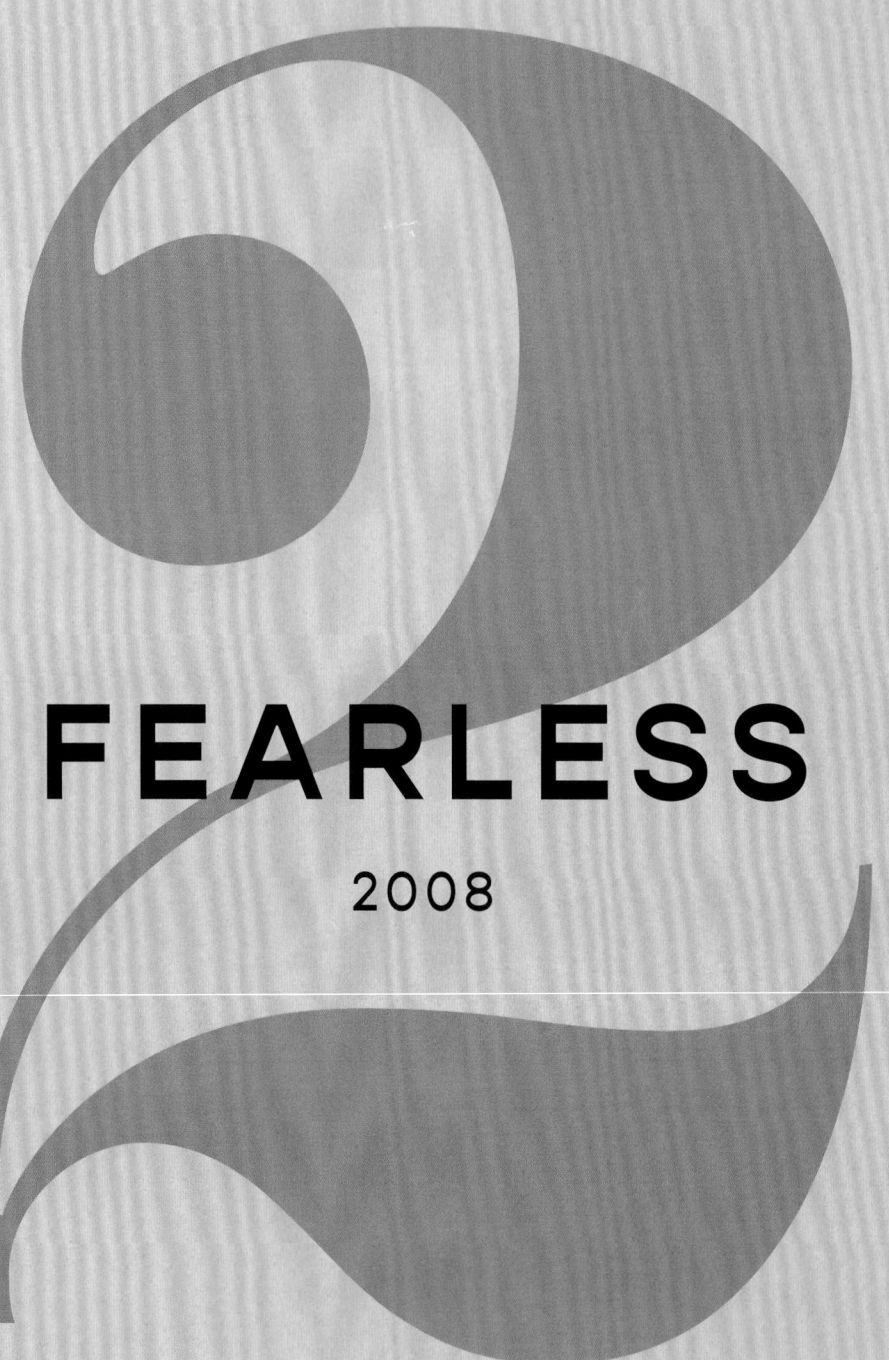

FEARLESS

2008

COURAGE IS KIND

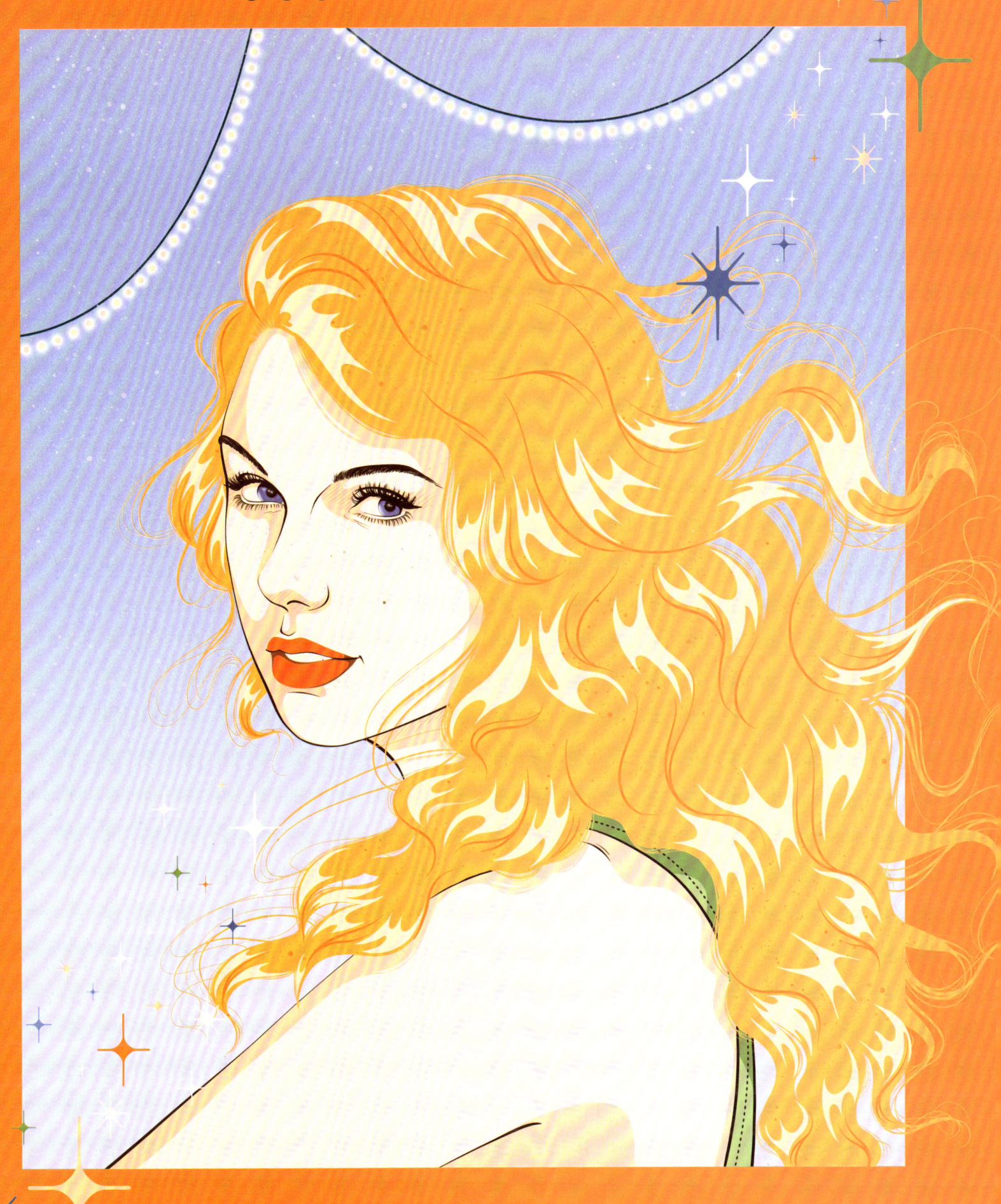

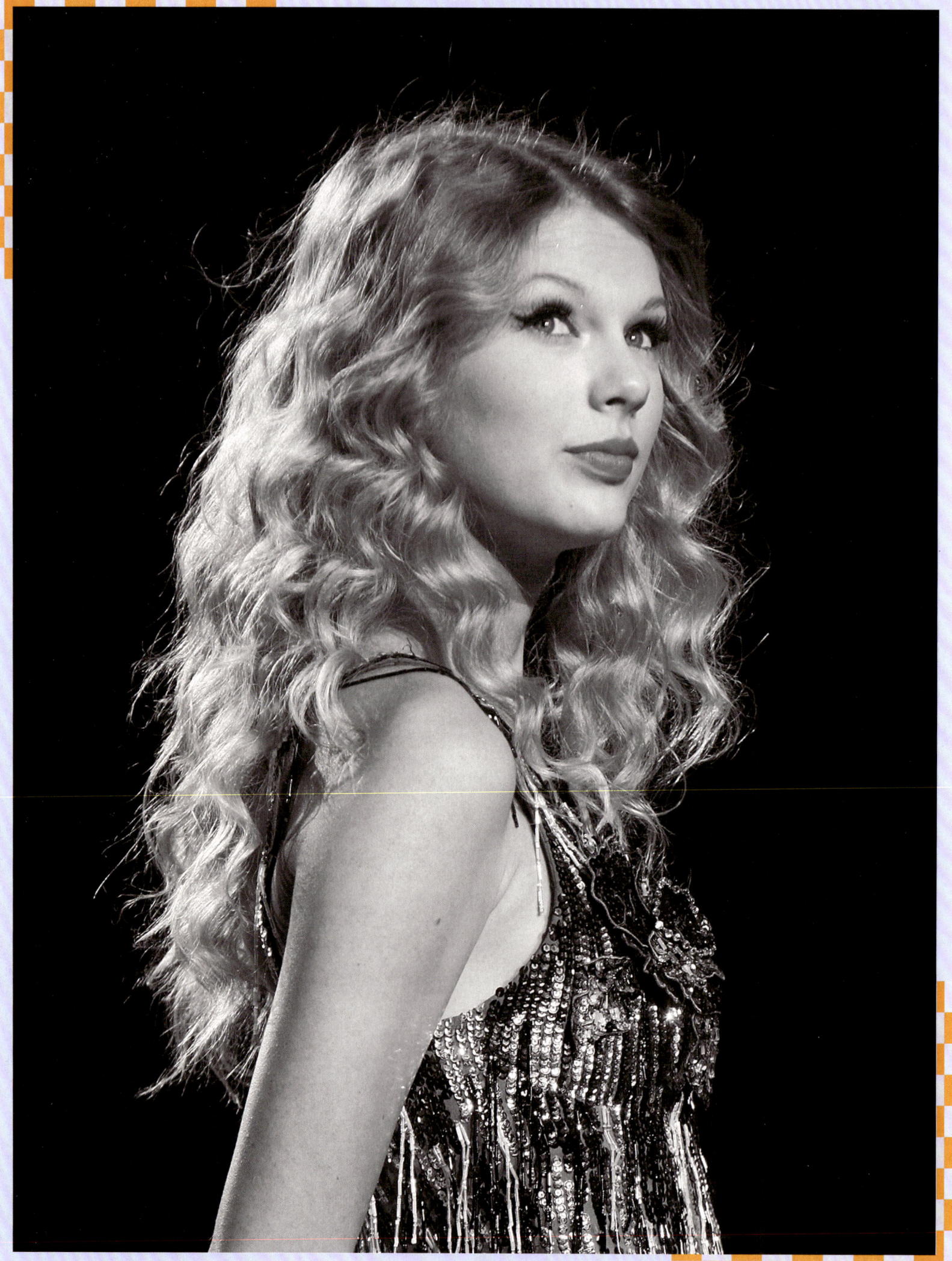

> # "To me, fearless is living in spite of those things that scare you to death."
>
> Taylor, 2008

THE JOURNEY THAT MADE HER FEARLESS

Following the success of her debut release, Taylor fearlessly jumped in headfirst and turned from up-and-coming country start into full-on global superstar with the release of her sophomore album, *Fearless*. At midnight on November 8, 2008, Taylor went to the Hendersonville Walmart in Tennessee to buy her new album. Hundreds of fans showed up, also to buy the Fearless album, and got the surprise of a lifetime upon meeting Taylor, who stayed to sign albums and take photos with fans. She was amazed that something she'd created was in stores and that people came out late at night to buy it.

Her hard work was paying off. *Fearless* ended up selling 592,000 copies in the first week and spent eleven nonconsecutive weeks at the No. 1 spot on the Billboard 200, the longest run of any female country album. Her singles "Love Story"

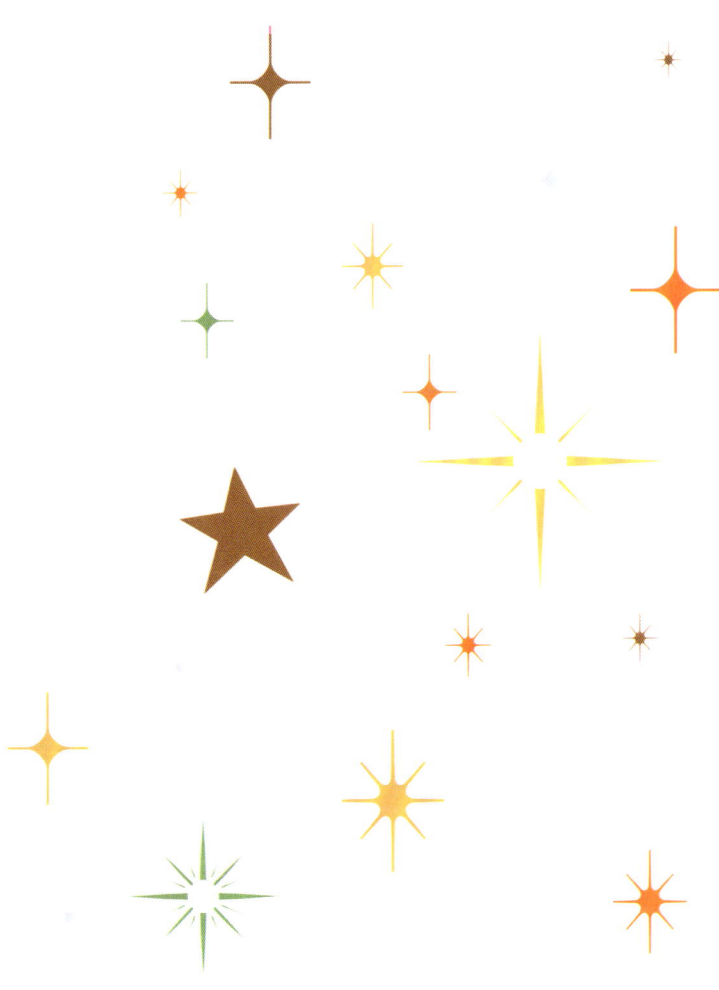

SO HIGH SCHOOL

Fearless has been dubbed Taylor's high-school album—a coming-of-age record with songs reminiscent of fairy-tale love stories, heartbreak, and self-discovery. While *Fearless* came out as a country album, it crossed over into the pop charts with "Love Story" and "You Belong with Me," both of which charted on country as well as pop charts.

"Love Story" reimagines Shakespeare's *Romeo and Juliet*, giving listeners a hopeful twist, while "You Belong with Me" captures the feeling of being a nerdy outsider crushing on a popular guy who likes someone else, as well as the desire to win someone's love and affection. "White Horse" is a gut-punch ballad about a fairy-tale love coming to an end.

While most of the songs are autobiographical, Taylor wrote "Fifteen" about her best friend Abigail and her experience of navigating first love and the heartbreak that comes when you give it all away. Abigail was even featured in the music video for this song.

Cherished songs like "The Best Day," which pays homage to Taylor's mom, dad, and brother, showcase that no matter fame or fortune, the best days are spent with the ones you love.

While *Fearless* incorporates banjos, fiddles, and acoustic guitars as a nod to Taylor's country roots, the album also embraces polished pop sounds, making it a crossover success in both the country and pop categories.

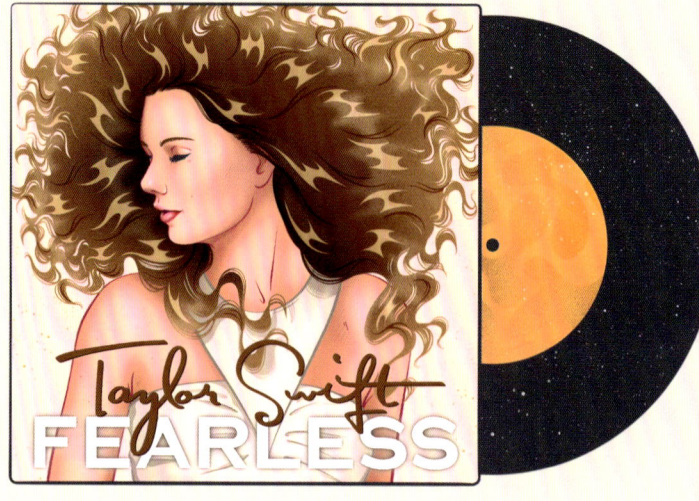

ALBUM
Fearless

DATE LAUNCHED
November 8, 2008

FIRST SINGLE
"Love Story" (September 15, 2008)

OTHER SINGLES
"White Horse" (December 8, 2008),
"You Belong with Me" (April 20, 2009),
"Fifteen" (August 31, 2009), and
"Fearless" (January 4, 2010)

TOUR
Fearless Tour (April 2009 to July 2010)

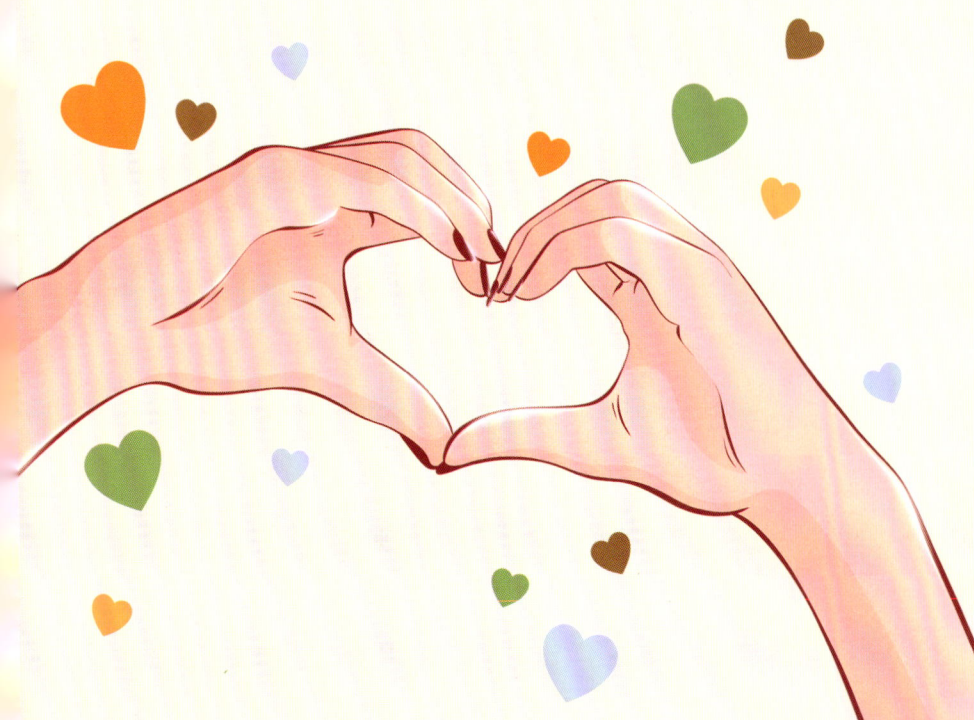

Taylor positions herself as a songwriter and embraces storytelling as her favorite way to connect with her audience. Her ability to capture universal emotions has helped her build a strong connection with her audience, from high schoolers to grandparents and beyond.

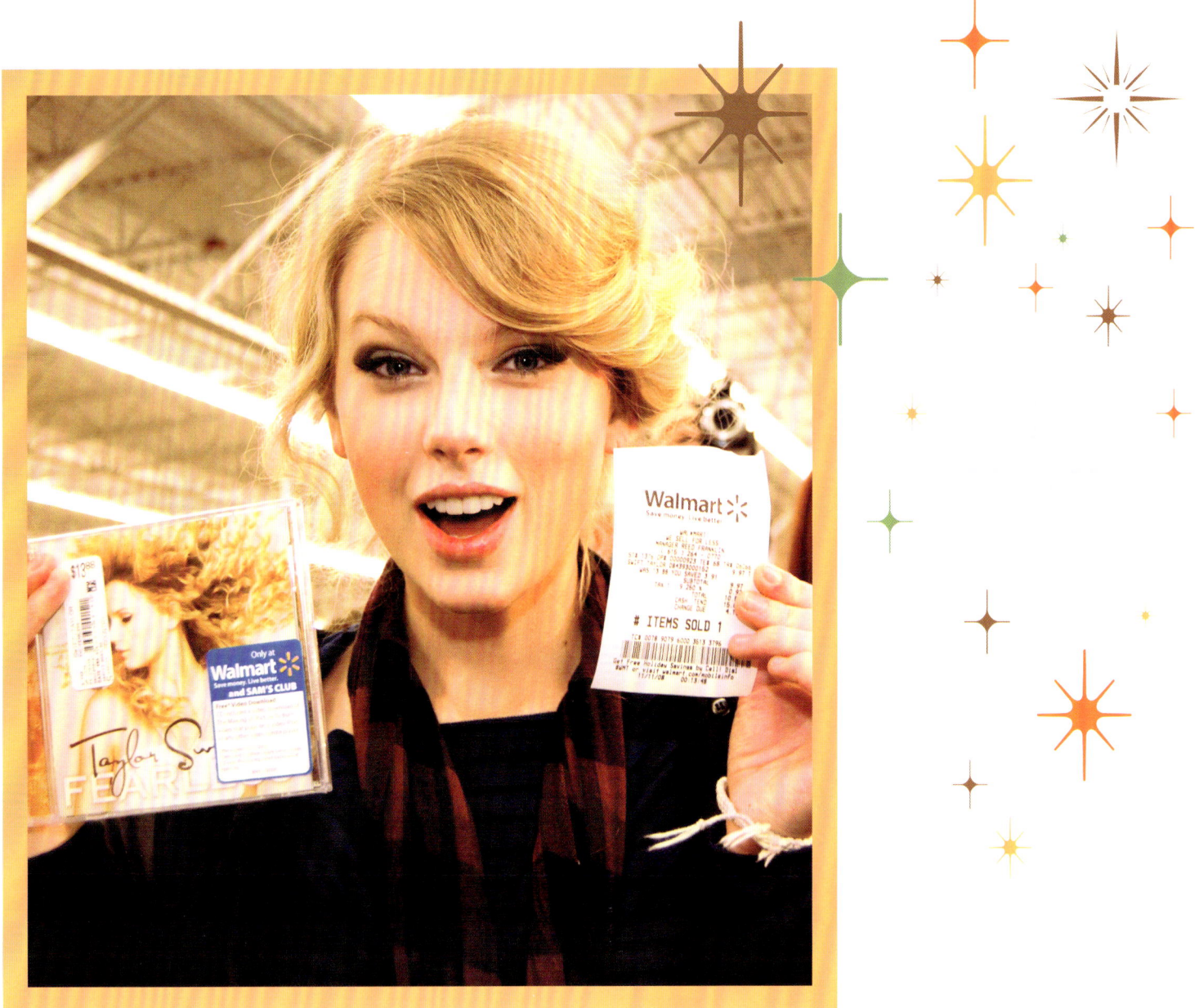

and "You Belong with Me" became crossover pop favorites for non-country listeners and gave Taylor an entry into the pop genre.

In October 2009, Taylor released a special *Fearless Platinum Edition* of the album, which included six bonus tracks, a DVD of music videos, behind-the-scenes content, and photos that her brother had taken of her. During a late-night interview with Jimmy Fallon, she joked that she wanted to call it "The Hardcore Ninja Jedi Version," but they went with "Platinum Edition" instead. This type of mixed media in the world of music, like adding videos or behind-the-scenes content, was new at the time and showed that Taylor wasn't afraid to do things differently.

This success wasn't by chance or luck—it was due to the hard work that Taylor had put into her career for years at that point. Taylor laid the groundwork for her achievements by opening for acts such as Rascal Flatts, Brad Paisley, and Keith Urban; doing radio tours across country to get more radio stations to play her songs; and connecting with her fans on social media. She earned a top spot on both the country and pop charts and was getting ready to headline her first world tour. This era is when Taylor fully stepped into her own.

ABOVE: Taylor stops in to Walmart to pick up her new *Fearless* CD on the day of its release.

PAGE 34: No fear here: Taylor performs at Madison Square Garden in New York City during the Fearless Tour, August 27, 2009.

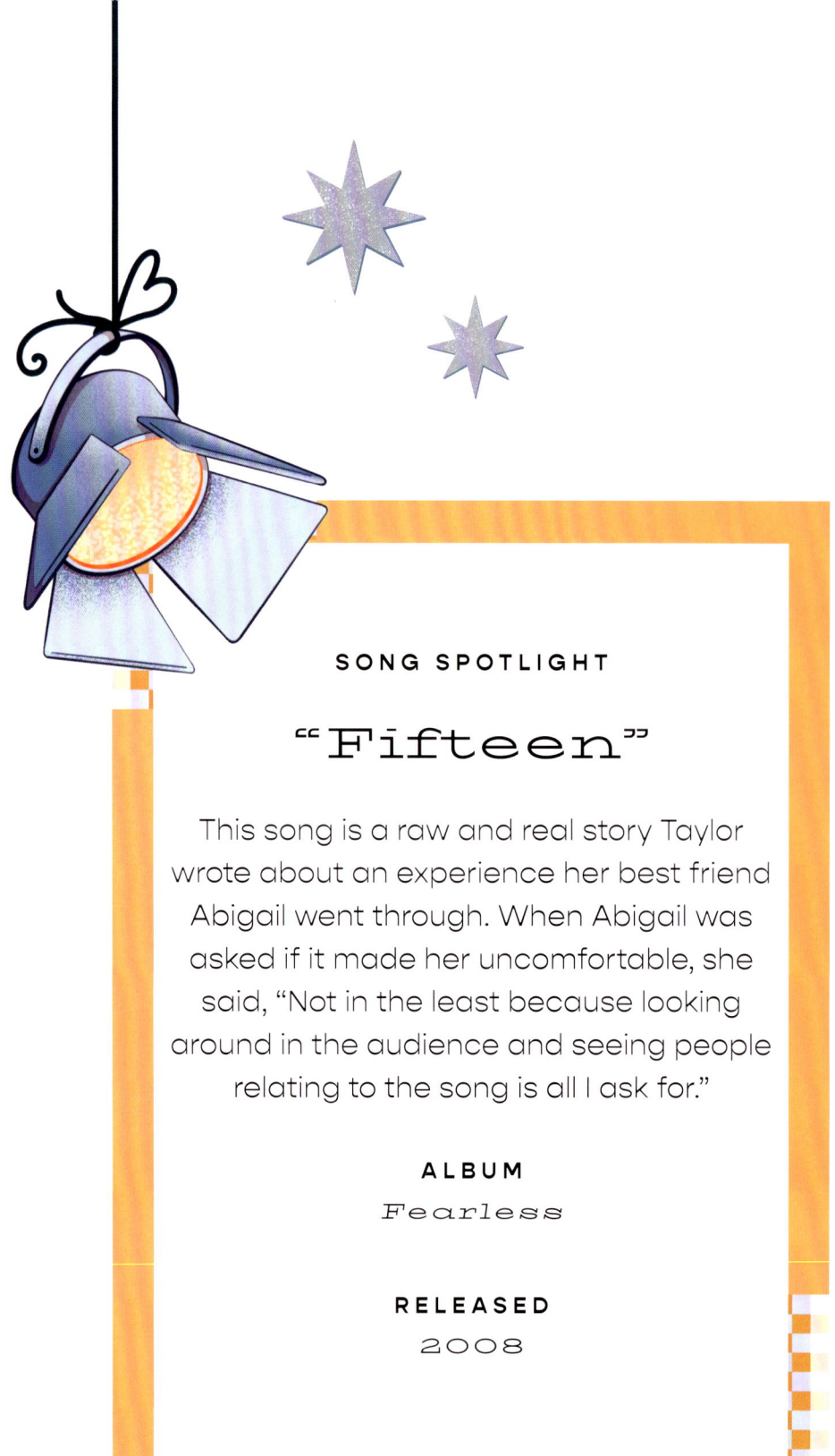

SONG SPOTLIGHT

"Fifteen"

This song is a raw and real story Taylor wrote about an experience her best friend Abigail went through. When Abigail was asked if it made her uncomfortable, she said, "Not in the least because looking around in the audience and seeing people relating to the song is all I ask for."

ALBUM

Fearless

RELEASED

2008

On Tour

From writing her own songs to coming up with the tour concepts and music videos, Taylor has always taken front row at creative direction, ensuring that no detail is left untouched. The Fearless Tour was no different. This two-hour show combined graphics, theatrical performances, and thoughtful, special fan moments.

The show opened with Taylor Swift coming up from the stage in a marching band uniform and the number "13" written on her hand, looking at the crowd, before going into "You Belong with Me." Halfway through the song, Taylor would move downstage and open her arms, and her dancers would pull off the marching band uniform to reveal a black, sequin, sparkly dress. This sequence perfectly sums up Taylor—a band geek at heart with a love of sparkles and sequins.

The stage theatrics were impressive. Her set looked like a big spiral staircase and a castle, but the castle columns were also digital video monitors that could transform the fairy-tale classroom into a school library in seconds. Taylor was inspired by theater, storytelling, and what she saw in her head when she wrote the songs.

Taylor also brought dancers on this tour, marking a big shift for country music at the time. Most country-music stars kept their sets minimal, featuring just the band and maybe some screen visuals, but Taylor chose to include dancers on the Fearless Tour to add a storytelling effect. She also used the stage to clap back at the media controversy she experienced for writing songs about men and sometimes including their names.

During a set change, Taylor debuted a short film she made called *Crimes of Passion*, the film was a spoof show featuring a detective, who hunted down the guys she wrote songs about and then found out how their lives were

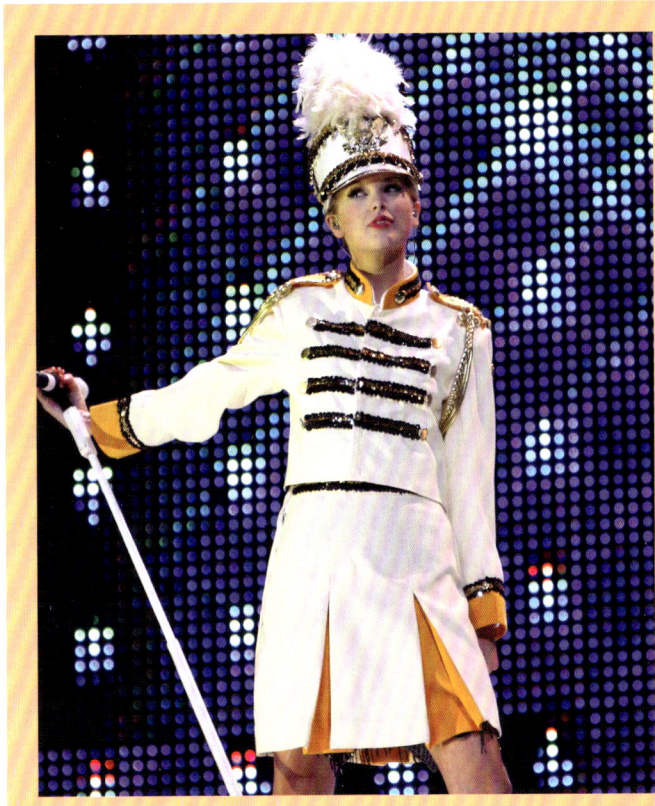

Her Journey to Fearlessness

WHAT
A three-part miniseries detailing Taylor's journey from her small-town beginnings to the making of the Fearless Tour.

AIRED
As a three-part series on The HUB starting October 22, 2010.

RELEASED
Released on DVD on October 11, 2011.

impacted. Tim McGraw himself made a cameo as "Taylor Swift's first victim." It added a funny element to the show and gave Taylor a voice to address the controversies in her own way.

Also in the show was a mock interview with Hoda Kotb, during which Hoda asked Taylor why any man would want to date her if they knew that she'd write a song about them afterward. This question referenced an actual interview in which someone asked Taylor that question, and this reference was her way of clapping back at the double standard of asking women questions like this. Taylor responded that the men shouldn't do bad things and offered the perfect segue into the song "Should've Said No." During the set, Taylor started on a red interview chair, similar to the one in the music video, and eventually threw the chair off the stage in a rage. She was not only using her songs to communicate her feelings and experiences; she was now using her tours to

continue the conversation and dive a little deeper into the media controversies as well.

One of the most noteworthy special touches of this tour, however, was finding ways to give back to her fans. In the *Journey to Fearless* documentary, Taylor mentioned her amazement at how much her fans have done for her, and how that inspires her to make sure they feel seen in every way possible at her shows.

About halfway through the show, she would jump down into the crowd and walk through the people, hugging fans and taking photos with as many fans as she could. She would eventually make her way to a stage in the back, where she performed a few songs, giving the audience farther from the stage a closer view of the show. She said that she wanted people who thought they got the worst seats in the house to get the best seats too, and this act of kindness was her way of ensuring that.

ABOVE: Taylor in the drum major outfit she wore to sing "You Belong to Me," the opening song of the Fearless Tour concerts.

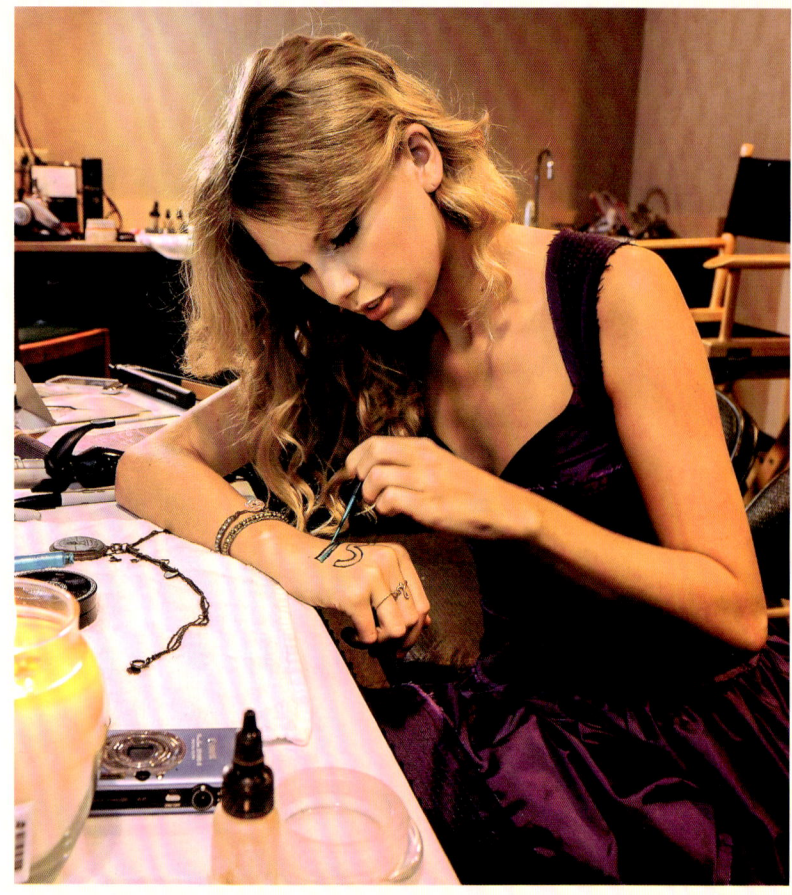

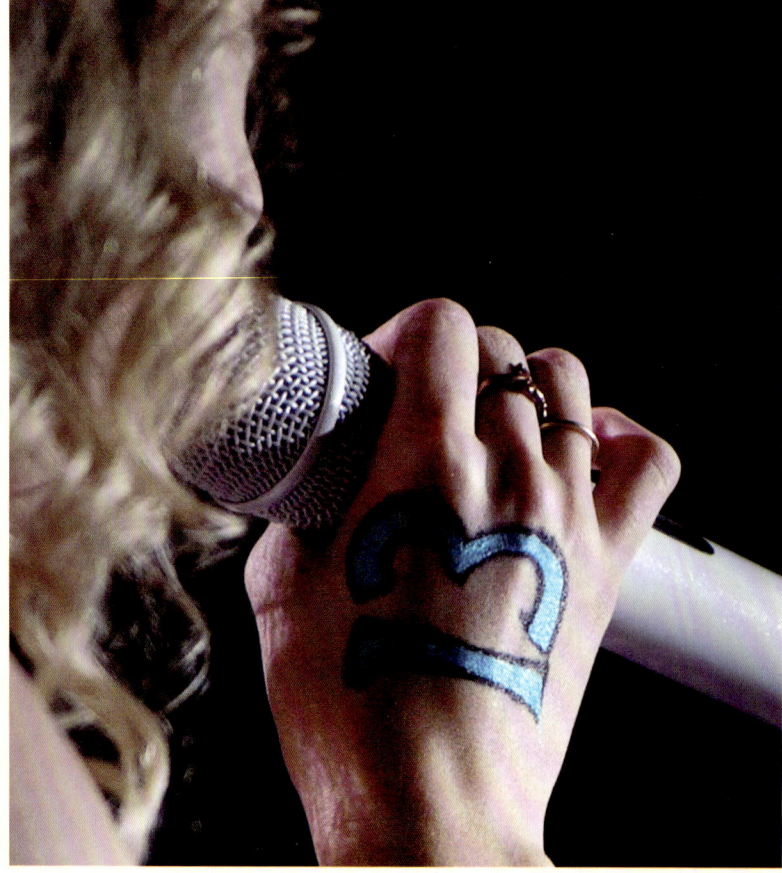

During a set change, Taylor would run across the arena, seeing fans at concession stands and in various areas of the stadium, only to land at one of the lower sections of the stadium and perform an acoustic song right in the stands, right next to fans at their seats. This offered Taylor yet another way to feel close to her fans and ensure that everyone left with something special.

As if that wasn't enough, instead of doing traditional meet-and-greets and charging audience members to attend, Taylor instead started what she called "T Parties." She had her mom and other people on her team find the wildest, danciest, most over-the-top fans with the best costumes or signs, and they would be invited backstage to a T Party. Backstage, there was an enchanting space filled with TVs, foosball, pink-pong, pizza, drinks, and snacks. Taylor would surprise them with her appearance and hang with them for hours after her shows. This was a way for Taylor to meet her fans, learn about them, and let them know how grateful she was for all their support. These fan-forward touches have been reimagined in various ways throughout all her tours.

As a final celebration for her fans, Taylor debuted a music video for "Fearless" on January 4, 2010, that featured real footage from the Fearless Tour. In it, she can be seen interacting with fans, hugging, signing autographs, and sharing moments with them. Several fans are holding signs and showing off their costumes. She wanted to make sure the fans knew they were an integral part of the *Fearless* story.

Taylor's success continued. She received countless accolades, including Country Music Association Entertainer of the Year in 2009 (the youngest ever to win), and *Fearless* became the most awarded country album in history.

With so much success and stardom, media controversy was soon to follow.

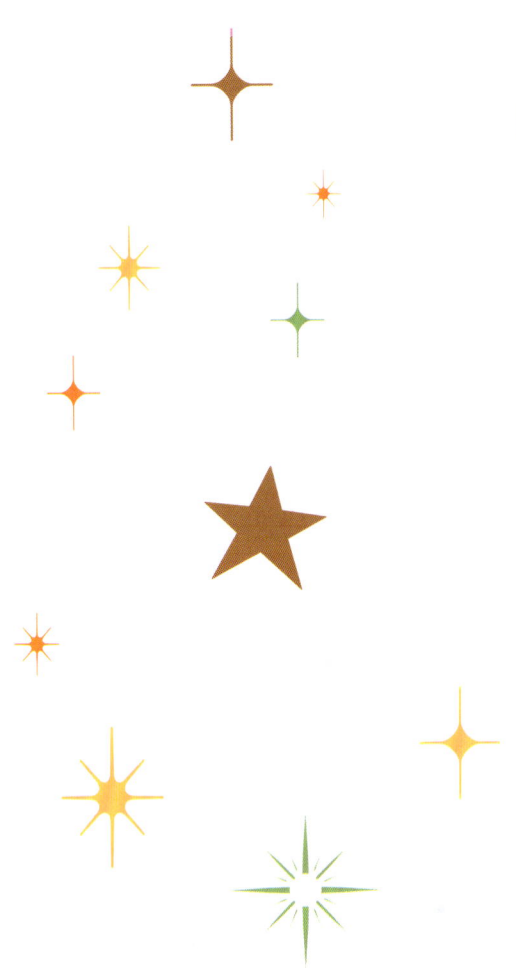

RISING FAME—BUT REMAINING GROUNDED

Despite a sold-out world tour, a record-breaking album, and numerous accolades and awards, Taylor has remained a down-to-earth woman. When asked during a 2009 interview with Dave Berry at *The Hot Desk* how the fame had impacted her, she said, "You have to have a perspective change when your life shifts into the gear of everyone knows who you are. You have to focus on thinking about it in the perspective of, I'm going to go shopping right now and it's not going to take the same amount of time it used to take before people know who I was, it's going to take double, and I'm cool with that because this is what I wanted and I'm one of the lucky people who actually got what they wanted in life, and it's a good thing."

MTA VMAs

Enter the 2009 MTV Video Music Awards, held on September 13, 2009, at Radio City Music Hall in New York City. Taylor was nominated for Best Female Video for her hit song "You Belong with Me." This was her first VMA nomination and a huge honor, coming at a time when Taylor was slowly crossing over from country music into mainstream.

Nineteen-year-old Taylor arrived in a horse-drawn carriage that looked straight out of a fairy tale wearing a sparkling, floor-length silver gown. Her date that evening was her mother, Andrea.

When it came time to announce the award for Best Female Video, singer Shakira and actor Taylor Lautner, who had been romantically linked to Taylor Swift, took the stage to present.

The category highlighted songs from prominent women artists, including Beyoncé's "Single Ladies (Put a Ring on It)," Lady Gaga's "Poker Face," Katy Perry's "Hot N Cold," Kelly Clarkson's "My Life Would Suck Without You," and Pink's "So What."

Shakira and Taylor Lautner opened the envelope and excitedly announced Taylor Swift as the winner. The crowd erupted in cheers; "You Belong with Me" started to play; and Taylor looked visibly shocked, saying, "WHAT!" before heading to the podium.

Taylor stepped onto the stage, completely stunned, staring at her new moon person trophy. "I always dreamed about what it would be like to maybe win one of these someday," she said, "but I never thought it would actually happen."

OPPOSITE: Bringing the positivity: Taylor draws her lucky number on her hand before a performance.

FOLLOWING PAGES: Taylor performing "You Belong with Me" at the 2009 MTV Video Music Awards. She would win the award for Best Female Video for the song later that night.

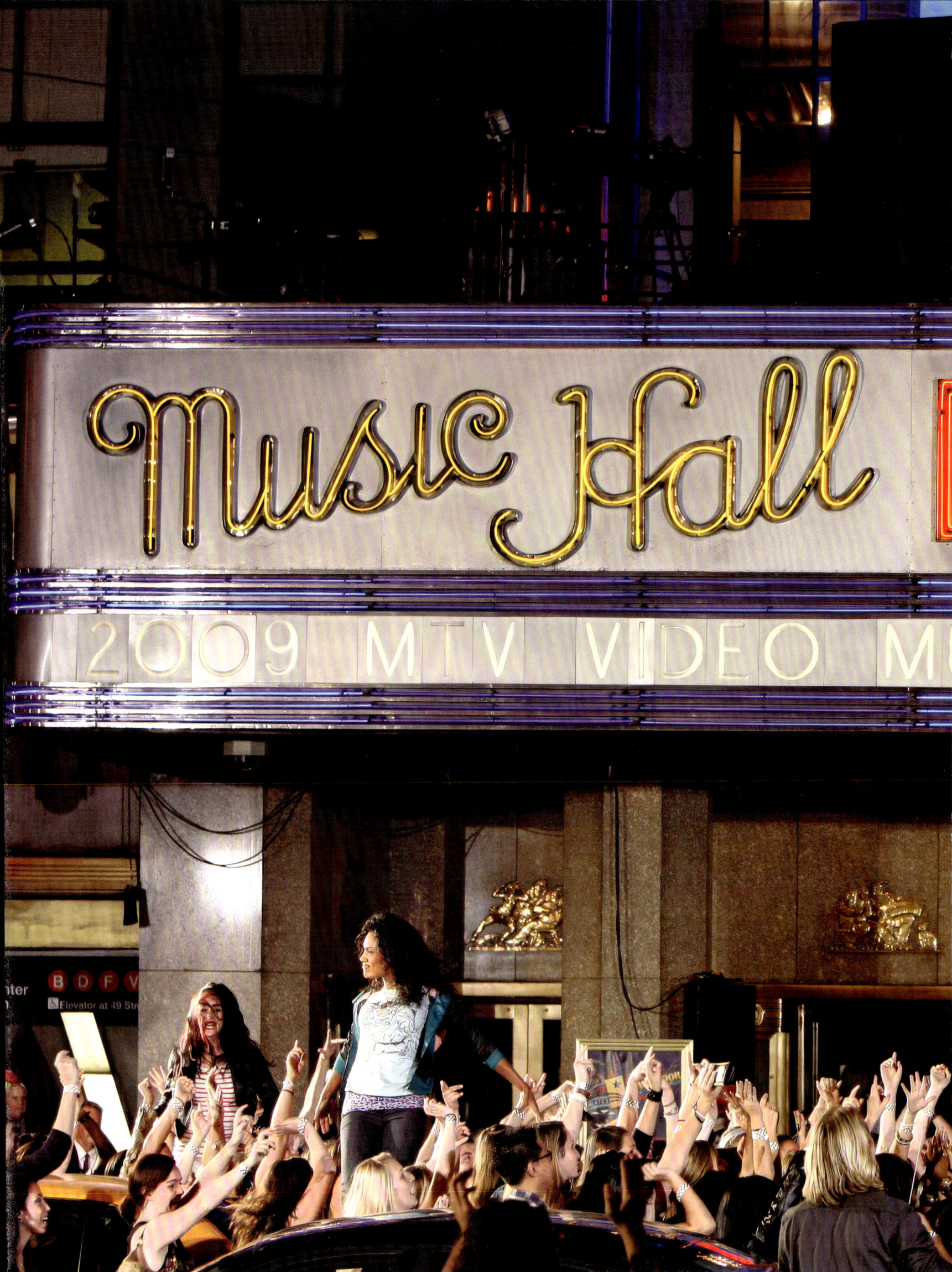

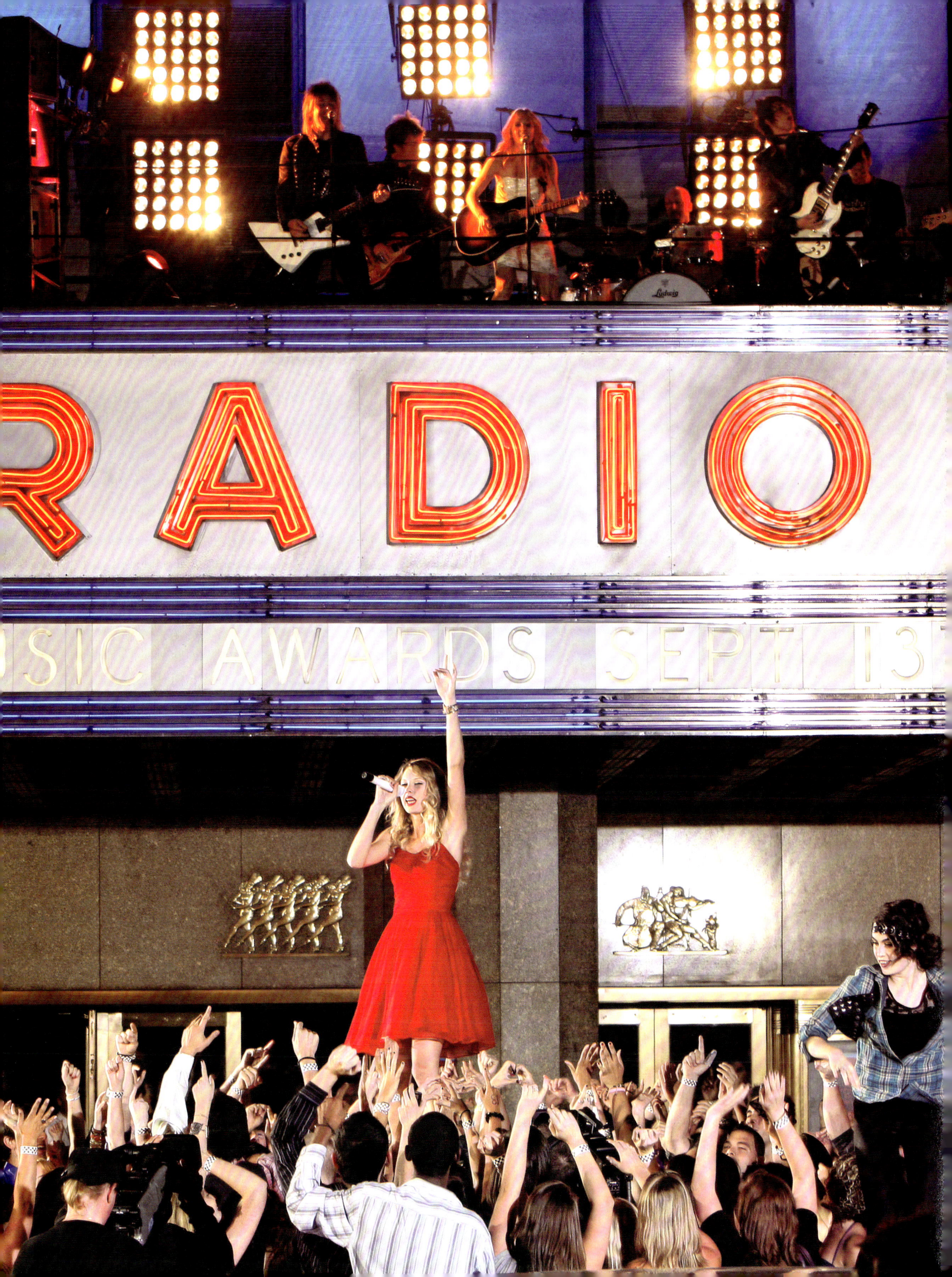

SNL MONOLOGUE SONG

Coming off the infamous MTV VMAs, Taylor hosted Saturday Night Live on November 7, 2009. She captivated audiences immediately as she opened the episode with a song called "Monologue Song (La La La)." Taylor is credited with writing the song herself, bringing it to the writer's room, and performing it on the first day of rehearsals. The SNL staff had no notes.

With her acoustic guitar in hand, not only did Taylor name names, but she also addressed the VMAs incident and her then-relationship with Taylor Lautner, all while maintaining an incredible sense of humor. Yet again, Taylor did what she does best: turn her feelings into songs and uses her storytelling to do so.

Her delivery offered the perfect balance of humor and relatability, and showed that Taylor's talents extend beyond music. It also proved that she could laugh at herself and handle the pressure of fame with a sense of humor. This moment became a milestone in Taylor's career, demonstrating that she could thrive with challenges and that her talent knows no bounds.

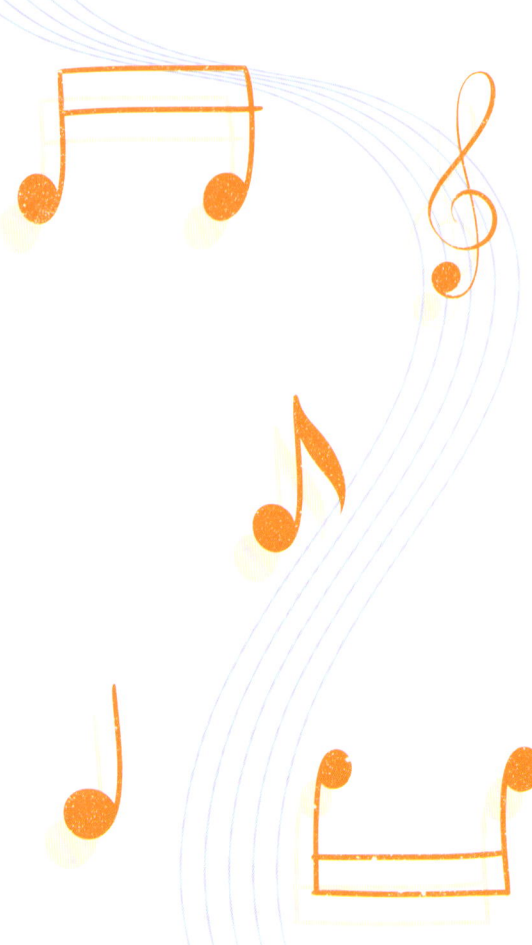

Before Taylor could finish, Kanye West jumped onstage, interrupted her win, grabbed a microphone, and said, "Yo, Taylor, I'm really happy for you, I'ma let you finish, but Beyoncé had one of the best videos of all time!"

The crowd was stunned. There were boos and gasps and Taylor just stood there, unsure how to react. Kanye handed the microphone back to Taylor, but she didn't get to finish her speech. The show quickly cut to a commercial.

For the final award of the show, Beyoncé won Video of the Year for "Single Ladies" and used her time to invite Taylor back onstage to have her moment. Taylor was able to accept her award, and this act of kindness signaled solidarity between Beyoncé and Taylor.

This incident took social media by storm and made headlines across traditional media for weeks (if not years) afterward. Kanye received a ton of backlash from fans and celebrities. Even President Barack Obama called him a "jackass."

Taylor went on ABC's *The View* just two days after the awards show to discuss the incident. She explained that she had no idea what was happening and thought maybe it was a planned skit. It wasn't until later that she thought the crowd was booing her and not Kanye West. She shared that Kanye called her to personally apologize and she felt it was genuine, accepted his apology, and appreciated that he reached out.

OPPOSITE: La la la: Taylor jokes about herself (and Kanye) during her SNL "Monologue Song," November 7, 2009.

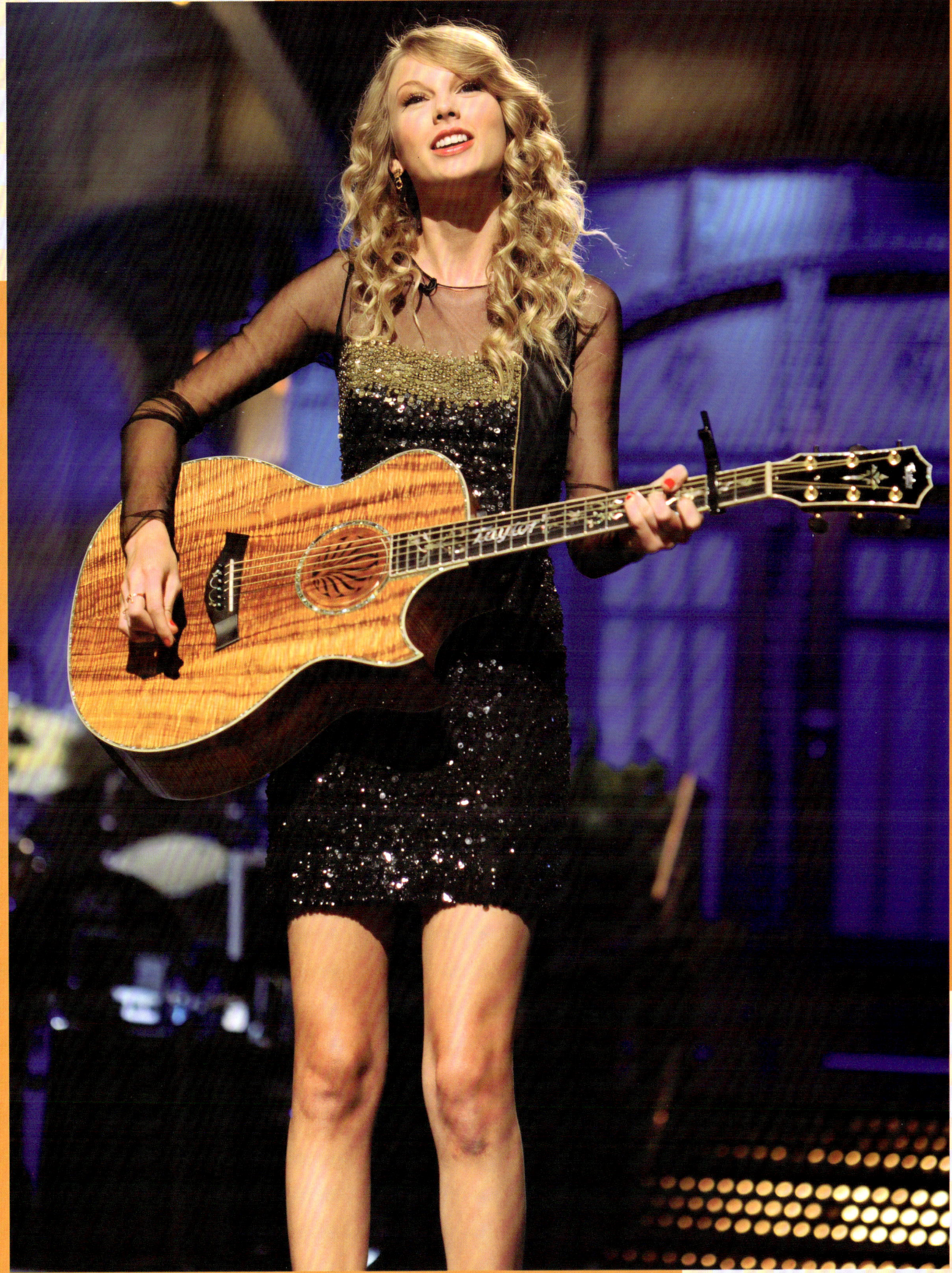

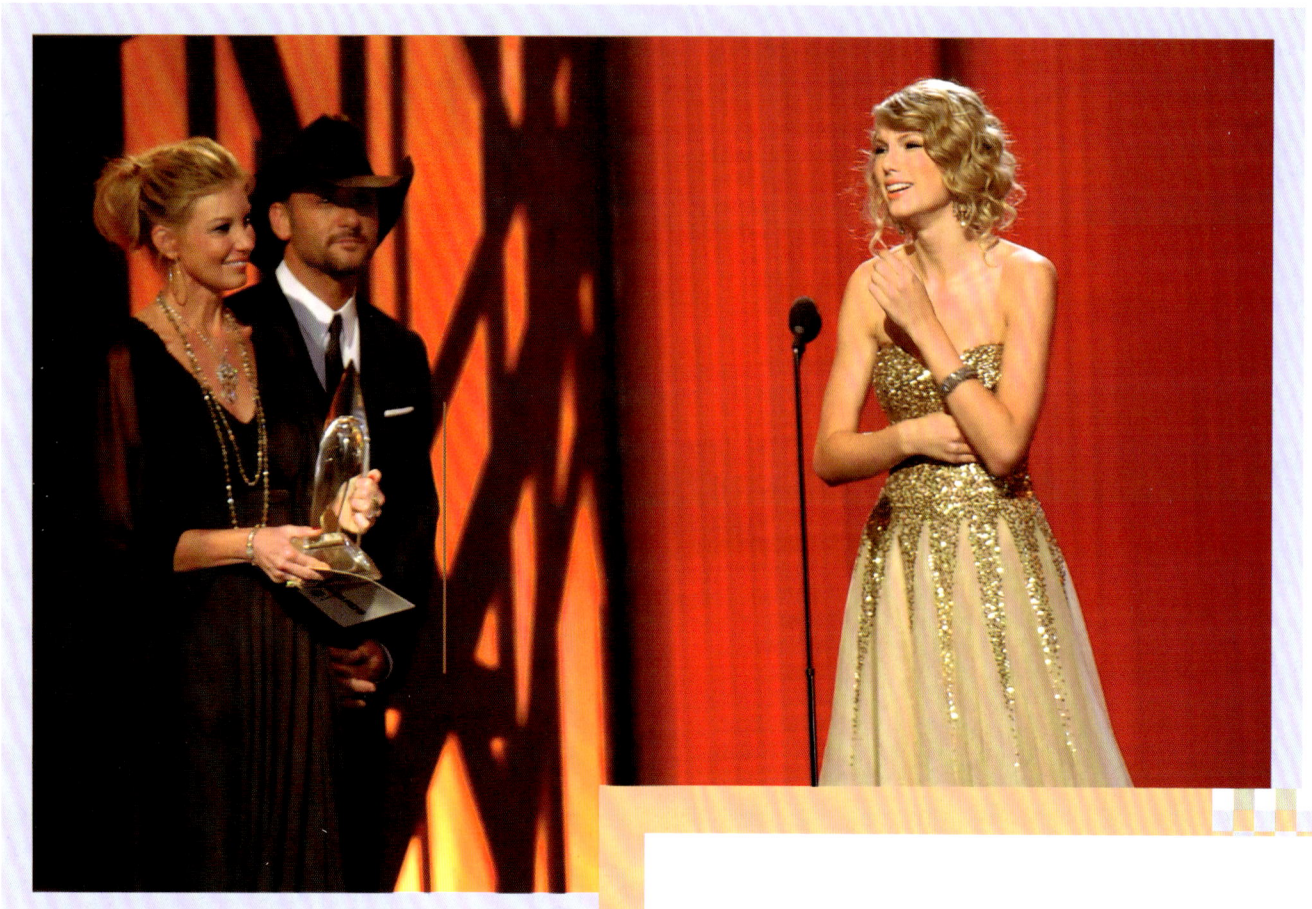

Grammy Award– Winning Album

WHEN

January 31, 2010

Not only did *Fearless* go on to become the top-selling album for two years in a row, it also won the 2010 Grammy Award for Album of the Year, making twenty-year-old Taylor the youngest artist at the time to win this prestigious award.

Taylor later went on Ellen DeGeneres's and Oprah Winfrey's programs and discussed the incident. Throughout this time, Taylor maintained her grace and composure, focusing on the support she received from fans and the love from fellow artists. She wanted to move on without engaging further. One thing that became apparent at this time—and that Taylor was praised for—was how well she handled this experience. More people than just her fans saw Taylor in a new light, as someone who took a humiliating experience and treated it with grace and resilience.

On her MySpace page, she wrote, "I've loved my fans from the very first day, but they've said things and done things recently that make me feel like they're my friends—more now than ever before. I'll never go a day without thinking about our memories together." While Taylor didn't explicitly call out the incident, she acknowledged how her fans remained in her corner and helped her through her own dark time.

While this became a defining point in her career, she did not let it stop her from continuing to stay fearless. It's important to note that Taylor was already selling out arenas and stadiums at this time and was well on her way to becoming the icon she is today.

After the media appearances, Taylor returned to the Fearless Tour and started writing her next album, channeling many of those present feelings into future songs, of course.

Not only did *Fearless* go on to become the top-selling album for two years in a row, it also won the 2010 Grammy Award for Album of the Year, making twenty-year-old Taylor the youngest artist at the time to win this prestigious award.

Her tour had more than 1.2 million attendees and brought in $66.5 million. Despite media scrutiny and backlash, she continued to establish an unparalleled connection with her fans through her fearless courage and creative fan connection. The *Fearless* era was a defining chapter for Taylor, laying the foundation for her evolution as an artist and cultural icon. It was the moment she truly became a household name.

Coming off the financial success of her world tour, a Grammy win, and a best-selling album, Taylor was asked during an interview with Dave Berry at *The Hot Desk* how she chose to be extravagant with her money.

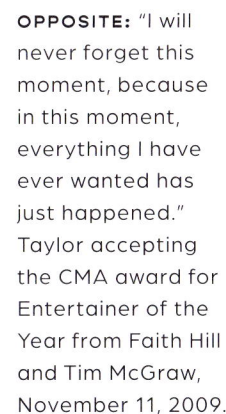

"I just hope that you know how much this means to me, and to Nathan my producer . . . that we get to take this back to Nashville."

Taylor, 2010

OPPOSITE: "I will never forget this moment, because in this moment, everything I have ever wanted has just happened." Taylor accepting the CMA award for Entertainer of the Year from Faith Hill and Tim McGraw, November 11, 2009.

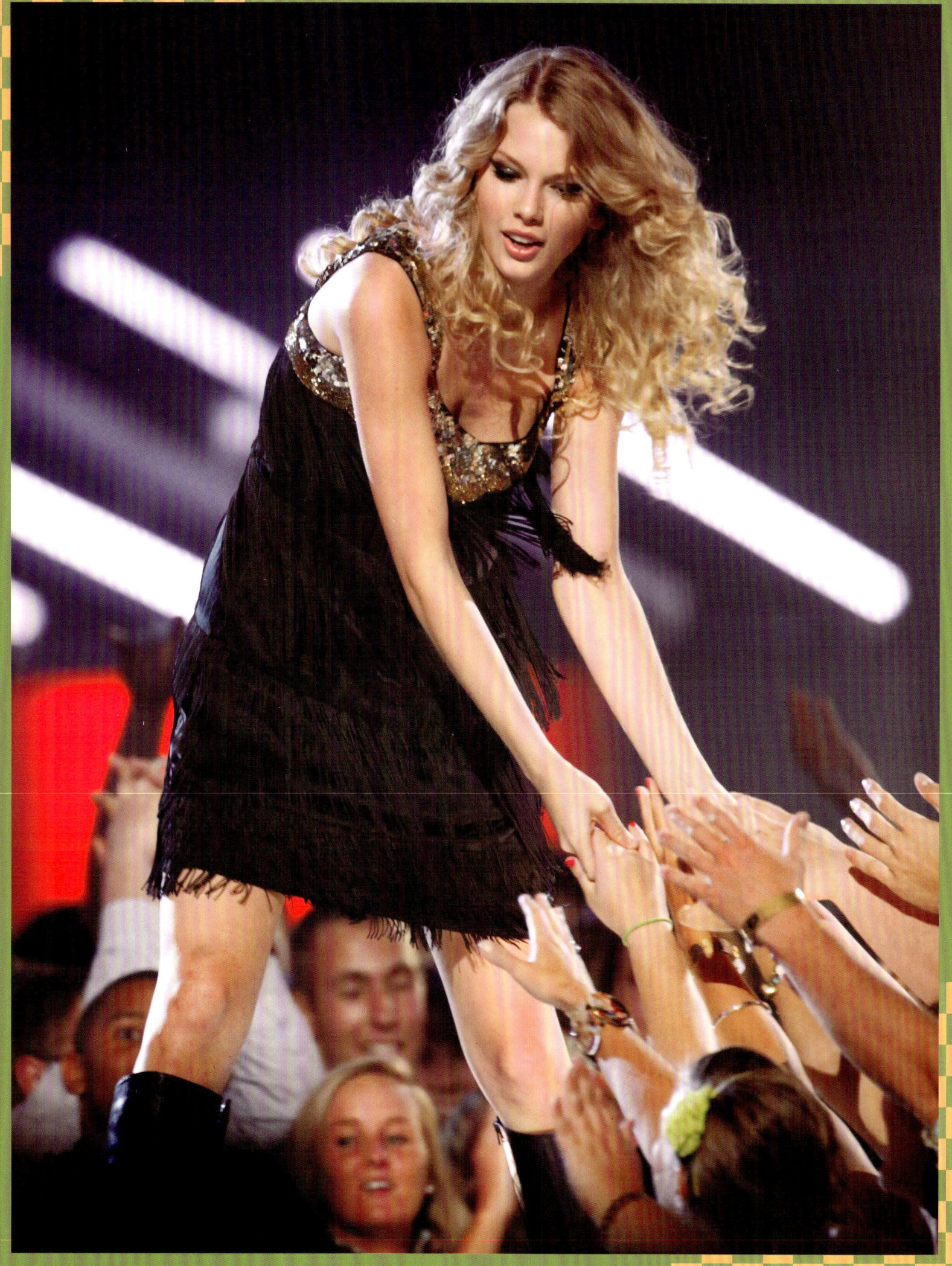

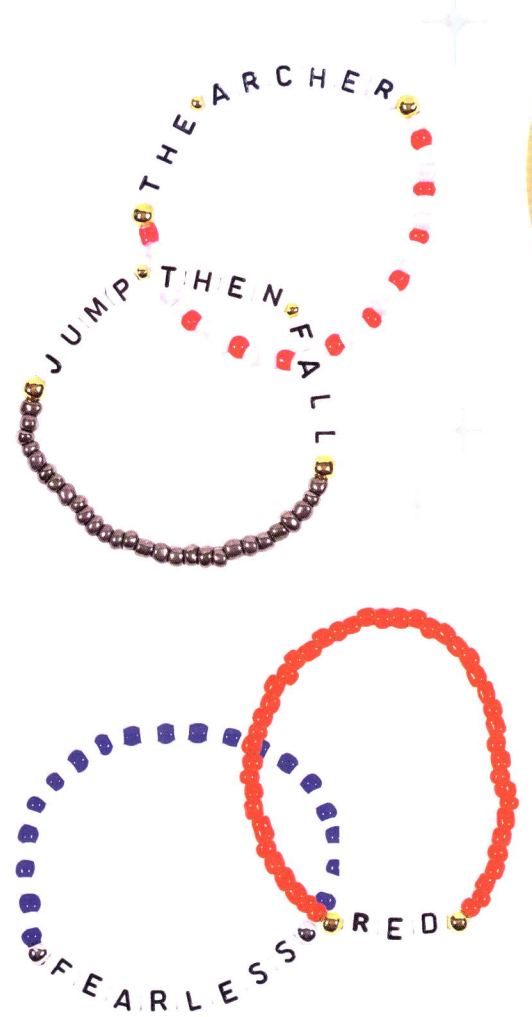

BEFORE THE FRIENDSHIP BRACELETS

Before the infamous friendship bracelets of The Eras Tour, Taylor gave her own bracelets to fans when she met them. In return, fans made special bracelets and gifted them to her. Taylor often wore fan-made bracelets for shows as a sign of appreciation.

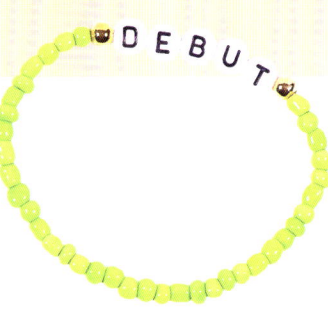

Taylor, at just nineteen years old, said, "I try to take care of my band and my crew and just, you know, for me that's the most fun thing in the world, you know, rather than buying a Lamborghini, I just make sure like everyone feels like they're in the right place. You know, I make sure that everyone feels like they're really taken care of and paying them well, bonusing them well, and also fun things for me, I like being a good tipper at restaurants . . . and just random things that you do because you've been given a really, really good lot in life and I am just really grateful, so I try to just kind of help other people when I can."

This is just one of the many reasons why Taylor remains when so many others fade. She's a fearless leader not just as an artist, but as a businesswoman as well, and through her kindness, she gives back to her band, her crew, her fans, and even strangers at Starbucks.

The last show of the Fearless Tour took place on June 5, 2010, at Gillette Stadium in Foxborough, Massachusetts, one of Taylor's favorite places to play.

The *Fearless* era was pivotal not just in her rise to fame but also in establishing the deep, personal bond between her and her fans—a bond that has only grown stronger over the years. In many ways, fans felt that they were part of Taylor's journey, experiencing the highs and lows with her, all while her music offered a backdrop to their own feelings and journeys. The courage she showed throughout her controversies, and her thoughtfulness along the way, made the *Fearless* era a golden age of connection—one that cemented the Swiftie universe.

OPPOSITE: Taylor connects with her fans during a performance at the CMT Music Awards, June 16, 2009.

COLLABORATION OVER COMPETITION

As Taylor's fame rose, so did her collaborations with other artists. From writing music and performances to hilarious videos, Taylor wasn't afraid to invite people to the table and branch out of her comfort zone.

From country to rock, pop to rap, here is a collection of just some of the people with whom Taylor has worked.

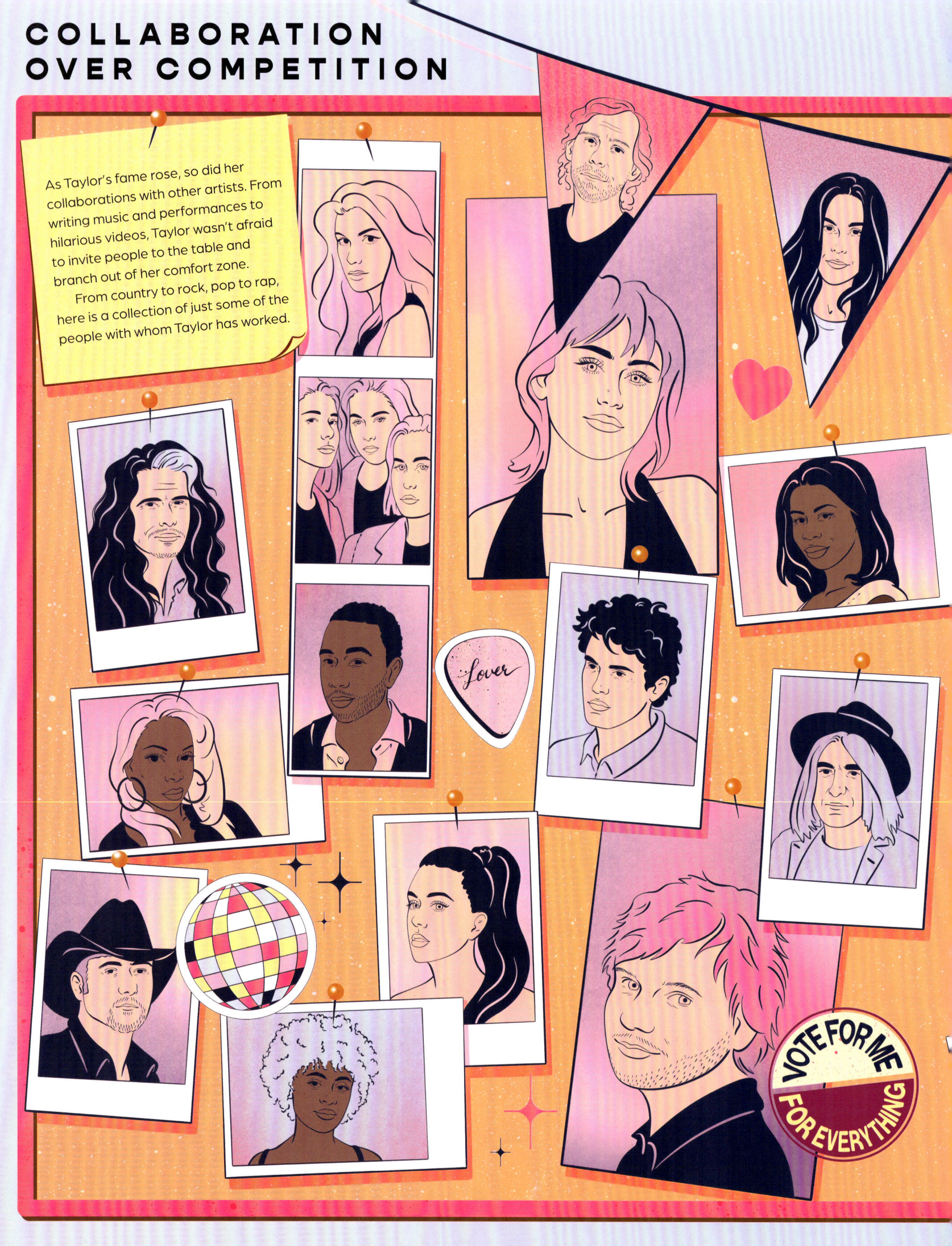

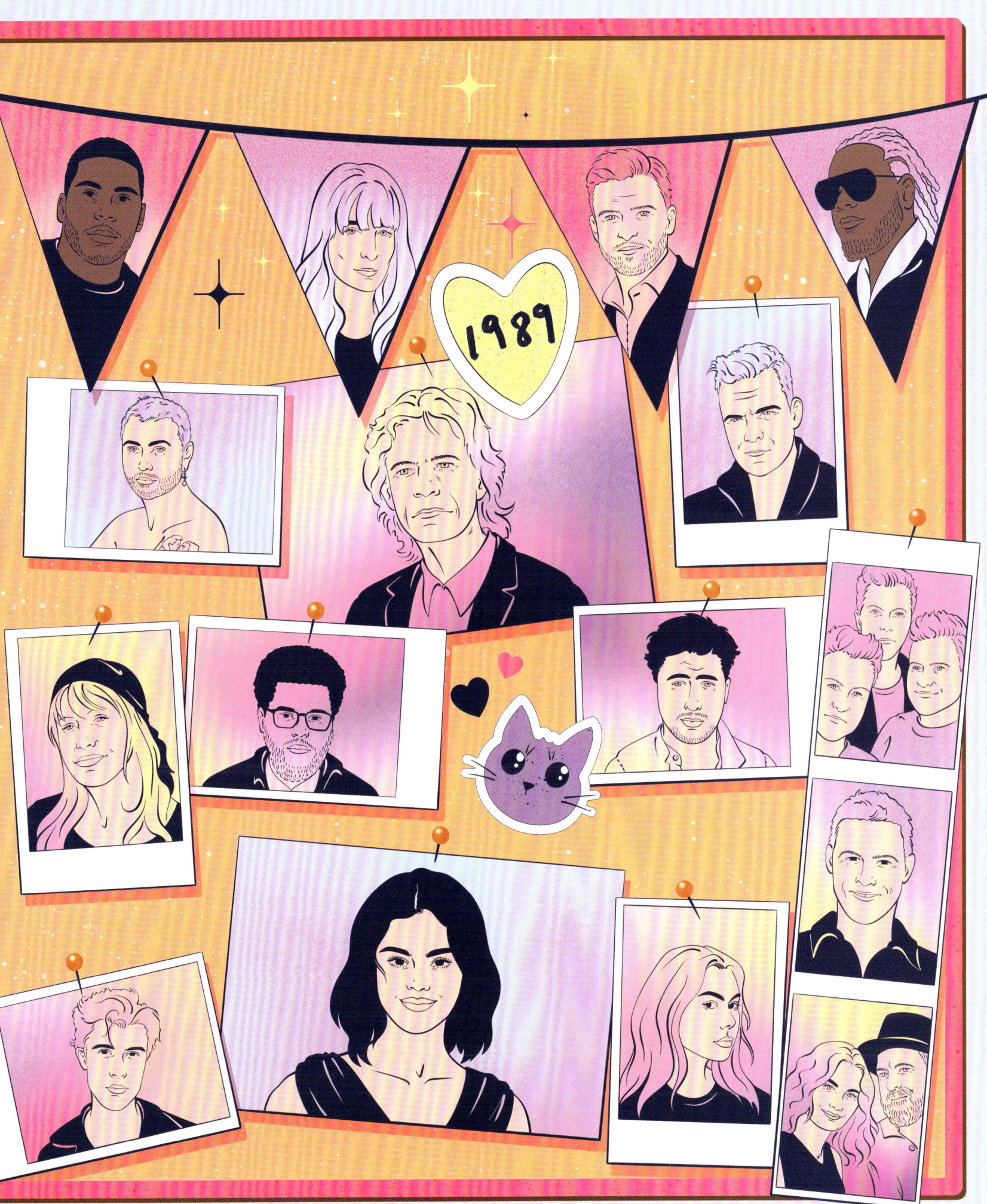

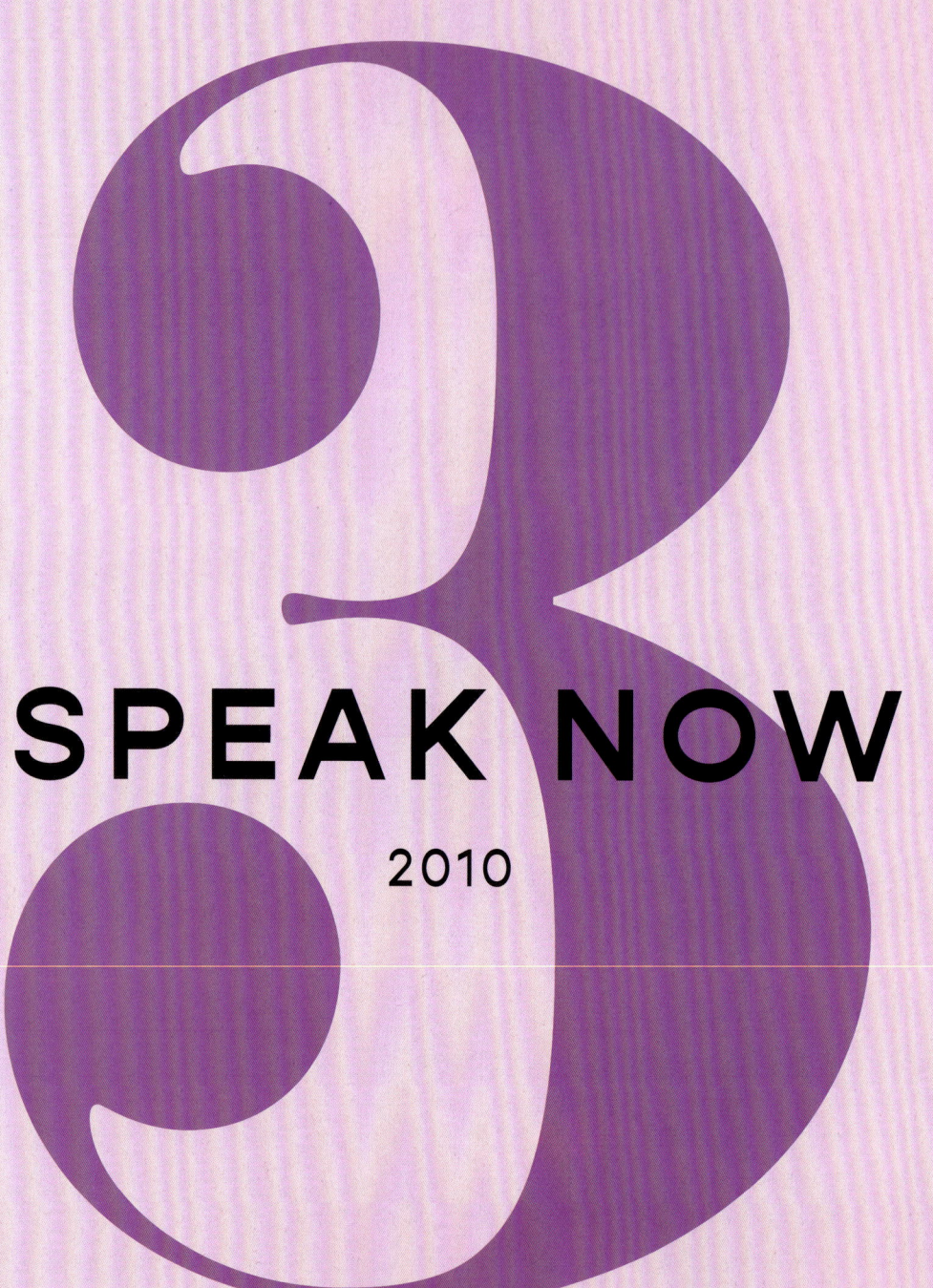

SPEAK NOW

2010

TRUTH IS KIND

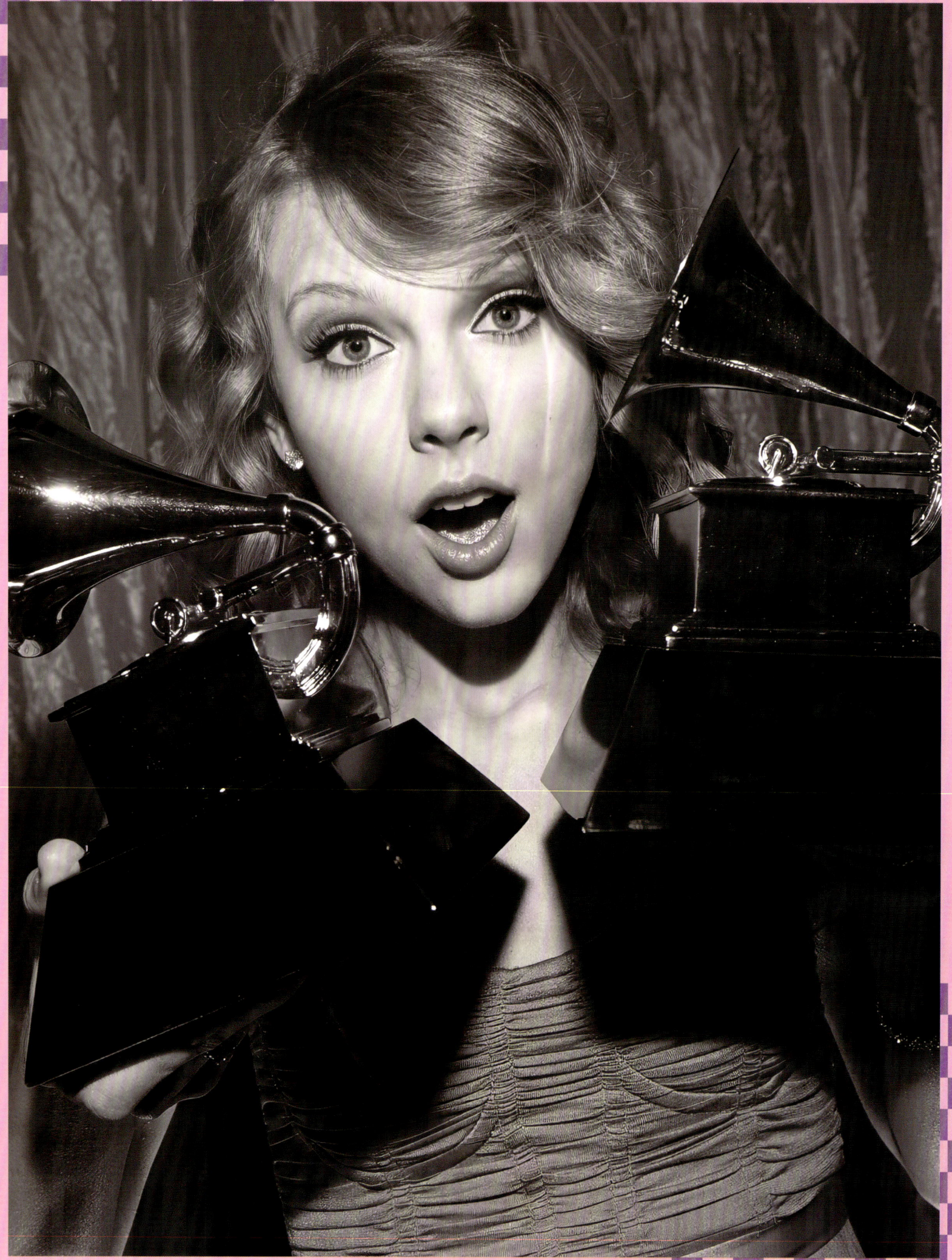

"I don't think you should wait. I think you should speak now."

Taylor, 2010

A WOMAN CAPABLE OF USING HER VOICE

This was the era during which Taylor claimed her validity as a songwriter and a woman capable of using her voice.

Taylor's wildly successful *Fearless* era was a mix of exciting new highs (her first Grammy, a hugely successful tour, and a record-breaking album release) and lows (Taylor's first big media controversy with the infamous MTV VMAs incident).

Aside from the mic-grab seen around the world, Taylor was receiving more and more criticism from the media and music critics alike. In her personal life, media outlets clung to her romantic life and speculated about whom she was dating and whom she'd broken up with and why. She was constantly criticized for writing songs about her relationships and questioned as to what that meant for the guys she dated.

SHE'S THE MAN

Taylor is not only an incredible artist and a creative; she is also an incredible boss and a businesswoman. The *Speak Now* era marked a pivotal moment in her career, transitioning her from an artist to a businesswoman making movies.

Taylor created *Fearless: The Platinum Edition* following the success of the record, but with *Speak Now*, she started out with an exclusive fan experience album from the beginning. She decided to release a special edition of *Speak Now*, available exclusively at Target.

The album featured a special red cover and six additional tracks, including fan favorites like "Ours" and "If This Was a Movie," as well as acoustic versions of songs and behind-the-scenes content that dove deeper into her process as a songwriter. Target produced TV ad campaigns to highlight the partnership. The relationship between Taylor and Target showcased her business acumen and demonstrated her ability to foster mass-market appeal with exclusive licensing. The partnership continues to this day.

Around the same time, Taylor debuted Wonderstruck Taylor Swift, her first-ever perfume, working with the cosmetic company Elizabeth Arden. Its floral scent with notes of raspberry, vanilla, and honeysuckle were designed to make a "sparkling first impression." The perfume name is inspired by a lyric in her song "Enchanted." Its purple bottle—adorned with gold charms of a Moravian star, a dove, and a birdcage—all fit the magical, fairy-tale vibes of that song.

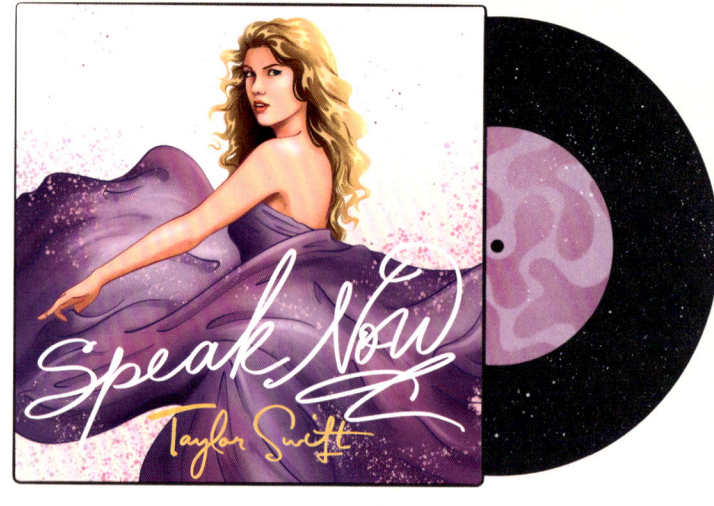

ALBUMS
Speak Now (2010) and *Speak Now World Tour–Live* (2011)

DATE LAUNCHED
October 25, 2010, and November 21, 2011

FIRST SINGLE
"Mine" (August 4, 2010)

OTHER SINGLES
"Back to December" (November 15, 2010), "Mean" (March 7, 2011), "The Story of Us" (April 19, 2011), "Sparks Fly" (July 18, 2011), and "Ours" (December 5, 2011)

TOUR
Speak Now World Tour (February 2011 to March 2012)

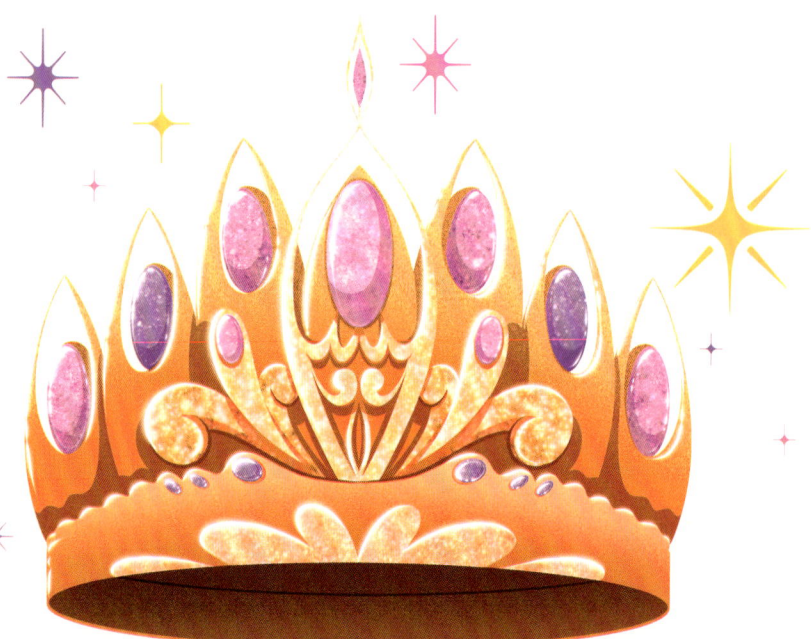

"A fragrance can help someone shape someone's first impression and memory of you," Taylor said. "It's exciting to think that Wonderstruck will play a role in creating some of those memories."

These business decisions highlight Taylor's ability to not only create products that people want, but to do it in an intentional way that truly means something to her fan base.

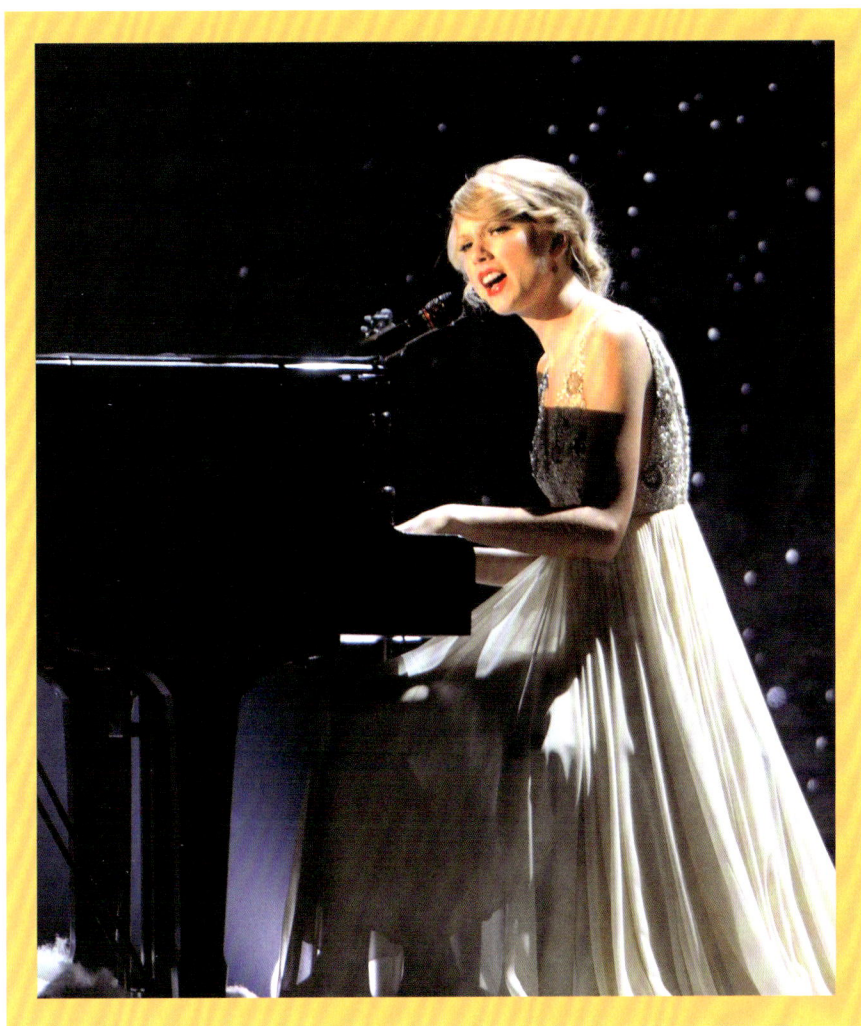

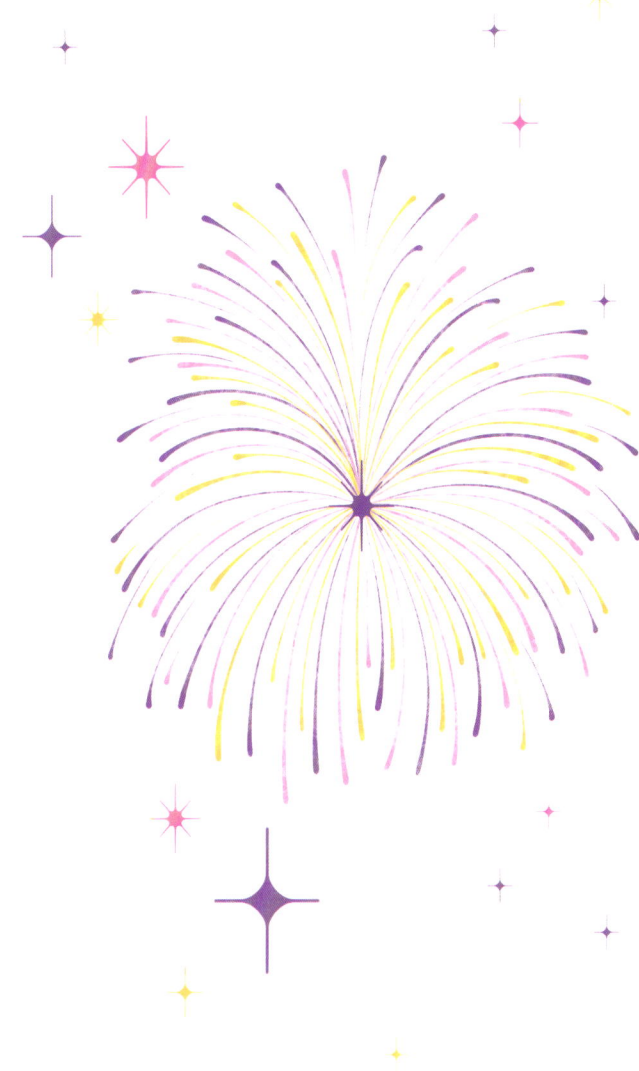

On the career side, Taylor was criticized for her vocal ability, often being compared to other performers of the time. The biggest gut-punch of all was questioning whether she wrote her own music. Taylor had said for years that she wrote her own songs, but people were quick to discredit her. They argued that she featured co-writers on her previous records and, thus, brought a new wave of controversy to whether she was actually as talented a writer as she claimed to be.

Her fairy-tale coming-of-age journey was now moving into early adulthood, a time at which the shelter of protection tends to disappear. Taylor's wide-eyed dreams were slowly colliding with the reality of the world. While she no longer dealt with bullies at school,

from where she could run home to her mom, she was now dealing with real-life bullies—this time, with an entire world stage looking at her, wondering what she was going to say or do. While she could still run home to Mama Swift, she was forced to confront these challenges differently. She needed to start using her voice in a different way.

Taylor accepted this challenge and did what she does best. As she traveled around the world on the Fearless Tour between 2009 and 2010, she was feverishly writing and recording new songs, turning all the experiences, raw emotions, pain, hurt, and grief into artistry. She was not just writing songs; she was crafting her response to things that she had not spoken about in public.

PAGE 54: Taylor at the 52nd Grammy Awards, January 31, 2010. She was nominated for eight awards and won four, including Album of the Year (for *Fearless*).

ABOVE: Taylor performs "Back to December" at the 44th Annual CMA Awards, November 10, 2010.

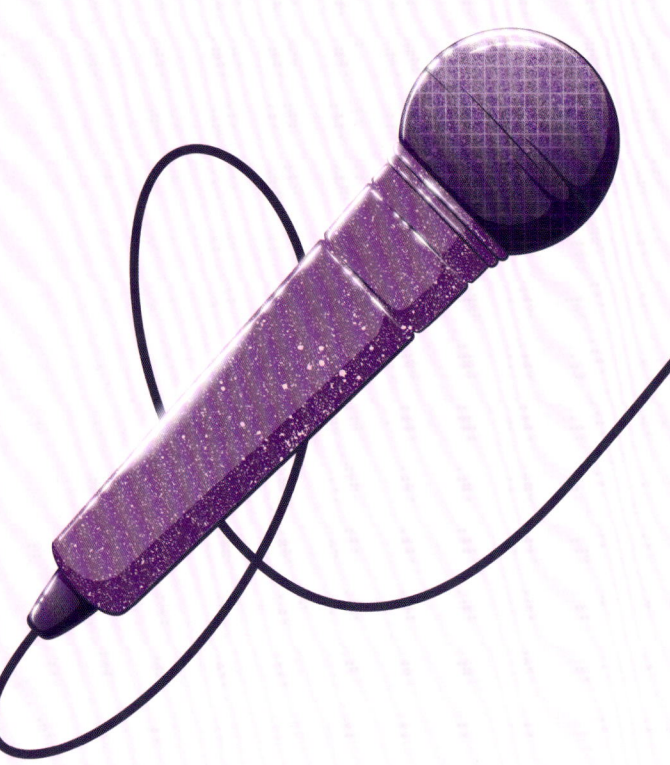

Enter: *Speak Now*

This was an era during which Taylor leaned all the way into using her voice.

In the prologue to *Speak Now*, Taylor wrote, "In the years since, I have developed a thicker skin about public criticism and the cynicism with which people approach the music I make. At that time, it leveled me. I had these voices in my head telling me that I had the perfect chance and I blew it. I hadn't been good enough. I had given it all I had and been found wanting. I wanted to get better, to challenge myself, and to build on my skills as a writer, an artist, and a performer. I didn't want to just be handed respect and acceptance in my field, I wanted to earn it. To try and confront these demons, I underwent extensive vocal training and made a decision that would completely define this album: I decided I would write it entirely on my own."

She went on to say, "I had the nagging sense that in the most intense moments of my life, I had frozen. I had said nothing publicly. I still don't know if it was out of instinct, not wanting to seem impolite, or just overwhelming fear. But

I made sure to say it in all these songs. I decided to call the album *Speak Now*. It was a play on the 'speak now or forever hold your peace' moment in weddings, but for me it symbolized a chance to respond to the chatter and commentary around my own life."

Vocal Training

"I had been widely and publicly slammed for my singing voice." —Taylor Swift

WHEN

After the success of Taylor's *Fearless* album, criticism quickly followed, especially when it came to both her writing and her singing ability. To combat that criticism, Taylor decided to not only write all the songs on *Speak Now* herself, but she also underwent intense vocal training. She said, "I wanted to get better, to challenge myself, and to build on my skills as a writer, an artist, and a performer." While she has likely worked with several vocal coaches over the years, most notable are Norma Garbo and Brett Manning.

OPPOSITE: Taylor sporting the lyrics from "Long Live" on her arm during her Madison Square Garden concert on the Speak Now World Tour, November 21, 2011.

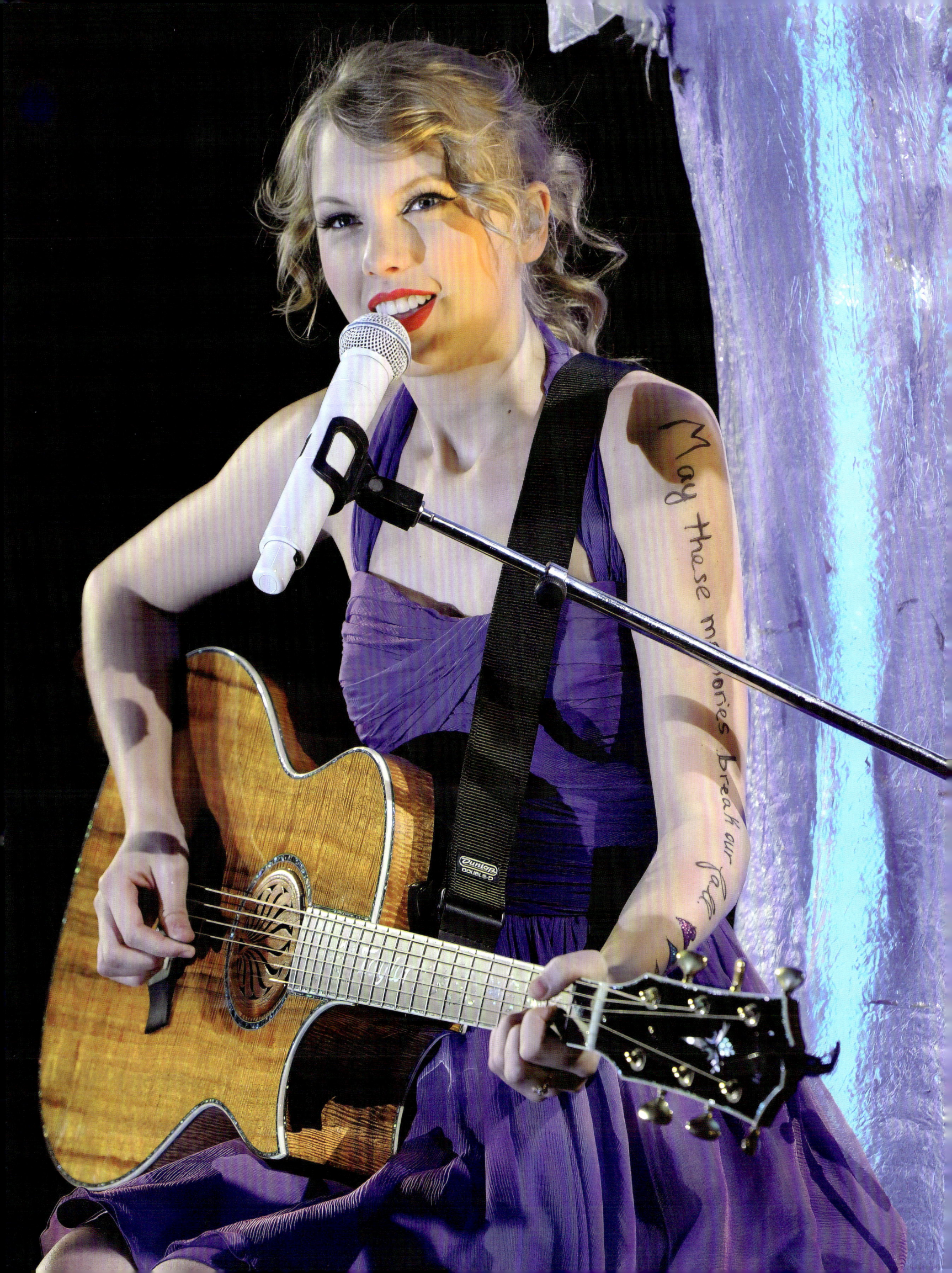

In recent interviews, Taylor has said that people often underestimate how much she will inconvenience herself to make a point. The *Speak Now* era may be when this concept began for her and will influence how she responds to criticism in future eras. While she isn't afraid to speak up and use her voice, especially as she gets older, Taylor knows when to remain quiet and use her art to respond. She wants her words to hold weight, and she's careful about when to use them to do so.

In *Speak Now*, Taylor uses her voice, complete with the addition of vocal lessons, to finally tell her side of the story, in her own words. The album is her most rock, heavy metal–leaning album, featuring more rock sounds than country or pop.

The storytelling, however, is where this album really shines through, as does her voice. The emotions are raw and often extreme.

The title track, "Mine," leans into the adolescent love reminiscent of her debut release. In the fan-favorite "Back to December," Taylor owns her part in a relationship that ended and issues an apology.

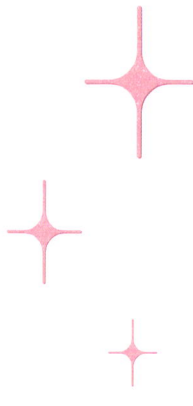

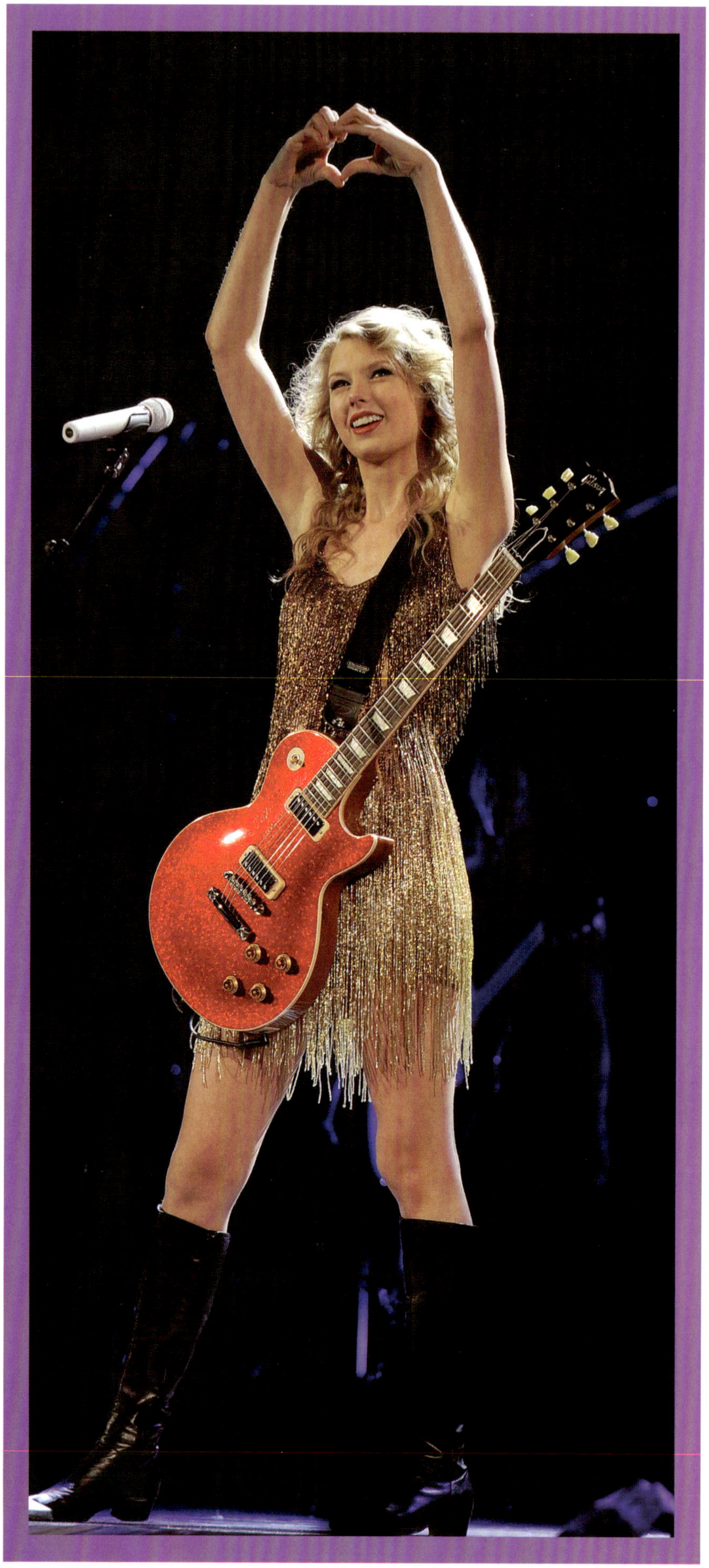

RIGHT: Taylor in the outfit she wore for the opening set of songs on the Speak Now World Tour, 2011.

TRACK FIVE

Track five has become a phenomenon in the Swiftie community. Fans first noticed it during the *Speak Now* era, and over time, it's become apparent that the fifth song on her albums is often the most raw, vulnerable, and heartbreaking one. Track five on *Speak Now* is "Dear John," and on her following album, *Red*, "All Too Well" marks one of her most gut-wrenching, fan-favorite songs to date. Seeing those two songs as track five back-to-back signaled a pattern for Swifties. Most track five songs tend to be softer, leaning into acoustic guitars or pianos to emphasize the heightened emotional toll.

When Taylor caught wind of this fan theory, she said it wasn't intentional but that the fans were spot-on with their assessment. On an Instagram live in 2019 when promoting the *Lover* album, Taylor said, "Track five is kind of a tradition that really started with you guys because I didn't realize I was doing this, but as I was making albums, I guess—I don't know why—but instinctively I was just kind of putting a very vulnerable, personal, honest, emotional song as track five."

She went on to say, "So, because you noticed this, I kind of started to put the songs that were really honest, emotional, vulnerable, and personal as track five. So, that has definitely happened in the case of track five on this album, *Lover*."

Now, when Taylor shares the track list for an upcoming album, fans love to speculate on how soul crushing the track five will be based on the title alone and eagerly await the first listen when an album launches.

TRACK FIVES LIST

"Cold As You," *Taylor Swift* (2006)

"Fifteen," *Fearless* (2008)

"Dear John," *Speak Now* (2010)

"All Too Well," *Red* (2012)

"All You Had to Do Was Stay," *1989* (2014)

"Delicate," *reputation* (2017)

"The Archer," *Lover* (2019)

"My Tears Ricochet," *folklore* (2020)

"Tolerate It," *evermore* (2020)

"You're on Your Own, Kid," *Midnights* (2022)

"So Long, London," *The Tortured Poets Department* (2024)

Track five is just another example of how Taylor connects deeply with her fans. She acknowledged the accuracy in the fan theory and continued to ensure her track-five songs delivered the vulnerability and emotional depth fans have come to love and appreciate.

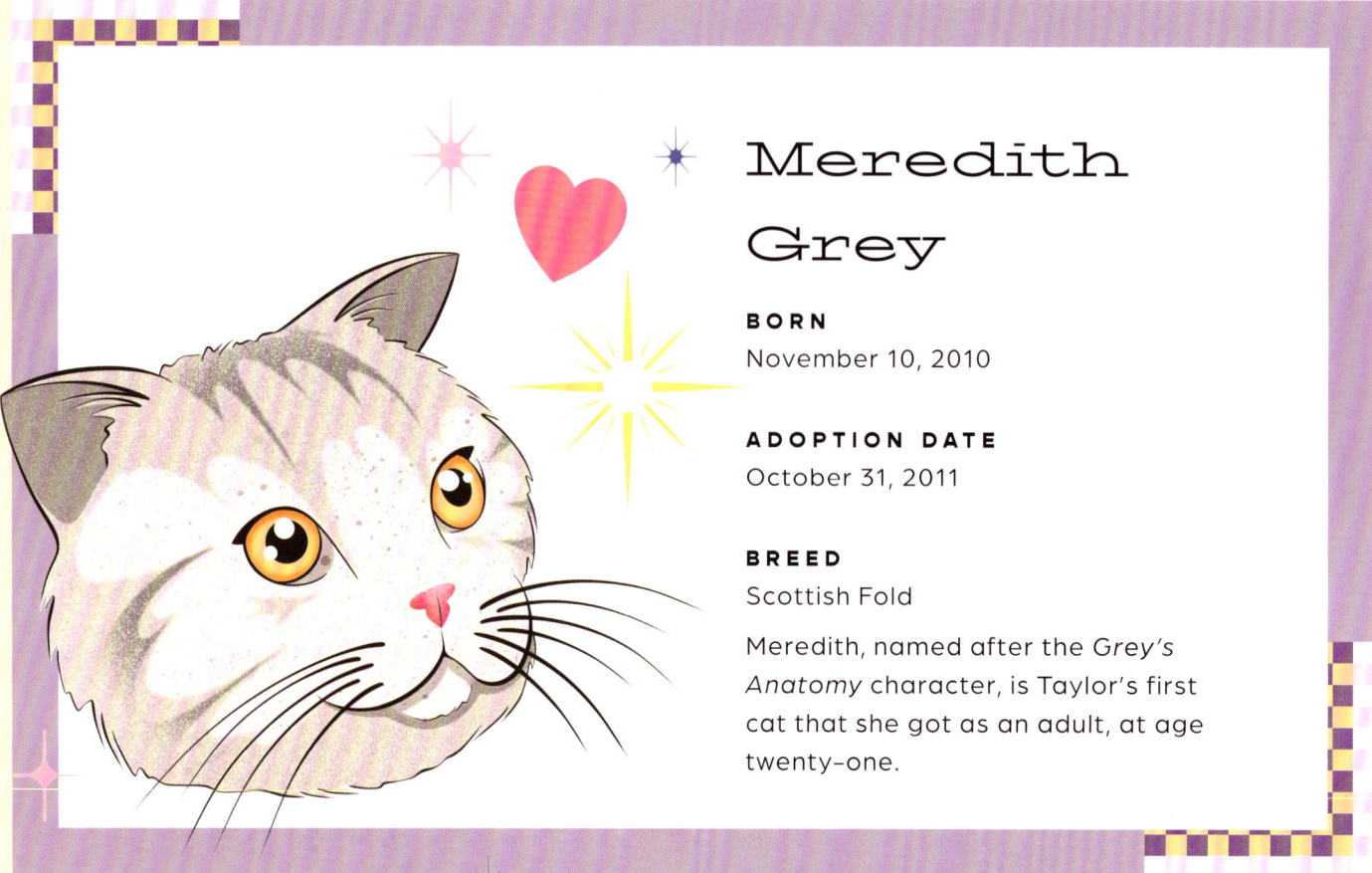

Meredith Grey

BORN
November 10, 2010

ADOPTION DATE
October 31, 2011

BREED
Scottish Fold

Meredith, named after the *Grey's Anatomy* character, is Taylor's first cat that she got as an adult, at age twenty-one.

Taylor explores the hurt caused by critics on the track "Mean," in which she sings about being ridiculed by someone who thinks they are superior. By the end of the song, she flips the narrative and realizes that the bully is, ultimately, powerless. This song had a significant impact on fans. It served as a reminder that bullies often act out their own insecurities and that fans should keep going because they would ultimately rise above it all. With the rise of online bullying during that time, this song became an anthem in which many fans found comfort. While their experiences with bullying might have been completely different, fans connected with the song and were reminded that Taylor shared their feelings.

In a twist of extremes, the song "Innocent" addresses the MTV VMAs incident, but from the perspective of someone looking on with empathy and trying to understand why people might be mean and do the things they do. At the end of the song, you can hear Taylor showing forgiveness by saying who you are is not what you did.

"Dear John" is one of the most scathing tracks on the entire album, according to Taylor herself. Allegedly about musician John Mayer, it's just detailed enough that he'd realize it.

"Long Live" was written during the *Fearless* era on the very last day of the tour. A tribute to her band, it has since become a love letter between Taylor and her fans.

This era really centers around Taylor's words. *Speak Now* is a completely self-written album that addresses her pain, relationships, and experiences in unexpected, introspective detail.

Speak Now
World Tour

Taylor wasted no time between the album release and getting back on tour. The Speak Now World Tour ran from February 2011 to March 2012 and spanned 111 shows across 19 countries.

As the show began, the stage lit up and concertgoers heard Taylor's voice say, "There's a time for silence and a time for waiting your turn. But if you know how you feel and you so clearly know what you need to say, you'll know it. I don't think you should wait; I think you should *Speak Now.*"

This was Taylor's most theatrical and immersive concert experience yet. Her favorite Broadway musical, *Wicked*, inspired some of the set design, which included large video screens, pyrotechnics, confetti, dancers, and special stage setups. She rang a massive bell tower during "Haunted," and a glittering, flying balcony for "Love Story" brought her around the stadiums to ensure that every fan had a great seat.

A fan favorite of this tour included her acoustic performances, which were different in each city. Taylor sat under a large, lit tree for this set, with just her and a ukulele. Fans could not wait to see what surprise song their stop would get, and this became big talk in the Swiftie-verse. She even invited special guests like Justin Bieber, Usher, and Nicki Minaj onto the stage, demonstrating her star power and love of collaboration over competition.

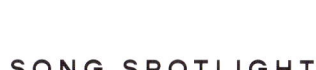

SONG SPOTLIGHT

"Speak Now"

This title track was inspired by one of Taylor's friends, who told her that her childhood sweetheart/crush was getting married. Taylor said she randomly said to her friend, "Ha, are you going to speak now? You know, like storm the church. Speak now or forever hold your peace. I'll go with you, I'll play guitar." And that's how the song and album title, *Speak Now*, was born.

ALBUM

Speak Now

RELEASED

2010

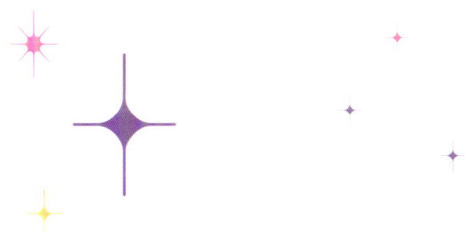

FOLLOWING PAGES: Taylor and lead guitarist Grant Mickelson during the Columbus, Ohio, concert on the Speak Now World Tour, June 7, 2011.

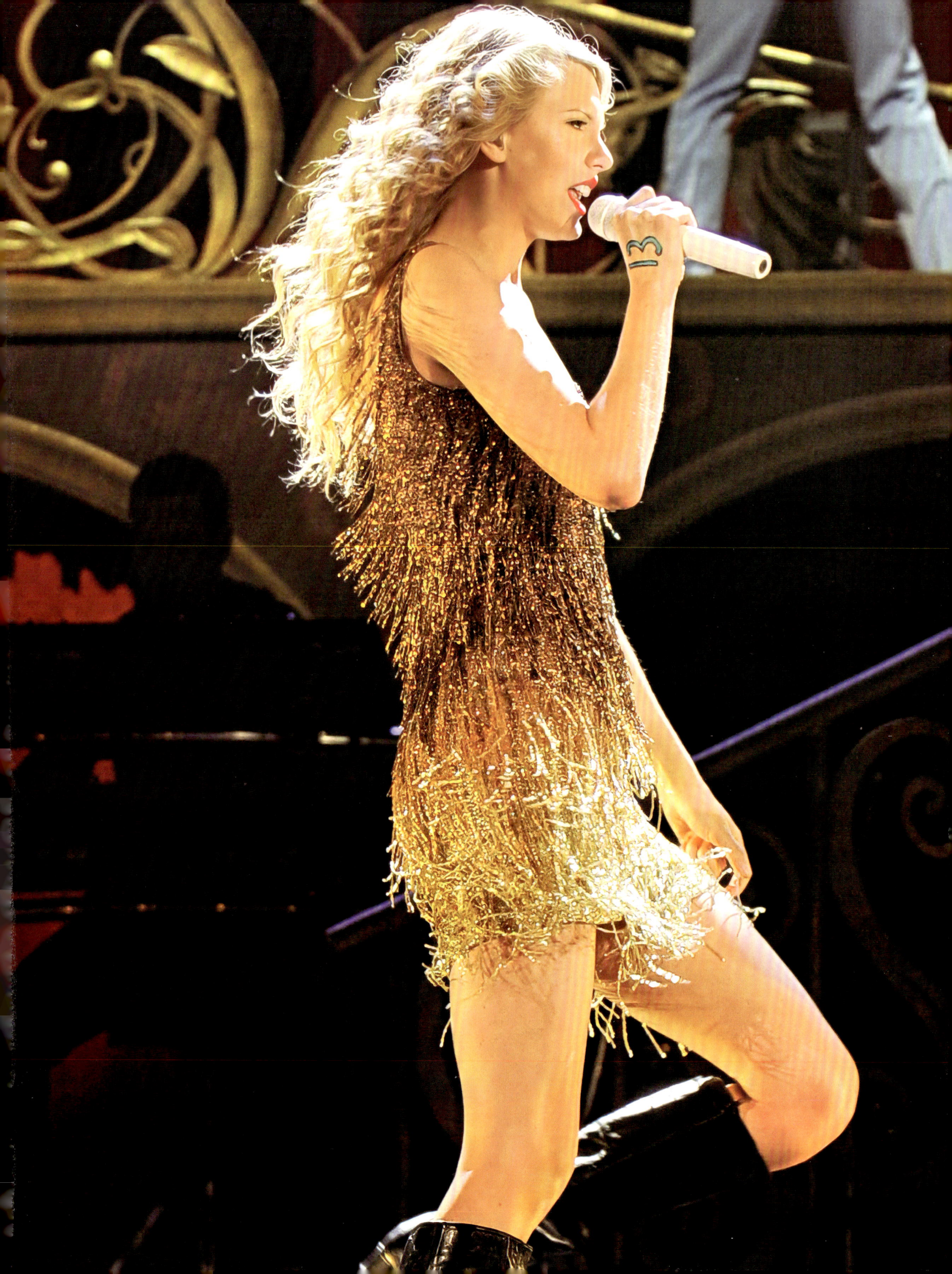

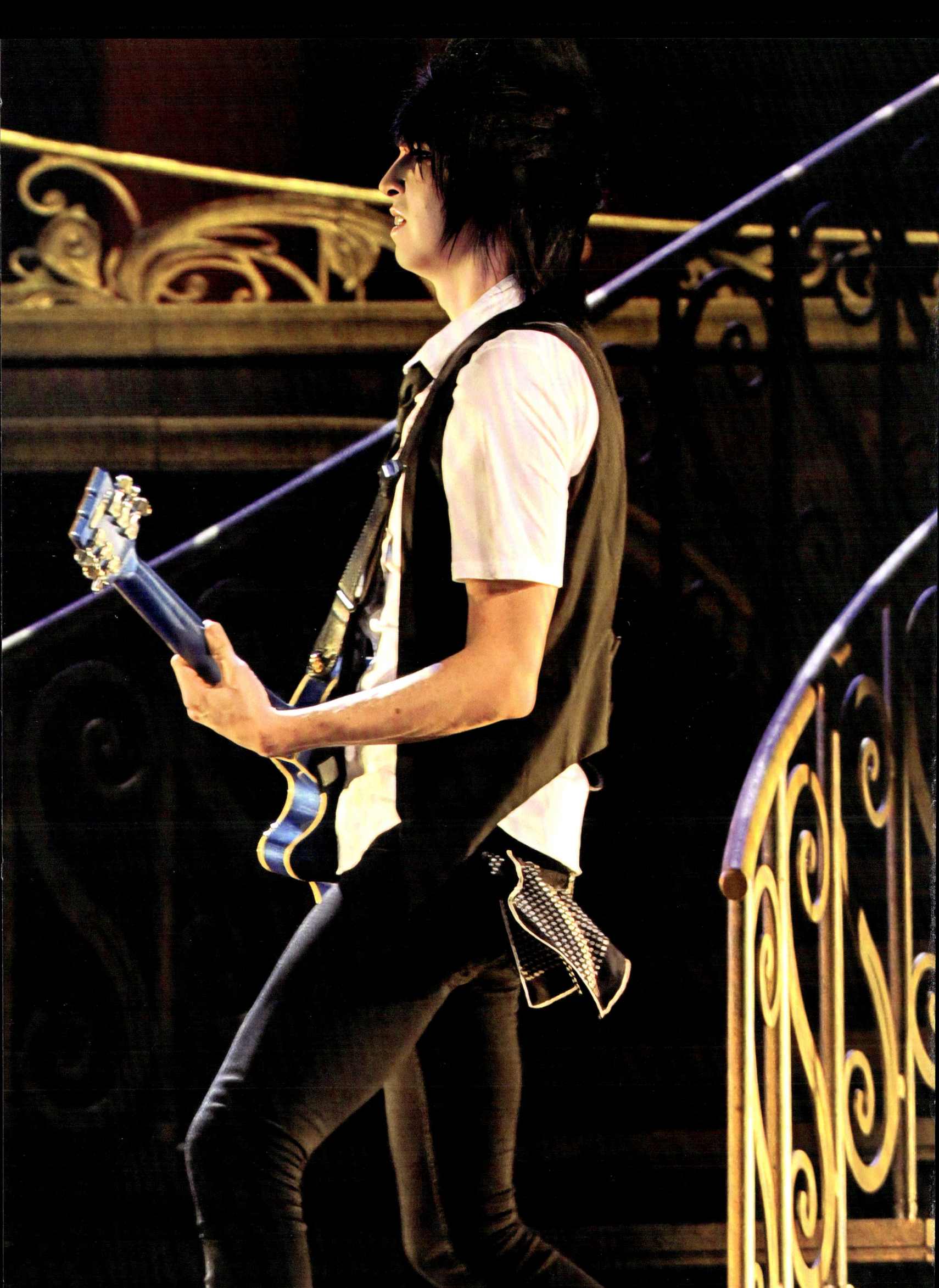

"LONG LIVE"

"Long Live" is one of Taylor's most beloved fan anthems, originally released on the album *Speak Now*. Taylor wrote the song during the *Fearless* era as a tribute to her band and crew to capture the feeling, perseverance, and gratitude she shares with those who helped her along the way.

Over the years, "Long Live" took on a deeper meaning, evolving from a celebration of her bandmates to a love letter to her fans. The *Speak Now* CD lyric book even featured an Easter egg in the form of a secret message spelled out in the lyrics that said "For You."

Reflecting on the song, Taylor said, "This song for me is like looking at a photo album of all the award shows, and all the stadium shows, and all the hands in the air in the crowd. It's sort of the first love song that I've written to my team."

The Speak Now World Tour grossed $123.7 million, cementing Taylor's status as a global superstar. Her authenticity and connection to her fans mixed with her theatrics and willingness to work hard were all praised by critics.

The *Speak Now* era included a wide range of accomplishments, including the album selling more than six million copies in the United States alone and achieving multi-platinum status. The album debuted at No. 1 on the Billboard 200 with more than one million copies sold in its first week, making Taylor the youngest artist at the time to achieve this feat.

Most notably, her song "Mean" went on to win Grammy Awards for Best Country Solo Performance and Best Country Song in 2012. She also earned a Billboard Music Award for Top Country Album and an American Music Award for Favorite Country Album, and she won Entertainer of the Year at the Academy of Country Music Awards.

Aside from the awards and accolades, Taylor credits her fans with helping her get through this tough time. In the prologue to *Speak Now*, Taylor wrote, "The outstretched hands of those bright and beautiful faces of the fans. Their support was like an open palm that reached out and helped me up off the ground when others were, frankly, mean."

Taylor continued to host T Parties after her concerts, but she was also looking for new

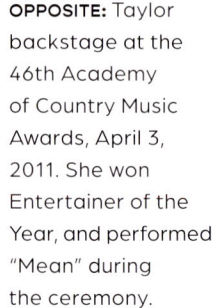

OPPOSITE: Taylor backstage at the 46th Academy of Country Music Awards, April 3, 2011. She won Entertainer of the Year, and performed "Mean" during the ceremony.

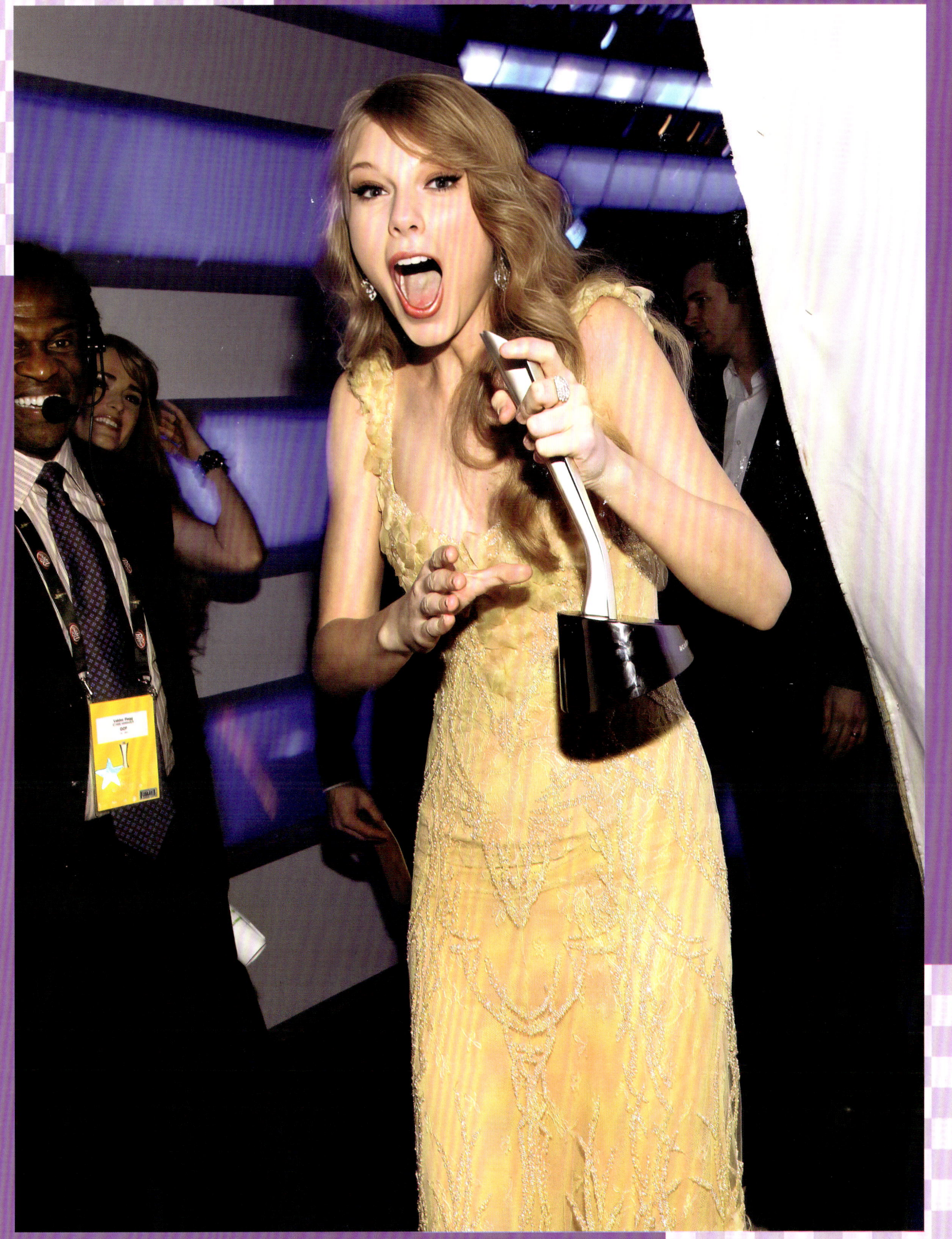

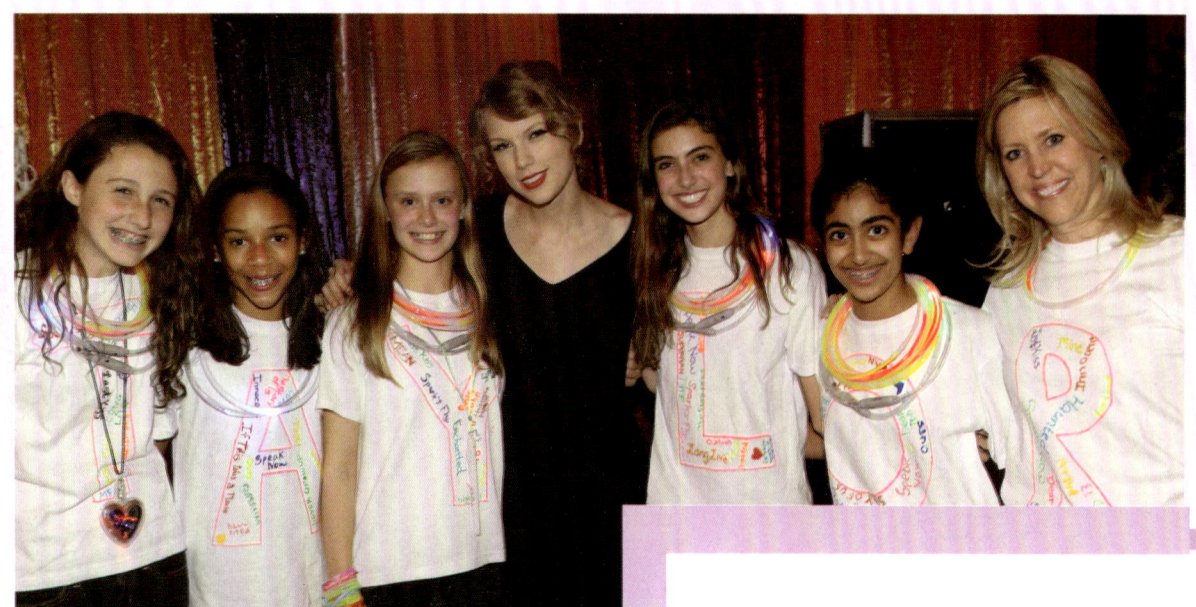

The T Party Room

The T Party room was a special backstage area created during each tour stop. Taylor's mom, Andrea, would invite fans to hang after the show and meet Taylor, at no additional cost.

EST.

T Parties started on the Speak Now World Tour and ran through the Reputation Stadium Tour.

OTHER NAMES

She changed the names of each T Party room in connection with the tour. The Red Tour room was called "Club Red"; The 1989 World Tour room was called "Loft '89"; and the Reputation Stadium Tour room was called "Rep Room."

ways to connect with more fans. While social media platforms like Twitter were still new, Taylor created "Taylor Connect," a forum that ran until 2013 and allowed Taylor to connect directly with her fans. This dedicated platform, run on her website, acted as both a social network and a forum. Taylor and her team would post first looks and exclusive content, and for many, the site offered a chance to connect with fellow Swifties who often transformed into real-life friends.

Taylor also used these platforms to learn about her fans and help those in need. While it was not always publicized, she helped fans pay for college textbooks and sent money to fans going through illnesses or financial hardships. She would respond with words of encouragement to fans

Equipped with her pen in hand, Taylor was writing her own story.

who let her know that they were going through a breakup. Often, she would create care packages or handwritten notes and send them to fans to celebrate their accomplishments or give them encouragement if they were struggling.

Taylor's actions during this time were often private and personal. Whether through handwritten letters, conversations on the forum, thoughtful snail-mail gifts, or invites to a T Party, she constantly went out of her way to ensure that her fans felt loved and appreciated. This helped her form an intimate and close bond with her fans, who appreciated the empathy and kindness from Taylor.

In addition to helping her fans, she gave back in other ways by supporting causes she believed in and aiding communities that supported her. In 2011, she donated six thousand books to the Berks County Public Libraries in her native Pennsylvania. Librarians got to choose books based on their needs, and Taylor took care of the bill.

Before the Speak Now World Tour, there were devastating tornadoes that tore through

the southern United States. One of Taylor's dancers lived in Alabama and shared photos of some of the damage done. Without hesitation, Taylor decided to turn her tour rehearsal into a benefit show. She said, "Here we are at a rehearsal, in an arena, with empty seats. What if we fill those seats? And give the proceeds to the victims of the tornadoes?"

The benefit, which was called, "Speak Now . . . Help Now," took place on May 21, 2011, at the Nashville Bridgestone Arena in Nashville, Tennessee. The stadium held 13,700 fans, raised $750,000 in ticket sales, and 100 percent of sales were donated to the Community Foundation of Middle Tennessee to help aid in relief.

Equipped with her pen in hand, Taylor was writing her own story, in her own words, and was ready to speak her mind more boldly. She confronted the critics head-on with her resilience and her artistry. But more than anything, she continued to use her voice in other big ways—encouraging her fans, fostering empathy for others, and speaking her mind when it mattered most.

OPPOSITE: Taylor meets her fans backstage in the T Party room after her Madison Garden performance on the Speak Now World Tour, November 21, 2011.

GO DOWN THE RABBIT HOLE

Taylor Swift's Easter eggs started early in her career and have become a defining connection between her and her fans. She hides messages, symbols, and clues to share a special message, hint at upcoming albums, reference things in her personal life, and more. She began by placing secret messages in her liner notes, and now anything is up for Easter-egg speculation, including social media posts, outfits, interviews, speeches, and even her nail polish.

Go down the rabbit hole of Easter eggs throughout the eras.

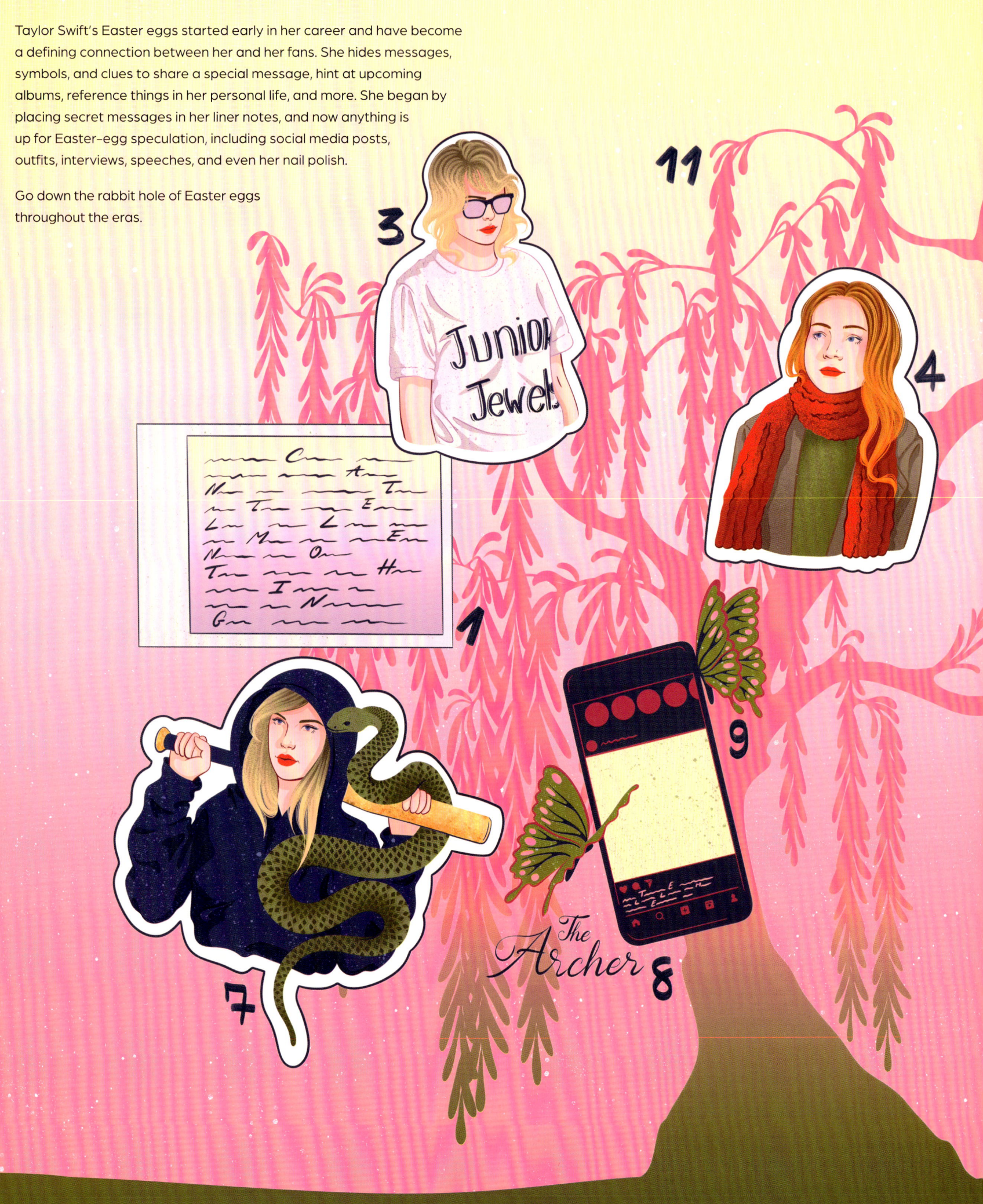

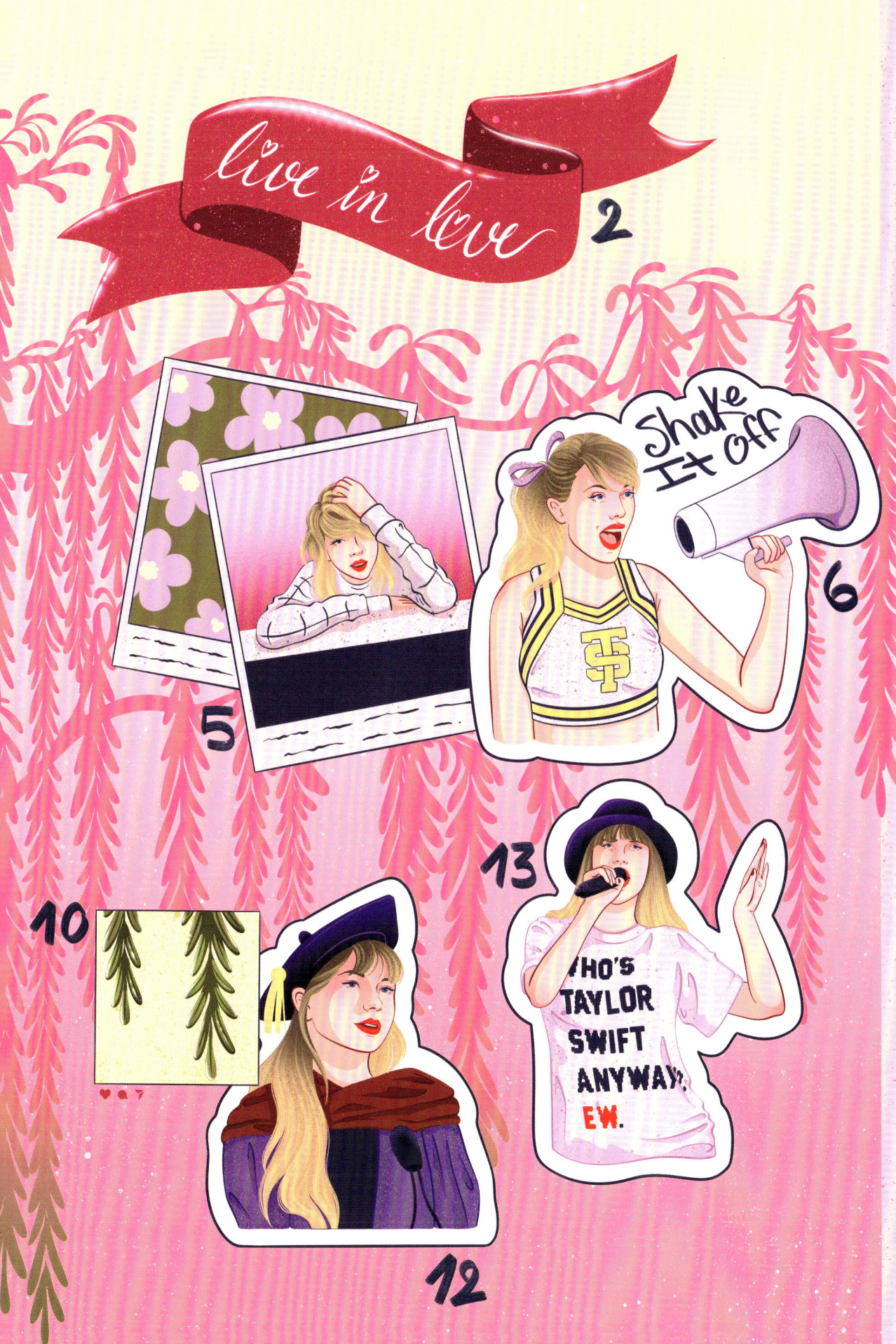

live in love

1 In the album's liner notes, she used capitalized letters in her lyrics to spell out secret messages for each song. For example: "Tim McGraw" spelled out: CAN'T TELL ME NOTHING.

2 In the "You Belong with Me" video, Taylor wore a shirt with the name "Junior Jewels" on it. The shirt features a lot of different names.

3 Red scarf worn by actress Sadie Sink in the "We Are Never Ever Getting Back Together" video.

4 Social Media Teases: Taylor began using Instagram and Twitter to drop hints about upcoming singles and albums by posting cryptic nods to future lyrics and emojis to build anticipation.

5 Polaroids in the Album Packaging: Each Polaroid included a unique lyric or caption inviting fans to piece together a deeper story.

6 The "Shake It Off" Video: Hidden throughout the choreography and set design were nods to Taylor's previous eras, from her country roots to her transition into pop.

7 Snake Imagery: The snake became the defining symbol of *reputation*. This was Taylor's opportunity to reclaim the narrative after being labeled a "snake" online. She teased this transformation with cryptic Instagram posts of snake scales before announcing the album.

8 "ME!" Video Clues: This music video hinted at track titles like "The Archer," and the painting on the wall was a nod to The Chicks. Plus, Taylor adopted her cat Benjamin from this music video!

9 Capitalized Letters in Posts: Moving away from liner notes, Taylor started capitalizing letters in captions on Instagram, leading fans to speculate about lyrics, titles, and even release dates.

10 Album Announcements: Taylor surprised fans with *folklore* in July 2020, but there'd been subtle hints in her prior social media posts, such as woodsy aesthetics and poetic captions.

11 "Cardigan" Video: Easter eggs in the video pointed to the *evermore* follow-up via the presence of a willow tree and recurring nature motifs.

12 NYU Graduation Speech: Taylor was presented with an honorary doctorate degree from New York University. She served as the commencement speaker and used her speech to drop hints to lyrics from an upcoming album.

13 Eras Tour Merch and Set List: The tour itself is a playground for Easter eggs, with costumes, visuals, and transitions hinting at future projects. Illustrate the "22" shirt or the "who is taylor swift anyway EW" T-shirt.

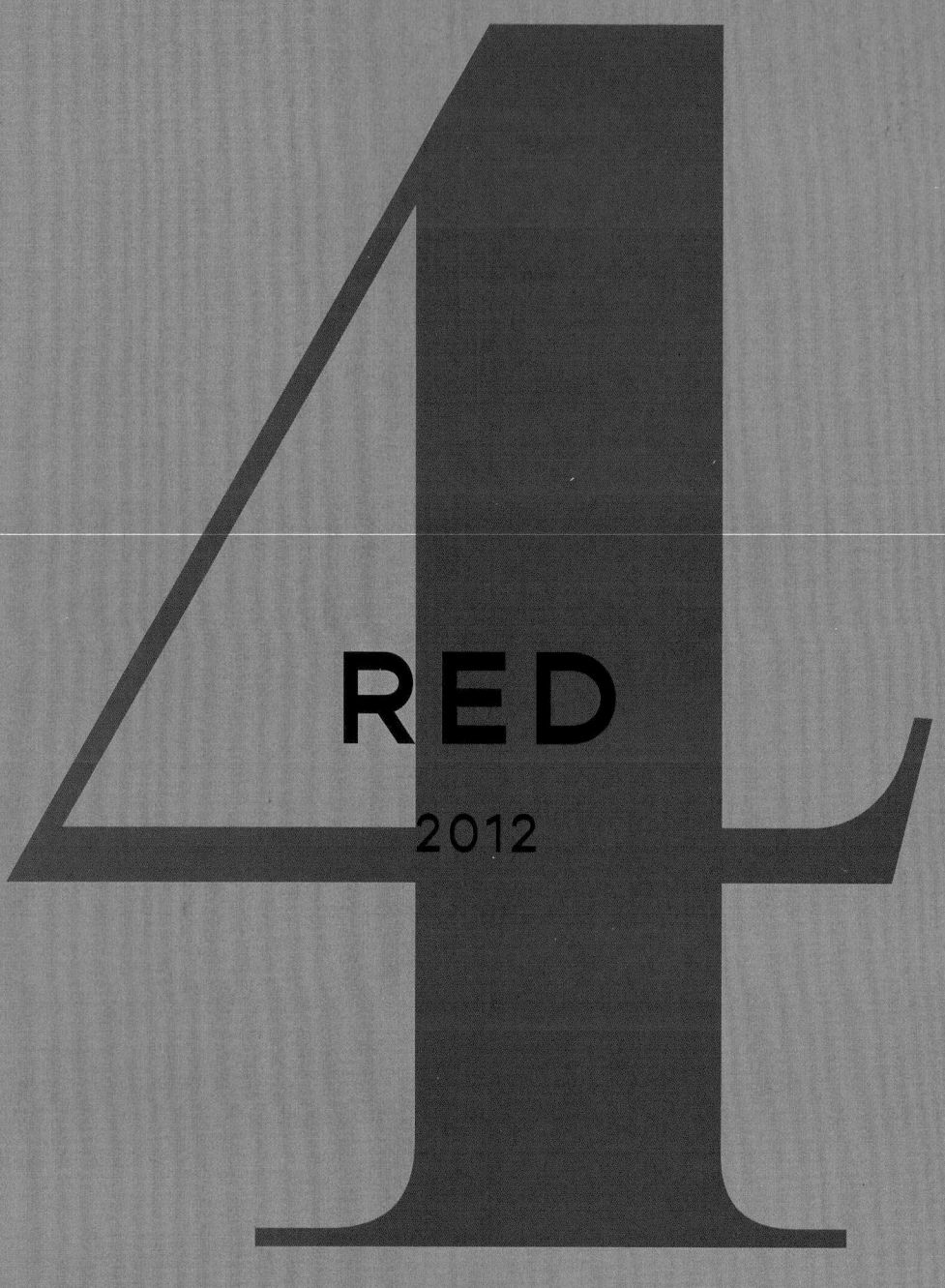

RED

2012

VULNERABILITY IS KIND

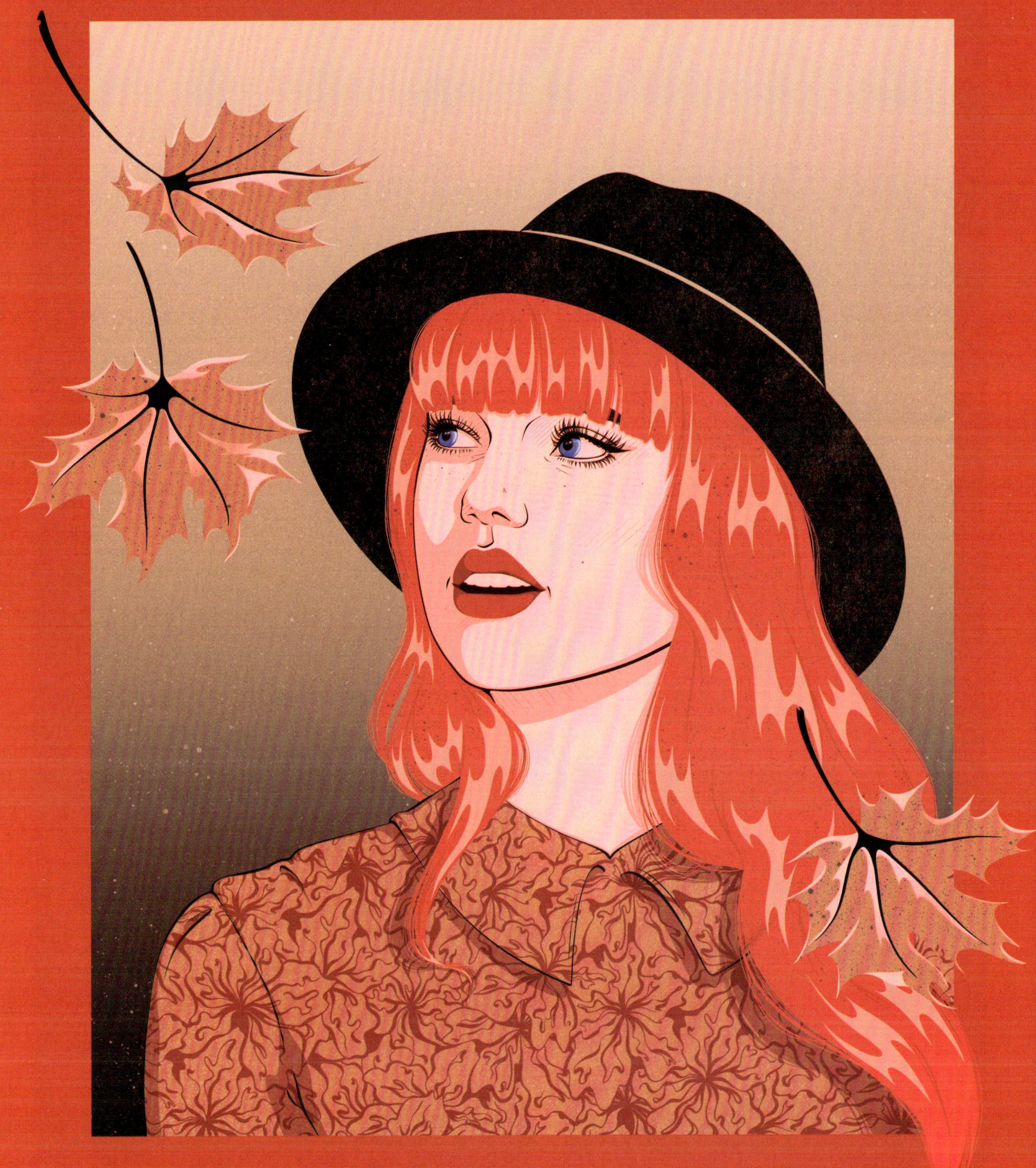

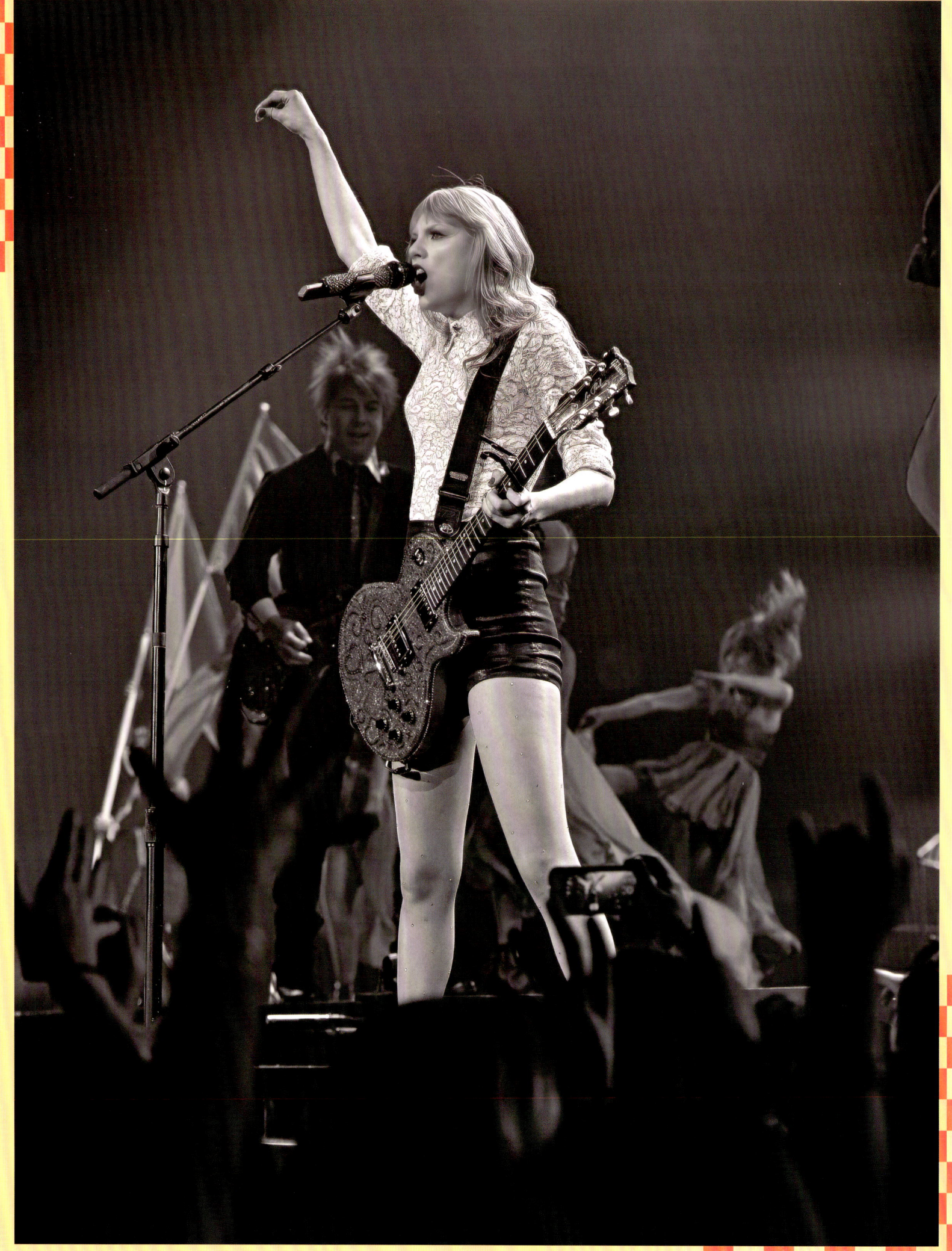

"I cannot put up protective walls, because it's my job to feel things."

Taylor, 2012

A LYRICAL GENIUS

This was the era that bridged the gap between Taylor's country and pop lines and solidified her status as a lyrical genius.

Fresh off the *Speak Now* era, Taylor solidified her aptitude as a writer during this time. Equipped with her pen (likely three types: quill, fountain, and gel), Taylor leaned all the way into her lyrical superpower. *Red* contains her most heartbreaking, raw, and vulnerable lyrics yet. Featuring devastating themes of loss, regret, abandonment, and pain, *Red* is unmistakably a breakup album.

The journey to make *Red* took about two years. The first year, Taylor wrote enough songs for an album, but she felt that the album wasn't different enough from what she'd done previously. This was her fourth studio album, and she wanted to shake things up.

She said, "You can either do things the way that you have always done them, and then you're forming a pattern of doing things the same way, or you can switch it up and go outside your comfort zone. And for me, my comfort zone is writing songs alone. So I just thought, what if I were to indulge those curiosities that I've always had?"

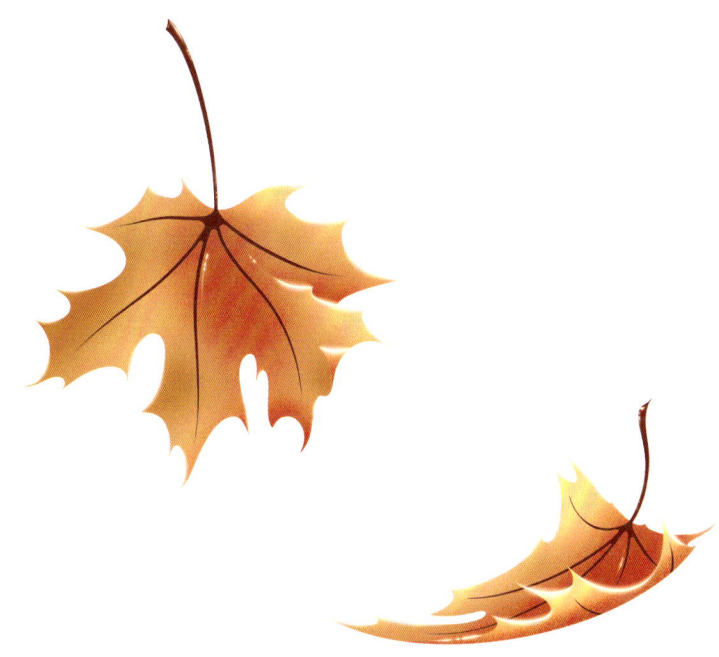

"ALL TOO WELL"

Despite never being a single, the track five song "All Too Well" immediately became a fan favorite and cultural phenomenon. This raw, vulnerable track encapsulated Taylor's strength as a storyteller and took listeners through an almost cinematic display of utter heartbreak. The imagery of a forgotten scarf, as well as the sense of betrayal and lingering heartbreak described in the song, felt both specific and universal, allowing fans to see their own experiences reflected in the song.

Taylor has described "All Too Well" as the song that came together almost accidentally. It began during a band rehearsal when Taylor, reeling from heartbreak, started improvising lyrics over a chord progression. In an interview, she said that one of the engineers recorded the improvisation and gave her the recording. The raw version of the song ran for about ten minutes, and Taylor said she obviously had to pare it down because "you can't put a ten-minute song on an album." She worked with frequent collaborator Liz Rose to shape the initial draft, trimming it down into a five-and-a-half-minute song that still retained its emotional depth.

Taylor performed "All Too Well" during The Red Tour, and it became clear that it was more than just an album track—it was a defining moment. Fans would scream the lyrics back to her, and the emotional weight of her performances created a sense of shared catharsis. In 2014, Taylor performed a piano version of "All Too Well" at the Grammy Awards after fans requested it. She received a standing ovation and demonstrated the power and the life of the song.

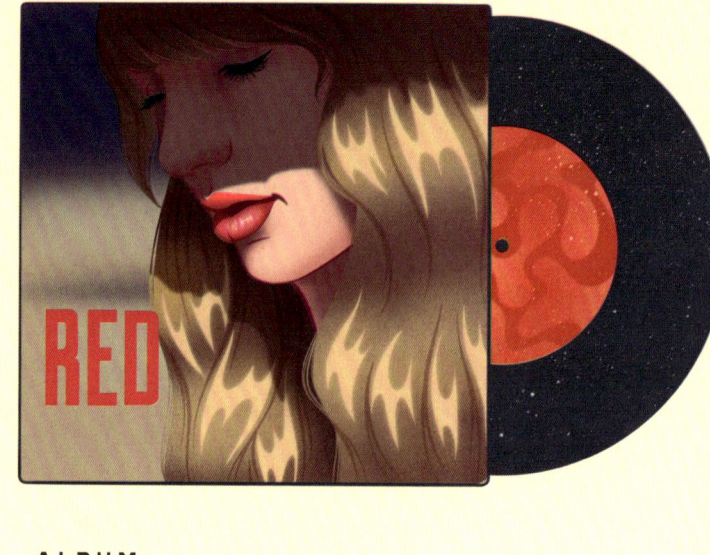

ALBUM
Red

DATE LAUNCHED
October 22, 2012

FIRST SINGLE
"We Are Never Ever Getting Back Together" (August 13, 2012)

OTHER SINGLES
"Begin Again" (October 1, 2012), "I Knew You Were Trouble" (November 27, 2012), "22" (March 12, 2013), "Red" (June 24, 2013), "Everything Has Changed" (July 14, 2013), and "The Last Time" (November 4, 2013)

TOUR
The Red Tour (March 2013 to June 2014)

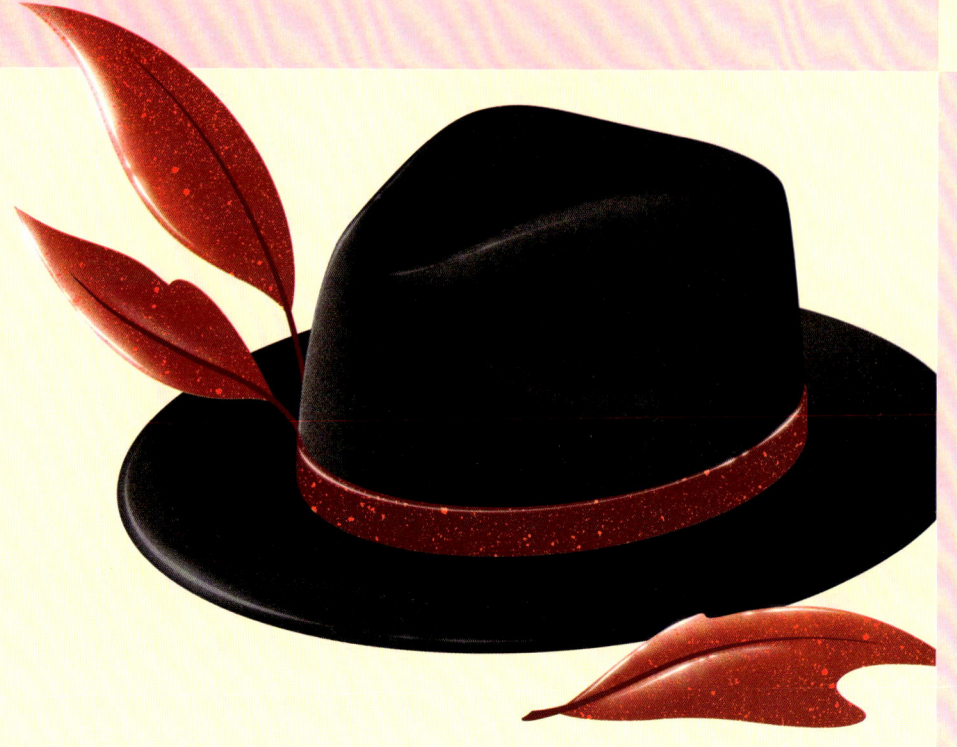

During the Reputation Stadium Tour, before performing "All Too Well," Taylor said, "It's weird because I feel like this song has two lives to it in my brain. In my brain, there's the life of this song, where this song was born out of catharsis and venting and trying to get over something and trying to understand it and process it. And then there's the life where it went out into the world, and you turned this song into something completely different for me. You turned this song into a collage of memories of watching you scream the words to this song, or seeing pictures that you post to me of you having written words to this song in your diary, or you showing me your wrist, and you have a tattoo of the lyrics to this song underneath your skin. And that is how you have changed the song 'All Too Well' for me."

By the time Taylor began re-recording her albums to reclaim her masters, the cultural significance of "All Too Well" had only grown. Recognizing the song's importance to her fans, Taylor included a highly anticipated ten-minute version of "All Too Well (10-Minute Version)" on

Red (Taylor's Version) in 2021. This extended version, with its additional lyrics and expanded storytelling, was the ultimate gift to fans who had championed the song for nearly a decade. It was accompanied by a short film written and directed by Taylor herself, starring Sadie Sink and Dylan O'Brien, which brought the song's narrative to life and further cemented its legacy. Taylor even performed the ten-minute version live on The Eras Tour, marking a much-anticipated part of the evening for Swifties.

While the song was never a lead single, "All Too Well" has achieved something far greater: It has become a cornerstone of Taylor Swift's career, a song that defines her as an artist, and one that has taken a life of its own in all the best ways.

PAGE 74: Taylor opening The Red Tour in Atlanta, April 18, 2013.

LEFT: Red on tour: Soldier Field, Chicago, August 10, 2013.

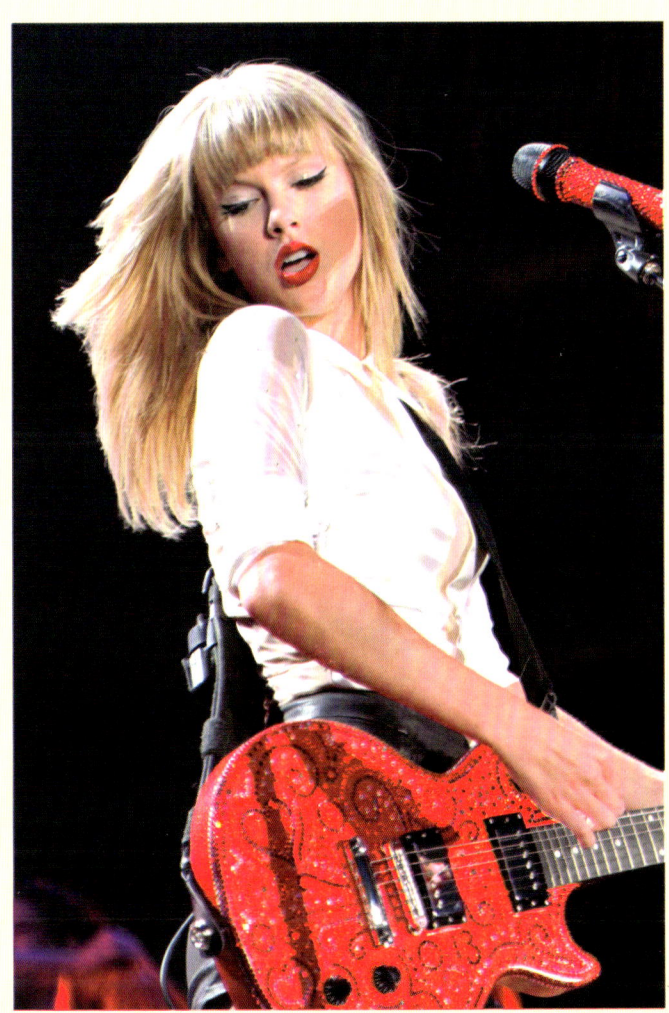

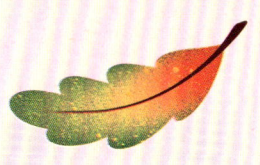

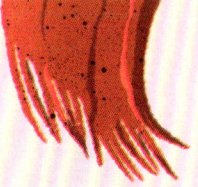

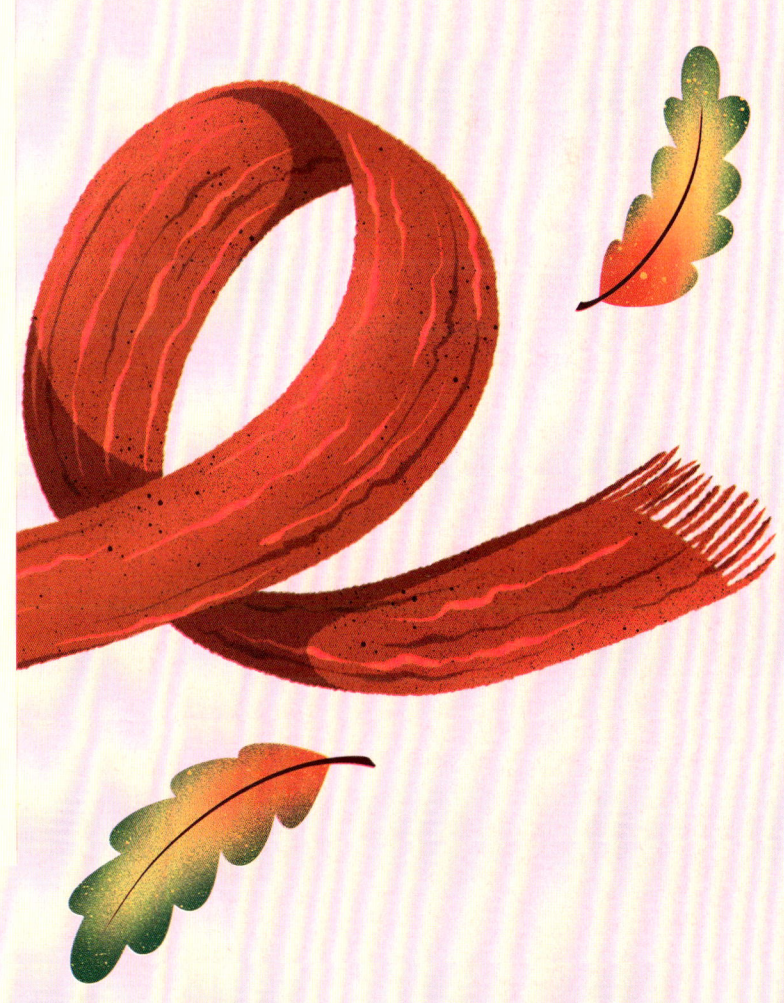

THE PUZZLE PIECE PROJECT

About a hundred Swifties from different countries came together and decorated one piece of a puzzle for a venture called the "Puzzle Piece Project." Each puzzle piece was decorated with something special as a token of appreciation for Taylor. During each tour stop, a fan would give her a new piece of the puzzle. When she'd received all of the pieces and put them together, Taylor saw that the puzzle formed a giant heart with a special message from her fans that read, "Taylor, your music connects people all over the world and ties them together with a smile. Love love love, your fearless fans." She framed the piece and hung it on a wall, and mentioned how wonderful and organized her fans were to make it happen.

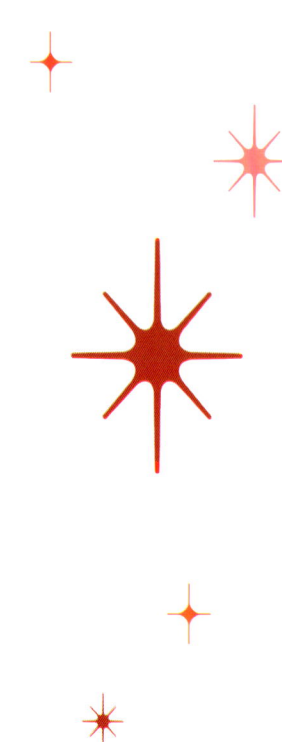

Taylor had previously worked with her longtime collaborator Nathan Chapman, but for this album, she opted to bring on new collaborators, both to learn from them and to see what sounds she could create. She worked with Dann Huff, Max Martin, Shellback, Jeff Bhasker, Dan Wilson, Jacknife Lee, and Butch Walker.

While that might seem like a lot of collaborators with various sounds and expertise, Taylor was less worried about having a cohesive sound. Rather, she aspired to produce an album that reflected her often conflicting feelings, such as being sad, happy, lonely, and confused—occasionally all at the same time.

On August 13, 2012, in another nod to her social-savvy ways, Taylor hosted a live webchat on Google Hangouts and announced *Red*. Describing the album's namesake, Taylor said, "Red is such an interesting color to correlate with emotion, because it's on both ends of the spectrum. On one end, you have happiness, falling in love, infatuation with someone, passion—all that. On the other end, you've got obsession, jealousy, danger, fear, anger, and frustration. All those emotions—spanning from intense love, intense frustration, jealousy, confusion, all of that—in my mind, all those emotions are red. You know, there's nothing in between. There's nothing beige about any of those feelings, it all comes back to me, and it's red."

The album's lead single, "We Are Never Ever Getting Back Together," is arguably Taylor Swift's most pop song to date. With its catchy melody and spoken-word bridge, the song became an instant favorite—one that Taylor famously wrote by accident. While she was at the studio working on a different song with Max Martin and Shellback, a friend of an ex-boyfriend of

OPPOSITE: Taylor performs "We Are Never Ever Getting Back Together," "Red," and "Love Story" on *Good Morning America* as part of the release-day promotion for *Red*, October 23, 2012.

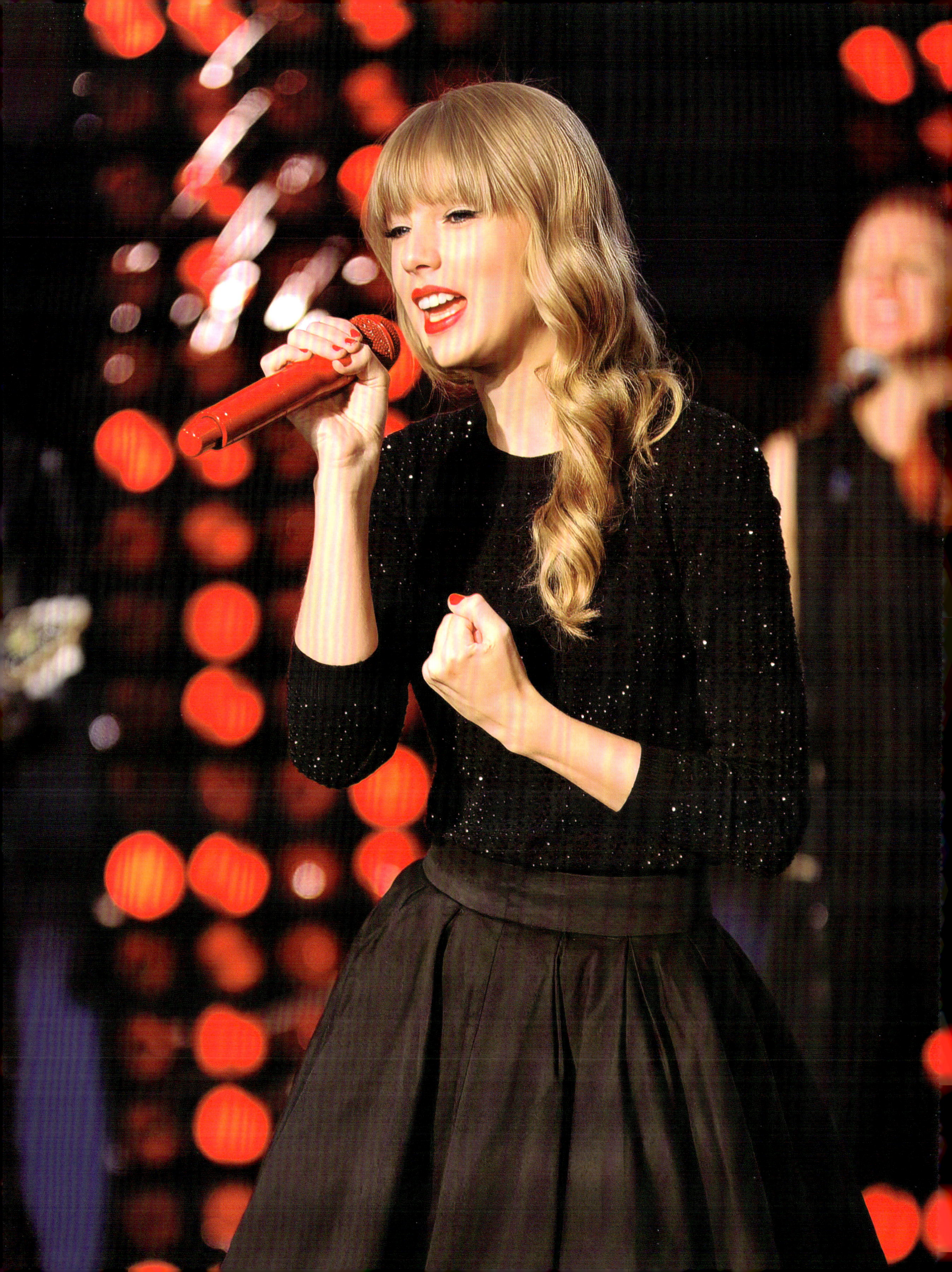

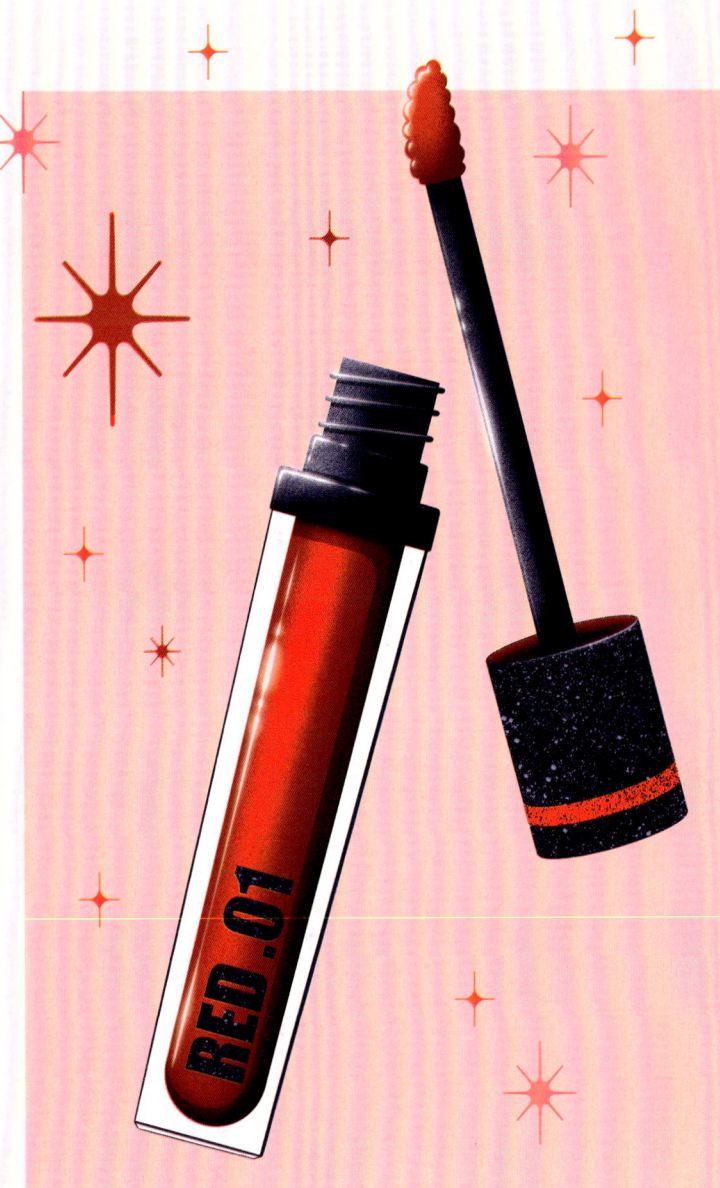

Her Signature Style

ESTABLISHED
March 16, 2009

THE RED LIP

Taylor first debuted her red lip on a cover of *Allure* magazine in 2009. Gucci Westman, the makeup artist on the cover shoot said she had to get permission from Taylor's mom and her management team to let her try the bold new red lip look. Taylor loved it so much that the makeup artist sent her home with a tube of her very own, a very history-in-the-making event! A month after the *Allure* magazine feature, Taylor embarked on the Fearless Tour where she debuted her new red lip that has since become a signature look. Her current signature lip shade? Pat McGrath Labs LiquiLUST Legendary Wear Lipstick in Elson 4.

hers happened to stop by and mentioned that he'd heard that Taylor and her ex were getting back together. After he left, she went on a rant about the interaction and said that they were never getting back together, like ever, ever, ever. Max Martin told her they needed to turn that into a song, and from there, Taylor immediately started working on the song.

Doing things differently worked out. *Red* debuted at No. 1 on the Billboard Hot 100, making it her first track to hit the No. 1 spot. The album sold 1.21 million copies in its first week, the highest debut of her career at the time. The album went on to win Favorite Country Album at the 2013 American Music Awards and Top Country Album at the 2013 Billboard Music Awards.

Taylor was also nominated for Grammy Awards for both Album of the Year and Best Country Album; however, she went home empty-handed. While she was lauded for her lyrical depth and vulnerability in *Red*, other critics described this album as "not quite country" and "not quite pop," unsure which genre to use to categorize her. After the Grammy loss, Taylor did what most of us might do: She skipped the after-parties, binged In-N-Out Burger, and cried a little. While she is a superstar, she is also still a human. At the time, this seemed like a setback, but really, it fueled her. That very night, her next album, *1989*, came to her, and Taylor decided that she would lean all the way into the pop genre.

OPPOSITE:
Everybody loves pretty: Taylor wore this spectacular red gown to sing "The Lucky One" in The Red Tour concerts.

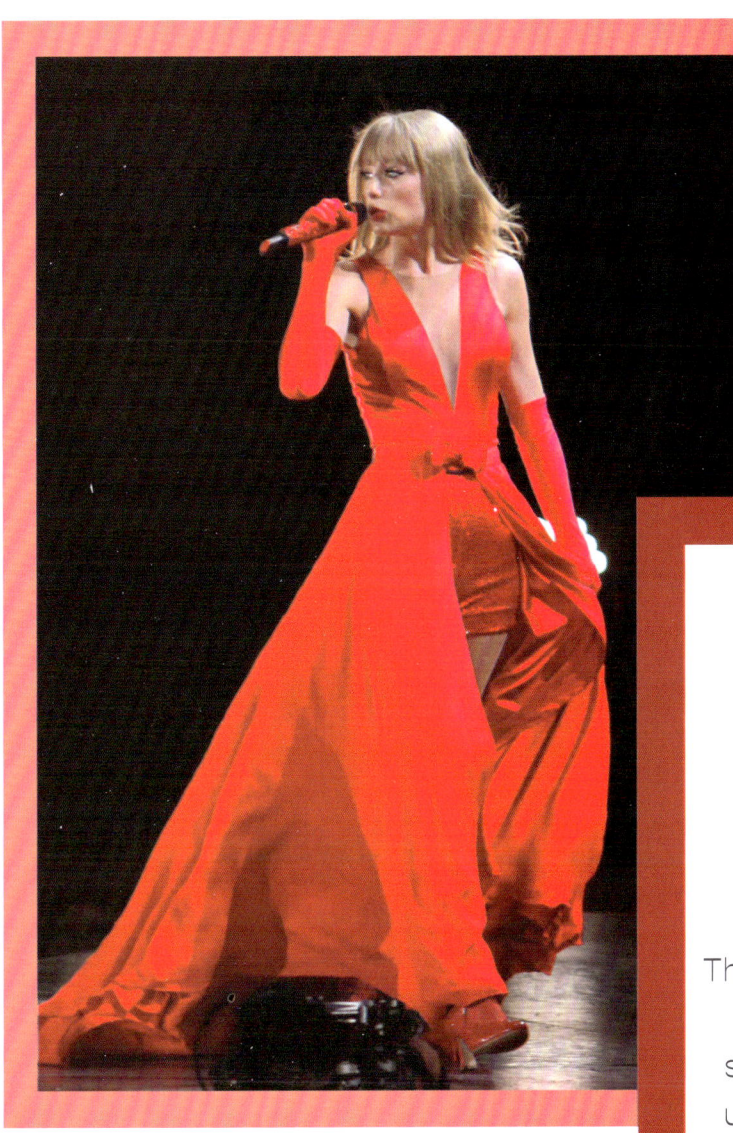

The album Red spent seven weeks at No. 1 on the Billboard 200.

"Red"

The song "Red" was the catalyst for Taylor's transition from country to pop. The *Red* album originally started in Taylor's signature country style, but she wasn't satisfied and was ready to shake things up sonically. Swedish pop producer Max Martin was called in, and the first song the two worked on together was the song "Red." While he was not the final producer on the song, he and fellow producer Shellback ended up producing three songs on *Red*. The songs include "I Knew You Were Trouble," "22," and "We Are Never Ever Getting Back Together."

ALBUM

Red

RELEASED

2012

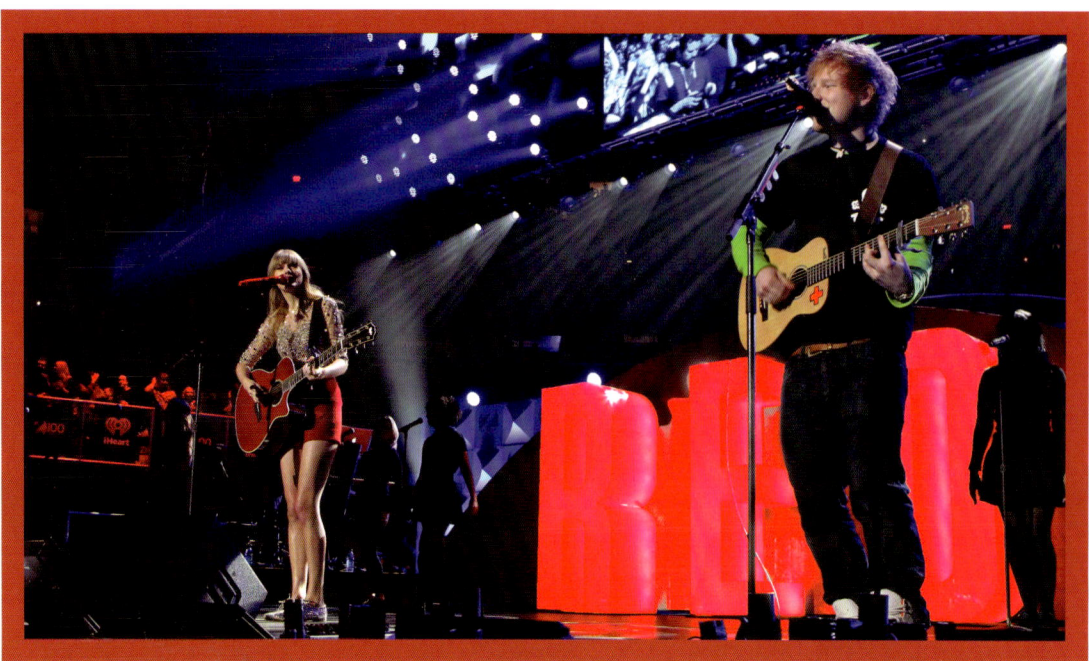

Always in Love

As Taylor's fame continued to rise, the media switched its focus from whether she could sing or write to whom she was dating. One of the most talked-about relationships was her brief romance with Harry Styles. The pair was first linked in late 2012, around the time that *Red* was released, and their relationship became tabloid fodder almost immediately. From their public outings in New York City to their infamous snowmobile accident during a trip to Utah, their romance captured both the media and their fans' imaginations.

It wasn't all fun and games, however. Tabloids and late-night hosts frequently joked about Taylor's relationships, painting an unfair image of her as someone who dated men just to write songs about them. Her lyrical and musical ability was often reduced to a punch line about a boy-crazy girl who can't keep a guy and writes a song about him. In other cases, they would ask why anyone would want to date her since she would just use them as songwriting fuel.

Taylor often called out these double standards in playful ways, like when she was on *The Ellen DeGeneres Show* in 2012. She appeared with Zac Efron and was asked multiple times by Ellen if they were dating. The two performed a song together to the beat of "Pumped Up Kicks" by Foster the People—but with their own lyrics, lovingly calling out Ellen. One of Taylor's verses goes, "She always asks me who I'm dating every time I'm on this show, and I don't even know why."

In a 2012 interview with *Glamour* magazine, Taylor was pressed to admit if she was dating Conor Kennedy. She responded, "I don't talk about my personal life in great detail. I write about it in my songs, and I feel like you can share enough about your life in your music to let people know what you're going through."

While the media remained fixated on her love life, Taylor focused on doing the one thing she most looks forward to when releasing a new album: connecting with her fans on tour. After the press tour ended, the world tour began. Taylor embarked on The Red Tour, which spanned eighty-six shows from March 13, 2013, to June 12, 2014.

ABOVE: Taylor debuts "Everything Has Changed" with Ed Sheeran at Z100's Jingle Ball in New York City, December 7, 2012. The song, thought to be about her relationship with Conor Kennedy, was to promote both the *Red* album and upcoming tour; shortly after, Taylor would announce Ed as her first opening act for the tour.

FOLLOWING PAGES: Performing her Red Tour opening set to a sold-out crowd in Denver, June 2, 2013.

CHAI COOKIE RECIPE

Taylor is known for her love of baking and says it's one of her favorite things to do when she's not on the road touring. During her radio tour to promote her debut album, *Taylor Swift*, she would visit radio stations with freshly baked cookies for the hosts. On the "Fifteen" music–video set, Taylor shared two different versions of her homemade "hybrid" chocolate–chip cookies with the crew and asked which cookie they liked best. As recently as 2024, she baked "Victory Pop–Tarts" for the Kansas City Chiefs on game day.

For the 1989 Secret Sessions (a series of previews of her record that she hosted in her home, exclusively for hand–selected fans), Taylor made chai cookies. After the album was released, fans who attended the Secret Sessions shared how much they loved the cookies. To ensure that all her fans could enjoy the cookies, she posted the recipe in November 2014 to her social media. These cookies have become a staple for Swifties, who often make them during the fall season and in celebration of new album launches.

Taylor's Chai Sugar Cookies & Icing

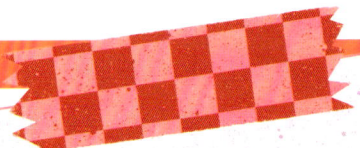

INGREDIENTS

½ cup unsalted butter, at room temperature

½ cup vegetable oil

½ cup sugar, plus more for topping

½ cup powdered sugar

1 large egg

2 teaspoons vanilla extract

2 cups flour

½ teaspoon baking soda

¼ teaspoon salt

1 chai tea bag

DIRECTIONS

1. Oven at 350°F, grease cookie sheet.
2. Beat butter and add vegetable oil.
3. Add sugar, powdered sugar, egg, and vanilla.
4. Stir in flour, baking soda, salt, and loose tea from the tea bag.
5. Chill the soft dough for about 1 hour.
6. Line cookie sheet with 12 tablespoons dough drops.
7. Press evenly and cover with sugar.
8. 9ish minutes in the oven.
9. Cover with icing when cool completely.

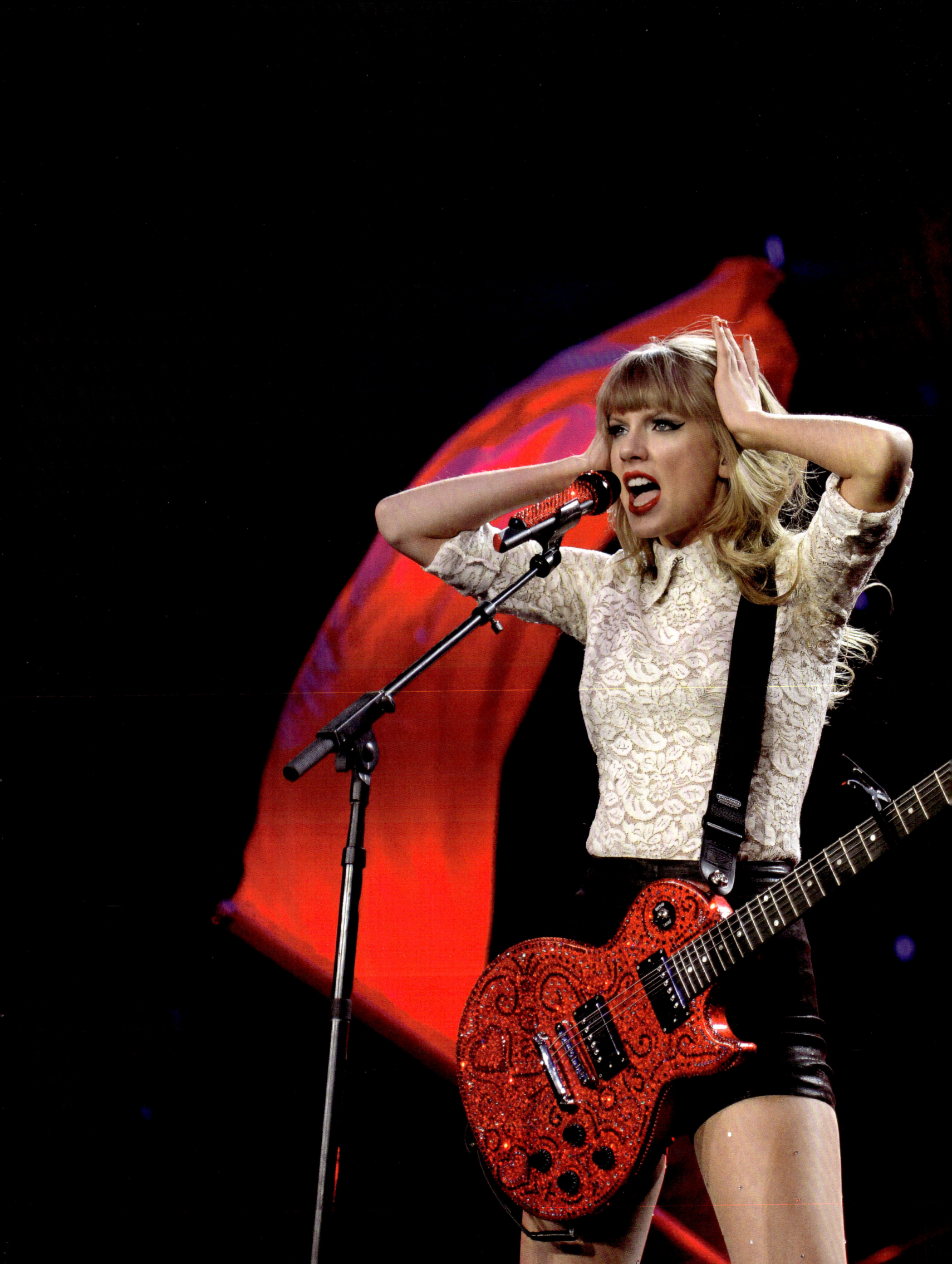

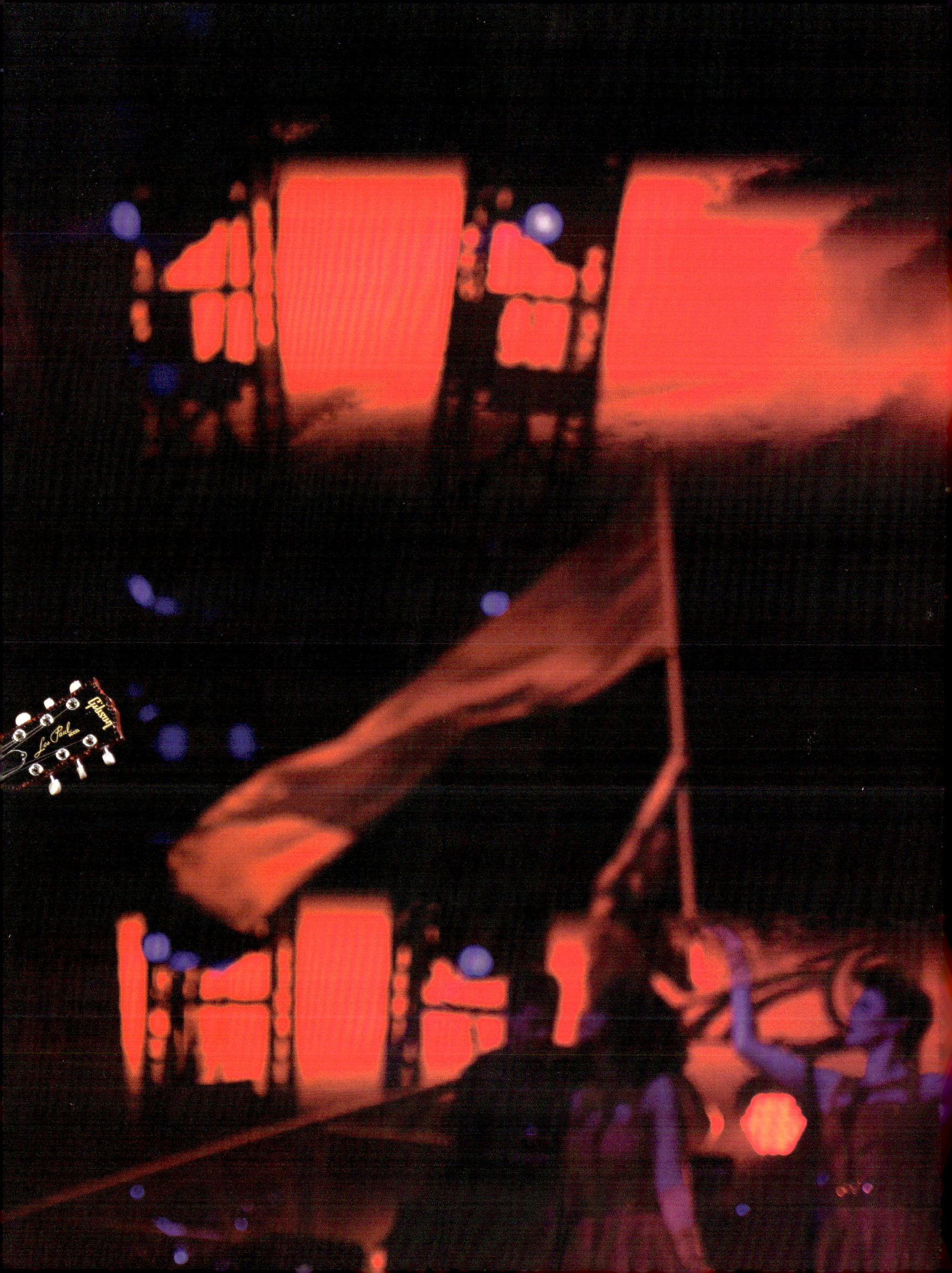

The Red Tour

A silky red backdrop lined the stage, and as "State of Grace" began to play, the silhouette of Taylor in her signature "22" hat appeared, illuminated behind the fabric. The crowd let out an electric scream. The set spanned eighteen songs during a two-hour set, including one surprise song each night. During the US tour, she performed a duet of "Everything Has Changed" that featured opening act Ed Sheeran.

Always thinking about ways to connect with her fans, Taylor chose a U-shaped stage with a catwalk down the middle, allowing for two pits so that more fans could be close to the stage. And, in her signature style, during the song "22," her dancers lifted her up and carried her through the crowd as she sang and gave high-fives all the way to the other stage at the back of the venue. She finished "22" and performed a surprise acoustic song, ensuring that the audience in the back also had a great view of the show. Once Taylor finished with the acoustic set, she started singing "Sparks Fly" and moved back through the crowd on foot, singing face-to-face and high-fiving fans. These close stage connections at shows continued to mean a lot, both to Taylor and her fans.

While Taylor was onstage, her mom, Andrea, roamed the crowd looking for the most decorated and passionate fans she could find to invite them to Taylor's T Party room meet-and-greet. This newer tradition started during the Fearless Tour and carried through to The Red Tour. This time, Taylor renamed it to Club Red, in a nod to the *Red* album. The T Party room was completely redesigned and now included a bar area with nonalcoholic drinks, candy machines, and high-top seats and barstools for guests to relax. A special memorabilia section included iconic dresses worn by Taylor during the Fearless Tour, and she took photos with fans in a designated photo area. She brought her T Parties to a whole new level.

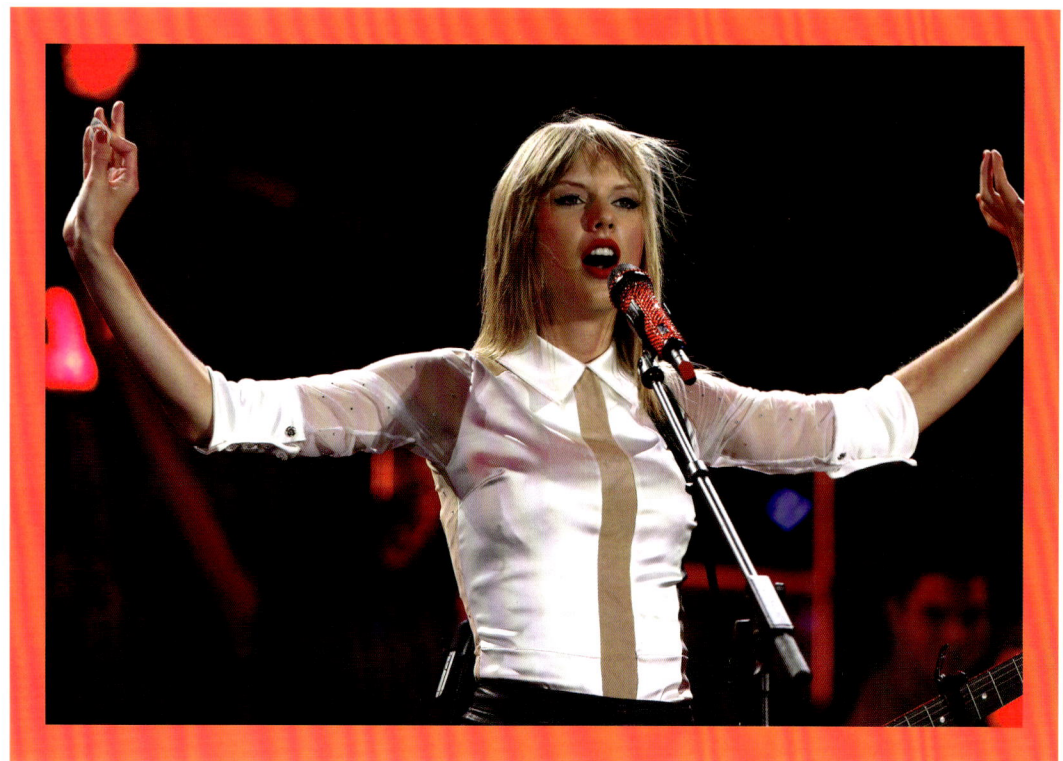

LEFT: Performing at the Gillette Stadium in Foxborough, Massachusetts, July 26, 2013.

OPPOSITE: Taylor's holiday house on Watch Hill in Westerly, Rhode Island.

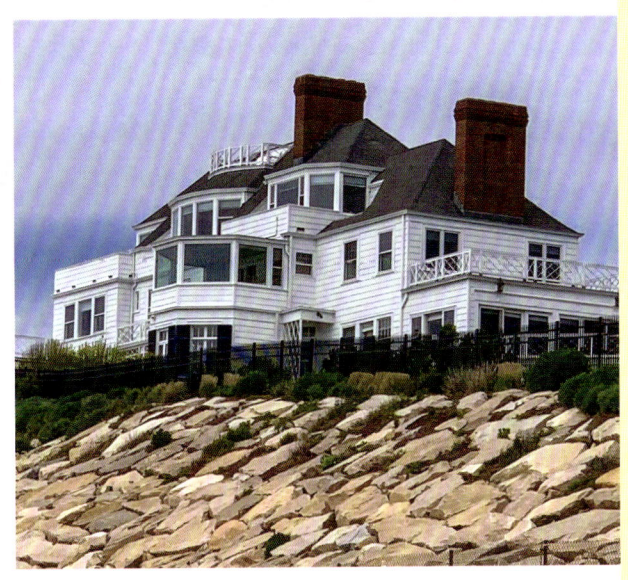

Holiday House

Taylor's Rhode Island residence, known as the "Holiday House," is the most expensive private home in Rhode Island.

EST.

Purchased in 2013.

Taylor is known for throwing star-studded and Instagram-worthy Independence Day parties with many major celebrities in attendance over the years. Taylor also hosted "Secret Sessions" for her albums *1989* and *reputation* at this residence.

Knowing how much her beloved fans enjoyed dressing up at concerts inspired Taylor to feature as many weird costumes as she could in her music videos for the *Red* album. In the "We Are Never Ever Getting Back Together" music video, her band dressed in furry costumes as a squirrel, bear, and donkey. For Taylor's concerts, fans dressed up with everything from homemade costumes out of her iconic music videos, like the "not a lot going on at the moment" shirt from the "22" video and the red light-up tutus and homemade T-shirts bedazzled with the word "Swiftie."

The term "Swiftie" had been lightly used up to this point. During a 2011 interview on *The Tonight Show Starring Jimmy Fallon*, Jimmy lovingly described himself as a Swiftie and asked Taylor if people call her that, to which she replied, "A lot more people now." During the *Red* era, "Swiftie" really took off and solidified the name for her fan base. In a 2012 interview with music-video network Vevo, Taylor said, "My fans came up with a name for themselves, and it's so cute. They call themselves 'Swifties.' And it's adorable because they made it up on their own."

During the *Red* era, Taylor embraced certain collaborations different from those in eras to come. She launched her third perfume, Taylor by Taylor Swift, a fruity floral fragrance with a pearl-adorned bottle. She also collaborated with Keds and created an entire shoe line inspired by patterns, colors, and things she likes. The shoes featured design elements like heart sunglass patterns, sparkly rhinestones, and heart- and guitar-pick charms. Her concerts included activation stations that promoted both collaborations.

Growing Up

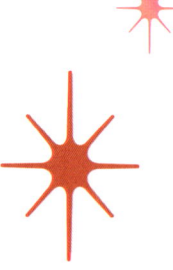

Personally, this was a coming-of-age time for Taylor. Not only was she now a young adult of drinking age; she was also starting to lean into her style, her home, and her friendships. During a photoshoot with *Vogue* magazine, one of the directors asked if she would be open to cutting her hair for the shoot, and she excitedly said, "YES!" This was the moment when Taylor officially got bangs, and they became an important element of her iconic looks over the years. She also leaned more into her personal style and embraced wearing heels, as she noted in the *Red* album liner notes for the song "Begin Again."

Then there was her "housewife era," which she described during her 2022 honorary doctorate speech at New York University. She said, "I promise you: You're probably doing or wearing something right now that you will look back on later and find revolting and hilarious. You can't avoid it, so don't try to. For example, I had a phase where, for the entirety of 2012, I dressed like a 1950s housewife. But you know what? I was having fun. Trends and phases are fun. Looking back and laughing is fun."

Taylor was all about exploring her personal style and having fun with it. She described her personal home style at the time as "Tim Burton–*Alice in Wonderland*–pirate ship–*Peter Pan*." She loves pairing antiques with new things. Something she will never buy secondhand, though? A couch. Why? Because there could be bugs in it. Instead, Taylor likes to go antiquing for knickknacks and home décor to pair with her modern-day comforts.

As far as her friendships, Taylor kept the circle close, often hanging out with her childhood best friend Abigail, as well as A-list stars like Emma Stone, Selena Gomez, and Hayley Williams. Taylor was never a partier or club-goer, opting instead to spend time with friends having dinners and quiet nights in.

As she gravitated toward moments of solace, Taylor purchased her Rhode Island home, often referred to as "Holiday House" as referenced in the song "The Last Great American Dynasty" from the *folklore* album. Located in the quiet town of Watch Hill, the house signified a place of retreat from the outside world for Taylor and provided additional privacy as she navigated needing increased security due to her fame.

BELOW:
Taylor and Selena Gomez at the Teen Choice Awards, July 22, 2012.

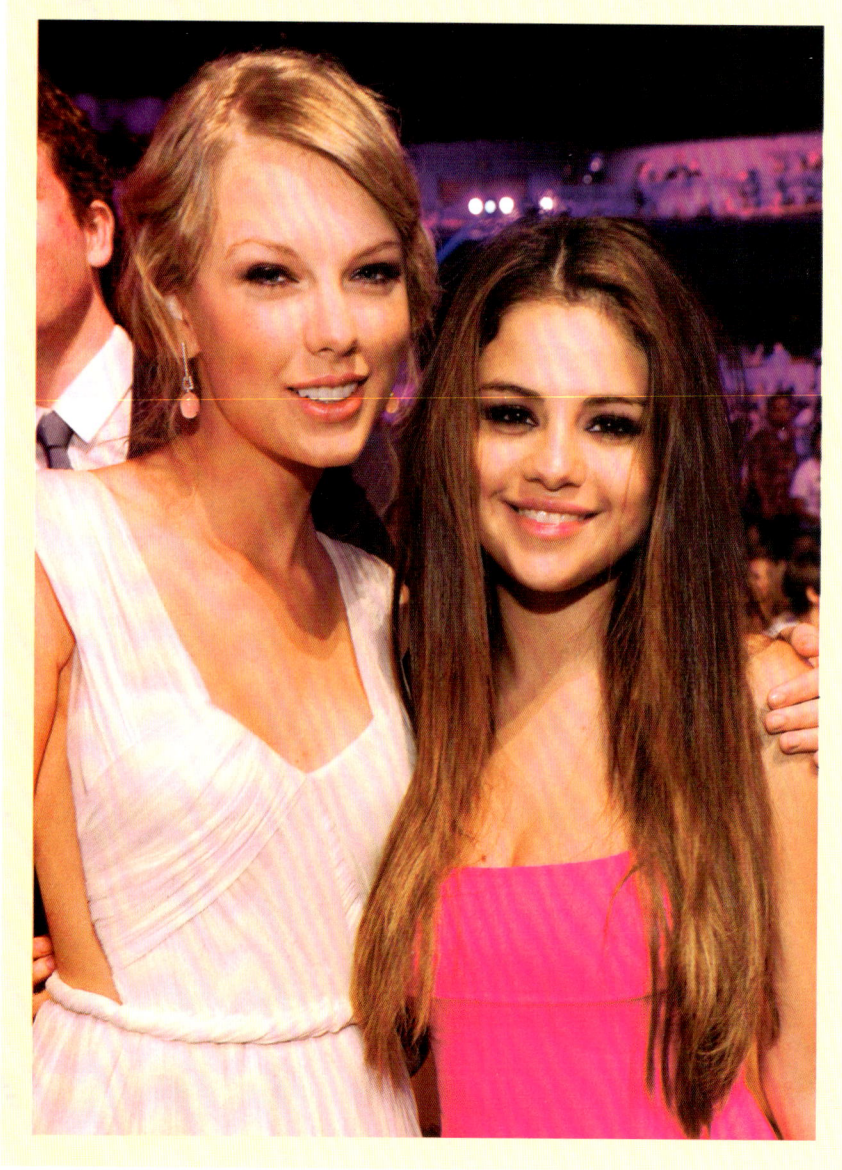

RONAN'S SONG

In 2010, Maya Thompson wrote a blog called *Rockstar Ronan*. It detailed her three-year-old son Ronan's diagnosis with neuroblastoma, an aggressive form of childhood cancer. Maya wrote about their journey and eventually her grief after losing Ronan just nine months after his initial diagnosis. Little did Maya know that Taylor religiously read Maya's blog and fell in love with both Maya and Ronan. Taylor invited Maya and her family to the Speak Now World Tour, and then about one year later, Taylor called Maya out of the blue and told her that she wrote a song for Ronan and asked for Maya's permission to perform it during a Stand Up To Cancer event in September 2012. Taylor gave Maya a writing credit on the song, since she drew lyrics and inspiration from Maya's blog, and also pledged that all the proceeds from the track would be donated to children's cancer charities.

Taylor has only performed the song "Ronan" twice: once at the Stand Up To Cancer event, and the other as a surprise song during The 1989 World Tour in Glendale, Arizona, where Maya and her family were present. Before performing the song at The 1989 World Tour, Taylor said, "I think that in my opinion, one of the bravest things a human being can ever do is to go through something absolutely unbearable and then share their experience with the world." She went on to say, "There is a woman here tonight named Maya Thompson, and she has lived in this area and brought her kids up in this area, and I wouldn't know half as much as I know about childhood cancer and childhood cancer research if she wouldn't have shared her story about her son Ronan. A few years ago, when I was reading her blog, I decided that her account of things was so heart-wrenching and so honest that I took a lot of the things that she said and I put them into a song and I put her as a co-writer because she is the rightful co-writer of the song called 'Ronan,' and when we put it out, all the proceeds of that song went to The Ronan Thompson Foundation and other childhood cancer research."

When Taylor re-recorded *Red (Taylor's Version)*, she personally reached out to Maya and asked for her permission to officially include "Ronan" on the re-release. Maya shared part of the letter that Taylor sent, and it said, "I've recently completed the re-recording of my fourth album, *Red*. It's really exceeded my expectations in so many ways, and one of those ways is that I thought it would be appropriate to add 'Ronan' to this album. *Red* was an album of heartbreak and healing, of rage and rawness, of tragedy and trauma, and of the loss of an imagined future alongside someone. I wrote 'Ronan' while I was making *Red* and discovered your story as you so honestly and devastatingly told it. My genuine hope is that you'll agree with me that this song should be included on this album. As my co-writer and the rightful owner of this story in its entirety, your opinion and approval of this idea really matters to me, and I'll honor your wishes here."

Maya agreed to include the song on the album, cementing a permanent home for "Ronan" on *Red (Taylor's Version)*. Ronan's story continues to be a source of love, grief, hope, and healing for Swifties and beyond.

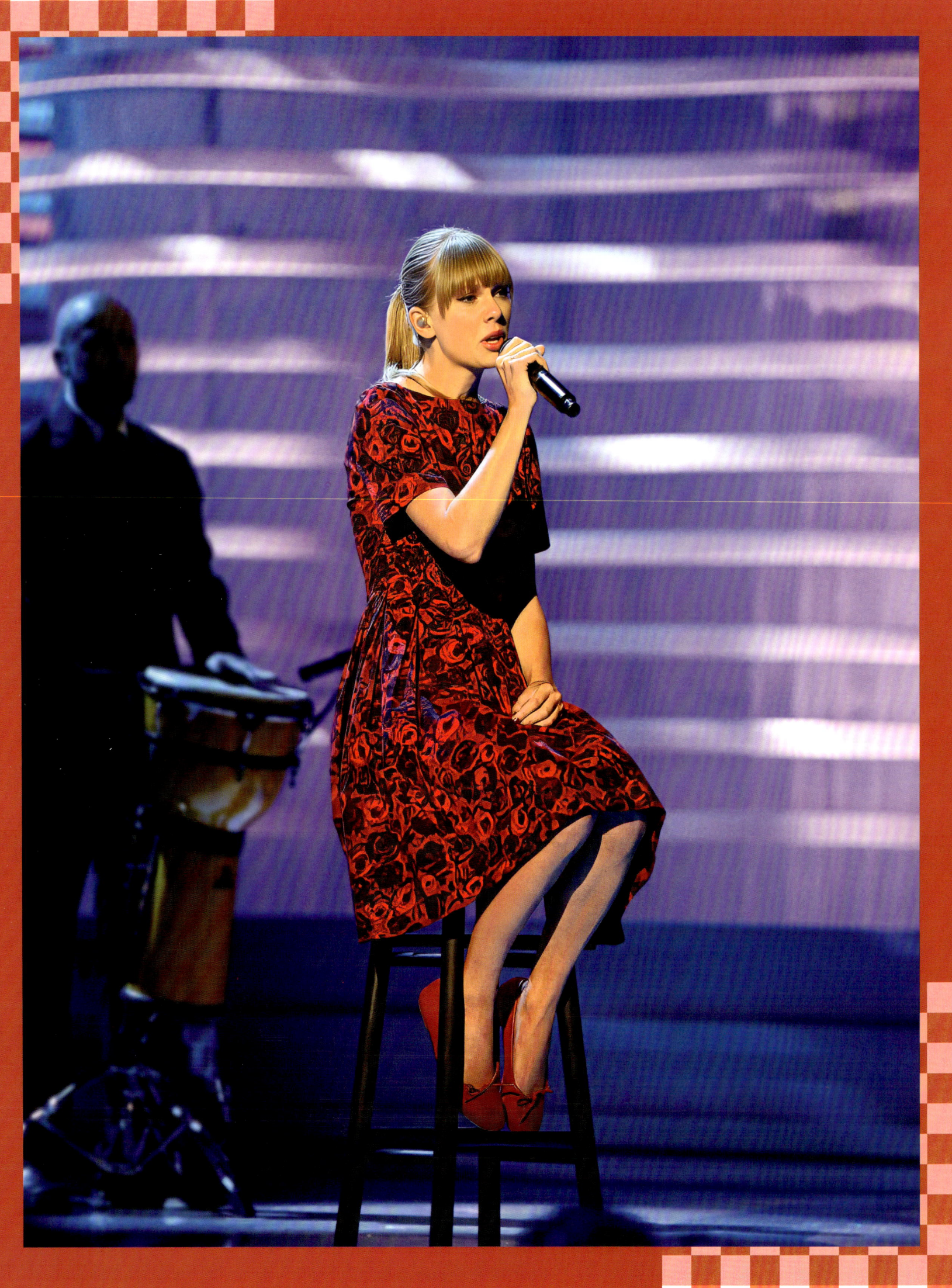

"I'm living a life, I know I'm going to make mistakes. I'm just going to try to handle those mistakes as a good person."

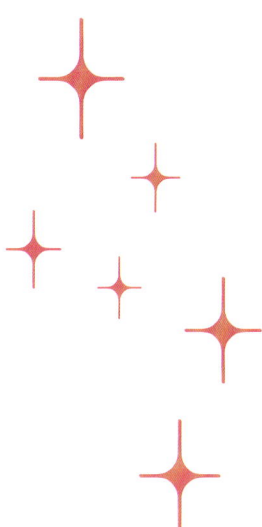

Taylor, 2012

One thing that didn't change was Taylor's giving heart. In 2012, she donated $4 million to the Country Music Hall of Fame to start the Taylor Swift Education Center. The center includes classrooms, exhibits, and programs designed to teach children and aspiring musicians about music history, songwriting, and performing. It remains one of the most impactful gifts in the museum's history and underscores Taylor's dedication to education and preserving the legacy of country music.

Known to act swiftly in times of natural disasters, Taylor donated $500,000 to the flood-relief effort in Nashville in 2012, and in 2013, she donated $100,000 to the American Red Cross to help support those impacted by tornadoes in Oklahoma.

Perhaps one of the most touching things during the *Red* era was a charity single that Taylor released on September 12, 2012, called "Ronan." The song was written in honor of a boy named Ronan, who died of childhood cancer in 2011. His mother, Maya, wrote a blog journeying their story from his diagnosis to the grief of losing her son only nine months later. Taylor read the blog and became incredibly invested in their story, even using the blog as inspiration for the song's lyrics. She not only gave Maya a writing credit on the song, but she also pledged that all the proceeds from the track would be donated to children's cancer charities.

Ultimately, the *Red* era was a formative period for Taylor. She experienced the sting of heartbreak and the challenges of living under the microscope of fame. Yet she channeled these experiences into her art, creating an album that resonated deeply with fans and marked a turning point in her career. This era solidified Taylor's resolve to embrace vulnerability while finding solace in her independence, friendships, and connection with her fans.

OPPOSITE: Taylor performs "Ronan" at the Stand Up To Cancer telethon, September 12, 2012. She released the single soon after this performance, with all the proceeds going to cancer charities.

TAYLOR'S HAIR OVER THE YEARS

From her signature curly locks and Vogue magazine bangs to "bleachella," Taylor has evolved and changed her hair many times over the years.

"I look out at the stadiums full of people and see them all knowing the words to songs I wrote. And curling their hair! I remember straightening my hair because I wanted to be like everybody else, and now the fact that anybody would emulate what I do? It's just funny. And wonderful."

Taylor, 2012

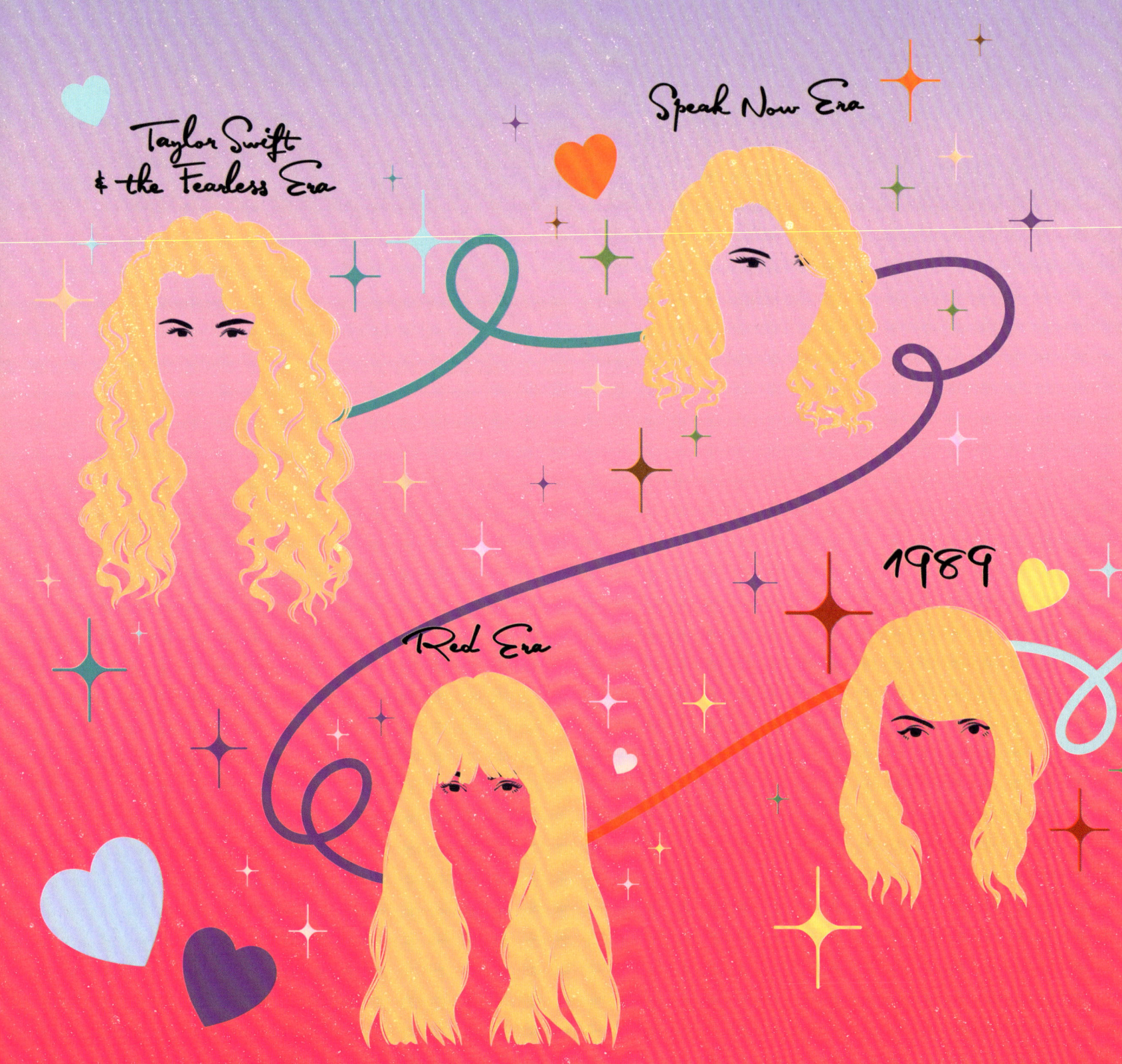

Taylor Swift & the Fearless Era

Speak Now Era

Red Era

1989

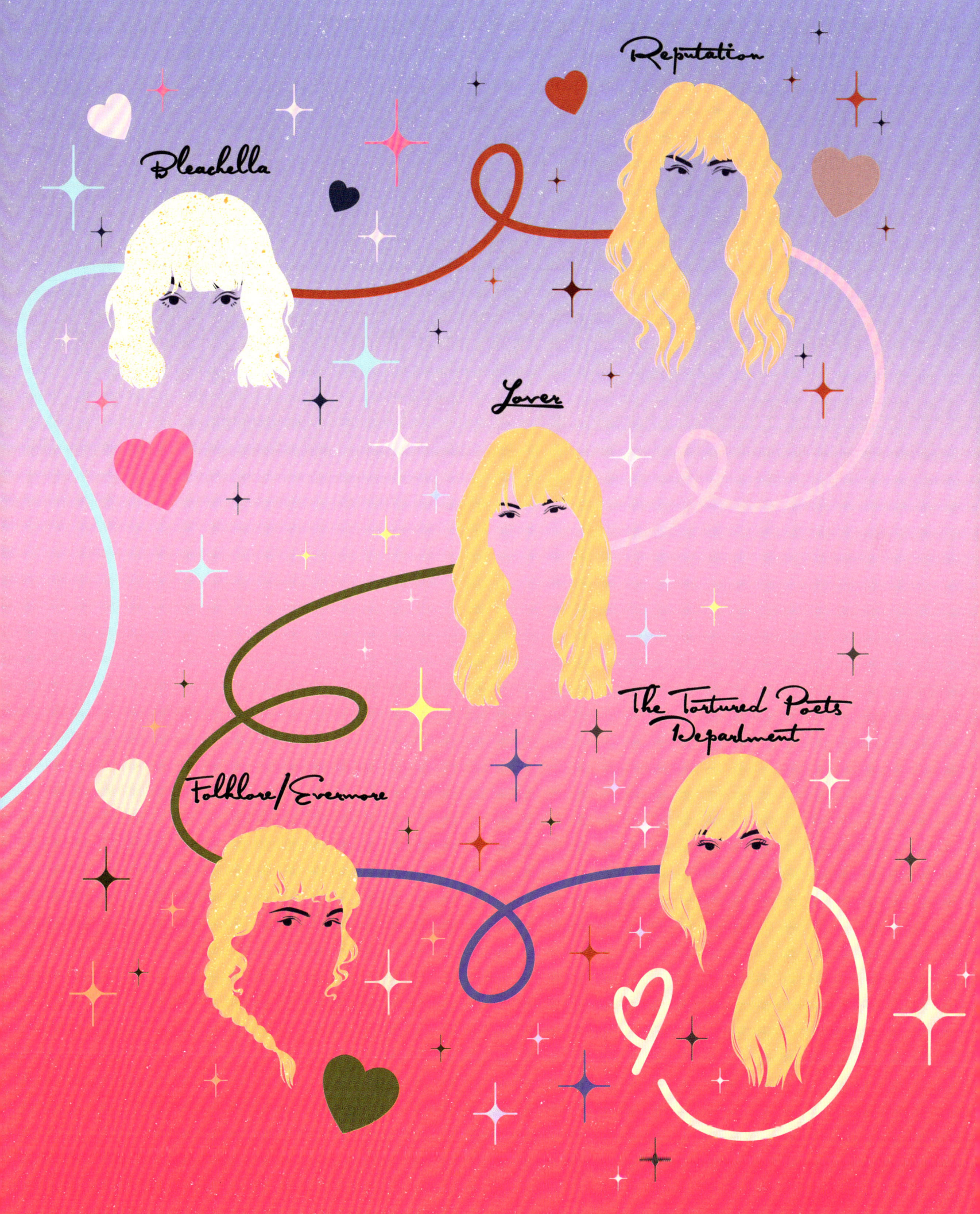

Bleachella

Reputation

Lover

Folklore/Evermore

The Tortured Poets Department

5

1989

2014

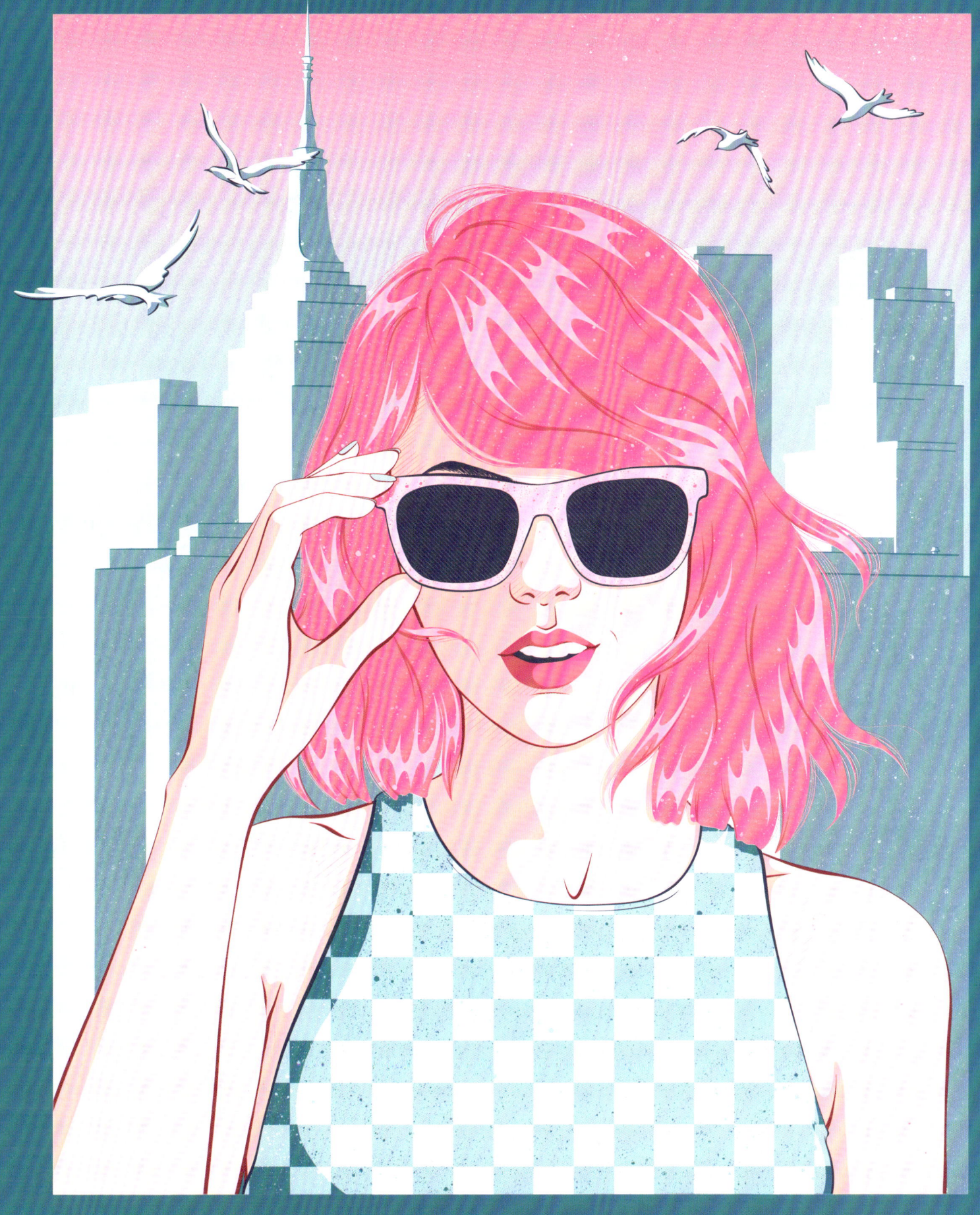

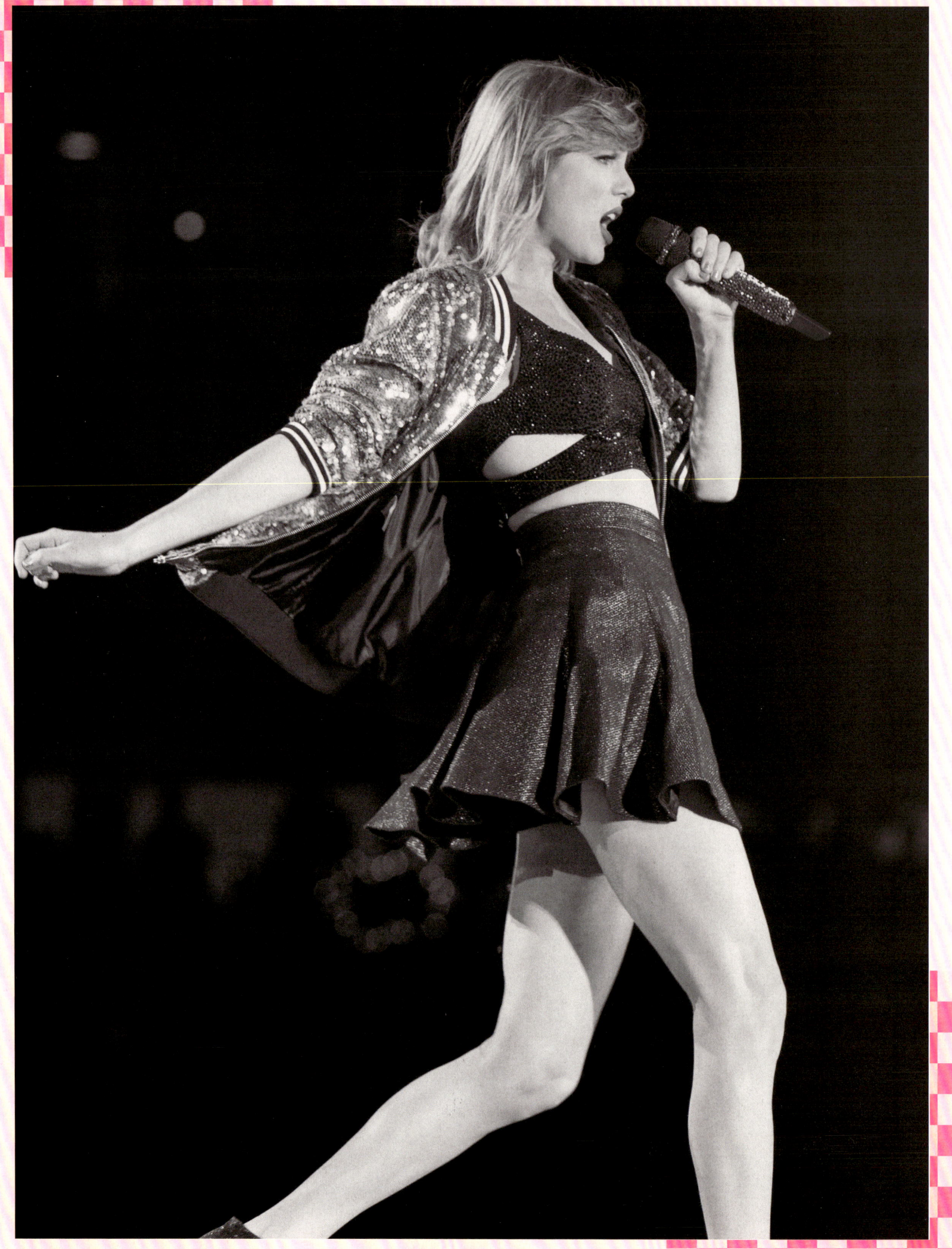

"I feel no need to burn down the house I built by hand."

POP-STAR STATUS

This was the era during which Taylor stepped into her pop-star status.

During this time, Taylor shook off past versions of herself and stepped fully into her pop-star status. She marked the momentous occasion not only with a brand-new, fully pop album, *1989*, but also by sporting a fresh bob and welcoming New York City as her home. She also embraced her friendship circles and put dating on the back burner. This was an era of self-discovery, with Taylor learning from her past and choosing a new way forward.

When describing why she wanted to lean into a full-pop album, she told *Rolling Stone*, "At a certain point, if you chase two rabbits, you lose them both." Losing a Grammy Award for *Red* was a big catalyst.

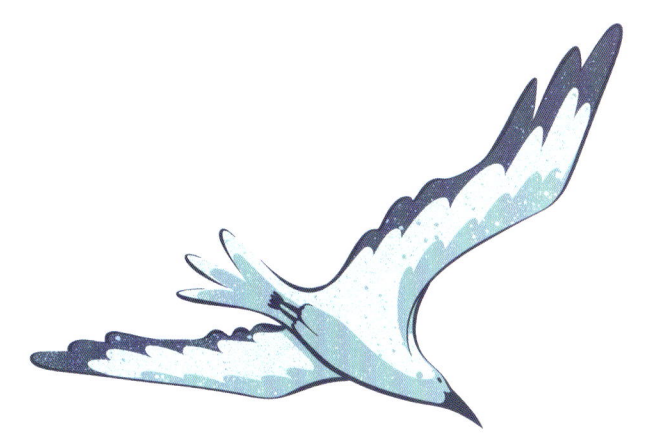

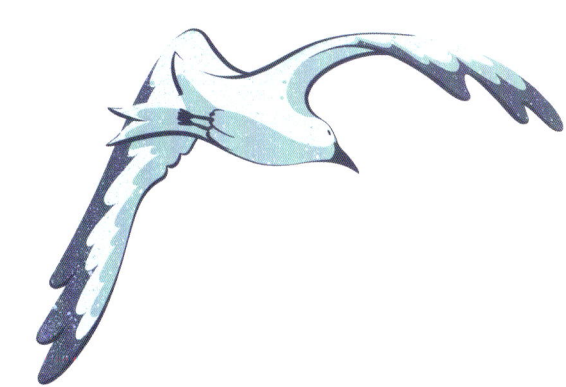

THE INTRODUCTION OF JACK ANTONOFF

Jack Antonoff, the former guitarist for the band Fun and lead singer for Bleachers, first crossed paths with Taylor around 2013. Taylor reached out to Jack because of his reputation as someone who could seamlessly combine introspective songwriting with innovative pop production.

The first collaboration between the two was for "Sweeter than Fiction," a song written for the 2013 film *One Chance*. While the song wasn't a chart-topping hit, their creative chemistry clicked, and it set the stage for deeper collaboration on Taylor's groundbreaking fifth studio album, *1989*.

"Out of the Woods" was the first song the two wrote together. Jack sent Taylor a finished instrumental track while she was on an airplane. About thirty minutes later, she sent him a voice memo containing the lyrics for the song. This was Taylor's first time writing a song to an existing instrumental track—something with which she would eventually get more comfortable.

The two work well together: Taylor brings her personal, universally relatable storytelling, and Jack creates dynamic soundscapes to amplify those emotions. They have been able to take creative risks together and have found a mutual trust in each other.

Jack credits Taylor with being the first person who's allowed him to produce music. When discussing the process of working with Taylor, he said, "And when, in the past, where someone would say, 'Now we'll hand it off to so-and-so, who has a proven track record,' she just

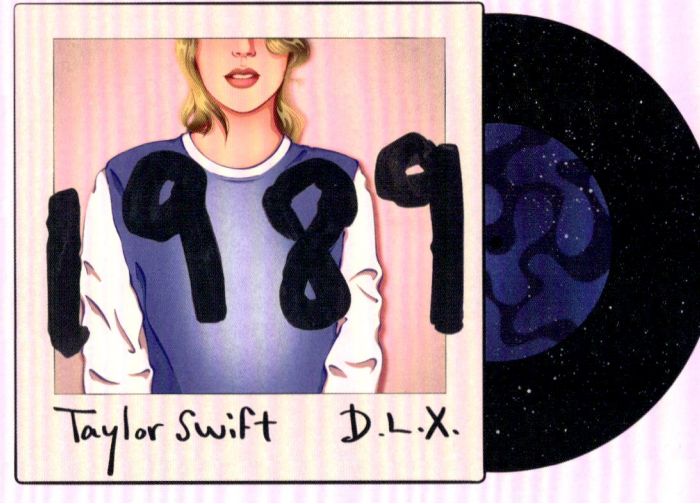

ALBUMS
Speak Now (2010) and *Speak Now World Tour—Live* (2011)

DATE LAUNCHED
October 25, 2010, and November 21, 2011

FIRST SINGLE
"Mine" (August 4, 2010)

OTHER SINGLES
"Back to December" (November 15, 2010), "Mean" (March 7, 2011), "The Story of Us" (April 19, 2011), "Sparks Fly" (July 18, 2011), and "Ours" (December 5, 2011)

TOUR
Speak Now World Tour (February 2011 to March 2012)

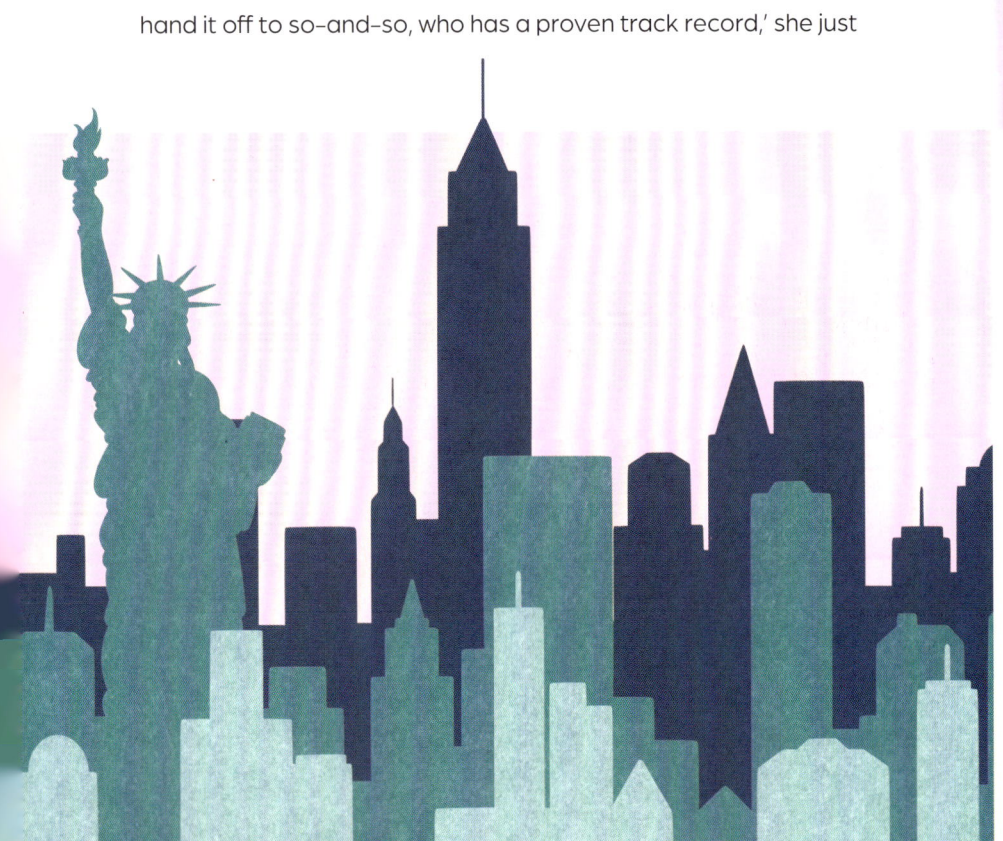

said, 'It's done.' I was sort of shocked—and thrilled! She hears what I hear, cool. She didn't think twice. I think that's part of the reason why we've had such an incredibly long and beautiful collaboration."

Taylor even wrote the *1989* song, "You Are in Love," about Jack and his then-partner, Lena Dunham. Taylor said she

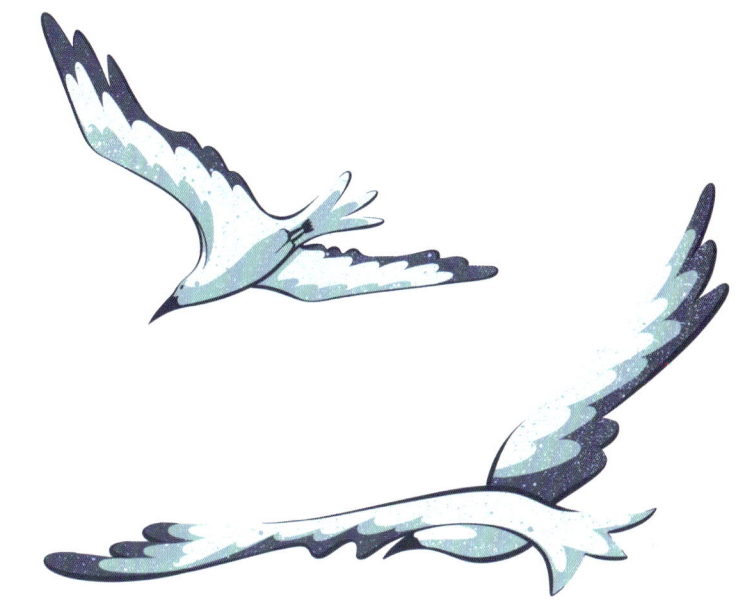

never had that best-friend feeling in a partner and so the song and lyrics were inspired by what Lena told her about the pair. Taylor said, "And I think that that kind of relationship—God, it sounds like it would just be so beautiful—would also be hard. It would also be mundane at times."

One of their most iconic song collaborations is "Getaway Car." Fans got a behind-the-scenes look at the creation of the song in the documentary *Miss Americana*. Taylor and Jack were seen in the studio, trying to get the lyrics to the song right. They piggybacked off each other, each providing new lyrics, and soon, Taylor finished the new verse and screamed, "AHHH!"

They nailed it.

During her 2023 MTV Video Music Awards acceptance speech for Song of the Year for "Anti-Hero," Taylor said, "I'm really, really lucky that I get to write songs with one of my best friends in the world. His name is Jack Antonoff."

The respect is mutual, and Jack isn't afraid to come to Taylor's defense. In 2022, musician Damon Albarn went on record to say that Taylor doesn't write her own songs. Jack immediately clapped back and defended Taylor. In an interview later talking about that experience, he said, "But you come after my friend Taylor, you're toast to me."

Jack and Taylor have since worked on every subsequent album together, from *1989* through to *The Tortured Poets Department*, and have collaborated on eighty-eight songs to date.

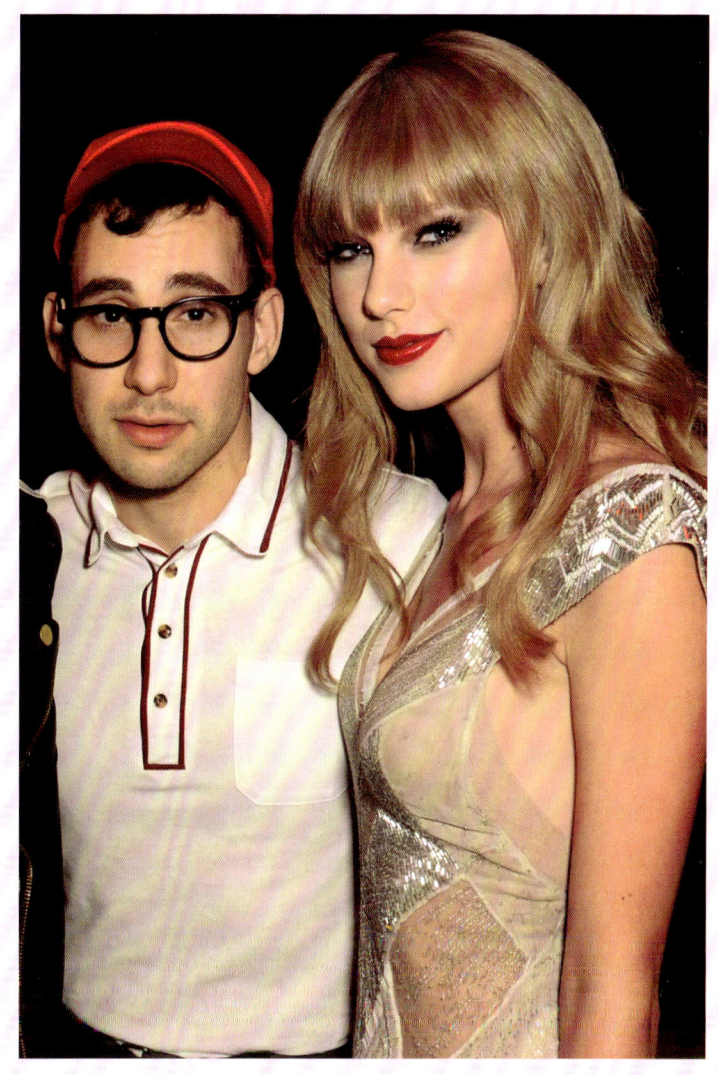

PAGE 96: Welcome to the Windy City: Taylor opens her 1989 World Tour concert with "Welcome to New York" at Chicago's Soldier Field, July 19, 2015.

RIGHT: Taylor and Nate Reuss, front man for the band Fun, at MTV's Europe Music Awards in Germany, November 11, 2012.

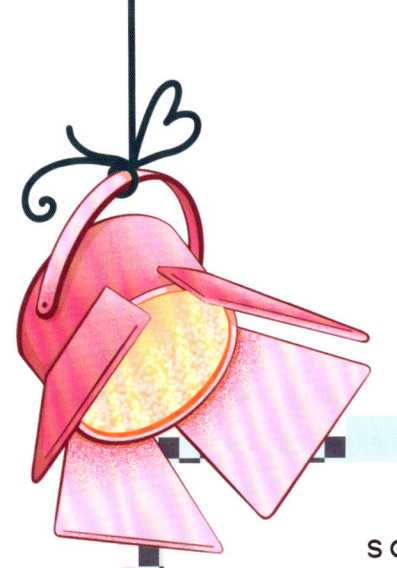

"All You Had to Do Was Stay"

Taylor wrote this song after she woke up from a really embarrassing dream about an ex-boyfriend. In a 2014 *Time* interview, she discussed the dream and said, "In the dream, my ex had come to the door to beg for me to talk to him or whatever, and I opened up the door and I went to go say, 'Hi,' or 'What are you doing here?' or something—something normal—but all that came out was this high-pitched singing that said, 'Stay!' It was almost operatic. So I wrote this song, and I used that sound in the song. Weird, right?"

ALBUM

1989

RELEASED

2014

She said, "We don't make music to win a lot of awards, but you have to take your cues from somewhere if you're going to continue to evolve." Taylor realized that her last two albums were like "patchwork quilts" and not sonically cohesive like her breakthrough album *Fearless*. After the Grammy loss, she woke up at four in the morning with the foundation of *1989*, including the title of the album, in her mind. She decided to make it a full pop record that embraced synth sounds from the 1980s and determined that she was not going to listen to any feedback from her record label. She opted instead to move forward and started working on the album the very next day.

Listening to her gut worked out: *1989* debuted at No. 1 on the Billboard 200 and sold more than 1.28 million copies in its first week. It was the only album to go platinum in 2014. Of the most notable awards, Taylor took home three Grammy Awards for *1989*, including Album of the Year, Best Pop Vocal Album, and Best Music Video for "Bad Blood" (featuring Kendrick Lamar). She was also named Billboard's Woman of the Year for the second time in 2014.

When asked by Barbara Walters whether she was worried that she would lose some of her country fans, Taylor confidently said, "I am not worried about that. I am really in touch with my fans, and I know what they like. What my fans in general were afraid of is that I would start making pop music and I would stop writing smart lyrics or I would stop writing emotional lyrics. And when they heard the new music, they realized that that wasn't the case at all."

Switching from country to pop brought skepticism and challenges for Taylor, who had built her entire career in the country-music scene. However, these milestones also showed the world that Taylor was here to stay and that she would continue to evolve and make music on her own terms.

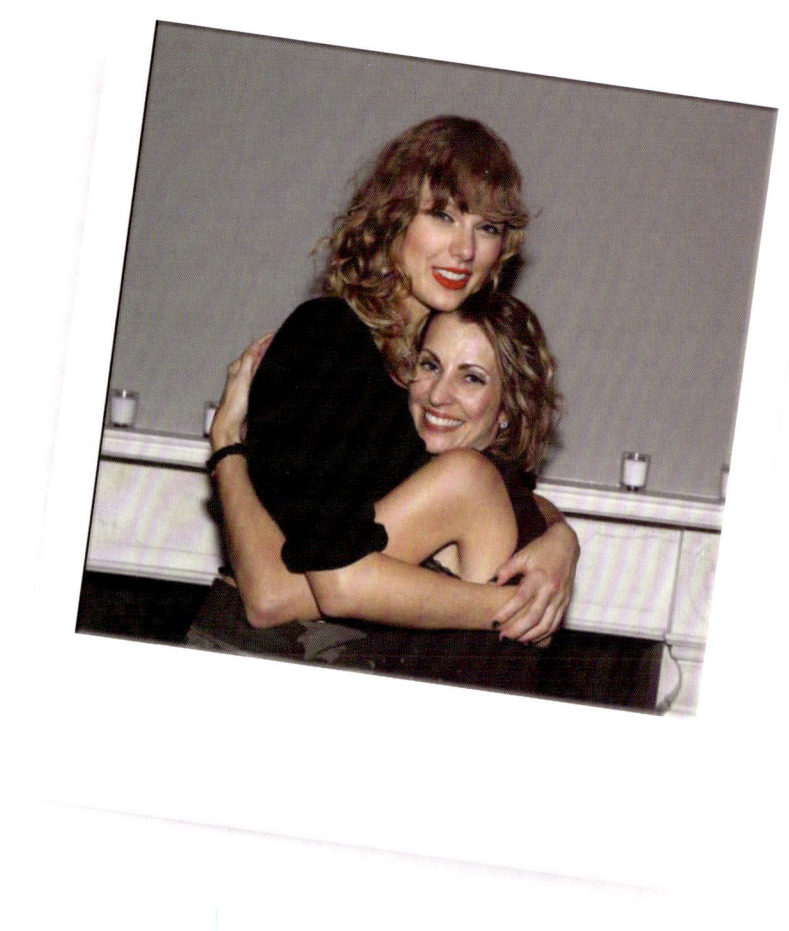

Secret Sessions

Before Taylor released *1989* into the world, she hosted what have become known as "Secret Sessions." Always thinking of ways to pour back into her fans for their love and support, she wanted to do something special for this album release. Long before the album came out, she handpicked fans from around the world and hosted eighty-nine of them at intimate gatherings in each of her homes.

The process of selecting these fans became known as "Taylurking." Taylor would lurk on social media (she was especially active on Tumblr during this era) for months, taking note of the most die-hard fans. She would learn about them: their interests, their families, and any other information she could find. Taylor has been known to greet her most loyal fans by name, often saying it's nice to finally meet them or asking them about certain things she knows about them.

Once selected, fans got a message from her fan platform, Taylor Nation, inviting them to a "top-secret" event. On the day of the event, the fans met in a parking lot, checked in their cell phones, and were bused off to a secret location, which happened to be one of Taylor's houses.

When the fans arrived at Taylor's home, they were greeted by members of the Taylor Nation team and treated to drinks, snacks, and homemade baked goods like Taylor's famous pumpkin-chocolate cookies and chai cookies.

Once everyone had mingled for a bit, Taylor came in and surprised the fans with a "Hi, guys!" Screams erupted and the fans got the surprise of a lifetime. Taylor played her new record from start to finish, singing and dancing with her fans and sharing behind-the-scenes information and, of course, taking lots of Polaroid photos with everyone.

Describing the importance of these events, Taylor said, "I want to come up with as many ways we can spend time together and bond because it keeps me normal, and it keeps my life feeling manageable."

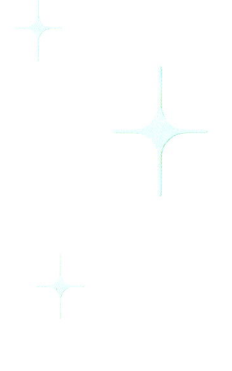

ABOVE:
Suzy Hackbarth was one of the lucky fans who attended a Secret Sesson.

A WHITE VEIL OCCASION

Taylor might barge in on some white veil occasions—but for good reason. One of the most heartwarming ways she has shown her fans love and generosity over the years is by surprising them during special moments in their life, such as engagements and weddings.

In April 2014, Taylor attended the bridal shower of longtime Swiftie Gena Gabrielle in Ohio. Gena had met Taylor at a past meet-and-greet and, on a whim, sent Taylor an invitation to her bridal shower, never expecting a reply. To her shock, not only did Taylor RSVP, but she also showed up to the event with thoughtful gifts in hand, including a KitchenAid stand mixer, handwritten recipes, and other personalized items.

In 2016, fan Max Singer and his bride, Kenya Smith, got married in a small ceremony at a hospital so that Max's dying mother could witness the wedding. His sister later wrote to Taylor, sharing the story and explaining how much Taylor's music, particularly the song "Blank Space," had meant to their family during this time. Max and Kenya planned a small wedding reception in New Jersey to celebrate with friends and family, and they got the surprise of a lifetime when Taylor showed up and performed an acoustic version of "Blank Space" for the newlywed couple. She even joked with the crowd that when she wrote the song, she never imagined performing it at a wedding.

In 2018, a longtime fan named Stephanie shared her emotional story of how Taylor stepped in during one of the hardest times of her life. Stephanie was pregnant when the house she lived in with her partner, Matthew, was condemned and Matthew lost his job, rendering them homeless and struggling to make ends meet. While attending the Reputation Stadium Tour concert, Stephanie was invited to the T Party room. Taylor was made aware of Stephanie's situation through the new fan app, The Swift Life, where Stephanie's mom told Taylor what was going on. Stephanie said Taylor took her aside and said, "Stephanie, you've been in my life for a long time, and you've never asked me for anything. You could have reached out and I would have helped you. But you didn't. Your mum told me." Taylor told Stephanie that she wanted to reimburse her for the concert ticket, but instead, she stepped in and ensured that they had a house and all that they needed for their baby. Stephanie remembered Taylor telling her, "I want you to be able to enjoy your little girl, not have to worry about all this stuff."

While these stories stand out for good reason, they really are part of a broader invisible string of kindness that Taylor has weaved for years. She consistently goes above and beyond for her fans, building relationships with them that are genuine and personal, and always looking for ways to support them during their biggest milestones, just like so many of them have done for her.

Back on Tour

With the release of *1989* came the announcement of The 1989 World Tour, which spanned eighty-five shows in four continents and brought in more than $250 million. Taylor played her largest venues to date, and she got creative with this tour. The stage included massive LED screens that featured visual backgrounds for each song. The runway-style stage had a hydraulic lift that could cross the arena, ensuring that all her fans had a great view of the show. Each attendee received an LED wristband that lit up with varying colors for each song, creating a glittering arena full of magic and awe.

Her set list included seventeen songs, plus one surprise song each night, lasting a little over two hours. Opening acts were Vance Joy, Shawn Mendes, Rae Morris, and HAIM. One surprise of the tour was Taylor's different approach to the songs. For each stop of the tour, she asked a musician or someone special to share the stage with her. To her surprise, everyone agreed, and part of the excitement of attending a concert was wondering who would show up in your city. Guests included music stars like Mick Jagger, Alanis Morissette, and Wiz Khalifa. Actress Lisa Kudrow joined Taylor onstage and performed the infamous "Smelly Cat" from the television show *Friends*. Taylor's friends walked the catwalk, and the US Women's National Team for soccer graced the stage after winning the World Cup.

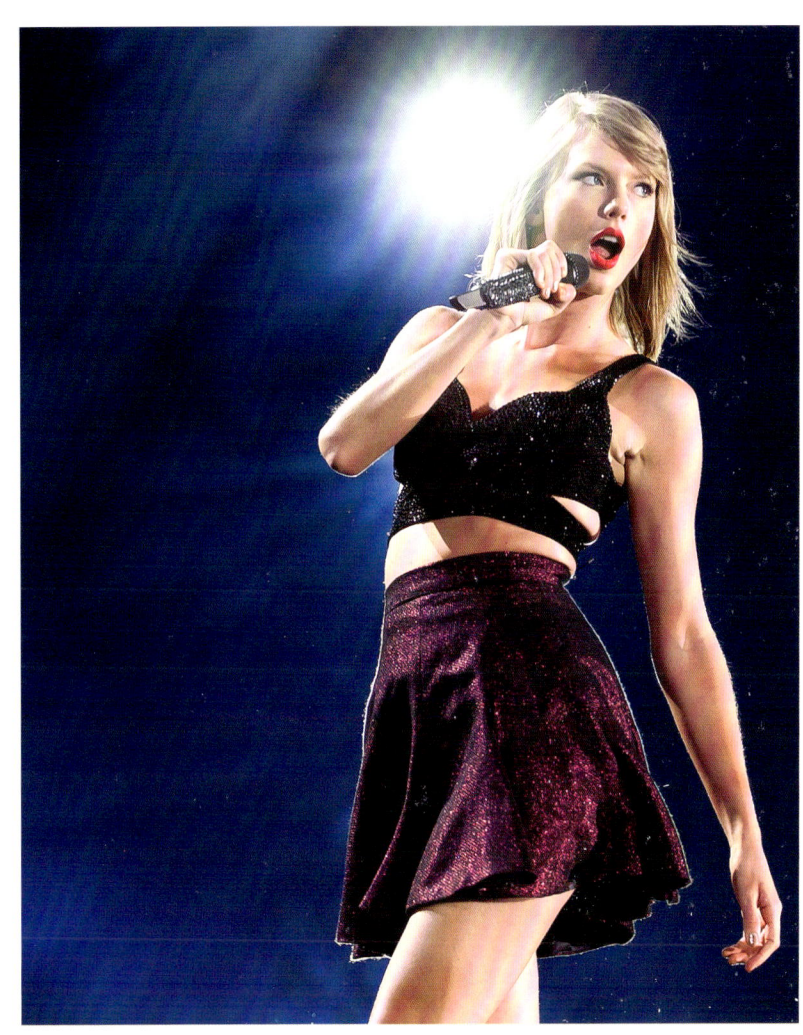

ABOVE: At the MetLife Stadium in New Jersey during The 1989 World Tour, July 11, 2015.

FOLLOWING PAGES: Headlining in Las Vegas at Rock in Rio USA, May 15, 2015. This was technically the first US date for The 1989 World Tour.

The intro to the song "Wildest Dreams" is Taylor's actual heartbeat.

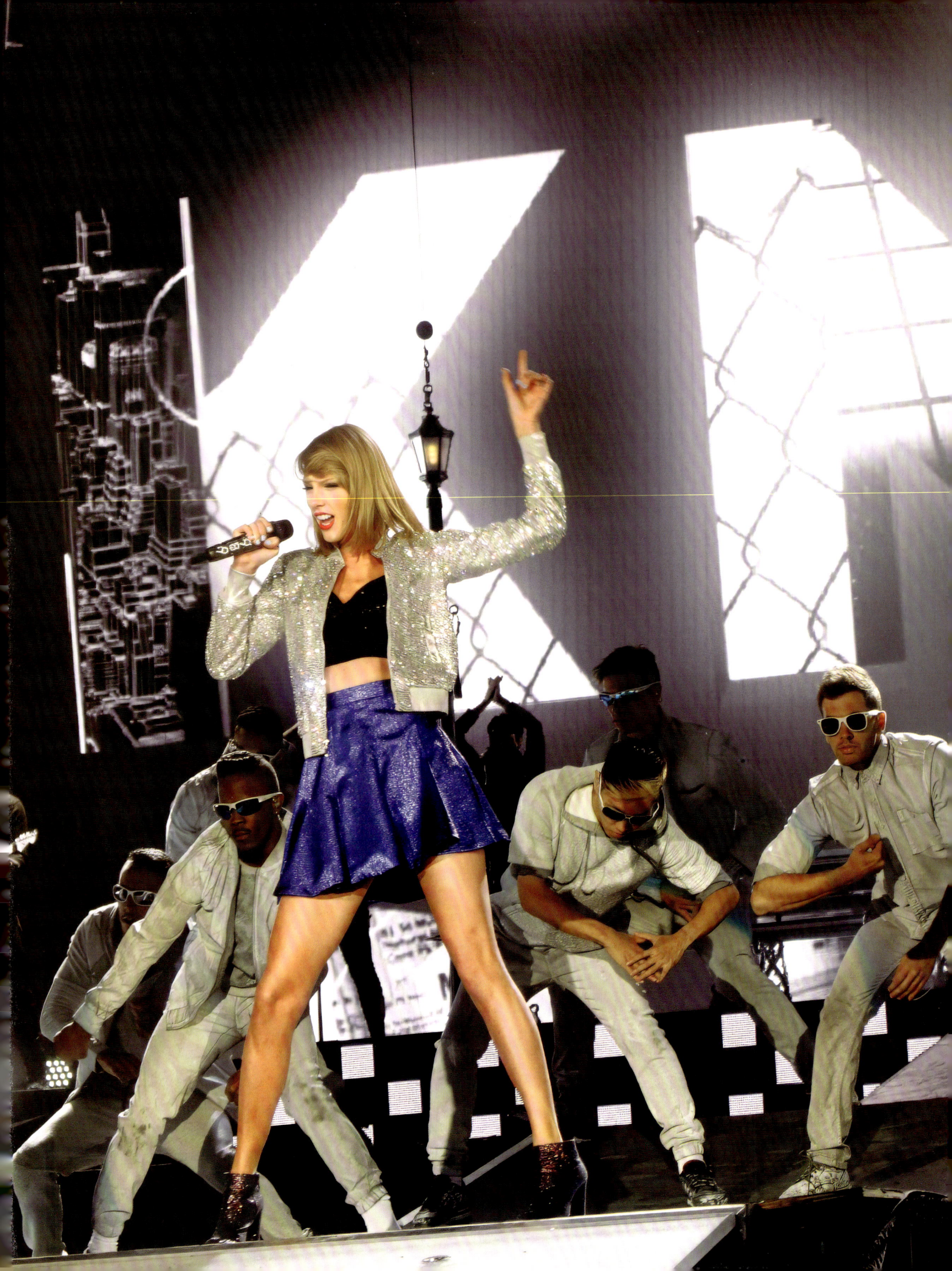

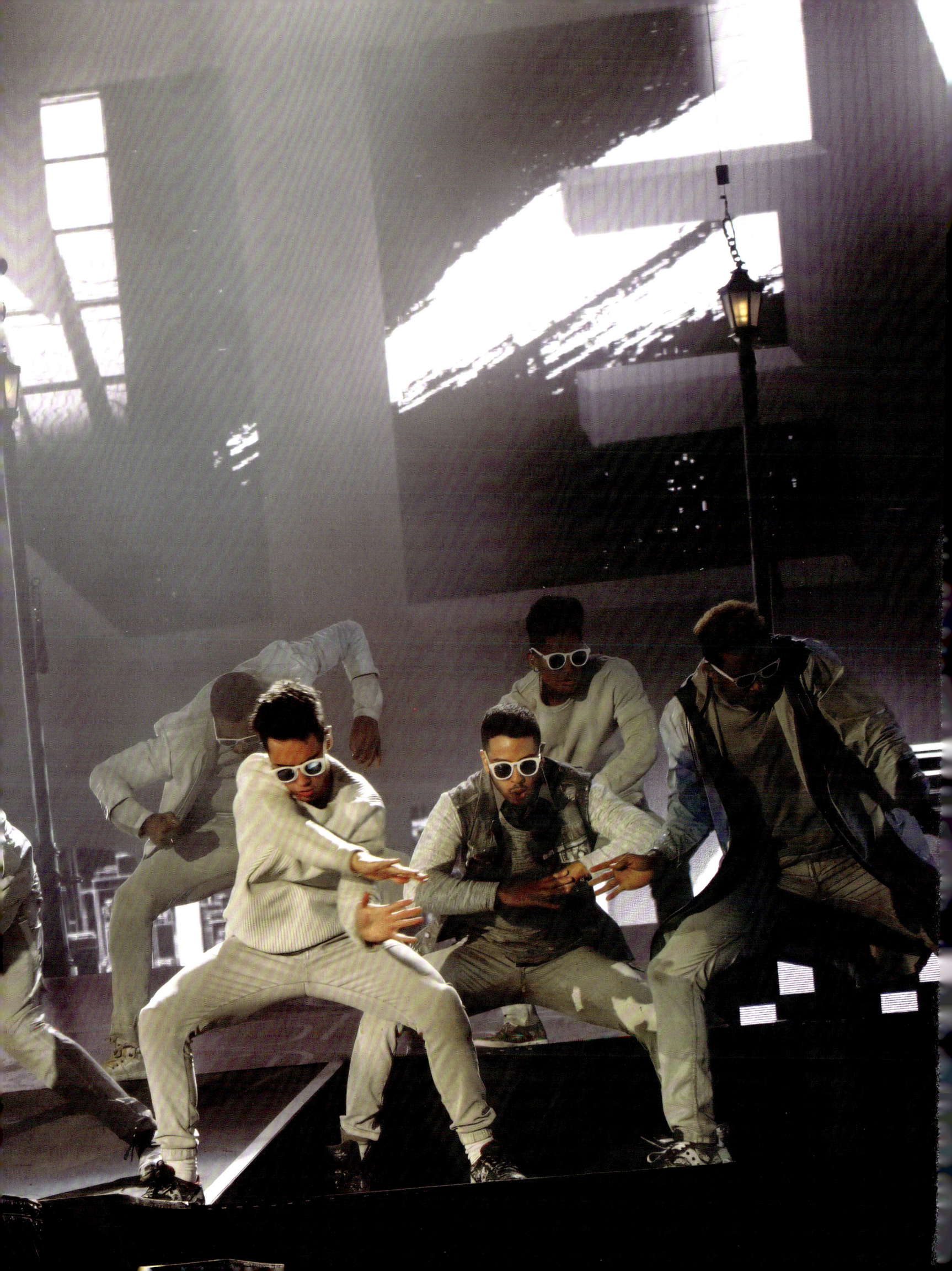

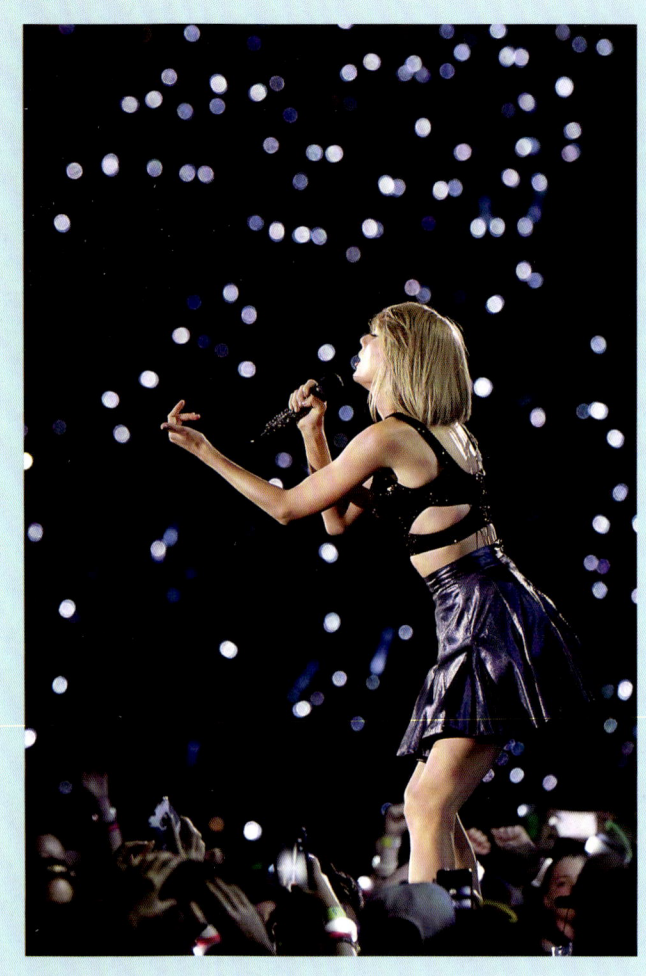

The LED Light-Up Bracelets

FIRST DEBUTED
The 1989 World Tour

A GLITTERING STADIUM

At the ticketing gate, every concertgoer was given an electronic bracelet to wear during the concert. During the show, the bracelet would light up different colors, creating a glittering effect across the entire stadium. The company that produces them is called "PixMob," and they use a special infrared technology called "Moving Head" to control the bracelets and "paint" designs across the stadium. Taylor is known for having surprise guests choose what color they want the color to light up during their moment.

Fans dressed their best and lit up the audience not just with LED bracelets, but also homemade signs and props. Knowing that the most outrageous costumes could possibly get them into the T Party room, renamed the 1989 Loft for this tour, fans got really creative, making visual representations of lyrics such as paper airplanes, as well as "hunters" and "foxes" as a nod to the song "Out of the Woods."

The 1989 Loft was set up to mimic a New Your City loft-style apartment, with faux brick backdrops and a living room area. A special photo station featured an oversize Polaroid cut-out in which Taylor and fans would snap photos to capture the evening.

To make the tour even more accessible, Taylor created *The 1989 World Tour Live*, a documentary that aired on Apple TV+ on December 20, 2015. The film showed the tour and included behind-the-scenes content and the special guest appearances for which the tour was known. As one of the first artists to make her entire tour available to at-home viewers, this film once again connected her already-supportive fan base and brought new fans to the table by letting them experience the concert at home.

ABOVE: The light-up bracelets in full effect during a performance in Sydney, Australia, on The 1989 World Tour, Novebmer 28, 2015.

Friends Forever

While Taylor credited her fans with helping to keep her life manageable, she also leaned on her friendships during this time. Now living in New York, a confident and stylish Taylor was often photographed hanging out in the city with what became known as "the squad." The squad was a star-studded group of Taylor's closest friends and included models, actors, and singers such as Selena Gomez, Gigi Hadid, Martha Hunt, Karlie Kloss, and Lena Dunham. The squad became one of the most talked-about social groups of the time, with the media hanging on every photo or outing. As someone who struggled to make friends in middle school and often channeled that into her storytelling, Taylor was now the life of the party, and she was happy to have a supportive friend group that had her back.

On social media, Taylor posted photos with her friends from birthday celebrations and her infamous Fourth of July parties at her Rhode Island home. The media and fans alike became enamored with Taylor's coveted Fourth of July parties and wondered who would attend and what moments would be shared on Instagram. Some of those moments shared online featured photos of the squad in matching bathing suits sliding down huge inflatable slides, giving social media onlookers serious FOMO. The squad even joined her onstage for The 1989 World Tour and in her "Bad Blood" music video.

A Few of Taylor's **Fourth of July** party 2015 guests: Gigi Hadid, Martha Hunt, the HAIM Sisters, Serayah, Calvin Harris, and Ed Sheeran.

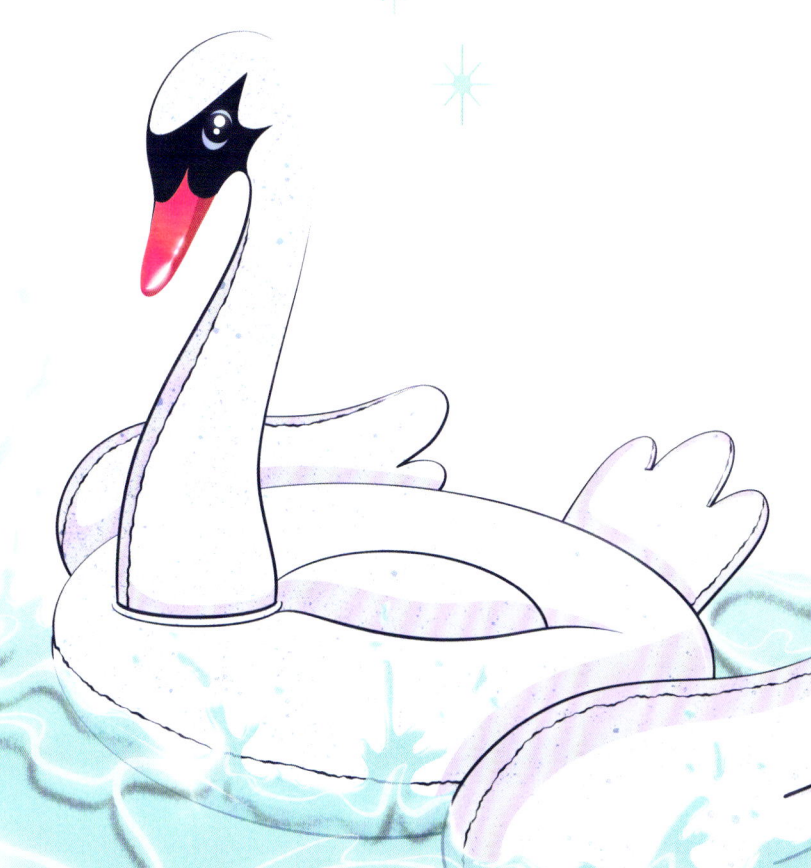

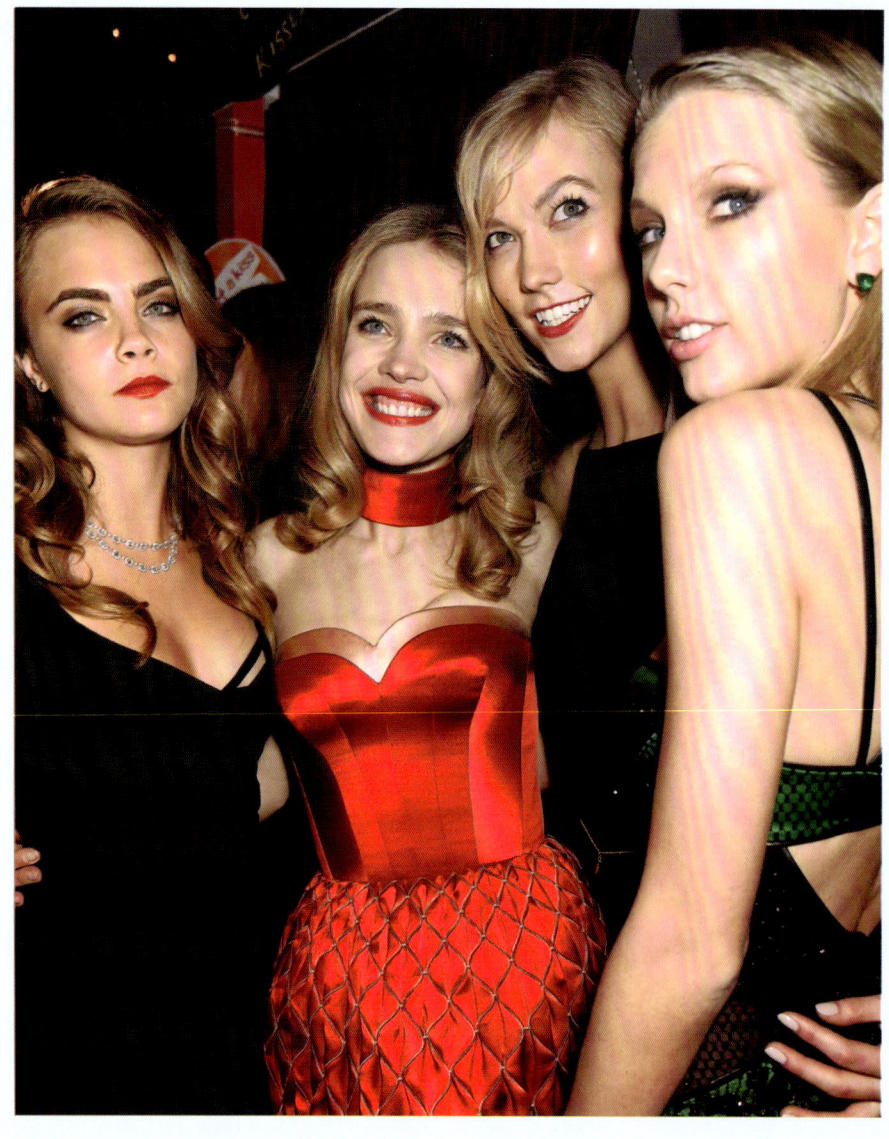

"My friendships are the most important thing to me right now because I can trust them."

Taylor, 2014

The squad didn't come without backlash, however. People questioned whether her group represented female empowerment and feminism, often commenting on Taylor's "model friends" and the unrealistic beauty standards that they represented.

Years later, in a 2019 *Elle* magazine article, Taylor shared thirty things she learned before turning thirty. She reflected on the infamous squad and spoke about what she'd learned, saying, "Realizing childhood scars and working on rectifying them. For example, never being popular as a kid was always an insecurity for me. Even as an adult, I still have recurring flashbacks of sitting at lunch tables alone or hiding in a bathroom stall, or trying to make a new friend and being laughed at. In my twenties, I found myself surrounded by girls who wanted to be my friend. So I shouted it from the rooftops, posted pictures, and celebrated my newfound acceptance into a sisterhood, without realizing that other people might still feel the way I did when I felt so alone. It's important to address our long-standing issues before we turn into the living embodiment of them."

ABOVE: Taylor attends the World's First Fabulous Fund Fair in London with (left to right) Cara Delevingne, Natalia Vodianova, and Karlie Kloss, February 24, 2015.

NEW YORK CITY 2014

In April 2014, Taylor settled into a penthouse in Tribeca. The song "Welcome to New York" is a nod to the move and the inspiration for a lot of the *1989* album. On *Good Morning America*, Taylor said, "I wanted to start the album with this song because New York has been an important landscape and location for the story of my life . . . The inspiration that I found in that city is kind of hard to describe and hard to compare to any other force of inspiration I've ever experienced."

EMPIRE STATE BUILDING

Iconic to the NYC skyline . . . and also the site of Taylor's *1989* album announcement via livestream. Their social media presence demonstrates that its staff are all huge Swifties.

THE HIGH LINE

Referenced in the song "cardigan," this beautiful, elevated greenway is located in Manhattan.

CHELSEA HOTEL

This hotel is referenced in the title track of *The Tortured Poets Department*. Part of the National Registry of Historical Places, this hotel was frequented by many famous writers, musicians, and poets, including Dylan Thomas and Patti Smith.

ELECTRIC LADY STUDIO

A recording studio in Greenwich Village founded by Jimi Hendrix in the 1960s. Taylor has recorded parts of her albums here since *Lover*.

APARTMENT ON CORNELIA STREET

Taylor rented an apartment on Cornelia Street while her Tribeca apartment was under construction and used it as the title of a song on the *Lover* album.

HOUSING WORKS BOOKSTORE

This is the location in the final scene of the *All Too Well: The Short Film*, where Taylor is seen doing a book reading for a novel called *All Too Well*. This bookstore is a nonprofit organization that helps fight the AIDS crisis and homelessness in NYC.

Taylor is often photographed going out with friends in NYC. She's been spotted at restaurants like Lucali, The Polo Bar, Banzarbar, and Waverly Inn, just to name a few.

SOON YOU'LL GET BETTER

Whether it's through hospital visits or her song "Ronan," it's no surprise that Taylor has shown generosity and support during fans' times of need, especially health challenges.

In 2015, eleven-year-old Naomi Oakes, a huge Taylor Swift fan, was diagnosed with acute myeloid leukemia. Naomi and her family made a video called "Naomi's Bad Blood" to promote the family's GoFundMe page and used Taylor's "Bad Blood" song in the background. The family shared that Naomi was heartbroken that she couldn't attend Taylor's The 1989 World Tour due to a hospital stay, but Taylor's song "Bad Blood" was her anthem to help her through the fight.

The video and story caught the attention of Taylor, and Taylor donated $50,000 to the GoFundMe campaign with a message of encouragement: "To the beautiful and brave Naomi, I'm sorry you have to miss it, but there will always be more concerts. Let's focus on getting you feeling better. I'm sending the biggest hugs to you and your family."

About a year later, Naomi was in remission and had the opportunity to finally see Taylor perform at a Formula 1 Grand Prix concert, and Naomi even got to meet Taylor after the show.

In 2018, a fan named Sadie Bartell posted on Tumblr that her mother had been in a coma for more than three years due to complications from a rare condition and that the medical expenses were overwhelming. Sadie shared her feelings of helplessness and financial strain on the family, and linked to a GoFundMe to ask for help.

Shortly after Sadie's post, Taylor donated $15,500 to their GoFundMe page and left a heartfelt note that said: "Love, Taylor, sending you and your family all my love."

In August 2019, fan Ayesha Khurram shared her struggles online with balancing her university tuition with her family's mounting medical bills due to her mother's battle with chronic kidney disease. Taylor saw her story and sent Ayesha $6,386.47 via PayPal to cover her tuition and expenses. Along with the money, Taylor included a message: "Ayesha, get your learn on, girl. I love you! Taylor."

So many of Taylor's charitable acts are done privately and involve her reaching out to fans or directly donating to their campaigns or through social media. While many include financial relief, these contributions also offer a deeply kind gesture that signals to fans that they are seen and valued by someone whom they deeply admire. Just like Taylor says, her fans have her back, and she wants to show them that she has theirs too.

Romantic Relationships

In mid-2015, the media shifted its focus from Taylor's squad to her romantic life. She'd embraced the single life for several years, until she was introduced to DJ Calvin Harris at the 2015 Brit Awards. The two began dating shortly after, and this became one of Taylor's first high-profile and long-term romances. The two attended the Billboard Music Awards together in May 2015 and stirred up a media storm with cameras always panning to them. The couple shared glimpses of their relationship online, like the popular photo of Taylor flipping sweet potatoes on the grill with Calvin's caption: "She cooks too." They also posted photos from a beach getaway, including a photo of "TS + AW" written in the sand. (Calvin's real name is Adam Wiles.)

While the couple captured the interest of the media and their fans, they eventually ended their relationship in June 2016, and it appeared amicable. Calvin tweeted, "The only truth here is that a relationship came to an end & what remains is a huge amount of love and respect," with Taylor retweeting the message.

Things took a dramatic turn just weeks later, when news surfaced that Taylor had co-written the Calvin Harris song "This Is What You Came For" (sung by Rihanna) under the pseudonym Nils Sjöberg. After initially denying her involvement, Calvin confirmed it in a now-deleted series of tweets, expressing frustration that Taylor's team had leaked the information post-breakup. Just a few weeks after the breakup, Taylor was spotted cozied up with actor Tom Hiddleston, sparking an even bigger media storm. Taylor continued to remain silent on the matter and, eventually, things with Tom fizzled out. In the fall of 2016, Taylor was linked to actor Joe Alwyn, who went on to become her long-term boyfriend of six years.

"I have rules for a lot of areas of my life. Love is not going to be one of them."

Taylor, 2012

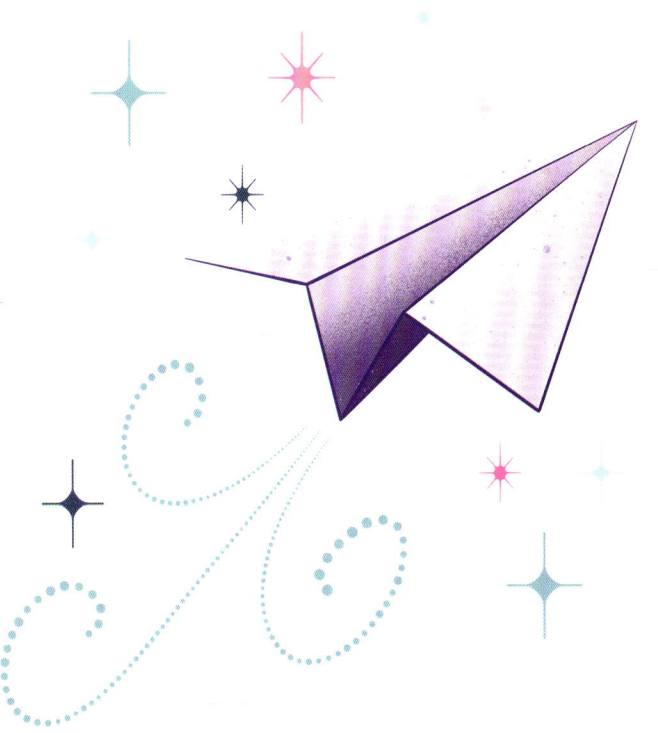

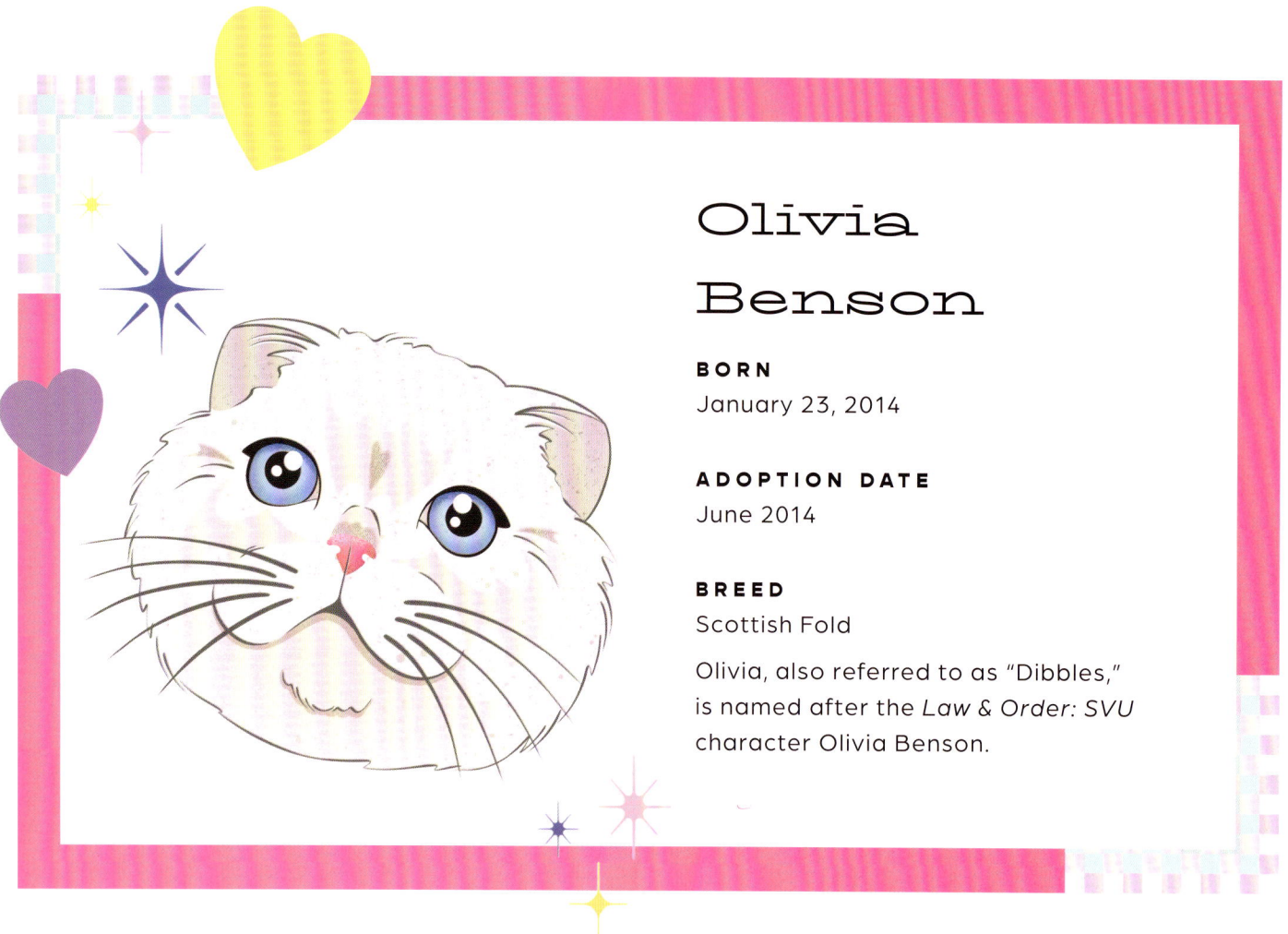

Olivia Benson

BORN
January 23, 2014

ADOPTION DATE
June 2014

BREED
Scottish Fold

Olivia, also referred to as "Dibbles," is named after the *Law & Order: SVU* character Olivia Benson.

Artist for Artists

Despite the media circus constantly surrounding her, on June 21, 2015, Taylor decided to use her voice for a cause that she believes deeply in: artists' rights. Taylor became a prominent voice for artists' rights in a high-profile dispute with Apple Music that ultimately led to significant changes in the streaming service's policies. The conflict arose as Apple prepared to launch its streaming platform with a three-month free trial period for new users, during which artists, producers, and songwriters would not be paid for their music.

Taylor, fresh off the success of her *1989* album, took a stand against the policy in a powerful open letter.

Posted on her Tumblr page, the letter was titled "To Apple, Love Taylor." It was professional but firm and expressed her disappointment with the decision and what it meant to artists. She made it clear that her speaking out was not about her, but on behalf of smaller independent artists, who deserve to be paid for their work. She wrote, "This is not about me. Thankfully I am on my fifth album and can support myself, my band, and my crew through live shows. This is about the new artist or band that has just released their first single and will not be paid for its success."

She revealed that she would withhold her album *1989* from the platform unless the policy

OPPOSITE:
Taylor meets her fans at the Narita International Airport in Japan during her press tour to promote *1989*, November 4, 2014.

was changed. She ended the letter with, "We don't ask you for free iPhones. Please don't ask us to provide you with our music for no compensation."

Less than twenty-four hours after her post, Apple's senior vice president, Eddy Cue, responded that Apple would reverse its policy and pay artists during the trial period. He said, "We hear you @taylorswift13 and indie artists. Love, Apple."

This is when the epithet "Taylor Swift *is* the music industry" came about. The swift response from Apple showcased Taylor's influence in the music industry and how her voice could be used to create better treatment for artists across the board. This incident also set a precedent for

companies to take artists' concerns seriously in the era of streaming, and it highlighted the evolving dynamics between musicians and major tech platforms.

This time in Taylor's life signified so much self-discovery. She had a new soundtrack to her life in every way, from her fashion style and her friendships to her music genre and new city. It was a time when Taylor experimented with who she was and what she stood for. One thing that didn't change, however, was the connection to her fans and her commitment to creating music on her own terms. She was no longer afraid to dance on her own or change the rules. For that and more, this was the era when Taylor Swift, the iconic pop star, was born.

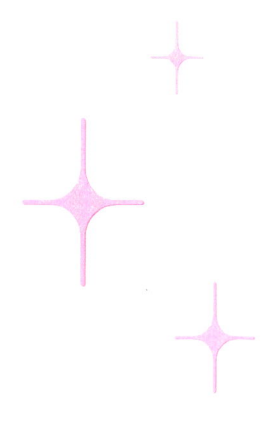

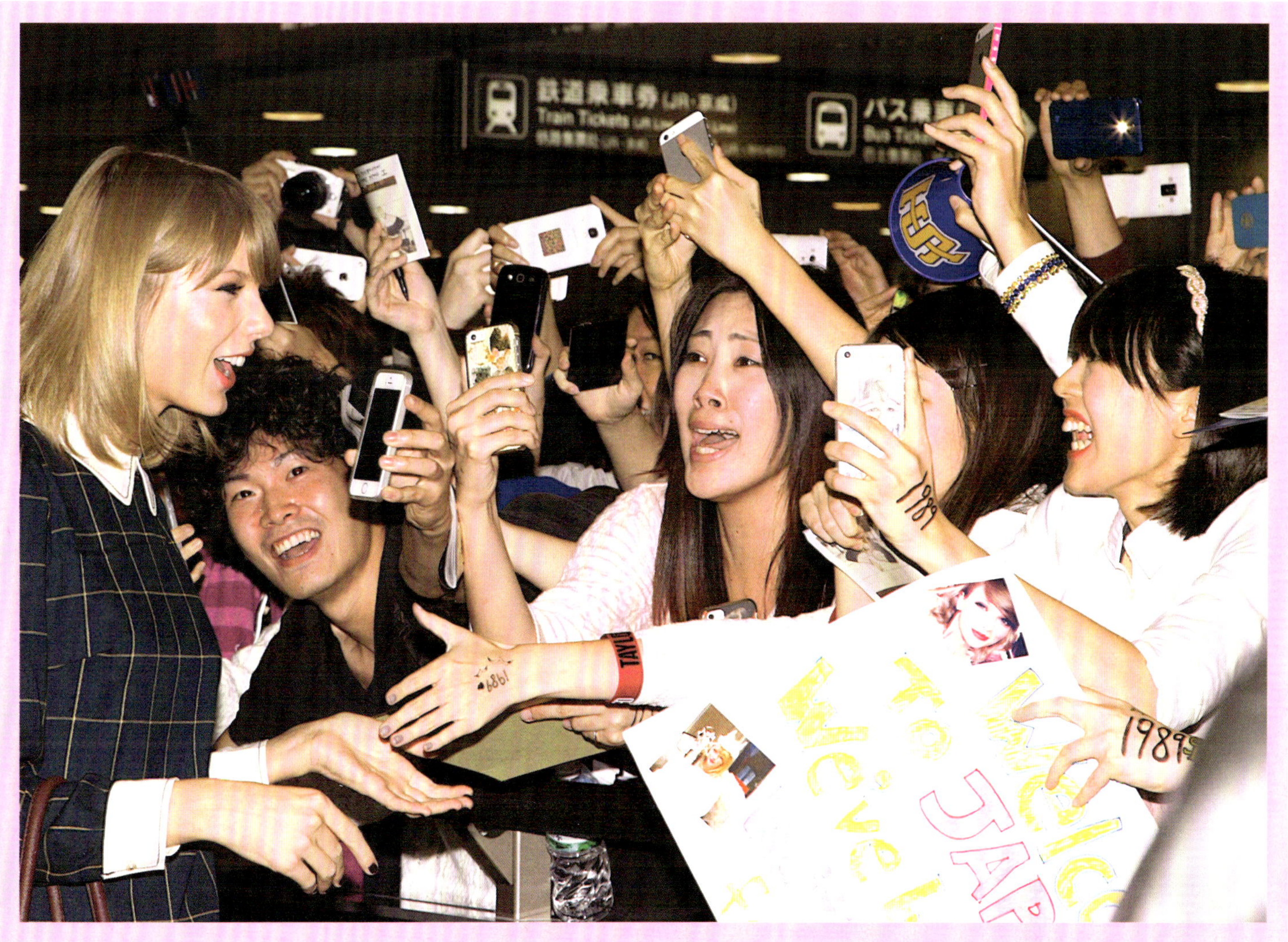

THE ERAS OF TAYLOR'S FOOTWEAR

From her debut days of only wearing cowboy boots to custom Louboutin on The Eras Tour, Taylor's footwear has evolved throughout the years.

A Cowboy Like Me
2005–2008

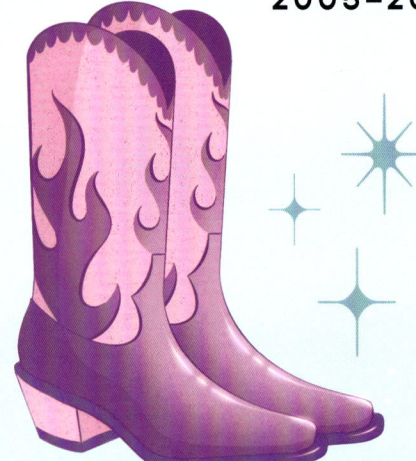

"I wear cowboy boots so that when I walk down the stairs I won't fall. I have this fear of falling in front of large groups of people. That's why I tend not to wear heels. I'm like 6'2 when I wear heels, so I tend to wear cowboy boots a lot." —Taylor Swift

From classic leather to custom bedazzled, Taylor rocked cowboy books as a nod to her country-music roots.

SO HIGH SCHOOL
2009–2011

"I promise you, you're probably doing or wearing something right now that you will look back on later and find revolting and hilarious. You can't avoid it, so don't try to. For example, I had a phase where, for the entirety of 2012, I dressed like a 1950s housewife. But you know what? I was having fun. Trends and phases are fun." —Taylor Swift

Even though Taylor was no longer in high school and was now as a young adult, she traded in her cowboy boots for Mary Janes with short heels, giving vintage schoolgirl vibes.

She Wears High Heels AND Sneakers
2012–2014

"I WEAR HEEELS NOW!" —Red Liner Notes in the song "Begin Again"

Even though her height used to stop her from wearing high heels, she started embracing them in this era. Of course, she also still had tried and true Keds that she would wear on more casual outings. She even designed a shoe line in collaboration with Keds during The Red Tour.

ROCK N' ROLL
2015–2016

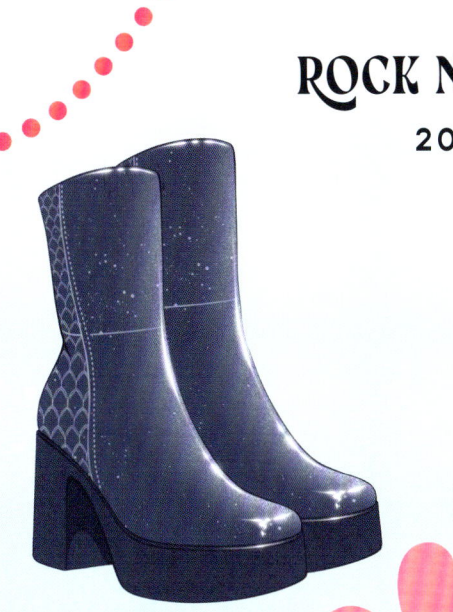

I'm thrilled that it's Taylor Swift, who's my co-chair this year at the Met Gala, and we very much wanted to give Taylor a new look, make her into a sort of a rock n' roll chick." —Anna Wintour

Taylor leaned all the way into rock star status during The 1989 World Tour. She wore lots of thick, chunky leather boots and heels that matched her new short haircut.

Big Reputation
2017–2019

"Style is such a personal thing; it's your way to be an individual." —Taylor Swift

Taylor opened her Reputation Stadium Tour sporting thigh-high boots made by Christian Louboutin. This is where we see Taylor lean more into thigh-high boots, high fashion, and making more bold choices in her looks.

IF THE SHOW FITS, WALK IN IT
2020–2024

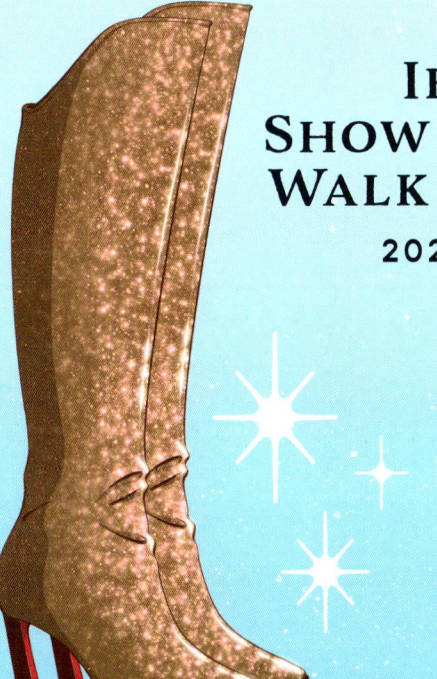

"My style advice to other girls is to be experimental but always have a 'home base' and stick with your comfort style." —Taylor Swift

Since 2020, we see Taylor fully embracing her style, shimmering at every angle. From lacy, glimmering stilettos to chunky heels to thigh-high boots, Taylor is expressing herself across all her eras and embracing a style that is her own. During The Eras Tour, Christian Louboutin designed over 250 pairs to compliment her entire tour wardrobe.

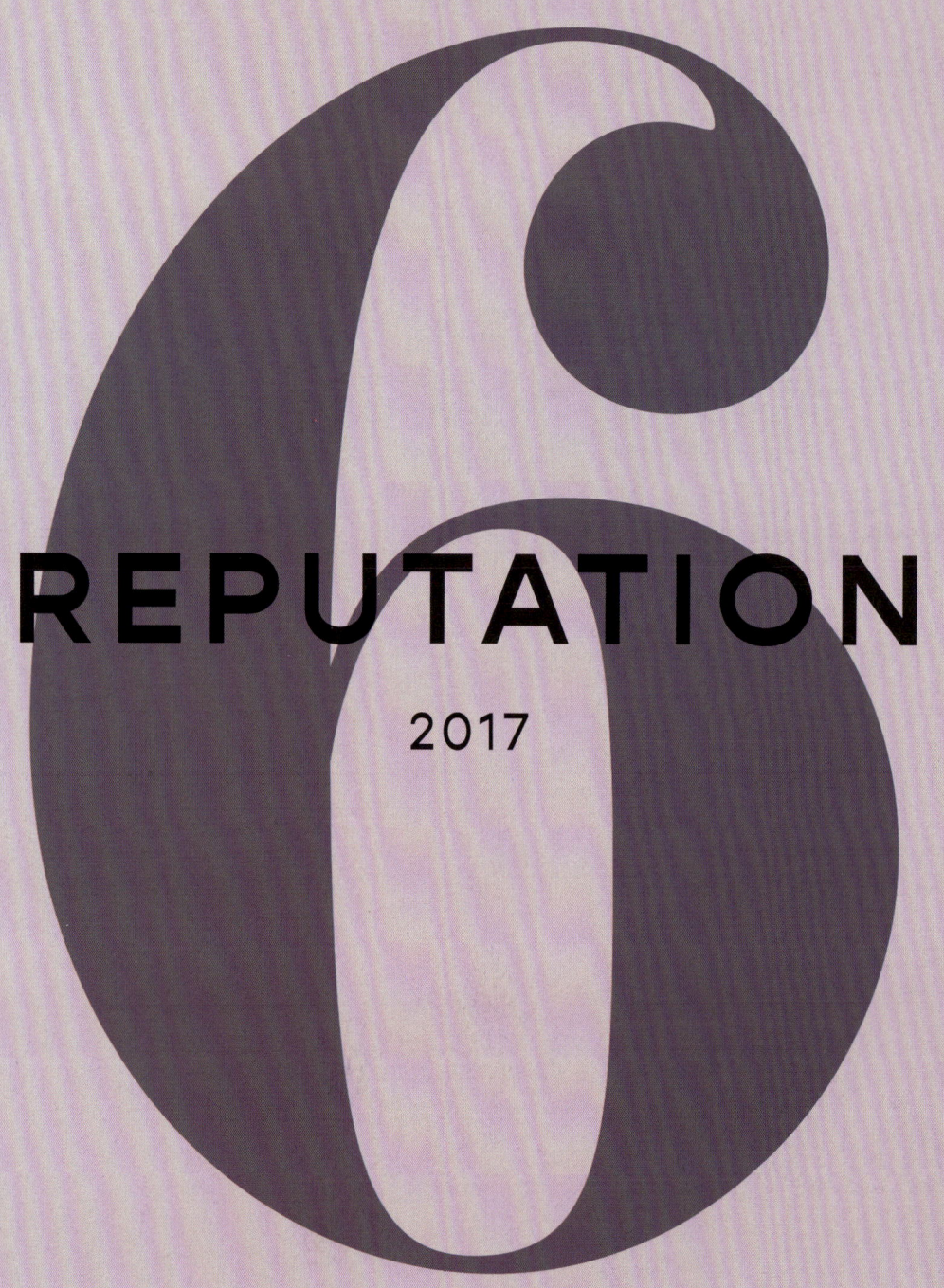

REPUTATION

2017

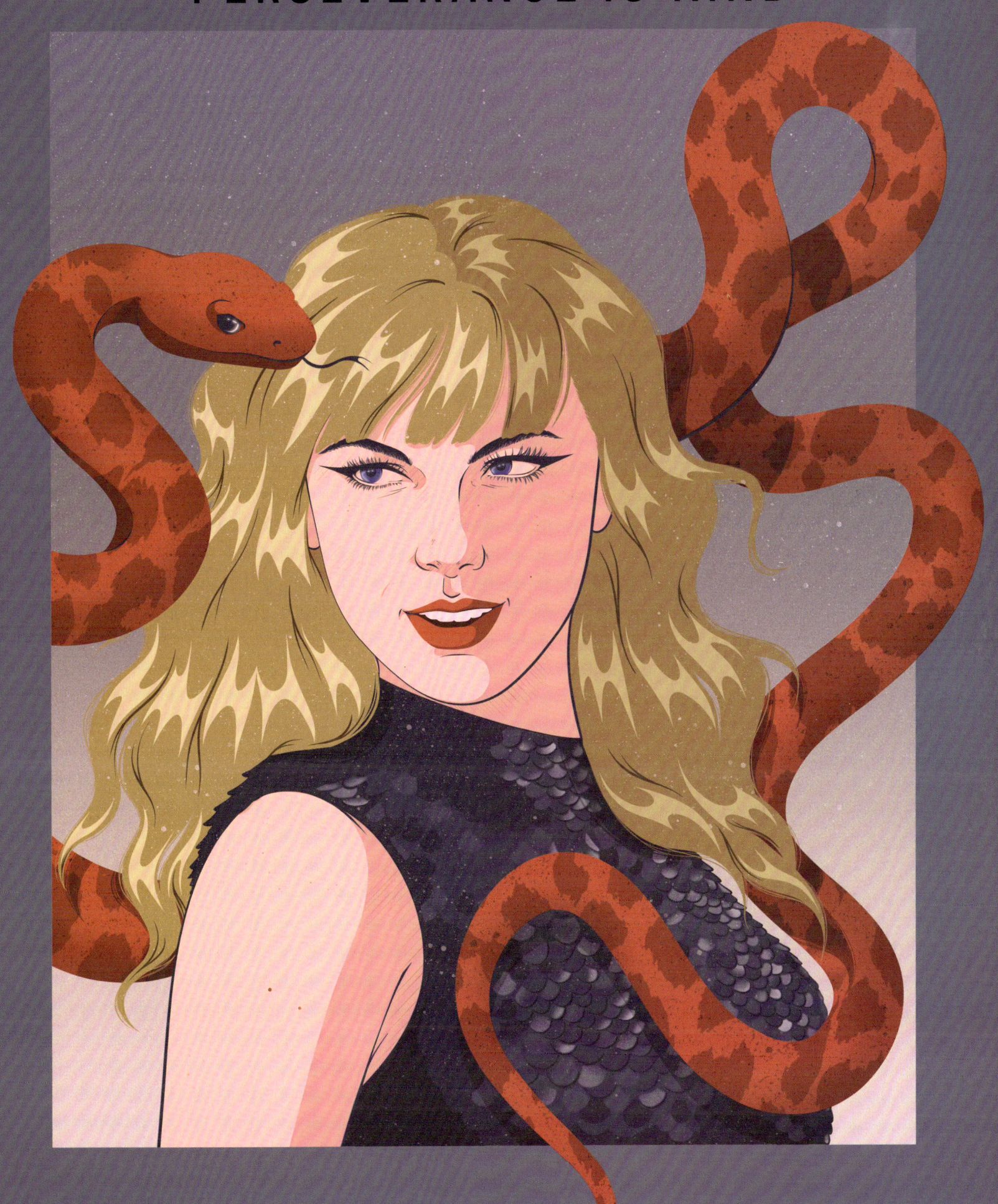

PERSEVERANCE IS KIND

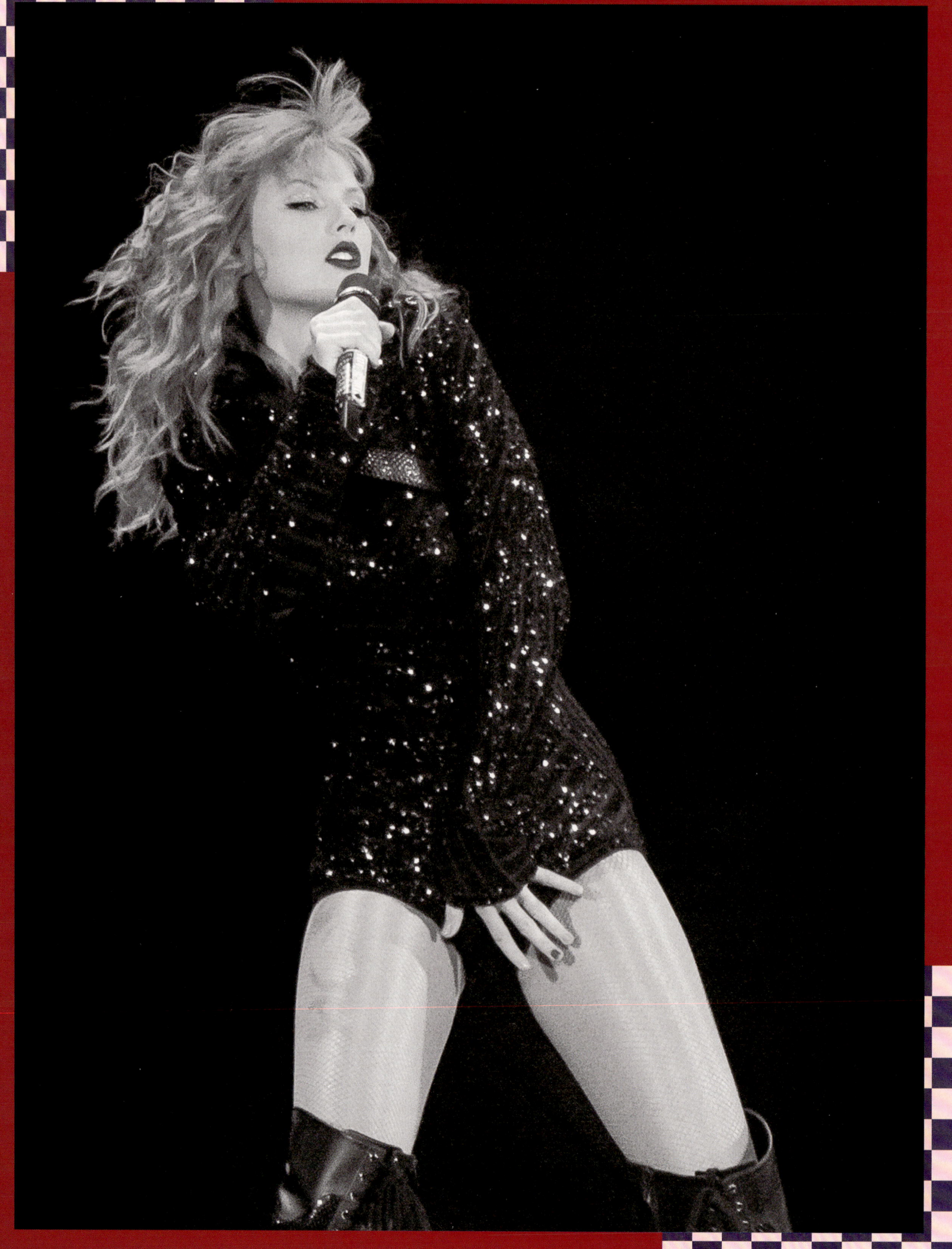

"There will be no further explanation. There will just be reputation."

Taylor, 2017

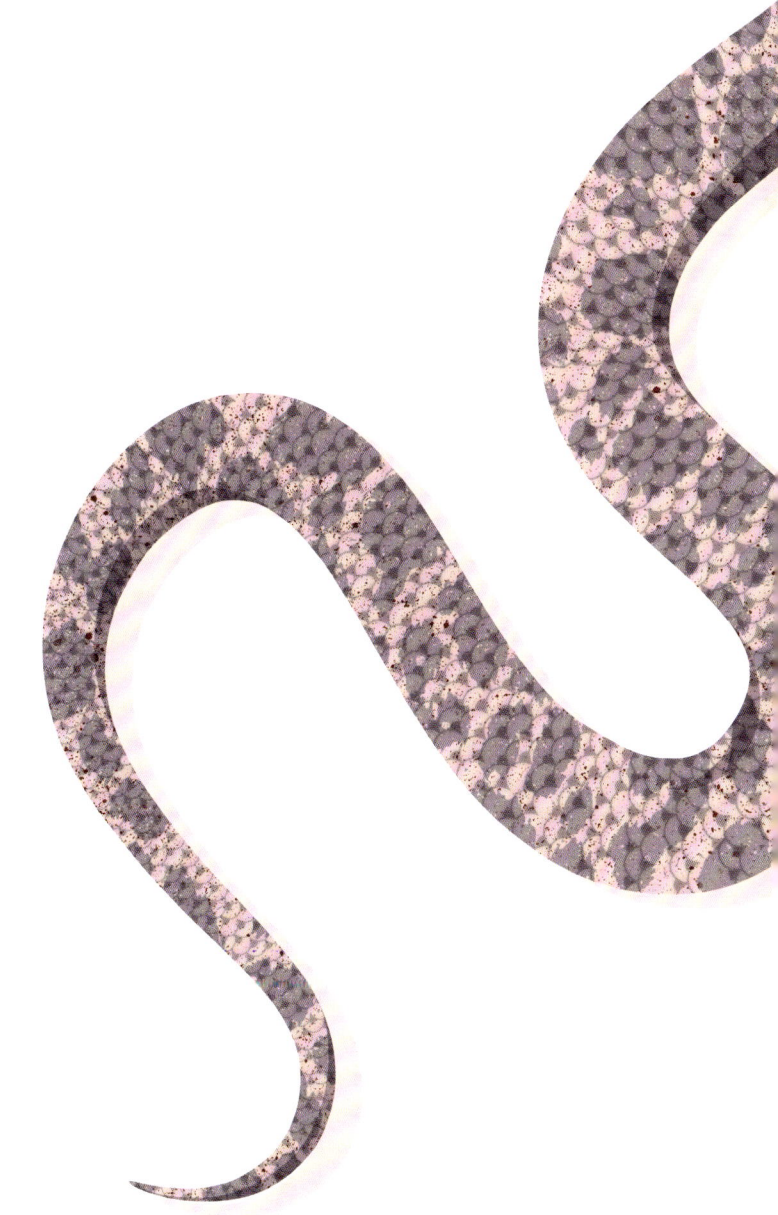

BIG REPUTATION

This era defined her reputation.

The record-breaking and cultural success of *1989* put Taylor at the top of her game. With adoring fans, huge sales, and star-studded friendships, she ended 2015 in a healthy new relationship and finished an incredible world tour.

By the end of 2015, Taylor and Kanye West seemed to squash their beef, when Taylor presented West with MTV's Michael Jackson Video Vanguard Award at the Video Music Awards. All seemed to be right in the world.

Things took a turn in February 2016, however, when Kanye released the song "Famous" on *The Life of Pablo* album. The song included the controversial line: "I feel like me and Taylor might still have sex. Why? I made that bitch famous."

The line sparked immediate backlash. Many viewed it as misogynistic and disrespectful, particularly given Kanye's previous history with Taylor, which dated back to the 2009 VMAs, when he interrupted her award-acceptance

NEW YEAR'S DAY & JIMMY FALLON

In November 2017, Taylor Swift performed her song "New Year's Day" on *The Tonight Show Starring Jimmy Fallon*. This was Jimmy's first show back hosting following the death of his mother, Gloria. Taylor wasn't scheduled to do the show, but the staff wanted to do something special for Fallon's return and since Taylor was in town preparing for *Saturday Night Live* later that week, they asked her. She agreed!

Her set list for the show included the debut of the song "New Year's Day." Unbeknownst to Taylor, earlier that day, Jimmy shared a story about his mother and how she used to squeeze his hand three times to say, "I love you."

There is a line in "New Year's Day" about squeezing a hand three times, and upon hearing those lyrics, it struck an emotional chord with both Jimmy and the audience. While the connection between the song and Jimmy's story was purely coincidental, it made the performance feel deeply personal and raw. Jimmy was visibly moved and teared up during and after the performance. After the song concluded, Jimmy and Taylor embraced. With his voice quivering, Jimmy can be heard saying, "Thank you, Taylor," over the microphone before turning back to address the audience. The crowd cheered and gave them a standing ovation.

The show's producer Mike DiCenzo said, "That hug between Jimmy and Taylor after the song was 100% real emotion. Whatever you think of Taylor, she did something beautiful for Jimmy and our show today, and we're forever grateful."

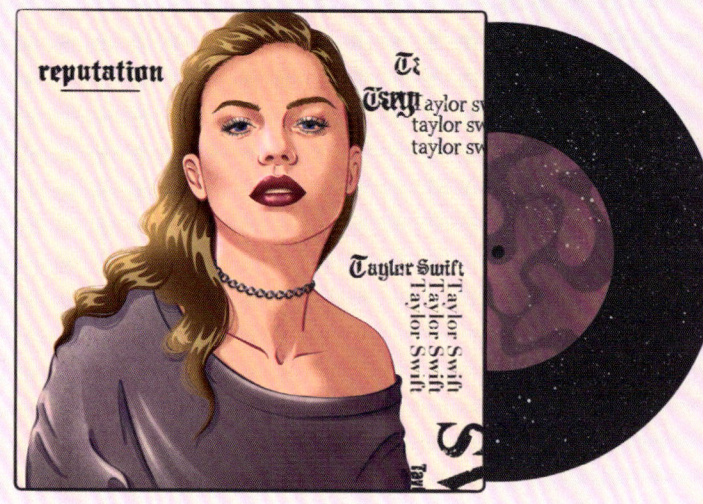

ALBUM
reputation

DATE LAUNCHED
November 10, 2017

FIRST SINGLE
"Look What You Made Me Do"
(August 24, 2017)

OTHER SINGLES
". . . Ready for It?" (September 17, 2017), "End Game" (November 14, 2017), "New Year's Day" (November 27, 2017), "Delicate" (March 12, 2018), and "Getaway Car" (September 7, 2018)

TOUR
Reputation Stadium Tour (May 2018 to December 2018)

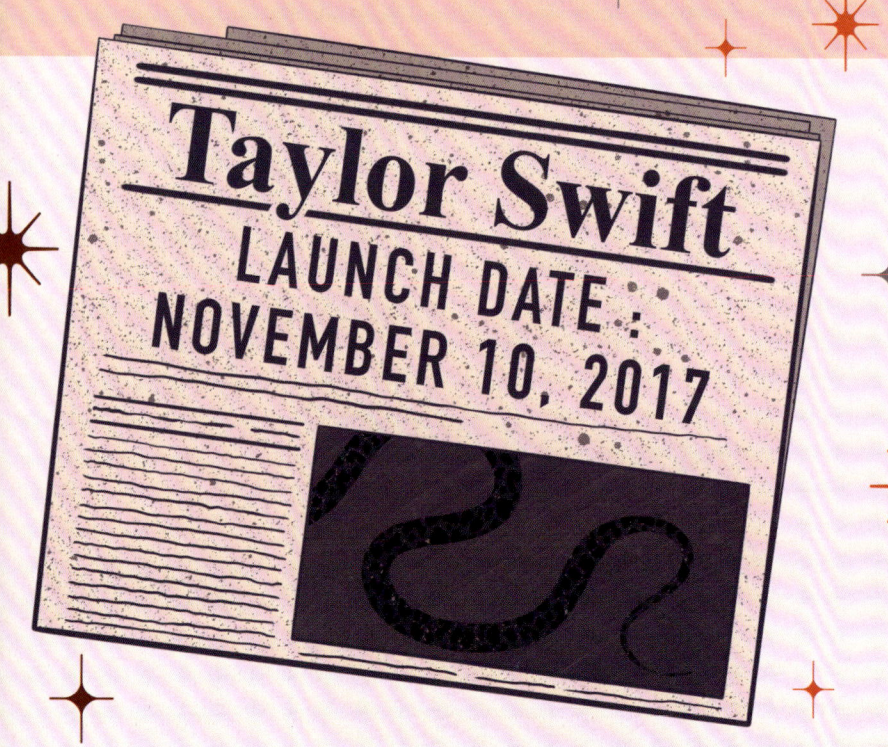

Even Questlove of The Roots, the official house band for *The Tonight Show Starring Jimmy Fallon*, said, "I'm just realizing Taylor didn't readjust the song's lyrics for tonight's performance. But the narrative literally applies to the words Jimmy spoke of his mother. Wow. You can't plan these things."

The moment offers a testament to the power of music and how lyrics can move and connect people through different emotions and experiences.

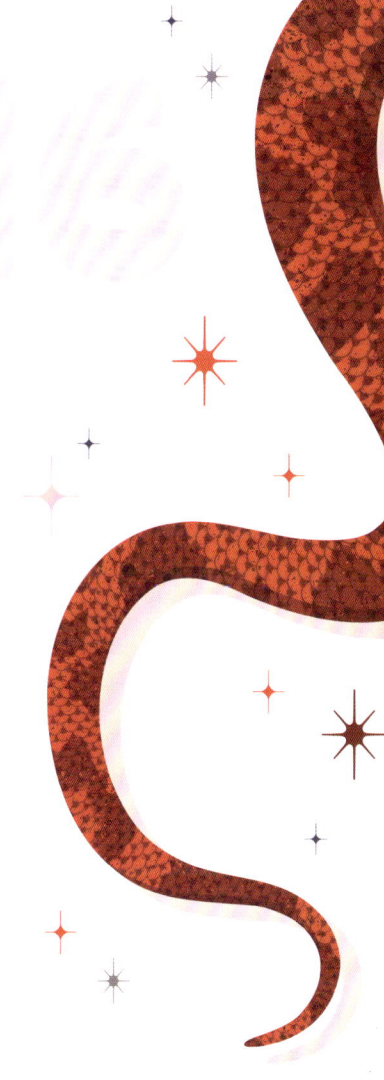

speech. Taylor's team released a statement shortly after the song's release, saying that she had not approved the lyrics. Taylor's squad, including Gigi Hadid, Jaime King, and her brother, all came to her defense on social media and called out Kanye.

While Taylor herself remained silent and didn't name the incident, her acceptance speech for Album of the Year at the Grammys spoke volumes. She said, "[A]s the first woman to win album of the year at the Grammys twice, I want to say to all the young women out there, there are going to be people along the way who will try to undercut your success or take credit for your accomplishments or your fame. If you just focus on the work, and you don't let those people sidetrack you, someday when you get where you're going, you'll look around and you will know that it was you and the people who love you who put you there, and that will be the greatest feeling

in the world. Thank you for this moment."

Then, in June 2016, Kim Kardashian, Kanye West's then-wife, got involved during an interview with *GQ*. Kim claimed that Taylor approved the line during a phone call with Kanye and accused Taylor of playing the victim. Kardashian said, "She totally knew that that was coming out. She wanted to all of a sudden act like she didn't. I swear, my husband gets so much shit for things [when] he really was doing proper protocol and even called to get it approved."

Taylor's team responded with a statement: "Taylor does not hold anything against Kim Kardashian, as she recognizes the pressure Kim must be under and that she is only repeating what she has been told by Kanye West. However, that does not change the fact that much of what Kim is saying is incorrect. Kanye West and Taylor only spoke once on the phone while she was on vacation with her family in January of 2016 and

PAGE 118: Gorgeous style: Taylor performs her opening set of songs of the Reputation Stadium Tour in Toronto, August 3, 2018.

RIGHT: Picking up the eighth Grammy of her career, Album of the Year for *1989*. She would also win Best Pop Vocal album that night. February 5, 2016.

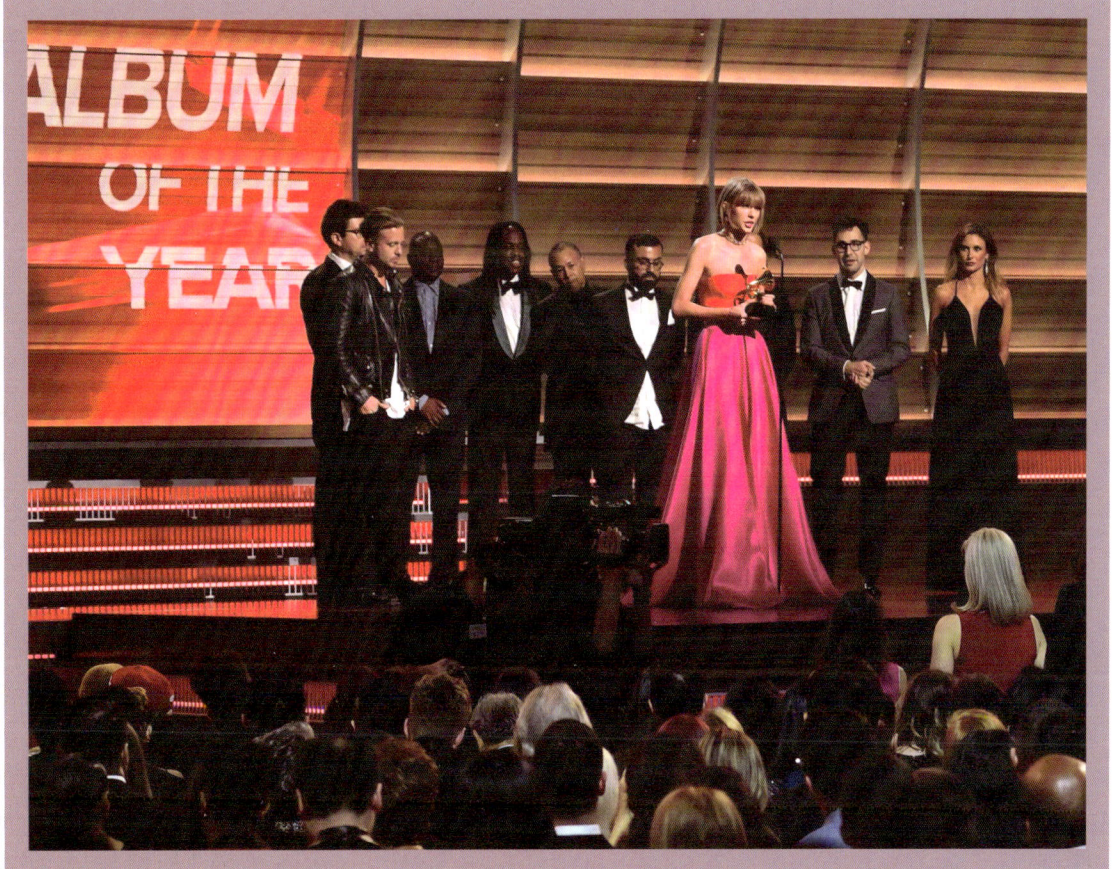

they have never spoken since. Taylor has never denied that conversation took place. It was on that phone call that Kanye West also asked her to release the song on her Twitter account, which she declined to do."

Just a week later, Kanye dropped the music video for "Famous," which featured a naked wax figure of Taylor Swift next to Kanye and other naked wax celebrities together in a bed. The music video stirred up even more controversy, both from a misogynistic standpoint and by raising the ethics around revenge porn and consent since the wax figures were naked.

On July 17, 2016, Kim escalated the situation further by posting clips on Snapchat of the phone call between Taylor and Kanye. In the clips, Kanye can be heard telling Taylor about the lyric "I feel like me and Taylor might still have sex." Taylor is heard responding, "I really appreciate you telling me about it. That's really nice. I mean, it's like a compliment, kind of."

> "I would very much like to be excluded from this narrative, one that I have never asked to be a part of, since 2009."
>
> Taylor, 2016

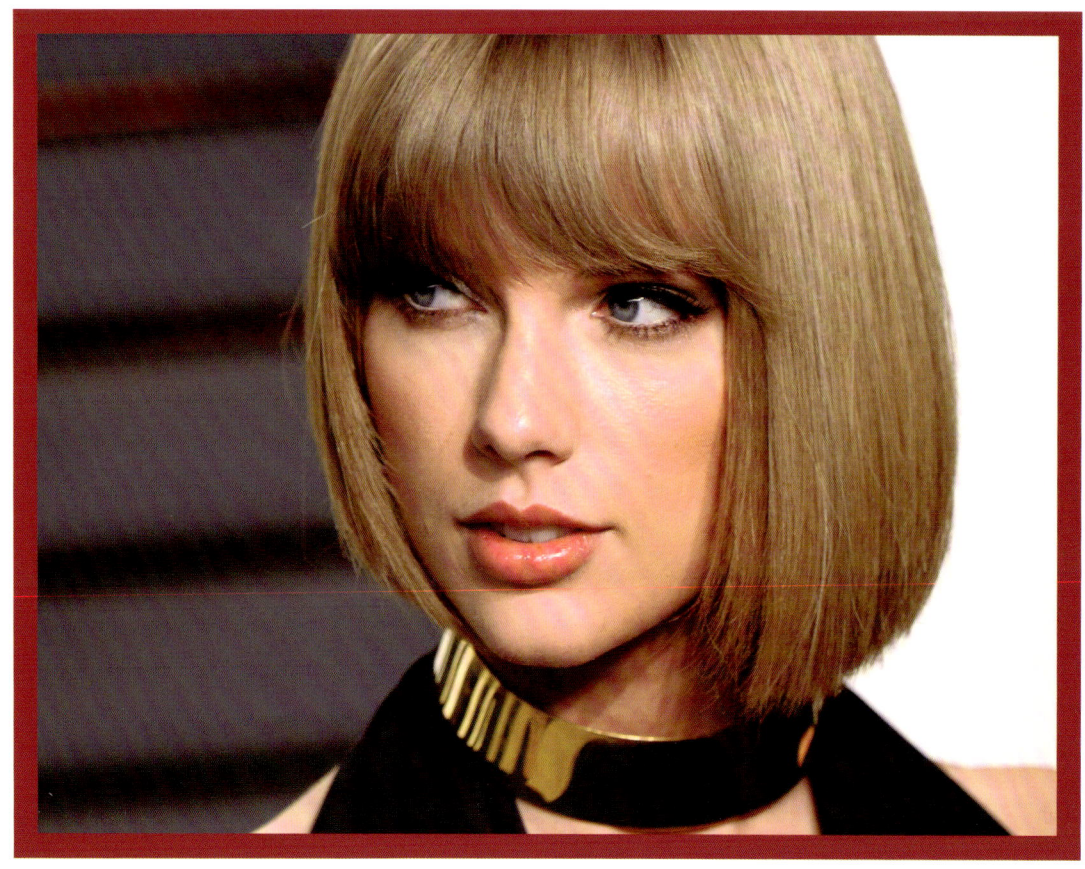

LEFT: Taylor stepped up her chic game for the 2016 Vanity Fair Oscars party, appearing in a sleek Alexandre Vauthier gown and a smoldering new look.

1, 2, 3, LGB!

If you have attended a Taylor Swift concert since May 2018 or have seen videos of shows online, you might be keen to hear the infamous "1, 2, 3, LGB!" chant during the song "Delicate." It all started at the Reputation Stadium Tour in Pasadena, California, in May 2018, when Swiftie Emily Valencia shouted, "1, 2, 3, Let's go, bitch!" during the song "Delicate" and later posted the video to Twitter.

While she posted several videos from the evening, this video and chant took off with fans, who then started saying it at future shows. While at first this chant confused Taylor, wondering what the fans were screaming, she eventually caught on. Just a few weeks later, Taylor herself participated by mouthing the chant onstage at a tour stop in Wembley Stadium in England. Fans went wild, knowing Taylor was now in on it too.

Nearly five years after the chant was popularized, Swifties made sure it would be one of the many fan-based chants featured at The Eras Tour. From opening night until the very last tour stop, the chant has become a staple during the performance of "Delicate." Taylor even used her fingers to count out "1, 2, 3" while gleefully chanting along with the crowd, cementing its place in the Swiftie-verse.

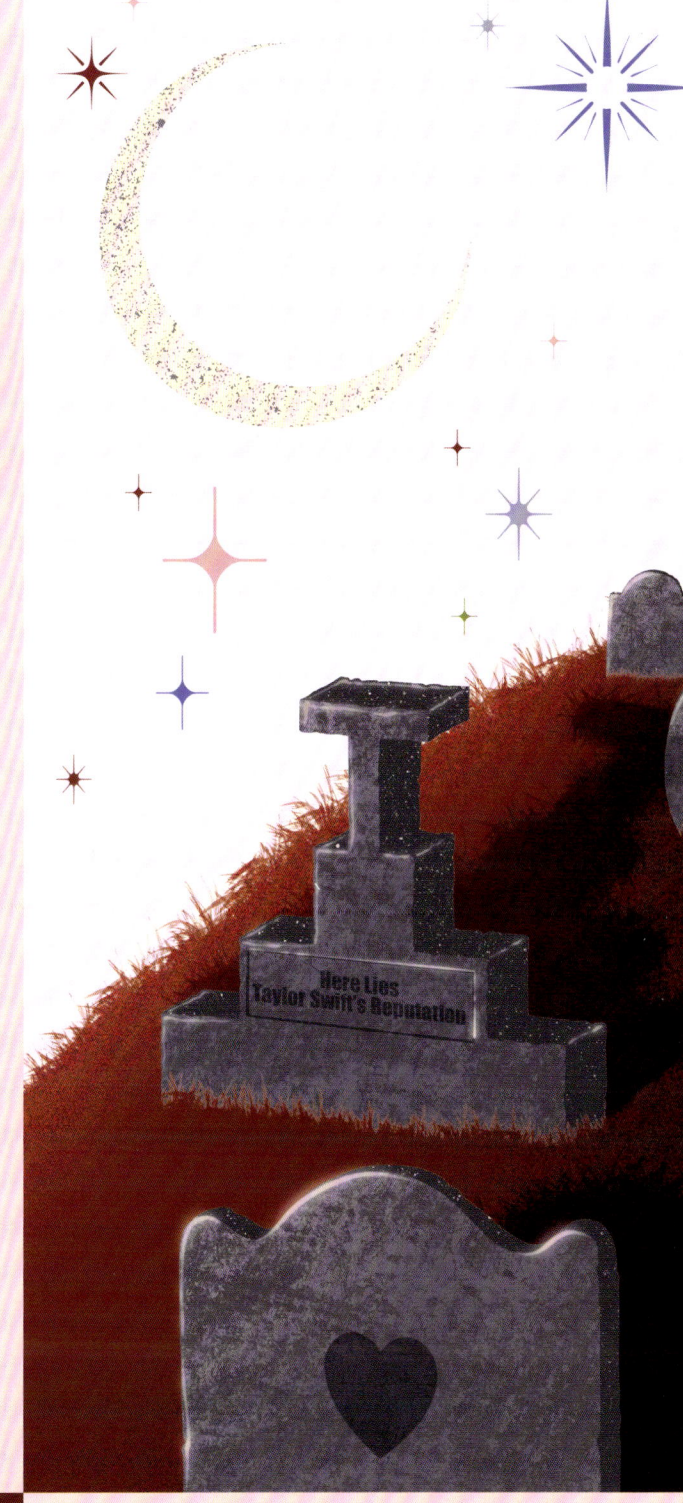

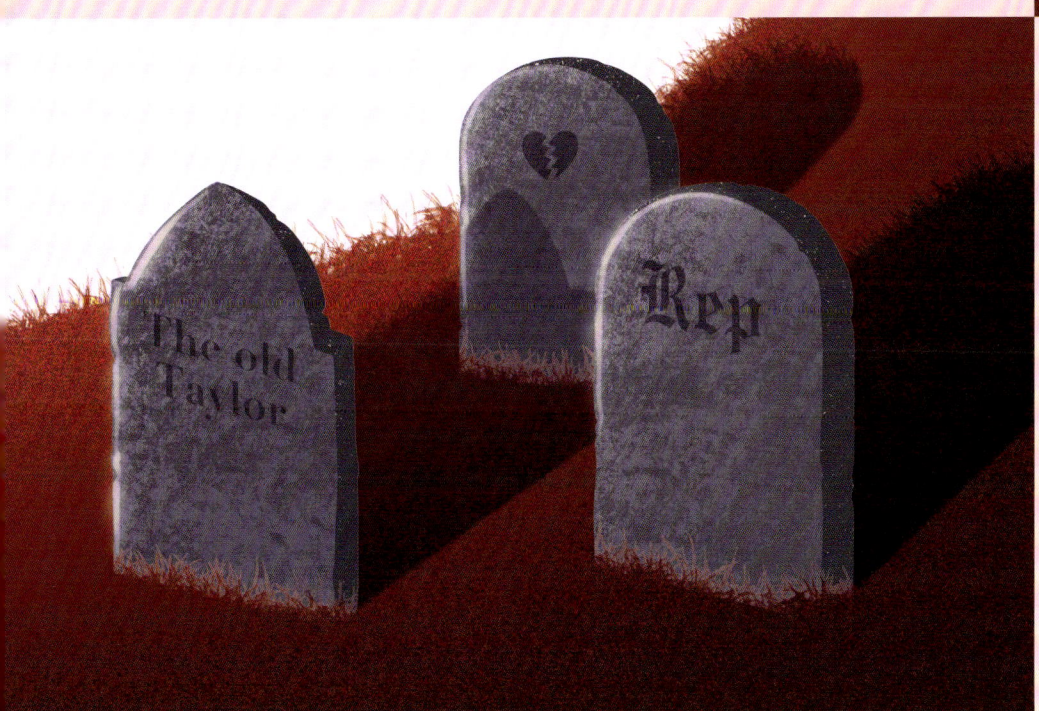

This is just one of the many traditions Swifties have started over the years that are now synonymous with Taylor's songs as well as her live shows. And like the class act that she is, Taylor always gives credit where credit is due. Emily, the originator of the chant, was later invited to the Secret Sessions for the *Lover* album, and Taylor acknowledged the chant and thanked Emily for it.

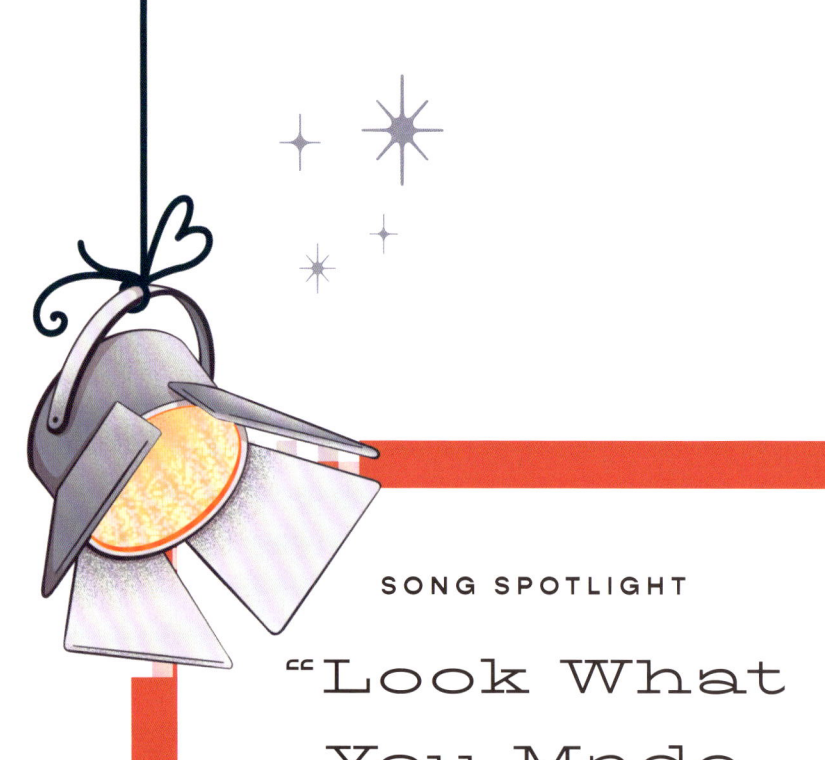

"Look What You Made Me Do"

The lead single "Look What You Made Me Do" is a catchy and repetitive chorus that was sampled and inspired by the song "I'm Too Sexy" by Right Said Fred. Taylor, always one to give credit where credit is due, added them as co-writers to the song. Front-man Richard Fairbrass said, "She [Taylor] and all the people that work with her have been incredibly friendly. I've got a huge bunch of flowers here from them in the house. It's been a rewarding experience, and very flattering."

ALBUM

reputation

RELEASED

2017

The leaked video painted Taylor as complicit in the creation of the lyrics and led to a massive social media backlash against her. Kim Kardashian posted on X (formerly known as Twitter), "Wait it's legit National Snake Day?!?!? They have holidays for everybody, I mean everything these days!" The hashtag #KimExposedTaylorParty trended worldwide, and Taylor became the subject of intense ridicule and online bullying.

Shortly after the Snapchat clips surfaced, Taylor posted a statement on Instagram defending herself. She clarified that Kanye West had not informed her of being referred to as "that bitch" in the song and that she never would have approved such language. She wrote: "You don't get to control someone's emotional response to being called 'that bitch' in front of the entire world. Of course I wanted to like the song. I wanted to believe Kanye when he told me I would love the song. I wanted us to have a friendly relationship. He promised to play the song for me, but he never did. While I wanted to be supportive of Kanye on the phone call, you cannot 'approve' a song you haven't heard. Being falsely painted as a liar when I was never given the full story or played any part of the song is character assassination." She then said, "I would very much like to be excluded from this narrative, one that I have never asked to be a part of, since 2009."

The damage was done, however, and most people seemed to side with Kanye and Kim. Taylor became the target of online harassment, was branded a liar, and was inundated with snake emojis on her social media platforms.

The backlash was so intense that Taylor pulled off an unprecedented move for a global pop star: She disappeared from the public eye

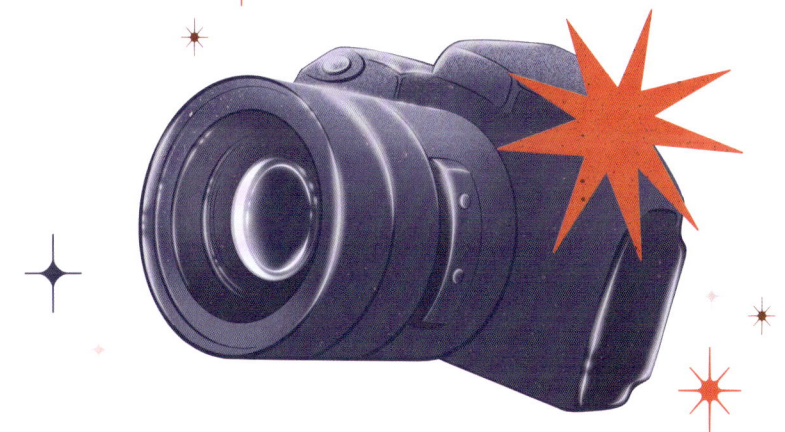

for nearly a year. She stopped attending award shows, avoided the paparazzi, and limited her public outings to essential commitments. The squad photos and Fourth of July parties were no longer served up, and she eventually stopped posting on social media altogether.

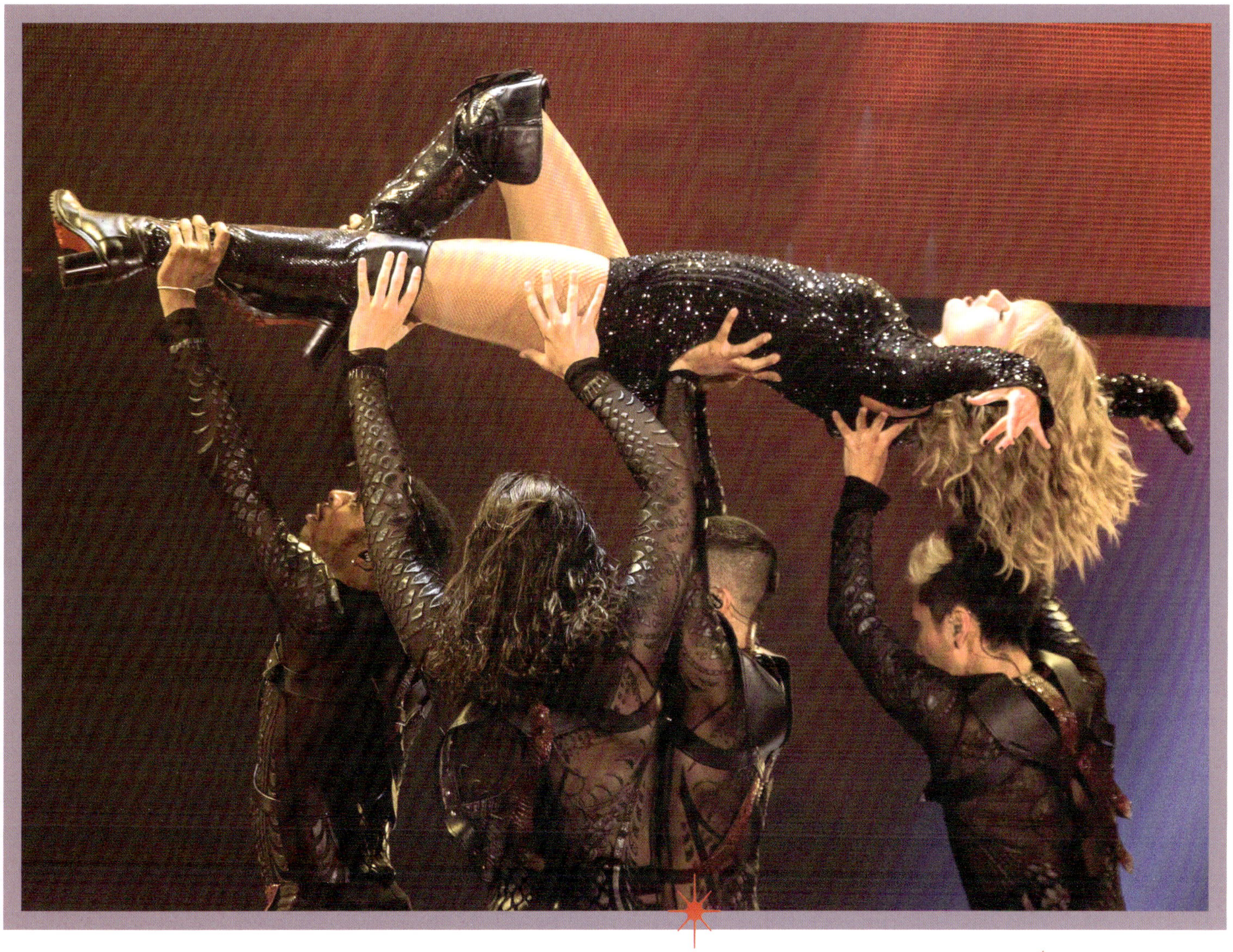

The mystery of where Taylor was deepened when even paparazzi images became scarce. Taylor, known for navigating paparazzi-dense areas like New York City with ease, was rarely photographed. Fans noted her potential use of creative tactics to avoid being seen and even speculated that she traveled in a large suitcase to avoid detection.

In August 2017, after almost a year of radio silence, Taylor wiped her social media accounts entirely, replacing them with cryptic snake videos. The move marked her reentry into public life, the start of her *reputation* era, and the launch of her sixth studio album.

ABOVE: Dancers lift Taylor during the "I Did Something Bad" segment of the The 1989 World Tour concert.

Back Out There

By the time Taylor reemerged for *reputation*, fans were ready for her.

Swifties celebrated with an outpouring of love and support. Her absence had created a sense of longing, and her comeback made the *reputation* era feel even more significant. Fans appreciated that she had used the time to prioritize herself and interpreted her return as a statement of resilience and artistic reinvention.

The snake imagery was Taylor's direct response to being labeled a "snake" by critics during her feud with Kim Kardashian and Kanye West. It was a moment of reclamation, as Taylor leaned into the persona her haters had crafted for her and turned it into an empowering motif, one that has since been taken back by Swifties.

While much of her life during this time was shrouded in mystery, Taylor's deliberate departure from her more public-facing *1989* era offered glimpses at how she dealt with the controversy and what was going on in her personal relationships as shown through her

songwriting. Songs like "Look What You Made Me Do" and "This Is Why We Can't Have Nice Things" were widely interpreted as responses to the ordeal with Kanye West and Kim Kardashian. The album also touched on her newfound love with and loyalty to her long-term boyfriend, Joe Alwyn, via songs like "King of My Heart" and "Delicate." These tracks revealed a deep sense of gratitude and vulnerability, and highlighted Joe's steady presence during a tumultuous time in Taylor's life.

Taylor's relationship with Joe became a cornerstone of her personal life during this time. The pair reportedly began dating in late 2016, but they kept their relationship private. While Taylor had previously been open about

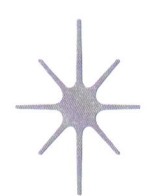

RIGHT: Taylor, wearing Stella McCartney, and Joe Alwyn attend the British *Vogue* Fashion and Film BAFTA party in London, February 10, 2019.

FOLLOWING PAGE: The Reputation Stadium Tour in Perth, Australia, October 19, 2018.

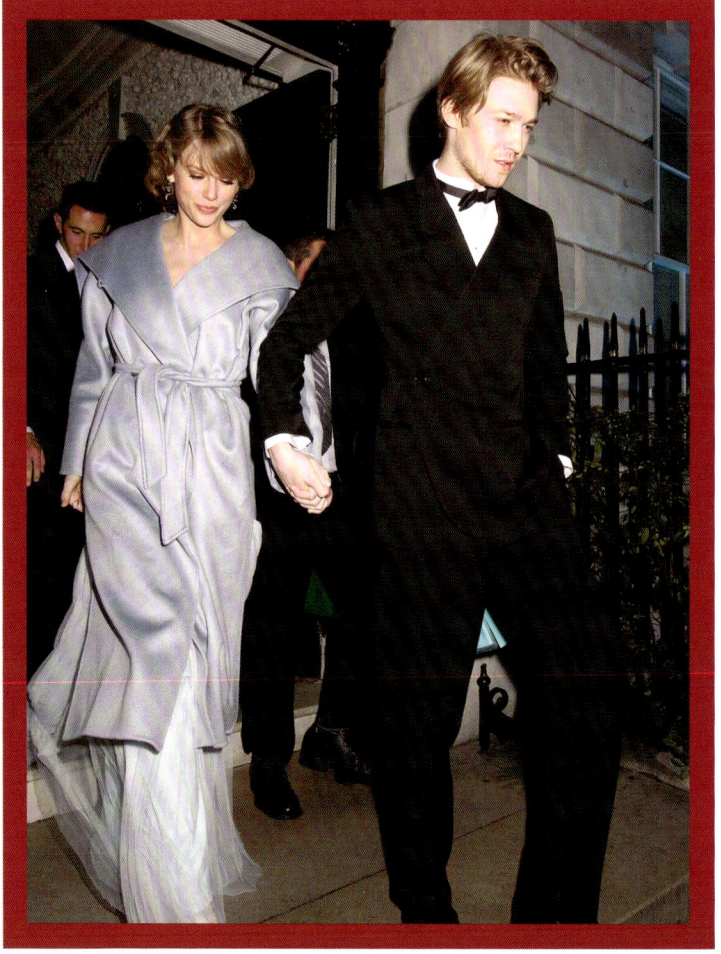

A SYMBOLIC $1

In 2017, Taylor got involved in a legal battle with former radio DJ David Mueller, who was accused of groping her during a 2013 meet-and-greet at a Denver concert. At the time of the incident, Taylor and her team dealt with the matter privately and kept it out of the public eye. They informed Mueller's employer and shared the evidence with them directly, resulting in David Mueller being fired from his job.

Then, in 2015, David Mueller filed a lawsuit against Taylor for defamation, claiming that her accusation had cost him his career. Taylor countersued for sexual assault, seeking a symbolic one dollar in damages as a statement that the case was not about money but accountability. Her decision to file a countersuit was also significant because it encouraged other victims of sexual assault to come forward, particularly in light of the common fear that speaking out would result in retaliation.

The case went to trial in 2017, and during the proceedings, Taylor was praised for her willingness to speak openly about the experience. She testified that she had been in shock after the assault and was initially unsure how to respond, saying, "It was a very shocking thing that never happened to me before."

When asked why her skirt doesn't appear to be lifted in the photo of the alleged incident, Taylor clapped back and said, "Because my ass is in the back of my body." This sentence became iconic and a rally cry for sexual assault victims.

In August 2017, the jury ruled in Taylor's favor, finding that David Mueller had indeed groped her and awarding her the symbolic one dollar in damages.

The "Look What You Made Me Do" music video featured a symbolic one-dollar bill. This alluded to Taylor's significant victory and offered a broader statement against sexual assault and victim-blaming.

In her documentary film *Miss Americana*, Taylor talks about how this moment deeply changed her. She had witnesses and photographic evidence, but she realized that many women do not have the evidence needed to come forward. Since the trial, Taylor became even more outspoken about issues related to women's rights and sexual assault. She expressed support for the #MeToo and Time's Up movements, and has advocated for systemic changes to better support survivors of sexual harassment and assault.

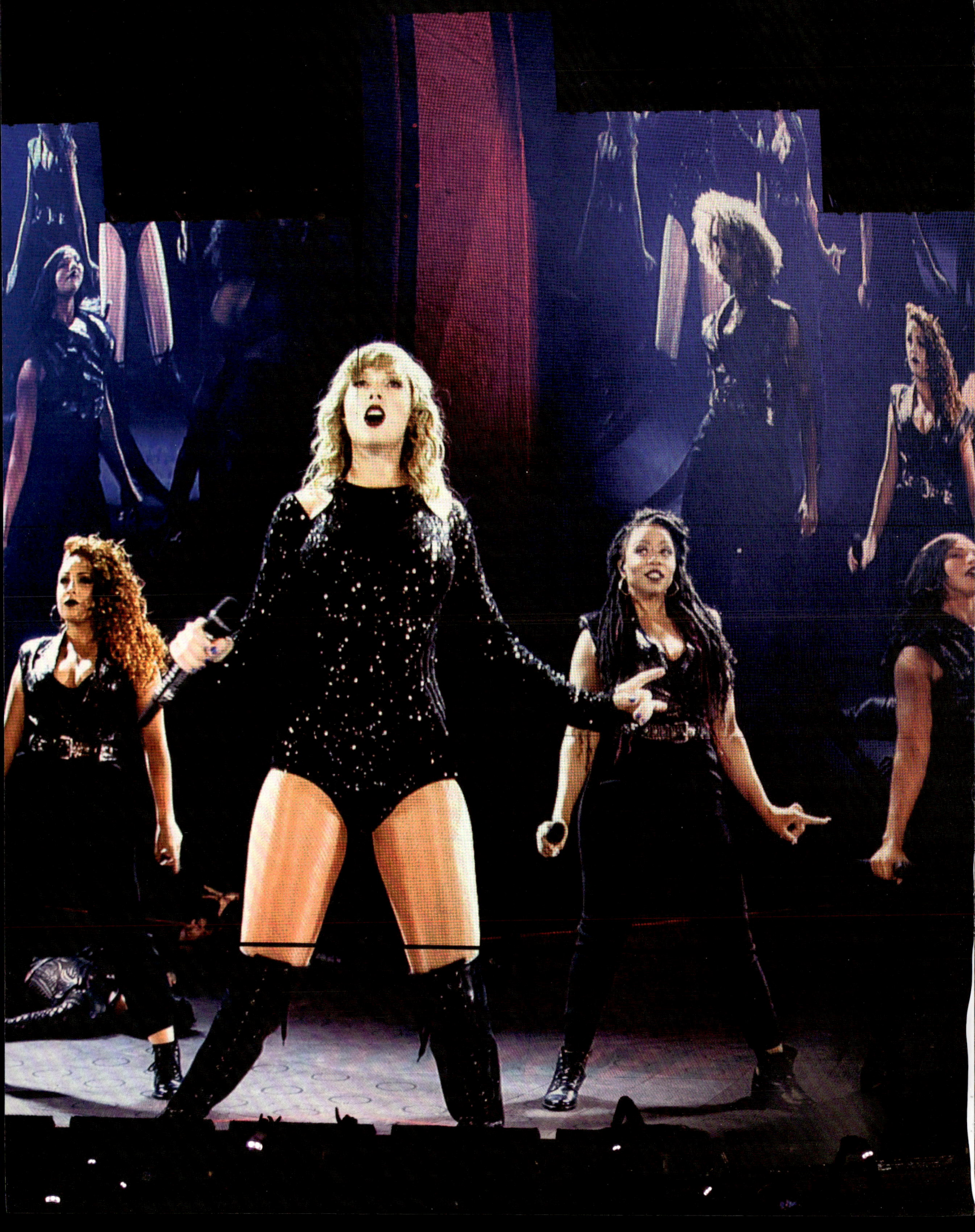

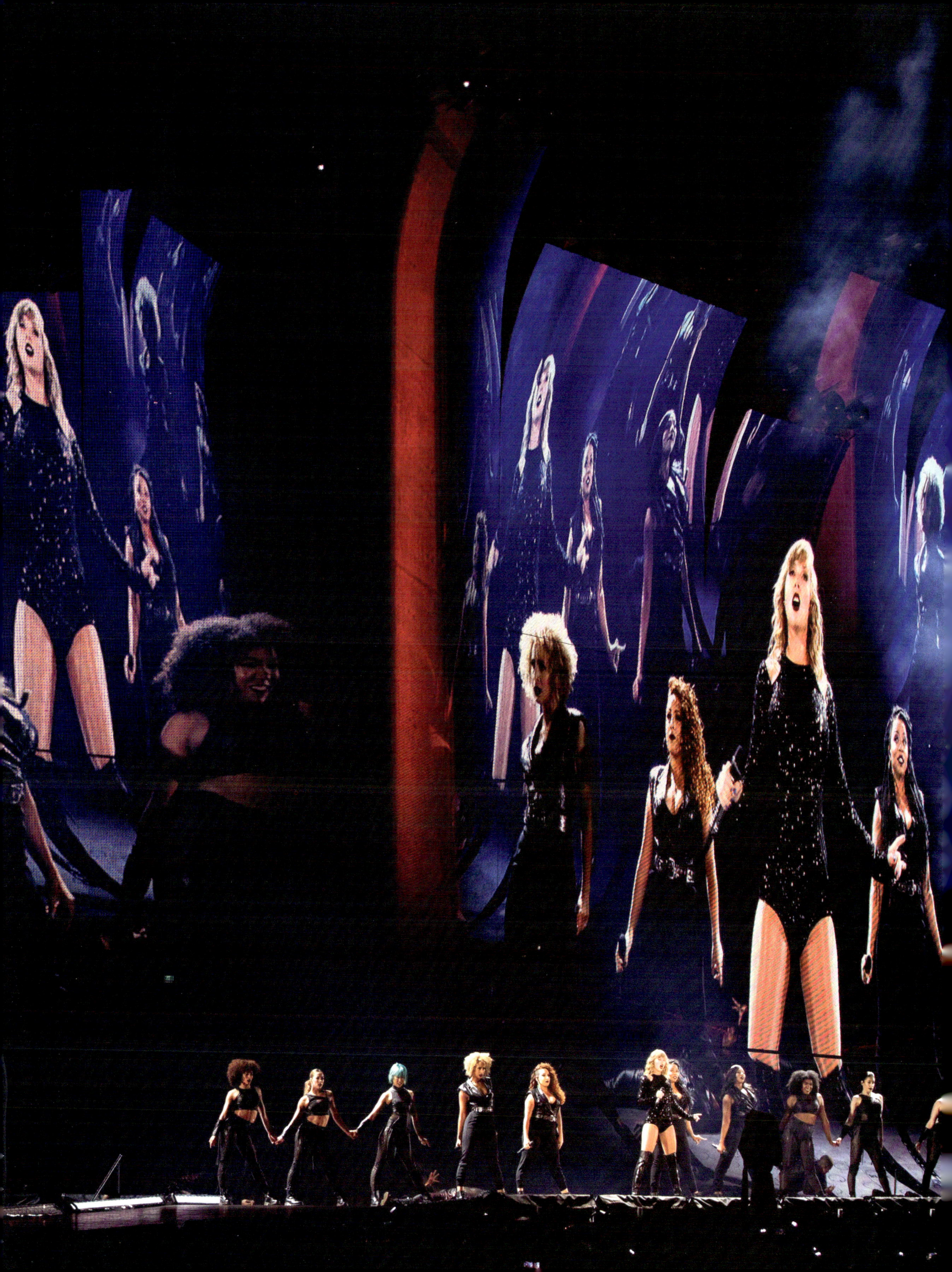

her love life through public outings and media narratives, she chose a different approach with Joe, shielding their romance from the spotlight. She took this opportunity to redefine her boundaries with the public and media.

Taylor appeared to scale back her previously publicized "squad" of celebrity friends, which had been a major focus of her *1989* era. While the media often speculated that her friendships had dissolved, the truth was more nuanced. Taylor chose to prioritize deep, private connections over the performative nature of her former "squad goals" narrative.

She maintained close relationships with a core group of friends that included Blake Lively and Ryan Reynolds, Ed Sheeran, Selena Gomez, and Martha Hunt. These friends remained loyal supporters during a time when Taylor faced intense media scrutiny. Blake and Ryan were particularly present in her life, even lending

their daughter's voice to the intro of "Gorgeous." Selena publicly defended Taylor, often sharing heartfelt messages of support. Their bond remained strong, with Selena describing Taylor as a source of encouragement and stability.

After the backlash and betrayal that she faced during the *1989* era, Taylor became more selective about whom she trusted. In interviews, she later reflected on this time, noting that she learned who her real friends were and how important it was to surround herself with people who genuinely cared for her.

While fans and friends understood that Taylor Swift was here to stay, critics were unsure how she could bounce back after her reputation seemed to sour, with some people even predicting that the upcoming tour would flop. The album debuted at No. 1 on the Billboard 200, however, selling more than 1.2 million copies in the United States in its first week alone.

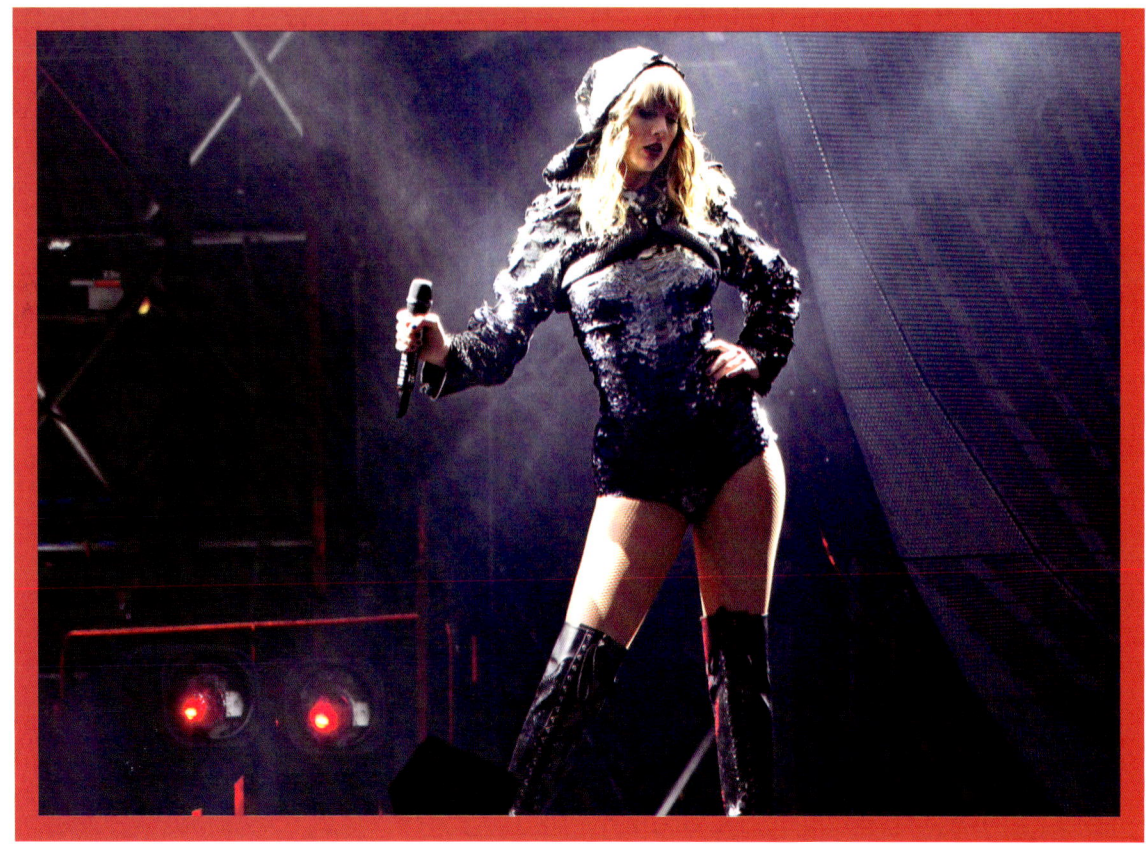

LEFT: Ready for it: The Reputation Stadium Tour makes its way to Manchester, UK, June 8, 2108.

SUPPORTING SURVIVORS

Taylor Swift's support for Kesha during her legal battles with music producer Dr. Luke became a public display of solidarity and empathy, demonstrating how Swift used her platform to advocate for another artist facing significant personal and professional challenges.

In 2014, Kesha filed a lawsuit against Dr. Luke, accusing him of sexual assault, harassment, and emotional abuse during their professional relationship. The case garnered widespread attention as Kesha sought to be released from her contract with Dr. Luke, alleging that he had abused her physically, sexually, and emotionally for years. The legal proceedings were highly publicized, and Kesha's emotional struggles became a focal point in the conversation about sexual harassment and abuse within the music industry.

In 2016, as Kesha's legal battle intensified, Taylor Swift offered her support by donating $250,000 to help Kesha with her legal fees. While Taylor made the donation privately, Kesha publicly thanked her in a heartfelt Instagram post, writing: "Thank you @taylorswift for your support. You have been a huge inspiration to me and my fans for years. Your kindness is a light in the dark, and I am beyond grateful to you."

Taylor's gesture was notable not only for the monetary support but also because of her public stance on the issue. At the time, the music industry was largely silent on Kesha's claims. Taylor's donation was a significant show of solidarity for Kesha. It demonstrated that powerful figures in the music industry could use their platforms to support artists who were fighting for their rights and dignity.

"I spoke to Kesha, and it really helped to talk to someone who had been through the demoralizing court process."

Taylor, 2017

THESE ARE NOT MY TENNESSEE VALUES

On October 7, 2018, a month before the United States midterm elections, Taylor broke her political silence. For years she'd said that people wanted to hear her sing, not talk about her political views. Additionally, coming up in the country-music scene, there was often an understanding that you didn't want to get political because of what happened to The Chicks, who were famously "canceled" for speaking out against the Bush administration.

On the cusp of her sexual assault lawsuit, however, Taylor changed her mind. She took to Instagram and penned a post about her views. She said, "In the past I've been reluctant to publicly voice my political opinions, but due to several events in my life and in the world the past two years, I feel very differently about that now." She promised to vote for candidates who support human rights, including LGBTQ, civil, and women's rights.

She ended the post by encouraging others to make their voices heard and to register to vote before the deadline. Within twenty-four hours of her post, Vote.org reported that 65,000 Americans between the ages of eighteen and twenty-nine had registered to vote. Just a few days later, that number jumped to 102,000.

This courageous move won over Taylor's fan base even more and paved the way for Taylor to become more vocal about politics and voting, including putting her support behind Democratic candidates such as Joseph Biden and Kamala Harris.

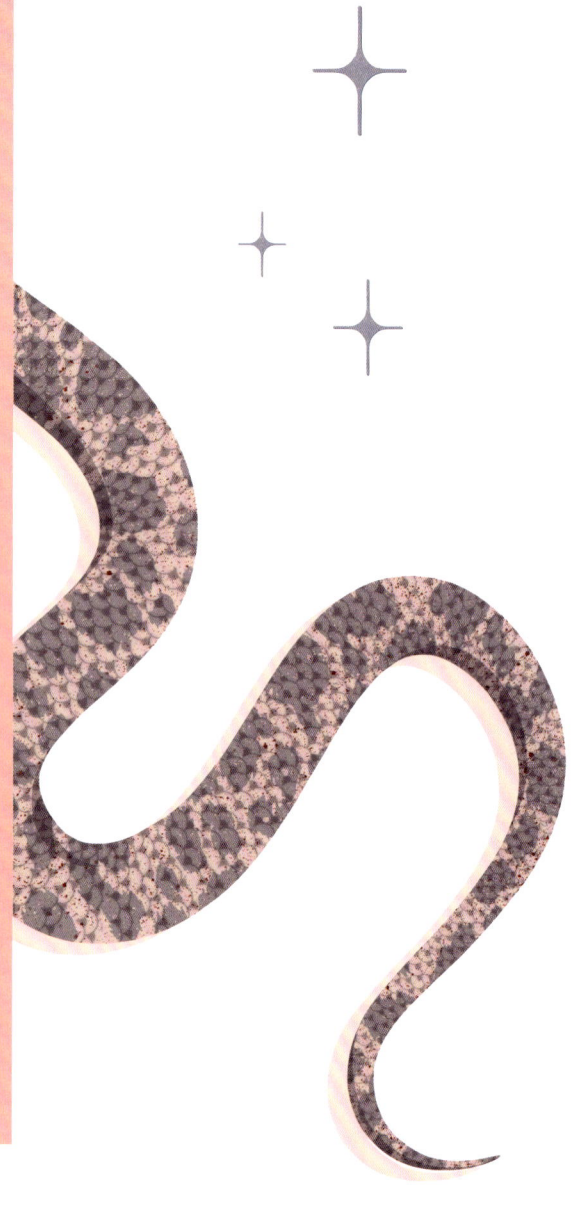

Singles like "Look What You Made Me Do," ". . . Ready for It?," and "Delicate" became major hits, with the "Look What You Made Me Do" music video breaking YouTube records for views (43.2 million in twenty-four hours).

During the release of *reputation*, Taylor famously said, "There will be no further explanation. There will just be reputation." She refrained from media appearances and instead let the songs, artwork, and music videos speak for themselves.

For the release of the album, each CD came with a magazine that looked like a salacious tabloid magazine. Inside, however, it featured poetry, paintings, handwritten lyrics, and photos.

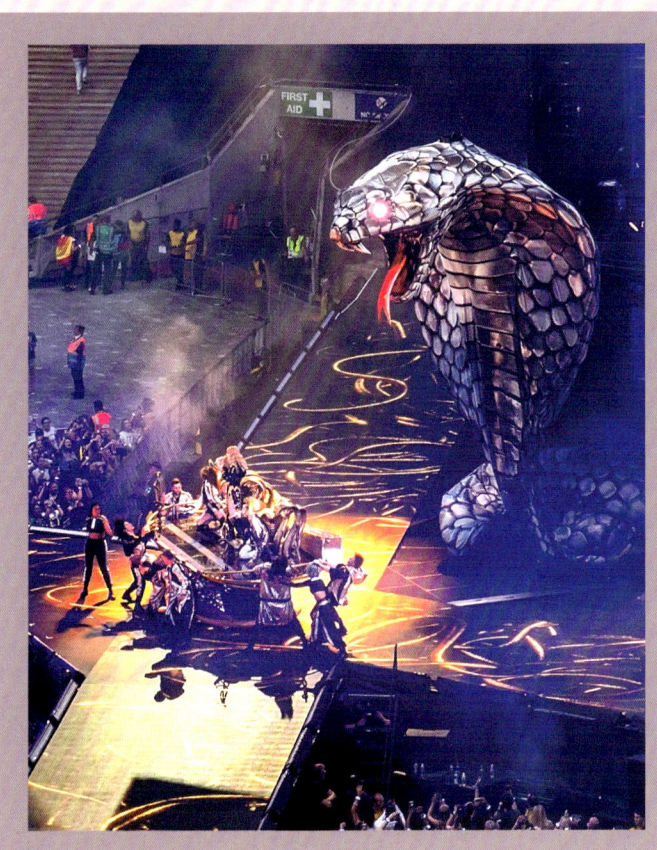

Karyn

ESTABLISHED
May 8, 2018

THE INFLATABLE SNAKE
Karyn, a giant inflatable snake, graced the stage for the "Look What You Made Me Do" set of the entire Reputation Stadium Tour. She was part of Taylor's performance at the American Music Awards show to the song "I Did Something Bad" and became so popular that she trended on X, formerly known as Twitter.

On Tour Again

Taylor used the Reputation Stadium Tour itself to continue to tell a story. In the introduction to the tour, she featured a montage of people discussing how she sought attention for donations and was getting what she deserved. The audience heard "Baby, let the games begin," and the stage opened to a hooded Taylor gliding down the stage. She turned to the side and said, "Are you ready for it?"

During "Look What You Made Me Do," a sixty-three-foot inflatable cobra named Karyn floated onstage, acting as a mascot for Taylor's reclamation of her reputation. On Tumblr, Taylor wrote about Karyn: "There once was a snake known by everyone and no one. Her name was Karyn. No one understood her, or tried to. Most people were scared she was going to swallow them whole. This made Karyn sad. No one wanted to be her friend. So she just hid

away in her underground world where no one could find her. But then one day word came around to her that there was someone just like her. Someone misunderstood by the world. Someone people didn't bother getting to know before judging them. This made Karyn feel less alone. She met up with this person and they both instantly got along. Karyn and Taylor; two misunderstood souls that felt so understood by each other. Taylor told Karyn about her tour. And her plan to turn people's words around so they didn't bite them. Karyn loved the idea and now they're happily on tour together."

In an interview later with *Elle* magazine, Taylor discussed the controversy at the time and said, "I learned that disarming someone's petty bullying can be as simple as learning to laugh." She continued, "I can't tell you how hard I had to keep from laughing every time my

NO MORE BAD BLOOD

While the feud between Taylor and Kanye West had been at the forefront since 2009, Taylor has also publicly feuded with other celebrities, including Katy Perry and Nicki Minaj.

Katy and Taylor seemed to be friends throughout the years, often supporting each other in various ways. Katy even joined Taylor onstage to perform "Hot N Cold" during the Fearless Tour, and Taylor was on record saying it was one of her favorite songs of the year. However, in 2014, when Taylor was interviewed by *Rolling Stone*, she was asked about the song "Bad Blood" and who it was about. Taylor revealed that the song was actually about a friendship.

She said, "For years, I was never sure if we were friends or not. She would come up to me at awards shows and say something and walk away, and I would think, 'Are we friends, or did she just give me the harshest insult of my life?' She did something so horrible. I was like, 'Oh, we're just straight-up enemies.' And it wasn't even about a guy! It had to do with business. She basically tried to sabotage an entire arena tour. She tried to hire a bunch of people out from under me. And I'm surprisingly nonconfrontational—you would not believe how much I hate conflict. So now I have to avoid her. It's awkward, and I don't like it."

Fans weren't theorizing that this was about Katy Perry until she posted on social media a day after the article went live and said, "Watch out for the Regina George in sheep's clothing . . ." People then started speculating that the song was aimed toward Katy.

In May 2015, Taylor released the "Bad Blood" music video. It featured a star-studded lineup. The video was nominated for several MTV Video Music Awards and went on to win Video of the Year and Best Collaboration.

Shortly after the nominations were announced, Nicki Minaj, who was not nominated for her infamous "Anaconda" video, took to social media to clap back and said, "If your video celebrates women with very slim bodies, you will be nominated for vid of the year."

Taylor, thinking this was a jab at her, responded with, "I've done nothing but love & support you. It's unlike you to pit women against each other. Maybe one of the men took your slot."

Nicki clarified that the comment wasn't about Taylor and said that she was missing the point. Then Katy entered the chat and said, "Finding it ironic to parade the pit women against other women argument about as one unmeasurably capitalizes on the takedown of a woman . . ."

A few days later, Taylor publicly issued a public apology to Nicki: "I thought I was being called out. I missed the point, I misunderstood, then misspoke. I'm sorry, Nicki."

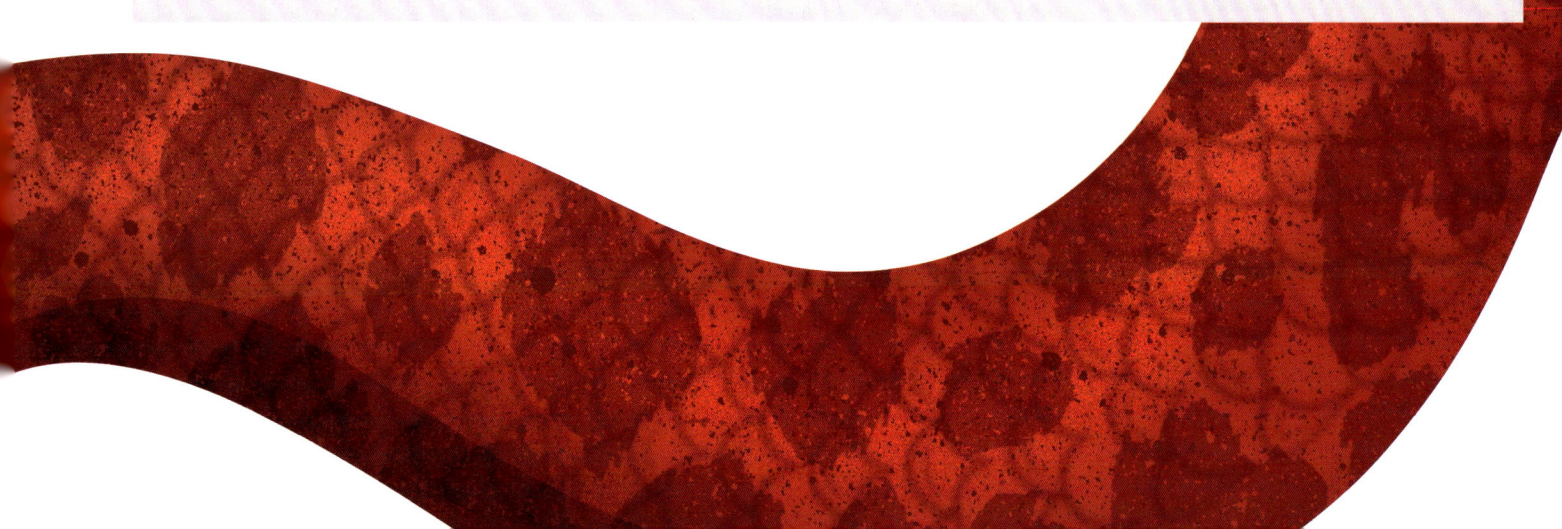

Nicki accepted the apology and said, "I've always loved her. Everyone makes mistakes. She gained so much more respect from me. Let's move on."

Nicki and Taylor went on to perform a mash-up of "Bad Blood" and "The Night Is Still Young" at the MTV VMAs, proving that their beef was officially squashed.

Katy and Taylor's beef continued, however, and even seemed to snowball through possible diss tracks and cryptic social media posts over the years. But then, in 2018, there was a change of heart. Katy sent Taylor an actual olive branch before the first show of Taylor's Reputation Stadium Tour. Taylor posted it on social media and thanked Katy.

A year later, Katy joined Taylor in her music video for "You Need to Calm Down." Katy, dressed as a cheeseburger, and Taylor, dressed as french fries, embraced each other.

Taylor discussed writing the script for the music video and said, "When I thought of this concept for the video, and I wrote the treatment, I thought of this idea and was like, I'm just going to ask her if she'd be interested in this, but I would be totally fine if she'd rather keep it private and keep it between us. But I sent it to her, and she was like, 'I would love for us to be a symbol of redemption and forgiveness.' And I feel the same way about it."

Knowing when to apologize and when to forgive is a powerful thing, and these women showed publicly how to do just that.

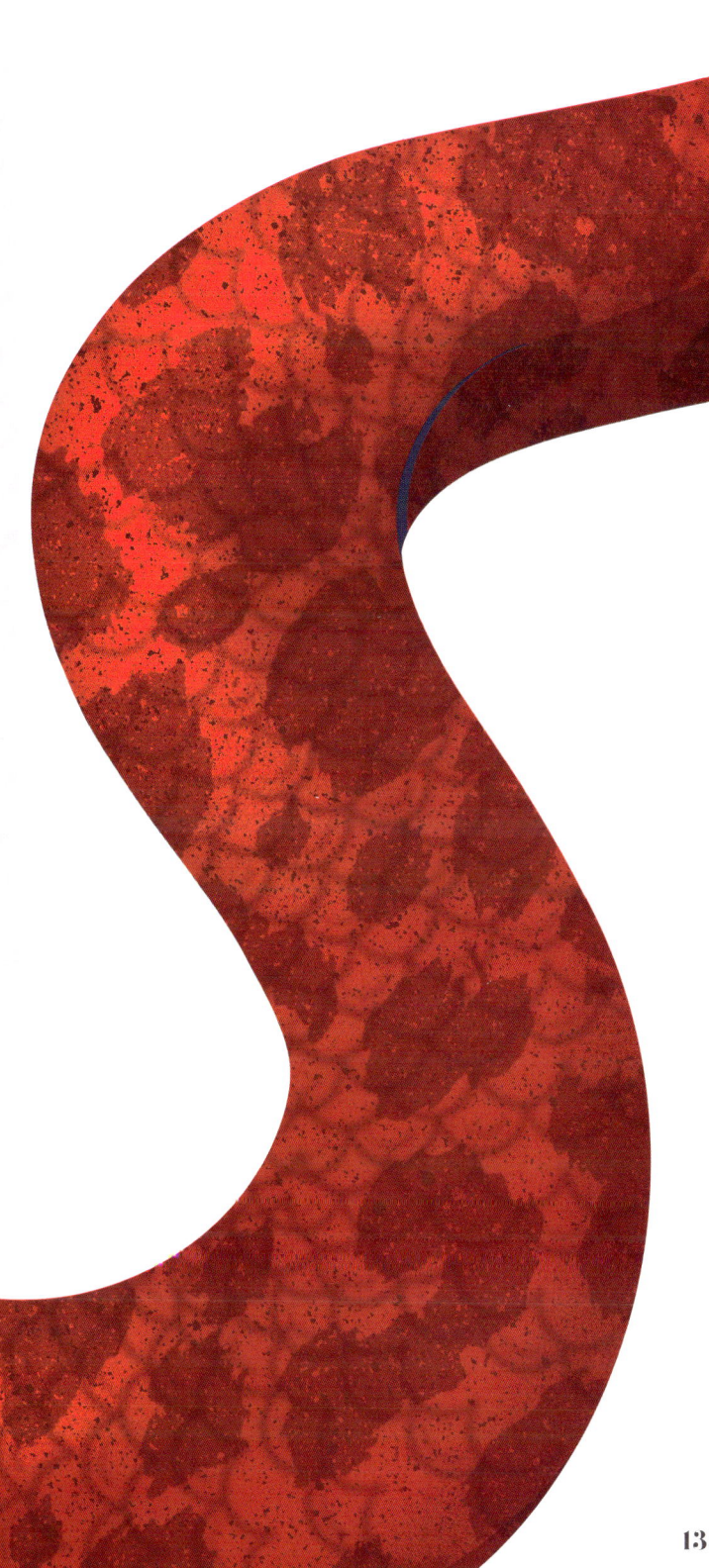

sixty-three-foot inflatable cobra named Karyn appeared onstage in front of sixty thousand screaming fans. It's the Stadium Tour equivalent of responding to a troll's hateful Instagram comment with 'LOL.'"

The album and reclamation of Taylor's reputation worked. The tour was a massive commercial success, becoming the highest-grossing US tour of all time (until Taylor herself later beat it with The Eras Tour), earning $345.7 million globally. The Reputation Stadium Tour won Tour of the Year at the 2018 iHeartRadio Music Awards.

In her acceptance speech for the award, Taylor discussed how for six months leading up to the tour, every headline she read predicted it to be a flop. She went on to say, "I've learned a lot, and one of the things I learned is that life is really unpredictable. And people can make forecasts and predictions, but those predictions and forecasts may not come true if there's an unforeseeable factor involved, and that unforeseeable factor in this case was my fans. I honestly owe everything in my life to you."

She ended by saying, "And I also just wanted to say before I go that I love your passion, I love your attention to detail, I love how much you care. I love seeing all the things that you're voicing online, and I just wanted to let you know that when there's new music, you will be the first to know."

During one of the most difficult times in Taylor's life, she recognized how much her fans were there for her through it all. She continued the T Party tradition with the Rep Room, and her mother, Andrea, continued to handpick fans to come backstage and meet Taylor after the show. The *reputation* era solidified the bond between Taylor and her fans in a way that transcended the traditional artist-fan relationship. While the media often portrayed her as a snake or a misunderstood figure, her fans saw through the noise and continued to support her. Taylor's vulnerability, transparency, and kindness toward her fans over the years only helped strengthen this connection and transformed the *reputation* era into a powerful chapter in the history of Swiftie fandom.

Official "Taylor Swift Day"

Minneapolis Governor Mark Dayton proclaimed it "Taylor Swift Day" in Minnesota during Taylor's visit on the Reputation Stadium Tour.

EST.

The proclamation was officially set for Friday, August 31, 2018.

A MOVEMENT

Other states and cities have officially or unofficially called for similar days when Taylor's tour hit town. For example, Glendale, Arizona, proclaimed the city be named "Swift City" during her two nights of The Eras Tour. Other cities named streets after her or renamed their stadiums to be "(Taylor's Version)."

Back on Top

In March 2020, a longer version of the infamous phone call video was leaked online, proving that Kanye West did not explicitly mention the "that bitch" line to Taylor. This revelation sparked a wave of support for Taylor, as it appeared to vindicate her claims that she had not been fully informed about the song's content. Fans trended hashtags like #TaylorToldTheTruth, and Kanye and Kim were criticized for selectively editing and releasing the original clips in 2016.

The infamous phone call was the catalyst for this era, and Taylor solidified her ability to turn personal struggles into artistic expression, as she channeled the fallout into one of her most defiant and creatively ambitious eras with *reputation*.

While Swifties didn't need the confirmation to know that Taylor was telling the truth, it was clear that this era had not only marked a shift in Taylor's music and public persona; it also deepened the relationship between her and the loyal fan base that had stood by her side through thick and thin. More than just fans, Swifties were a vital part of her journey, and Taylor's recognition of their unwavering love played a significant role in her continued success.

BELOW: The second of two sold-out shows at Wembley Stadium, London, June 23, 2018.

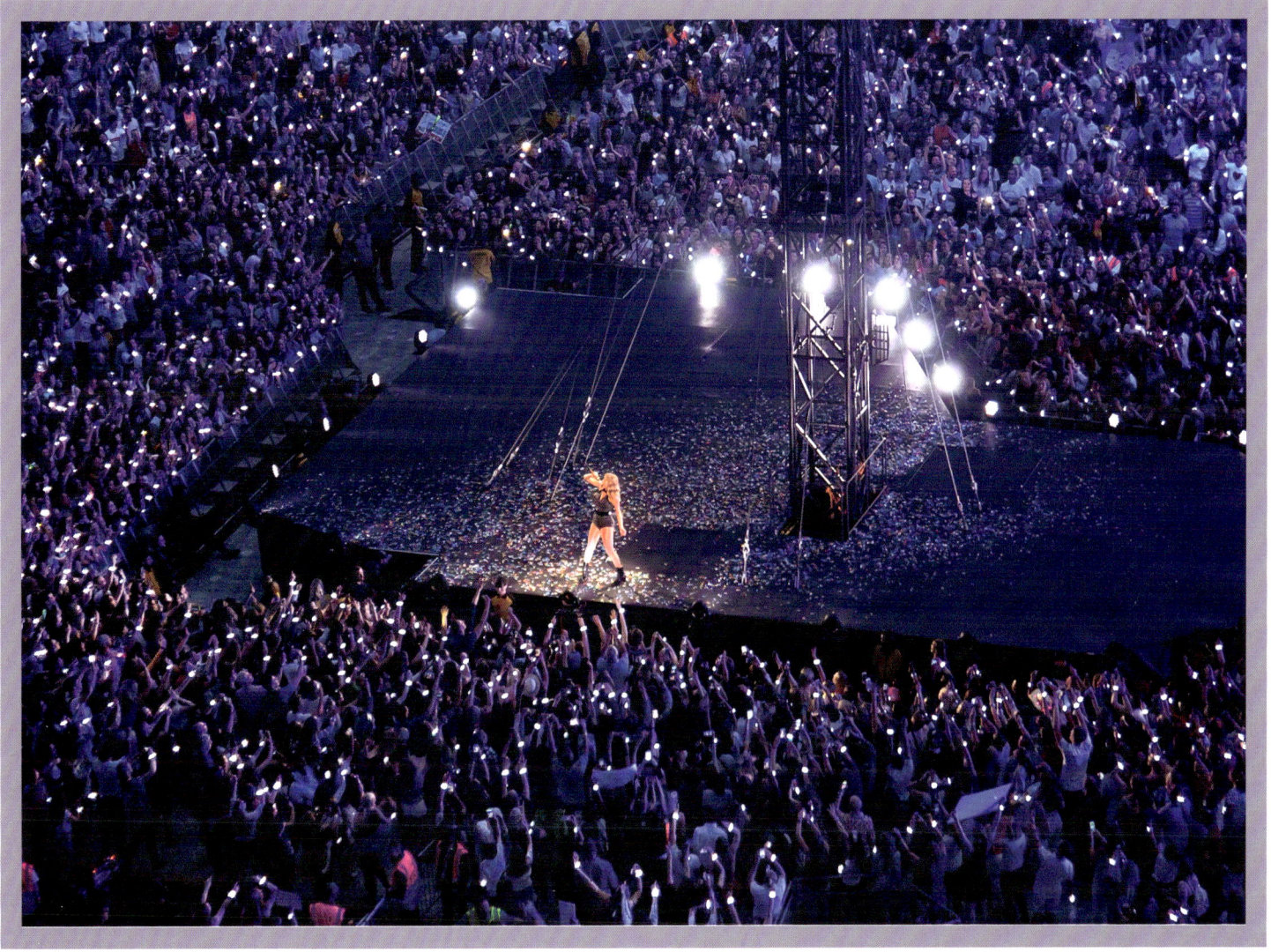

AWARDS BY THE NUMBERS

Taylor won her first music award in 2007. To date, she has been nominated for 1,386 awards and has won 874. Here are some of her statistics for the biggest awards in the business.

Grammys   NOMINATIONS: 58   WINS: 14

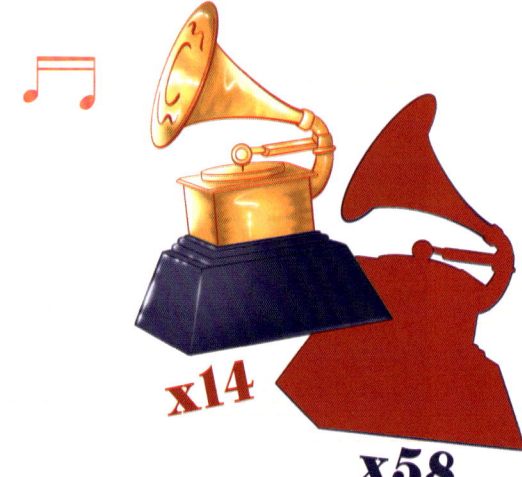

NOTABLE MILESTONES:

- First woman solo artist to win Album of the Year four times: *Fearless* (2010), *1989* (2016), *folklore* (2021), and *Midnights* (2024)

- Youngest winner of Album of the Year at age twenty for *Fearless*

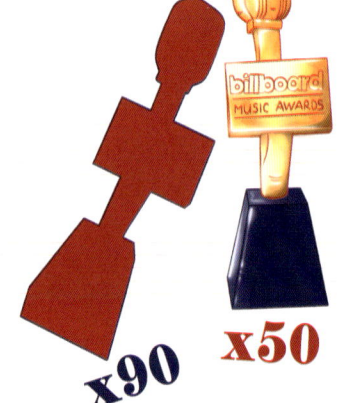

Billboard Music Awards   NOMINATIONS: 90   WINS: 50

NOTABLE MILESTONES:

- Holds the record for the most wins by a female artist, including multiple wins for Top Artist and Top Female Artist

- Also won four Billboard Live Music (Touring) Awards, as well as the Billboard Women in Music Award for Woman of the Year twice, plus Woman of the Decade in 2019

American Music Awards (AMAs)   NOMINATIONS: 48   WINS: 40

NOTABLE MILESTONES:

- Artist of the Decade in 2019
- Record holder for most AMA wins

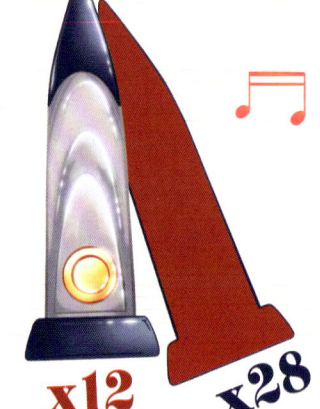

Country Music Association Awards (CMAs)   NOMINATIONS: 28   WINS: 12

NOTABLE MILESTONES:

First female artist to win Entertainer of the Year twice consecutively

MTV Video Music Awards (VMAs)   NOMINATIONS: 60   WINS: 30

NOTABLE MILESTONES:

- Holds the record for the most Video of the Year wins (four),
  including for *All Too Well: The Short Film*

- Holds the record for the most MTV Europe Music Awards,
  with nineteen

x30   x60

BRIT Awards   NOMINATIONS: 11   WINS: 2

NOTABLE MILESTONES:

First woman to win the Global Icon Award in 2021

x2

x11

IHeartRadio Music Awards   NOMINATIONS: 62   WINS: 25

NOTABLE MILESTONES:

Taylor is the most-awarded artist in the history of the
iHeartRadio Music Awards

x25

x62

People's Choice Awards   NOMINATIONS: 39   WINS: 20

NOTABLE MILESTONES:

Tied with Ellen DeGeneres as the most-awarded person, with twenty awards

x39

x20

Other:

- Holds 118 Guinness World Records, including fastest-selling digital album by a
  female artist, most simultaneous US Hot 100 entries by a female artist, and the
  only artist to occupy the entire top ten of the Billboard Hot 100

- Won eleven Nickelodeon Kids' Choice awards, second only to Adam Sandler and
  Ariana Grande (who both have twelve)

- Taylor is the first woman to be named *Time*'s Person of the Year for two years
  (2017 and 2023) and the first entertainer to be named Person of the Year

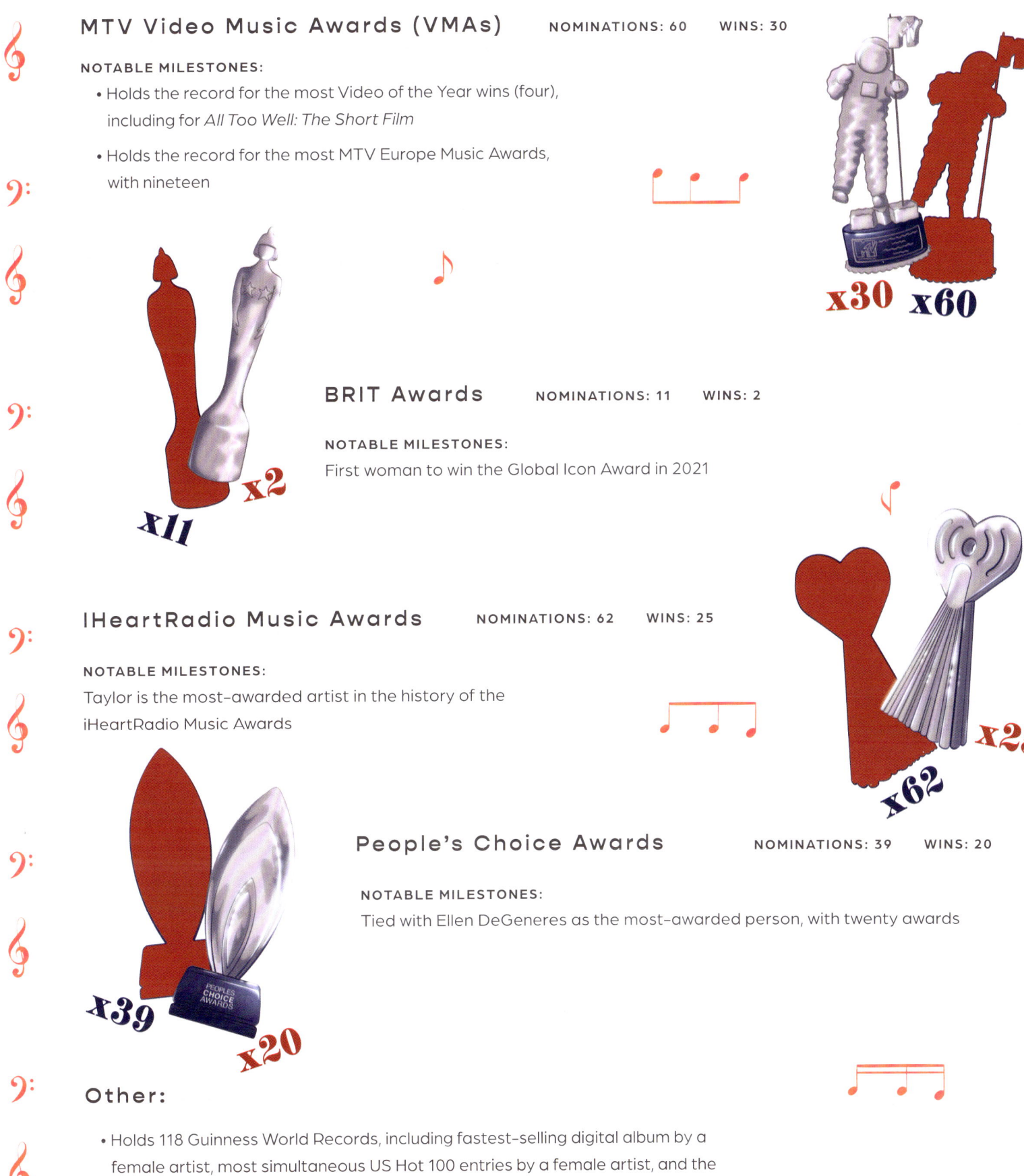

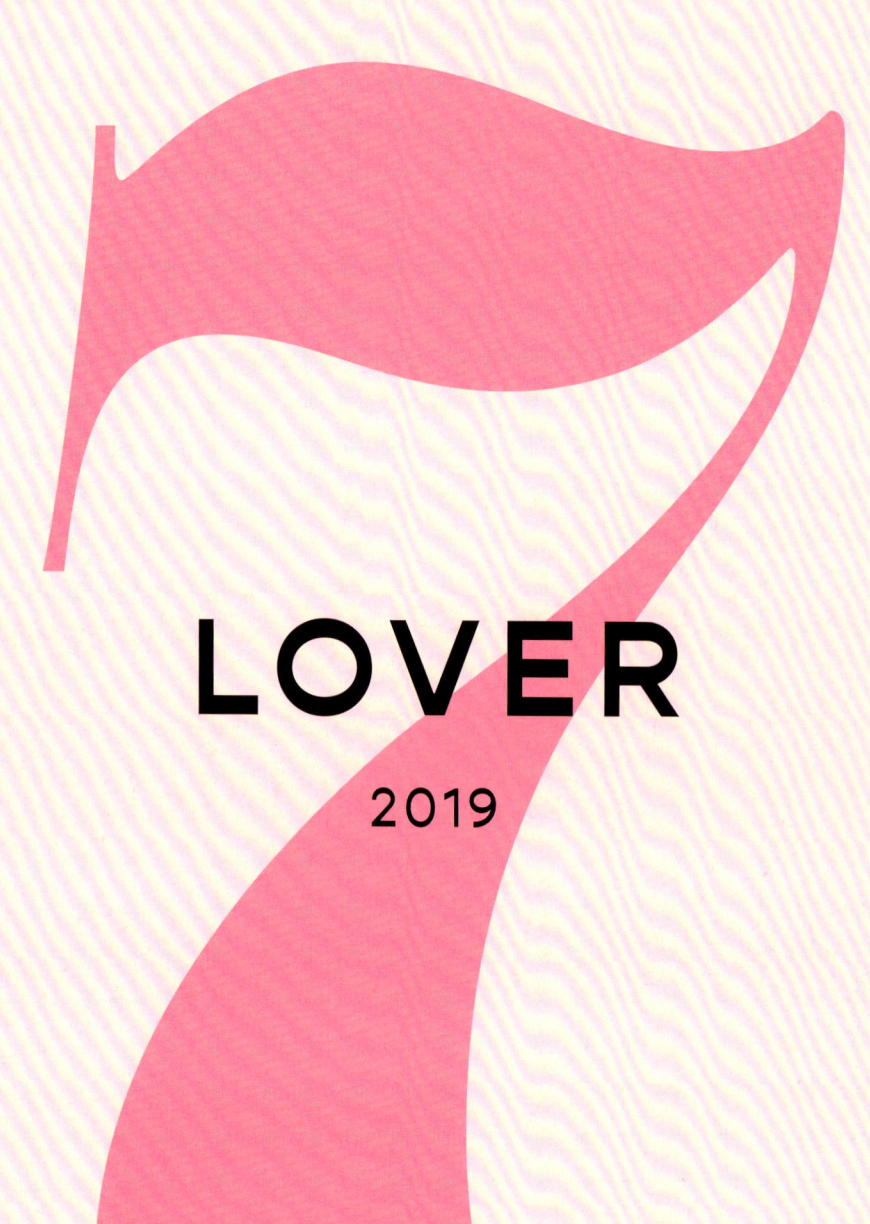

LOVER

2019

EQUALITY IS KIND

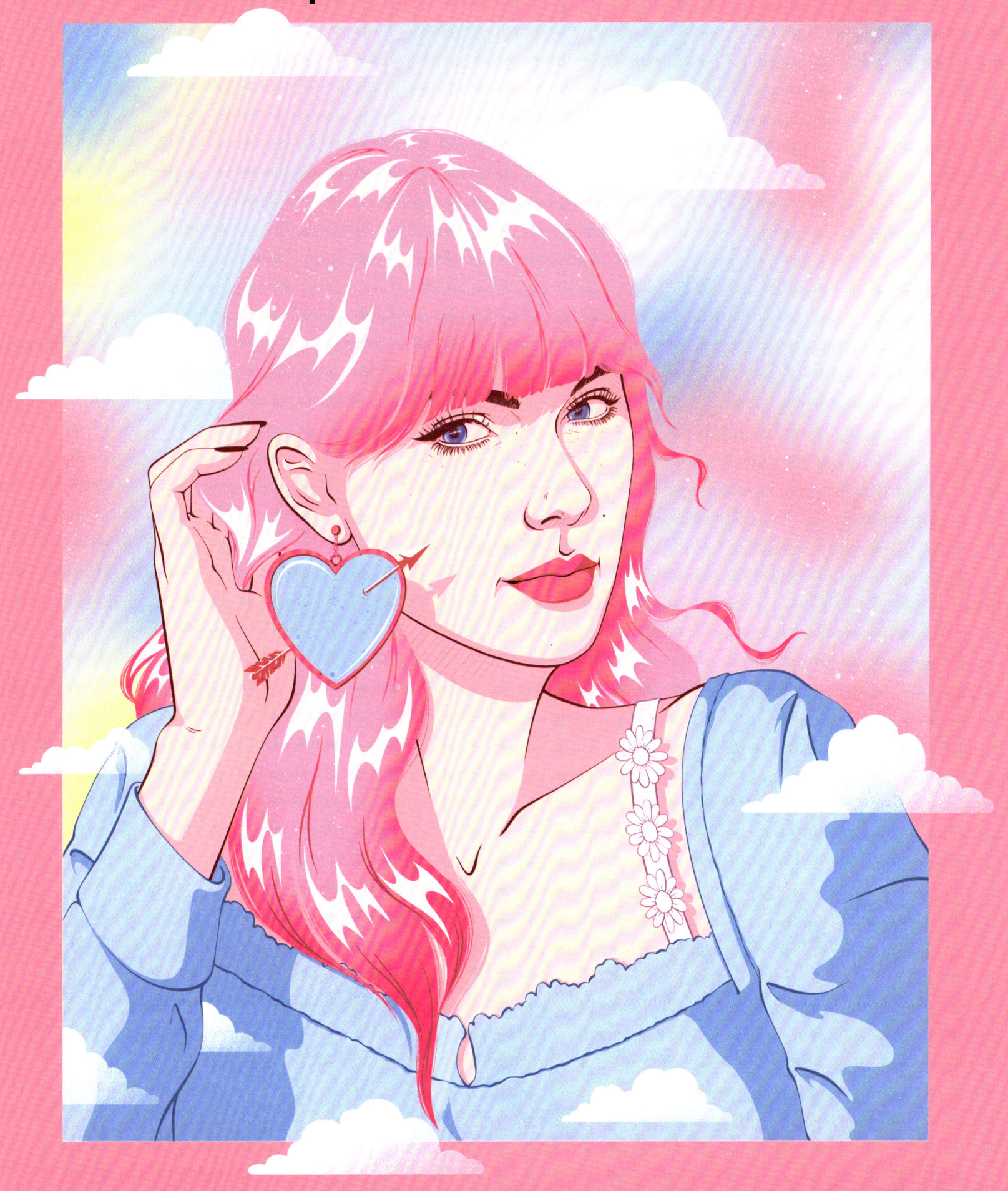

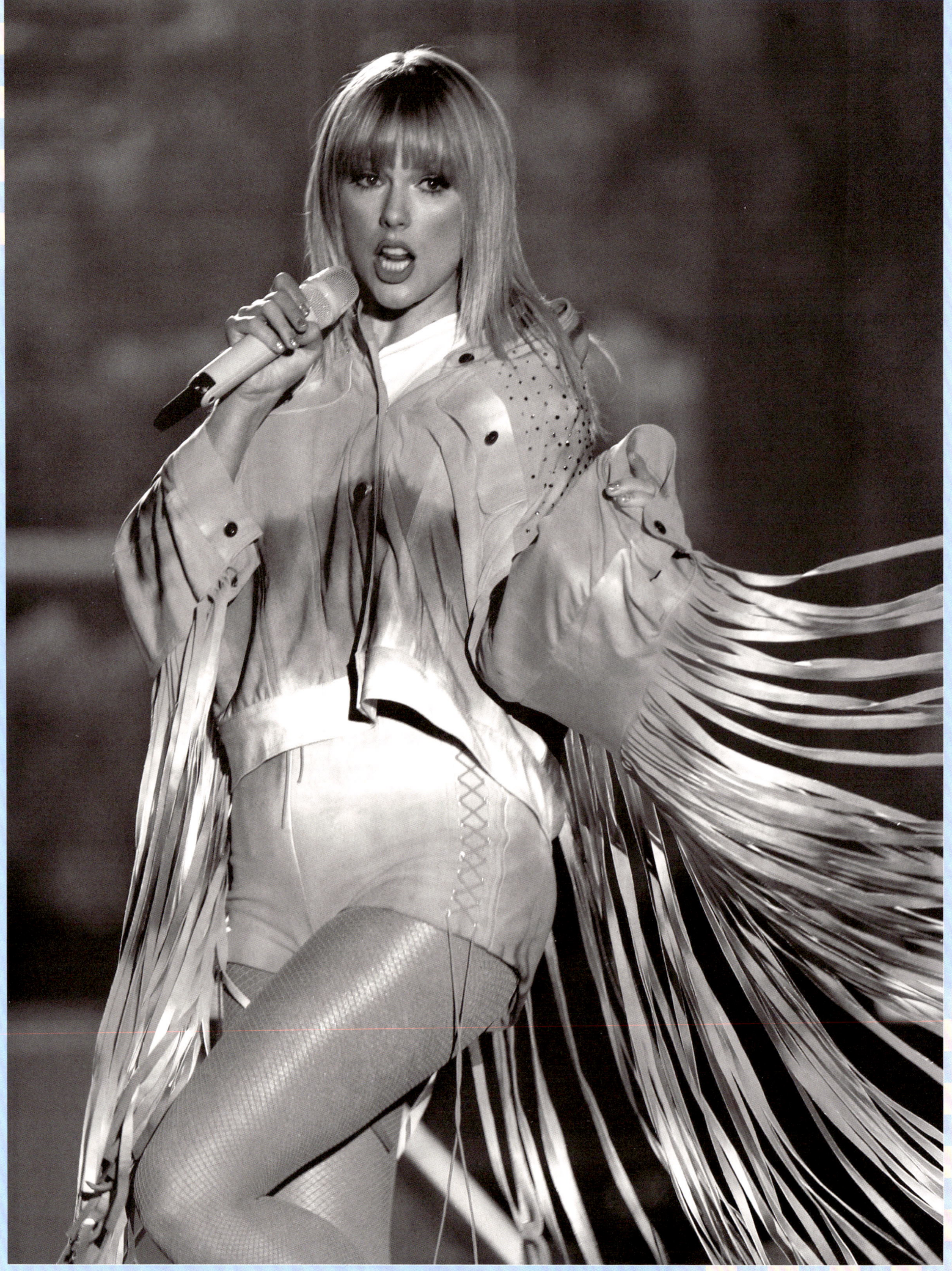

> "I believe that everyone should be able to live out their love story without fear."
>
> Taylor, 2020

USING HER VOICE FOR GOOD

This was the era during which Taylor fully owned and used her voice for the causes she cares about.

The dark imagery and snakes of the *reputation* era had, by now, transformed into dreamy clouds of blue and pink skies, with the snakes transitioning into beautiful butterflies. In 2018, Taylor left Big Machine Label Group and signed a new deal with Republic Records. This move enabled Taylor to own her masters, which was extremely important to her. The *Lover* album was especially liberating for her, as this was an album she fully owned. In many ways, this era symbolized Taylor's growth, and it's when she was able to fully step into using her voice, both by reclaiming her music and by standing up for others.

IT'S A CRUEL SUMMER

There were four singles on the *Lover* album: "ME!," "You Need to Calm Down," "Lover," and "The Man."

During The Eras Tour in 2023, Taylor opened the show with the song "Miss Americana," swiftly followed by "Cruel Summer," arguably a fan-favorite song that wasn't made a single. Things changed in June 2023, however, when Taylor announced during a show in Pittsburgh, Pennsylvania, that "Cruel Summer" would become her next single—because of the fan support and love for the song.

Onstage before "Champagne Problems," Taylor took to the microphone and said, "A magical thing is happening. It never happened to me in the whole time of doing this. 'Cruel Summer' is a song that I just played a second ago. The one with the bridge where we all screamed.

"So basically, 'Cruel Summer' was on the *Lover* album," she continued. "That album came out four years ago, and I just need to let you know something. 'Cruel Summer'—that song was my pride and joy on that album. It was my favorite song. And you know, you have conversations before the album comes out, and everybody around weighs in on what they think should be singles, and I was finally about to have my favorite song become the single off of *Lover*. And I'm not trying to blame the global pandemic, but that is something that happened that stopped 'Cruel Summer' from ever being a single. So what's happening right now, thanks to you,

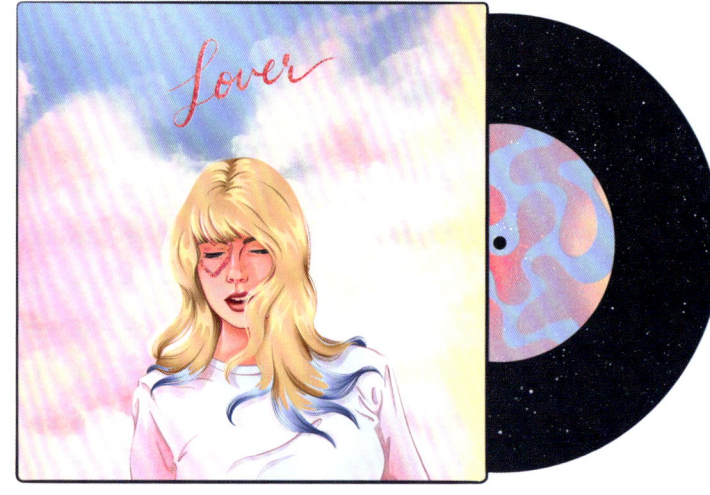

ALBUM
Lover

DATE LAUNCHED
August 23, 2019

FIRST SINGLE
"Me!" (April 26, 2019)

OTHER SINGLES
"You Need to Calm Down" (June 14, 2019), "Lover" (August 16, 2019), "The Man" (January 27, 2020), and "Cruel Summer" (June 13, 2023)

TOUR
Lover Fest (RIP)

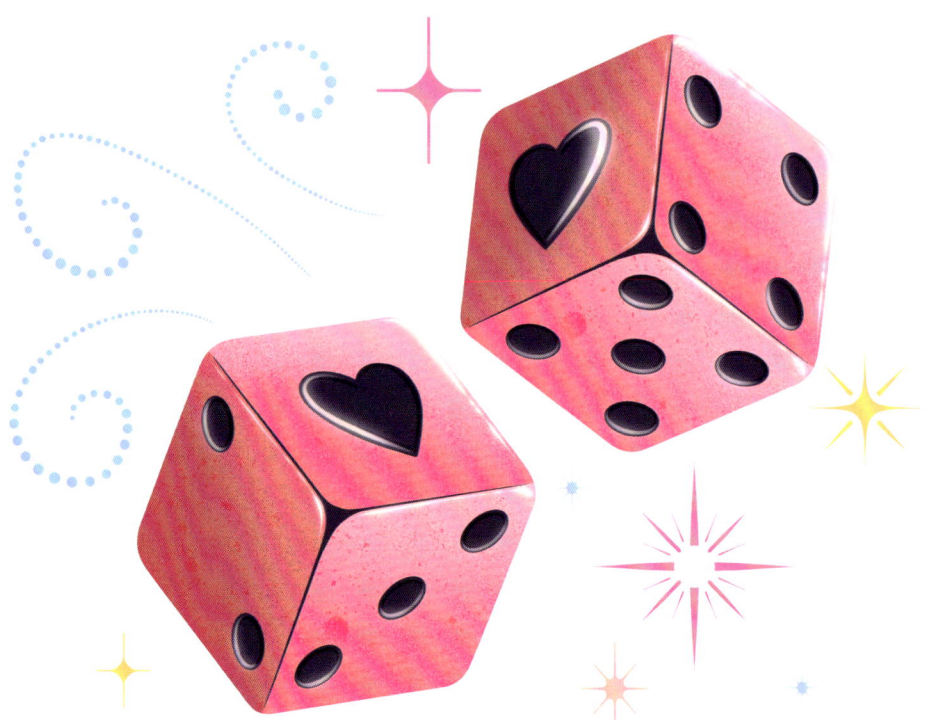

and honestly no one understands how this is happening, but you guys have, like, streamed 'Cruel Summer' so much right now in 2023, it's like at the top, it's like rising on the streaming charts so crazy that my label just decided to make it the next single."

The fans started screaming, and Taylor continued, "It's just truly, truly perplexing to me because this is just, I just haven't had something like this happen in my career, so thank you to anyone who's been listening to that song, like, 500 times a day because it's my favorite one."

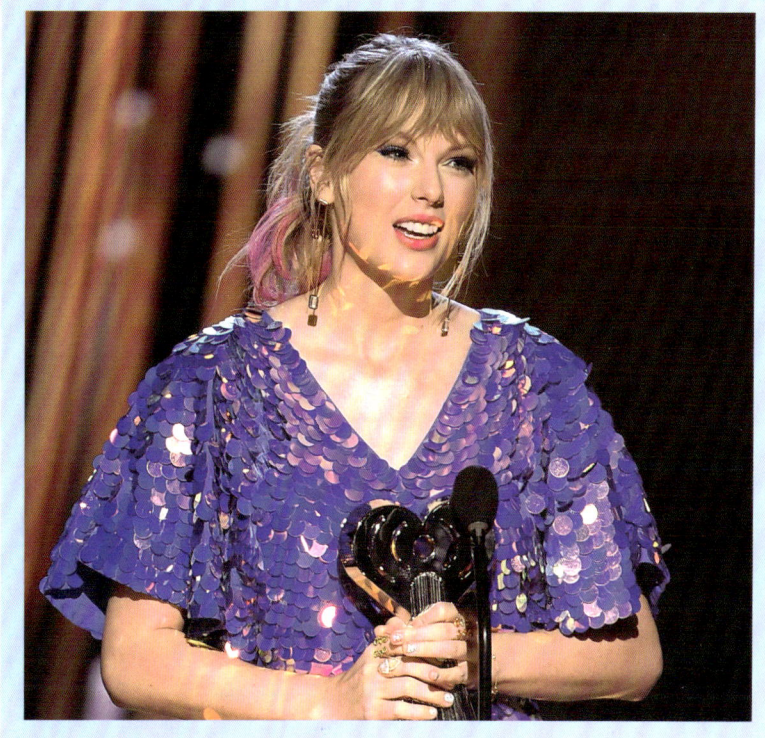

Taylor sprinkled Easter eggs for *Lover* as early as *reputation*. When the Reputation Stadium Tour won Tour of the Year at the 2019 iHeartRadio Music Awards, Taylor wore a purple sequined romper, with her hair in a ponytail and the ends of her hair dyed pink, and butterflies on her shoes. Butterflies later became a signature of the *Lover* era. When she took to social media to announce *reputation*, Taylor wore a rainbow sequined mini dress with a matching jacket. The rainbow aesthetic was a contrast to the *reputation* era that she was entering, but it served as a very early Easter egg for eagle-eyed Swifties.

During the *Lover* era, Taylor embraced traditional media, appearing on *CBS News Sunday Morning*, *The Ellen DeGeneres Show*, and *The Tonight Show Starring Jimmy Fallon* in connection with album announcements and song releases—something she'd shied away from during the *reputation* era. However, she continued her tradition of connecting with fans through her "Secret Sessions." Taylor hosted surprise *Lover* album release parties at her homes in London, Nashville, and Los Angeles. She also remained active on social media, regularly engaging with her followers and expressing gratitude for their support.

The first social media clues pointing to this new era came when Taylor posted pastel-colored images, palm trees, and fences, signaling a shift toward a lighter aesthetic and leaving fans speculating what it all meant—even counting the number of posts in the fence. (After all, Swifties believe that everything in the Taylor-verse can have meaning!) She started dropping different hints, including mentioning the butterfly migration in Southern California. Fans wondered what was going on when a butterfly mural, created by artist Kelsey Montague, appeared in Nashville. The mural's colors seemed to match the new colors that Taylor was posting, and fans were quick to notice seven flowers (a nod to her seventh studio album), thirteen hearts (her favorite number), and, of course, cats.

Fans flocked to the mural, and eventually it was updated with the word "Me!" in the middle. Taylor visited the mural and ended up meeting with fans and taking photos for forty-five minutes. She later posted a photo standing inside the butterfly mural and thanked the fans for showing up. She said, "I've never been more proud of your FBI-level detective skills."

PAGE 142: Taylor performing as the closing act for iHeartRadio's Wango Tango. Panic! at the Disco's Brendon Urie would join her for her final song, "ME!"

ABOVE: Accepting the 2019 iHeartRadio Music Award for Tour of the Year, for her Reputation Stadium Tour. She would also win Best Music Video for "Delicate."

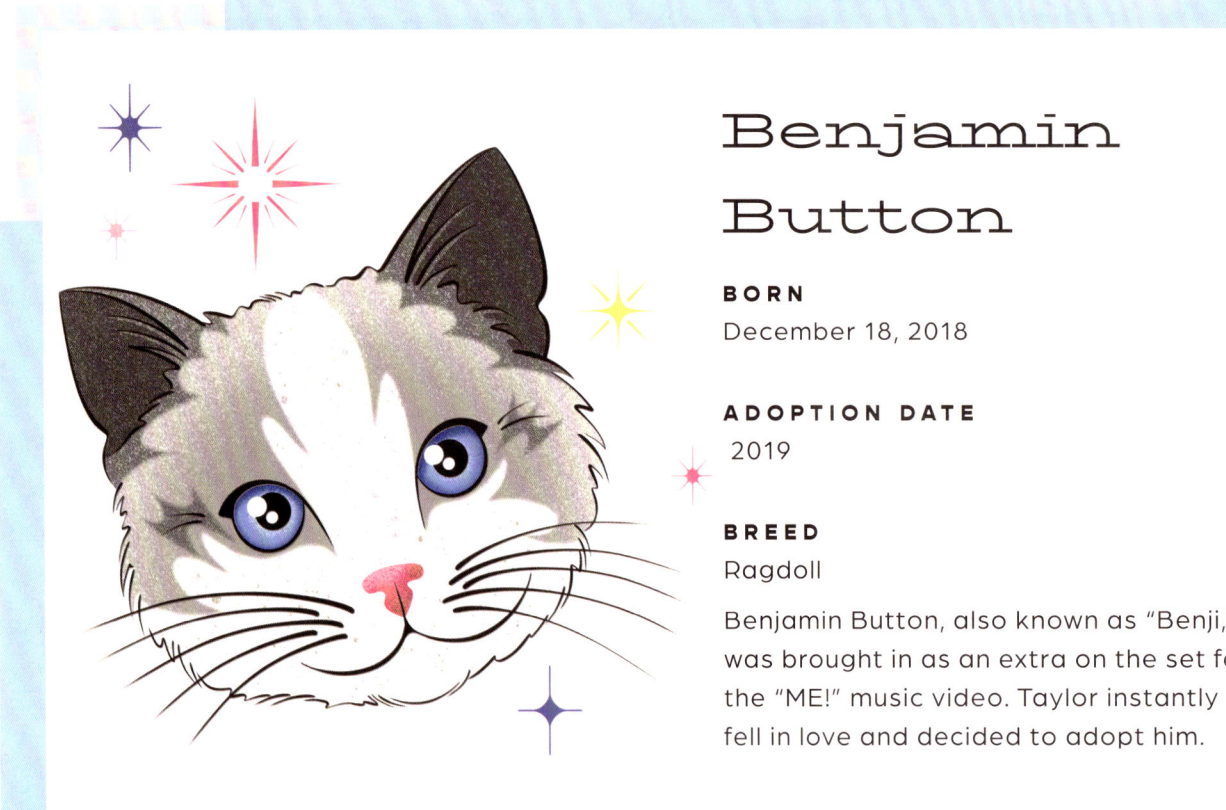

Benjamin Button

BORN
December 18, 2018

ADOPTION DATE
2019

BREED
Ragdoll

Benjamin Button, also known as "Benji," was brought in as an extra on the set for the "ME!" music video. Taylor instantly fell in love and decided to adopt him.

Later that day, she joined Robin Roberts on *Good Morning America* and announced the first single "ME!" from her new album. Featuring Brendon Urie of Panic! At The Disco, the song was to drop the next day, on April 26, 2019. When asked about the song, Taylor said, "'ME!' is a song about embracing your individuality and really celebrating it and owning it. With a pop song, we have the ability to get a melody really stuck in people's heads, and I just want it to be one that makes them feel better about themselves."

When the music video dropped, fans went wild looking for a plethora of Easter eggs, trying to guess the album's title, title tracks, potential features, and more. The video offered a treasure trove of Easter eggs, including right at the beginning when a pink and white snake suddenly burst into beautiful butterflies. This was seen as confirmation that *reputation* was behind Taylor. The video also featured wall portraits of baby

chicks and a photo of the band The Chicks. This clue was later confirmed when The Chicks were featured in the song "Soon You'll Get Better." Also in the video, Taylor was shown receiving several gifts and not liking them, but then being gifted a new kitten that she was overjoyed about. That joy transferred to real life, as Taylor ended up adopting that adorable kitten and naming him Benji (short for Benjamin Button).

Fans were anxiously awaiting more news about the album when on June 13, 2019, Taylor went live on Instagram and thanked them for caring about her Easter eggs. Mentioning that they found many of them, she discussed how fans speculated about the word "calm" and that she was excited to announce that she was releasing a new single called "You Need to Calm Down." The song was to release the next day, followed by a music video a few days later. Taylor said she wanted fans to listen to the song first and take it in before viewing the visuals.

HEART-SHAPED VINYL

The *Lover (Live from Paris)* performance took place on September 9, 2019, the Olympia, an iconic venue known for its intimate, historic atmosphere. The event celebrated the release of Lover and featured stripped-down, acoustic versions of Taylor's songs. The performance captured the raw emotion and personal connection that the Lover era emphasized, creating an experience cherished by those lucky enough to attend. For those who weren't in attendance, the concert was later aired on ABC as a one-hour special called *Taylor Swift: City of Lover Concert*. The performances can still be found online and listened to on streaming.

On February 14, 2023, Taylor released the *Lover (Live from Paris)* Heart-Shaped Vinyl, which was a shortened version of the concert, featuring only the songs performed from the *Lover* album. This vinyl became a coveted collectible among fans because of the unique heart-shaped design, in the pastel colors of pink and blue, both a direct nod to the album's namesake. Plus, they actually work on the turntable!

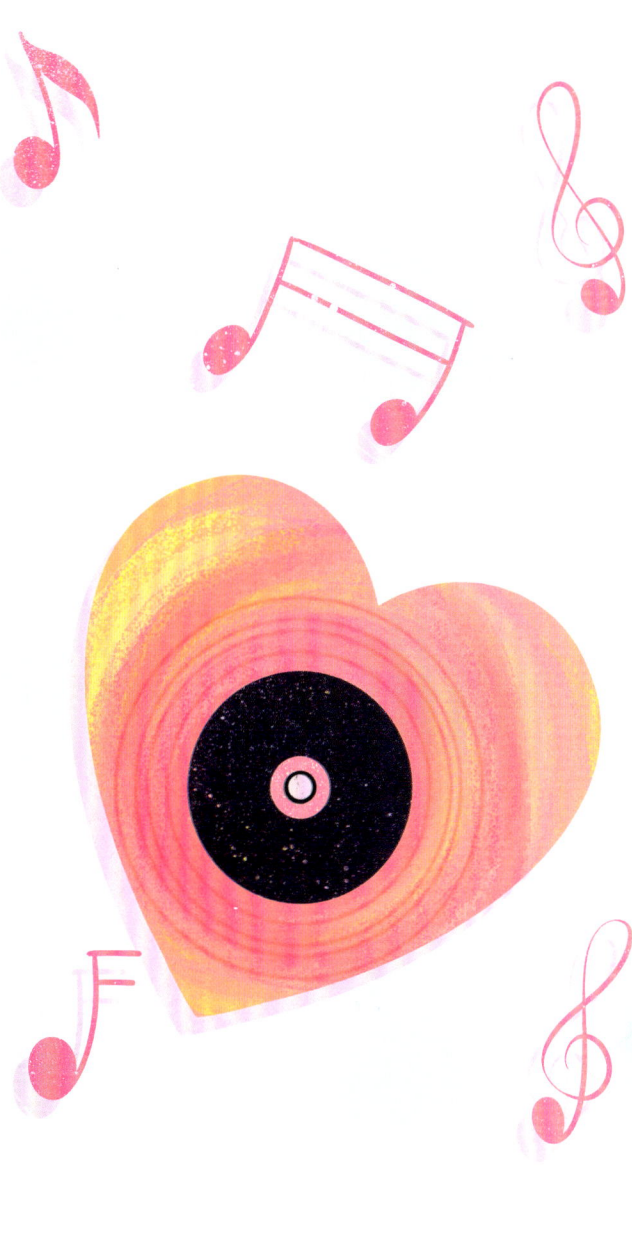

The heart-shaped vinyl records were released in limited quantities. It's estimated that the first pressing was around thirteen thousand copies, a fun nod at Taylor's favorite number. The combination of rarity and unique design caused an immediate frenzy, and the album sold out in minutes. Taylor did another re-pressing of the records in 2025 with an updated swirl pastel pattern. It's estimated that around one hundred thousand copies were pressed and again, they also sold out in minutes.

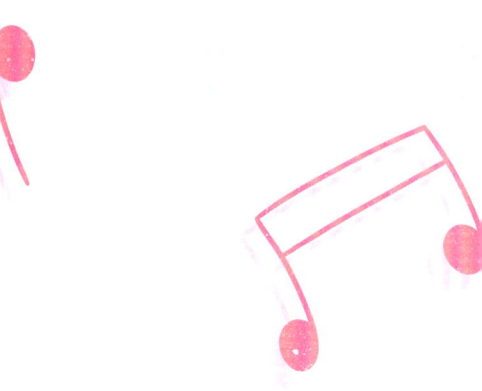

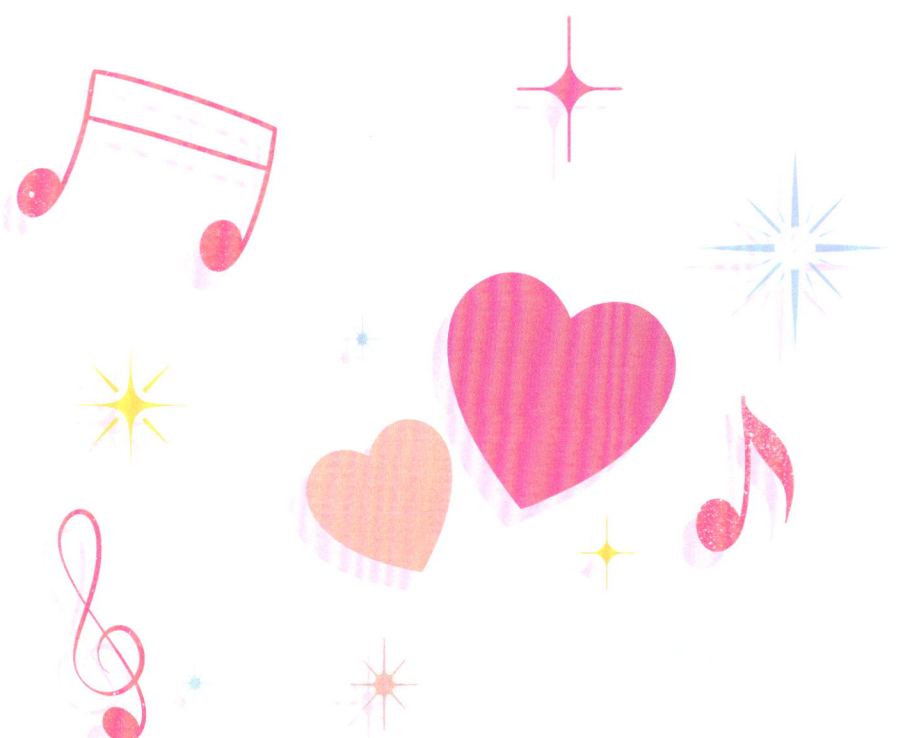

For fans, these heart-shaped vinyl records encapsulate the magic of the *Lover* era, the romance of Paris, and the intimate connection that Taylor always strives to foster through both her music and the merchandise she creates with her fans in mind. Whether displayed as art or played on turntables, they remain a cherished item for many Swifties.

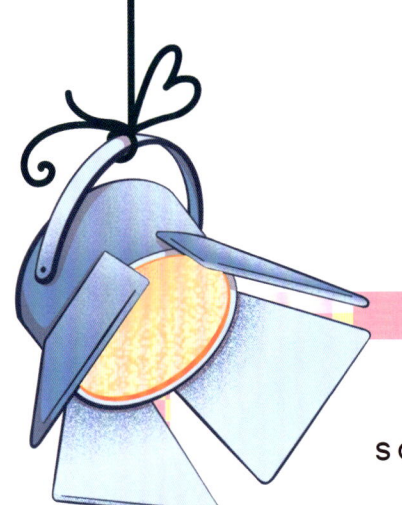

"Death by a Thousand Cuts"

There was a bit of an invisible string connection between the movie *Someone Great,* written and directed by Jenn Kaytin Robinson and Taylor. Taylor credits the movie to being the inspiration behind the song "Death by a Thousand Cuts." In an interview with Elvis Duran, Taylor said, "I cried watching the movie and for about a week, I started waking up from dreams that I'm living out that scenario . . . I'd have these lyrics in my head based on the dynamics of these characters."

ALBUM

Lover

RELEASED

2019

You Need to Calm Down

The "You Need to Calm Down" music video was co-directed by Todrick Hall and featured a star-studded cast of drag queens and Taylor's friends, many of whom were part of the LGBTQ+ community. The cast included A'keria Davenport, Adam Lambert, Adam Rippon, Adore Delano, Antoni Porowski, Billy Porter, Bobby Berk, Chester Lockhart, Ciara, Delta Work, Dexter Mayfield, Ellen DeGeneres, Hannah Hart, Hayley Kiyoko, Jade Jolie, Jesse Tyler Ferguson, Jonathan van Ness, Justin Mikita, Karamo Brown, Katy Perry, Laverne Cox, Riley Knoxx, RuPaul, Ryan Reynolds, Tan France, Tatianna, Todrick Hall, Trinity K. Bonet, and Trinity Taylor.

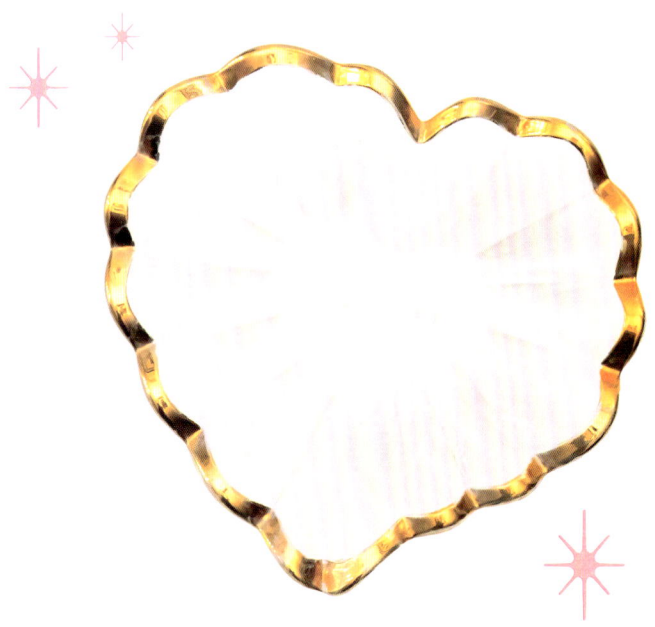

London 2023

In 2023, Taylor expanded her real-estate portfolio and bought a mansion in North London, planting some roots in a city she is known to love. While she was no longer dating a London boy at the time of the purchase, it's clear that she loves and appreciates all that the city has to offer.

HAMPSTEAD HEATH

Another spot reference in "London Boy," this is a beautiful green space in London.

HIGHGATE

This area was referenced in the song "London Boy" off the *Lover* album.

KENTISH DELIGHT

A small kebab shop that was featured in the "End Game" music video. The owner had a few cameos in the video and has a selfie with Taylor hanging on the wall of the shop.

CAMDEN MARKET

Filled with shops and food vendors, this place is one where Taylor enjoys walking in the afternoon.

SHOREDITCH

A part of East London, known for art, music, restaurants, and vintage shops, this is another area referenced in the song "London Boy."

HACKNEY

Taylor doesn't need to be in the infamous posh areas of London, as she also prefers Hackney, which is home to a lush park called London Fields.

WEST END

London's theater and entertainment district, also referenced in "London Boy." Most notably, Taylor attended a performance of *Cabaret* at the Kit Kat Club to see her pal Cara Delevingne perform.

THE SAVOY HOTEL

This art deco hotel was used as the backdrop for a 2015 photoshoot featuring Taylor in *Vanity Fair*. It was also featured in the "End Game" music video, and it's a hotel where Taylor stayed the night, making it a hot spot for Swifties.

THE BLACK DOG

This pub was referenced in *The Tortured Poets Department* in a song by the same name. This is a pub in South London that recently created a Taylor Swift–themed menu for her fans.

Taylor has been vocal about lots of things she loves in London, including Ed Sheeran, Topshop, rose and violet cream chocolates, Squashies candies, and, of course, her fans.

BRIXTON

This area of south London has a strong musical heritage (it's the birthplace of David Bowie!) and was another spot mentioned in "London Boy."

100% Hers

On November 19, 2018, Taylor announced that she found a new home for her music at Republic Records after her previous deal with Big Machine Records expired earlier that same month.

FIRST ALBUM SHE OWNS

Lover is the first album completely owned by Taylor. Taylor said, "It's the first album of mine that I've ever owned, and I couldn't be more proud."

RECORD-BREAKING

Upon the release of *Lover*, all of the album's eighteen tracks simultaneously charted on the Billboard Hot 100, breaking the record for the most simultaneous chart entries for a female artist.

The video showcased themes of love, inclusivity, and acceptance. It embraced queer love, accepting yourself for who you are, and forgiveness, as Taylor and Katy Perry hugged it out dressed as a burger and french fries, showing that they too had squashed their beef.

The music video included subtitles with the lyrics written out, leading fans to notice that the word "glad" was actually spelled "GLAAD," in support of the LGBTQ advocacy group that "works to ensure fair, accurate, and inclusive representation and creates national and local programs that advance LGBTQ acceptance." Afterward, the organization reported receiving a spike in thirteen-dollar donations, in a gesture from Swifties showing their support.

The end of the video featured a call to action: "Let's show our pride by demanding that, on a national level, our laws truly treat all our citizens equally. Please sign my petition for Senate support of the Equality Act on Change.org." This was one of Taylor's first instances of calling for political action and cemented her stance on LGBTQ+ rights.

Anthony Ramos, GLAAD's director of talent engagement at the time, issued a statement saying, "The fact that she continues to use her platform and music to support the LGBTQ community and the Equality Act is a true sign of being an ally. 'You Need to Calm Down' is the perfect Pride anthem, and we're thrilled to see Taylor standing with the LGBTQ community to promote inclusivity, equality, and acceptance this Pride month."

Shortly after the song was released, Taylor surprised fans by performing an acoustic set of "Shake It Off" during Jesse Tyler Ferguson's cabaret show at the Stonewall Inn, honoring the fiftieth anniversary of the Stonewall Uprising. Jesse joined her onstage for the bridge and final chorus, and the crowd went wild.

Masters Controversy

While the launch to *Lover* started off full of rainbows and butterflies, things quickly changed. On June 30, 2019, Taylor got word that Scooter Braun's company, Ithaca Holdings, had bought her former record label, Big Machine Label Group, for $300 million. This deal included the master recordings of Taylor's first six albums and set off a firestorm, with Taylor taking to Tumblr to share her disappointment and anger over the situation.

In her Tumblr post, Taylor expressed feeling blindsided and heartbroken by the deal. She revealed that she had been trying to regain ownership of her masters for years but was only offered the chance to "earn" them back by signing another contract with Big Machine, which she declined. Instead, she chose to leave the label and start fresh with Universal Music Group.

Taylor described Scooter's acquisition as her "worst-case scenario," citing past experiences of feeling bullied by him and his clients, including Justin Bieber and Kanye West. Her post also called out Big Machine's founder, Scott Borchetta, whom she accused of betraying her by selling the label—and her life's work—to Scooter. Taylor said that she was not given the opportunity to purchase her masters outright, even though she had asked numerous times.

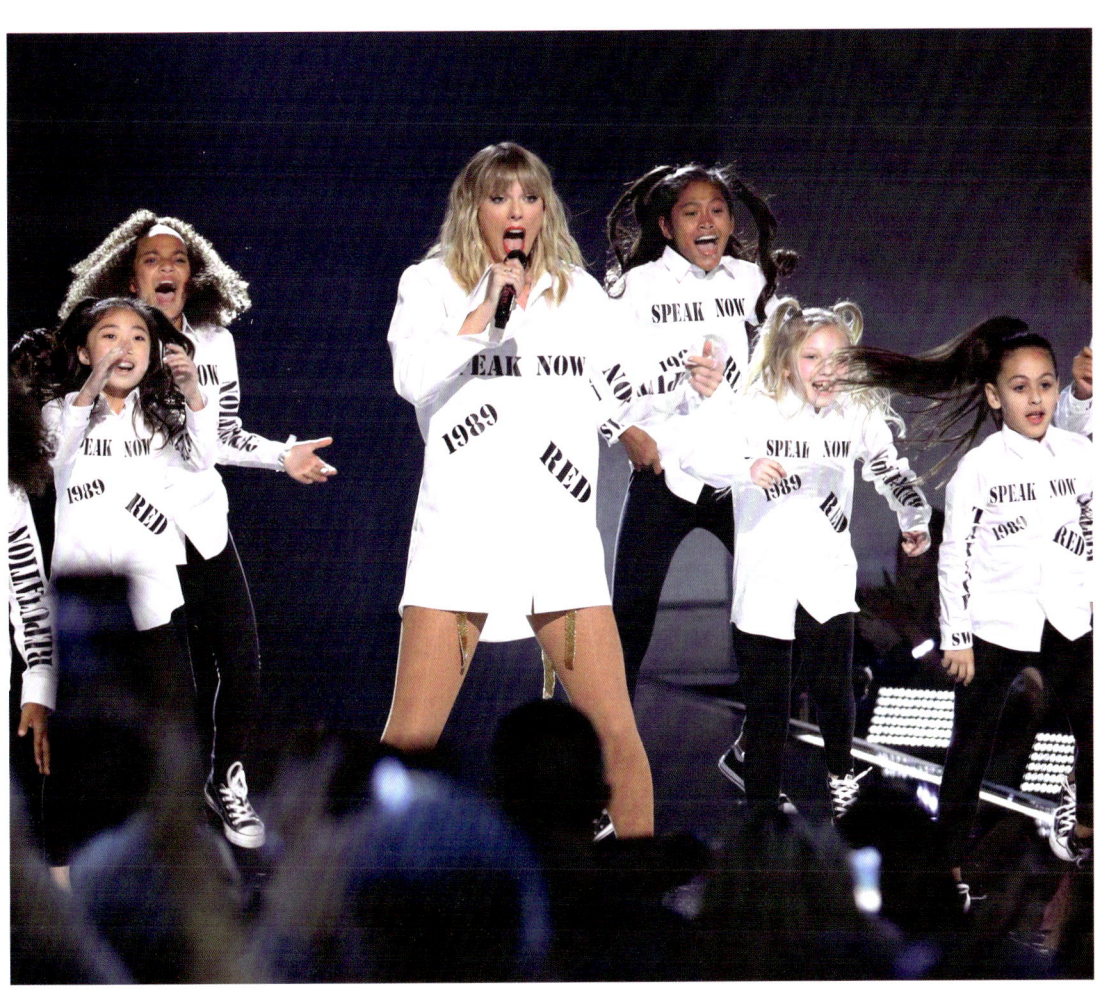

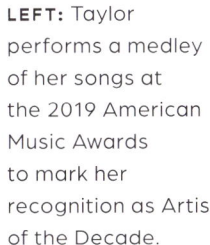

LEFT: Taylor performs a medley of her songs at the 2019 American Music Awards to mark her recognition as Artist of the Decade.

FOLLOWING PAGES: Taylor performs on *Good Morning America* from New York City's Central Park, to promote the release of *Lover*, August 22, 2019.

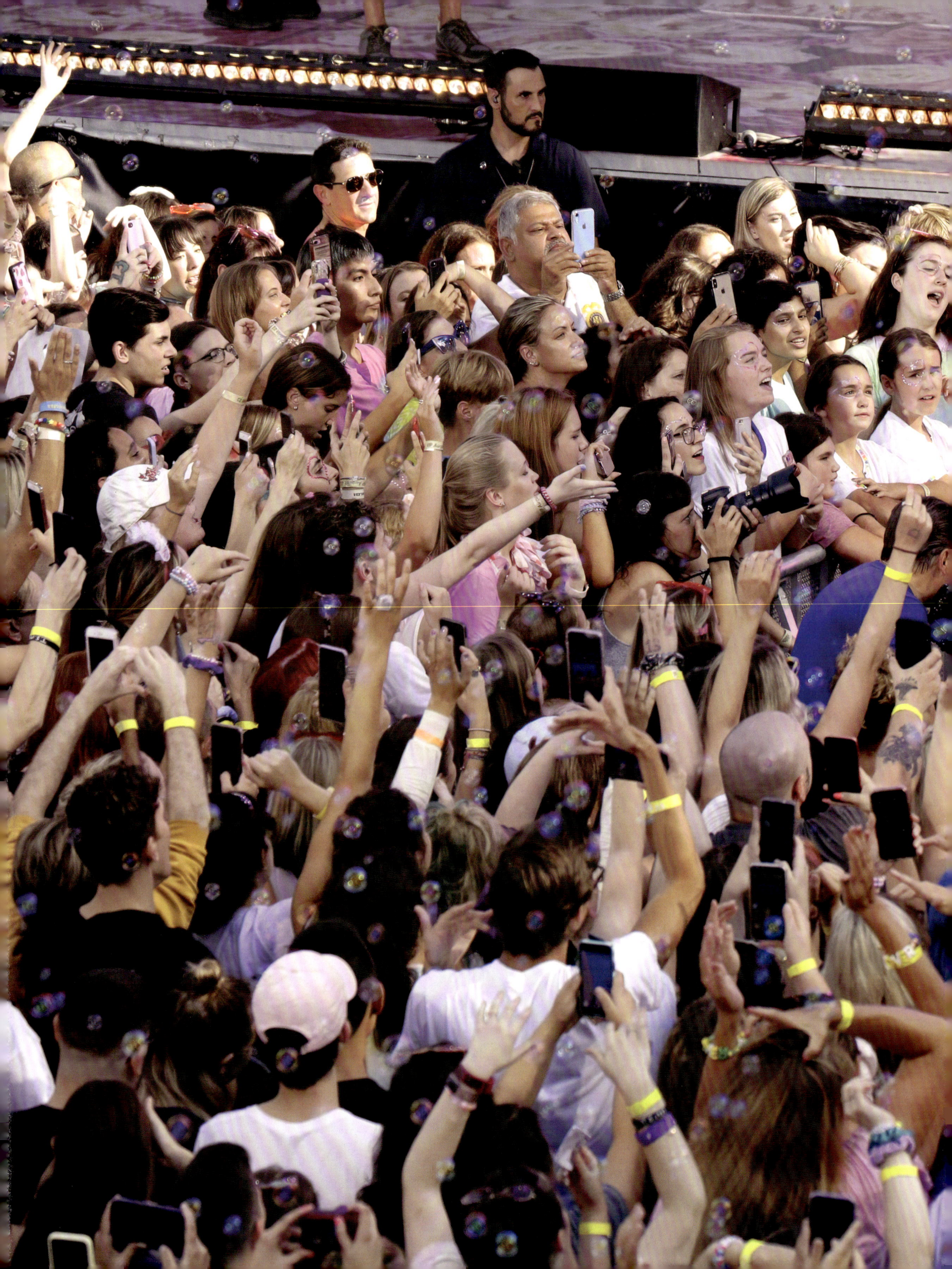

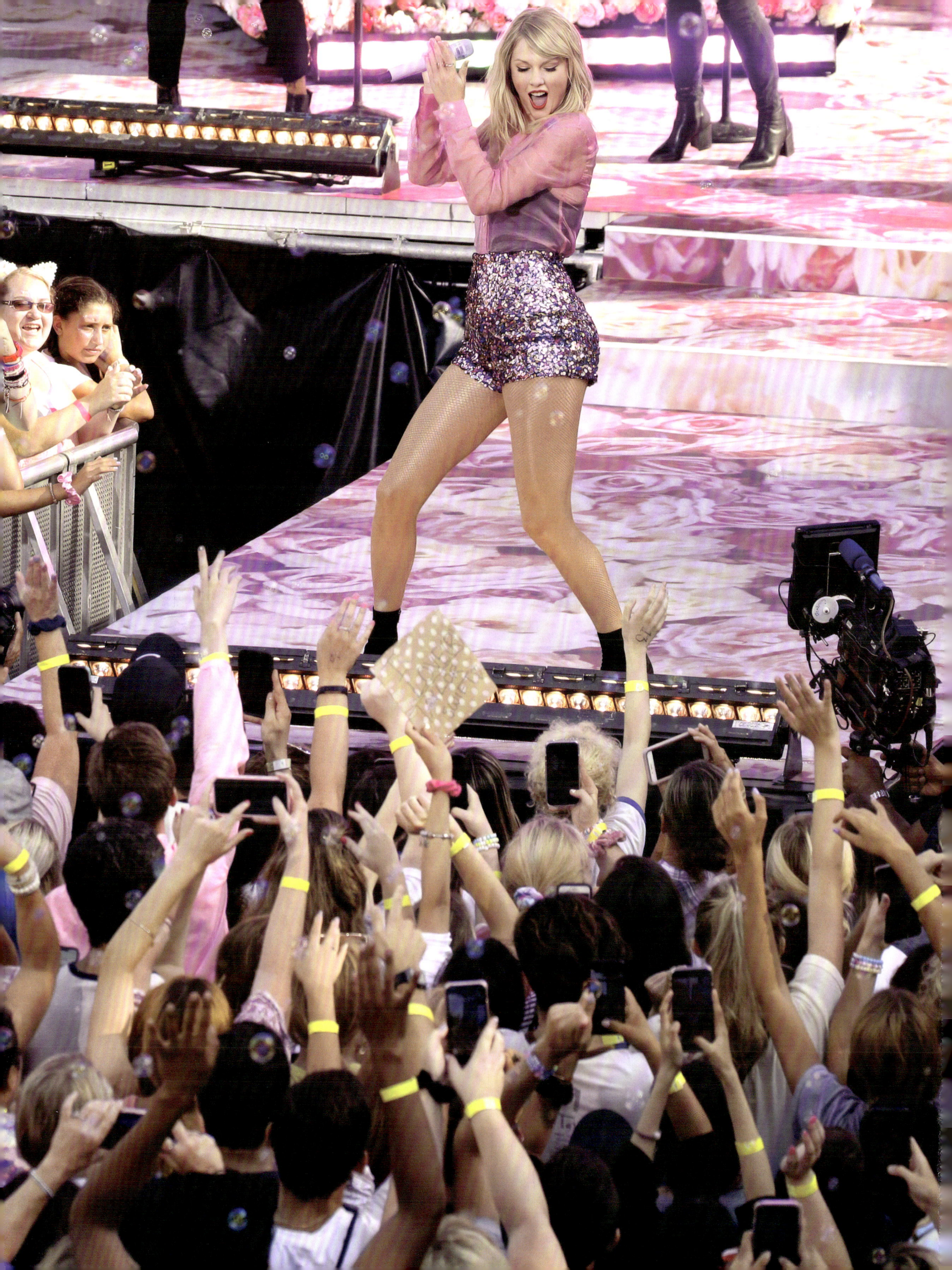

Taylor ended her Tumblr post by saying, "Thankfully, I am now signed to a label that believes I should own anything I create. Thankfully, I left my past in Scott's hands and not my future. And hopefully, young artists or kids with musical dreams will read this and learn about how to better protect themselves in a negotiation. You deserve to own the art you make."

The Tumblr post sparked a cultural conversation about the music industry, including artists' rights and control over their work. It also caused a media storm of people rallying behind Taylor, while others defended Scooter.

She shared that while she was proud of her past work, fans were encouraged to buy *Lover* in August for a "healthier option." Taylor was responding to the acquisition news in real time and had no plans (at least not publicly) to re-record her old albums at the time. There was chatter that she might re-record, however, and most famously, singer Kelly Clarkson took to X (formerly known as Twitter), tagged Taylor, and said, "@taylorswift13 just a thought, U should go & re-record all the songs that U don't own the masters on exactly how U did them but put brand new art & some kind of incentive so fans will no longer buy the old versions. I'd buy all the new versions just to prove a point." Pretty soon, fans caught on and agreed that they, too, would support this.

"I love how kind she is, though; she's a very smart businesswoman."

Kelly Clarkson

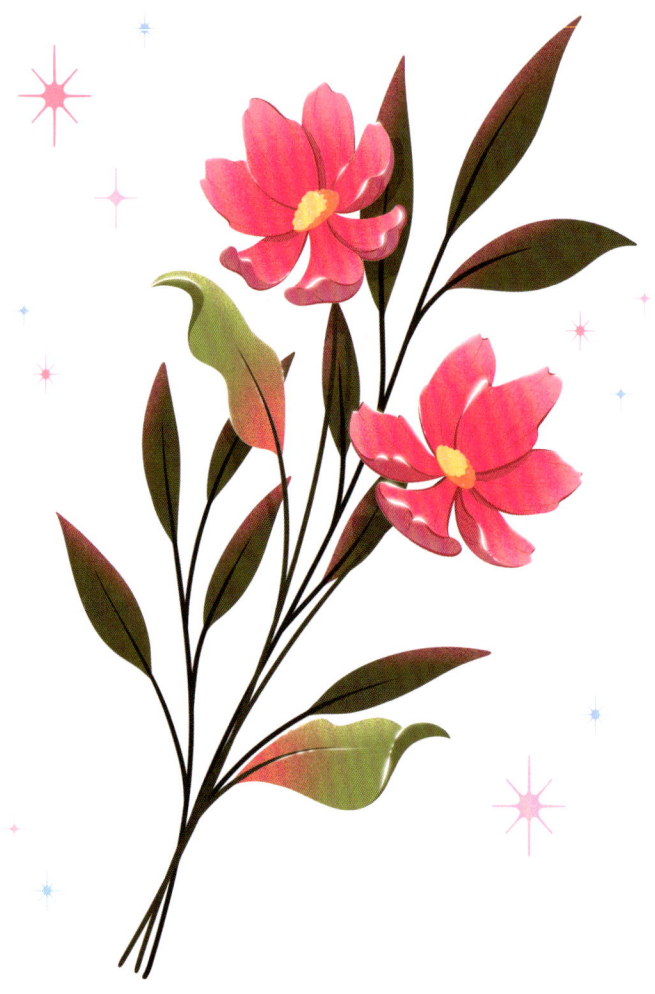

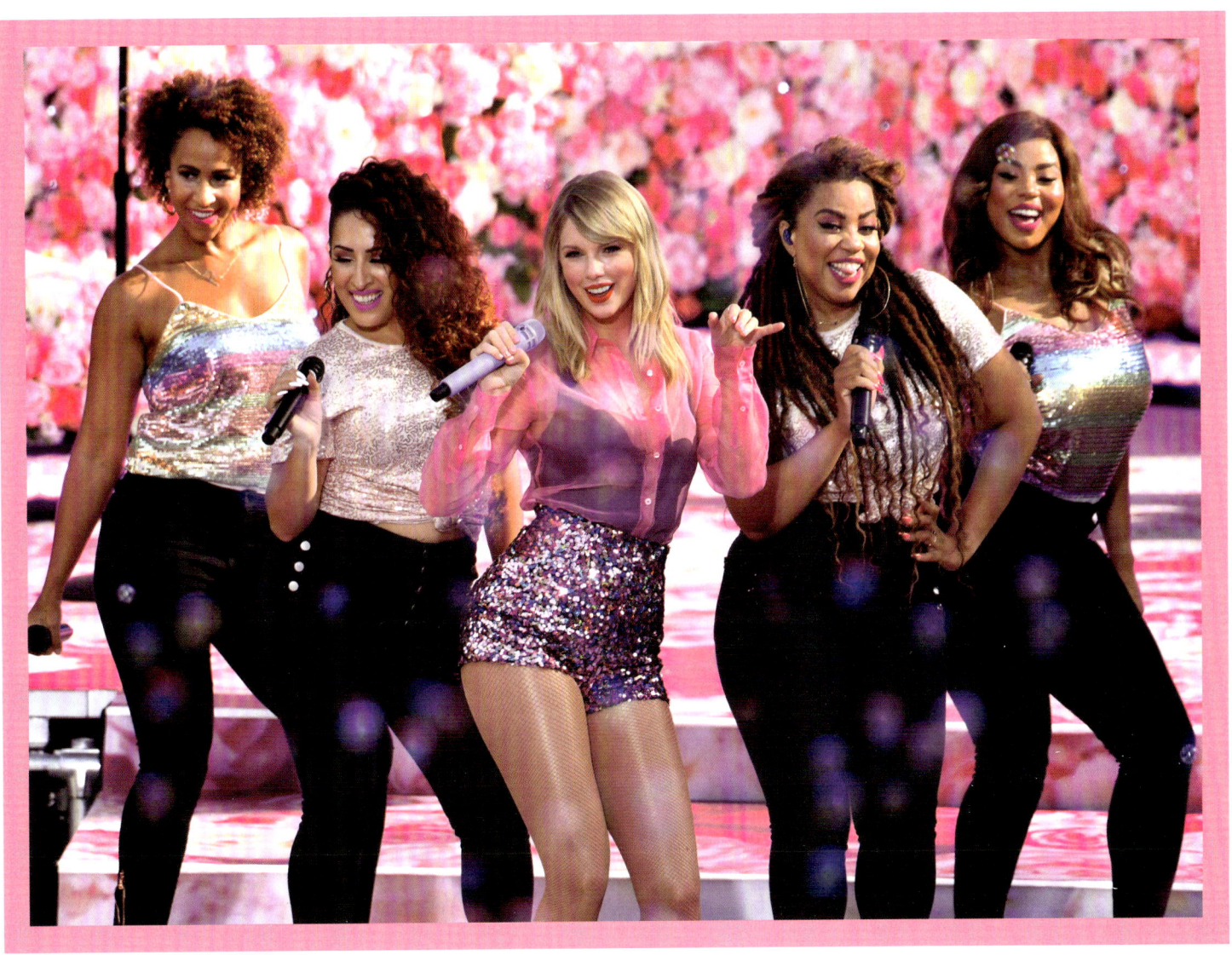

Lover Release

Taylor kept moving forward with the release of *Lover*, and on August 16, 2019, she released the album's title track and new single "Lover." The single was accompanied by a whimsical, vintage-inspired music video, released on August 22, 2019, just one day before the full album dropped. The video, directed by Taylor herself, depicted what became known as "The Lover House" by Swifties. It was a colorful house, inside a snow globe, and each room was thought to represent various eras and reflected a different mood and season of a couple's relationship, symbolizing the complexity and beauty of love in all phases. Of course, the video was packed with Easter eggs that fans continue to decipher to this day.

On the launch day of *Lover*, Taylor appeared on *Good Morning America* for an interview with Robin Roberts and to perform songs from her album onstage in New York's Central Park. During the interview, Robin asked Taylor if she could provide a few lyrics from the new album. Instead, Taylor shared something even more meaningful. She said, "One thing about this album that's really special to me, that it is the first one that I will own of my work." The crowd erupted with a

ABOVE: Above: Performing "ME!" for *Good Morning America*'s Concert in the Park series, August 22, 2019.

FOLLOWING PAGE: Taylor accepts the first-ever Icon Award at the 2019 Teen Choice Awards. The trademark surfboard trophy is decorated with her three cats, Meredith Grey, Olivia Benson, and Benjamin Button.

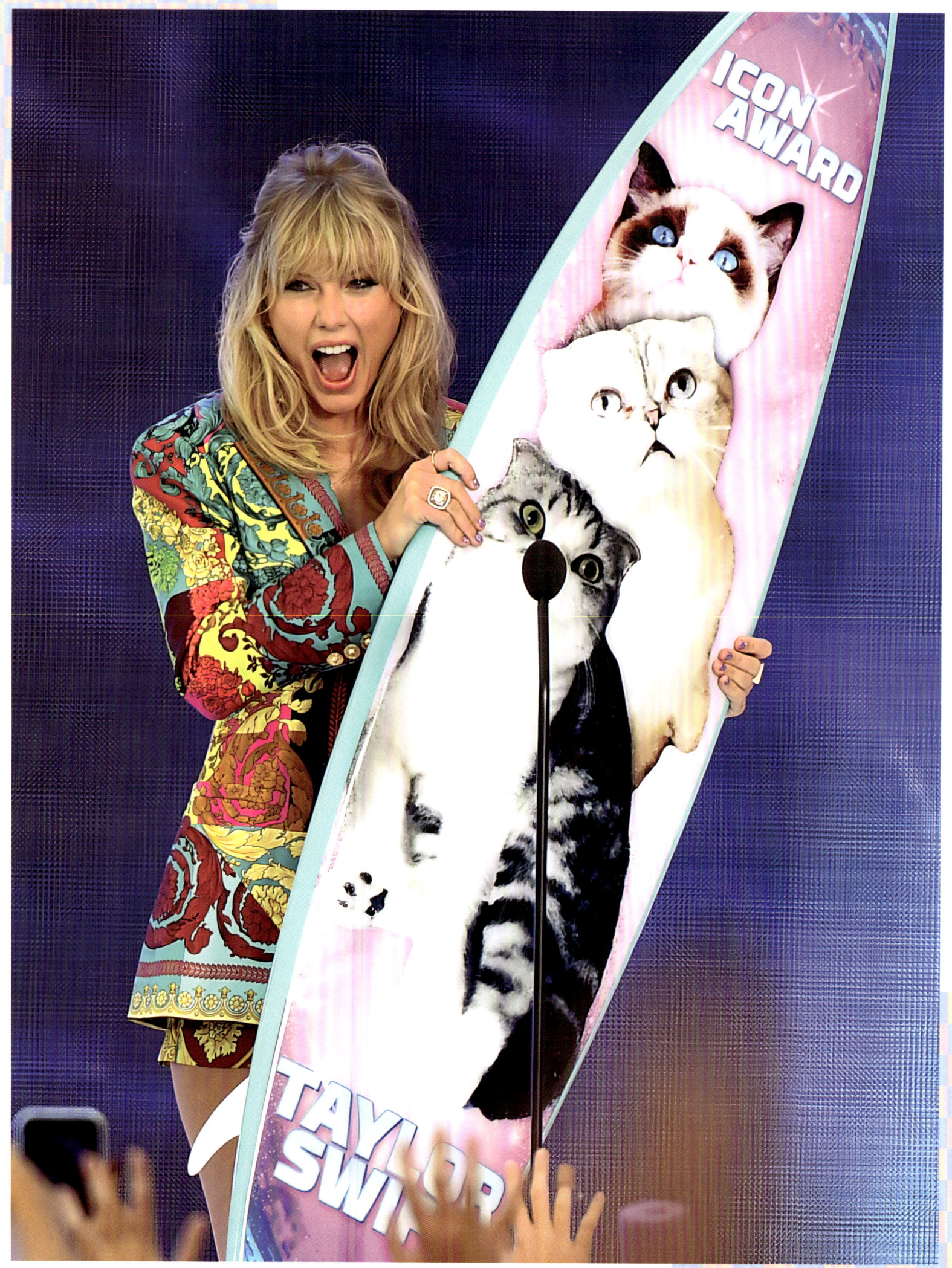

THE ITTY-BITTY PRETTY KITTY COMMITTEE

"When in doubt, ask the itty-bitty pretty-kitty committee. When they shun you with silence, ambivalence, and judgmental brush-offs . . . just put the song out, anyway." —Taylor Swift

It's no secret that Taylor is the ultimate cat lady. Her cats have made appearances across her social media; they've been referenced in her songs and in interviews; and they were featured in her music videos. In 2024, Taylor voiced her support for Kamala Harris in the upcoming election and signed her online statement with "Childless Cat Lady."

Meet the cats who have inspired Taylor and the world over the years.

MEREDITH GREY

Meredith is the oldest sibling and the cat who initiated Taylor's journey as an official cat lady. Taylor wrote in her diary about the moment she got Meredith, and that entry was later shared in the deluxe version of the *Lover* album. She wrote, "Guess what I'm doing tomorrow? Getting a kitten! I've wanted a cat for so long and I'm finally doing it. I love Scottish Folds. I look up Internet videos of them. They're so cute and they love humans. So I'm going to get this little kitten tomorrow morning. I'm naming her Meredith. Meredith Grey because she's gray."

Meredith is known to be the well-behaved one and is Taylor's frequent travel companion. Fans have seen glimpses of her traveling on planes and in stadiums.

In 2020 to 2021, fans grew worried about the lack of Meredith's internet presence for over a year, so Taylor set the record straight and said that Meredith just hates having her photo taken. While she might be a bit camera shy, Meredith appeared in the "ME!" music video alongside her sister Olivia.

OLIVIA BENSON

Olivia is known for her acrobatic skills and was featured in several of Taylor's commercials and music videos, including a Diet Coke commercial and the music videos for "Blank Space," "ME!," and "Karma." In 2023, Olivia won the Nickelodeon's Kids' Choice Award for Favorite Pet. Olivia has an estimated net worth of $97 million, making her the richest of Taylor's three cats.

BENJAMIN BUTTON

Taylor met Benjamin Button (also known as "Benji") on the set of her music video for "ME!" As she petted him before the scene, she asked, "Can I have him?" The cat's handler responded, "He's available." Taylor gasped and brought him to each of her parents, commenting on his purrs. She decided to adopt him, making Benjamin the only brother of the crew and the cat who cemented Taylor's title as "cat lady."

Benjamin was also famously wrapped around Taylor's shoulders in the 2023 Time Person of the Year cover photo.

Honorable Mentions: Indy and Eliehsen, family cats of Taylor's while growing up.

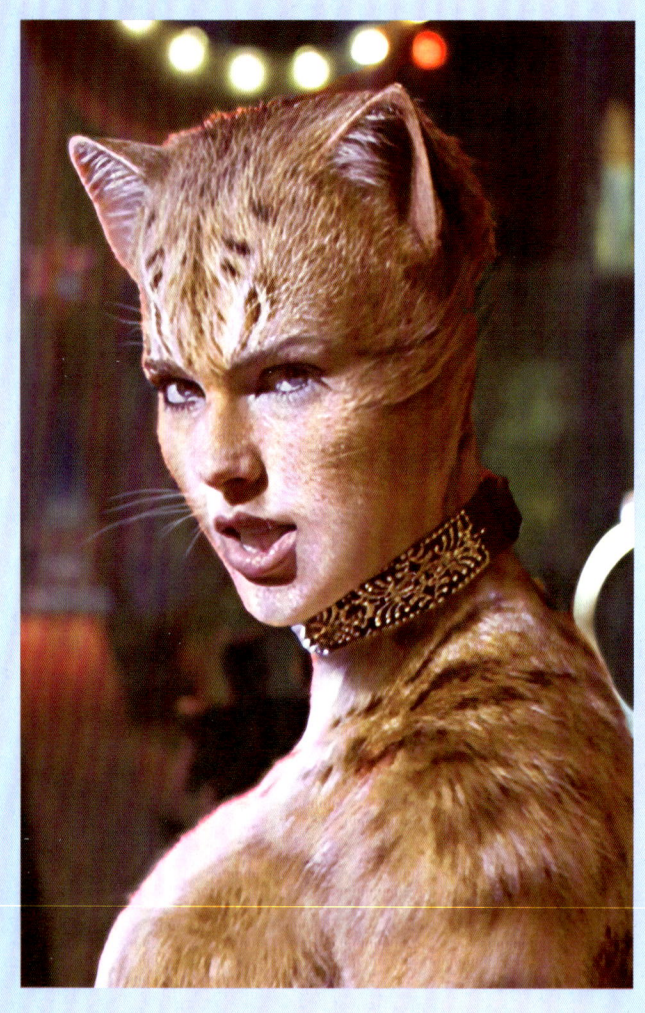

Taylor as a Cat

RELEASE DATE
December 20, 2019

THEATRICAL DEBUT
In 2019, Taylor joined the star-studded cast of the film adaptation of Andrew Lloyd Webber's *Cats*, portraying Bombalurina, a flirtatious and confident feline with a mischievous edge. Taylor took fans behind the scenes of "cat school," where she was trained how to embody the physicality of a cat. She also co-wrote the film's new original song "Beautiful Ghosts" with Andrew Lloyd Webber. While the film ultimately received mixed reviews and faced criticism for its visual effects, Taylor described the experience as "weird and wonderful," marveling at the dedication required to bring such a unique production to life.

huge cheer, to which Taylor continued, "Which is a concept they're very supportive of," alluding to the fans' excitement. The album marked a significant milestone in her career. It was her first release under Republic Records and Universal Music Group, and for the first time, she had full ownership of her master recordings. When Robin asked her if she planned on re-recording her music, she said, "Yes, absolutely," and confirmed her plans to re-record her albums, starting with the first five since contractually she could do so by November 2020.

When asked why this was so important to her, she said, "I think that artists deserve to own their work, and I feel very passionately about that." She explained that owning her masters had always been a priority for her, and creating *Lover*, an album she described as a "love letter to love itself," was particularly empowering because it represented her artistic freedom and ownership.

The announcement electrified fans and shifted the narrative around the music industry. By deciding to re-record her albums, Taylor was reclaiming control over her earlier work in a way that was both creative and business-savvy. This bold move also served as a statement about artists' rights and inspired conversations about the importance of musicians having control over their own intellectual property.

During the interview, Taylor mentioned that the whole launch week was a team effort that included fans, partners, and her family. Her dad even handed out pizza to fans who camped out for her performance the night before. Taylor said, "As a family, it blows our mind that people would want to do that."

Following the interview, Taylor gave a dazzling performance for the *Good Morning America* audience, singing "You Need to Calm Down" and "ME!" and ending with fan-favorite "Shake It Off." The energy of the performance reflected the celebratory tone of the *Lover* era.

Commercially, *Lover* was a massive success, debuting at No. 1 on the Billboard 200 chart with more than 867,000 album-equivalent units sold in its first week in the United States alone.

Aside from media appearances, Taylor also did a merchandise deal with Capital One, airplay deals with SiriusXM and iHeartMedia, and other partnerships with YouTube Music and Amazon. She continued her long-standing relationship with Target and created four deluxe editions of the album. These editions

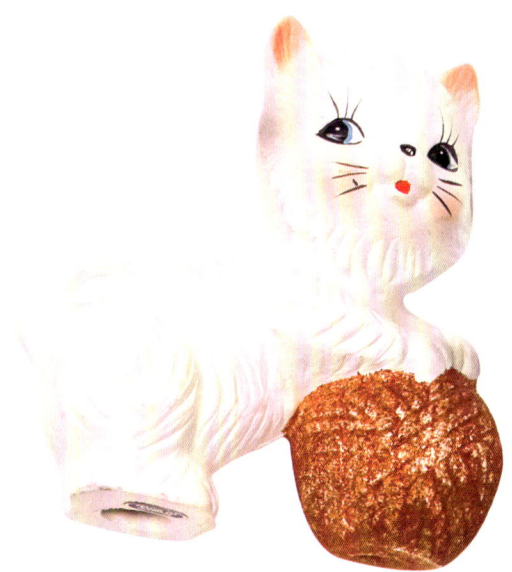

included two bonus audio memos, a blank journal, a poster, and bonus content taken straight from Taylor's old diaries and photos. Fans loved the personal touches and could not wait to share and get some insights into her old journal diaries. Taylor also collaborated with friend and designer Stella McCartney to offer a limited-edition merchandise collection. These extras made fans feel special and especially connected.

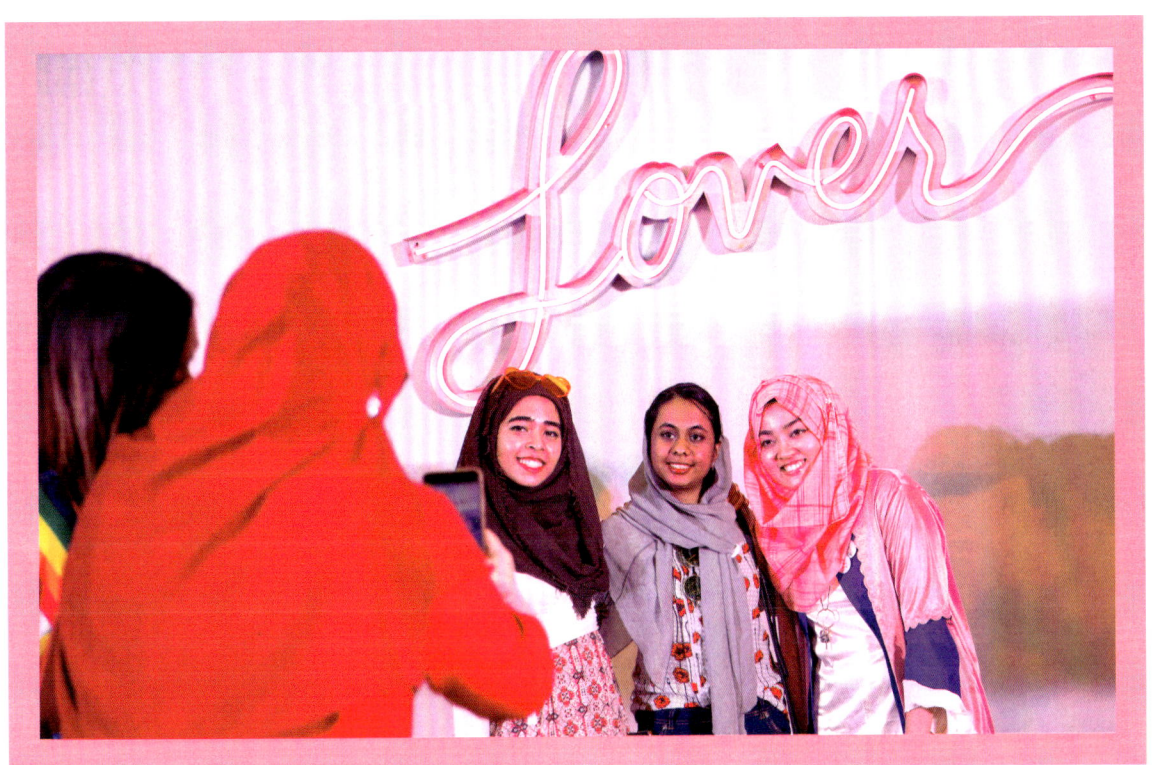

OPPOSITE: Taylor as Bombalurina in *Cats* (2019).

LEFT: Fans gather at a mall in Kuala Lumpur to celebrate the release of *Lover* in Malaysia, October 12, 2019.

Taylor's Triumph

In September 2019, Taylor announced Lover Fest, planning two dates in Los Angeles and two in Foxborough, Massachusetts, in the summer of 2020. Unlike her previous tours, Lover Fest would be just four domestic performances, as well as appearances at international festivals. At the time, Taylor's mother was undergoing treatment for cancer, and Taylor didn't want to do an extensive tour to promote the record. This slower pace seemed better suited for her life and family at the time. The tour was eventually canceled altogether, however, due to the COVID-19 pandemic.

All the promotion and fan support went far; *Lover* became the bestselling album of 2019 and produced several hit singles, including "ME!," "You Need to Calm Down," and "Lover." The album received multiple awards and nominations, including several Grammy nominations. Taylor brought home the Album of the Year award at the People's Choice Awards and was honored at the 2019 American Music Awards as Artist of the Decade.

At the American Music Awards, Taylor gave a very special performance for her award. She started the set singing the chorus of "The Man" while wearing a white button-up shirt featuring the titles of the albums controlled by Scooter Braun. The sound of glass shattering erupted and a little girl joined her onstage, wearing the exact same shirt. Several other little girls in matching outfits all joined them for a choreographed dance to finish out "The Man," and then they hugged Taylor before exiting the stage while she continued to perform a selection of songs from her discography. Fans speculated

"A man does something, it's 'strategic'; a woman does the same thing, it's 'calculated.' A man is allowed to 'react'; a woman can only 'overreact.'"

Taylor, 2019

that this iconic opening served as a clap back to her stolen masters, as well as a demonstration of the importance of looking out for a younger generation of artists.

The song "The Man" became a fan favorite for many looking to make a statement about sexism. The song uses a bit of a satirical lens to discuss the sexism that women often face, especially those in a position of authority. Taylor made the song her next single in January 2020 and debuted a music video for it. The video featured a male supervisor acting in heightened and stereotypical ways like showing no regard for his surroundings, yelling at people on the phone, surrounding himself by women on a huge yacht, getting praise for simply being a dad, and more. The big reveal comes at the end of the video, when it's shown that "the man" featured in the video is actually Taylor Swift herself. She transformed to look and act like a man for the making of the music video. The ending credits say: "Directed by Taylor Swift, Written by Taylor Swift, Owned by Taylor Swift, Starring Taylor Swift," which was the icing on the cake for the song and video and thrilled fans with her creativity in both the songwriting and music video processes.

Beyond the music, the *Lover* era was notable for its positivity. It encapsulated a new chapter in Taylor's life and career, one surrounded by more light than during her darker past. It represented her stepping into her power as an artist who not only writes and performs, but also takes control of her creative and professional goals. She became a role model to her fans and other artists and showed that using your voice is important, especially when it's for good.

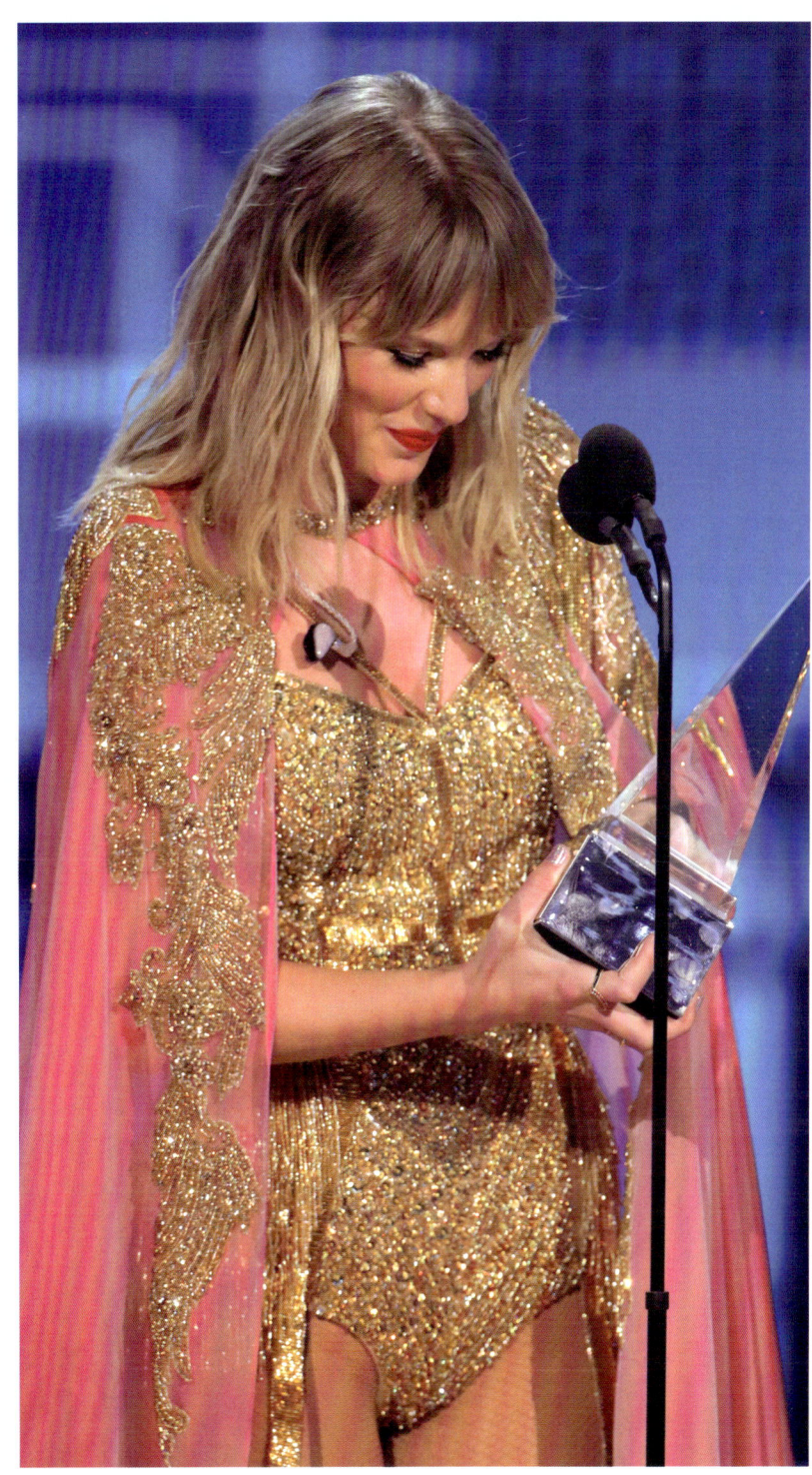

ABOVE: Taylor accepts the Artist of the Decade award at the 2019 American Music Awards. She won a total of six awards that night, including Artist of the Year and Favorite Pop/Rock Album for *Lover*.

WORLD TOUR COSTUMES

Across every tour, Taylor's costumes have become as iconic as her music, charting the evolution of both her storytelling and her style. Whether channeling a fairy–tale romance, an indie–folk hipster, or a tortured poet, Taylor uses fashion to thread together the complete story of her music. From tear–off outfit changes during the Fearless Tour to the black sequin bodysuits during the Reputation Stadium Tour, each ensemble has served as a visual scrapbook of both an era of her album cycles and her growth as an artist. On The Eras Tour, we witness her complete journey, with costumes that serve as nods to her past while elevating them to the present day.

Let's take a journey through some of Taylor's most iconic outfits from her tours.

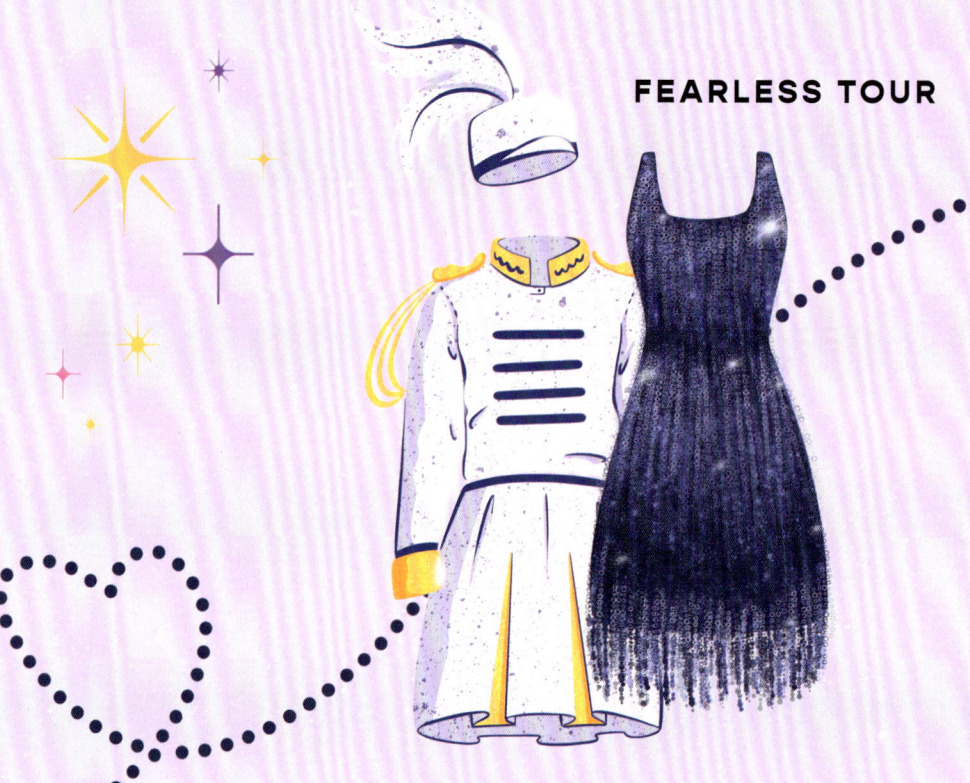

FEARLESS TOUR

This era was full of glittering gold dreams and high school vibes. Taylor was still grounded in her country roots, often sporting cowboy boots and an acoustic guitar. However, she started leaning into sequins, glitter, and gold hues, capturing the pop–star energy that she was stepping further and further into.

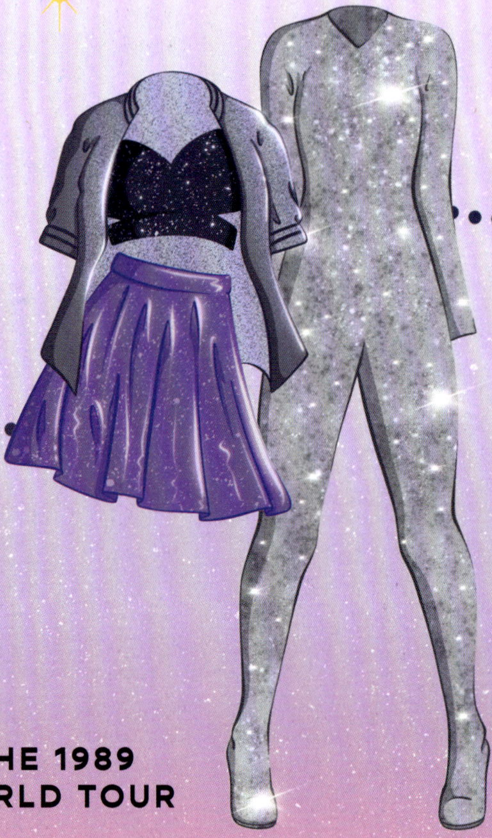

THE 1989 WORLD TOUR

This tour reflected Taylor's shift to full–blown pop star. The set was sleek and structured, signifying her move to New York City, and the costumes of shimmering sequined sets and bold colors brought the synth–pop era to life on the stage.

REPUTATION STADIUM TOUR

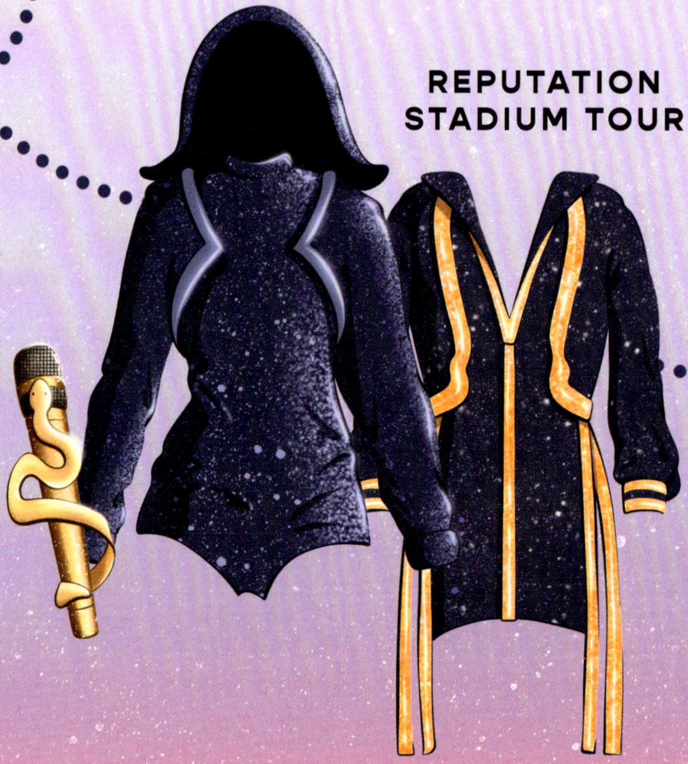

Dark, edgy, and unapologetic, the Reputation Stadium Tour aesthetic acted as both a shield of armor and a statement piece. Featuring snakes, black sequins, over-the-knee boots, bodysuits, and sharp silhouettes, Taylor projected her power as an artist reclaiming her narrative.

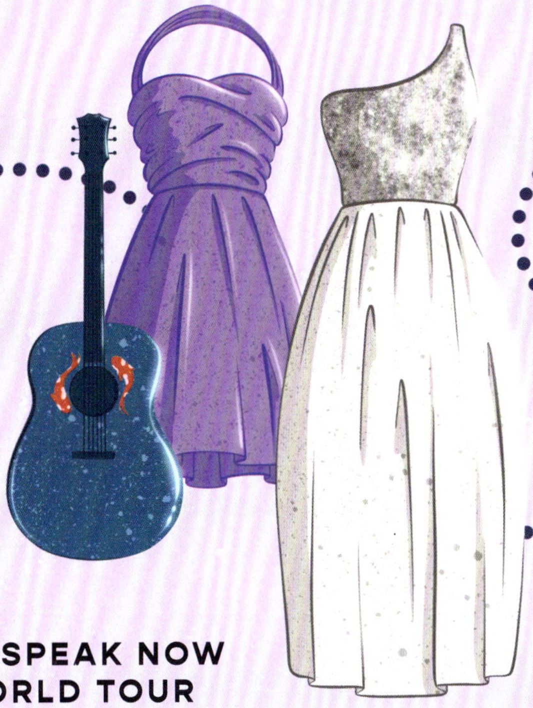

THE SPEAK NOW WORLD TOUR

A more theatrical Taylor emerged on this tour, weaving her dramatic storytelling into both the stage set and her outfits. The costumes of this era were all dresses, including her iconic purple dress that matched the album colors. She also debuted her signature koi fish guitar, which made a return on The Eras Tour.

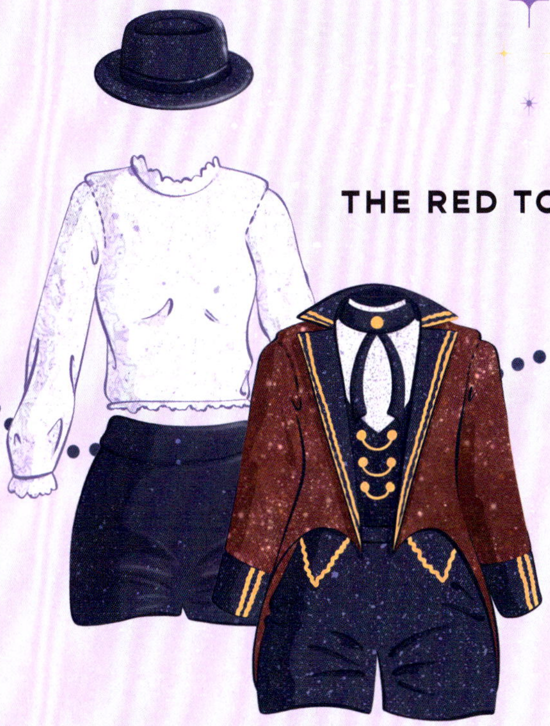

THE RED TOUR

During The Red Tour, Taylor debuted a more relaxed, vintage-meets-modern look, which was a shift in style from the many sequin dresses from previous tours. Her costumes included high-waisted shorts, fedoras, sneakers, and of course, her signature bold red lipstick.

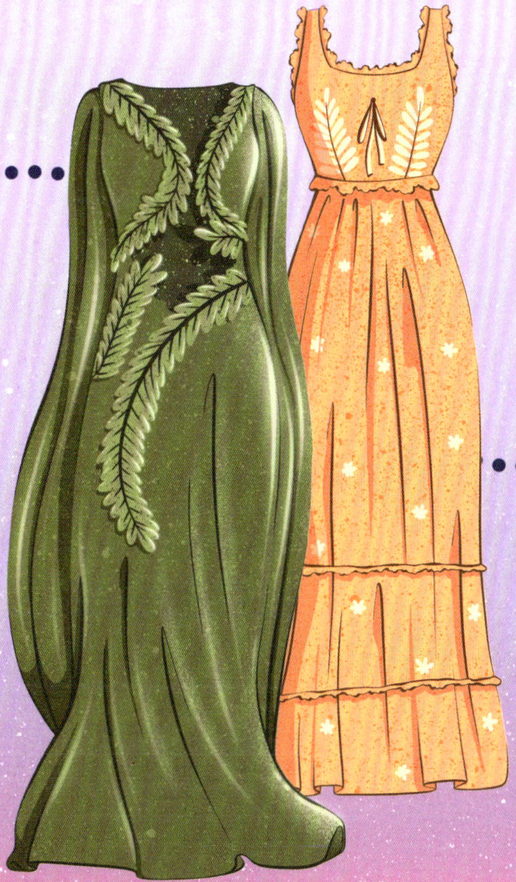

THE ERAS TOUR

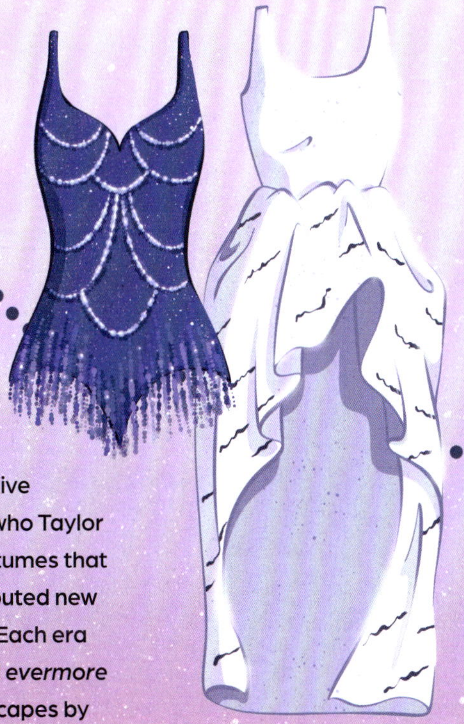

The Eras Tour unfolded like a live autobiographical journey reflecting who Taylor was and who she's become, with costumes that both honored the past eras and debuted new eras that never got their own tour. Each era had its own distinct look: *folklore* and *evermore* featured chiffon gowns and witchy capes by Alberta Ferretti (left) and Etro (right) that flowed perfectly across the stage. The *Midnights* era was reflected in a dark-blue Oscar de la Renta sequined bodysuit, while *TTPD* featured a dramatic black-and-white Vivienne Westwood gown and gloves. The shimmering Versace bodysuit and a glittery blazer created for *Lover* became an instant icon for the tour.

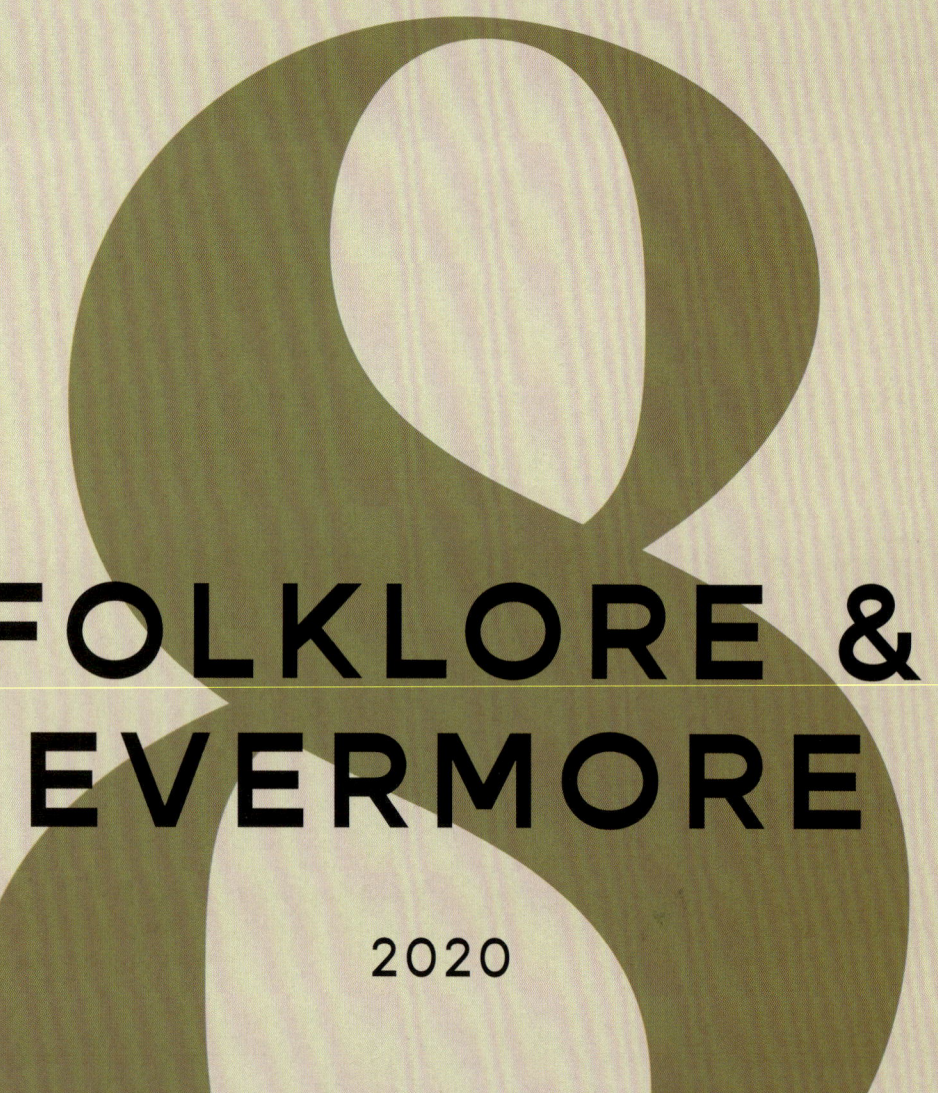

FOLKLORE & EVERMORE

2020

INTROSPECTION IS KIND

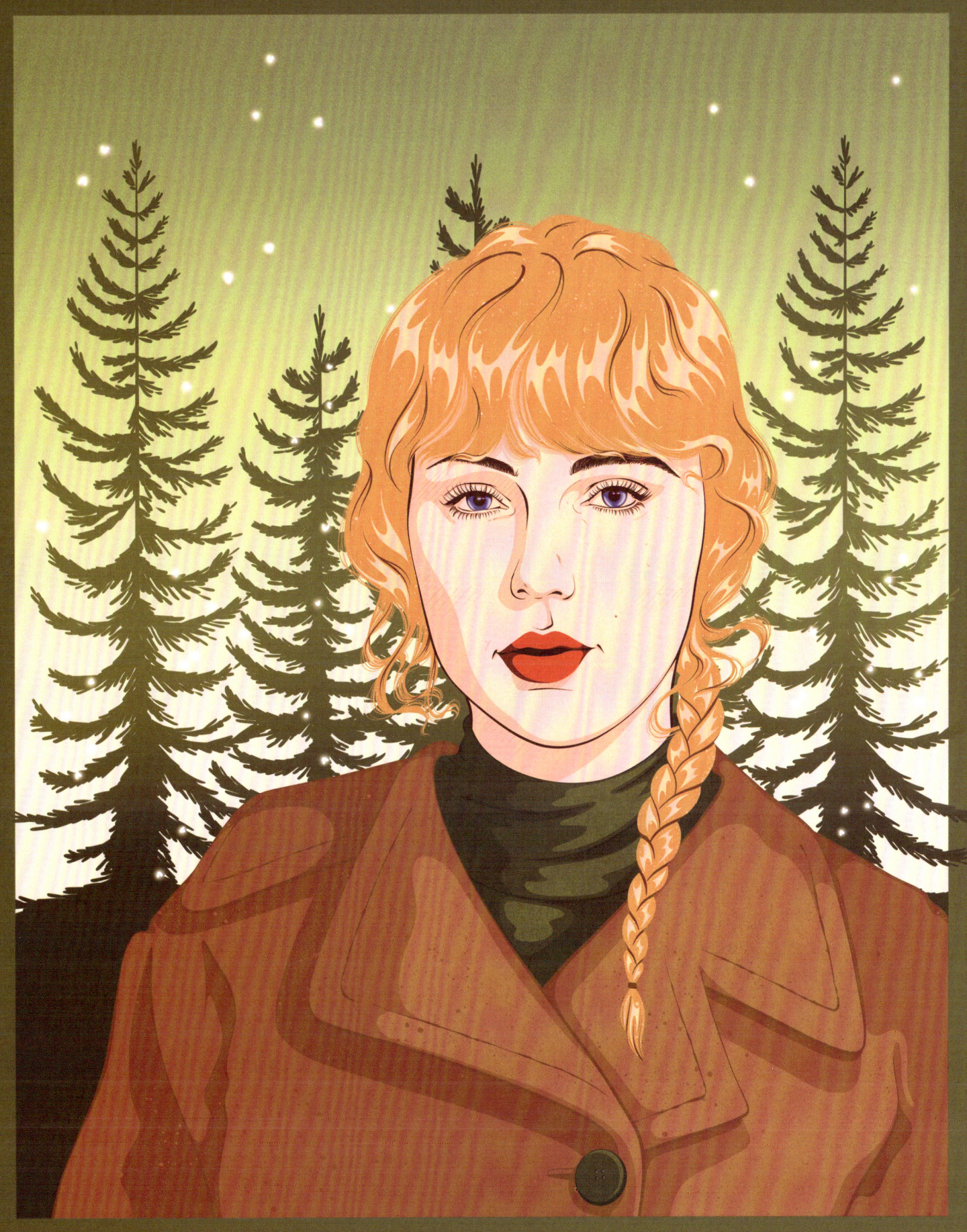

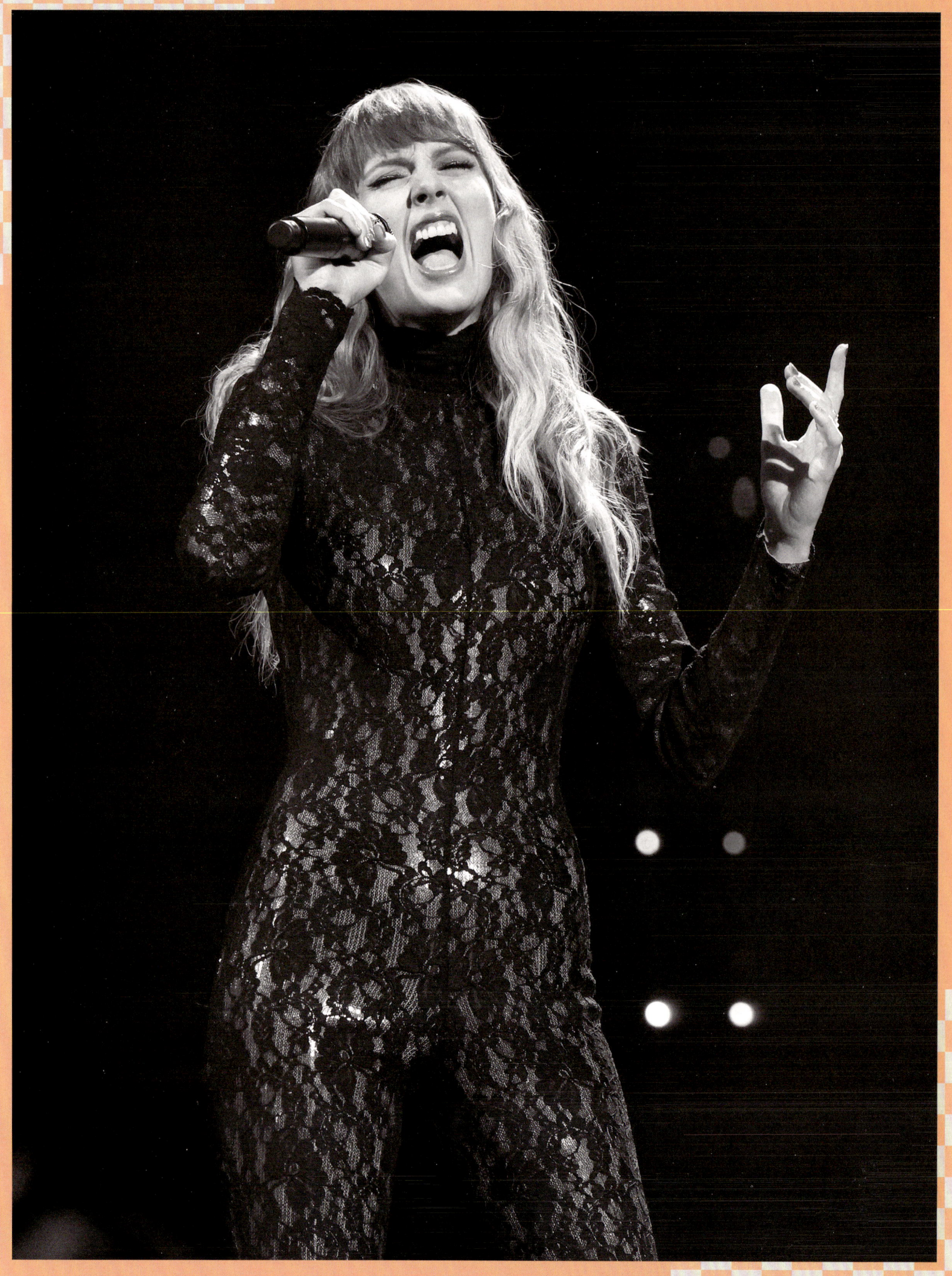

> **"When you put your whole heart into something, and if it is met with cynicism, let it fuel you."**
>
> Taylor, 2021

LOTS OF UNEXPECTED SURPRISES

This was the era during which Taylor surprised everyone, including herself.

Since the beginning of her career, Taylor made it clear that she wanted to evolve as an artist. She wouldn't be pigeonholed into genres or styles; instead, she strove for her creativity to shine through in whatever she made.

This era was no different.

2020 started off with a big win: the launch of *Miss Americana*. Directed by Lana Wilson, the documentary gave fans an inside look at Taylor's life over the course of several years and showed her most vulnerable side yet. The documentary dove into topics such as body dysmorphia and disordered eating, her mother's cancer diagnosis, her sexual assault trial, her support of the LGBTQ+ community, and her decision to speak out about politics for the first time. Scenes featured Taylor writing songs at home and in the

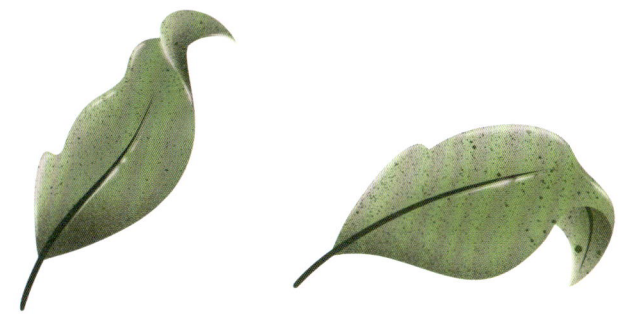

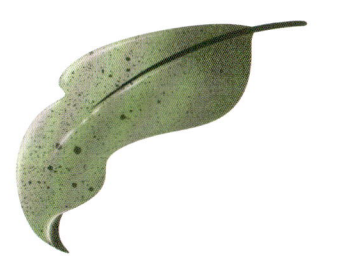

WOODVALE THEORY

Eagle-eyed Swifties got to work when one of the eight vinyl variations of *folklore*, titled "Hide and Seek," had the word "woodvale" lightly printed in the top corner. Since the album didn't have the title printed on it for any of the other variations, fans started speculating on what it could mean. At first, fans thought it might be the name of the next album. Then, once the release of *evermore* was confirmed, fans thought that "woodvale" was an Easter egg for a third album, making this era a trilogy.

In December 2020, however, Taylor finally gave fans the real reason for the word "woodvale." In an interview on *Jimmy Kimmel Live!,* Taylor explained that she wanted to keep the title of the record a secret from even her closest team and management. To do this, she came up with the codename "woodvale," since it included the same number of letters as *folklore*. She used the code name as a placeholder when mocking up designs to see if she wanted to include the album name on the cover. She eventually decided that the album wouldn't include the name, but she forgot to remove it from the cover file before sending it off to print.

In the interview, she said, "So, I tend to be sort of annoyingly secret agent-y about dropping clues and hints and Easter eggs. And it's very annoying. But it's fun for fans and it's fun for me because they like to pick up on things. And they'll notice things in music videos or whatever. Then, sometimes, I take it too far and I make a mistake."

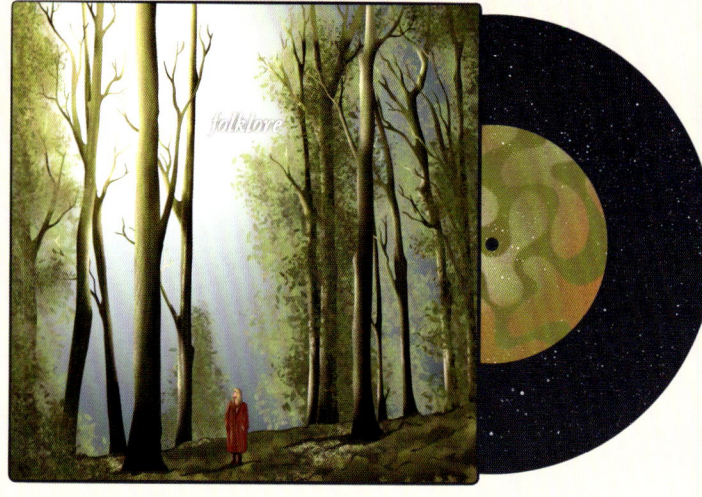

ALBUM
folklore

DATE LAUNCHED
July 24, 2020

FIRST SINGLE
"cardigan"

OTHER SINGLES
"exile" and "betty"

TOUR
None

OTHER MEDIA
Lover (Live from Paris) (May 19, 2020); *Folklore: The Long Pond Studio Sessions* (2020), *Miss Americana* (January 31, 2020), *Fearless (Taylor's Version)* (April 9, 2021), and *Red (Taylor's Version)* (November 12, 2021)

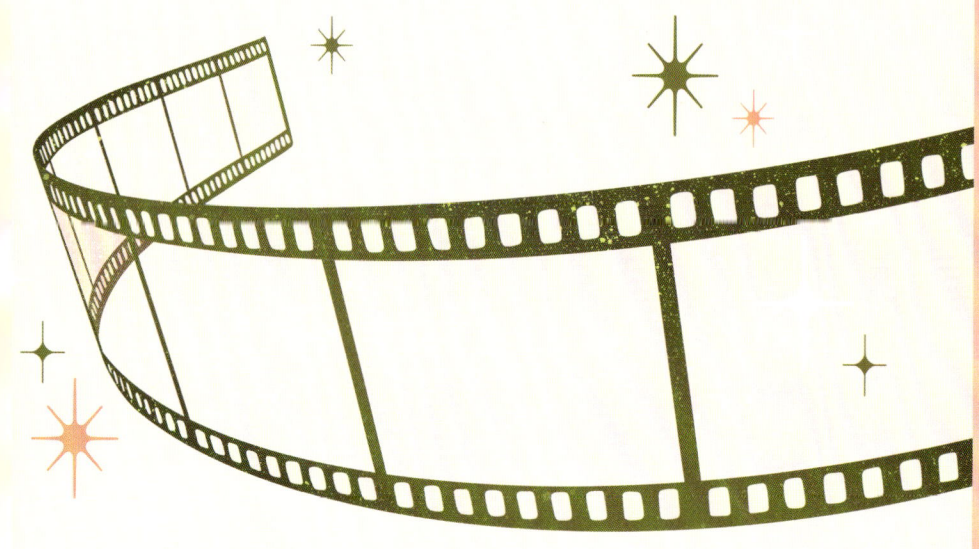

While "woodvale" was a simple mistake that never materialized as a real project, the theory itself became a part of Swiftie culture, showcasing the depth of fan engagement and Taylor's legendary use of Easter eggs.

studio, making dinner with her childhood best friend, and gracefully avoiding the paparazzi. We also see how Taylor reacted when she found out that she didn't receive a Grammy nomination for the *reputation* album. Her voice quivering, she said, "I just need to make a better record."

One of the most commonly re-shown clips from the documentary showed Taylor talking about how she sought to be as educated as she could about respecting people and how she had to actively work on rewiring misogyny in her own brain. She shared how passionately she felt about this topic and then said, "Sorry, that was a real soapbox. Why did I say, 'Sorry'?" She and the director discussed how women were trained to say sorry, and Taylor jokingly remarked, "Sorry was I loud? In my own house that I bought? With the songs that I wrote about my own life?" We saw her in real time, working on practicing what she actively strove to break through.

When describing the film, director Lana Wilson said, "I see the movie as looking at the flip side of being America's sweetheart." Seeing Taylor come up in the public eye, we have always seen a polished and polite "good girl." However, with more life experience thrown at her, we saw her start to understand the power of using her voice for good. Taylor said, "I still think it's important to be polite, but not at all costs. Not when you're being pushed beyond your limits, and not when people are walking all over you. I needed to get to a point where I was ready, able, and willing to call out bullshit rather than just smiling my way through it."

One major aspect shown in this documentary was Taylor's introspection. She absorbed and processed all that had happened to her throughout her eras and gave fans (and non-fans) a look into that world. We might not understand what it's like to live life as a pop star in the spotlight, but Taylor revealed herself as completely human—a person who's grown, changed, and evolved, and who has many of the same anxieties, fears, and feelings that we do.

PAGE 166: Taylor performs "Will You Still Love Me Tomorrow" at the 2021 Rock and Roll Hall of Fame induction ceremony as part of a tribute to inductee Carole King.

BELOW: Before the world falls: Taylor attends the Sundance Film Festival in Park City, Utah, January 23, 2020.

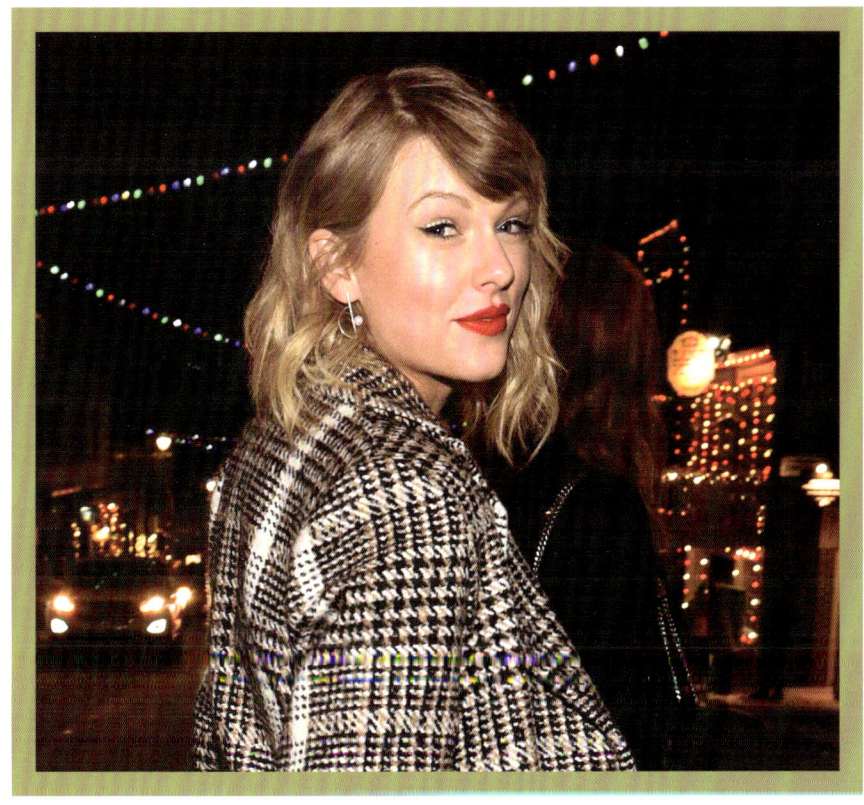

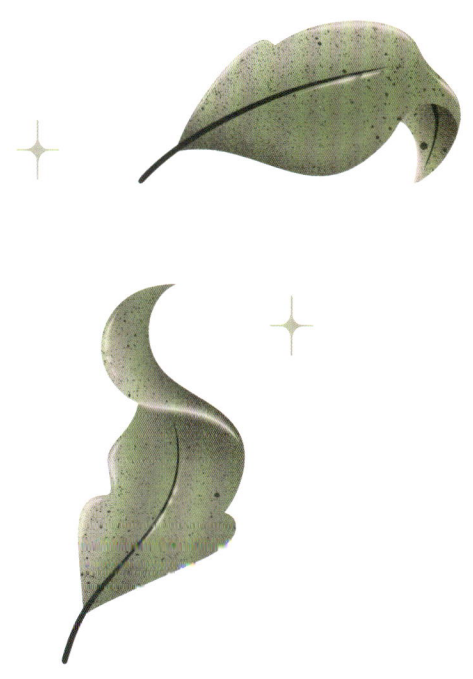

A Global Pandemic Strikes

After the release of *Miss Americana*, Taylor geared up for more promotion of her *Lover* album, as well as the upcoming Lover Fest. However, the world had different plans. In March 2020, the COVID-19 pandemic caused a worldwide shutdown. Touring musicians canceled their performances at record speeds, and so much of the world was uncertain.

During the shutdown and uncertainty of the world, Taylor leaned into using her resources for good. On April 18, 2020, she performed an at-home performance of the song "Soon You'll Get Better" during the "One World: Together at Home" event hosted by Global Citizen. Taylor had said that she would likely never perform this song because it was about her mother's cancer journey and was very emotional for her. Choosing to perform this song during a global health crisis was appreciated by fans, however, and they felt like Taylor stood in solidarity with the health issues so many were facing.

Taylor didn't just use her music for good; she also performed charitable acts of giving. Throughout the pandemic, Taylor matched donations to fans' GoFundMe pages and sent money to help cover rent for many fans in need. She would look through social media, messaging fans who were struggling and asking if she could send them money to help. One of her messages to a fan read, "Leah, I'm so sorry this situation has caused you so much stress and I hope my gift of $3,000 will help. Can you send me your PayPal account please? Love, Taylor."

Taylor even took to local businesses, reaching out to Grimey's New & Preloved Music in Nashville and offering to pay for the salaries and healthcare of the entire staff for three months. Aside from musical and financial contributions, Taylor also sent care packages to frontline workers and fans. With so much uncertainty in the world, Taylor tried to help as many individual fans and institutions as she could to find a little more joy and stability.

"I miss you terribly and can't wait till we can all safely be at shows together again."

Taylor, 2021

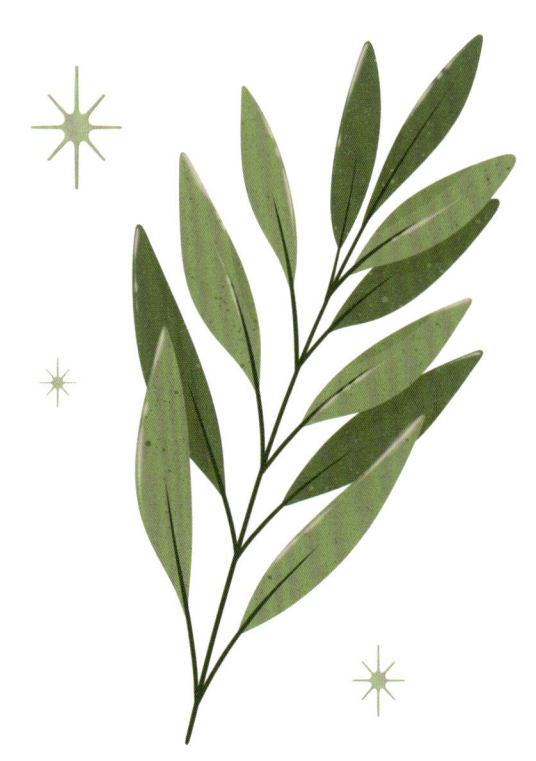

"MARJORIE"

The namesake of the song "marjorie" is Taylor's grandmother Marjorie Finlay. Marjorie was her mother's mother and a famous singer in her own right. An opera singer, she was known for hitting high notes and winning talent contests. She toured with ABC's *Music with the Girls* and eventually landed a hosting gig for *El Show Pan-Americano*, a variety show in Puerto Rico. Taylor pays a beautiful tribute to her grandmother's star power and influence by including her backing vocals on the song.

Taylor even made sure to include the song in The Eras Tour set list, with her grandmother's vocals reaching thousands of Swifties each night. Then something unexpected happened during the show in Atlanta on April 29, 2023. Fans lit up the entire stadium with their phone flashlights during the song "marjorie" to honor Taylor's grandmother and create a special moment for her.

Taylor was visibly touched by this (and teary-eyed). When she came back out onstage for her piano set of "champagne problems," she addressed the crowd, saying, "How are you going to go and do that to me on a song about my grandmother who passed away? I just completely—like, my knees went weak, genuinely, like that physically. I physically felt them. That was so beautiful of you to do that."

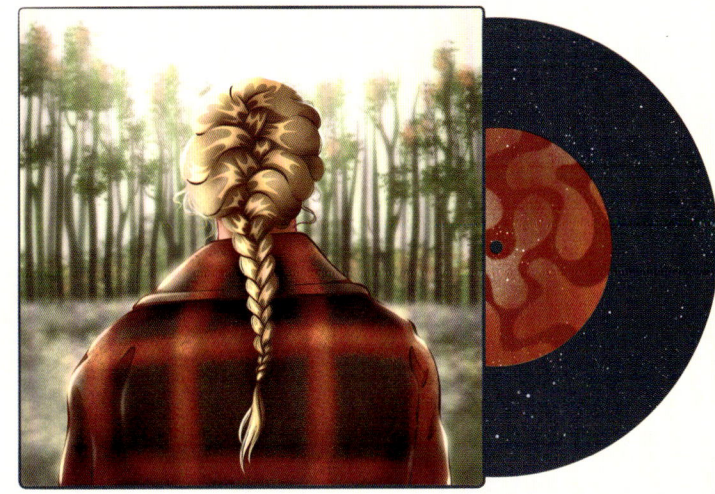

ALBUM
evermore

DATE LAUNCHED
December 11, 2020

OTHER SINGLES
"willow," "no body, no crime" (featuring HAIM), and "Coney Island"

TOUR
None

OTHER MEDIA
Lover (Live from Paris) (May 19, 2020); *Folklore: The Long Pond Studio Sessions* (2020) and *Miss Americana* (January 31, 2020), *Fearless (Taylor's Version)* (April 9, 2021), and *Red (Taylor's Version)* (November 12, 2021)

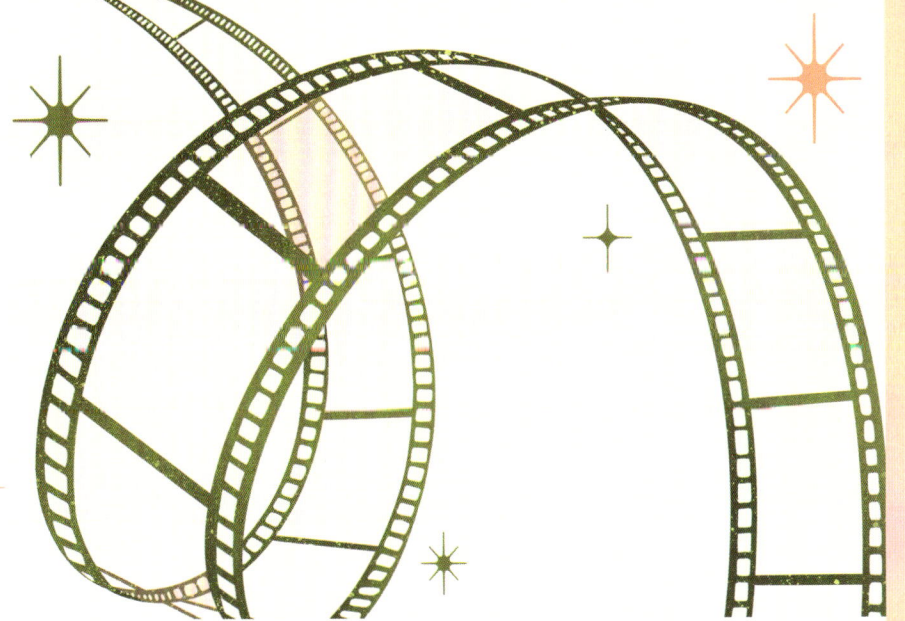

Taylor's mom, Andrea, was also deeply touched by this act of fan kindness. She was later seen holding up her phone, lit up with a photo of her late mother, during the song. This created a nightly tradition that continued throughout the rest of The Eras Tour, cementing Taylor's grandmother in the hearts of Swifties worldwide.

NIKKI GLASER & TAYLOR SWIFT

Nikki Glaser and Taylor Swift have a connection that stems from mutual admiration and a bit of controversy. Nikki, a stand-up comedian known for her public roasts and self-deprecating humor, has long been a vocal fan of Taylor Swift. However, their relationship took an unexpected turn when Nikki appeared, unknowingly, in Taylor's 2020 documentary *Miss Americana*.

In the film, an old clip shows Nikki making a comment about Taylor's body during the *1989* era, saying, "She's too skinny; it bothers me . . . all of her model friends, and it's just like, c'mon!" This part of the documentary touched on Taylor's struggles with body image and disordered eating, including Nikki's remark, as an example of the kind of criticism Taylor faced in the public eye. When Nikki saw the documentary, she was mortified that she had contributed to Taylor's pain.

Nikki quickly took to Instagram to issue a heartfelt public apology, expressing deep regret for her words and explaining that she, too, had struggled with body-image issues. She posted a photo of herself in a T-shirt from the *Red* era, and Nikki wrote, "I love Taylor Swift. Unfortunately, I am featured in her new documentary as part of a montage of asshats saying mean things about her, which is used to explain why she felt the need to escape from the spotlight for a year. It's insanely ironic because anyone who knows me knows I'm obnoxiously obsessed with her and her music.

"I really have no need to post this other than to apologize to someone who seriously means SO much to me," she continued, ending with, "I love you Tay, and I can't wait to watch 99.97% of your new doc, *Miss Americana*."

Taylor noticed and not only liked Nikki's post, but also commented on it. She said, "Wow. I appreciate this so much, and one of the major themes about the doc is that we have the ability to change our opinions over time, to grow, to learn about ourselves. I'm so sorry to hear that you've struggled with some of the same things I've struggled with. Sending a massive hug."

Since then, Nikki has continued to share her admiration for Taylor and even attended twenty-two of The Eras Tour shows, forever cementing her love and support for Taylor.

Their connection serves as an example of how public figures can acknowledge their missteps, take accountability, and still be met with understanding and kindness.

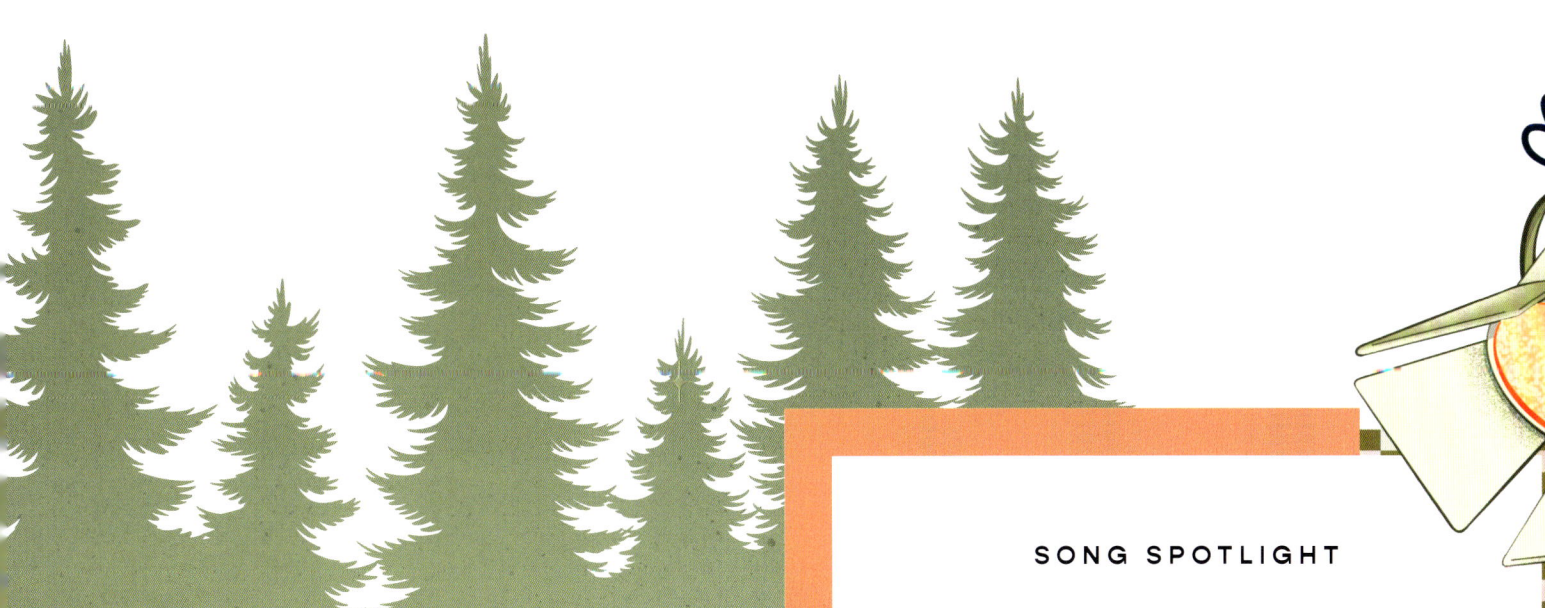

Once a Writer, Always a Writer

While Taylor's personal and professional plans were forced to take a pause, Taylor continued to do what she does best: write. Taylor reached out to Aaron Dessner of The National (one of Taylor's favorite bands) to ask how their band was able to continue to create while being apart. This encounter turned out to be the spark that both Taylor and Aaron needed to fuel their creativity, and the two began collaborating about two days into the pandemic. Taylor described it as "one of the most effortless collaborations," and in July 2020, fans got the surprise of a lifetime with the launch of her new studio album, *folklore*. This surprise release was announced just a few short hours before it went live and was the first time Taylor departed from her typical planned rollout strategy.

She took to social media and said, "Most of the things I had planned this summer didn't end up happening, but there is something I hadn't planned on that DID happen. And that thing is my eighth studio album, *folklore*. Surprise!

"Invisible String"

The "invisible string theory," a spiritual concept, argues that certain people are connected to each other by fate or destiny by inevitable meetings or encounters that happen to bring them together at the same time and place. Taylor vividly portrays this theory in her song "invisible string" but linking all the fate-like encounters her and her boyfriend at the time, Joe Alwyn, experienced. Fans have continued to use the term, making it part of the pop culture zeitgeist.

ALBUM

folklore

RELEASED

July 24, 2020

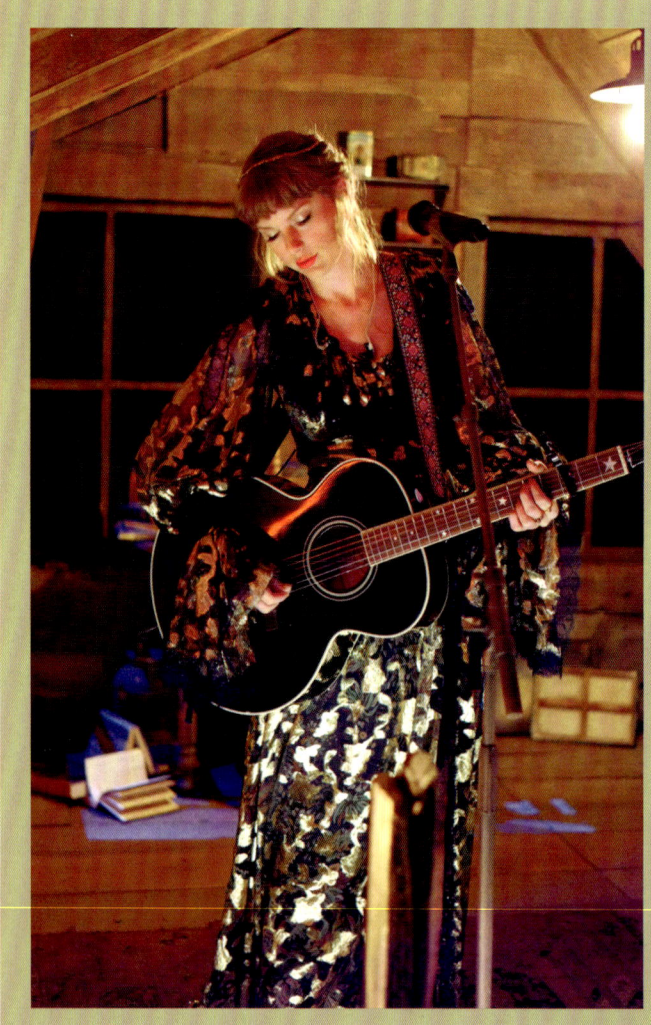

The *folklore* Cabin

ESTABLISHED
March 14, 2021

AN INTIMATE SETTING

The iconic *folklore* cabin was first introduced at the 2021 Grammy Awards. Taylor, Aaron Dessner, and Jack Antonoff performed a mash-up of "cardigan," "august," and "willow" in an offset A-frame cabin adorned with green moss and twinkly lighting. The cabin set had a cozy, cottagecore, woodsy vibe reminiscent of the *folklore* and *evermore* albums. Taylor brought the *folklore* cabin from the Grammys to The Eras Tour, complete with a chimney that featured smoke puffs coming out throughout the set. Even though the *folklore* cabin was only onstage for one era, it added a cozy, intimate setting to each night of The Eras Tour.

Tonight at midnight I'll be releasing my entire brand-new album of songs I've poured all of my whims, dreams, fears, and musings into.

"Before this year," she continued, "I probably would've overthought when to release this music at the 'perfect' time, but the times we're living in keep reminding me that nothing is guaranteed. My gut is telling me that if you make something you love, you should just put it out into the world. That's the side of uncertainty I can get on board with. Love you guys so much."

folklore marked a pivot to indie folk and alternative styles. Taylor collaborated not just with Aaron Dessner but also Jack Antonoff, Justin Vernon (of Bon Iver), and "William Bowery," who was later discovered to be the pseudonym for her boyfriend at the time, Joe Alwyn.

Critics praised the album for its introspective storytelling, lush production, and emotional depth. It also came at a time when Taylor was touching on themes that so many were collectively experiencing: loneliness, isolation, and uncertainty.

Fact & Fiction

The lead single "cardigan" debuted at No. 1 on the Billboard Hot 100, and *folklore* debuted at No. 1 on the Billboard 200, making Taylor the first artist to debut atop both charts simultaneously. This was also the first time we heard Taylor publicly talk about how she leaned more into fictional storytelling on this album. This was a departure from her usual autobiographical tropes. However, plenty of songs blended personal and fictional. Writing the entire album in quarantine, Taylor said, "I was inspired by the feeling of isolation and how that can either be freeing or terrifying, and how it causes you to reminisce on the past."

The *folklore* era came with carefully curated aesthetics: soft, muted tones; cozy textures; and cottagecore vibes. As part of the album's promotion, Taylor sent a limited-edition cream-colored cable-knit cardigan with black piping and embroidered stars on the sleeves to close friends, collaborators, and select fans. Celebrities like Gigi Hadid and Jennifer Hudson, as well as her longtime friend Abigail, proudly shared photos wearing the sweater. Taylor eventually released these for sale to her fans and they became a coveted item, selling out almost immediately. The popularity of these cardigans prompted her to create custom cardigans for other eras and specialty releases. Other bands, including Green Day and Weezer, took notice and began creating specialty cardigans for their band merchandise too.

A few months later, in November 2020, Taylor gifted fans with another intimate look into *folklore* with *Folklore: The Long Pond Studio Sessions*, a Disney+ documentary and live-performance film. Recorded at Aaron Dessner's Long Pond Studio in upstate New York, the film featured Taylor, Aaron, and Jack Antonoff. The trio performed every song on the album while reflecting on its creation. It gave fans a deeper understanding of *folklore*'s themes and lyrical depth while showcasing Taylor's stripped-down, organic approach to music-making during the pandemic.

The *folklore* era, with the song "cardigan" and cardigans as its centerpiece, became a defining moment in Taylor's career, one that embraced fictional storytelling, emotional rawness, and a sense of intimacy with her audience, all while wrapping it in the warmth of a cozy, star-embroidered sweater. And just as fans were getting cozy in their cardigans, Taylor announced that her ninth studio album, *evermore*, the sister album to *folklore*, would be released at midnight on December 11, 2020.

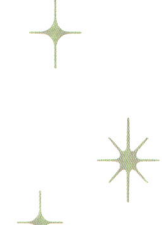

OPPOSITE AND FOLLOWING PAGES: Taylor performing a mash-up of songs from *folklore* at the 2021 Grammy Awards.

BELOW: A poster for the Disney+ streaming release of the *Long Pond Studio Sessions*.

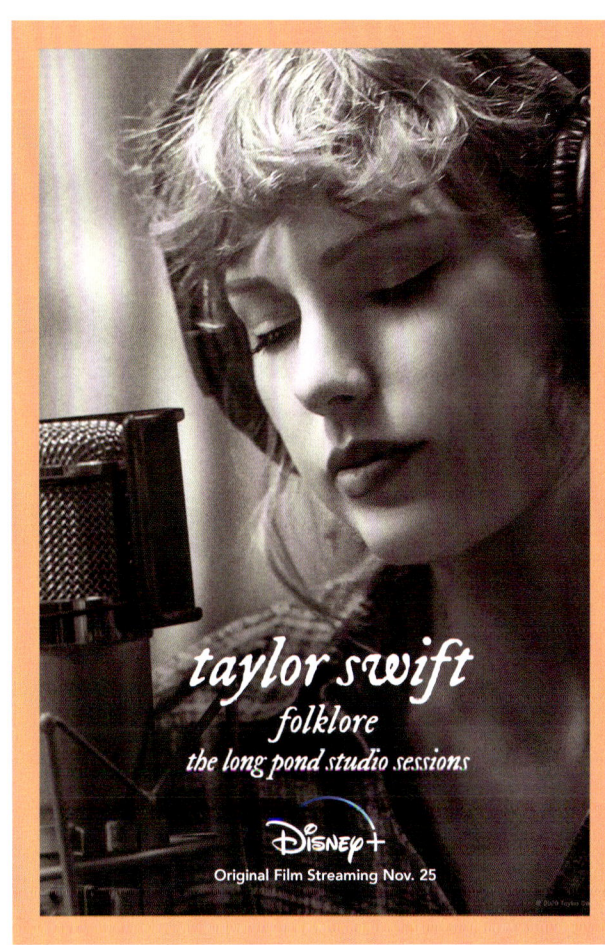

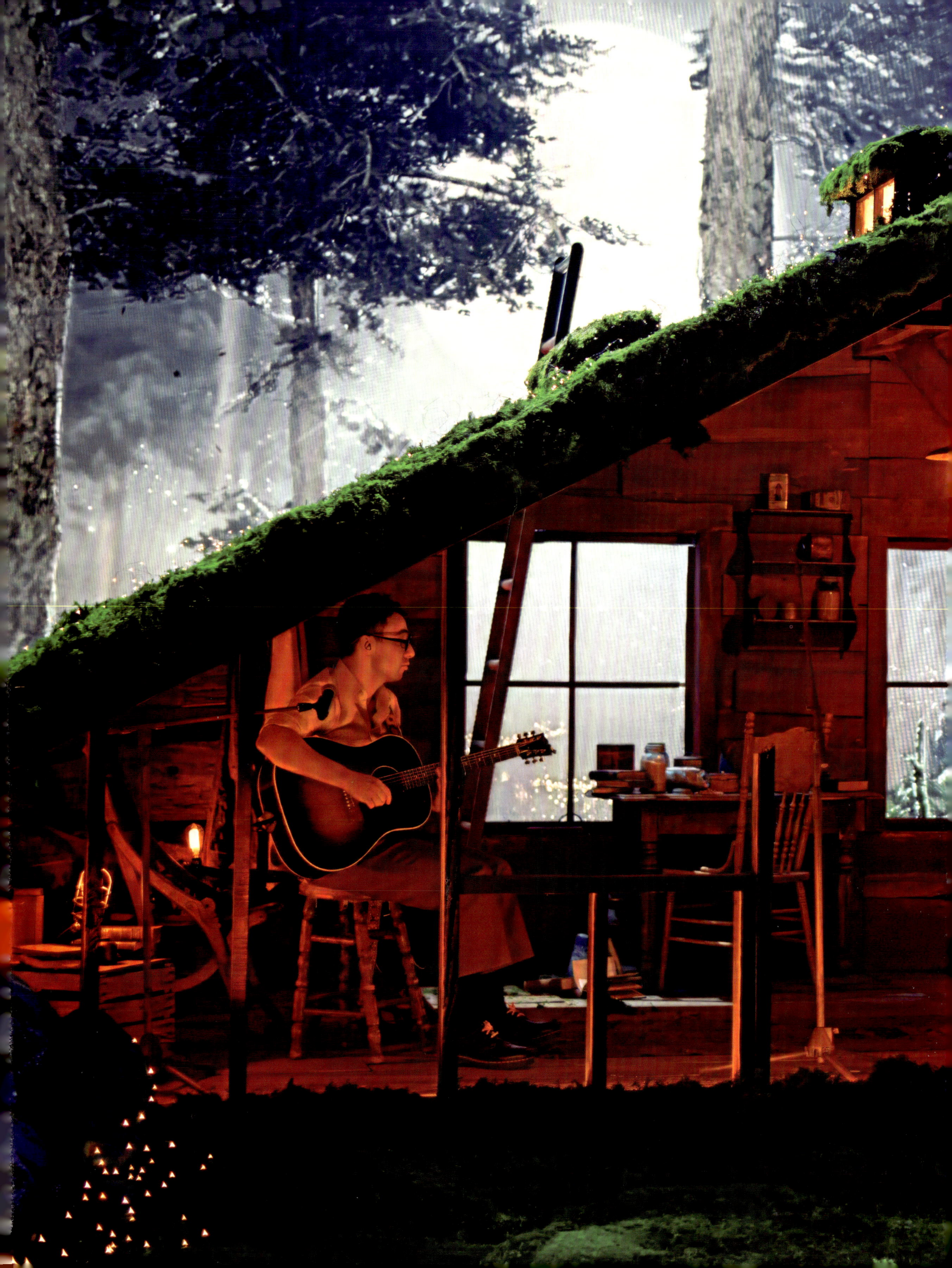

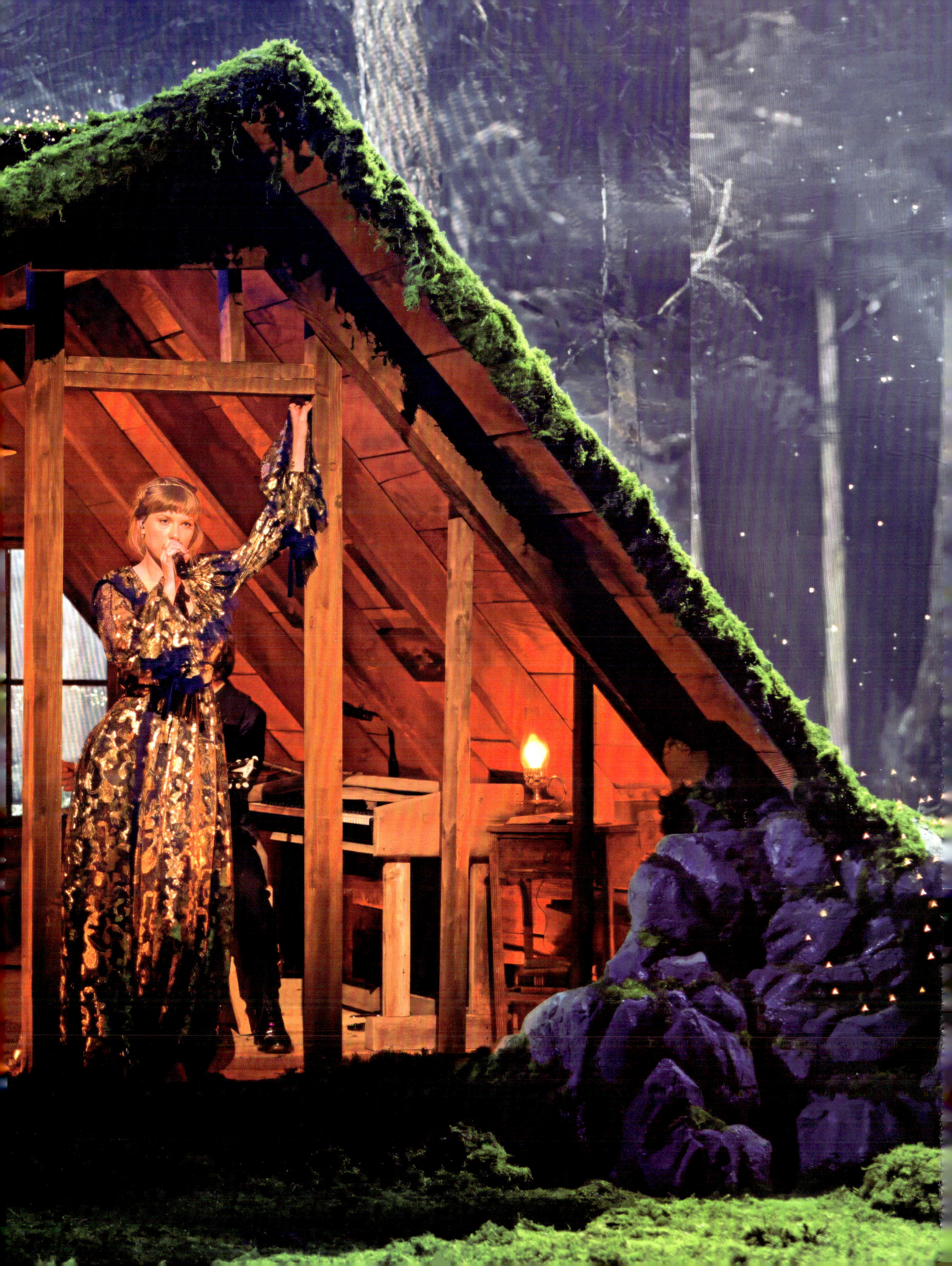

Another Album

Taylor once again took to social media, saying, "I'm elated to tell you that my ninth studio album, and *folklore*'s sister record, will be out tonight at midnight eastern. It's called *evermore*. To put it plainly, we just couldn't stop writing songs. To try and put it more poetically, it feels like we were standing on the edge of the folklorian woods and had a choice: to turn and go back or to travel further into the forest of this music. We chose to wander deeper in. I've never done this before. In the past I've always treated albums as one-off eras and moved onto planning the next one after an album was released. There was something different with *folklore*. In making it, I felt less like I was departing and more like I was returning. I loved the escapism I found in these imaginary/not imaginary tales. I loved the ways you welcomed the dreamscapes and tragedies and epic tales of love lost and found into your lives. So I just kept writing them. And I loved creating these songs with Aaron Dessner, Jack Antonoff, WB, and Justin Vernon."

Arriving just five months after its predecessor, *evermore* continued the introspective, indie-folk sound that Taylor was exploring. While *folklore* felt like a quiet, introspective retreat, *evermore* carried a slightly more experimental tone. Songs like "gold rush" and "long story short" had a poppier edge, while tracks like "cowboy like me" and "no body, no crime" (featuring HAIM) leaned into storytelling rooted in country and murder-mystery narratives, a favorite genre of Taylor's.

The album debuted at No. 1 on the Billboard 200. The title track, "willow," also debuted at No. 1 on the Billboard Hot 100, making Taylor the first artist in history to top the charts for an album twice and single simultaneously, as she had previously achieved both No. 1 spots with *folklore* and "cardigan" in July 2020.

Because of the close release of the two albums, fans speculated that Taylor didn't like *evermore* as much as *folklore*, as it didn't seem to get the same amount of love or airtime. At The Eras Tour, during the performance of "champagne problems," Taylor addressed the rumors by saying, "You have a really good sense

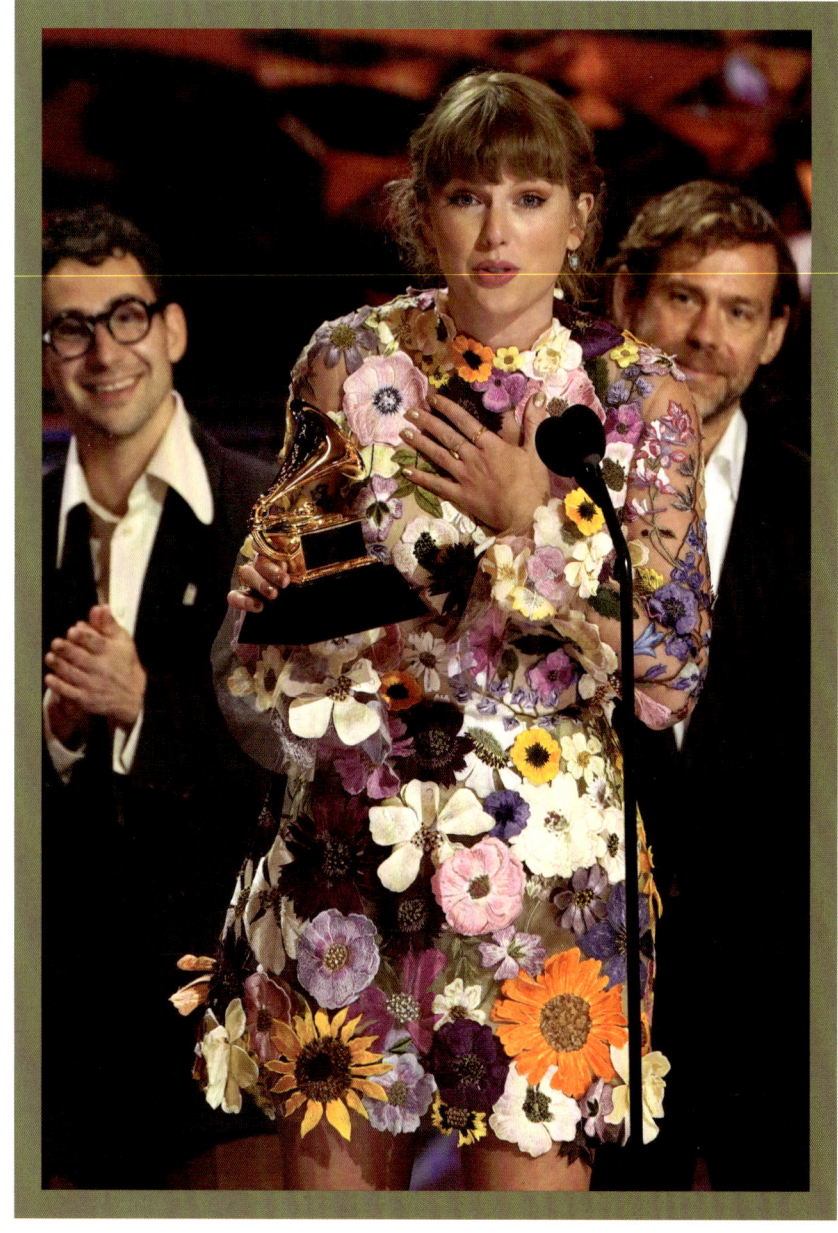

KINDNESS

A WOMAN OF HER WORD

Taylor has built a big reputation for her unwavering commitment to her fans, rarely canceling shows throughout her career, even in the face of challenging circumstances. When given a choice, Taylor has always chosen to postpone first, ensuring she can make up the date to fans. All things considered, she has only postponed a handful of shows throughout her career, mainly due to illness.

As of 2024, the only shows she has canceled have been to extenuating circumstances beyond her control and in which she canceled to ensure the health and safety of her fans first. The first was a show she canceled in Bangkok, Thailand, during The Red Tour. The stop was canceled due to political unrest in the country. Taylor canceled Lover Fest in 2021 due to the COVID-19 pandemic. And most recently, Taylor canceled three shows in Vienna on The Eras Tour due to a terrorist plot by ISIS.

This dedication and commitment has signaled to fans that when they buy a ticket to her concert, she and her team will do everything in their power to show up and deliver an unforgettable experience to all.

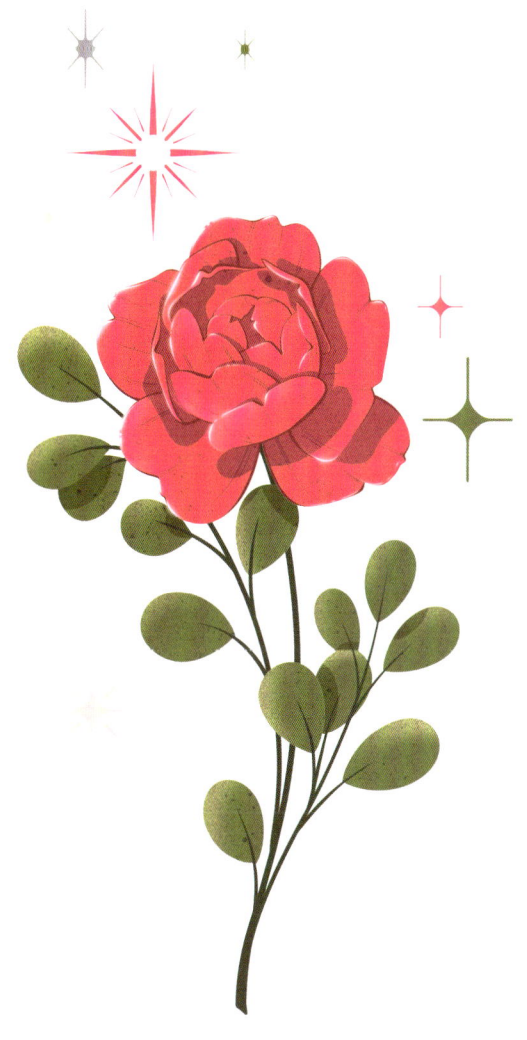

of humor, and sometimes you like to tease me about things, and the really hilarious thing that you were on for a while was saying, 'Taylor hates *evermore*.' I am here to dispel the rumors and prove wrong the allegations that I hate *evermore* because I actually love that album and I'm so proud of it, and I'm so happy that you like it too."

While the two albums were not on Taylor's radar at the start of the year, the pandemic unearthed this newly found creativity that continued to catapult her career. *folklore* went on to win Album of the Year at the 2021 Grammy Awards, making Taylor the first female artist to win this award three times.

The year 2020 was an unprecedented and tumultuous time, with the whole world facing a pandemic and much uncertainty, and Taylor's music not only reflected the times, but also provided so many with comfort and solace during a time of introspection and isolation. Together, *folklore* and *evermore* represent one of Taylor's most artistically daring periods, proving her ability to evolve and surprise her audience (and even herself) by continuing to genre-bend and go with her gut.

By the time 2021 started, fans speculated what would come next. Would there be a follow-up to *folklore* and *evermore*, or would we finally

OPPOSITE:
Taylor accepts the award for Album of the Year for *folklore* at the 63rd Grammy Awards, March 14, 2021.

KELLY CLARKSON

In 2019, Taylor found out that her masters were sold out from under her by her former record label, Big Machine Label Group. Taylor publicly shared her disappointment in public statements, and many came to her support. Singer Kelly Clarkson was one of those people. She took to X (formerly known as Twitter), tagged Taylor, and said, "@taylorswift13 just a thought, U should go & re-record all the songs that U don't own the masters on exactly how U did them but put brand new art & some kind of incentive so fans will no longer buy the old versions. I'd buy all the new versions just to prove a point."

She was the first celebrity to publicly share this idea of re-recording her albums and showed big support for Taylor early on. After Taylor released her first re-release, *Fearless (Taylor's Version)*, she sent Kelly flowers, and she continues to send Kelly flowers for every re-release.

Kelly expressed her admiration for how Taylor handled the situation, noting that Taylor's business decisions are empowering for artists navigating the complexities of the music industry. She joked that she wasn't sure if her suggestion had any real impact, but regardless, she was thrilled to see Taylor reclaim her work.

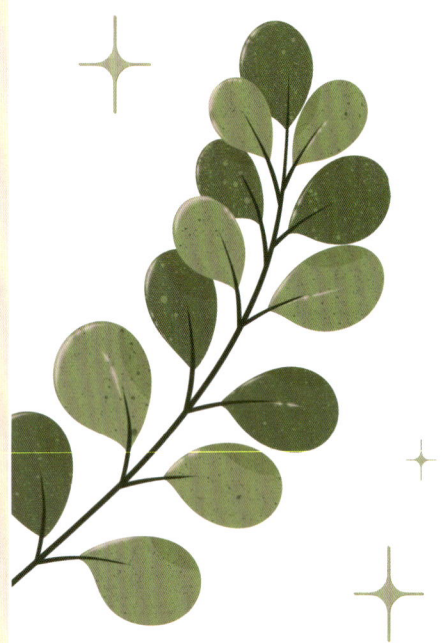

get some of her re-recordings? With these two surprise albums, fans realized that anything was now possible, and those surprises would be here sooner than anticipated.

In February 2021, Taylor officially announced her first re-recorded album, *Fearless (Taylor's Version)*, and dropped "Love Story (Taylor's Version)" that same night. This announcement marked the first step of Taylor reclaiming ownership over her first six albums. She made the official announcement on *Good Morning America* and then took to social media, where she shared a lengthy post about why she chose *Fearless* as her first re-recording. In true Taylor fashion, the announcement also came with a hidden message. Certain letters were capitalized, and if rearranged, they spelled "APRIL NINTH," officially confirming the album's release date.

In describing how she felt, Taylor said, "This process has been more fulfilling and emotional than I could've imagined and made me even more determined to re-record all my music."

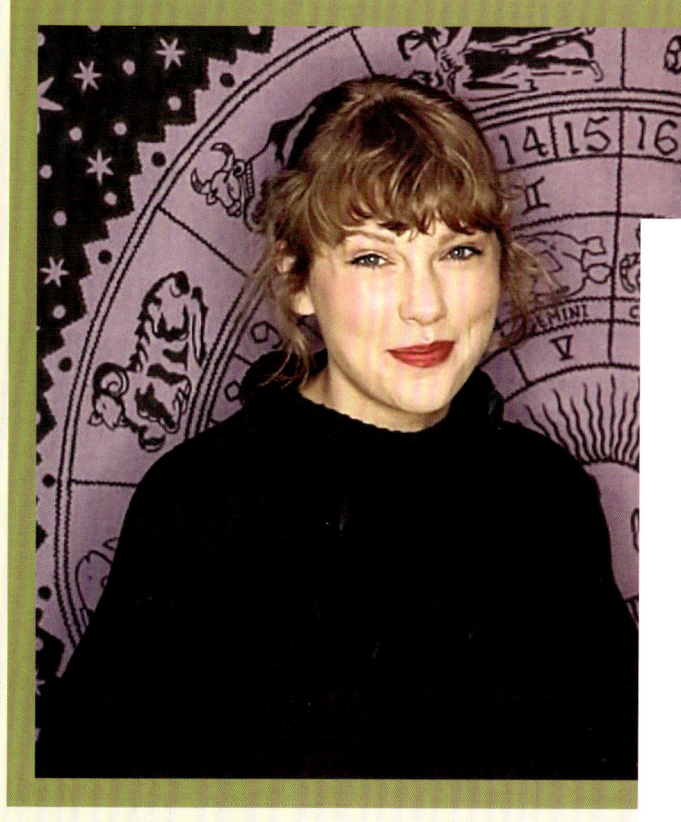

Swearing in Songs

The first time Taylor swore in an album was during her debut album, *Taylor Swift*. She said the word "damn."

ZERO SWEAR WORDS

The albums *Fearless* and *Speak Now* do not contain any swear words.

MORE SWEAR WORDS

While Taylor kept swear words to a minimum, they started increasing ever so slightly, typically with the words "damn" or "hell." However, she finally dropped an "f-bomb" during *folklore*, and she's been more consistently swearing in albums ever since.

The album itself contained new art, with a present-day image of Taylor featuring similar colors and vibes as homage to the original.

"Love Story (Taylor's Version)" debuted at No. 1 on the Billboard Hot Country Songs chart, making her the first woman to top the chart with a re-recording. When *Fearless (Taylor's Version)* dropped on April 9, 2021, it immediately topped the Billboard 200, with more than 291,000 album-equivalent units in its first week, making it the biggest debut of any country album in six years. The album contained 26 tracks, including six unreleased "From the Vault" songs, including "You All Over Me" (ft. Maren Morris) and "Mr. Perfectly Fine." The "From the Vault" tracks became instant fan favorites, giving fans even more insight into Taylor's world during her previous eras.

Fans immediately took a firm stance on where they stood with the re-recording issue:

They would only be streaming "Taylor's Version" from here on out. Radio stations—including iHeart, with more than 850 broadcast stations—declared that they too would only play "Taylor's Version" on the radio. In an interview on *The Graham Norton Show*, Taylor said, "I am thankful to radio stations across the United States that will only play my new versions. It is so heartwarming. It is something that I care about but don't expect other people to care about it."

ABOVE: Taylor, shocked the audience at the 2020 American Music Awards when she announced that she was accepting her award for Artist of the Year from "the studio where I am re-recording all my old music."

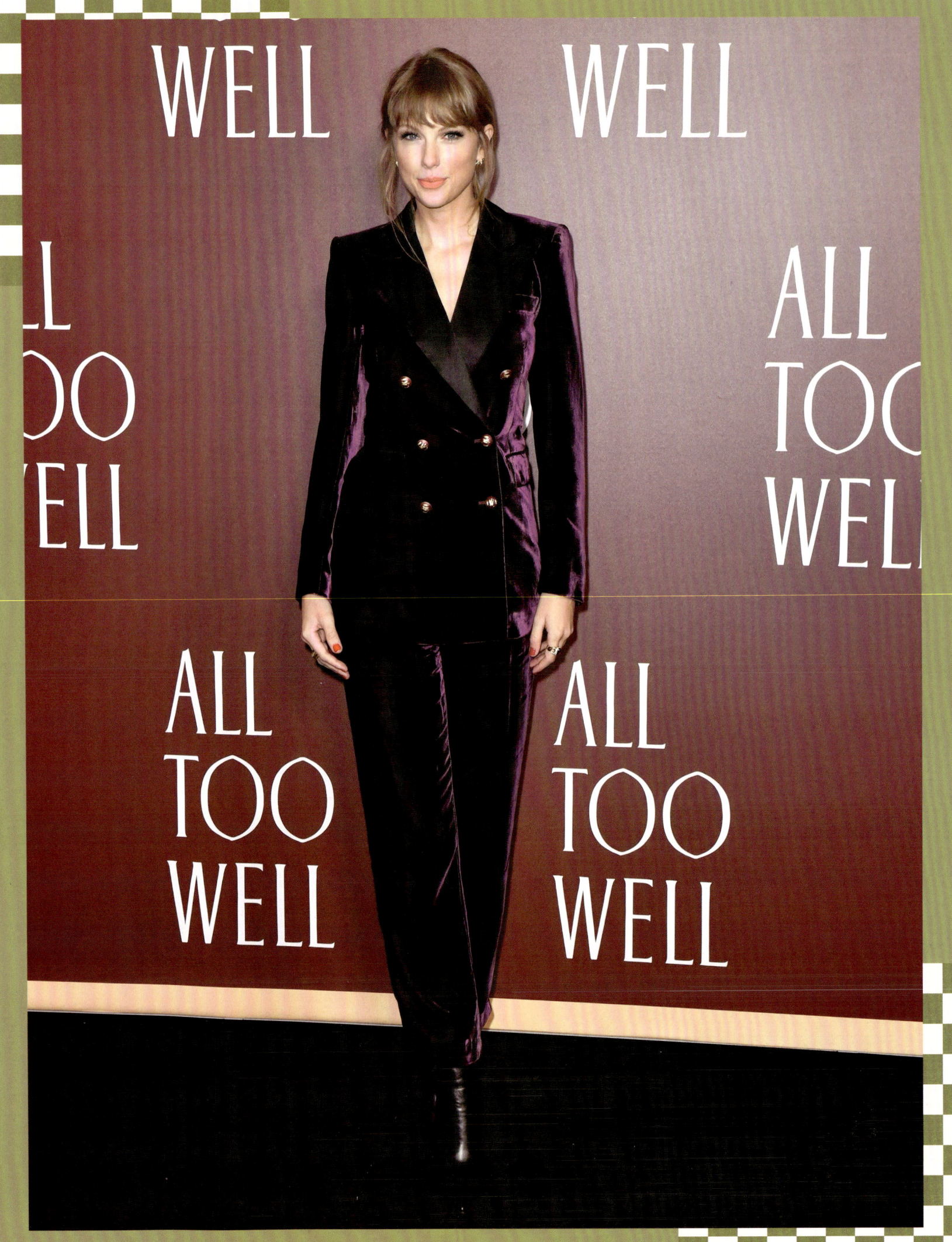

Seeing Red

Just two months after the launch of *Fearless (Taylor's Version)*, Taylor used Instagram to make another bombshell announcement: *Red (Taylor's Version)* would launch on November 19. (This date was later pushed up one week to November 12.) Taylor took to social media to announce what *Red* meant to her and said, "The next album that I'll be releasing is my version of *Red*, which will be out on November 19. This will be the first time you hear all thirty songs that were meant to go on *Red*. And hey, one of them is even ten minutes long."

Upon release, *Red (Taylor's Version)* quickly became one of the most successful re-recorded albums in history. It debuted at No. 1 on the Billboard 200 and sold 605,000 first-week units, making it Taylor's biggest sales week since *reputation* in 2017. Twenty-six songs charted on the Billboard Hot 100, and Taylor broke Spotify's record for the most-streamed album in a day by a female artist, at 90.8 million streams. It featured the original twenty-one tracks from *Red* plus nine "From the Vault" tracks, including collaborations with Phoebe Bridgers, Chris Stapleton, and Ed Sheeran.

The anticipated release of "All Too Well (10-Minute Version)" also came with a short film, directed by Taylor and starring Sadie Sink and Dylan O'Brien. The song was an instant fan favorite, and it became the longest track ever to top the Billboard Hot 100, dethroning Don McLean's "American Pie" after forty-nine years.

The addition of new songs on "Taylor's Version," and the care with which she rolled out each of the launches, made each new re-release exciting for fans. There was new content to listen to and new lyrics to dissect. This care, combined with the ownership stance, made Swifties not just excited for the re-releases, but ready to take action as well to support Taylor in taking back what is rightfully hers. This speaks volumes to the incredible connection she has built with her fans over the years.

Now, with two back-to-back sister records and the success of Taylor's versions, Taylor cemented her place as one of the most influential artists of the twenty-first century and set the stage for even bigger things to come in 2022 and beyond.

OPPOSITE: Taylor attends the premiere of *All Too Well*, the short film she wrote, directed, and starred in, November 12, 2021.

Taylor broke Spotify's record for the most-streamed album in a day by a female artist.

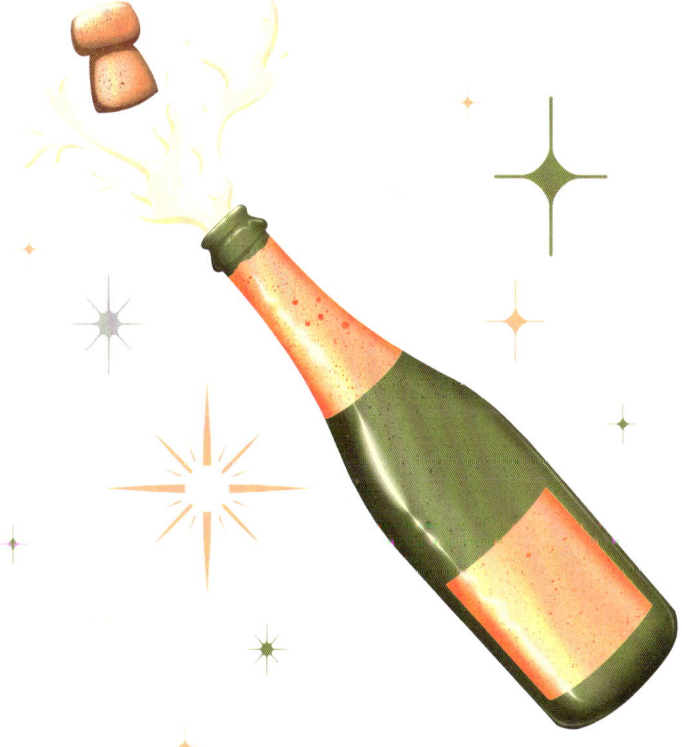

FLORALS IN SONGS

Taylor uses imagery from sources like nature, colors, and literature to set the scene and bring detail to her songs. Here are all the florals Taylor sings about in her songs:

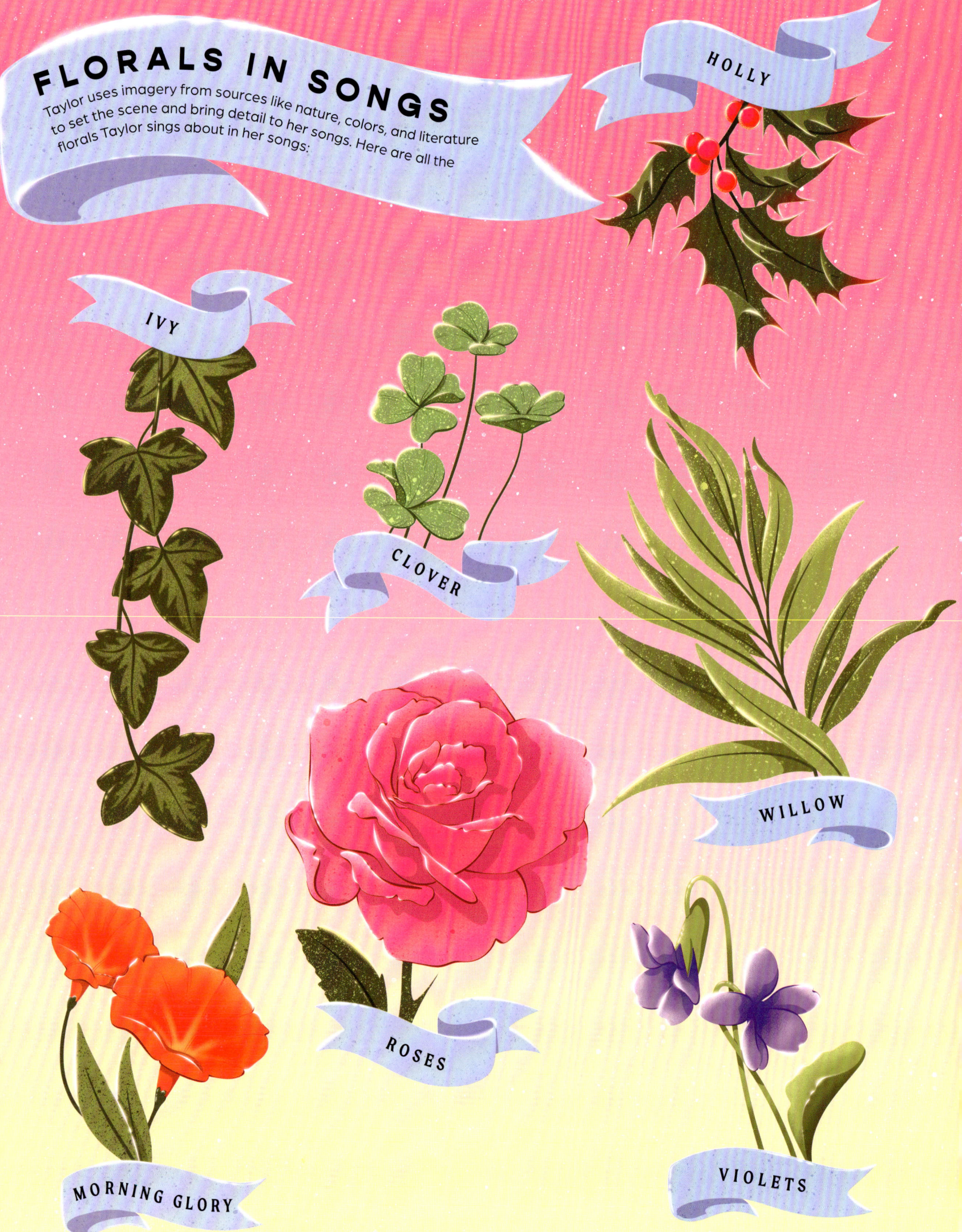

HOLLY

IVY

CLOVER

WILLOW

ROSES

MORNING GLORY

VIOLETS

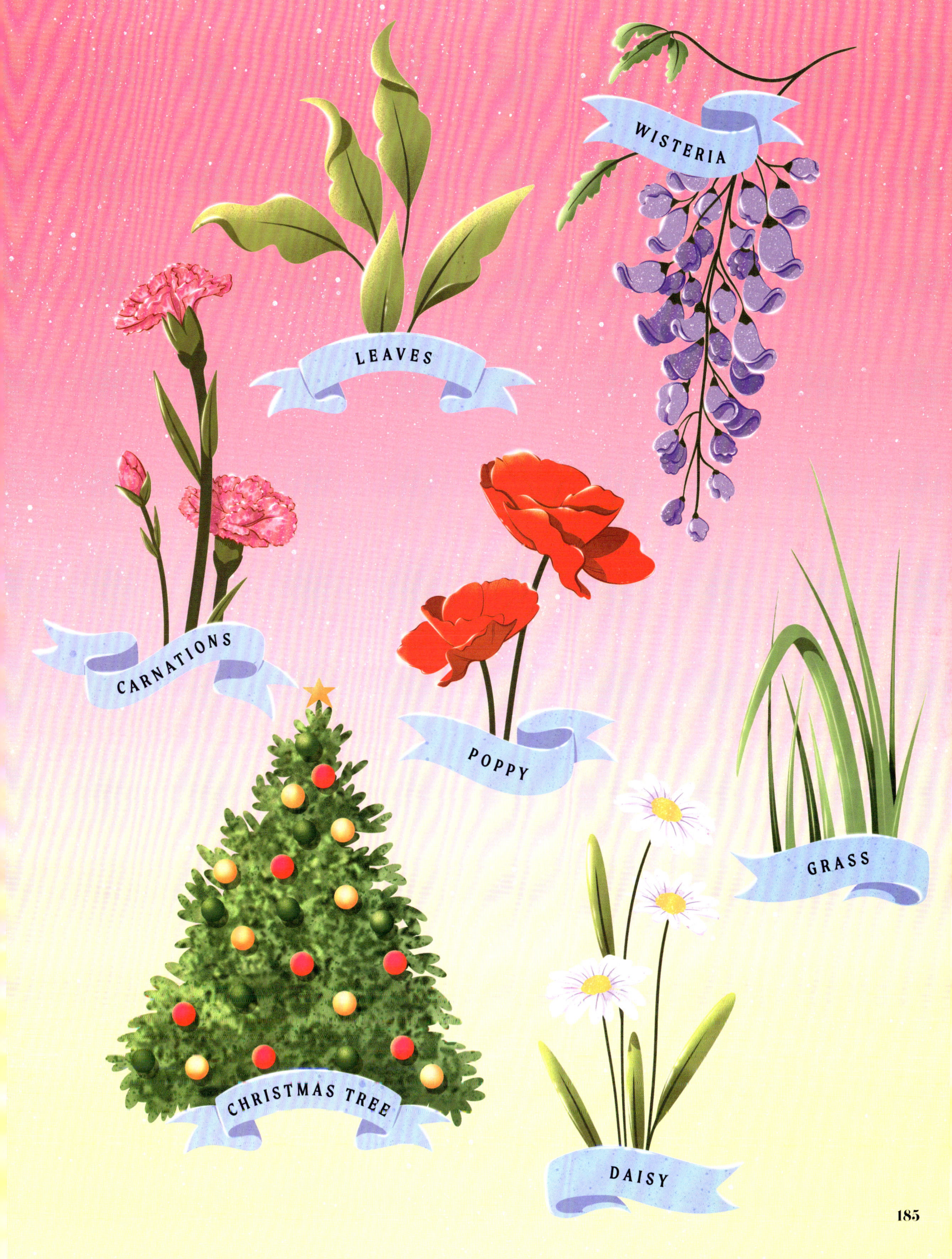

WISTERIA

LEAVES

CARNATIONS

POPPY

CHRISTMAS TREE

GRASS

DAISY

MIDNIGHTS

2022

THE ERAS OF KINDNESS

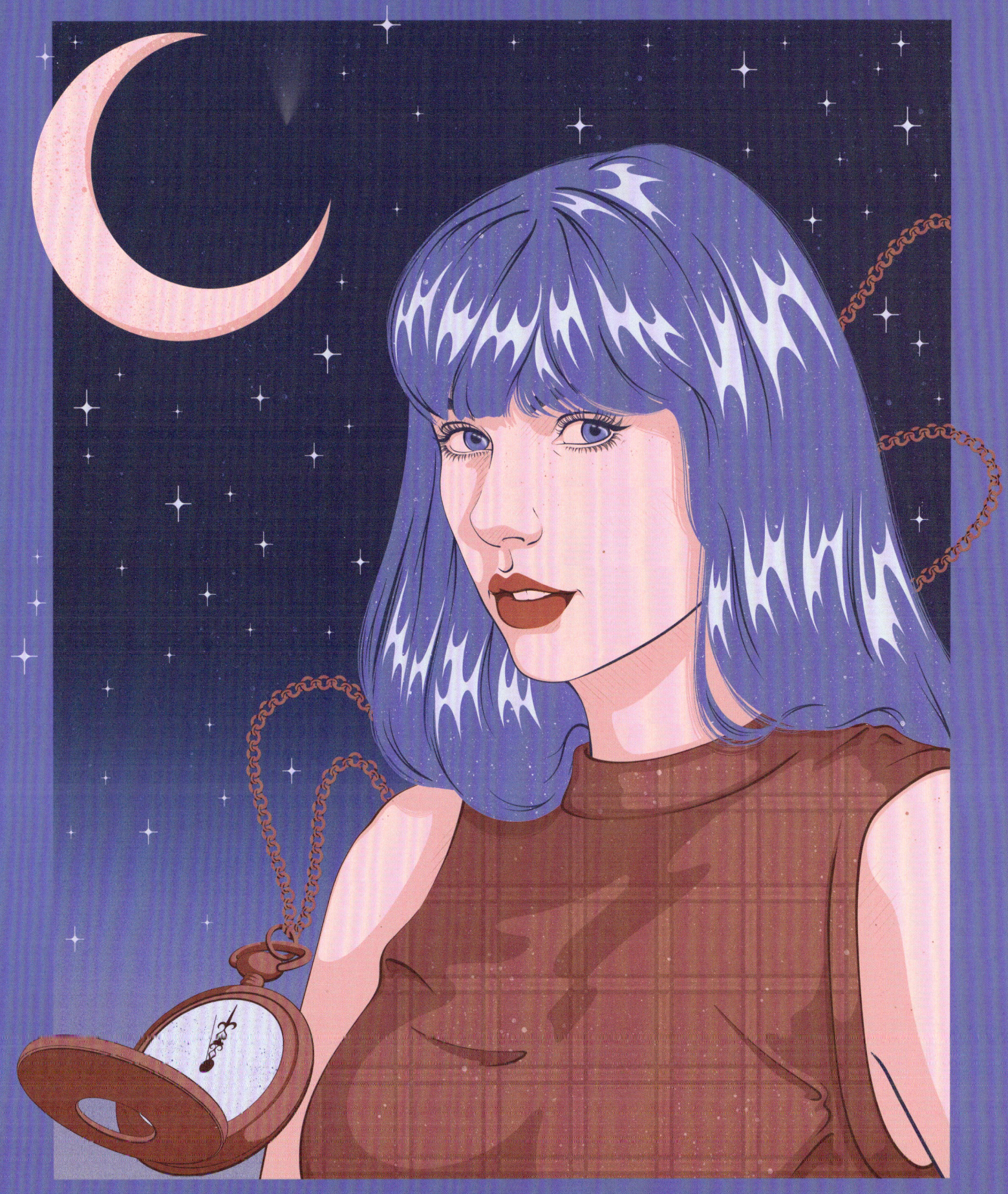

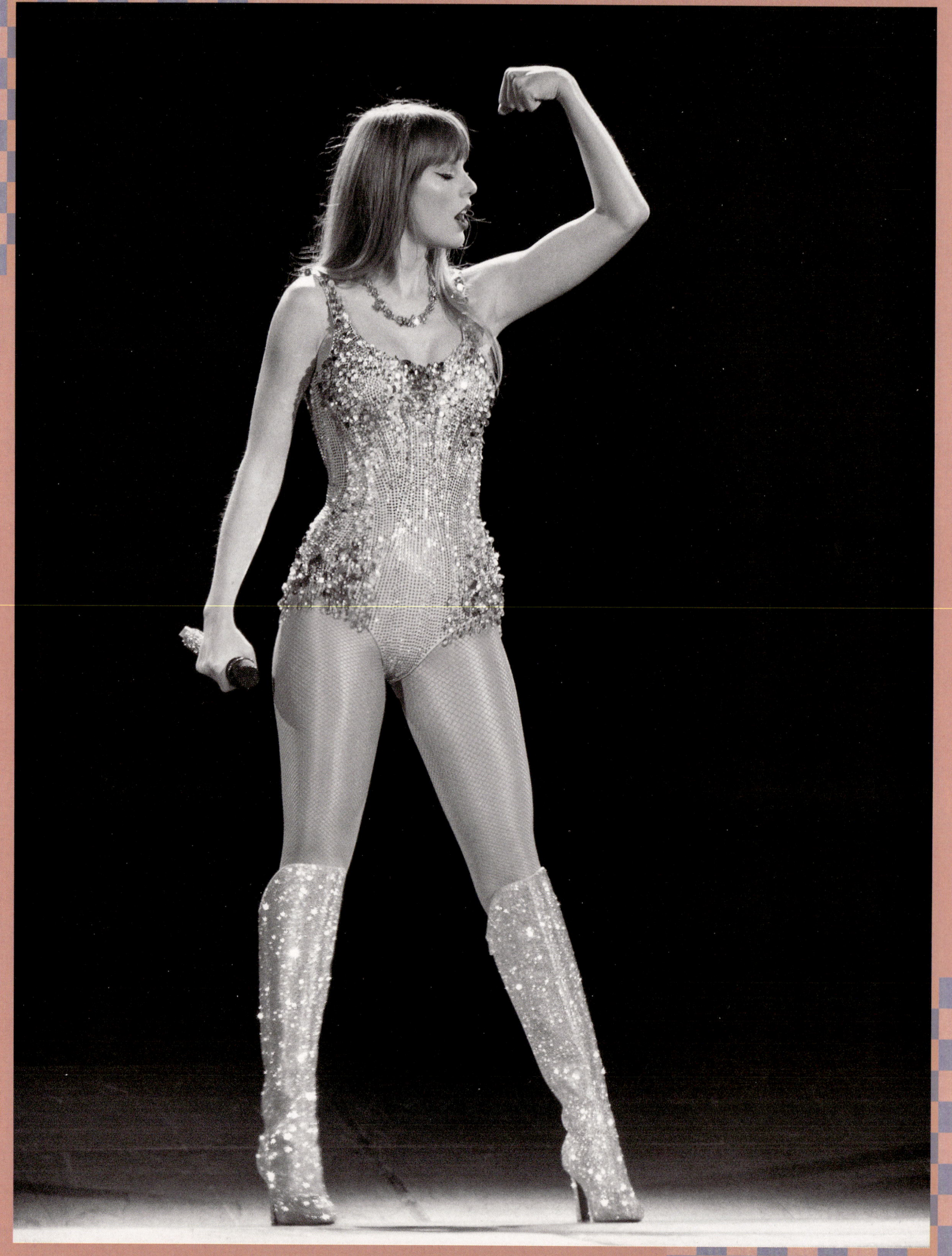

> "I believe that everyone should be able to live out their love story without fear."

Taylor, 2023

THIS ERA DEFINED ALL ERAS

After several years of back-to-back launches, both of new music and re-recordings, fans wondered what would happen next in the Swiftie-verse. Would this be the year of a tour announcement, a new re-recording, or new music altogether?

While 2022 got off to a bit of a slow start in the Swiftie-verse, in March 2022, Taylor posted on social media for the first time all year. She shared that she wrote the song "Carolina" (produced by Aaron Dessner) for the film adaptation of *Where the Crawdads Sing* by Delia Owens. Then, in May 2022, Taylor dropped another social media note to say that the song "This Love (Taylor's Version)" was featured in the trailer for the film adaptation of *The Summer I Turned Pretty* and that it would be released on May 6, 2022. Fans quickly speculated that *1989 (Taylor's Version)* might be the next release now that there was a new single out from that album.

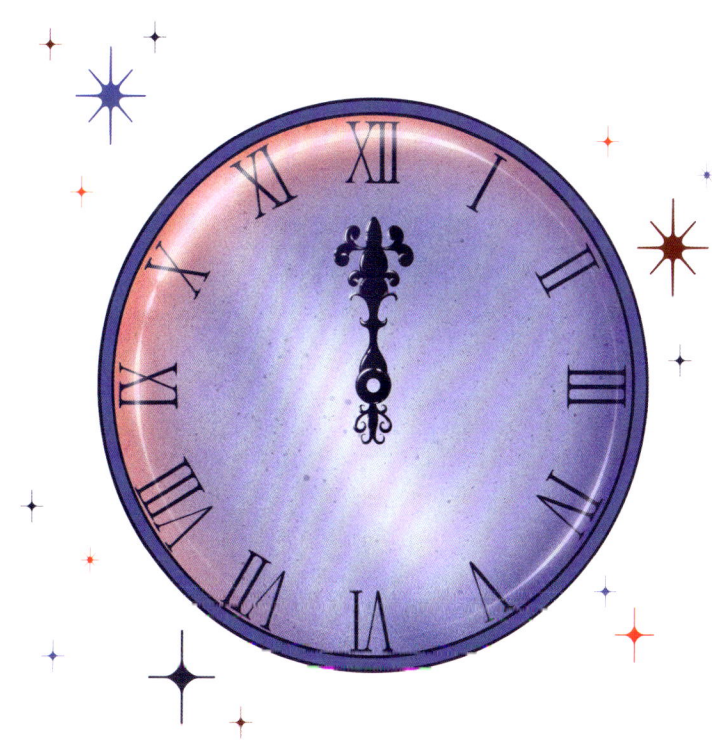

"BEJEWELED"

The "Bejeweled" music video was released on October 25, 2022, just a few days after the album dropped. Directed by Taylor, the music video reimagined the classic Cinderella story. However, in the end, Taylor ghosted the prince and ended up in a castle of her own. Taylor played the role of Cinderella, the evil stepmother was played by Laura Dern, her stepsisters were played by the HAIM sisters, and the prince was played by Jack Antonoff. The video even featured a burlesque performance by Taylor and the iconic Dita Von Teese, who played Taylor's fairy godmother. The two perform Dita's infamous "Martini Glass" routine.

Shortly after the song and music video premiered, Mikael Arellano, a Swiftie and content creator known for his fun dances, choreographed a short, sassy routine to part of the chorus of "Bejeweled." He strutted, twirled, and shimmered his hands to the song. This immediately went viral, and creators and celebrities alike posted videos of themselves doing the "bejeweled strut."

When the first The Eras Tour show debuted, fans were stunned and excited to see that Taylor included the "bejeweled strut" in her tour choreography. Mikael later went on social media and shared that Taylor's team reached out for permission, which he granted. Taylor's team invited Mikael to The Eras Tour show in Philadelphia, where he was chosen to receive the infamous "22" hat during the "22" set.

Mikael's dance remains a standout fan moment of the *Midnights* era. It not only took over TikTok; it also became part of the official

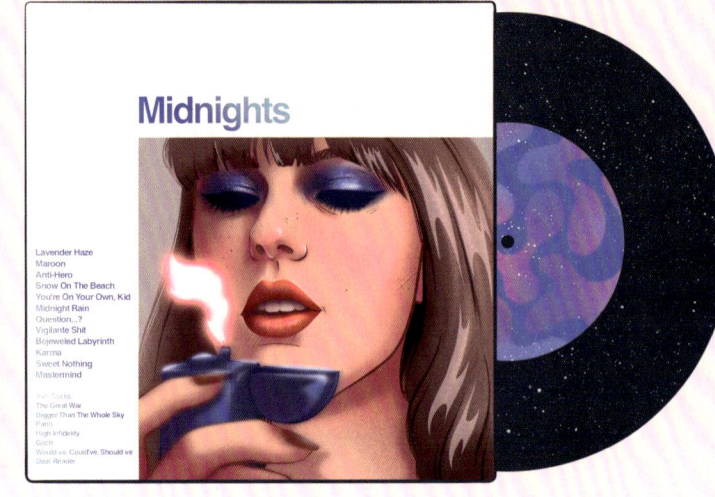

ALBUMS
Midnights, *Speak Now (Taylor's Version)*, and *1989 (Taylor's Version)*

DATES LAUNCHED
Midnights (October 21, 2022), *Speak Now (Taylor's Version)* (July 7, 2023), and *1989 (Taylor's Version)* (October 27, 2023)

FIRST SINGLES
Midnights: "Anti-Hero," *Speak Now (Taylor's Version)*: "I Can See You," and *1989 (Taylor's Version)*: "Slut!"

OTHER SINGLES
Midnights: "Lavender Haze" and "Karma"; *1989 (Taylor's Version)*: "Is It Over Now?"

TOUR
The Eras Tour (March 17, 2023 to December 8, 2024)

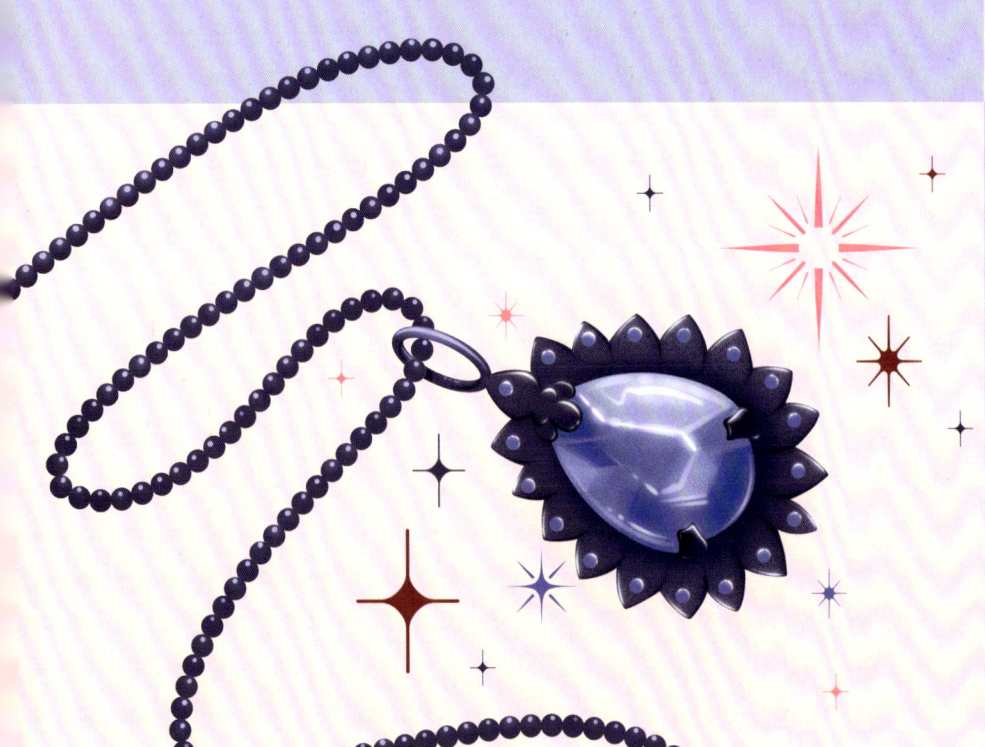

tour experience. Taylor's decision to seek permission instead of just using the dance set a positive example for proper crediting in the digital age, and it showed that fans and artists can influence each other in special and meaningful ways.

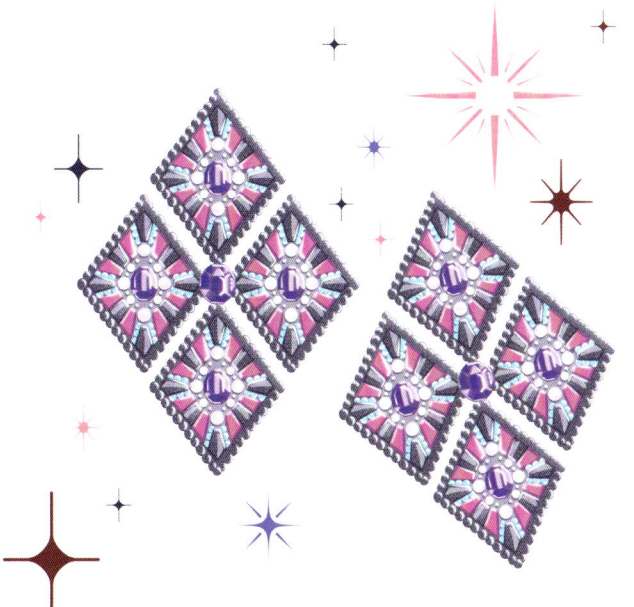

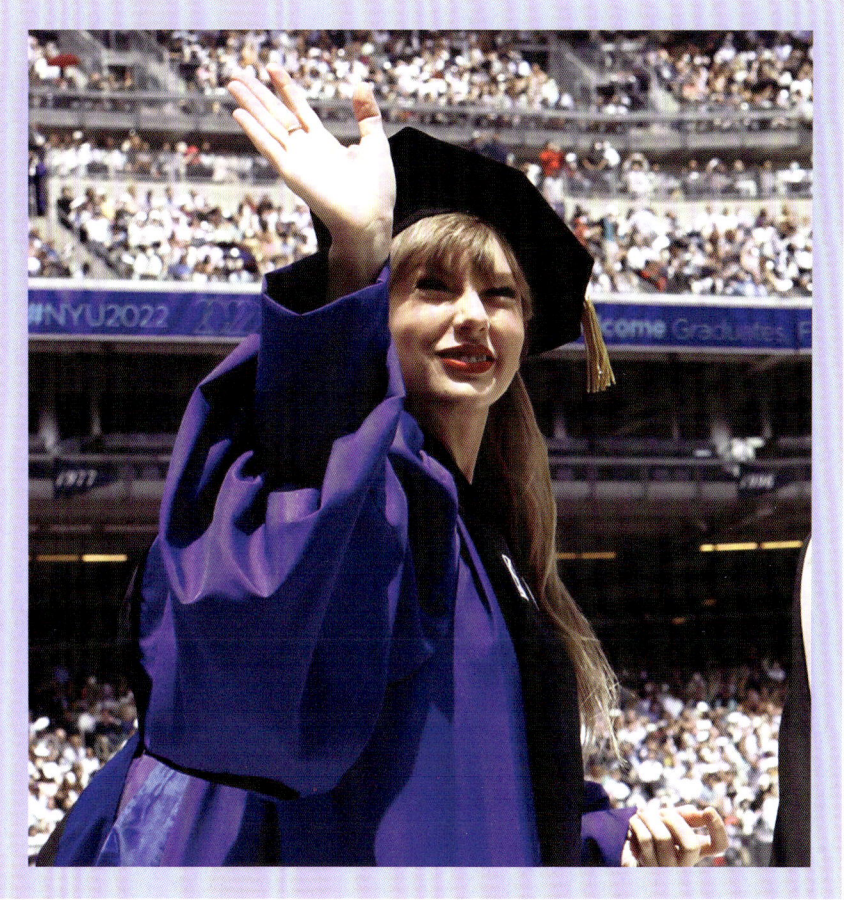

Just a few weeks later, the soon-to-be Dr. Taylor Swift made another announcement: that she was wearing a cap and gown for the first time and was on her way to New York University (NYU). On May 18, 2022, Taylor Swift was awarded an honorary Doctor in Fine Arts degree from NYU and delivered the commencement address at Yankee Stadium for the graduating class of 2022.

While Taylor never went to college, this honorary doctorate recognized her exceptional contributions to music, songwriting, and the arts. This was also a goal of hers, as she jokingly discussed in a *Vogue* magazine "73 Questions" interview. When asked one thing that she is determined to achieve in her lifetime, she responded with, "I really want an honorary doctorate degree because Ed Sheeran has one and I feel like he looks down on me now because I don't have one."

The ceremony was livestreamed, and fans tuned in to hear the commencement address from Dr. Taylor. She walked across the stage in a purple NYU cap and gown, but added a touch of her signature sparkle with rhinestone-studded heels. Her speech was humorous, heartfelt, and inspiring, and covered themes of growth, resilience, and embracing change. She also shared experiences from her own journey.

Taylor jokingly said, "I'm ninety percent sure the main reason I'm here is because I have a song called '22.'" She even welcomed the crowd to New York, as a nod to her *1989* track "Welcome to New York." She remained playful and humorous while also sharing personal experiences along the way.

She commented that while she didn't like to give anyone unsolicited advice, she would share some life hacks that worked for her and maybe they would work for them too. Her life hacks included "knowing what things to keep and what things to release," "learn to live alongside cringe," and "not hiding your enthusiasm." She also confronted perfectionism and stated, "My experience has been that my mistakes led to the best things in my life."

PAGE 188: The now-iconic outfit that defined The Eras Tour.

ABOVE: Now an honorary Doctor of Arts recipient, Taylor makes her way to the podium to deliver the commencement address to the graduates of New York University's class of 2022.

Midnights

She even managed to sprinkle in some Easter eggs for her future album *Midnights*, as fans realized in retrospect. And, in typical Taylor fashion, she ended it with another "22" reference by saying, "I hope you know how proud I am to share this day with you. We're doing this together. So let's just keep dancing like we're . . . the class of '22." Her speech quickly went viral, resonating with Swifties and non-Swifties alike.

Then, during the MTV Video Music Awards on August 28, 2022, not only did Taylor take home the Video of the Year award for "All Too Well (10-Minute Version) (Taylor's Version)," but during her acceptance speech, she also shocked fans by casually dropping her next album title: *Midnights*. Thanking the fans, she said, "I wouldn't be able to re-record my albums if it weren't for you. You emboldened me to do that, and I had sort of made up my mind that if you were going to be this generous and give us this, then I thought it might be a fun moment to tell you that my brand-new album comes out October 21. And I will tell you more . . . at midnight."

Shortly after the VMAs, Taylor posted the album cover on social media, along with a note describing *Midnights* as "the stories of thirteen sleepless nights scattered throughout my life." In the lead-up to the album release, Taylor kept fans engaged with her "Midnights Mayhem with Me," where over several weeks, she spun a gold bingo cage and revealed each track in random order. This playful rollout had fans speculating on what each song might be about. They were eager to hear the album. As part of the marketing efforts, Taylor revealed four limited-edition vinyl variants featuring different artwork, which, when pieced together, formed a clock face—one of many

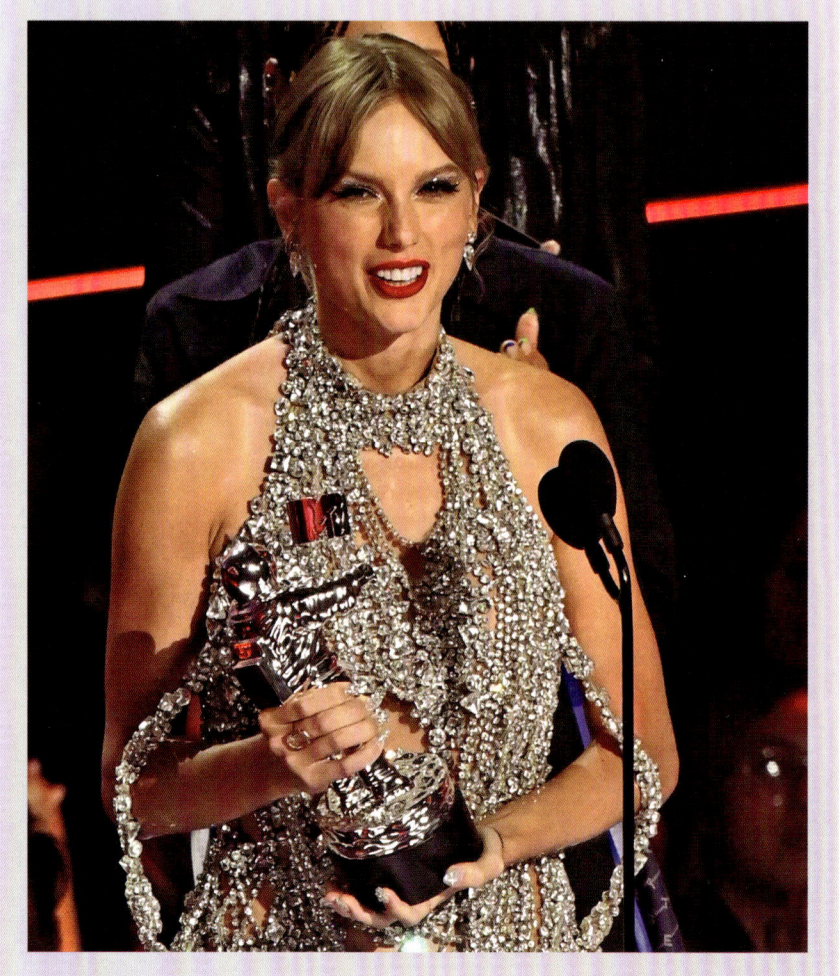

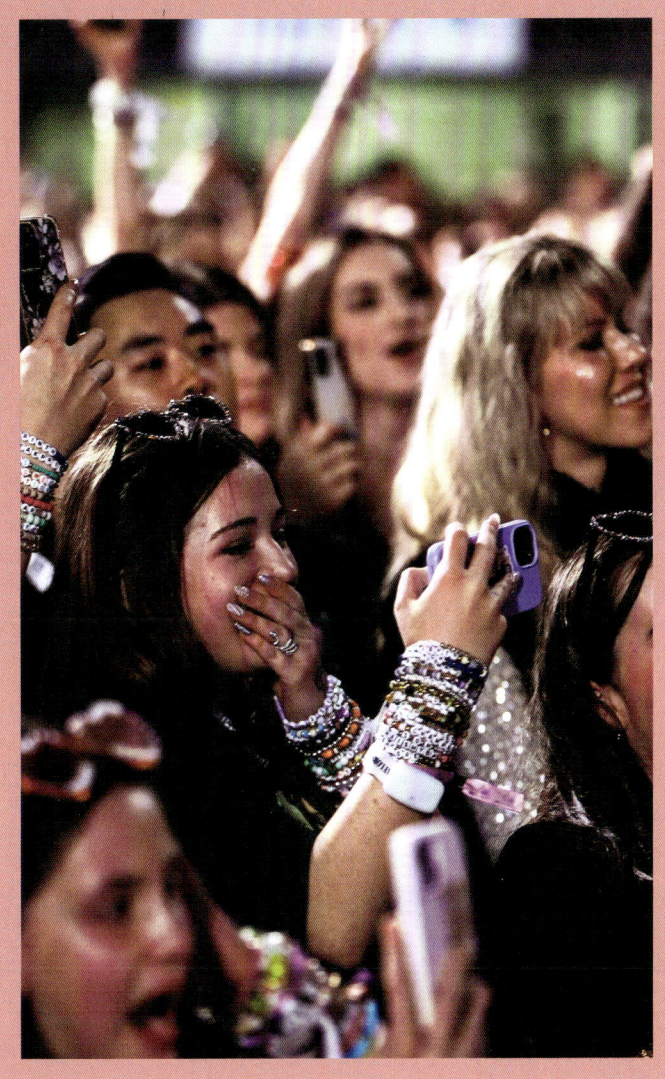

In Her Wildest Streams

ESTABLISHED
March 17, 2023

LIVESTREAM ERA
The Eras Tour quickly became a cultural phenomenon. The high demand also meant that tickets were extremely hard to get. That didn't stop Swifties, though. Several content creators took it upon themselves to curate livestreams for each tour stop. It caught on, and thousands of fans tuned into the grainy livestreams in each city. Many livestreams even had a special countdown until the coveted surprise songs each night. Taylor acknowledged the fans watching on livestreams by saying, "We're very lucky to have a lot of people that like to watch this on the Internet and care about these shows even if they're not here."

Easter eggs in this era. She even sold a clock set so the albums could be hung as wall art and made into a real, working clock.

Fans met her at midnight on October 21, 2022, for the release of *Midnights*. But the surprises didn't stop there. Three hours later, at three o'clock in the morning, she announced and released *Midnights (3am Edition)* with five additional tracks, all produced by Aaron Dessner.

Taylor chose "Anti-Hero" as the lead single, describing the song as one of her most personal, as it explores self-doubt, insecurity, body

dysmorphia, and imposter syndrome. She released it simultaneously with a music video that she self-directed. The video featured two versions of Taylor: herself and the version that confronted every turn, usually bringing up some sort of insecurity or deep vulnerability. The video cited specific insecurities, like betrayal, when she pointed at a chalkboard with the words "Everyone will betray you," as well as body-image issues when she stepped on a scale, only for her other version to be disappointed with her. There was even a "larger-than-life"

OPPOSITE: Taylor accepts the MTV Music Video Award for Video of the Year for *All Too Well (10 Minute) (Taylor's Version)*. This is the fourteenth MTV award of her career.

ABOVE: Fans at Taylor's final performance of The Eras Tour, Vancouver, British Columbia, December 8, 2024.

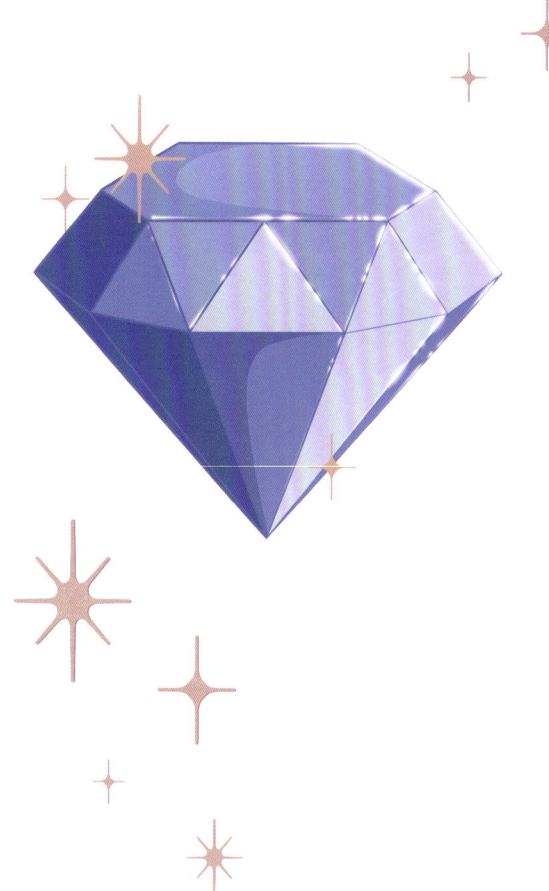

SONG SPOTLIGHT

"You're on Your Own, Kid"

The song "You're on Your Own, Kid" not only inspired the friendship-bracelet trading phenomenon; it was also the most played surprise song during the two-year run of The Eras Tour. Taylor played the song either in full or as a mash-up eleven times.

ALBUM

Midnights

RELEASED

2022

OPPOSITE: It's me, hi: Taylor accepts the Song of the Year award for "Anti-Hero" at the 2023 iHeartRadio Music Awards. The song also won the award for Best Lyrics.

Taylor that took up a lot of space when in the room with others, as a metaphor about some of Taylor's insecurity with her fame.

Toward the end of the video, the music stopped, and a fictional future scenario unfolded. It showed Taylor's funeral, and her two fictional sons and daughter-in-law going over her will. The scene featured Mike Birbiglia, John Early, and Mary Elizabeth Ellis, who play greedy, exaggerated versions of her supposed heirs. They read the will and realized that Taylor only left them with thirteen cents, to which the offspring thought that there must be a secret encoded message that meant something else. As they continued reading the will, Taylor said that there was no secret encoded message. While the video itself hit on so many deep insecurities, it also managed to bring a playful humor.

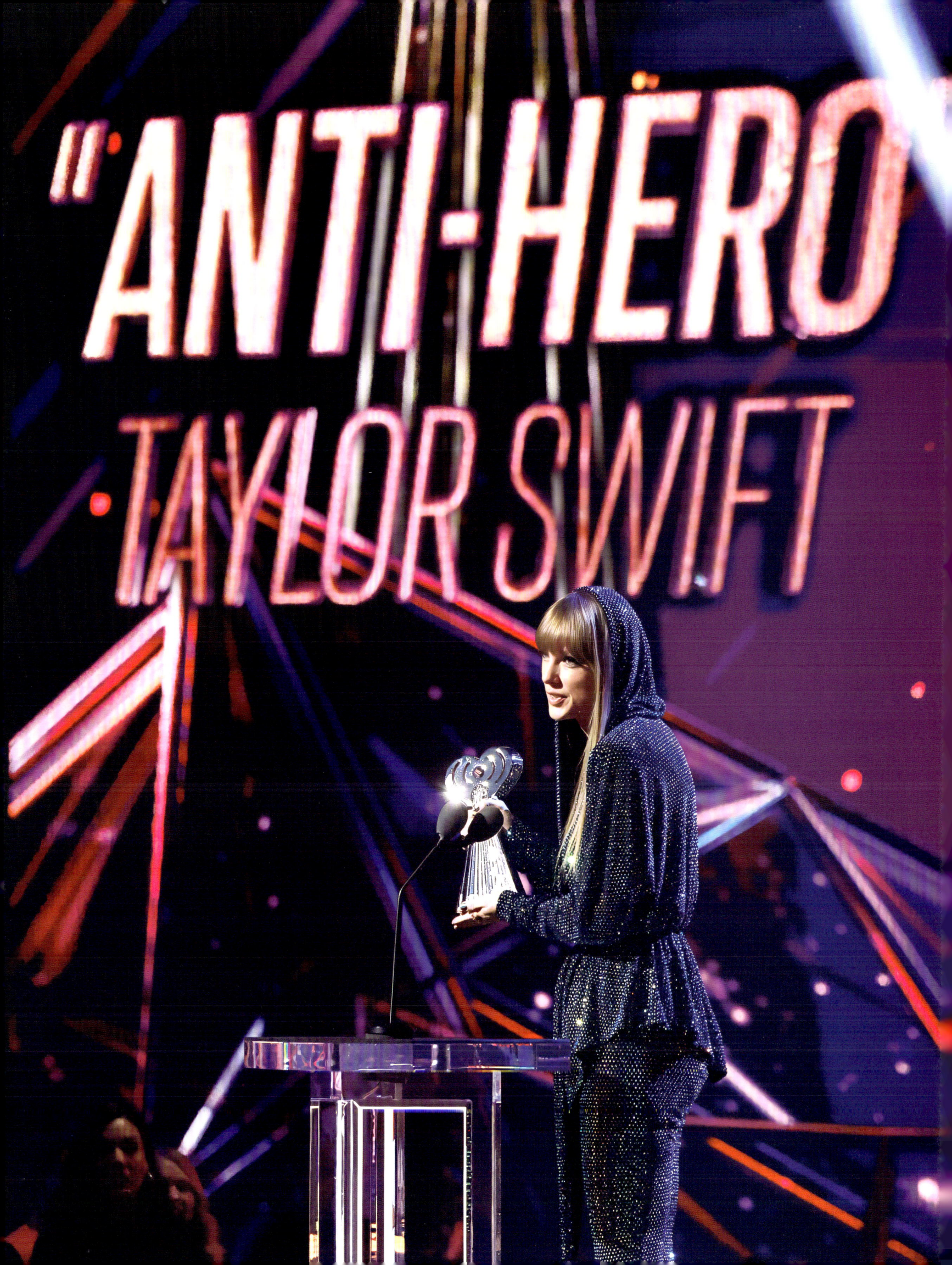

IT'S A LOVE STORY: FROM A FRIENDSHIP BRACELET TO THE ERAS TOUR STAGE

On July 8, 2023, Travis Kelce, tight end for the football team the Kansas City Chiefs, attended The Eras Tour in Kansas City. He later took to his podcast, *New Heights*, and revealed that he had tried to give Taylor a friendship bracelet with his number on it, but he was unsuccessful. At the time, this was mostly seen as a lighthearted and playful comment.

While there was some lingering speculation about a possible Taylor-and-Travis romance, nothing was confirmed. However, things took a turn on September 24, 2023, when Taylor was spotted at Arrowhead Stadium in Kansas City, Missouri, cheering on the Kansas City Chiefs as they played against the Chicago Bears. She was in a suite with Travis's mother, Donna Kelce, and the sighting caused a media frenzy among the NFL, Swifties, and almost every media outlet. After the game, Taylor and Travis were seen driving off in Travis's convertible, with the top down. Fans dubbed this the "getaway car."

Travis reflected on that moment on his podcast and said, "I just thought it was awesome how everybody in the suite had nothing but great things to say about her, the friends and family—she looked amazing. Everybody was talking about her in great light and on top of that, the day went perfect for Chiefs fans, of course. To see the slow-motion chest bumps, to see the high-fives with Mom, to see how Chiefs Kingdom was all excited that she was there.

Then we just slid off in the getaway car at the end. Took my Chevelle to the game."

Taylor continued to be a staple at any game she was able to attend, and Swifties started to embrace football, causing NFL views and sales to skyrocket. Female viewership alone increased by 24 percent, and Travis Kelce's jersey sales went up 400 percent. Fans started referring to Taylor's presence as "TayVooDoo," because of how many games the Chiefs won and how well Travis performed when Taylor was in the crowd.

Their love story continued to blossom, and things became onstage official on November 11, 2023, when Travis was spotted at The Eras Tour show in Buenos Aires, Argentina. During the show's finale song "Karma," Taylor changed the lyrics to say, "guy on the Chiefs," and the fans went wild. Between games and practice, Travis made sure to attend as many shows as he could. On June 23, 2024, Travis even made his debut on The Eras Tour stage. During the "I Can Do It With a Broken Heart" performance, Travis carried Taylor across the stage, brushing her with makeup and trying to coach her how to dance by doing a little dance from *Dumb and Dumber*. This hilarious and playful addition had both Swifties and Taylor swooning.

It was safe to say that both Taylor and Travis were on winning streaks—in their careers and together as a couple.

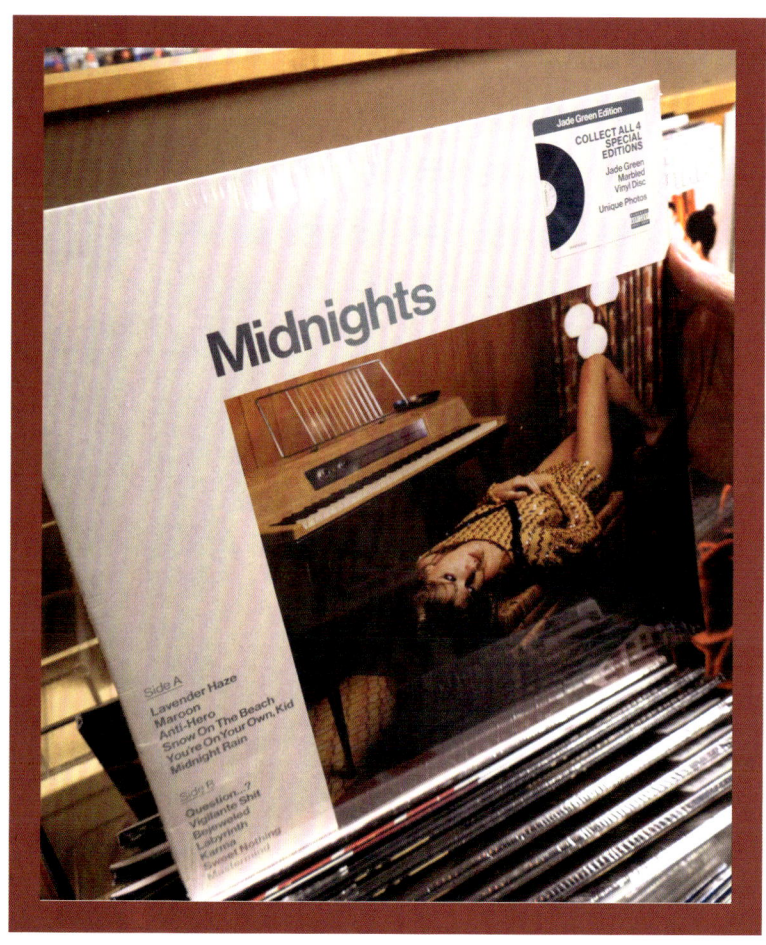

In just one day of record sales, *Midnights* became the top-selling record of the year.

Another Success

The album's first single "Anti-Hero" became an instant cultural success. Spending eight weeks at No. 1 on the Billboard Hot 100, it was the longest-running No. 1 hit of her career at the time. The beginning lyric to the song became a viral trend, with people posting embarrassing moments and mishaps to playfully own up to their chaos with a bit of humor. Celebrities and brands also jumped on to the trend, and it took social media by storm.

The album itself shattered records. *Midnights* was the biggest Spotify streaming debut of all time, with 185 million streams in twenty-four hours. It also boasted the biggest album sales of 2022, selling 1.568 million copies in the first week. It was the fastest-selling album of Taylor's career, and she was the first artist to ever occupy all top ten spots on the Billboard Hot 100.

On November 1, 2022, just days after *Midnights* shattered records, Taylor officially announced The Eras Tour, her first stadium tour in nearly five years. The announcement, made via social media, immediately sent fans into a frenzy, marking the beginning of what would become one of the biggest tours in music history.

Taylor posted a photo of the tour poster that included a mix of iconic photos and colors reminiscent of her ten studio albums. She then shared, "I'm enchanted to announce my next tour: Taylor Swift | The Eras Tour, a journey through the musical eras of my career (past and present!)."

ABOVE: *Midnights* had four versions, each with a different album cover, sleeve, eight-page lyric booklet, and vinyl color.

Ticketmaster Fiasco

Within minutes, The Eras Tour was trending worldwide. A few weeks later, the ticket-sale process became a historic event itself, with Ticketmaster's presale crashing due to overwhelming demand. Unable to get tickets, many fans were upset and united against Ticketmaster. Taylor even took to social media to address the issue.

She wrote, "Well. It goes without saying that I'm extremely protective of my fans. We've been doing this for decades together and over the years, I've brought so many elements of my career in-house. I've done this SPECIFICALLY to improve the quality of my fans' experience by doing it myself with my team who care as much about my fans as I do. It's really difficult for me to trust an outside entity with these relationships and loyalties, and excruciating for me to just watch mistakes happen with no recourse. There are a multitude of reasons why people had such a hard time trying to get tickets, and I'm trying to figure out how this situation can be improved moving forward. I'm not going to make excuses for anyone because we asked them, multiple times, if they could handle this kind of demand, and we were assured they could. It's truly amazing that

The First Fans Act

During the verified fan presale for The Eras Tour, Ticketmaster's website crashed due to the high demand, leaving many fans frozen in queues or logged out entirely.

THE NUMBERS

There were 2.6 million seats for the tour. There were 3.5 million people registered for the verified fan presale program, of which 1.5 million received a presale code. However, due to scalper bots and website visits, a reported 3.5 billion user requests led to the crash.

THE RESPONSE

The outrage led to lawsuits and bills being put forward, including the "Fans First Act," which is a bipartisan bill to help reform the live-event ticketing system.

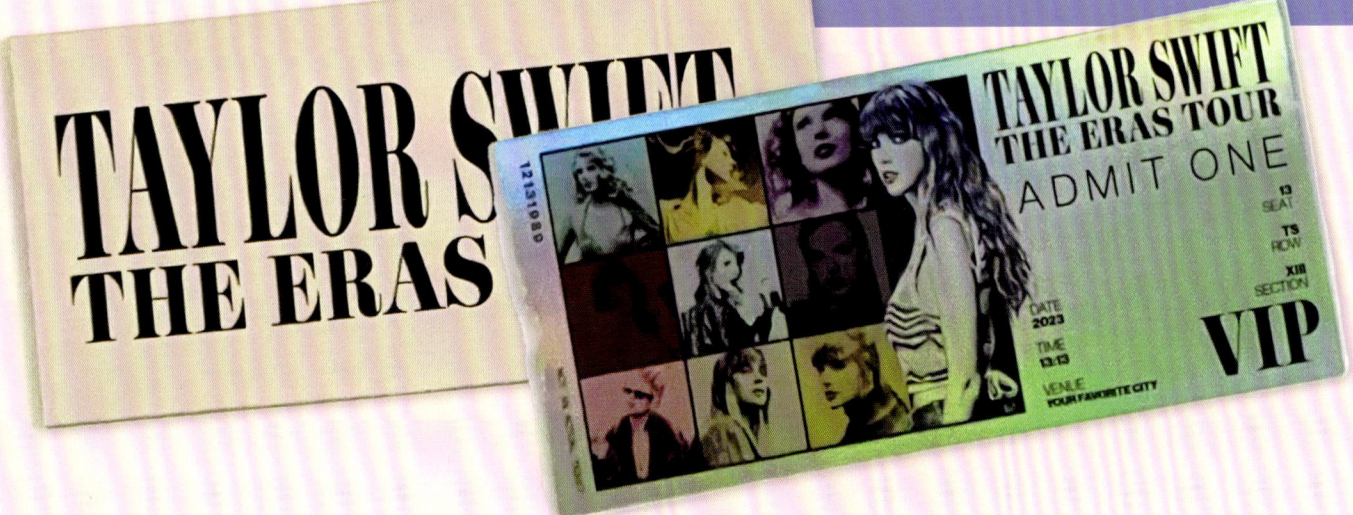

CHANGING FOR THE BETTER

As a songwriter, words matter to Taylor. As societal conversations around inclusivity and sensitivity have evolved, Taylor has demonstrated her own growth and willingness to reflect, listen, and revise when necessary.

The song "Picture to Burn," featured on her debut album, contained a lyric that, at the time, was intended as a dismissive, teenage burn but was later recognized as problematic for using queerness as an insult. While Taylor did not publicly announce the change, in later editions of the song, she adjusted the lyrics to remove the reference altogether.

Another notable change was on the release of *Speak Now (Taylor's Version)*. One of the lyrics in the song "Better Than Revenge" was often criticized for its misogynistic undertones and slut-shaming. For the new version, Taylor changed the lyrics so that she kept the spirit of the song intact without those previous undertones.

Even though she wrote both songs as a teenager, Taylor showed her fans her commitment to changing for the better and ensured that her music reflects her values by making these subtle, but impactful, changes.

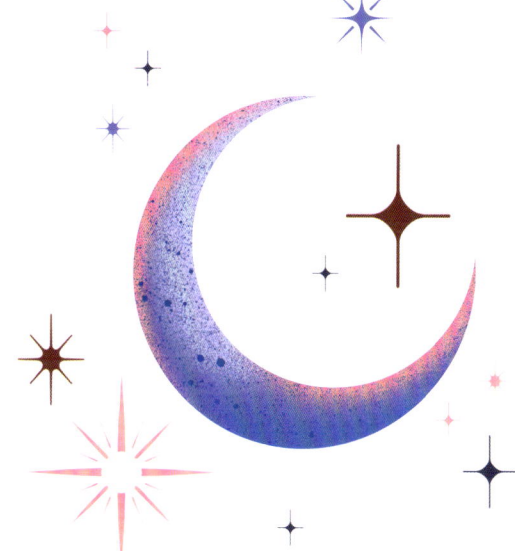

2.4 million people got tickets, but it really pisses me off that a lot of them feel like they went through several bear attacks to get them. And to those who didn't get tickets, all I can say is that my hope is to provide more opportunities for us to all get together and sing these songs. Thank you for wanting to be there. You have no idea how much that means."

Because of Ticketmaster's mishandling of the launch, many Swifties filed lawsuits against Ticketmaster, accusing them of fraud, antitrust violations, and price gouging. Even the US Department of Justice began investigating Live Nation's monopoly over the live-events industry. Despite the setbacks at the start, The Eras Tour sold more than 2.4 million tickets on its first day of presales, making it the largest ticket sale for an artist in a single day in history.

FOLLOWING PAGES:
Next stop, Argentia:
The Eras Tour at
the Estadio Mas
Monumental Antonio
Vespucio Liberti,
Buenos Aires,
November 9, 2023.

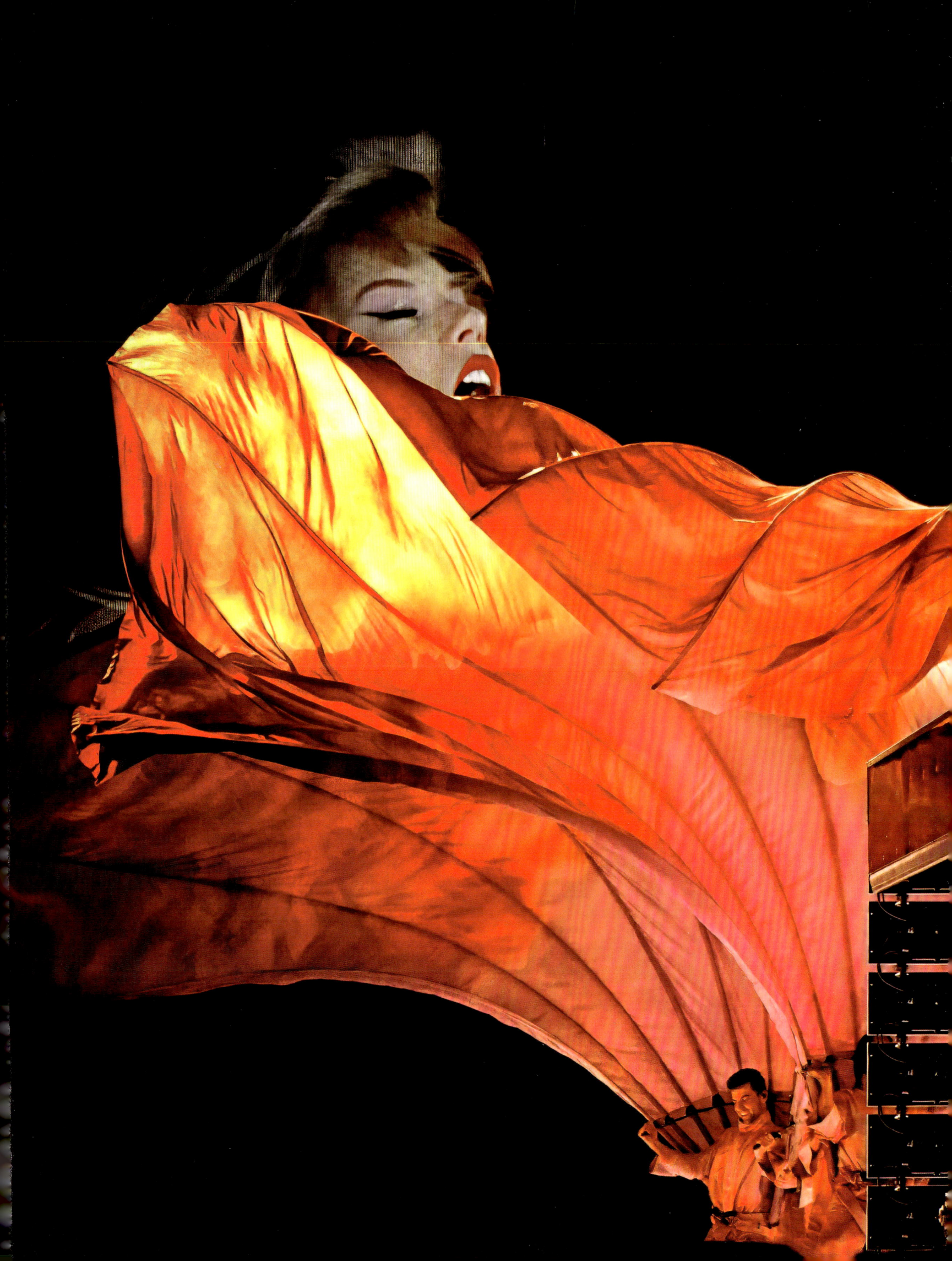

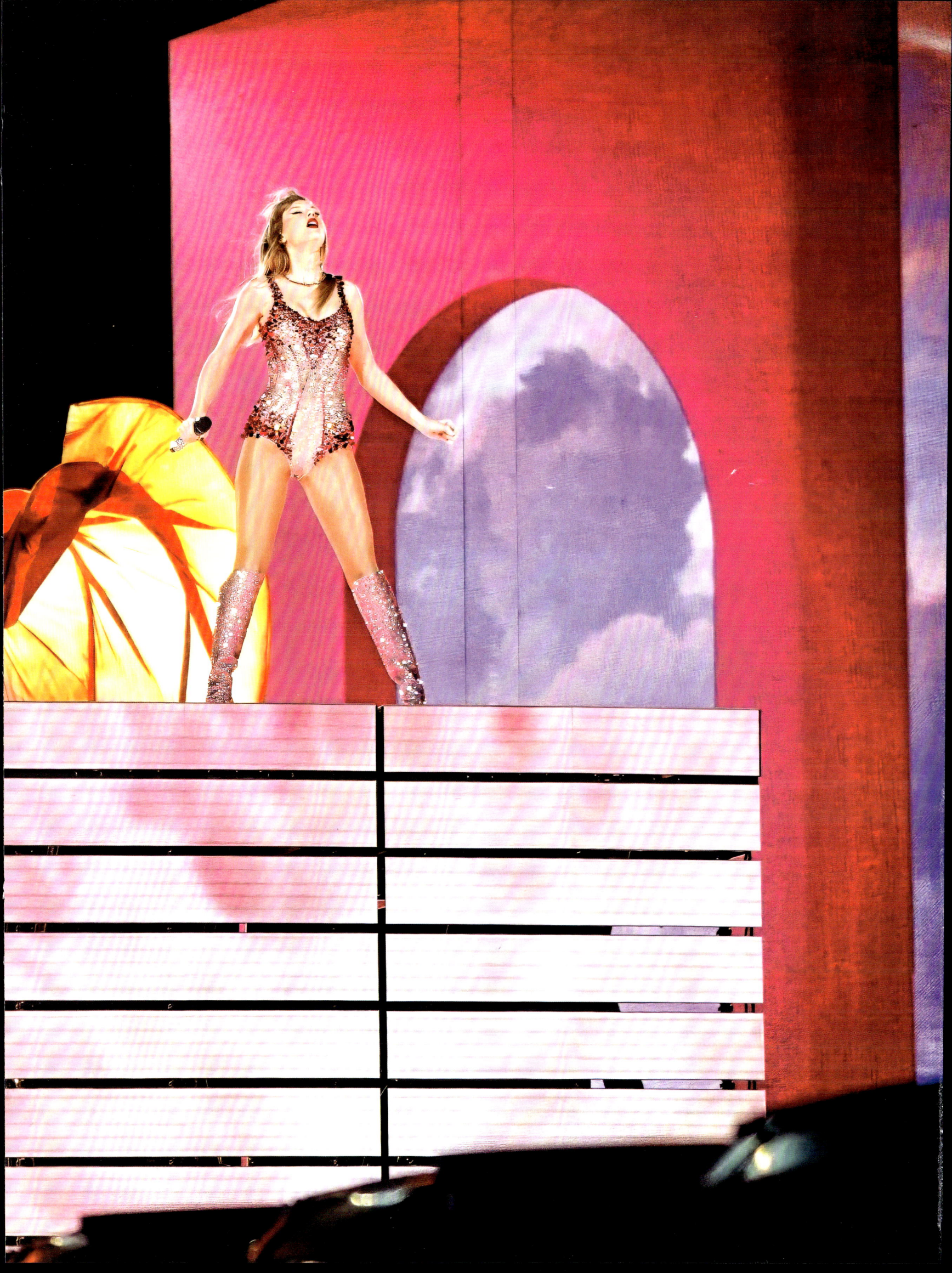

THE "22" HAT

One of the most heartwarming traditions on The Eras Tour took place during the *Red* performance on the song "22." At every tour stop, Taylor and her team choose a special fan from the audience to receive her black fedora hat, reminiscent of the one she wore in the "22" music video. The tradition quickly became one of the most anticipated parts of the show, with fans wondering each night who would be the lucky recipient.

Taylor would sing and dance to the end of the stage, where the lucky recipient was waiting. Many times, the recipient gave Taylor a friendship bracelet and Taylor put the hat on them, giving hugs and high-fives. Some of the recipients were young Swifties attending their first concert, while others had special connections to Taylor throughout the years. Some of the "22" hat recipients include:

- Mikael Arellano: the creator of the "bejeweled strut."
- Scarlett Oliver: a nine-year-old from Australia who was battling an aggressive brain cancer.
- Bianka Bryant: Kobe Bryant's daughter. Kobe talked about his respect for Taylor and even presented her with a "champion" banner at the Staples Center in Los Angeles during The 1989 World Tour to celebrate Taylor for having sixteen sold-out shows there.
- Eloise: Eloise's mother, Cindy, is a huge Swiftie. And in 2017, Taylor "tay-lurked" on one of Cindy's livestream videos during which she introduced her newborn, Eloise. On the livestream, Taylor commented, "She's a tiny baby and I will totally meet her and A when they're not three months old and jus tryna GET SOME REST." Taylor made good on that promise, inviting Eloise to receive the "22" hat. Taylor could even be seen onstage during the moment saying, "I knew you since you were a baby."

The "22" hat giveaway highlights Taylor's deep connection with her fans. While The Eras Tour was a massive, record-breaking tour in huge stadiums, this small, personal gesture was Taylor's way of remaining close to her fans and giving them something special each night.

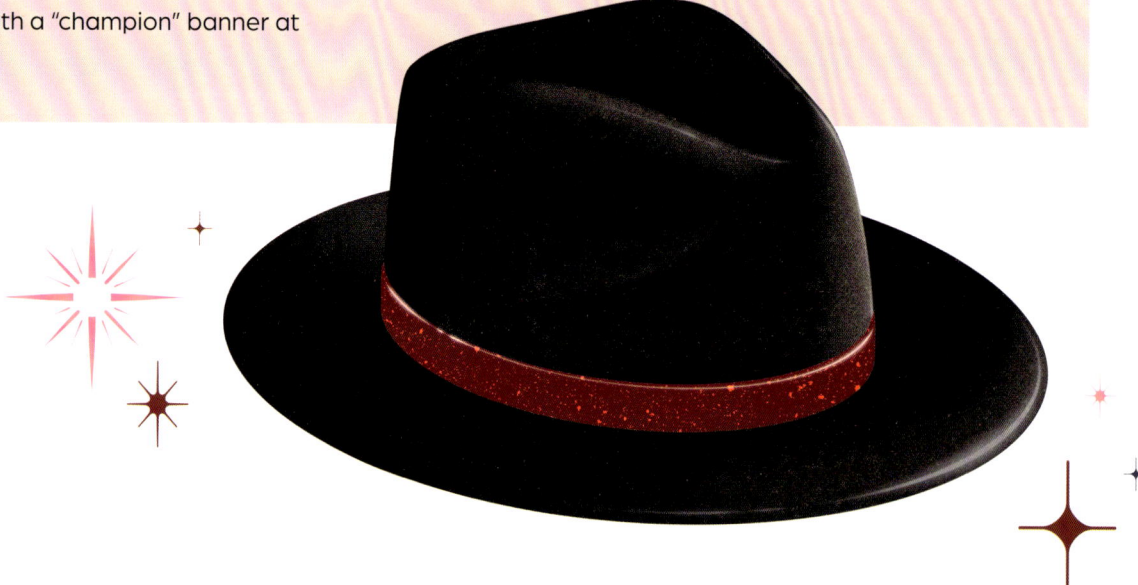

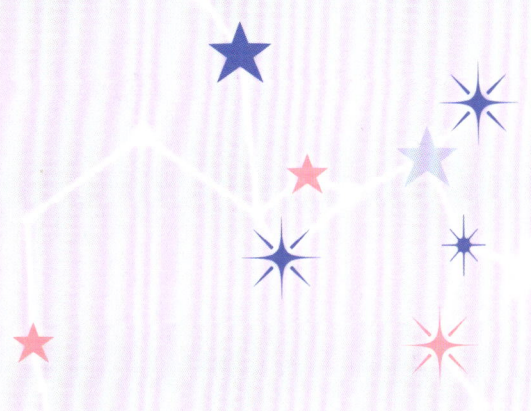

"I'm a Sagittarius, and it says one of our major qualities is that we're blindly optimistic."

Taylor, 2021

The Eras Tour

The Eras Tour officially kicked off on March 17, 2023, in Glendale, Arizona (temporarily renamed "Swift City" for the occasion). It marked the beginning of one of the most ambitious, record-breaking, and culturally significant tours in music history. Designed as a retrospective of Taylor's nearly two-decade-long career, the tour was a love letter to her fans, celebrating every musical era she had ever created.

From the very first show, it was clear that The Eras Tour was unlike anything Taylor had ever done before. The set list was an unprecedented three-and-a-half hours long and featured more than forty songs spanning ten albums, with each section dedicated to a different "era" of her career. The visual storytelling, elaborate costume changes, and massive stage production transformed stadiums into immersive worlds. One moment evoked the whimsical forests of *folklore;* the next flashing neon for *1989;* and then she shifted into the dark, futuristic aesthetic of *reputation.*

Fans played a huge role in making the tour an experience beyond just the music.

A tradition of trading friendship bracelets, inspired by a lyric from "You're on Your Own, Kid," swept through every venue, turning concerts into community-building events. Attendees dressed up as their favorite Taylor era, and the crowds roared so loudly that seismologists recorded earthquake-like activity in Seattle. In many cities, thousands of fans without tickets would take seats outside the venues to listen to the concert and sing and dance along with other Swifties in an event known as "Taylor-gating." At a tour stop in Munich, Germany, it was estimated that fifty thousand fans listened to the show from a hillside outside the stadium.

Taylor added to the excitement each night by introducing "The Acoustic Set," during which she would play two surprise acoustic songs, one on guitar and one on piano, and she aimed to play a different song every night. Eventually she let go of that rule and started doing mash-ups of multiple songs, including some repeat songs.

Beyond the music, the economic and cultural impact of the tour was staggering. The tour

WHEN CONFETTI FALLS TO THE GROUND

When confetti falls to the ground at her concert or comes out of a package from an order from her store, Swifties delight in the extra detail that Taylor puts into something as tiny as confetti. Many fans collect their confetti as a keepsake to represent concerts attended, merchandise ordered, and memories created.

One of the most iconic pieces of confetti came about during the Reputation Stadium Tour, where Taylor dropped confetti that looked like a tabloid newspaper reminiscent of the imagery in the *reputation* era. She included moon and star confetti in *Midnights* packages, butterfly and flower confetti in *Lover* mail, and autumn leaves during the *Red (Taylor's Version)* release. For several years between tours, this confetti served as a reminder to Swifties that confetti would fall to the ground in a stadium again soon.

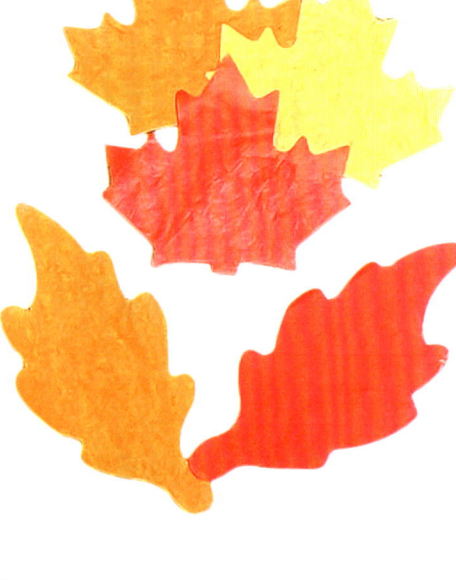

shattered records at every turn. It became the highest-grossing tour of all time, eventually surpassing $2 billion in revenue. Fans traveled from around the world, spending thousands on tickets, hotels, and outfits and boosting local economies at every stop. In the United States alone, it was estimated that the tour contributed billions of dollars to the economy. Politicians and businesses alike acknowledged its influence, with even the Federal Reserve Board citing The Eras Tour as a factor in consumer spending surges.

While the tour was off to a strong start, fans noticed that Taylor's long-term boyfriend, Joe Alwyn, was missing from the debut shows. People started speculating. On April 8, 2023, it was announced that the two split amicably, marking the end of their six-year relationship—a romance largely defined by its privacy. Of course, Swifties quickly noticed that Taylor had made a subtle but noticeable change to The Eras Tour set list. A week before the announcement, Taylor swapped out the love song "invisible string" and replaced it with "the 1," a breakup song, leading to speculation that the breakup had occurred earlier than publicly revealed.

Taylor used The Eras Tour stage not only to make subtle statements through her own grief, but also as a way to share jokes, stories, and even surprises. During the tour, she announced the re-recordings of *Speak Now (Taylor's Version)* and *1989 (Taylor's Version)*. Taylor announced *Speak Now (Taylor's Version)* on May 5, 2023, during a stop on The Eras Tour in Nashville, Tennessee. During the surprise acoustic set, she told the audience she had been planning something for a while

and said "You know how I love to surprise you with the things that I've been planning. It's my love language with you. I think rather than me speaking about it, I thought I would just show you." She then directed the crowd to look at the screen behind her, where the album cover and release date (July 7, 2023) of *Speak Now (Taylor's Version)* were revealed.

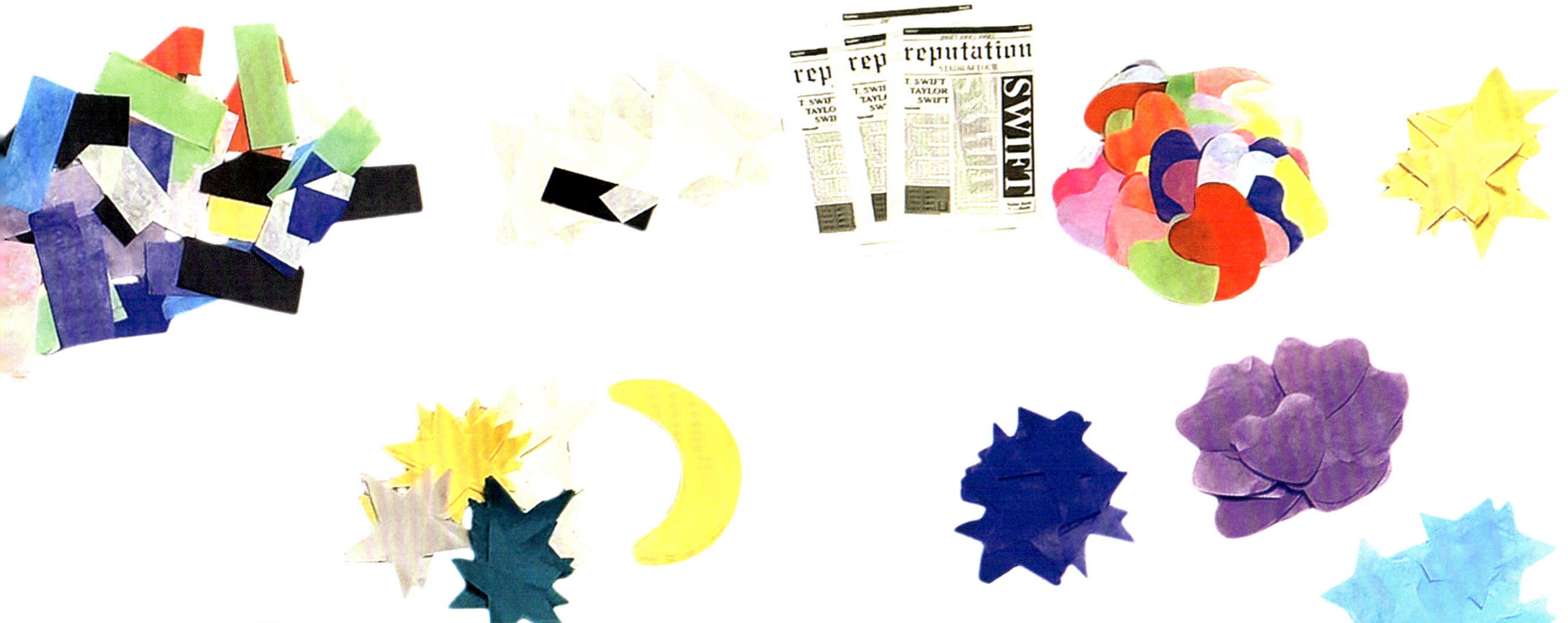

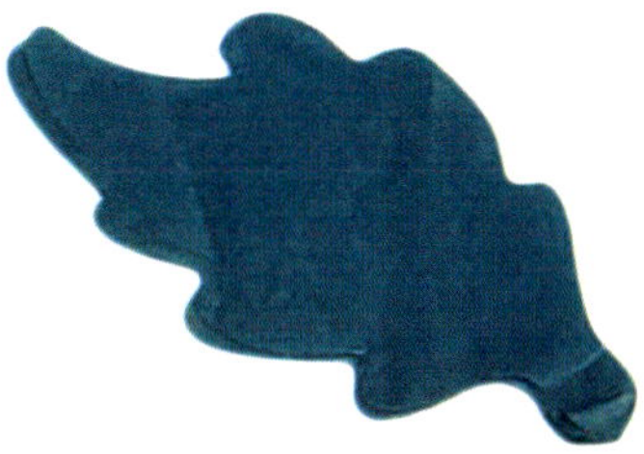

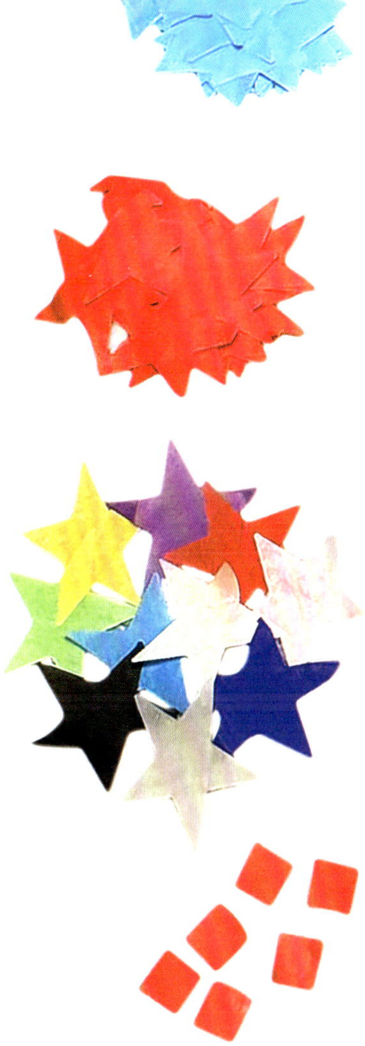

Speak Now (Taylor's Version) featured twenty-two tracks, including six previously unreleased "From the Vault" songs written during the original *Speak Now* era that didn't make the final cut. Among them were collaborations, like with Fall Out Boy on "Electric Touch" and Hayley Williams of Paramore on "Castles Crumbling," highlighting Taylor's deep-rooted love for pop-punk influences that shaped her during that time.

The first promotional single "I Can See You (Taylor's Version)" (From the Vault) was released alongside a music video starring Joey King, Taylor Lautner, and Presley Cash, all of whom had connections to Taylor's past. The three were invited onstage for the music video premiere

during The Eras Tour stop in Kansas City. Taylor Lautner even famously performed a series of backflips onstage.

Speak Now (Taylor's Version) was an instant success, debuting at No. 1 on the Billboard 200, with more than 716,000 album-equivalent units. It became Taylor's twelfth No. 1 album, surpassing Barbra Streisand for the most No. 1 albums by a female artist. The album broke streaming records, with Spotify reporting it as the most-streamed album in a single day in 2023 upon its release.

Since this album was completely self-written and included deeply personal themes, Taylor reminded fans to practice kindness before the album's release. During a surprise set on The Eras Tour, before playing the song "Dear John," rumored to be about John Mayer, Taylor said, "I'm putting this album out because I want to own my music, and I believe that any artist who has the desire to own their music should be able to." She continued, "I'm 33 years old. I don't care about anything that happened to me when I was 19 except the songs I wrote and the memories we made together. So what I'm trying to tell you is that I'm not putting this album out so that you can go and feel the need to defend me on the internet against someone you think I might have written a song about 14 billion years ago when I was 19."

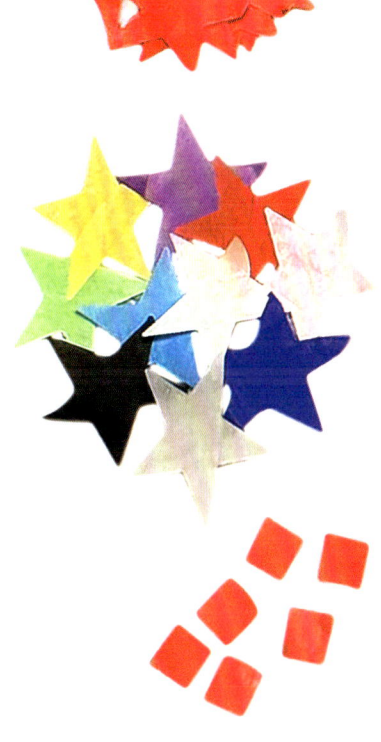

ABOVE: The eras of keepsakes: a collection of confetti from Taylor's tours.

THE TAYLOR EFFECT

The "Taylor Effect" refers to the massive cultural, economic, and industry-shaping impact of Taylor Swift. Whether it's boosting local economies, breaking streaming records, influencing political engagement, or shifting industry norms, Taylor's presence creates ripple effects far beyond music.

Here are just some of the effects she has had:

- The economic Eras boom: Perhaps the most visible example of the "Taylor Effect" is the financial windfall cities experience when she arrives. The Eras Tour became an economic powerhouse, generating an estimated more than $2 billion in global revenue and giving cities a tourism boost. In the United States, her 2023 shows alone contributed an estimated $4.6 billion to the economy.

- The music industry: Taylor completely changed the game for artists' rights with her stances against Spotify and Apple and with her decision to re-record her old albums and own the rights to her work. Her success has influenced younger artists to renegotiate contracts, own their masters, and re-record their own music to maintain control of their art.

- The political impact: In 2018, when Taylor broke her political silence and encouraged fans to vote, Vote.org reported that 65,000 Americans between the ages of eighteen and twenty-nine registered to vote, and just a few days later, it jumped to 102,000. In 2023, when she encouraged fans to register to vote again, the website Vote.org saw a 1,226 percent spike in registrations in a single day.

- Small-business impact: From the posture-correcting bra Forme that Taylor was seen wearing at The Eras Tour rehearsals to the glitter freckles by Fazit that Taylor sported during a Chiefs game, Taylor embraces indie brands and small businesses, often wearing products for dinners out or at football games. Many of these small businesses are women-owned and have seen significant sales, often selling out their products in minutes.

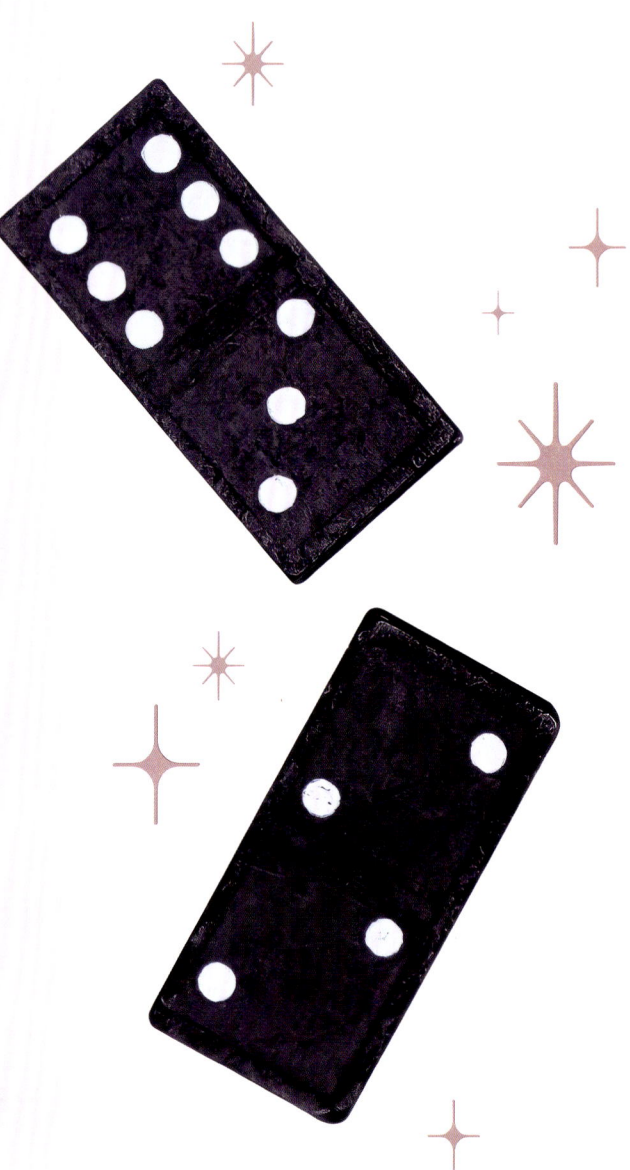

A New Era for *1989*

Then, just a month after *Speak Now (Taylor's Version)* launched, Taylor surprised fans yet again on the last US show of the first leg of The Eras Tour in Los Angeles, California. During the acoustic set, she thanked fans for being so supportive of Taylor's versions and for making her fight their fight too. She mentioned how the day happened to be the "eighth month" and the "ninth day," and that she'd been planning something for a "ridiculously long time." She said, "I think instead of telling you about it, I think I'll just sort of show you something." She directed fans to a screen behind her and unveiled that *1989 (Taylor's Version)* would be out on October 27, 2023.

This re-recording was arguably one of the most anticipated re-recordings to date,

as *1989* was the album that cemented her transition from country singer to full-fledged pop superstardom. The announcement sent fans into a frenzy, especially when Swift teased that the album would include five previously unreleased "From the Vault" tracks.

The album release leaned into the aesthetic of the *1989* era. Special edition vinyls in pastel colors of blue, rose garden pink, aquamarine green, and Sunrise Boulevard yellow were released in limited quantities. The marketing campaign also included a Google vault puzzle challenge. Fans had to collectively solve thirty-three million puzzles to unlock the titles of the unreleased tracks. Swifties were able to complete this in just a matter of hours.

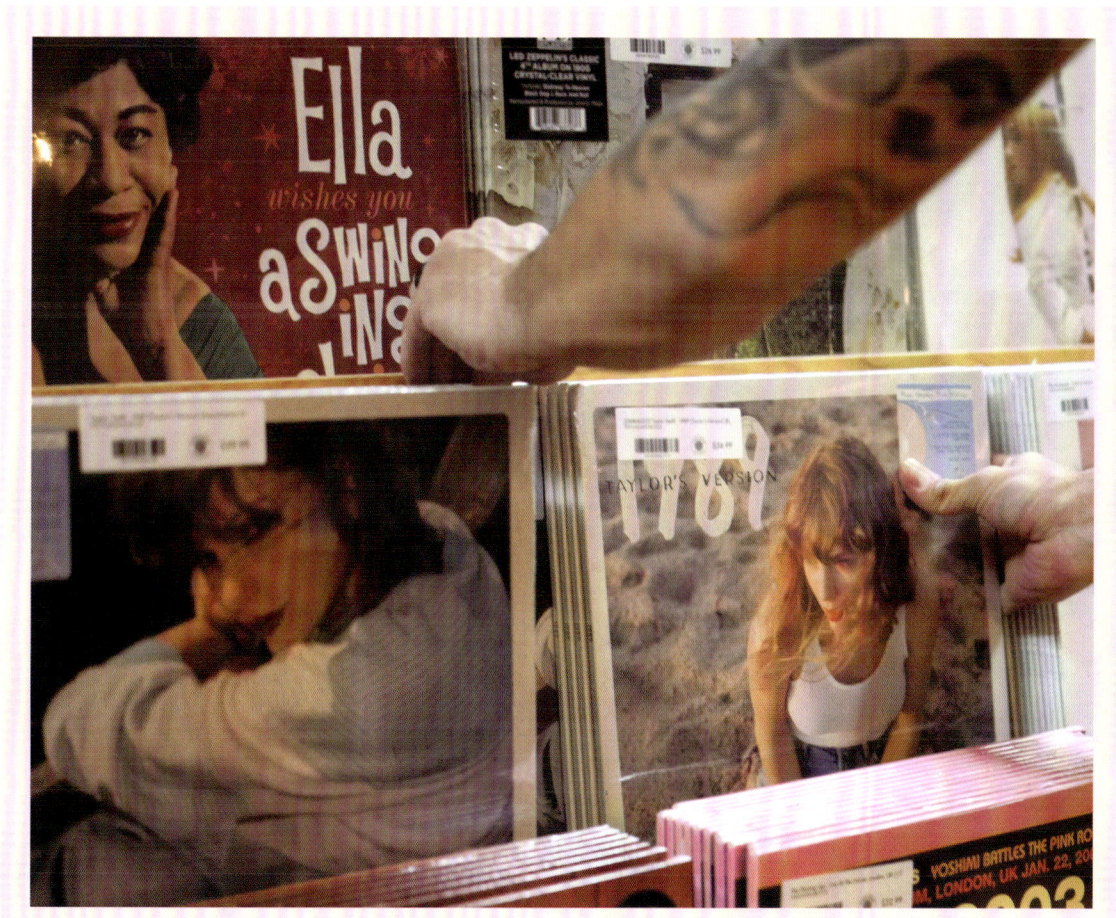

LEFT: An employee of Plaid Room Records in Loveland, Ohio, stocks the bins with *1989 (Taylor's Version)*, October 27, 2023.

1989 (Taylor's Version) was a massive commercial success, debuting at No. 1 on the Billboard 200 with 1.653 million album-equivalent units, making it Taylor's biggest album debut ever. It broke Spotify's record for the most-streamed album in a single day in 2023 and made Taylor the first artist to occupy the entire top ten of the Billboard Hot 100 twice, thanks to the popularity of the "From the Vault" tracks.

To wrap up an incredible year, Taylor surprised fans yet again, announcing that *Taylor Swift: The Eras Tour* movie would be coming to theaters on October 13, 2023. Now fans who didn't have the opportunity to score tickets could still experience the show.

The film also proved to be a savvy business move. Taylor worked directly with AMC Theatres for distribution, essentially cutting out the middlemen. This move allowed her to release the film exactly as she wanted and meant that she could keep more profits. Plus, this decision gave struggling movie theaters an economic boost, as many theaters were still trying to bounce back from the pandemic.

Within twenty-four hours, the film had shattered the record for the biggest first-day presales in AMC history, earning $26 million and surpassing previous record-holder *Spider-Man: No Way Home*. Upon its official release, the movie opened to $92.8 million domestically and $123.5 million globally, making it the highest-grossing concert film debut in history. To date, the film has earned $261.6 million globally. Fans treated screenings like live concerts, dressing up in their favorite Eras Tour outfits, trading friendship bracelets, singing along, and ensuring that they scored the special collectors' popcorn buckets and drink cups that were available during showings.

"I'm feeling very overwhelmed by the fans' love for the record. I'm also feeling, like, very soft and fragile."

Taylor, 2023

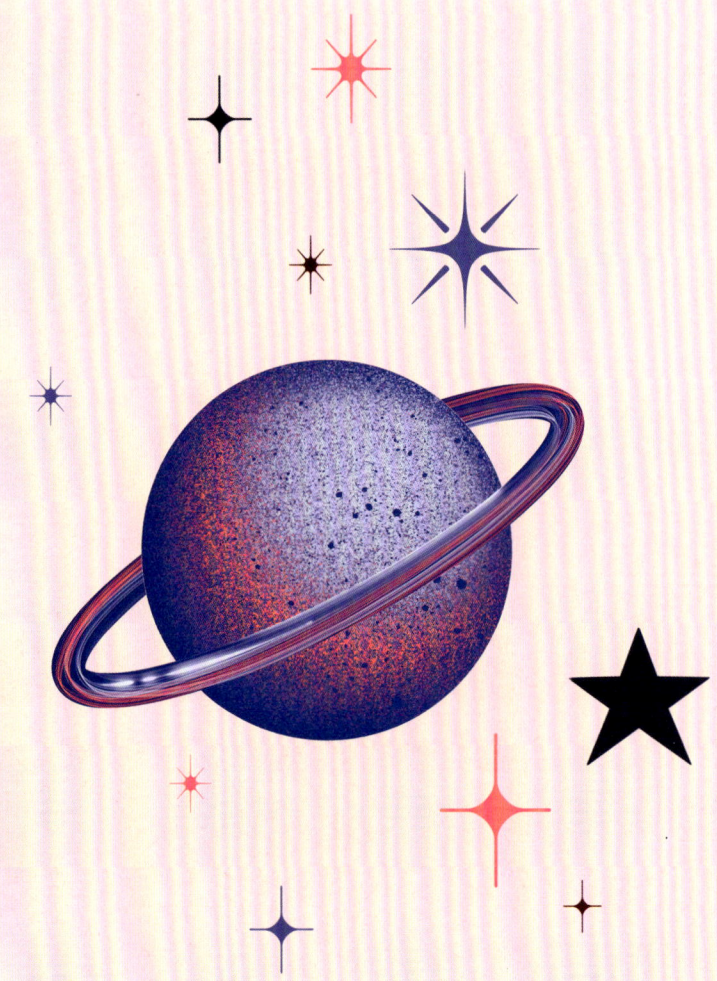

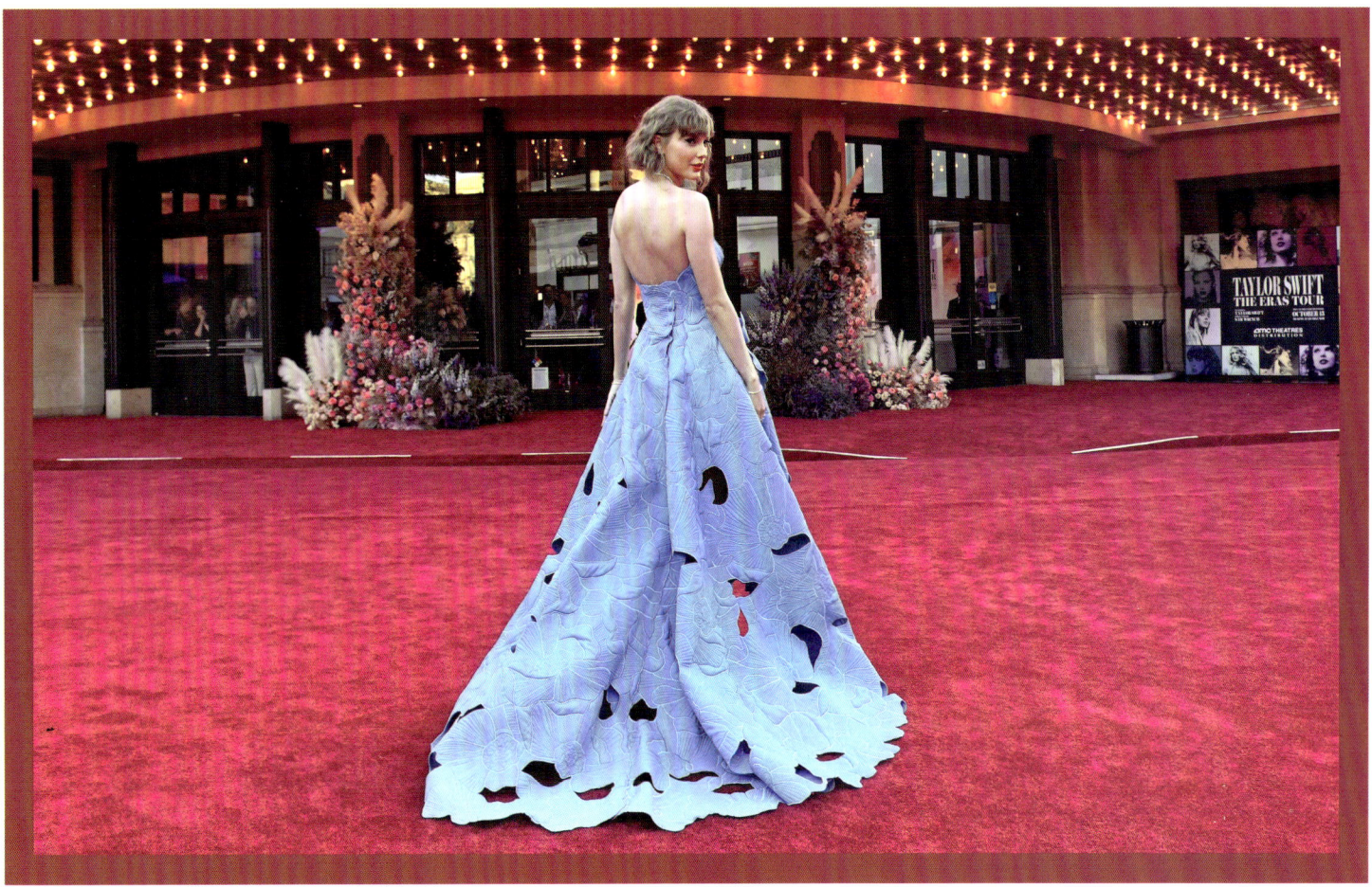

Taylor eventually released the film to the Disney+ streaming service. It included several new songs not featured in the theater version. It became the most streamed music film on their platform at 4.6 million views in the first three days. After seeing the success of Taylor's release, Beyoncé followed suit, partnering with AMC for her Renaissance tour film release. Taylor even showed her support and attended Beyoncé's tour film premiere and posted about it on social media.

With several record-breaking years and the wildly successful The Eras Tour, in December 2023, Taylor was named *Time* Person of the Year. She was recognized for her many groundbreaking achievements and influence in pop culture. *Time* magazine featured a cover story about Taylor, and fans got a deeper look into her challenges and misrepresentations over the years, including her public feuds. The magazine also featured three different covers—most notably, one where Taylor had her cat Benji wrapped around her neck like a scarf.

By the end of 2023, Taylor solidified her place in history as an artist who transcended music to become an icon of empowerment, authenticity, innovation, and kindness. As the year concluded, there was a sense of excitement and anticipation for what would come next—whether it was the ongoing The Eras Tour, new Taylor's versions, a new album, or something else. One thing was certain: Taylor's influence was far from over, and her best eras were yet to come.

ABOVE:
Taylor arriving at the premiere of the concert movie *Taylor Swift: The Eras Tour*, at The Grove in Los Angeles, October 11, 2023.

★ ERAS TOUR ★ BY THE NUMBERS

149 tour dates

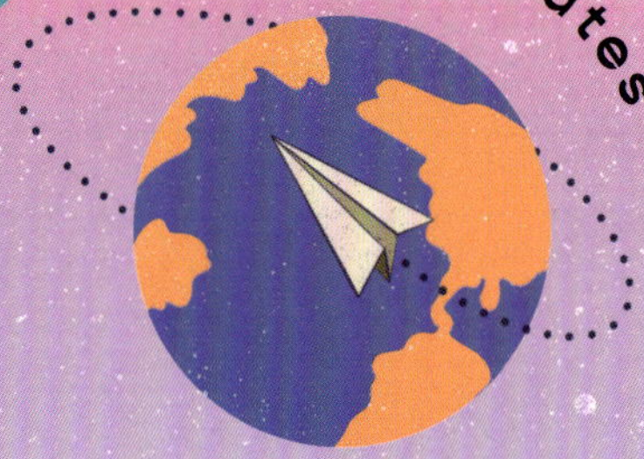

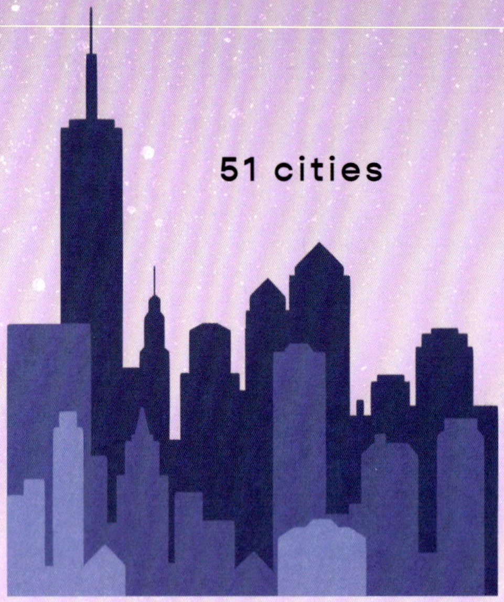

21 countries

51 cities

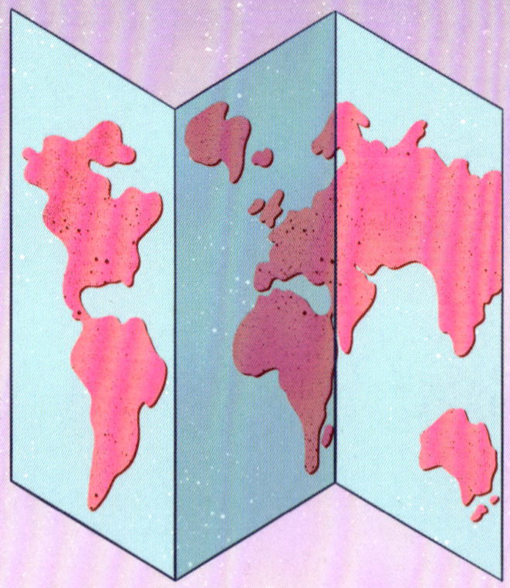

3 canceled shows in Vienna

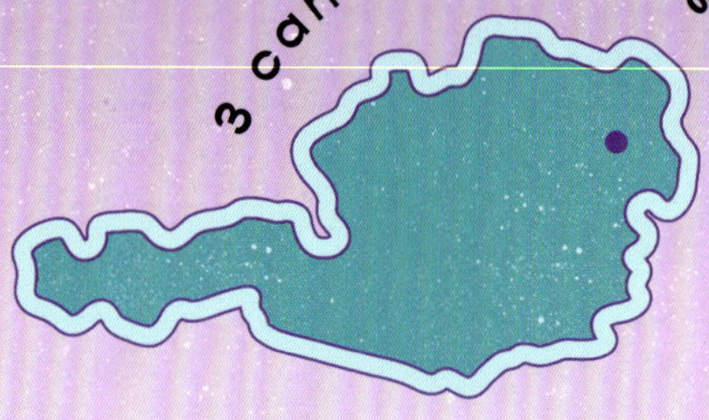

18 opening acts

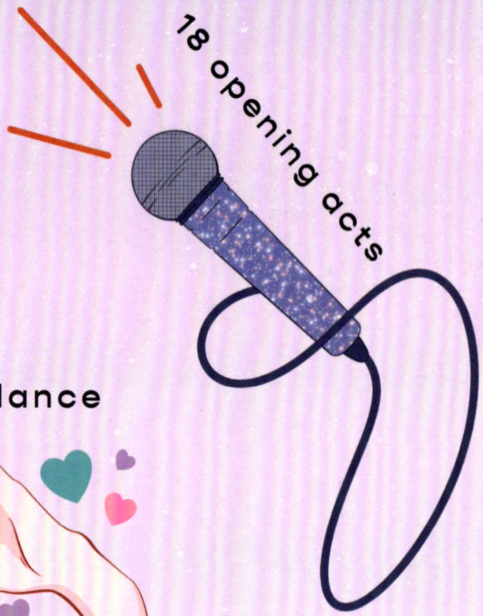

10,168,008 people in attendance

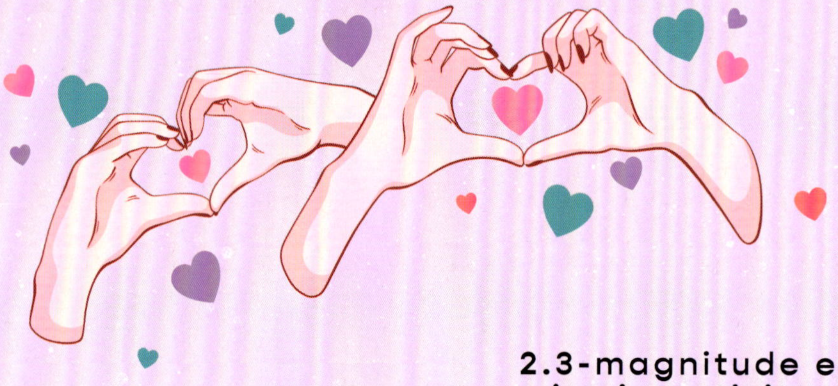

60+ outfits

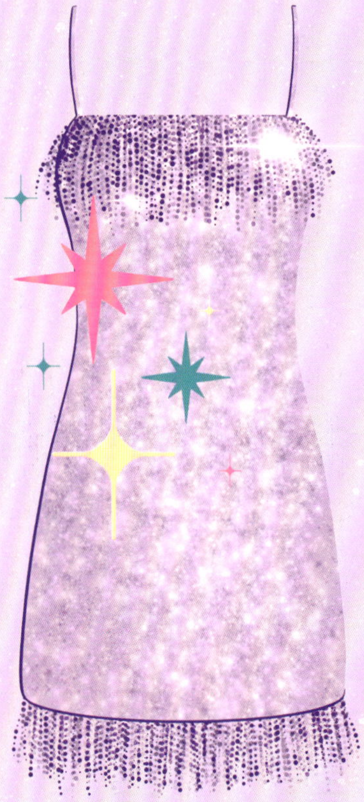

2.3-magnitude earthquake seismic activity recorded in Seattle from fans dancing

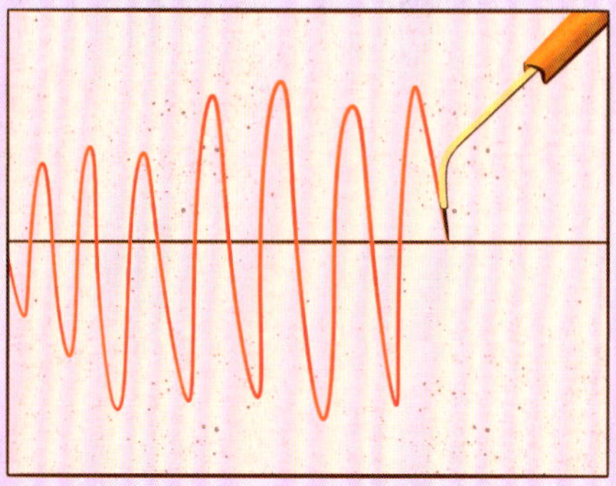

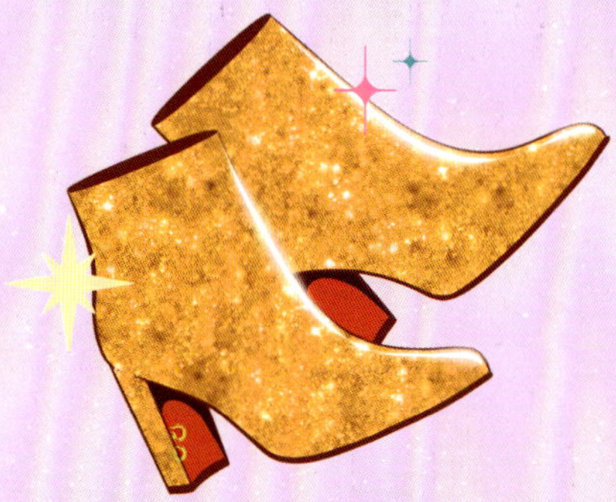

250+ custom shoes

2.9 million tickets sold in first presale

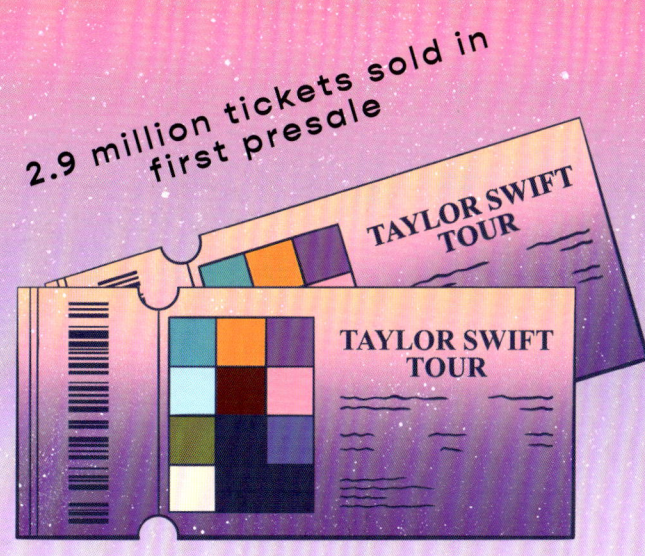

$2 billion in revenue

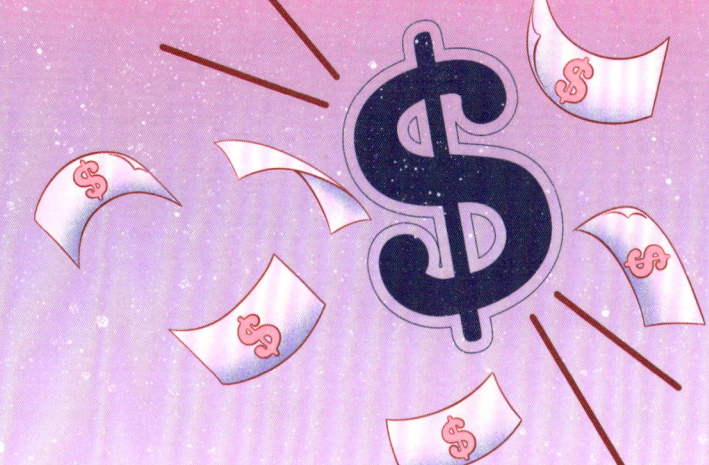

$197 million in bonuses to performers, crew, and staff

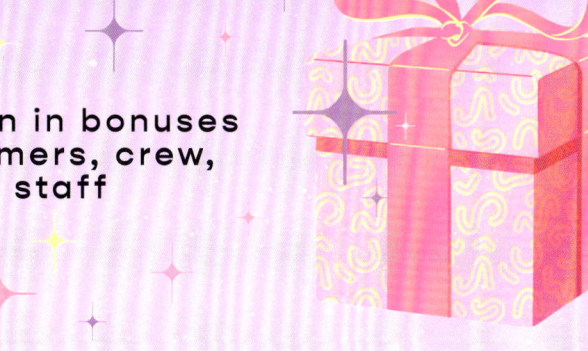

Food bank donations on every stop

96,000 people at the biggest crowd in Melbourne Cricket Ground in Australia

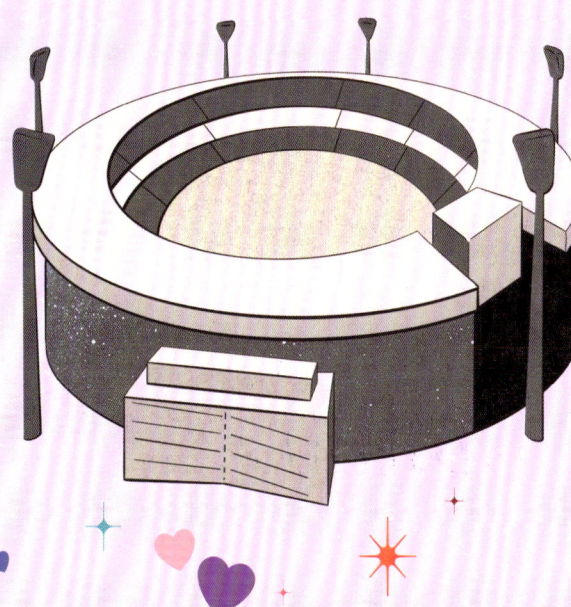

2 Taylor's Version album announcements

Millions of friendship bracelets traded

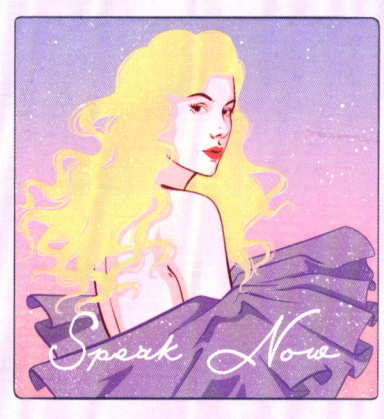

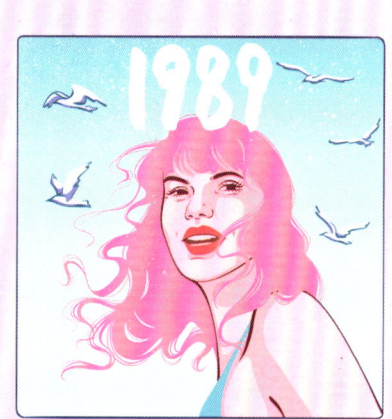

SPEAK NOW (TAYLOR'S VERSION) AND 1989 (TAYLOR'S VERSION)

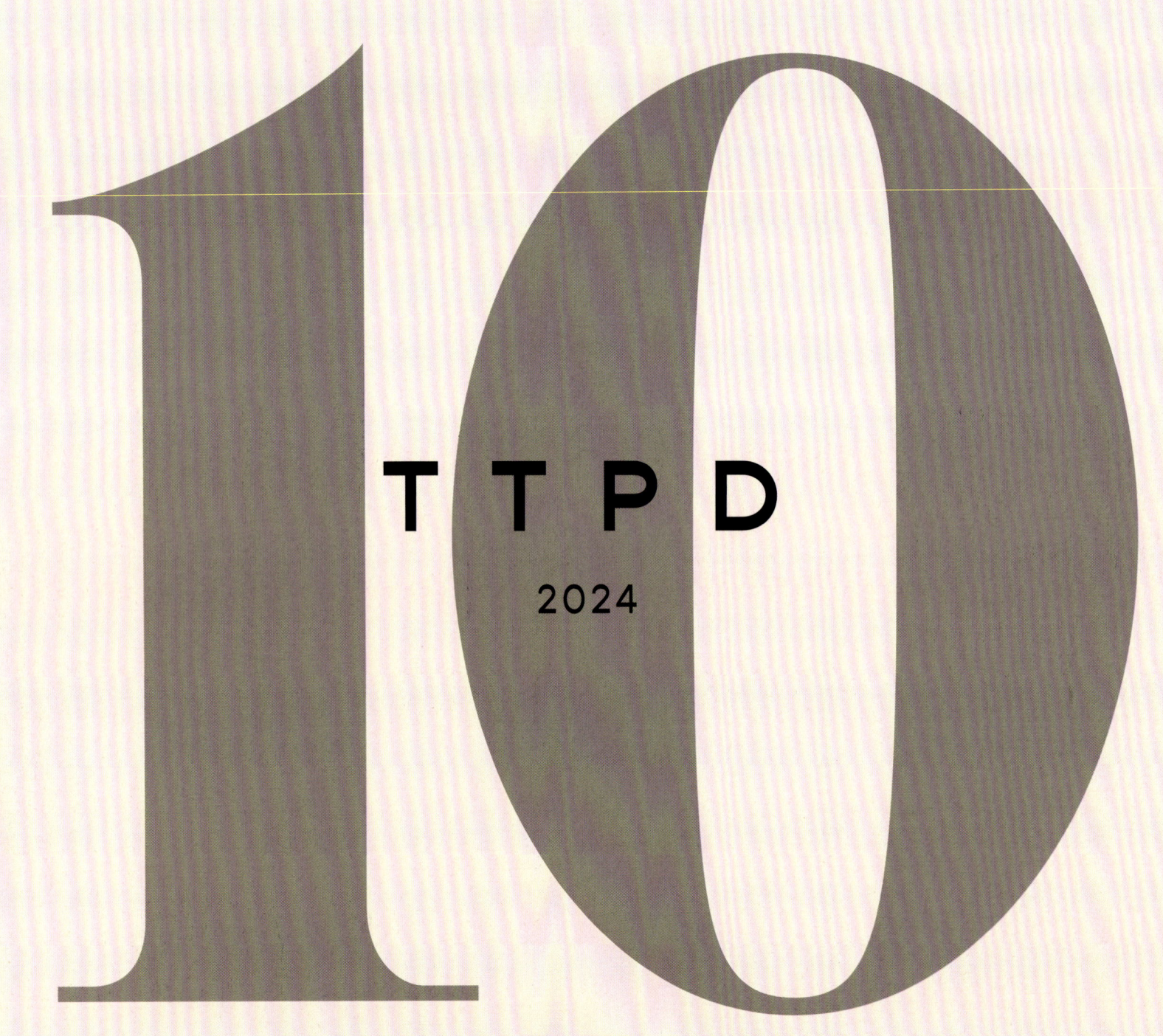

TTPD

2024

EMPATHY IS KIND

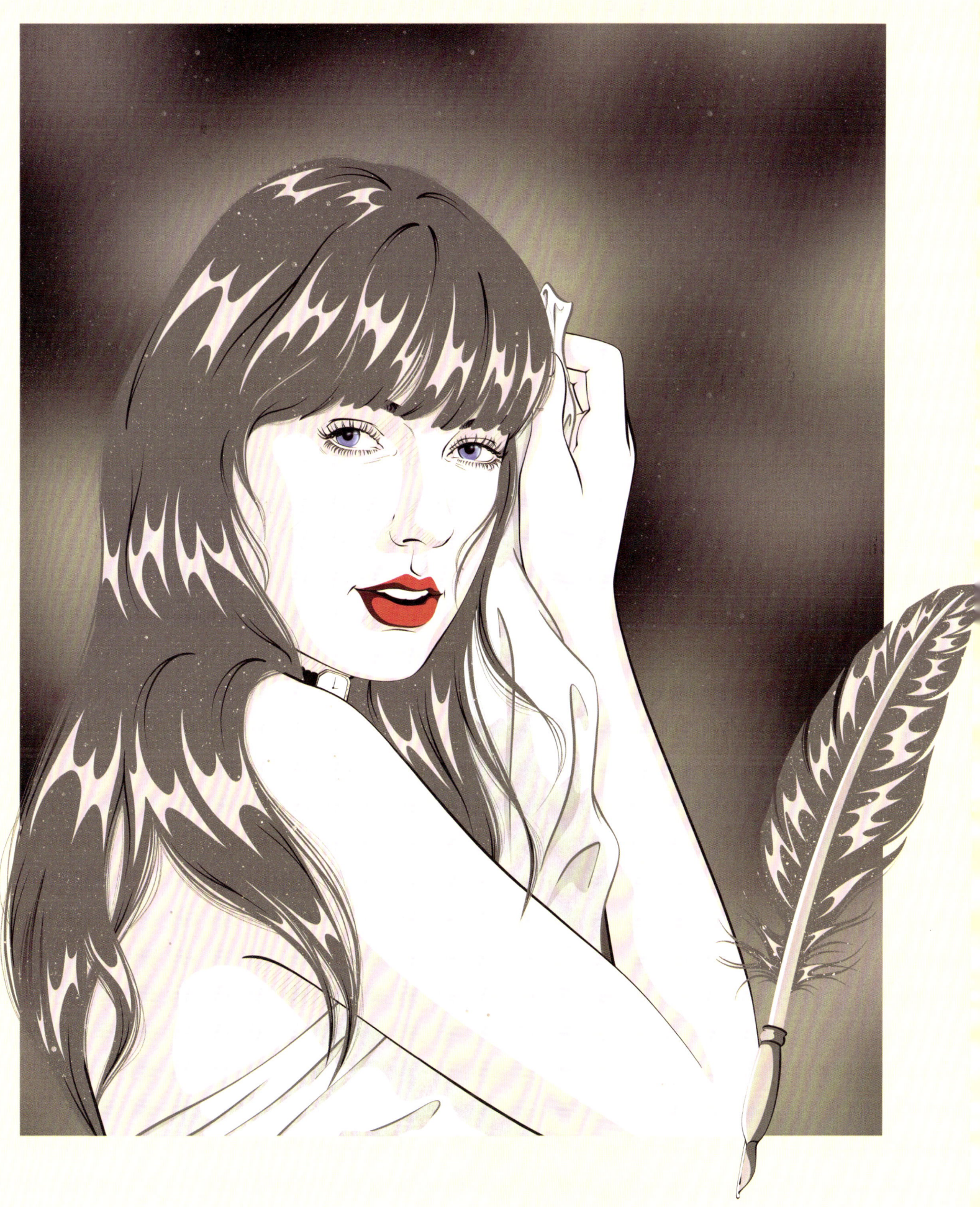

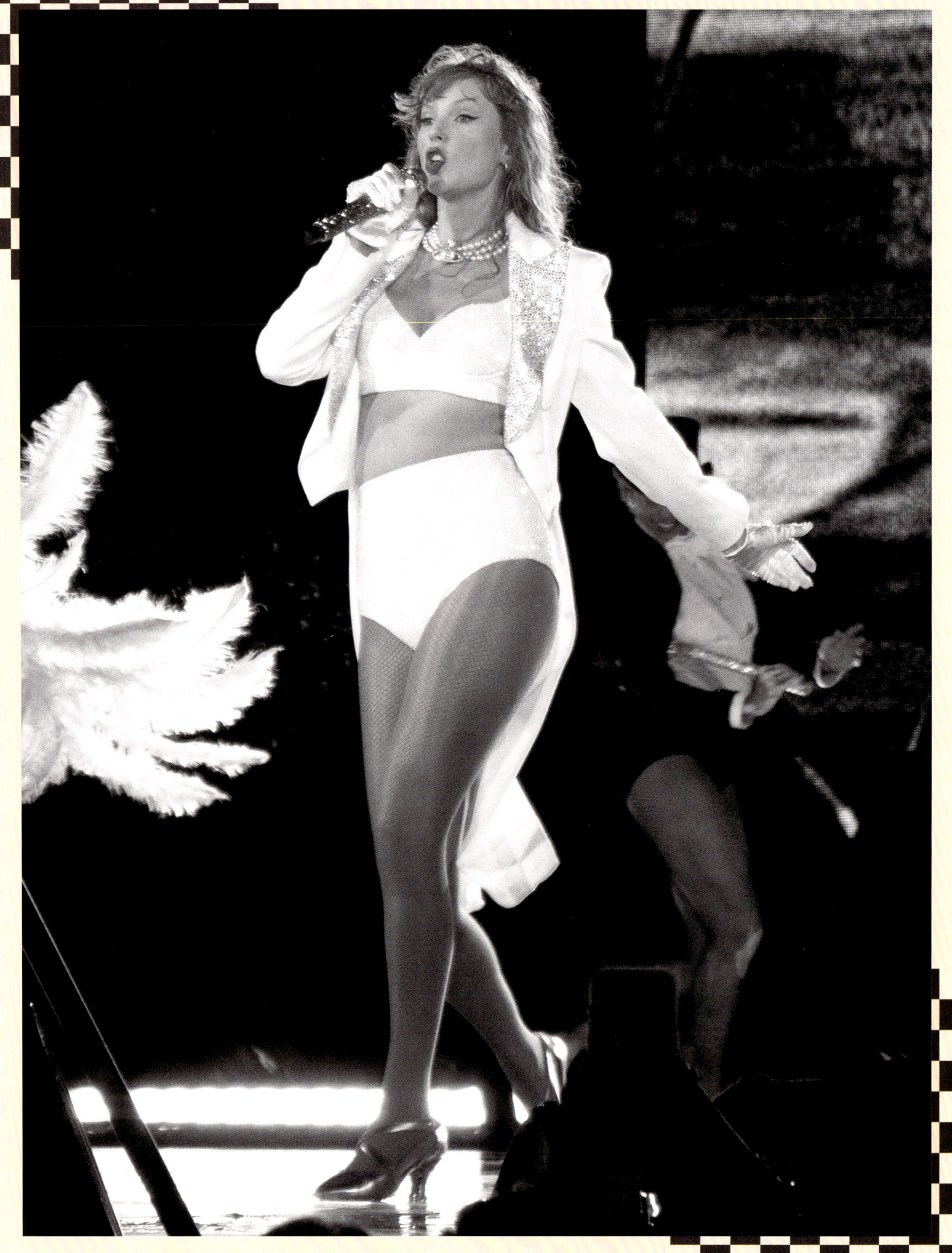

TAYLOR'S POETIC SIDE

This was the era during which Taylor embraced being her most cathartic, vulnerable self, while also embodying her strongest and most empowered self.

Seeing black and white popping up on Taylor's feed, her friends' feeds, and through her outfit choices made fans speculate that the highly anticipated release of *reputation (Taylor's Version)* was going to be announced next. When Taylor showed up to the 66th Grammy Awards on February 4, 2024, wearing a white dress with long black gloves, fans flipped out, thinking this was a nod to the black-and-white imagery found in *reputation*.

Taylor went on to win two Grammys that evening for her album *Midnights*, but that wasn't the only surprise she had in store. During her acceptance speech for Best Pop Vocal Album, Taylor gave fans the plot twist of a lifetime. She took to the stage and said, "OK, this is my thirteenth Grammy, which is my lucky number.

"The hundreds of dumb ideas are what lead me to my good ideas. You have to give yourself permission to fail."

Taylor, 2023

"CLARA BOW"

"Clara Bow" was named after the actress and the first "it girl," Clara Bow, who rose to fame in the 1920s, during the silent film era. She was featured in fifty-seven movies throughout her career and was the face and a sex symbol of the flapper period. With her fame, however, she was both highly praised and widely criticized.

Clara Bow's family responded to the news that there was a song named after their family member. While they were initially nervous of what the song might entail, they were filled with gratitude once they heard it. Nicole Sisneros, the great-granddaughter of Bow's said, "It is hauntingly beautiful the way Taylor uses her songwriting ability and her artistry to draw parallels between Clara's life and her own. It's a really beautiful testament to both of their legacies."

The song also name drops Stevie Nicks, who Taylor has long admired and considers Stevie one of her mentors in the music industry. Stevie wrote a poem that was included in the prologue of *The Tortured Poets Department* physical album copies. It was titled "For T and me..." Stevie has a mutual respect for Taylor saying, "This girl writes the songs that make the whole world sing, like Neil Diamond or Elton John. She sings, she writes, she performs, she plays great guitar."

Featuring these women was intentional as the song was inspired by how Taylor felt the industry treats women. Reflecting on the inspiration for the song in an Apple Music exclusive Taylor said,

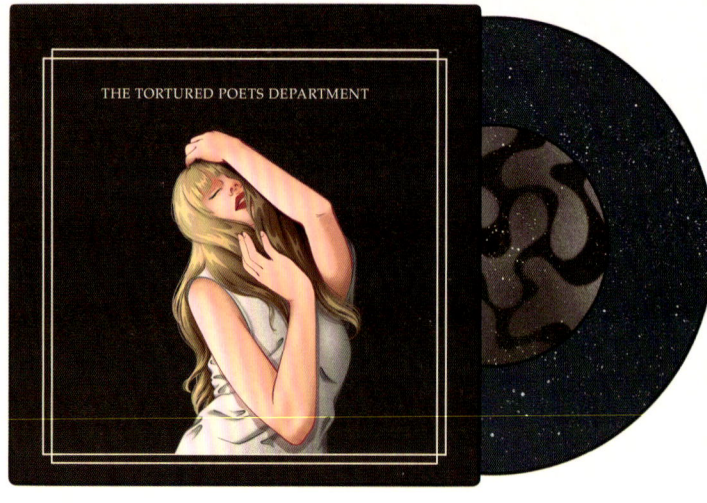

ALBUM
The Tortured Poets Department

DATE LAUNCHED
April 19, 2024

FIRST SINGLE
"Fortnight"

OTHER SINGLES
"I Can Do It with a Broken Heart" and "Clara Bow"

TOUR
The Eras Tour

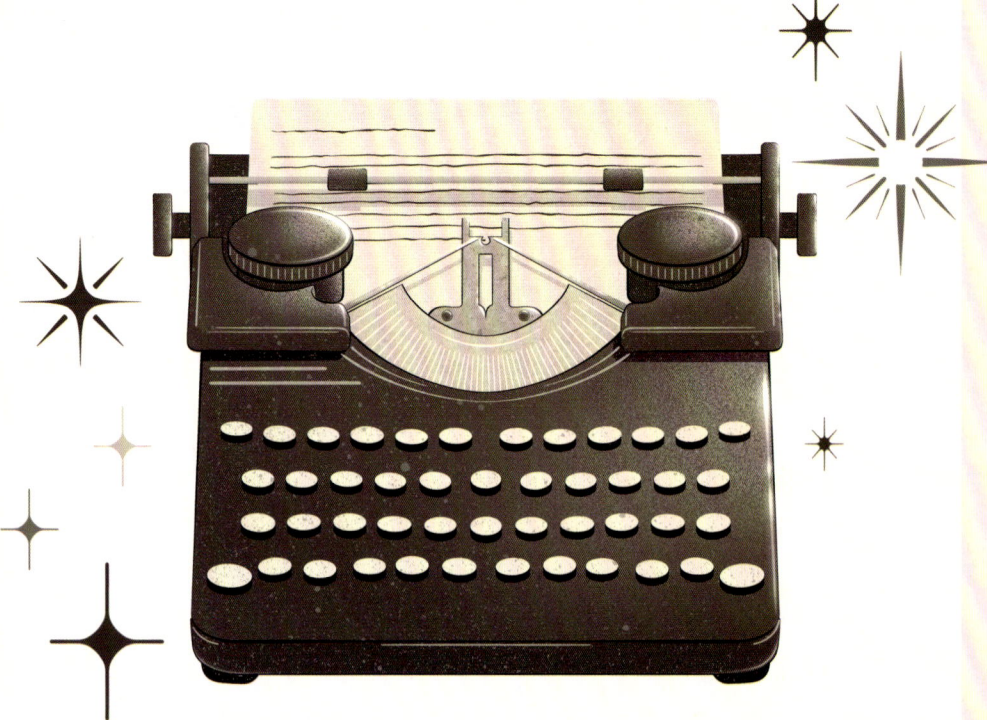

"I used to sit in record labels trying to get a record deal when I was a little kid. And they'd say, 'you know, you remind us of' and then they'd name an artist, and then they'd kind of say something disparaging about her, 'but you're this, you're so much better in this way or that way.' And that's how we teach women to see themselves, as like you could be the new replacement for this woman who's done something great before you.

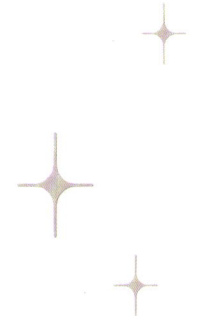

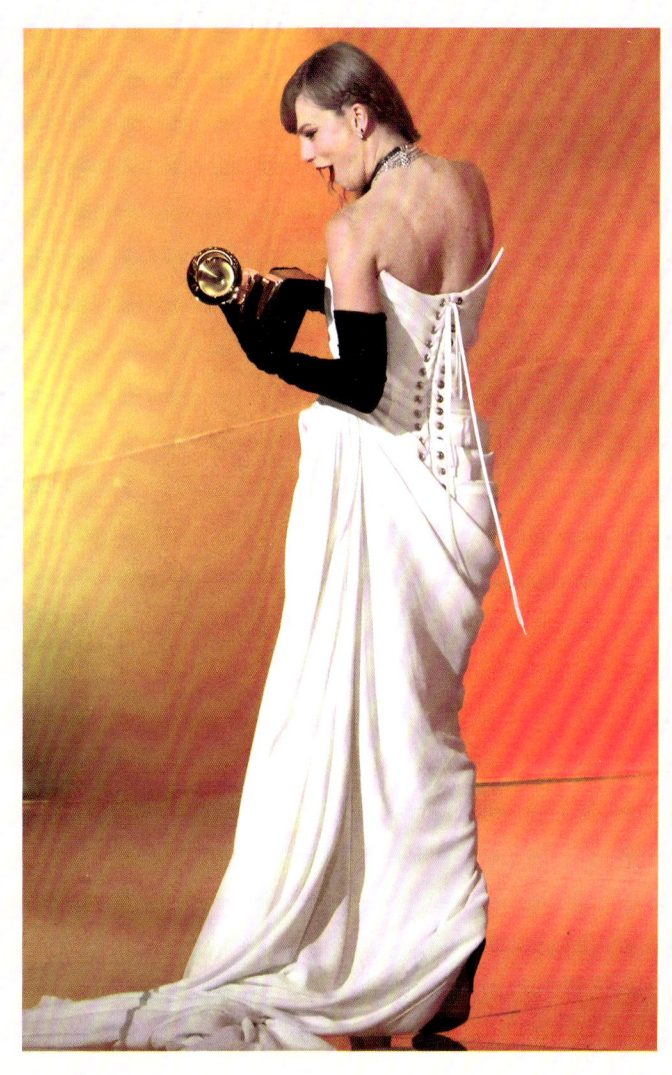

I don't know if I ever told you that." She went on to thank the recording academy for their selection and said that she knows that part of the reason is because of the passion of her fans.

While looking down and polishing the Grammy Award with her glove, she said, "I want to say thank you to the fans by telling you a secret that I've been keeping from you for the last two years, which is that my brand-new album comes out April 19. It's called *The Tortured Poets Department*. I'm gonna go and post the cover right now backstage. Thank you. I love you. Thank you."

This announcement had Swifties gasping, and it was one of the biggest red herrings in the Swiftie universe. All signs pointed to *reputation (Taylor's Version)*, but Taylor had other plans—an entirely new album. The album's title immediately intrigued fans (as soon as they could remember the entire title by heart), with many speculating on themes of heartbreak and introspection. Some believed that the album would reflect on her long-term relationship and breakup with Joe Alwyn. The title itself also sparked curiosity by Swifties because of Joe's rumored group chat with friends called "The Tortured Man Club," a detail that fans connected to the album's name.

There would be main album art, and Taylor also announced four collectible vinyl variants, each featuring different bonus tracks. This fueled speculation and excitement about whether there would be bonus content or an entire bonus album. With *The Tortured Poets Department*, Taylor crafted an entire aesthetic that leaned deeply into literary and poetic imagery, as well as classic black-and-white imagery. The album had typewriter-style fonts, and typewriters were a pervasive theme. The album prologue was written in the form of a poem and signed with, "All's fair in love and poetry. Sincerely, The Chairman of The Tortured Poets Department."

PAGE 214: It's an art: Performing "I Can Do It with a Broken Heart" in Miami on the final leg of The Eras Tour, October 17, 2024.

ABOVE: Taylor taking home her fourteenth Grammy Award for *Midnights*. The album won Best Pop Vocal Album and Album of the Year.

Even More Easter Eggs

In typical Taylor fashion, the promotion for the album rolled out in unique ways, with fans looking for clues and Easter eggs at every angle. The album was promoted on digital platforms, and Taylor made special Apple Music playlists inspired by the five stages of grief. Each playlist was made up of her previous work and had fans preparing for an emotionally raw album, given the aesthetics and subtle details.

At a pop-up library at The Grove in Los Angeles, hosted by Spotify, there were books with song titles and nods to lyrics on them. The pop-up leaned into the poetic aesthetic that the tone of this album was setting, with typewriters and quill-pen vibes. Fans could drop letters and share which songs they were looking forward to, making this an even more immersive experience. QR codes popped up in various cities across the world and took fans to an unlisted YouTube shorts page on Taylor's channel. Fans eagerly tried to put all the clues together.

The album officially released at midnight on April 19, 2024, and two hours later, fans got another surprise with the announcement of *The Anthology*, containing fifteen bonus tracks—essentially an entire bonus album.

"Fortnight" featuring Post Malone was the lead single for the album, and the official music video launched the same day as the album. The video features not only Post Malone, but also "mad scientists" played by Ethan Hawke and Josh Charles, actors who performed in *Dead Poets Society* movie in a fun nod to an Easter egg in Taylor's poet era.

The album was speculated to be about the breakup with her long-term boyfriend Joe, her brief romance with The 1975 singer Matty Healy, and her new romance with Travis Kelce. The song "thanK you aIMee" is rumored to be about the drama with Kanye West and Kim Kardashian because Taylor capitalized "KIM" in the album and then shared it again online with the spelling "thank You aimEe," which is thought to be aimed at "YE," or Kanye West. Taylor addressed her fame in songs like "Clara Bow," and in "I Can Do It With a Broken Heart," she addressed how she handled devastating grief and loss while also performing on The Eras Tour, where she appeared to be happy and cheery all night. In this album, we get the entire range of emotions that any poet explores and the most intricate poetic lyrics we've seen from Taylor yet.

"I've got like 100. Good luck!"

Taylor, 2015

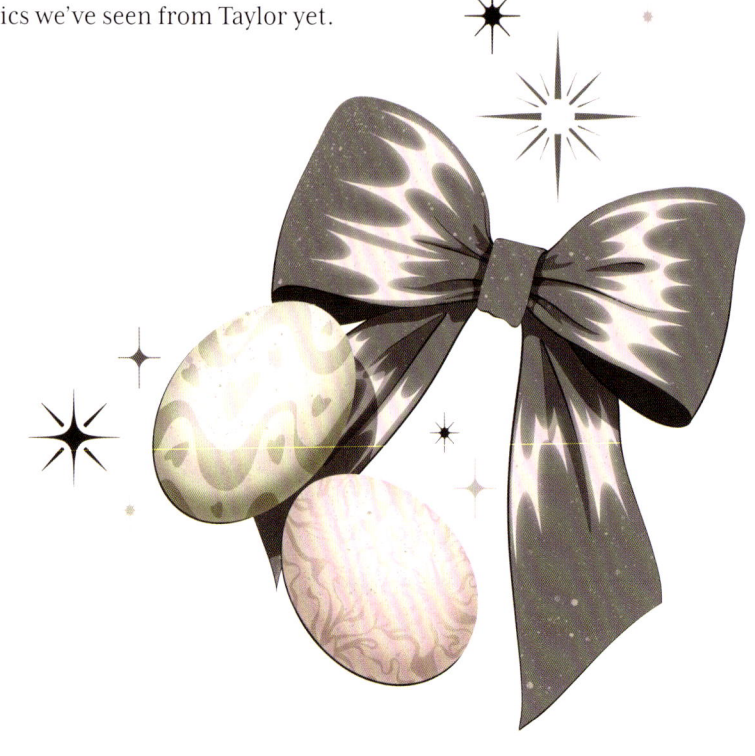

THE BEST THING THAT'S EVER BEEN . . . HERS

It's declared: May 30, 2025, is Swiftie Independence Day. It's the day that Taylor announced she bought back her entire musical catalog and she now owns ALL of her music, music videos, concert films, album art, photography, and unreleased songs. Everything is now hers.

She wrote, "I really get to say these words: All of the music I've ever made . . . now belongs to me."

Taylor posted a photo on her social media platform of her surrounded by the original version of her six albums: *Taylor Swift, Fearless, Speak Now, Red, 1989,* and *reputation*. She then directed folks to review a lengthy letter on her website detailing out the big news.

She first credited the fans, then goes on to say, "To say this is my greatest dream come true is actually being pretty reserved about it. To my fans, you know how important this has been to me—so much that I meticulously re-recorded and released 4 of my albums, calling them Taylor's Version. The passionate support you showed those albums and the success story you turned The Eras Tour into is why I was able to buy back my music. I can't thank you enough for helping to reunite me with this art that I have dedicated my life to, but have never owned until now."

Fans immediately took to social media when the news broke to congratulate her and celebrate with her, referring to the previously titled "stolen" albums now as the "reclaimed" albums. Many also posted videos, memes, and "how it started vs how it's going" photos, showcasing how monumental this was to both Taylor and her fans. Longtime friend and collaborator, Jack Antonoff, even posted a video of him and Taylor re-creating the iconic "Getaway Car," video they captured when they originally recorded the song with the caption, "rep forever guilt free listening!"

The goal for Taylor has always been to own her own music. While this fight was hers (and in many ways became her fans' too), it opened up bigger conversations in the music industry, helping pave the way for a fairer treatment of artists. Reflecting on this Taylor said in her letter, "Every time a new artist tells me they negotiated to own their own master recordings in their record contract because of this fight, I'm reminded of how important it was for all of this to happen. Thank you for being curious about something that used to be thought of as too industry-centric for broad discussion."

Few musicians in history have attempted to re-record their records as a way to take ownership back. Many artists that decide to re-record, select only a handful of their most famous tracks as it is not an easy task for artists to re-record and recapture such a unique moment in their musical career. But Taylor did it and it proved to be a monumental move in her career and is what ultimately led to her purchasing back the rights to all her music.

And on May 30, 2025, when she announced that she got her music back, fans realized they did too.

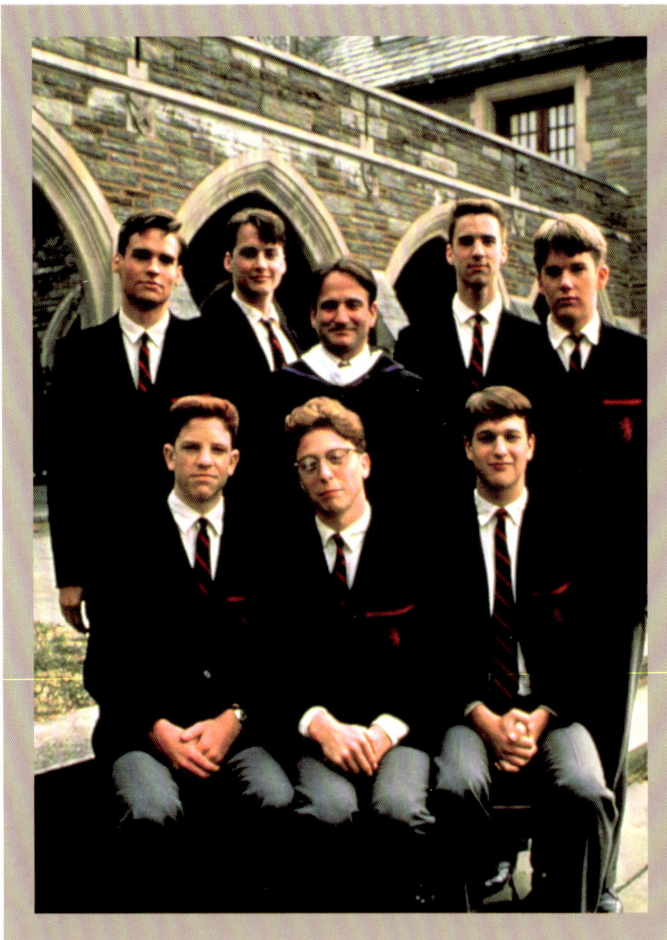

Tortured Poets Meet Dead Poets

ESTABLISHED
April 19, 2021

POETS OR POET'S
When *The Tortured Poets Department* was first announced and Taylor officially posted the title name online, some people pointed out that her spelling of the album title was not grammatically correct, using "Poets" instead of "Poet's." However, fans quickly realized that it was stylized like *Dead Poets Society,* a 1989 film starring Ethan Hawke and Josh Charles. Then, to fans' surprise, both actors were later featured in the "Fortnight" music video, confirming suspicions of the connection.

Lady in Love

While much of the album was about grief, heartbreak, loss, anger, and reflection, there were also moments of love and joy as featured on the songs "So High School" and "The Alchemy," which are thought to be about her new romance with Travis Kelce. Taylor continued to be seen with Travis throughout the end of 2023, cheering him on at games all the way to the 2024 Super Bowl LVIII.

Leading up to the Super Bowl, speculation swirled over whether Taylor would make it to the game due to The Eras Tour still happening. She performed in Tokyo, Japan, on February 10, and the media came up with various scenarios to see whether she could make the long-haul flight in time. Thanks to the time difference and a private jet, Taylor successfully landed in Las Vegas, Nevada, just hours before kickoff, solidifying her reputation as both a dedicated performer and a devoted partner. After the Kansas City Chiefs Super Bowl win, Taylor and Travis embraced on the field, where they shared a magical moment that quickly went viral. Taylor's presence in the NFL is credited with bringing a wave of new viewers, particularly among young women and international fans, who may not have watched football before. Thanks in part to her star

ABOVE: Robin Williams and the cast of *Dead Poets Society* (1989).

OPPOSITE: The Eras Tour.

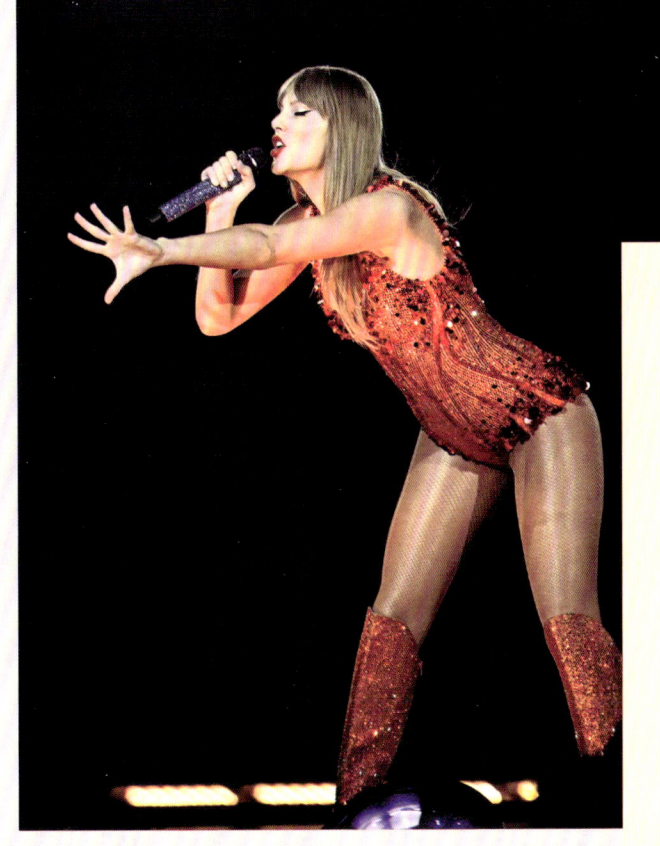

power, Super Bowl LVIII became the most-watched program ever in history.

The winning streak for Travis and Taylor continued. Not only did Travis win his third Super Bowl that year, but Taylor's new album also went on to break records. *The Tortured Poets Department* had the biggest album debut on Spotify of all time, surpassing 200 million streams on its first day. Fourteen songs charted on the Billboard Hot 100, making Taylor the first artist to hold that many spots. The album sold 1.6 million album-equivalent sales and more than seven hundred thousand vinyls, breaking her previous record.

"Who's Afraid of Little Old Me?"

Taylor referred to creating *The Tortured Poets Department* album as a "lifeline" for her and something she "needed to make" more than any other record of hers. While many of the songs on the album are descriptive and give fans theories as to whom they might be about, the song "Who's Afraid of Little Old Me?" is broader and critiques her public image and the way that people treat artists. She wrote this song alone at her piano and said it was one of those moments where she "felt bitter about just all the things we do to our artists as a society and as a culture."

ALBUM

The Tortured Poets Department

RELEASED

2024

QUILL LYRICS, FOUNTAIN PEN LYRICS & GLITTER GEL PEN LYRICS

In 2022, Taylor was named Songwriter-Artist of the Decade by the Nashville Songwriters Association International. During her acceptance speech, we learned about the "dorky" way that she categorizes her songs: quill lyrics, fountain pen lyrics, and glitter gel pen lyrics.

Quill Lyrics

These songs are super poetic, as though Taylor just finished reading a Charlotte Brontë novel or watched a film set in eighteenth-century Britain. Taylor described it in her acceptance speech as, "If my lyrics sound like a letter written by Emily Dickinson's great-grandmother while sewing a lace curtain, that's me writing in the quill genre."

Some songs written with Quill Lyrics include: "ivy," "epiphany," "Red," "Anti-Hero," and "Sad Beautiful Tragic"

Fountain Pen Lyrics

Most of Taylor's discography would be considered the "fountain pen lyrics" type. These are songs with a clear storyline and a slight poetic twist, usually at the end, something that she gets from her country-music roots. These songs take a common phrase, but they put modern references and vivid details to them. Taylor has described them as, "The songs I categorize in this style sound like confessions scribbled and sealed in an envelope, but too brutally honest to ever send."

Some songs written with fountain pen lyrics include: "All Too Well" (both versions), "Maroon," "Cruel Summer," "Cornelia Street," and "White Horse."

Glitter Gel Pen Lyrics

Taylor's most pop, bouncy, carefree, and fun songs fit into the glitter gel pen lyrics category. Taylor has described these lyrics as: "Glitter gel pen lyrics don't care if you don't take them seriously because they don't take themselves seriously. Glitter gel pen lyrics are the drunk girl at the party who tells you that you look like an angel in the bathroom. It's what we need every once in a while in these fraught times in which we live."

Some songs written with glitter gel pen lyrics include: "Shake It Off," "Bejeweled," "We Are Never Ever Getting Back Together," "You Belong with Me," and "You Need to Calm Down."

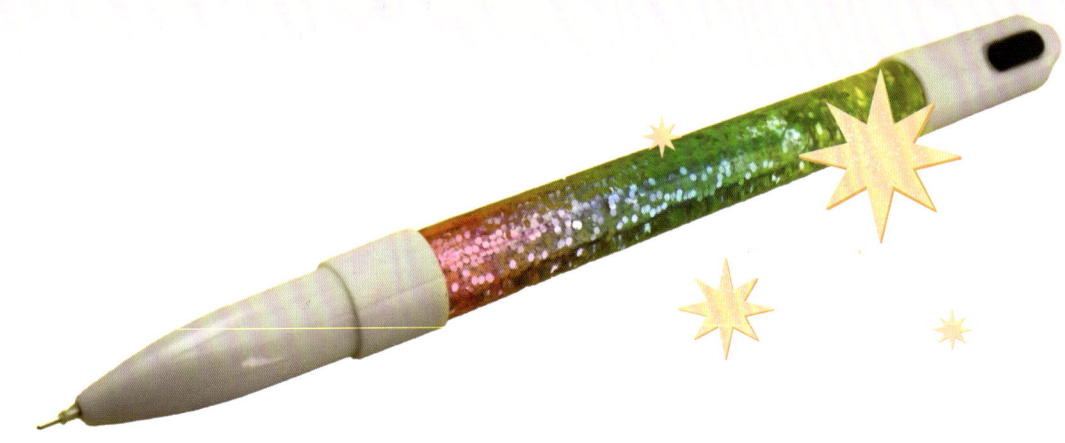

Updated Set

Taylor had some time off before the European leg of The Eras Tour, and fans speculated that she might change her set to include the newly added era of *The Tortured Poets Department*. On May 9, 2024, in Paris, fans attending The Eras Tour (either in-person or on grainy livestreams) realized that Taylor did, in fact, update the set. The entire show was shifted slightly to account for the entire new set dedicated to *The Tortured Poets Department*. The set included seven songs from the album, with a few shortened versions. For two shows, Taylor added and performed a special performance of the song "Florida!!!" featuring Florence Welch.

Fans were thrilled to see the addition, complete with updated costumes and stage theatrics. One of the most exciting updates was what fans lovingly call "the stage roomba," a raised block that Taylor stood on for the song "Who's Afraid of Little Old Me?" Taylor held onto a pole while singing a rage-filled performance and being guided around the stage on the "roomba." She even jokingly referred to that set as "Female Rage: The Musical." This section especially combined Taylor's vocal skills and her theater skills.

Another part of this set that fans loved was "I Can Do It With a Broken Heart." Taylor finished the "The Smallest Man Who Ever Lived," which she ended by "dying" in the middle of the stage. Two of her dancers would then go to retrieve her and bring her to the back of the stage, where Taylor collapsed dramatically onto a chaise lounge. Backup dancers Kam Saunders and Jan Ravnik, dressed in suits, physically picked her up, fluffed her hair, and pushed her to get ready for her performance. Taylor would fight back until she finally undressed, put on her jacket, and was then handed a mic and pushed back

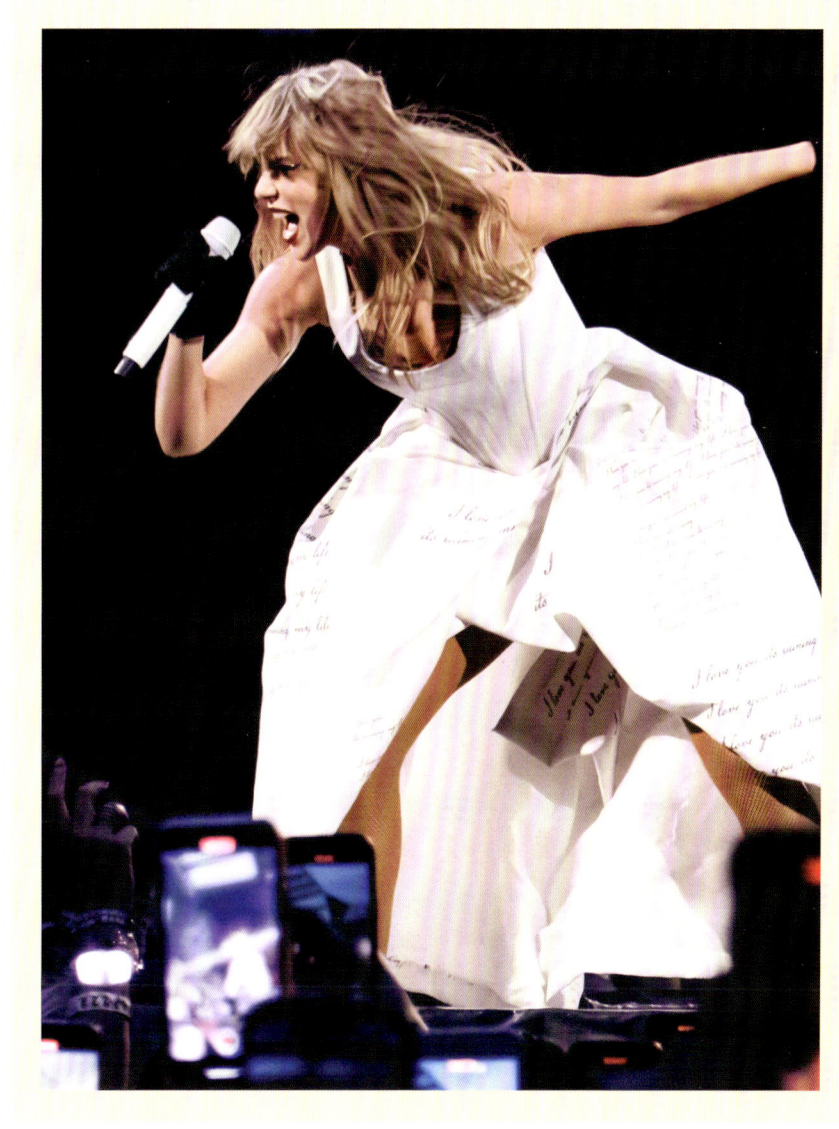

into performance mode. As soon as the song began, Taylor, who was just seen resisting, was right back into performance mode as if nothing had happened.

With the newly added set, The Eras Tour continued to be a cultural phenomenon, with fans now traveling overseas for a chance to be a part of this historical moment and to get a glimpse at the new additions made to the tour. For many, traveling overseas ended up being a less expensive option, where they got to not only travel to a different country but also to see the show. By the summer of 2024, this became known as the travel trend "gig tripping."

ABOVE: The dress worn for the *Tortured Poets* segment of The Eras Tour had lyrics from "Fortnight" written on it: "I love you it's ruining my life."

A Safe, Loving Experience

The Eras Tour has been described as one of the happiest places to be, full of love and joy. Fans often mentioned that they could truly feel like themselves and safe at these shows. Safety has always been a huge concern for Taylor and her team. Taylor has been subject to stalking, and someone even broke into her house and slept in her bed. Because of the threats, she has an entire security team, including a set of armored vehicles and people carrying QuikClot army-grade bandage dressing.

In an interview with *Elle*, Taylor described her fears around touring before *reputation*. She said, "After the Manchester Arena bombing and the Vegas concert shooting, I was completely terrified to go on tour this time because I didn't know how we were going to keep three million fans safe over seven months. There was a tremendous amount of planning, expense, and effort put into keeping my fans safe."

Safety efforts have always been a huge priority, and they came into play during The Eras Tour stop in Vienna, Austria. Taylor was scheduled to perform August 8 to 10, 2024, at the Ernst Happel Stadium. Just one day before the first performance was to take place, Austrian authorities, with intelligence assistance from the CIA, arrested two individuals linked to ISIS who were planning an attack. The suspects intended to cause mass casualties among the tens of thousands of fans, but the swift action of law enforcement prevented a potential tragedy.

Swifties had already taken over the city in preparation for these events, and the cancellation was a devastating blow for so many who spent time and money to get to the show. In times of tragedy comes beauty, however, and in the days that followed, Swifties took the streets of Vienna. They quite literally shut down an area next to a street named "Cornelia Street," paying homage to the same track title on the *Lover* album. Thousands of Swifties came together, sang Taylor songs, and traded friendship bracelets.

Businesses even came to show their support, gifting Swifties with free meals, museum entries, a free necklace from Swarovski, and much more. While The Eras Tour show would not happen, the city of Vienna wanted to ensure that Swifties, especially those who traveled long distances, could still find joy and connection during upsetting times.

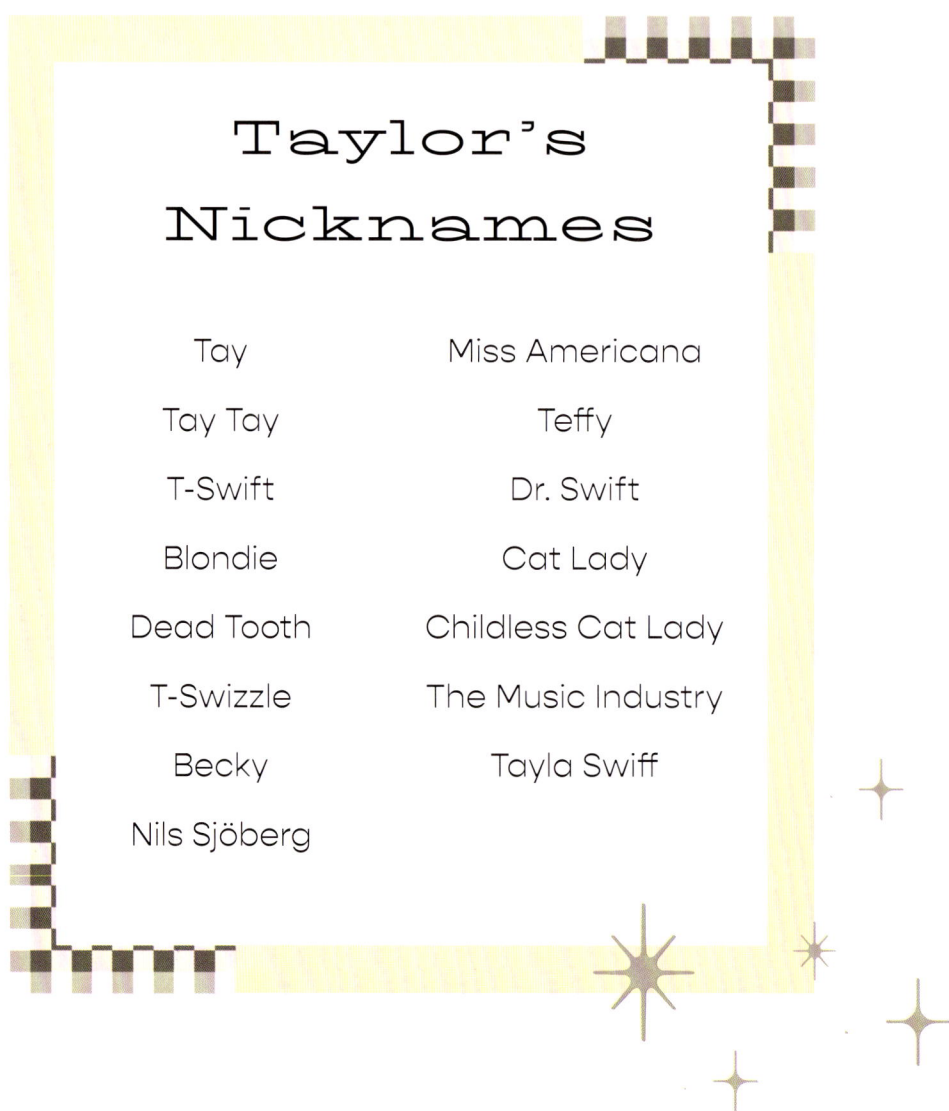

Taylor's Nicknames

Tay

Tay Tay

T-Swift

Blondie

Dead Tooth

T-Swizzle

Becky

Nils Sjöberg

Miss Americana

Teffy

Dr. Swift

Cat Lady

Childless Cat Lady

The Music Industry

Tayla Swiff

MEET ME IN THE POURING RAIN

"I think a rain show only chooses a crowd that is completely worthy and ready to party with us all night in the rain." —Taylor Swift

Rain has never stopped Taylor from showing up and performing. In fact, it's well-known that Taylor loves a rain show.

The rain-show love started during the Speak Now World Tour on June 25, 2011, in Foxborough, Massachusetts. Taylor's team was told that it was going to rain during her performance that evening. They considered canceling; however, the safety check was cleared, and they declared that the show must go on. But Taylor was still anxious about it. She wondered if people would even show up if it was raining. Or, worse yet, would they all leave when the rain started?

The first raindrops fell, and eventually it turned into a monsoon, soaking Taylor and everyone in the crowd. To her surprise, fans didn't leave; instead, they danced along in their best dresses, fearless of the rain coming down on them. Taylor said, "I saw girls with their perfectly curled hair turn sopping wet. I thought, 'They're all gonna leave.' Instead, they went nuts, dancing in the rain, screaming louder. It was awesome."

That moment cemented the rain show for both Taylor and her fans. Taylor's commitment to performing no matter the conditions strengthened the connection with her fans. There is a sense of "romantic camaraderie" that comes with a rain show, and for many Swifties, being part of a rain show has become a badge of honor.

Legendary rain shows include:
- Speak Now World Tour: June 11, 2011 (Foxborough, MA)
- Reputation Stadium Tour: July 21, 2018 (East Rutherford, NJ)
- The Eras Tour: May 7, 2023 (Nashville, TN), May 20, 2023 (Foxborough, MA) , and October 20, 2024 (Miami, FL)

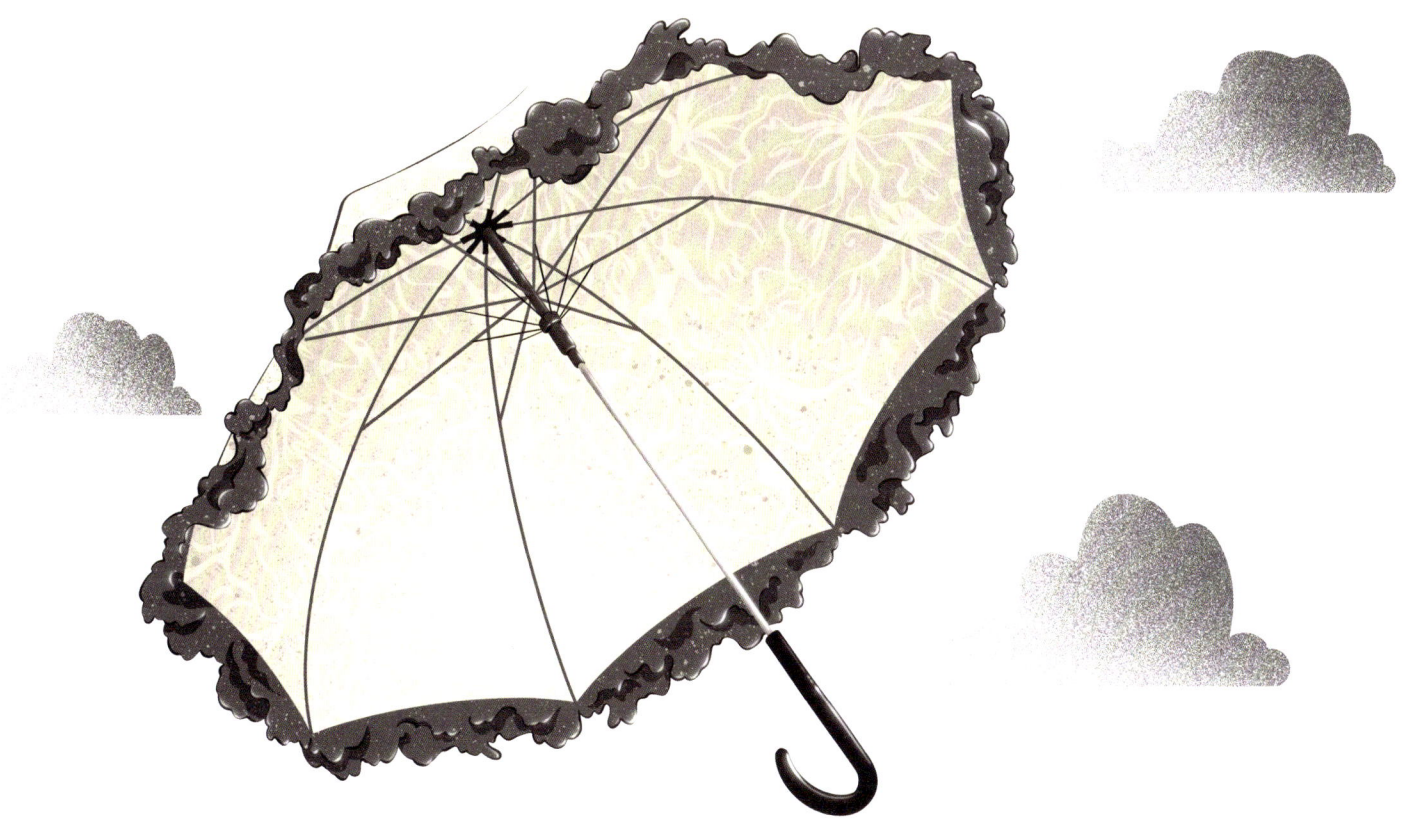

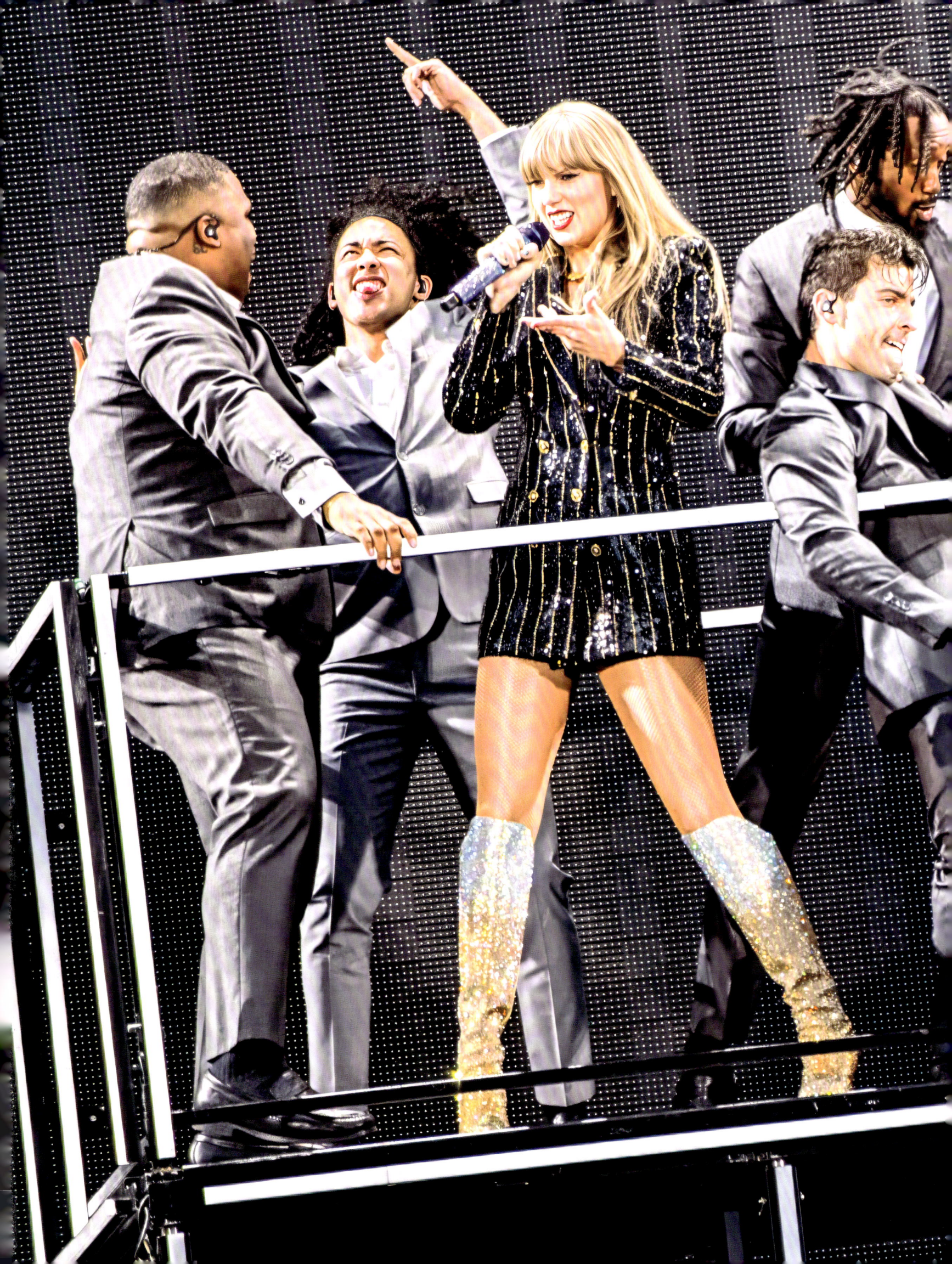

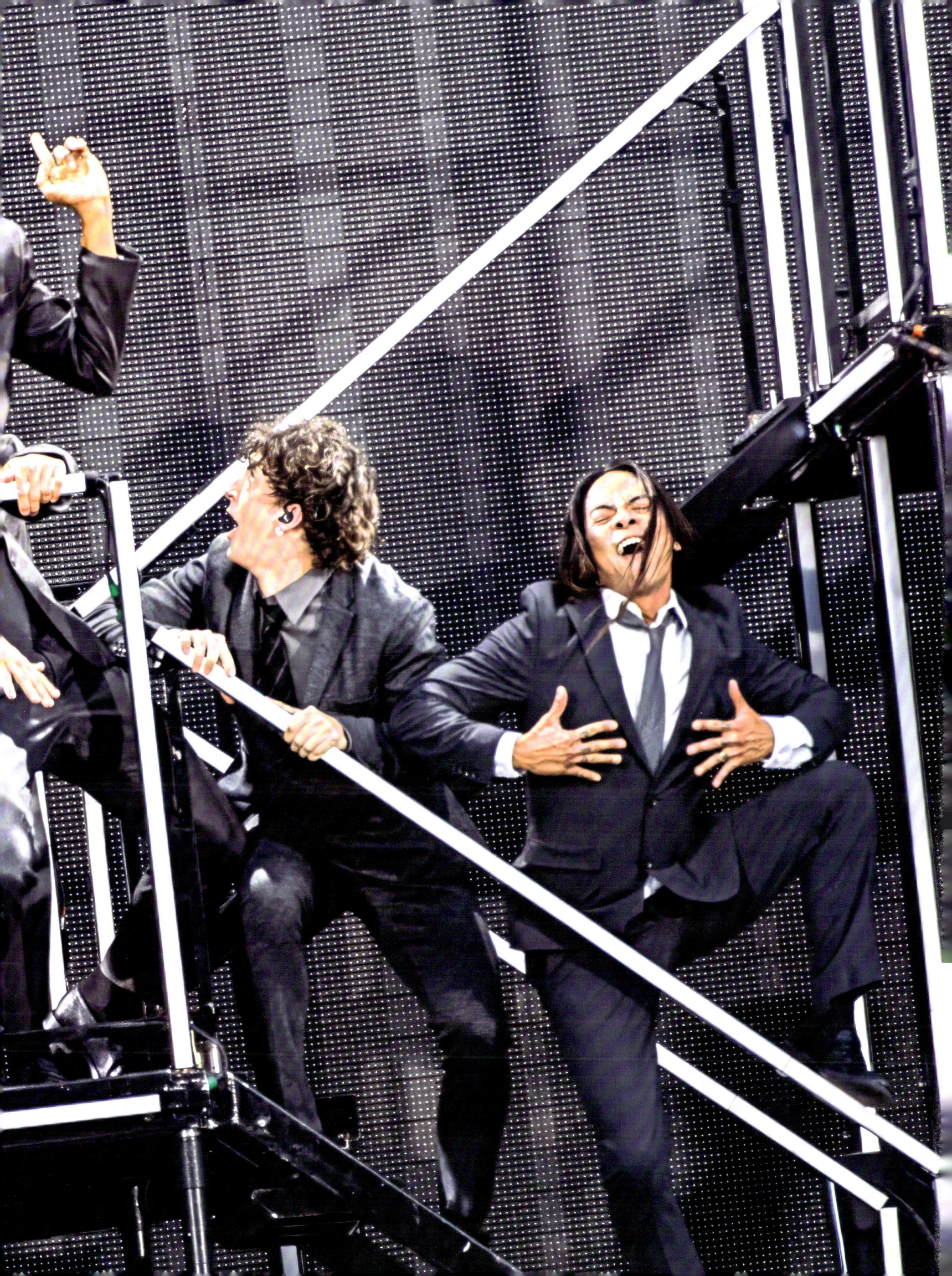

THE SPOTIFY STANDOFF

In November 2014, Taylor did something unprecedented. She pulled her music from the streaming platform Spotify. At the time, she had just released her record-breaking album *1989*, and this bold move set the stage for a greater conversation about the value of music and art in the digital age. While this announcement seemed to come as a shock, Taylor had hinted at this as early as her *Red* album, which she was hesitant to release on Spotify but eventually did.

In July 2015, just a few months before the announcement, Taylor penned an op-ed for *The Wall Street Journal*. She touched on the impacts of streaming and wrote, "Music is art, and art is important and rare. Important, rare things are valuable. Valuable things should be paid for. It's my opinion that music should not be free, and my prediction is that individual artists and their labels will someday decide what an album's price point is. I hope they don't underestimate themselves or undervalue their art."

This news didn't come without public debate. Many praised Taylor for taking a stance and standing up for artists' rights, while others criticized her for being greedy and alienating fans who relied on streaming.

When the news broke, Spotify put out a statement wishing that she would change her mind and help join them in "building a new music economy that works for everyone." They even created a playlist titled "Come Back, Taylor!" The playlist included song titles that spelled out the following message: "Hey Taylor, we wanted to play your amazing love songs and they're not here right now. We want you back with us and so do, do, do your fans."

But Taylor remained firm in her stance. This decision worked to her benefit and, eventually, other artists as well. By withholding *1989* from Spotify, she directed fans toward paid downloads and physical album purchases, helping the album become the bestselling album of the year. It also allowed her to negotiate her own terms when she eventually returned to streaming platforms in 2017, just as Spotify and others began to implement more artist-friendly models.

Ultimately, this stand wasn't just about Taylor. It was about remaining steadfast in the belief that artists should get paid for their work. This attention helped shine a spotlight on the financial challenges musicians face when it comes to streaming. Taylor shared in her op-ed, "My hope for the future, not just in the music industry, but in every young girl I meet . . is that they all realize their worth and ask for it."

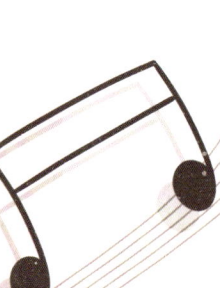
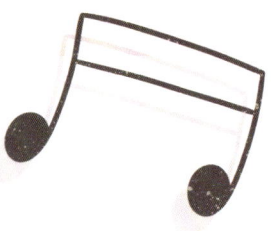
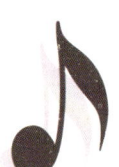

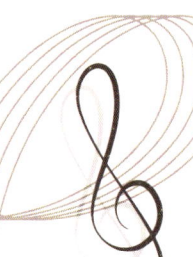

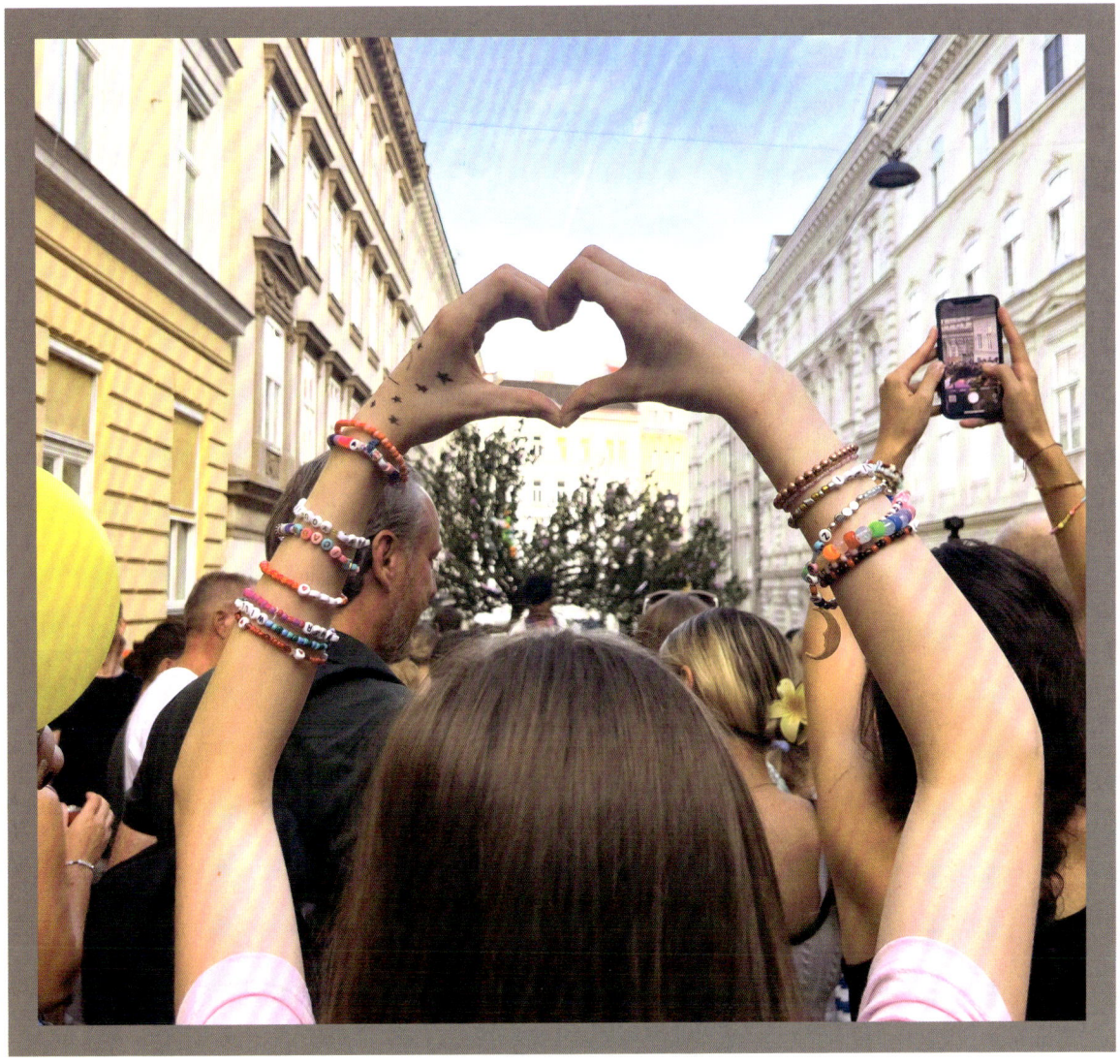

While Taylor initially kept quiet for the safety of herself, her crew, and her future shows, she eventually broke her silence on social media after the European leg of the tour wrapped. She said, "Walking onstage in London was a rollercoaster of emotions. Having our Vienna shows canceled was devastating. The reason for the cancellations filled me with a new sense of fear and a tremendous amount of guilt, because so many people had planned on coming to those shows. But I was also so grateful to the authorities because thanks to them, we were grieving concerts and not lives. I was heartened by the love and unity I saw in the fans who banded together. I decided that all of my energy had to go toward helping to protect the nearly half a million people I had coming to see the shows in London. My team and I worked hand in hand with stadium staff and British authorities every day in pursuit of that goal, and I want to thank them for everything they did for us. Let me be very clear: I am not going to speak about something publicly if I think doing so might provoke those who would want to harm the fans who come to my shows. In cases like this one, 'silence' is actually showing restraint, and waiting to express yourself at a time when it's right to. My priority was finishing our European tour safely, and it is with great relief that I can say we did that."

PREVIOUS PAGES: The fearless leader: Taylor performing "The Man" in Denver July, 14, 2023.

ABOVE: Fans in Vienna, Austria, show their love—and bracelets—for Taylor.

Well-Deserved Time Off

After the last leg of the European tour, Taylor had a few months off. She was seen out and about in New York with friends, attending the US Open (where she and Travis sang along to "I Believe in a Thing Called Love" by The Darkness) and, of course, attending Chiefs games to support her boyfriend. The relationship between Taylor and Travis blossomed even more. They attended events together and offered shoutouts to each other on Travis's podcast and at awards ceremonies. At the 2024 MTV Video Music Awards, during her acceptance speech for Video of the Year, she said, "Something that I'll always remember is that when I would finish a take, I would always just here, like, someone cheering and like 'wooooooo' from across the studio, and that one person was my boyfriend, Travis. Everything this man touches turns to happiness and fun and magic, so I want to thank

him for adding that to our shoot because all of us remember that." Fans love to see how the two are each other's biggest cheerleaders throughout the big moments of their lives.

During her time off, Taylor also took to social media to address her political stance after AI photos of her circulated. The photos appeared to show her supporting Donald Trump, and Taylor wanted to set the record straight. In her post, she said, "Recently I was made aware that AI of 'me' falsely endorsing Donald Trump's presidential run was posted to his site. It really conjured up my fears around AI, and the dangers of spreading misinformation. It brought me to the conclusion that I need to be very transparent about my actual plans for this election as a voter. The simplest way to combat misinformation is with the truth. I will be casting my vote for Kamala Harris and Tim Walz

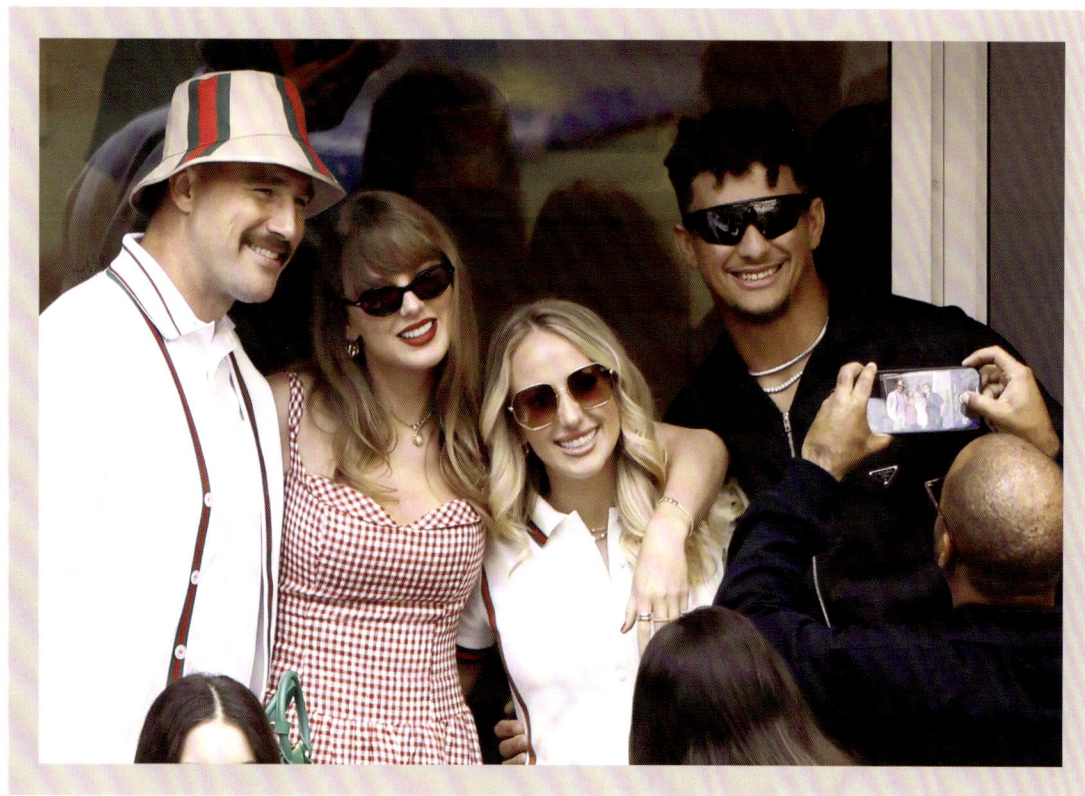

LEFT: Taylor and Travis Kelce pose for a picture with Patrick Mahomes and his wife, Brittany, during the men's singles finals at the 2024 US Open Tennis Championships in New York.

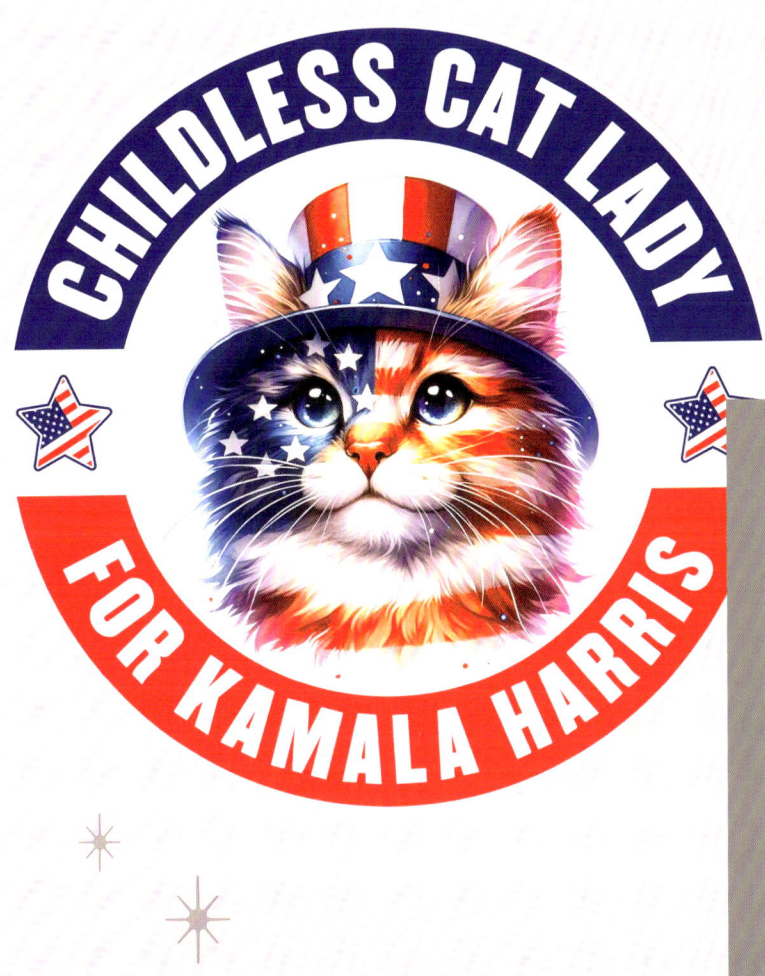

CHILDLESS CAT LADY
FOR KAMALA HARRIS

Childless Cat Lady

Taylor wrote a letter and posted it to her social media, confirming that she would be voting for Kamala Harris and Tim Walz in the 2024 presidential election.

EST.

On September 10, 2024, she signed the letter as "Childless Cat Lady" in reference to a comment JD Vance made about how the United States was being run by Democrats and referred to them as miserable, childless cat ladies.

A MOVEMENT

This clap back took social media by storm and gave many women the permission to own the "childless cat lady" status as a badge of honor, rather than a negative stereotype.

in the 2024 Presidential Election." She went on to share the many reasons why she was voting for the two and signed it, "With love and hope, Taylor Swift, Childless Cat Lady."

This post and signature caused a social media frenzy, with fans and followers embracing it as a symbol of independence and defiance against traditional expectations. Hashtags like #ChildlessCatLady started trending, and people across platforms posted memes, videos, and even merchandise that celebrated the label. For many, it became a playful way to reclaim a stereotype, shifting it from something negative to a badge of pride. Women in particular found solidarity in this statement, seeing it as a challenge to judgmental narratives about their personal lives, particularly when it comes to marriage, motherhood, and societal roles.

Back Onstage

After a few months off, Taylor got back to the "office" on the final leg of The Eras Tour, with only five cities left. While the tour was winding down, she surprised fans with one final surprise: *The Official Taylor Swift | The Eras Tour Book*. This book is a limited-edition photo book with more than five hundred photos, many never-before-seen, and reflections from Taylor herself. It was like a yearbook and love letter to the groundbreaking and beloved tour, and it has served a keepsake for Swifties.

One of the most surprising things about this book was that Taylor completely bypassed traditional publishers and instead published it under her own imprint, Taylor Swift Publishing. She partnered with Target for the exclusive distribution. This move showcased her savvy business skills and allowed her to not only retain the full rights to her final product, but also to release it on her terms. The book sold more than one million copies in the first week, making it one of the bestselling nonfiction books of 2024.

In the book, Taylor shared fun details about the tour, such as a look into the janitor cart that she got carted to and from stage in every night so that no one would see her before the first song. The inside of the cart looked a bit like a school locker, with décor that included an "Animal of the Day" poster. The animal featured in the photo was her cat Meredith. Fans also learned that the beloved "roomba" during *The Tortured Poets Department* set was actually driven around by someone inside of it.

The Eras Tour officially wrapped up on December 8, 2024, playing the final show in Vancouver, British Columbia. The final surprise songs included a mash-up of "Long Live," "New Year's Day," and "The Manuscript," all

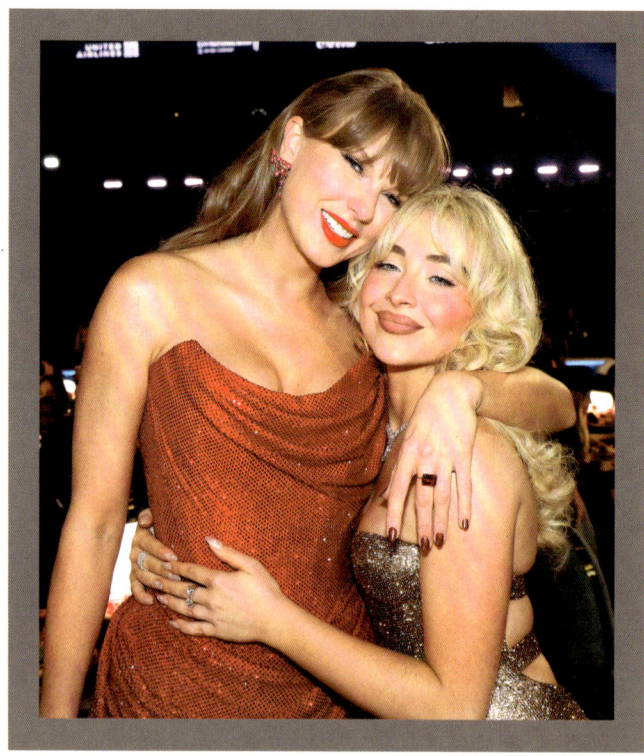

"To work with someone [who] cares about you as a person as well as an artist . . . that's been the biggest gift for sure."

Sabrina Carpenter,
on opening for The Eras Tour

MOVIES FEATURING TAYLOR SWIFT

From the stage to the screen, Taylor is no stranger to the spotlight. Here are all the movies, from documentaries to feature films, that she's been featured in over the years.

- *Jonas Brothers: The 3D Concert Experience* (2009)
- *Hannah Montana: The Movie* (2009)
- *Journey to Fearless* (2010)
- *Valentine's Day* (2010)
- *Speak Now World Tour–Live* (2011)
- *The Lorax* (2012)
- *The Giver* (2014)
- *The 1989 World Tour Live* (2015)
- *Taylor Swift Reputation Stadium Tour* (2018)
- *Bluebird* (2019)
- *Cats* (2019)
- *Miss Americana* (2020)
- *Taylor Swift: City of Lover Concert* (2020)
- *Folklore: The Long Pond Studio Sessions* (2020)
- *All Too Well: The Short Film* (2021)
- *Amsterdam* (2022)
- *Taylor Swift: The Eras Tour* (2023)

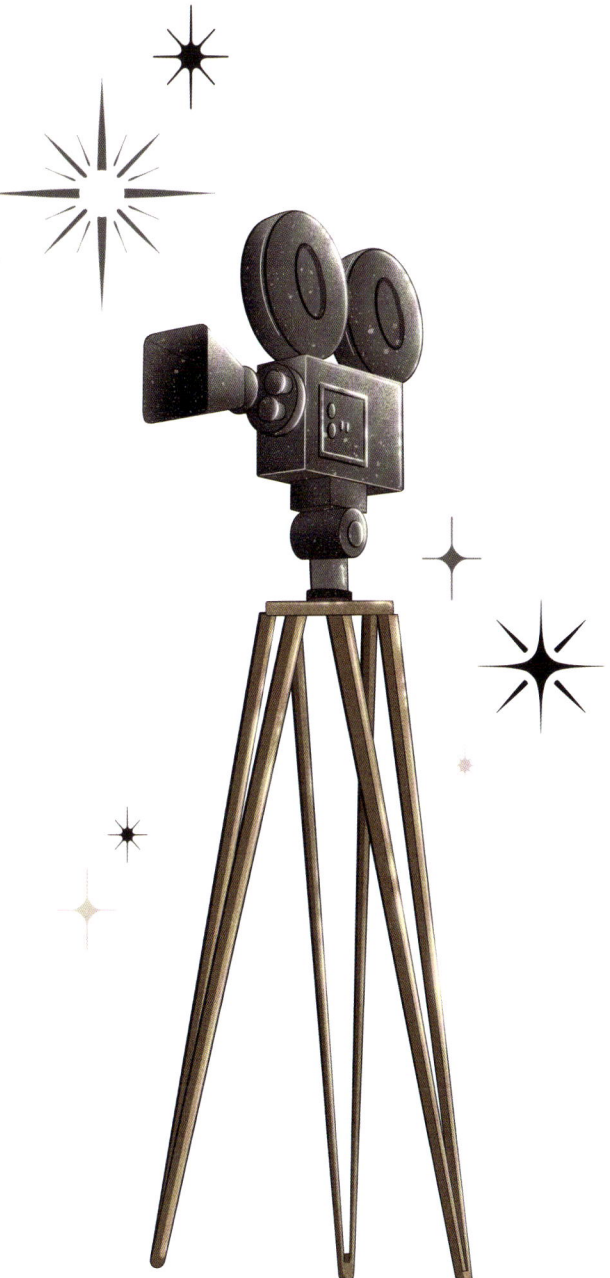

fan-centered and offering a way to encapsulate all that was The Eras Tour.

Just four days after the tour ended—on December 12, 2024, one day before her thirty-fifth birthday—Taylor stopped by Children's Mercy hospital in Kansas City, MO, to meet and bring gifts to the young patients and their families. In videos posted online, Taylor was seen joking and laughing with them and signing copies of her book. One child told her that they now like Travis Kelce, to which Taylor responded, "Me too. That's an absolute yes on that one."

The generosity didn't stop with the visit. As Taylor went around and talked to the young patients, she noted anything special they said they liked or wanted for Christmas. After the visit, she bought those gifts and sent them to the children, complete with a handwritten note.

Through her acts of kindness, whether she's surprising fans in hospitals, making donations on every stop of The Eras Tour, or speaking out on issues she believes in, Taylor continually uses what she's been given to help others. She might be the most successful pop star in the world, but Taylor has proven time and time again that no matter how big her success grows, she continues to show up with empathy and care. Taylor is the epitome of "karma."

OPPOSITE:
Taylor and Sabrina Carpenter at the 67th Grammy Awards, February 2, 2025. It was a big night for both: Taylor became the first woman to earn seven career nominations for Album of the Year, with *The Tortured Poets Department*, and Sabrina became the fourteenth artist in the history of the Grammys to earn nominations in all four main General Field categories in one night.

A TIMELINE OF GENEROSITY

Even from her earliest days, Taylor's generosity has shown through in so many ways. Here is just a sampling of how she has given back to her fans, and to people and organizations in need.

SEPTEMBER 2012

Ronan

Swift wrote and released the song "Ronan" in honor of a boy whose life and struggles with fatal neuroblastoma were documented in a blog by his mother, Maya. She then pledged to donate all of the proceeds of that single to cancer charities.

OCTOBER 2011

Donates books to her hometown library

Taylor donated six thousand books, worth approximately $70,000, geared for children and teens to the Reading Public Library in Pennsylvania.

AUGUST 2017

Helps survivors of sexual assault

Actress Mariska Hargitay's Joyful Heart Foundation, which helps those victimized by sexual assault, was the recipient of a generous pledge from Taylor after she won a countersuit against a former Denver DJ who allegedly groped her in 2013.

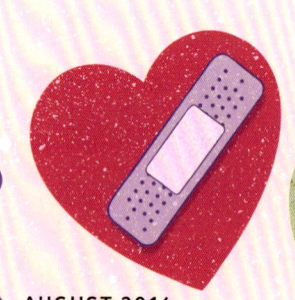

AUGUST 2016

Pledges to Louisiana flood relief

Taylor pledged $1 million to Louisiana flood relief after torrential rains caused massive flooding in the state, killing at least eleven people and damaging at least forty thousand homes.

SEPTEMBER 2017

Gives Hurricane Harvey survivors a helping hand

Following the devastation of Hurricane Harvey, Taylor made a very sizable donation to the Houston Food Bank in honor of her mother, Andrea Finlay Swift, who graduated from the University of Houston.

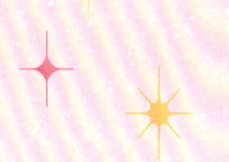

NO MEANS NO

APRIL 2018

Supports RAINN during Sexual Assault Awareness Month

The Rape, Abuse, and Incest National Network (RAINN) publicly thanked Taylor on Twitter for standing with survivors, saying, "Your generous donation this week during #SAAPM ensures that survivors and their loved ones get the help they need and deserve."

JULY 2018

Donates Reputation tour tickets

Taylor tried to help ease the pain after the death of Weymouth Sergeant Michael Chesna, who was shot and killed while investigating a car crash, by donating "a significant number of tickets" to the police department for her shows in Foxborough, Massachussetts.

DECEMBER 2014

Merry Swiftmas

Taylor spread holiday cheer by sending fans all over the world personalized presents. For one fan, a recent college graduate who had posted her worries about paying her student loans, she gifted $1,189 (a nod to her *1989* album) to help her start making payments—in addition to a personalized piece of art!

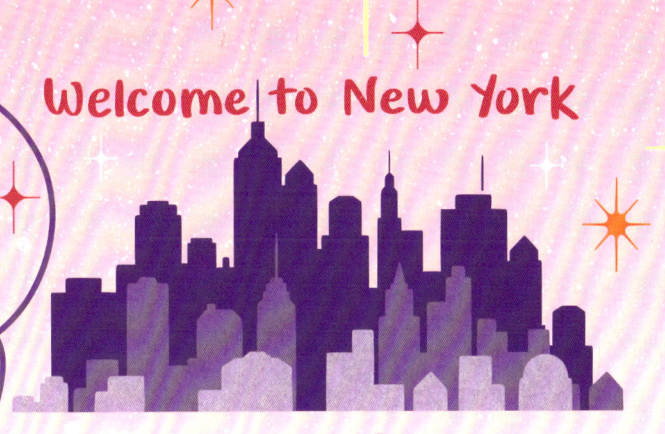

Welcome to New York

FEBRUARY 2015

Donates to NYC schools

To celebrate her move to New York City, Taylor released the single "Welcome to New York" (1989) and gave the proceeds—about $50,000—to the city's public schools.

SEPTEMBER 2015

Helps an animal foundation

Taylor donates the proceeds from her nature-themed "Wildest Dreams" video (another *1989* cut) to the African Parks Foundation of America, which focuses on nature conservation, eradicating poaching, and sustainable tourism.

AUGUST 2016

Gives thanks to doctors who saved her godson's life

Taylor made a significant donation to the doctors and team who saved her godson Leo's life after he was diagnosed with Transposition of the Great Arteries (TGA) at twenty weeks old.

FEBRUARY 2016

Helps out a fellow performer

Taylor gave fellow singer-songwriter Kesha $250,000 after she lost her court case in which she was petitioning to record music independently of producer Dr. Luke, to help her through the "trying time."

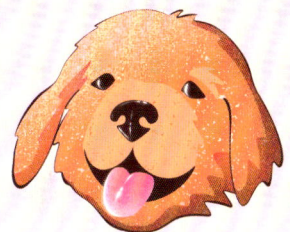

MARCH 2020

Donates $1M to Nashville tornado relief efforts

Taylor donated $1 million to the Middle Tennessee Emergency Response Fund after the tornadoes that destroyed homes and killed at least twenty-four people in Tennessee. Nashville being her home and a place close to her, she repeated this generosity in 2023 with another $1 million after tornadoes once again ripped through her beloved Nashville.

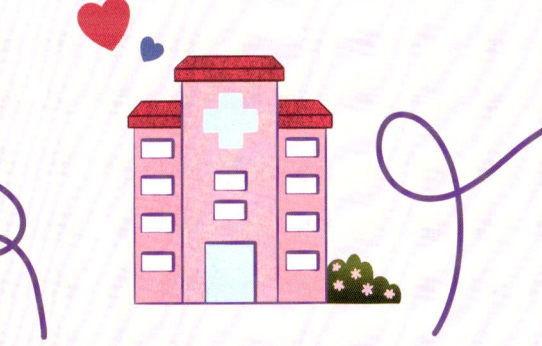

OCTOBER 2018

Helps a boy with autism get a service dog

Taylor donated $10,000 to Jacob Hill, a little boy with autism, so he could get a service dog. Two years later, Taylor invited him; his dog, Reid; and his family to her show at NRG Stadium in Houston.

SEPTEMBER 2019

Helps a fan battling cancer cover medical bills

Trinity Foster was diagnosed with stage-four osteosarcoma, which spread to her lung. The sixteen-year-old's GoFundMe page asked for help paying her medical bills, with a $10,000 goal. Taylor donated the entire $10,000.

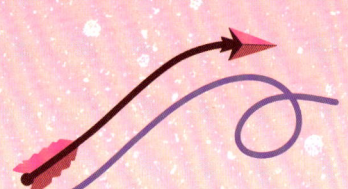

JUNE 2020

Donates to a Minneapolis fundraiser

Taylor gave $1,300 toward purchasing hair-care and skin-care products for people of color after seeing two fans post a video set to her song "Only the Young" asking for donations to help families in need in Minneapolis.

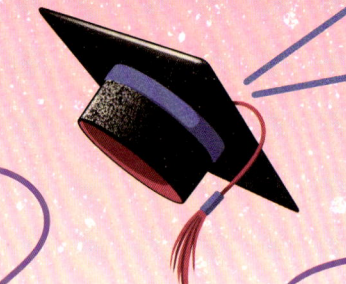

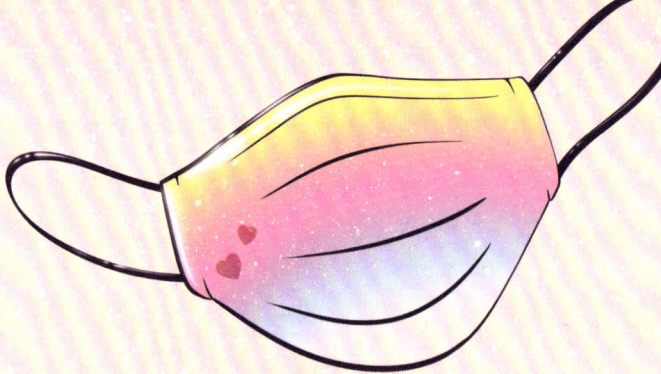

MARCH 2020

Helps fans during COVID

Several Swift fans took to social media to share that the superstar had personally sent them stimulus checks to help them get through the crisis.

AUGUST 2020

Helps out a student

Aspiring mathematician and European fan Vitoria Mario received a donation to her GoFundMe college fund campaign from Taylor, who gifted her about $30,000 to get her to her goal amount.

FEBRUARY 2024

Help Victim's Family of the Chiefs parade shooting

Following the death of radio DJ Lisa Lopez-Galvan at the shooting during the Kansas City Chief's 2024 Super Bowl victory parade, Taylor donated $100,000 to the GoFundMe set up by Lopez-Galvan's family.

NOVEMBER 2023

Supports the Mahomies Foundation

Taylor donated signed merchandise to the auction benefiting the Mahomies Foundation, started by her friends Kansas City Chiefs quarterback Patrick Mahomes and his wife, Brittany.

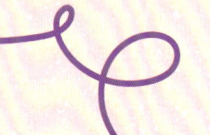

DECEMBER 2024

Eras bonuses, Part 2: World Tour

Taylor continued to give generous bonuses to every person who worked on the world tour—lighting, sound, production, assistants, security, choreographers, pyrotechnicians, you name it. The team put in the work, and in turn she rewarded them with bonuses of $142 million; with the bonuses for the North American leg, that's a total of $197 million.

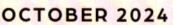

OCTOBER 2024

Donates to hurricane relief

Following the devastating hurricanes Helene and Milton that tore through Florida, Taylor sent $5 million to Feed America to help relief efforts in those areas.

DECEMBER 2020

Helps with rent

Taylor donated $13,000 to two mothers' GoFundMe pages after reading an article in the *Washington Post* about Americans falling behind on rent due to the government's lack of stimulus during the COVID-19 crisis.

DECEMBER 2020

Donates to a food bank

After Taylor saw the video of Ohio fan Sarah J. Bailey's elaborate holiday light display set to her song "Christmas Tree Farm" alongside a box for food bank donations, Taylor sent a donation to Our Community Hunger Center in Sarah's hometown—and a lovely note to Sarah.

MARCH 2021

Donates to a COVID-19 widow

Vickie Quarles—a mother of five whose husband died of COVID-19—was the beneficiary of Taylor's generosity when Taylor and her mother, Andrea, quietly donated the entire $50,000 of Vickie's GoFundMe goal amount.

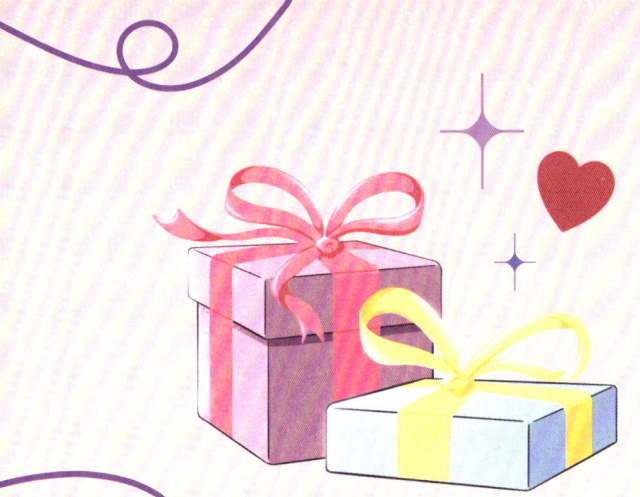

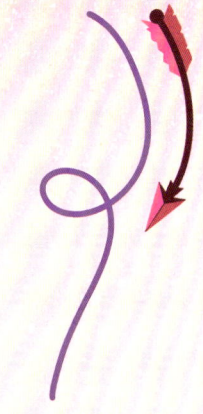

DECEMBER 2022

Supports pet rescue

Beth Stern's pet rescue foundation Beth's Furry Friends received a "sizeable donation" from Taylor to help her save more animal lives. Beth named one of the foster cats Angel Taylor in her honor.

AUGUST 2023

Era bonuses, Part 1: North America

Taylor proved to be a more-than-generous boss when she gave $55 million in bonuses to everyone on the tour, from caterers to dancers, including $100,000 bonuses to each of her Eras Tour truck drivers.

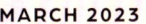

MARCH 2023

Helps food banks on the Eras tour

During The Eras Tour, Taylor quietly donated to local food banks in Glendale, Arizona, and Las Vegas, keeping her promise to leave a "positive impact" on the cities she planned to visit on the tour.

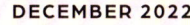

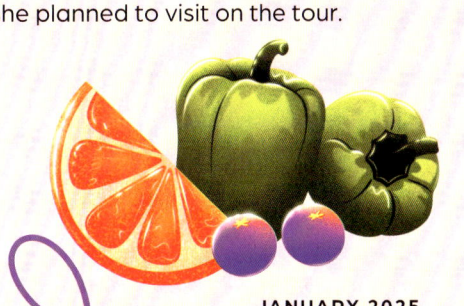

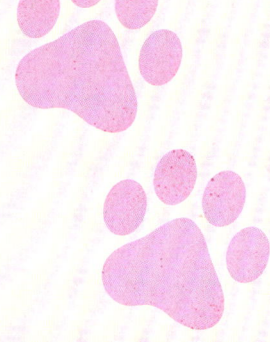

DECEMBER 2024

The giving season

Taylor spent a day with patients and employees at Kansas City's Children's Mercy Hospital, giving gifts, singing, posing for pictures. Later that month, she donated $250,000 to Operation Breakthrough, a Kansas City children's nonprofit organization.

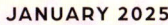

JANUARY 2025

Donates to LA wildfire relief efforts

Devastated by the horrible stories of families losing everything in the California wildfires, on January 16, Taylor shared on Instagram that she had donated to several organizations that were aiding in the wildfire relief.

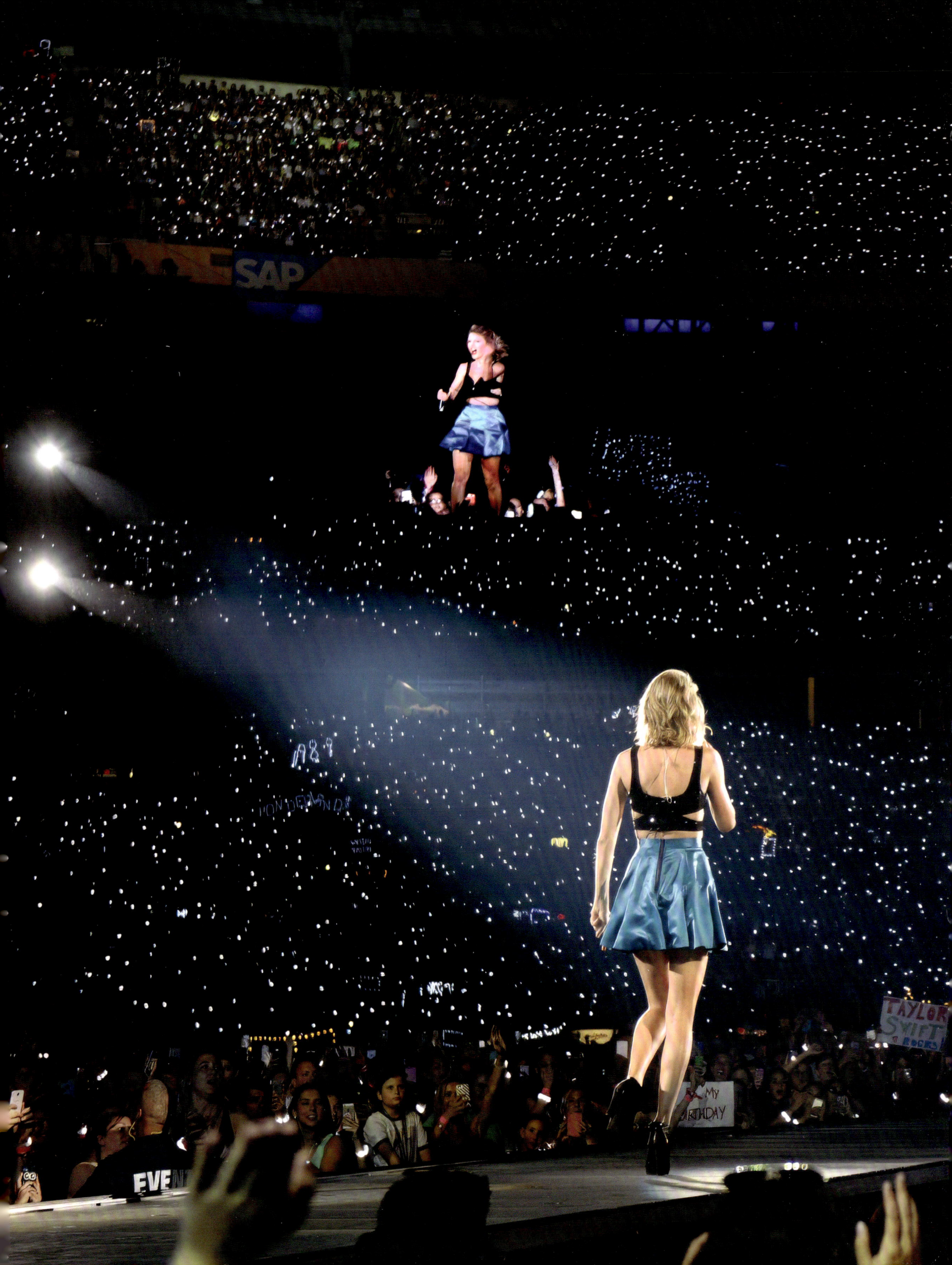

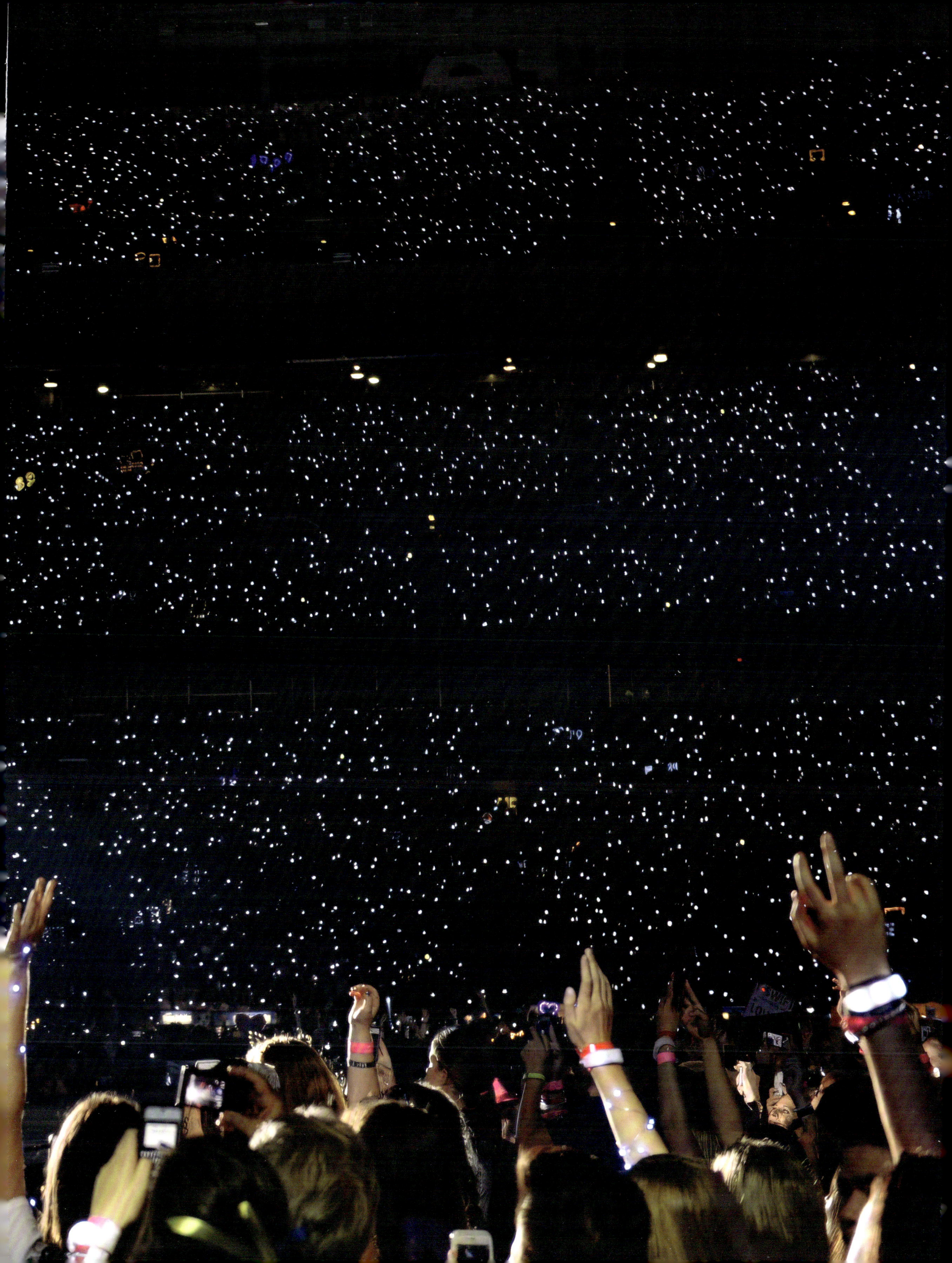

TAYLOR SWIFT'S COMPLETE DISCOGRAPHY
STUDIO ALBUMS

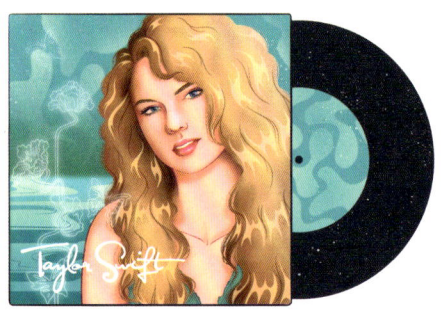

TAYLOR SWIFT
October 24, 2006
Big Machine Records

TRACK LIST
"Tim McGraw" (3:54)
"Picture to Burn" (2:55)
"Teardrops on My Guitar" (3:35)
"A Place in This World" (3:22)
"Cold As You" (4:01)
"The Outside" (3:29)
"Tied Together With a Smile" (4:11)
"Stay Beautiful" (3:58)
"Should've Said No" (4:04)
"Mary's Song (Oh My My My)" (3:35)
"Our Song" (3:24)

DELUXE EDITION BONUS TRACKS
"I'm Only Me When I'm With You" (3:35)
"Invisible" (3:25)
"A Perfectly Good Heart" (3:42)
"Taylor Swift's First Phone Call with
   Tim McGraw" (4:44)

DELUXE EDITION (ENHANCED) BONUS
TRACK
"Teardrops on My Guitar" (2:58)

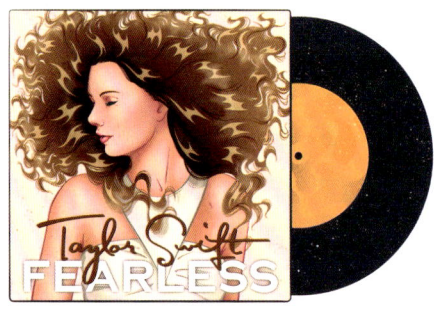

FEARLESS
November 11, 2008
Big Machine Records

TRACK LIST
"Fearless" (4:01)
"Fifteen" (4:54)
"Love Story" (3:55)
"Hey Stephen" (4:14)
"White Horse" (3:54)
"You Belong with Me" (3:51)
"Breathe" (featuring Colbie Caillat) (4:23)
"Tell Me Why" (3:20)
"You're Not Sorry" (4:21)
"The Way I Loved You" (4:03)
"Forever & Always" (3:45)
"The Best Day" (4:05)
"Change" (4:39)

PLATINUM CD + DVD
October 26, 2009

BONUS TRACKS
"Jump Then Fall" (3:56)
"Untouchable" (5:11)
"Forever & Always" (Piano Version) (4:27)
"Come In with the Rain" (3:58)
"SuperStar" (4:21)
"The Other Side of the Door" (3:57)
*The DVD comprised music videos ("Change,"
 "The Best Day," "Love Story," "White Horse,"
 and "You Belong with Me"), behind-the-
 scenes videos (for the latter three), more than
 fifty images (photographed by Austin K. Swift,
 the singer's younger brother) and backstage
 footage from the first concert of the Fearless
 Tour, and "Thug Story" (a video with rapper
 T-Pain filmed exclusively for the 2009 CMT
 Music Awards).*

NOTES
- Target-exclusive DVDs include behind-
  the-scenes recordings of "Breathe" and
  "Change."
- Target-exclusive Platinum Edition copies
  include live performances of "Untouchable" and "Fearless" from Clear Channel's
  Stripped.
- Walmart-exclusive copies include live performances of "Love Story" and "You Belong
  with Me" at the V Festival.
- Japanese CD copies include four bonus
  tracks: "Beautiful Eyes," "Picture to Burn"
  (2008 radio edit), "I'm Only Me When I'm
  with You," and "I Heart ?"

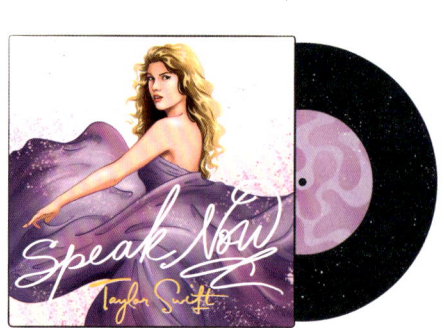

SPEAK NOW
October 25, 2010
Big Machine Records

TRACK LIST
"Mine" (3:50)
"Sparks Fly" (4:20)
"Back to December" (4:53)
"Speak Now" (4:00)
"Dear John" (6:43)
"Mean" (3:57)
"The Story of Us" (4:25)
"Never Grow Up" (4:50)
"Enchanted" (5:52)
"Better than Revenge" (3:37)
"Innocent" (5:02)
"Haunted" (4:02)
"Last Kiss" (6:07)
"Long Live" (5:17)

TARGET DELUXE EDITION
BONUS TRACKS
"Ours" (3:58)
"If This Was a Movie" (3:54)
"Superman" (4:36)
"Back to December" (Acoustic Version) (4:52)
"Haunted" (Acoustic Version) (3:37)
"Mine" (POP Mix) (3:55)
*Included thirty minutes of enhanced video
 content: the music video for "Mine," as well as
 behind-the-scenes footage of its production.*

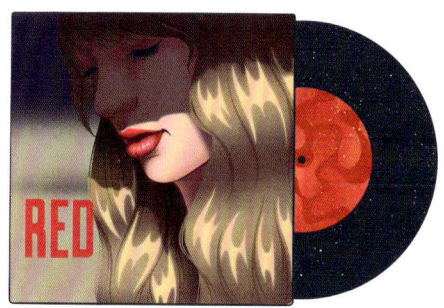

RED

October 22, 2012
Big Machine Records

TRACK LIST

"State of Grace" (4:55)

"Red" (3:43)

"Treacherous" (4:02)

"I Knew You Were Trouble" (3:39)

"All Too Well" (5:29)

"22" (3:52)

"I Almost Do" (4:04)

"We Are Never Ever Getting Back
Together" (3:13)

"Stay Stay Stay" (3:25)

"The Last Time" (featuring Gary
Lightbody) (4:59)

"Holy Ground" (3:22)

"Sad Beautiful Tragic" (4:44)

"The Lucky One" (4:00)

"Everything Has Changed" (featuring Ed
Sheeran) (4:05)

"Starlight" (3:40)

"Begin Again" (3:57)

DELUXE EDITION BONUS TRACKS

"The Moment I Knew" (4:46)

"Come Back . . . Be Here" (3:43)

"Girl at Home" (3:40)

"Treacherous" (Demo) (4:00)

"Red" (Demo) (3:47)

"State of Grace" (Acoustic Version) (5:23)

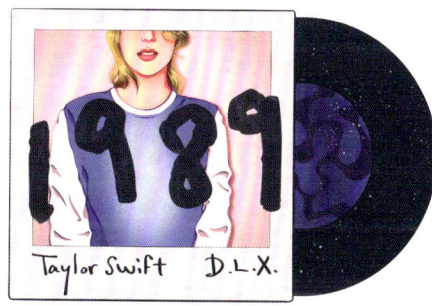

1989

October 27, 2014
Big Machine Records

TRACK LIST

"Welcome to New York" (3:32)

"Blank Space" (3:51)

"Style" (3:51)

"Out of the Woods" (3:55)

"All You Had to Do Was Stay" (3:13)

"Shake It Off" (3:39)

"I Wish You Would" (3:27)

"Bad Blood" (3:31)

"Wildest Dreams" (3:40)

"How You Get The Girl" (4:07)

"This Love" (4:10)

"I Know Places" (3:15)

"Clean" (4:30)

**TARGET DELUXE EDITION
BONUS TRACKS**

"Wonderland" (4:05)

"You Are in Love" (4:27)

"New Romantics" (3:50)

"I Know Places" (Voice Memo) (3:36)

"I Wish You Would" (Voice Memo) (1:47)

"Blank Space" (Voice Memo) (2:11)

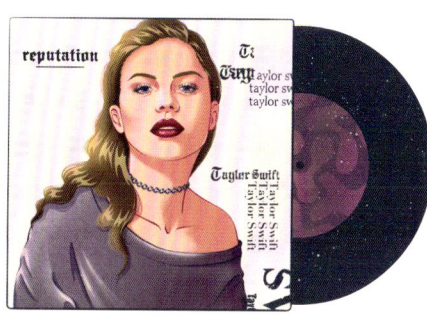

REPUTATION

November 10, 2017
Big Machine Records

TRACK LIST

". . . Ready For It?" (3:28)

"End Game" (featuring Ed Sheeran
and Future) (4:04)

"I Did Something Bad" (3:58)

"Don't Blame Me" (3:56)

"Delicate" (3:52)

"Look What You Made Me Do" (3:31)

"So It Goes" (3:47)

"Gorgeous" (3:29)

"Getaway Car" (3:53)

"King of My Heart" (3:34)

"Dancing with Our Hands Tied" (3:31)

"Dress" (3:50)

"This Is Why We Can't Have Nice Things" (3:27)

"Call It What You Want" (3:23)

"New Year's Day" (3:55)

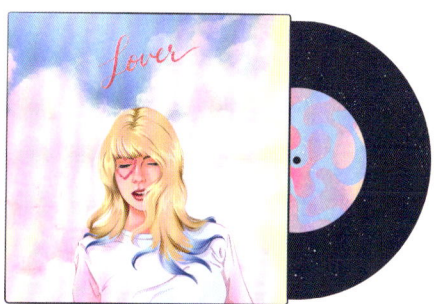

LOVER

August 23, 2019
Republic Records

TRACK LIST

"I Forgot That You Existed" (2:50)

"Cruel Summer" (2:58)

"Lover" (3:41)

"The Man" (3:10)

"The Archer" (3:31)

"I Think He Knows" (2:53)

"Miss Americana & the Heartbreak
Prince" (3:54)

"Paper Rings" (3:42)

"Cornelia Street" (4:47)

"Death By a Thousand Cuts" (3:18)

"London Boy" (3:10)

"Soon You'll Get Better" (featuring
The Chicks) (3:21)

"False God" (3:20)

"You Need to Calm Down" (2:51)

"Afterglow" (3:43)

"ME!" (featuring Brendon Urie) (3:13)

"It's Nice to Have a Friend" (2:30)

"Daylight" (4:53)

DELUXE EDITION BONUS TRACKS

"I Forgot That You Existed" (Voice Memo,
Piano/Vocal) (3:30)

"Lover" (Voice Memo, Piano/Vocal) (5:39)

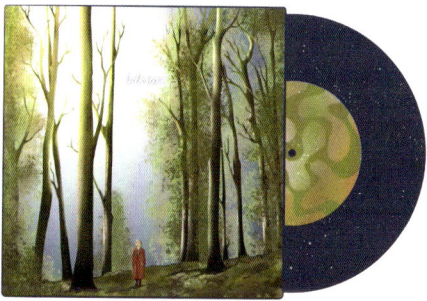

FOLKLORE

July 24, 2020
Republic Records

TRACK LIST

"the 1" (3:30)

"cardigan" (3:59)

"the last great american dynasty" (3:51)

"exile" (featuring Bon Iver) (4:45)

"my tears ricochet" (4:15)

"mirrorball" (3:29)

"seven" (3:28)

"august" (4:21)

"this is me trying" (3:15)

"illicit affairs" (3:10)

"invisible string" (4:12)

"mad woman" (3:57)

"epiphany" (4:49)

"betty" (4:54)

"peace" (3:54)

"hoax" (3:40)

TARGET EXCLUSIVE DELUXE EDITION BONUS TRACKS

"the lakes" (3:31)

On streaming platforms, four distinct EPs, called "chapters," featuring thematic compositions of songs from the album were released in August and September 2020.

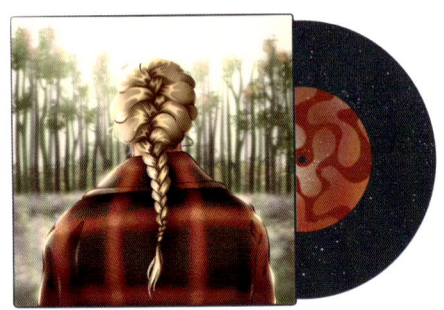

EVERMORE

December 11, 2020
Republic Records

TRACK LIST

"willow" (3:35)

"champagne problems" (4:04)

"gold rush" (3:06)

"'tis the damn season" (3:50)

"tolerate it" (4:05)

"no body, no crime" (featuring HAIM) (3:36)

"happiness" (5:15)

"dorothea" (3:46)

"coney island" (featuring The National) (4:35)

"ivy" (4:20)

"cowboy like me" (4:35)

"long story short" (3:35)

"marjorie" (4:17)

"closure" (3:01)

"evermore" (featuring Bon Iver) (5:04)

DELUXE EDITION BONUS TRACKS

"right where you left me" (4:05)

"it's time to go" (4:15)

On streaming platforms, three distinct EPs, called "chapters," featuring thematic compositions of songs from the album were released in January and February 2021.

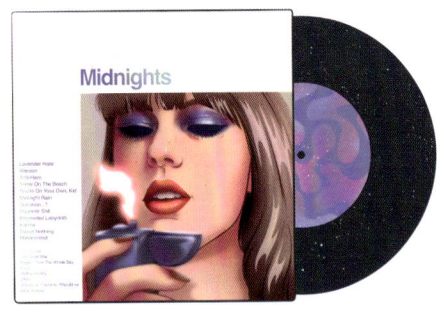

MIDNIGHTS

October 21, 2022
Republic Records

TRACK LIST

"Lavender Haze" (3:32)

"Maroon" (3:28)

"Anti-Hero" (3:20)

"Snow on the Beach" (featuring Lana Del Rey) (4:16)

"You're on Your Own, Kid" (3:14)

"Midnight Rain" (2:54)

"Question...?" (3:30)

"Vigilante Shit" (2:44)

"Bejeweled" (3:14)

"Labyrinth" (4:07)

"Karma" (3:24)

"Sweet Nothing" (3:08)

"Mastermind" (3:11)

3AM EDITION BONUS TRACKS

"The Great War" (4:00)

"Bigger Than The Whole Sky" (3:38)

"Paris" (3:16)

"High Infidelity" (3:51)

"Glitch" (2:28)

"Would've, Could've, Should've" (4:20)

"Dear Reader" (3:45)

TIL DAWN EDITION BONUS TRACKS

"Hits Different" (3:54)

"Snow On The Beach" (featuring more Lana Del Rey) (3:50)

"Karma" (featuring Ice Spice) (3:22)

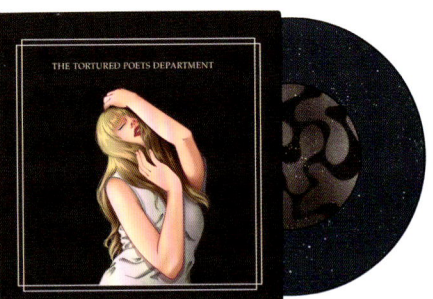

THE TORTURED POETS DEPARTMENT

April 19, 2024
Republic Records

TRACK LIST

"Fortnight" (featuring Post Malone) (3:48)

"The Tortured Poets Department" (4:53)

"My Boy Only Breaks His Favorite Toys" (3:23)

"Down Bad" (4:21)

"So Long, London" (4:22)

"But Daddy I Love Him" (5:40)

"Fresh Out The Slammer" (3:30)

"Florida!!!" (featuring Florence + the Machine) (3:35)

"Guilty as Sin?" (4:14)

"Who's Afraid of Little Old Me?" (5:34)

"I Can Fix Him (No Really I Can)" (2:36)

"loml" (4:37)

"I Can Do It With A Broken Heart" (3:38)

"The Smallest Man Who Ever Lived" (4:05)

"The Alchemy" (3:16)

"Clara Bow" (3:36)

THE ANTHOLOGY EDITION BONUS TRACKS

"The Black Dog" (3:58)

"imgonnagetyouback" (3:42)

"The Albatross" (3:03)

"Chloe or Sam or Sophia or Marcus" (3:33)

"How Did It End?" (3:58)

"So High School" (3:48)

"I Hate It Here" (4:03)

"thanK you aIMee" (4:23)

"I Look in People's Windows" (2:11)

"The Prophecy" (4:09)

"Cassandra" (4:00)

"Peter" (4:43)

"The Bolter" (3:58)

"Robin" (4:00)

"The Manuscript" (3:44)

LIVE ALBUMS

SPEAK NOW WORLD TOUR—LIVE

November 21, 2011
Big Machine Records

TRACK LIST

"Sparks Fly" (5:36)

"Mine" (4:19)

"The Story Of Us" (4:50)

"Mean" (4:06)

"Ours" (4:05)

"Back to December/Apologize/You're Not Sorry" (6:06)

"Better Than Revenge" (5:44)

"Speak Now" (4:08)

"Last Kiss" (6:09)

"Drops of Jupiter" (5:15)

"Bette Davis Eyes" (3:09)

"I Want You Back" (1:23)

"Dear John" (6:44)

"Enchanted" (6:29)

"Haunted" (4:52)

"Long Live" (6:16)

The special Brazilian Edition includes "Long Live" (featuring Paula Fernandes) (Remix).

FOLKLORE

THE LONG STUDIO POND SESSIONS

From The Disney+ Special
(Deluxe Edition)
November 25, 2020
Republic Records

TRACK LIST

"the 1" (3:39)

"cardigan" (3:50)

"the last great american dynasty" (3:52)

"exile" (featuring Bon Iver) (4:39)

"my tears ricochet" (4:55)

"mirrorball" (3:57)

"seven" (3:28)

"august" (4:20)

"this is me trying" (3:29)

"illicit affairs" (3:03)

"invisible string" (4:17)

"mad woman" (3:58)

"epiphany" (4:34)

"betty" (4:50)

"peace" (3:34)

"hoax" (3:41)

"the lakes" (3:19)

LOVER

LIVE FROM PARIS

February 14, 2019
Republic Records

TRACK LIST

"ME!" (Live from Paris) (3:33)

"The Archer" (Live from Paris) (3:30)

"Death By a Thousand Cuts" (Live from Paris) (3:30)

"Cornelia Street" (Live from Paris) (4:46)

"The Man" (Live from Paris) (3:39)

"Daylight" (Live from Paris) (4:22)

"You Need To Calm Down" (Live from Paris) (3:23)

"Lover" (Live from Paris) (3:49)

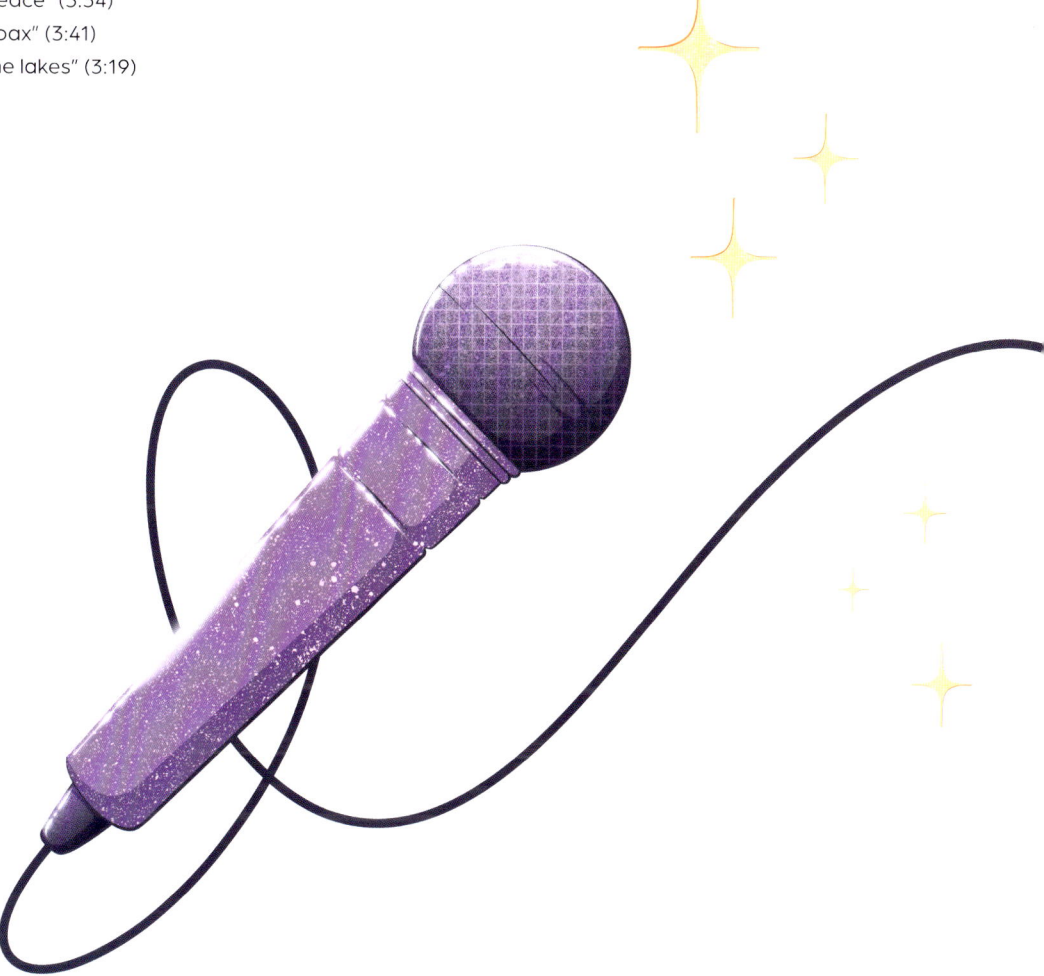

TAYLOR'S VERSIONS

FEARLESS (TAYLOR'S VERSION)
April 9, 2021
Republic Records

TRACK LIST
"Fearless (Taylor's Version)" (4:01)
"Fifteen (Taylor's Version)" (4:54)
"Love Story (Taylor's Version)" (3:55)
"Hey Stephen (Taylor's Version)" (4:14)
"White Horse (Taylor's Version)" (3:54)
"You Belong with Me (Taylor's Version)" (3:51)
"Breathe (Taylor's Version)" (featuring Colbie Caillat) (4:23)
"Tell Me Why (Taylor's Version)" (3:20)
"You're Not Sorry (Taylor's Version)" (4:21)
"The Way I Loved You (Taylor's Version)" (4:03)
"Forever & Always (Taylor's Version)" (3:45)
"The Best Day (Taylor's Version)" (4:05)
"Change (Taylor's Version)" (4:39)
"Jump Then Fall (Taylor's Version)" (3:57)
"Untouchable (Taylor's Version)" (4:39)
"Forever & Always (Taylor's Version)" (Piano Version) (4:27)
"Come In With The Rain (Taylor's Version)" (3:57)
"Superstar (Taylor's Version)" (4:23)
"The Other Side Of The Door (Taylor's Version)" (3:58)
"Today Was a Fairytale (Taylor's Version)" (4:01)
"You All Over Me (Taylor's Version)" (From the Vault) (featuring Maren Morris) (3:40)
"Mr. Perfectly Fine (Taylor's Version)" (From the Vault) (4:37)
"We Were Happy (Taylor's Version)" (From the Vault) (4:04)
"That's When (Taylor's Version)" (From the Vault) (featuring Keith Urban) (3:09)
"Don't You (Taylor's Version)" (From the Vault) (3:28)
"Bye Bye Baby (Taylor's Version)" (From the Vault) (4:02)

RED (TAYLOR'S VERSION)
November 12, 2021
Republic Records

TRACK LIST
"State of Grace (Taylor's Version)" (4:56)
"Red (Taylor's Version)" (3:43)
"Treacherous (Taylor's Version)" (4:02)
"I Knew You Were Trouble (Taylor's Version)" (3:39)
"All Too Well (Taylor's Version)" (5:29)

"22 (Taylor's Version)" (3:50)
"I Almost Do (Taylor's Version)" (4:04)
"We Are Never Ever Getting Back Together (Taylor's Version)" (3:13)
"Stay Stay Stay (Taylor's Version)" (3:25)
"The Last Time (Taylor's Version)" (featuring Gary Lightbody) (4:59)
"Holy Ground (Taylor's Version)" (3:22)
"Sad Beautiful Tragic (Taylor's Version)" (4:44)
"The Lucky One (Taylor's Version)" (4:00)
"Everything Has Changed (Taylor's Version)" (featuring Ed Sheeran) (4:05)
"Starlight (Taylor's Version)" (3:40)
"Begin Again (Taylor's Version)" (3:58)
"The Moment I Knew (Taylor's Version)" (4:45)
"Come Back … Be Here (Taylor's Version)" (3:43)
"Girl at Home (Taylor's Version)" (3:40)
"Ronan (Taylor's Version)" (4:24)
"Better Man (Taylor's Version)" (From the Vault) (4:57)
"Nothing New (Taylor's Version)" (From the Vault) (featuring Phoebe Bridgers) (4:18)
"Babe (Taylor's Version)" (From the Vault) (3:44)
"Message In a Bottle" (3:45)
"I Bet You Think About Me (Taylor's Version)" (From the Vault) (featuring Chris Stapleton) (4:45)
"Forever Winter (Taylor's Version)" (From the Vault) (4:23)
"Run (Taylor's Version)" (From the Vault) (featuring Ed Sheeran) (4:00)
"The Very First Night (Taylor's Version)" (From the Vault) (3:20)
"All Too Well (10 Minute Version) (Taylor's Version)" (From the Vault) (10:13)

SPEAK NOW (TAYLOR'S VERSION)
July 7, 2023
Republic Records

TRACK LIST
"Mine (Taylor's Version)" (3:51)
"Sparks Fly (Taylor's Version)" (4:21)
"Back to December (Taylor's Version)" (4:54)
"Speak Now (Taylor's Version)" (4:02)
"Dear John (Taylor's Version)" (6:45)
"Mean (Taylor's Version)" (3:58)
"The Story of Us (Taylor's Version)" (4:27)
"Never Grow Up (Taylor's Version)" (4:52)
"Enchanted (Taylor's Version)" (5:53)
"Better than Revenge (Taylor's Version)" (3:40)
"Innocent (Taylor's Version)" (5:01)
"Haunted (Taylor's Version)" (4:05)

"Last Kiss (Taylor's Version)" (6:09)
"Long Live (Taylor's Version)" (5:17)
"Ours (Taylor's Version)" (3:55)
"Superman (Taylor's Version)" (4:36)
"Electric Touch (Taylor's Version)" (From the Vault) (featuring Fall Out Boy) (4:26)
"When Emma Falls in Love (Taylor's Version)" (From the Vault) (4:12)
"I Can See You (Taylor's Version)" (From the Vault) (4:33)
"Castles Crumbling (Taylor's Version)" (From the Vault) (featuring Hayley Williams) (5:06)
"Foolish One (Taylor's Version)" (From the Vault) (5:11)
"Timeless (Taylor's Version)" (From the Vault) (5:21)

1989 (TAYLOR'S VERSION)
October 27, 2023
Republic Records

TRACK LIST
"Welcome to New York (Taylor's Version)" (3:32)
"Blank Space (Taylor's Version)" (3:51)
"Style (Taylor's Version)" (3:51)
"Out of the Woods (Taylor's Version)" (3:55)
"All You Had to Do Was Stay (Taylor's Version)" (3:13)
"Shake It Off (Taylor's Version)" (3:39)
"I Wish You Would (Taylor's Version)" (3:27)
"Bad Blood (Taylor's Version)" (3:31)
"Wildest Dreams (Taylor's Version)" (3:47)
"How You Get the Girl (Taylor's Version)" (4:07)
"This Love (Taylor's Version)" (4:10)
"I Know Places (Taylor's Version)" (3:15)
"Clean (Taylor's Version)" (4:31)
"Wonderland (Taylor's Version)" (4:05)
"You Are in Love (Taylor's Version)" (4:27)
"New Romantics (Taylor's Version)" (3:50)
"Slut! (Taylor's Version)" (From the Vault) (3:00)
"Say Don't Go (Taylor's Version)" (From the Vault) (4:39)
"Now That We Don't Talk (Taylor's Version)" (From the Vault) (2:26)
"Suburban Legends (Taylor's Version)" (From the Vault) (2:51)
"Is It Over Now? (Taylor's Version)" (From the Vault) (3:49)

DELUXE EDITION BONUS TRACK
"Bad Blood (Taylor's Version)" (featuring Kendrick Lamar) (3:20)

EPS

NAPSTER LIVE
October 24, 2006
Big Machine Records
"Tim McGraw (Album Version)" (3:54)
"Picture to Burn (Album Version)" (2:55)
"Baby, Don't You Break My Heart Slow" (3:40)
Only released as a digital download. No longer available on streaming platforms.

SOUNDS OF THE SEASON: THE TAYLOR SWIFT HOLIDAY COLLECTION
October 14, 2007
Big Machine Records
"Last Christmas" (3:28)
"Christmases When You Were Mine" (3:06)
"Santa Baby" (2:41)
"Silent Night" (3:32)
"Christmas Must Be Something More" (3:52)
"White Christmas" (2:34)

RHAPSODY ORIGINALS (RHAPSODY EXCLUSIVE)
November 6, 2007
Big Machine Records
"Tim McGraw" (3:54)
"Teardrops on My Guitar" (3:29)
"Our Song" (3:25)
"Should've Said No" (4:28)
Only released as a digital download. No longer available on streaming platforms.

LIVE FROM SOHO (iTUNES EXCLUSIVE)
January 15, 2008
Big Machine Records
"Umbrella" (1:29)
"Our Song" (3:29)
"Teardrops on My Guitar" (3:24)
"Should've Said No" (4:27)
"A Place In This World" (3:24)
"Mary's Song (Oh My My My)" (3:47)
"Tim McGraw" (4:00)
"Picture to Burn" (3:33)
Only released as a digital download. Currently available on iTunes.

BEAUTIFUL EYES
July 15, 2008
Big Machine Records
"Beautiful Eyes" (2:58)
"Should've Said No" (Alternate Version) (3:46)
"Teardrops on My Guitar" (Acoustic Version) (2:58)
"Picture to Burn" (Radio Edit) (2:54)
"I'm Only Me When I'm With You" (3:35)
"I Heart ?" (3:15)
Walmart Exclusive, included CD and DVD.

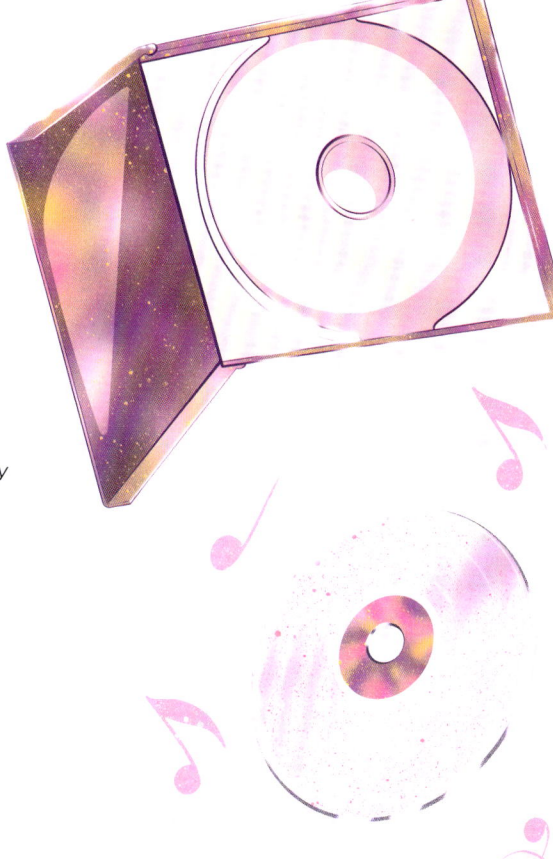

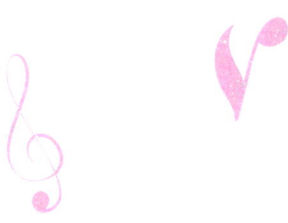

COMPILATIONS / STREAMING EXCLUSIVES

SPOTIFY SINGLES
April 13, 2018
Big Machine Records
A Spotify Exclusive (live acoustic versions)
"Delicate" Recorded at The Tracking Room Nashville (3:48)
"September" Recorded at The Tracking Room Nashville (3:07)

REPUTATION STADIUM TOUR SURPRISE SONG PLAYLIST
November 9, 2017
Big Machine Records
"All Too Well" (5:29)
"Wildest Dreams" (3:40)
"The Best Day" (4:06)
"Red" (3:43)
"Holy Ground" (3:22)
"Teardrops on My Guitar" Radio Single Remix (3:24)

"Our Song" (3:23)
"22" (3:42)
"I Knew You Were Trouble" (3:39)
"I Don't Wanna Live Forever (Fifty Shades Darker)" (4:07)
"Mean" (3:58)
"How You Get The Girl" (4:07)
"So It Goes..." (3:47)
"Fifteen" (4:56)
"Mine" (3:51)
"Sparks Fly" (4:22)
"State of Grace" (4:55)
"Haunted" (4:05)
"Never Grow Up" (4:52)
"Treacherous" (4:02)
"Babe" (3:35)
"Welcome to New York" (3:32)
"Fearless" (4:02)
"Enchanted" (5:53)
"Change" (4:41)
"Ours" (3:59)
"Out Of The Woods" (3:55)
"Come Back...Be Here" (3:43)

"A Place in This World" (3:22)
"This Love" (4:10)
"The Lucky One" (4:00)
"Invisible" (3:25)
"Breathe" (4:24)
"Better Man" (4:23)
"Jump Then Fall" (3:58)
"Begin Again" (3:59)
"Tied Together With a Smile" (4:11)
"The Story Of Us" (4:27)
"Forever & Always" (3:46)
"Hey Stephen" (4:16)
"Speak Now" (4:03)
"Wonderland" (4:05)
"White Horse" (3:55)
"I'm Only Me When I'm With You" (3:35)
"Starlight" (3:40)
"I Know Places" (3:15)

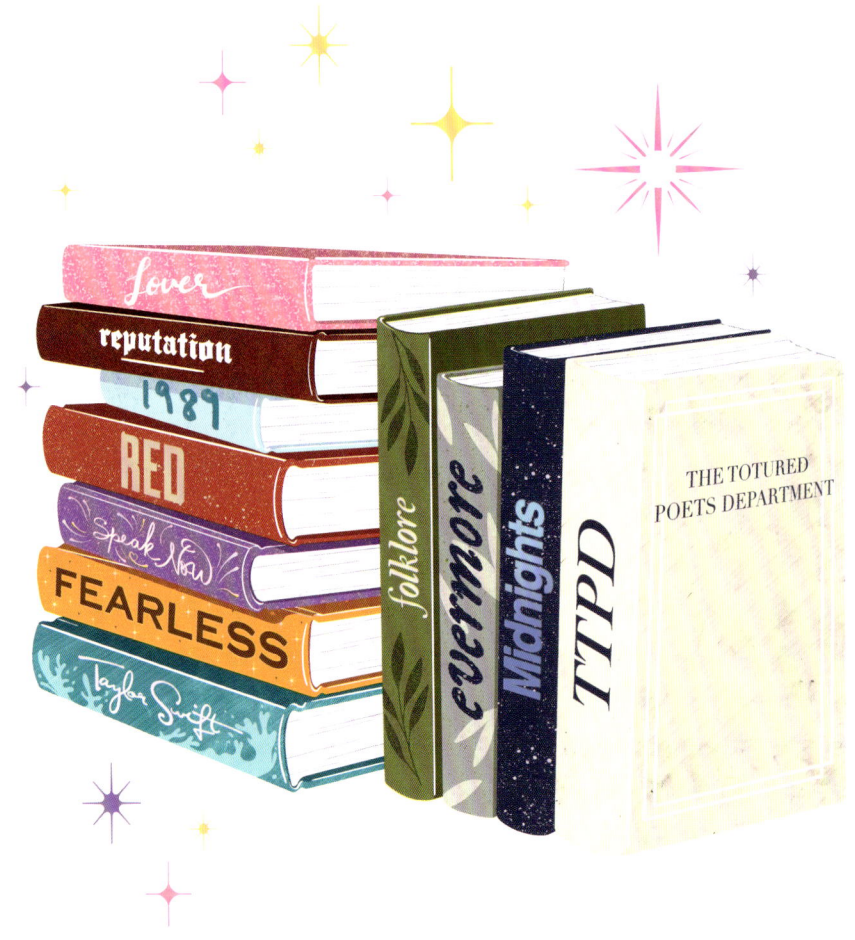

NON-ALBUM SINGLES

HANNAH MONTANA
THE MOVIE
March 20, 2009
Big Machine Records
"Crazier" (3:12)

"American Girl"
(4:10)
June 30, 2009
Big Machine Records

VALENTINE'S DAY
ORIGINAL MOTION PICTURE SOUNDTRACK
January 19, 2010
Big Machine Records
"Today Was A Fairytale" (4:02)

THE HUNGER GAMES
SONGS FROM DISTRICT 12 AND BEYOND
December 26, 2011
Big Machine Records
"Safe & Sound" (feat. The Civil Wars) (4:01)

THE HUNGER GAMES
SONGS FROM DISTRICT 12 AND BEYOND
March 12, 2012
Big Machine Records
"Eyes Open" (4:04)

RONAN
(4:25)
September 8, 2012
Big Machine Records
Single for charity—later added to Red *(Taylor's Version)*

ONE CHANCE
ORIGINAL MOTION PICTURE SOUNDTRACK
October 21, 2013
Big Machine Records
"Sweeter Than Fiction" (3:57)

FIFTY SHADES DARKER
ORIGINAL MOTION PICTURE SOUNDTRACK
December 9, 2016
Universal Music Group
"I Don't Wanna Live Forever" (with Zayn) (4:05)

CATS
HIGHLIGHTS FROM THE MAJOR MOTION PICTURE SOUNDTRACK
November 15, 2019
Polydor Records
"Beautiful Ghosts" (4:21)

"Christmas Tree Farm"
(3:52)
December 6, 2019
Republic Records

"Only the Young"
(2:37)
January 31, 2020
Republic Records
Promotional single for "Miss Americana"

"Christmas Tree Farm"
OLD TIMEY VERSION (3:52)
November 22, 2021
Republic Records

WHERE THE CRAWDADS SING
ORIGINAL MOTION PICTURE SOUNDTRACK
June 24, 2022
Republic Records
"Carolina" (4:24)

THE MORE LOVER CHAPTER
March 17, 2023 (backdated to August 23, 2019)
Republic Records
"All of the Girls You Loved Before" (3:41)

THE MORE FEARLESS
TAYLOR'S VERSION - CHAPTER
March 17, 2023 (backdated to April 9, 2021)
Republic Records
"If This Was a Movie (Taylor's Version)" (3:57)

GUEST APPEARANCES

Love Drunk
BOYS LIKE GIRLS
September 8, 2009
Sony
"Two is Better Than One" (4:02)

Hope For Haiti Now
VARIOUS ARTISTS
January 23, 2010
MTV Records
"Breathless" (3:51)

Strange Clouds
B.O.B
April 27, 2012
Grand Hustle Records, Rebel
Rock Entertainment, Atlantic
Records
"Both of Us" (feat. Taylor Swift) (3:36)

Two Lanes of Freedom
TIM MCGRAW
January 1, 2013
Big Machine Records
"Highway Don't Care" (feat. Taylor Swift and
    Keith Urban) (4:36)

Bigger
SUGARLAND
June 8, 2018
(single released on April 20,
2018)
Big Machine Records
"Babe" (3:35)

Women In Music Pt. III
HAIM
February 19, 2021
Columbia Records
"Gasoline" (3:13)

How Long Do You Think It's Gonna Last?
BIG RED MACHINE
August 27, 2021
Jagjaguwar
"Renegade" (4:14)

= (Tour Edition)
ED SHEERAN
May 27, 2022
Asylum, Atlantic Records
"The Joker and the Queen" (feat. Taylor Swift)
    (3:05)

First Two Pages of Frankenstein
THE NATIONAL
April 28, 2023
4AD
"The Alcott" (feat. Taylor Swift) (4:27)

The Secret of Us
GRACIE ABRAMS
June 21, 2024
Interscope Records
"us." (feat. Taylor Swift) (4:02)

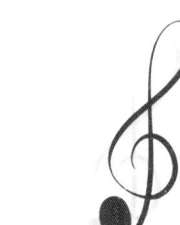
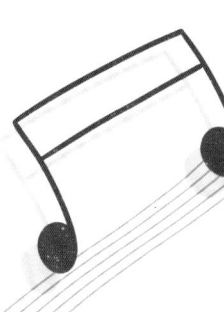
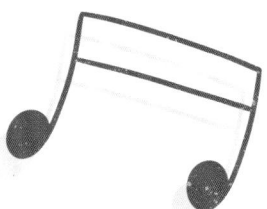
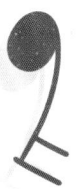
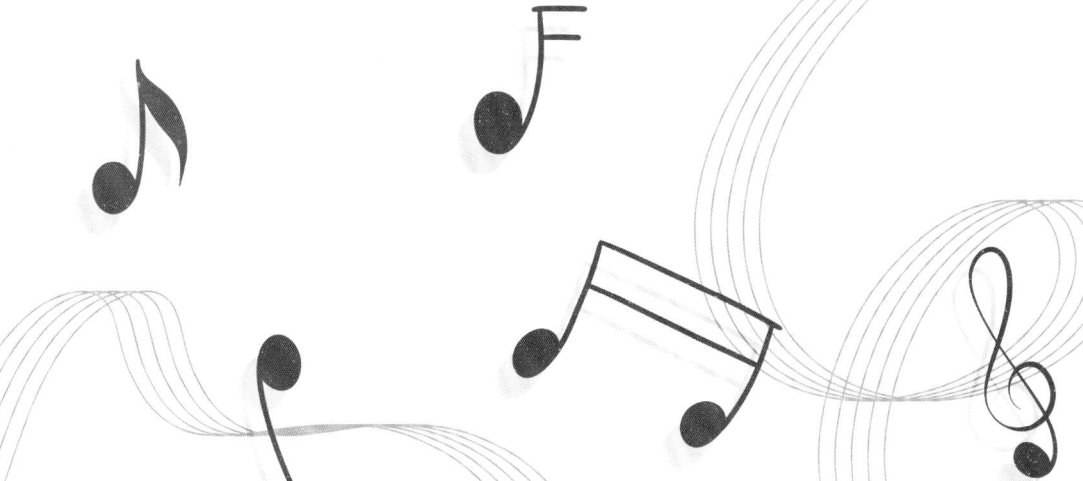

RESOURCES

ABC News. "Taylor Swift Barbara Walters Interview | Barbara Walters Most Fascinating People | ABC News." YouTube, December 15, 2014. https://www.youtube.com/watch?v=P-TFhUq3otQ.

ABC News. "Taylor Swift on What Inspired Her New Song, 'Welcome to New York,'" October 20, 2014. https://abcnews.go.com/Entertainment/taylor-swift-debuts-song-york/story?id=26316546.

ABC11 Raleigh-Durham. "Taylor Swift Donates $50,000 to 11-Year-Old Leukemia Patient with 'Bad Blood,'" July 8, 2015. https://abc11.com/taylor-swift-leukemia-bad-blood-patient-with/835561/.

Andriotis, Mary Elizabeth. "Here's the Story of the House behind Taylor Swift's 'the Last Great American Dynasty.'" House Beautiful, July 24, 2020. https://www.housebeautiful.com/design-inspiration/a33417436/taylor-swift-holiday-house-folklore-last-great-american-dynasty/.

Aniftos, Rania. "A Timeline of Taylor Swift & Travis Kelce's Relationship." Billboard, October 23, 2023. https://www.billboard.com/lists/taylor-swift-travis-kelce-relationship-timeline/july-8-kelce-attends-the-eras-tour/.

Armstrong, Holly, ed. Just Another Swift Story, Est. 2003.

Aswad, Jem. "Jack Antonoff on Lana Del Rey's 'Darkness' and Producing Taylor Swift." Variety, December 11, 2024. https://variety.com/2024/music/news/jack-anttonoff-lana-del-rey-darkness-taylor-swift-producing-1236245348/#.

Atkinson, Katie. "Taylor Swift's Luckiest Fan? Gena Gets Another Sweet Surprise | Billboard." Billboard, December 2014. https://www.billboard.com/music/music-news/taylor-swift-fan-anniverary-video-6334649/.

Bacon, Auzinea. "The End of an Era: How Taylor Swift Boosted the US Economy." CNN, December 8, 2024. https://www.cnn.com/2024/12/08/business/taylor-swift-eras-tour-economy.

Bailey, Alyssa. "Every Word of Taylor Swift's 4 History-Making VMAs Acceptance Speeches: 'This Is Unbelievable.'" ELLE, September 13, 2023. https://www.elle.com/culture/celebrities/a45085249/taylor-swift-speech-transcripts-vmas-2023/.

———. "Inside Taylor Swift's 'Tortured Poets' Spotify Pop-up Library." ELLE, April 16, 2024. https://www.elle.com/culture/music/g60503898/taylor-swift-tortured-poets-spotify-pop-up-library-photos/.

Barnes, Kelsey. "An Oral History of Taylor Swift's '1989' Secret Sessions." Nylon, October 26, 2023. https://www.nylon.com/entertainment/oral-history-of-taylor-swifts-1989-secret-sessions.

Bendlin, Karli. "Taylor Swift's Eras Tour: A Timeline of the Ticketmaster Fiasco." People, March 29, 2023. https://people.com/music/taylor-swift-eras-tour-ticketmaster-timeline/.

Berry, Brya. "Taylor Swift's Surprise Visit to Children's Mercy Hospital Brings Joy to Young Cancer Patient." KMBC, December 13, 2024. https://www.kmbc.com/article/eleven-year-old-battling-ewing-sarcoma-gets-surprise-taylor-swift-childrens-mercy-hospital-visit/63176732.

Berry, Dave. "The Hot Desk by Dave Berry Interview." YouTube, 2025. https://youtu.be/V3ZXAxfLap-M?si=UWvPVK8tYAbWpR3x.

Billboard. "'Hannah Montana' Trumps My Chem, Legend at No. 1." Billboard, November 1, 2006. https://www.billboard.com/music/music-news/hannah-montana-trumps-my-chem-legend-at-no-1-56784/.

———. "Taylor Swift." Billboard, 2024. https://www.billboard.com/artist/taylor-swift/.

———. "Taylor Swift Chart History." Billboard, 2025. https://www.billboard.com/artist/taylor-swift/chart-history/hsi/.

Billboard. "Taylor Swift on Winning Album of the Year at the 2016 Grammys: There Will Be People Who Try to 'Take Credit' for Your 'Fame,'" February 16, 2016. https://www.billboard.com/music/awards/taylor-swift-album-of-the-year-speech-credit-for-fame-6875390/.

Billboard. "Taylor Swift's 'Fearless' Flies at No. 1 with 592,000." Billboard, November 19, 2008. https://www.billboard.com/music/music-news/taylor-swifts-fearless-flies-at-no-1-with-592000-1301317/.

Blistein, Jon. "Taylor Swift's Album Re-Record Project Was a Massive Success." Rolling Stone, May 30, 2025. https://www.rollingstone.com/music/music-news/taylor-swift-album-re-record-project-success-1235351625/.

Bowenbank, Starr. "Taylor Swift Drops Heart-Shaped Vinyl of 'Lover (Live from Paris).'" Billboard, February 14, 2023. https://www.billboard.com/music/music-news/taylor-swift-heart-shaped-vinyl-lover-live-from-paris-1235253676/.

Breuninger, Kevin. "Voter Registrations Skyrocket after Taylor Swift's Get-Out-The-Vote Push." CNBC, October 9, 2018. https://www.cnbc.com/2018/10/09/voter-registrations-skyrocket-after-taylor-swift-instagram-post.html.

Burman, Theo. "Taylor Swift Eras Tour: Map Shows Which Countries Got Biggest Economic Boost." Newsweek, December 10, 2024. https://www.newsweek.com/taylor-swift-eras-tour-countries-economy-boost-1995919.

Callahan, Chrissy. "Scooter Braun Says He 'Learned an Important Lesson' after Taylor Swift Feud." TODAY.com, September 30, 2022. https://www.today.com/popculture/music/scooter-braun-taylor-swift-feud-rcna50205.

Calvario, Liz. "Taylor Swift Promises to 'Always' Advocate for LGBTQ+ Rights at 2020 Attitude Awards." CBS 8, December 2020. https://www.cbs8.com/article/entertainment/entertainment-tonight/taylor-swift-promises-to-always-advocate-for-lgbtq-rights-at-2020-attitude-awards/603-269b0ae4-213e-4ba4-99cc-a8f002bf2ca6.

Casey, Isabelle. "Exclusive: How Taylor Swift's Incredible Donation 'Saved' a Family from a 'Black Hole' of Despair." HELLO!, November 11, 2024. https://www.hellomagazine.com/celebrities/728714/taylor-swift-kindness-sadie-bartell/.

Caulfield, Keith. "Taylor Swift Scores 10th No. 1 Album on Billboard 200 Chart with 'Red (Taylor's Version).'" Billboard, November 21, 2021. https://www.billboard.com/music/chart-beat/taylor-swift-tenth-number-one-album-billboard-200-red-taylors-version-1235000860/.

———. "Taylor Swift Sells over 1 Million in Record Billboard 200 Debut." Billboard, November 3, 2010. https://www.billboard.com/music/music-news/taylor-swift-sells-over-1-million-in-record-billboard-200-debut-951902/.

CBS Boston. "Taylor Swift's Boston Children's Hospital Performance a Big Hit with Little Patient – CBS Boston," August 4, 2014. https://www.cbsnews.com/boston/news/taylor-swifts-boston-childrens-hospital-performance-a-big-hit-with-little-patient/.

CBS News. "Taylor Swift Awarded $1 in Groping Trial," August 14, 2017. https://www.cbsnews.com/news/taylor-swift-awarded-1dollar-in-groping-trial/.

CBS News. "Taylor Swift Donates 6,000 Books to Library," October 14, 2011. https://www.cbsnews.com/news/taylor-swift-donates-6000-books-to-library/.

Chan, Anna. "Taylor Swift's Brit Awards 2021 Speech." Billboard. Billboard, May 11, 2021. https://www.billboard.com/music/awards/taylor-swift-inspires-with-brit-awards-2021-speech-video-9570789/.

Chiu, Melody. "Taylor Swift Helped Formerly Homeless and Pregnant Fan Buy a House and Baby Gear." https://people.com/music/taylor-swift-helped-pregnant-fan-buy-house-baby-gear/. People Magazine, December 22, 2017. https://people.com/music/taylor-swift-helped-pregnant-fan-buy-house-baby-gear/.

———. "Taylor Swift's Rep Hits Back at Kim Kardashian after She Misquotes Her: 'Btw … That's Editing.'" People. com, March 24, 2020. https://people.com/music/taylor-swift-publicist-hits-back-kim-kardashian/.

Chron. "Taylor Swift Receives Her High School Diploma," July 27, 2008. https://www.chron.com/culture/main/article/taylor-swift-receives-her-high-school-diploma-1545672.php.

Crosbie, Eve. "Clara Bow's Family Reacts to Taylor Swift's 'Tortured Poets Department' Song." Business Insider, April 19, 2024. https://www.businessinsider.com/clara-bow-family-reaction-taylor-swift-song-tortured-poets-department-2024-4.

Dailey, Hannah. "Taylor Swift's NYU Commencement Speech: Read the Full Transcript." Billboard, May 18, 2022. https://www.billboard.com/music/music-news/taylor-swift-nyu-commencement-speech-full-transcript-1235072824/.

———. "Taylor Swift's NYU Commencement Speech: Read the Full Transcript." Billboard, May 18, 2022. https://www.billboard.com/music/music-news/taylor-swift-nyu-commencement-speech-full-transcript-1235072824/.

Dailey, Hannah, and Rania Aniftos. "A Timeline of Taylor Swift's Generosity." Billboard, December 21, 2023. https://www.billboard.com/lists/taylor-swifts-charity-donations-gifts-timeline/.

Dickey, Jack. "The Power of Taylor Swift." TIME, November 13, 2014. https://time.com/magazine/us/3583115/november-24th-2014-vol-184-no-20-u-s/.

Dominick, Nora. "Here Are 19 Behind-The-Scenes Facts about Taylor Swift's 'Lover.'" BuzzFeed, August 26, 2019. https://www.buzzfeed.com/noradominick/taylor-swift-lover-behind-the-scenes-facts#.

Draaisma, Muriel. "Taylor Swift Sends $6,386.47 to Ontario University Student to Help with Tuition." CBC, August 13, 2019. https://www.cbc.ca/news/canada/toronto/ayesha-khurram-taylor-swift-money-for-university-student-mississauga-1.5245678.

Dunkerley, Beville. "Taylor Swift Paints Pop-Laden Picture of Love Life on 'Red' (Exclusive Video Interview)." The Boot, October 22, 2012. https://theboot.com/taylor-swift-interview-red-album/.

Eells, Josh. "Cover Story: The Reinvention of Taylor Swift." Rolling Stone, September 8, 2014. https://www.rollingstone.com/music/music-news/the-reinvention-of-taylor-swift-116925/3/.

Elizabeth, De. "Taylor Swift Gave a Surprise Performance to Celebrate Fans' Engagement." Teen Vogue, February 24, 2019. https://www.teenvogue.com/story/taylor-swift-surprise-performance-celebrate-fans-engagement.

Enos, Morgan. "A Rough Guide to Taylor Swift's Tours to Date." Billboard, May 7, 2018. https://www.billboard.com/music/pop/taylor-swift-tour-guide-reputation-8454592/.

Fitzpatrick, Kevin. "Taylor Swift Dropped by Stonewall for a Surprise Pride Performance." Vanity Fair, June 15, 2019. https://www.vanityfair.com/style/2019/06/taylor-swift-stonewall-pride-surprise-performance?srsltid=AfmBOooo7ks2KbMn1RB6r9fx0yE-8ReV9JIsPTxXIokQVg6MAYOrjxrjG.

folkleric. "Taylor Thanking Fans Watching Online!" YouTube, February 22, 2024. https://www.youtube.com/shorts/rO36KK9PXmQ.

Gavilanes, Grace, and Sophie Dodd. "Inside Kanye West and Taylor Swift's 10-Year Feud: A Truly Comprehensive Timeline." PEOPLE.com, September 2, 2022. https://people.com/music/kanye-west-famous-inside-his-and-taylor-swifts-relationship-history/.

Gevinson, Tavi. "ELLE Cover Girl Taylor Swift Has No Regrets." ELLE, May 7, 2015. https://www.elle.com/fashion/a28210/taylor-swift-elle-june-cover-2015/.

Gibson, Kelsie. "Taylor Swift and Jack Antonoff's Friendship Timeline." People Magazine, April 19, 2024. https://people.com/music/taylor-swift-and-jack-antonoff-friendship-timeline/.

Gilbertson, Dawn. "Taylor Swift Treats Children to a Private Phoenix Concert, Pizza Party and Photo Op." The Arizona Republic. The Republic | azcentral.com, May 7, 2018. https://www.azcentral.com/story/entertainment/music/2018/05/07/taylor-swift-reputation-tour-phoenix-az-private-show-foster-children/586605002/.

Good Morning America. "Taylor Swift Says She'll Re-Record Her Old Albums | Live on GMA." YouTube, August 22, 2019. https://www.youtube.com/watch?v=ellK-CXh7B4.

Grigoriadis, Vanessa. "The Very Pink, Very Perfect Life of Taylor Swift." Rolling Stone, March 5, 2009. https://www.rollingstone.com/music/music-country/the-very-pink-very-perfect-life-of-taylor-swift-107451/.

Grow, Kory. "Taylor Swift Wins 2024 VMA for Video of the Year, Thanks Travis Kelce." Rolling Stone, September 12, 2024. https://www.rollingstone.com/music/music-news/taylor-swift-video-of-the-year-2024-vmas-fortnight-1235096115/.

Herrera, Monica. "Taylor Swift to Re-Release 'Fearless' with New Songs." Billboard, September 10, 2009. https://www.billboard.com/music/music-news/taylor-swift-to-re-release-fearless-with-new-songs-267429/.

iHeartRadio. "Taylor Swift Accepts the 2023 IHeartRadio Innovator Award!" YouTube, March 27, 2023. https://www.youtube.com/watch?v=I1di-djvvqTU.

IMDb. "Miss Americana," January 31, 2020. https://www.imdb.com/title/tt11388580/.

Jimmy Kimmel Live. "Taylor Swift on Turning 31, New Album, Fan Theories, Documentary & Boyfriend's Pseudonym." YouTube, December 17, 2020. https://www.youtube.com/watch?v=ionfV_r8s40.

Kellogg, Jane. "AMAs 2011: Winners and Nominees Complete List." The Hollywood Reporter, November 20, 2011. https://www.hollywoodreporter.com/news/general-news/ama-american-music-awards-katy-perry-bieber-264237/.

Kempin, Jason. "Read Taylor Swift's 2006 Diary Entry about Opening for Rascal Flatts." Taste of Country, August 27, 2019. https://tasteofcountry.com/taylor-swift-diary-entry-2006-rascal-flatts-tour/.

Kinane, Ruth. "Taylor Swift and Katy Perry: A Timeline of Their Feud." EW.com, April 5, 2024. https://ew.com/music/taylor-swift-katy-perry-timeline/?srsltid=AfmBOooa_64IT586-a9a-ODIxX-Ks93m9vad5IcIdy9BKF2DB-DqzriJ39.

Kreps, Daniel. "Kanye West Storms the VMAs Stage during Taylor Swift's Speech." Rolling Stone, September 14, 2009. http://www.rollingstone.com/music/news/kanye-west-storms-the-vmas-stage-during-taylor-swifts-speech-20090913?rand=84857.

Lansky, Sam. "Taylor Swift Is TIME's 2023 Person of the Year." TIME, December 6, 2023. https://time.com/6342806/person-of-the-year-2023-taylor-swift/.

Lewis, Randy. "Taylor Swift's '1989' Is 2015'S Highest Grossing Concert Tour by Far." Los Angeles Times, December 30, 2015. https://www.latimes.com/entertainment/music/posts/la-et-ms-taylor-swift-1989-tour-highest-grossing-concerts-pollstar-20151230-story.html.

Lewis, Rebecca. "Taylor Swift Fans Changed Meaning of Jake Gyllenhaal Song All Too Well." Metro, December 31, 2018. https://metro.co.uk/2018/12/31/taylor-swift-tells-fans-helped-change-meaning-heartbreaking-song-jake-gyllenhaal-8296924/.

Linshi, Jack. "Here's Why Taylor Swift Pulled Her Music from Spotify." Time, November 3, 2014. https://time.com/3554468/why-taylor-swift-spotify/.

Lipshutz, Jason. "Taylor Swift Accepts Tour of the Year at IHeartRadio Music Awards: Read the Full Speech." Billboard, March 15, 2019. https://www.billboard.com/music/awards/taylor-swift-iheartradio-speech-tour-of-the-year-new-music-8502632/.

———. "Taylor Swift Reveals 'Midnights' Album during 2022 VMAs Speech." Billboard, August 29, 2022. https://www.billboard.com/music/pop/taylor-swift-new-album-announcement-vmas-speech-1235132031/.

———. "Taylor Swift Reveals 'Never Ever' Inspiration." Billboard, September 24, 2012. https://www.billboard.com/music/music-news/taylor-swift-reveals-never-ever-inspiration-474960/.

Lutkin, Aimée . "All about Taylor Swift's Cats: Meredith, Olivia, and Benjamin." ELLE, June 12, 2024. https://www.elle.com/culture/celebrities/a60931239/taylor-swift-cats-explained/.

Lynch, Joe. "Taylor Swift Reacts to Minnesota's 'Taylor Swift Day' at Joyous Minneapolis Tour Stop." Billboard, September 1, 2018. https://www.billboard.com/music/pop/taylor-swift-minneapolis-reputation-tour-8473228/.

MacAskill, Ewen. "Obama Calls Kanye West a 'Jackass' over MTV Outburst." The Guardian, September 15, 2009, sec. US news. https://www.theguardian.com/world/2009/sep/15/obama-kanye-west-mtv.

Macke, Johnni. "Taylor Swift's 4th of July Squad through the Years." Us Weekly, July 3, 2024. https://www.usmagazine.com/celebrity-news/news/taylor-swifts-fourth-of-july-squad-through-the-years-w212178/.

Mann, Camille. "Taylor Swift and Zac Efron Cover 'Pumped up Kicks' on 'Ellen.'" CBS News, February 21, 2012. https://www.cbsnews.com/news/taylor-swift-and-zac-efron-cover-pumped-up-kicks-on-ellen/.

Mariah, D. "Taylor Swift Announces New Album after 13th GRAMMY Win at the 2024 GRAMMYs | GRAMMY.com." GRAMMY, February 4, 2024. https://www.grammy.com/news/taylor-swift-new-album-announcement-13th-grammy-win-2024-grammys.

Martin, Heather. "Taylor Swift's Chai Sugar Cookies Recipe and Review." TODAY.com. TODAY, October 5, 2023. https://www.today.com/food/recipes/taylor-swift-chai-sugar-cookies-rcna119005.

Martino, Andy. "EXCLUSIVE: The Real Story behind Taylor Swift's Guitar 'Legend': Meet the Computer Repairman Who Taught the Pop Superstar How to Play." New York Daily News, January 10, 2015. https://www.nydailynews.com/2015/01/10/exclusive-the-real-story-behind-taylor-swifts-guitar-legend-meet-the-computer-repairman-who-taught-the-pop-superstar-how-to-play/.

Mazzeo, Esme. "How Maya Thompson Got Her Son Ronan Back with Red (Taylor's Version)." Vulture, November 25, 2021. https://www.vulture.com/2021/11/maya-thompson-interview-taylor-swift-ronan-song-video.html.

McCluskey, Megan. "A Look Back at Taylor Swift's Record-Breaking Eras Tour." TIME, December 6, 2024. https://time.com/7199590/taylor-swift-eras-tour-final-numbers/.

McIntyre, Hugh. "Taylor Swift's Letter to Apple: Stern, Polite, and Necessary." Forbes, June 21, 2015. https://www.forbes.com/sites/hughmcintyre/2015/06/21/taylor-swifts-letter-to-apple-stern-polite-and-necessary/.

McNamara, Brittney. "Taylor Swift Said Talking to Kesha during Her Groping Trial 'Really Helped.'" Teen Vogue, December 6, 2017. https://www.teenvogue.com/story/kesha-taylor-groping-trial.

Mendez II, Moises. "'So Long, London' Is a Classic Taylor Swift Track 5 Song." TIME, April 19, 2024. https://time.com/6969042/taylor-swift-track-five-songs-tortured-poets-department/.

Meter, Jonathan Van, and Mario Testino. "Taylor Swift: The Single Life." Vogue, January 17, 2012. https://www.vogue.com/article/taylor-swift-the-single-life.

Mier, Tomás. "Aaron Dessner and Justin Vernon's Big Red Machine Announces New Album with Two Taylor Swift Songs." People Magazine, June 29, 2021. https://people.com/music/big-red-machine-announces-new-album-with-taylor-swift-songs/.

Mitra, Mallika. "Taylor Swift's New Song 'You Need to Calm Down' Drives Donations to LGBTQ Advocacy Group, but Not without Critics." CNBC, June 25, 2019. https://www.cnbc.com/2019/06/25/taylor-swifts-new-song-drives-donations-to-this-lgbtq-advocacy-group.html.

Morrow, Brendan. "All the Records Taylor Swift Has Broken in 2023." The Week, August 16, 2023. https://theweek.com/culture/entertainment/1025810/taylor-swift-records-2023.

Mullins, Jenna. "Taylor Swift's Rules about Love: A Comprehensive List." E! Online. E! News, February 4, 2014. https://www.eonline.com/news/507063/taylor-swift-s-rules-about-love-a-comprehensive-list.

Nashville Lifestyles. "Taylor Swift's Nashville Favorites." Nashville Lifestyles, December 13, 2012. https://nashvillelifestyles.com/entertainment/celebrities/taylor-swifts-nashville-favorites/.

Nast, Condé. "Taylor Swift Tells Glamour the Stuff She Usually Only Tells Her Girlfriends in Her November 2012 Interview." Glamour, October 1, 2012. https://www.glamour.com/story/taylor-swifts-november-glamour.

Naushad, Abdul Azim. "Taylor Swift & Nikki Glaser Relationship History." Yahoo Entertainment, September 2, 2024. https://www.yahoo.com/entertainment/taylor-swift-nikki-glaser-relationship-144050030.html.

NBC Connecticut. "For 10-Year-Old Connecticut Swiftie, This Concert Moment Hit All Too Well," May 22, 2023. https://www.nbcconnecticut.com/news/local/for-connecticut-swiftie-this-concert-moment-hit-all-too-well/3036258/.

Nesvig, Kara. "Taylor Swift Took Voice Lessons in 2010 after Intense Criticism." Teen Vogue, July 7, 2023. https://www.teenvogue.com/story/taylor-swift-criticism-voice-lessons-speak-now-letter.

Neugebauer, Cimaron. "Arizona Girl with Cancer Now in Remission, Gets to Meet Taylor Swift in Person." KUTV, October 25, 2016. https://kutv.com/news/local/arizona-girl-with-cancer-now-in-remission-gets-to-meet-taylor-swift-in-person.

Newman, Melinda. "Taylor Swift Leaves Big Machine, Signs New Deal with Universal Music Group." Billboard, November 19, 2018. https://www.billboard.com/music/music-news/taylor-swift-leaves-big-machine-signs-new-label-deal-universal-music-8485629/.

Nicholson, Jessica. "Taylor Swift Accepts Songwriter-Artist of the Decade Honor at Nashville Songwriter Awards: Read Her Full Speech." Billboard, September 21, 2022. https://www.billboard.com/music/country/taylor-swift-nashville-songwriter-awards-full-speech-1235142144/.

Nolfi, Joey. "Every Celebrity in Taylor Swift's 'You Need to Calm Down' Music Video." EW.com, June 22, 2022. https://ew.com/music/taylor-swift-you-need-to-calm-down-video-cameos/.

Norton, Graham. "Taylor Swift's Fans Demanded a 10 Minute Version of 'All Too Well' | the Graham Norton Show." YouTube. The Graham Norton Show, October 28, 2022. https://www.youtube.com/watch?v=MwNdxjnwr1A.

Olson, Samantha. "All of Taylor Swift's Albums in Order, from Debut to Taylor's Version." Cosmopolitan, April 18, 2024. https://www.cosmopolitan.com/entertainment/music/a60331387/taylor-swift-albums-in-order/.

Oxford Dictionary. "Swiftie, N. Meanings, Etymology and More | Oxford English Dictionary." Oed.com, 2024. https://www.oed.com/dictionary/swiftie_n.

PixMob. "Moving Head: How It Works | PixMob | All Wristbands," November 2, 2023. https://pixmob.com/stories/moving-head-how-it-works.

Pryor, Chloe, and Jorie Fawcett. "Nashville (Taylor's Version): A Tour of Nashville through Taylor Swift Lyrics – the Vanderbilt Hustler." The Vanderbilt Hustler – The official student newspaper of Vanderbilt University, February 17, 2023. https://vanderbilthustler.com/2023/02/17/nashville-taylors-version-a-tour-of-nashville-through-taylor-swift-lyrics/.

Quinlan, Erin. "Taylor Swift Sends Touching Instagram Message to Bullied Teen Fan." TODAY.com, September 4, 2014. https://www.today.com/popculture/taylor-swift-sends-touching-instagram-message-bullied-teen-fan-1d80126920.

Rapkin, Mickey. "Oral History of Nashville's Bluebird Cafe: Taylor Swift, Maren Morris, Dierks Bentley & More on the Legendary Venue." Billboard, July 27, 2017. https://www.billboard.

com/music/country/the-bluebird-cafe-taylor-swift-dierks-bentley-oral-history-7880979/.

Recording Academy / GRAMMYs. "Taylor Swift Accepting the GRAMMY for Album of the Year at the 52nd GRAMMY Awards | GRAMMYs." YouTube, February 2, 2010. https://www.youtube.com/watch?v=BFk2NjdJ1yY.

RIAA. "Gold & Platinum – RIAA," May 31, 2024. https://www.riaa.com/gold-platinum/?tab_active=default-award&ar=taylor+swift&ti=Taylor+Swift&lab=&genre=&format=Album&date_option=release&from=&to=&award=&type=&category=&adv=SEARCH#search_section.

Roberts, Madison. "Taylor Swift's Butterfly Mural Artist Kelsey Montague." People Magazine, April 26, 2019. https://people.com/travel/taylor-swift-butterfly-wings-mural-artist-kelsey-montague/.

Rogers, Alex. "Q&A: Why Taylor Swift Thinks Nashville Is the Best Place on Earth." Time, March 7, 2014. https://time.com/14933/taylor-swift-nashville-interview/.

Rogers, Katie. "It Was a Love Story, and Taylor Swift Just Said Yes." The New York Times, June 9, 2016. https://www.nytimes.com/2016/06/10/fashion/weddings/couples-love-story-draws-a-famous-romantic-taylor-swift.html.

Rolling Stone. "Taylor Swift Donates $4 Million to Country Music Hall of Fame," May 17, 2012. https://www.rollingstone.com/music/music-news/taylor-swift-donates-4-million-to-country-music-hall-of-fame-183102/.

Rosen, Christopher. "Taylor Swift Has No Regrets about Cats, a 'Weird-Ass Movie.'" Vanity Fair, January 21, 2020. https://www.vanityfair.com/hollywood/2020/01/taylor-swift-cats-weird-ass-movie?srsltid=AfmBOoqBhuKqSlyd-ND-ZltJf4DRRrg14Y4usjyad75Vh-GWZnxqY9ukd1.

———. "Taylor Swift Surprises Jimmy Fallon Audience with Emotional Live TV Debut of 'New Year's Day.'" Entertainment Weekly, November 14, 2017. https://ew.com/tv/2017/11/14/taylor-swift-jimmy-fallon-new-years-day/.

Rothman, Michael. "Taylor Swift Drops 'Lover' Album: 5 Things to Know about the Game-Changer." Good Morning America. ABC News, August 23, 2019. https://www.goodmorningamerica.com/culture/story/taylor-swift-drops-lover-album-things-game-changer-65143841.

Rubin, Rebecca. "Box Office: Taylor Swift's 'Eras Tour' Officially Opens to $92.8 Million in North America, $123.5 Million Globally." Variety, October 16, 2023. https://variety.com/2023/film/box-office/taylor-swift-eras-tour-box-office-final-opening-weekend-record-1235757568/.

Savage, Mark. "Taylor Swift and Kanye West's Phone Call Leaks." BBC News, March 23, 2020, sec. Entertainment & Arts. https://www.bbc.com/news/entertainment-arts-52003974.

Schocket, Ryan. "Taylors Swift Gives Mikael Arellano Hat at Eras Tour." BuzzFeed, May 14, 2023. https://www.buzzfeed.com/ryanschocket2/taylor-swift-mikael-arellano-hat-eras-tour.

Sciarretto, Amy. "Taylor Swift's Speak Now … Help Now Rehearsal Show Raises $750,000." Taste of Country, May 23, 2011. https://tasteofcountry.com/taylor-swift-speak-now-help-now-show/.

Segal, Corinne. "Taylor Swift Donates $250,000 to Kesha after Court Denies Injunction." PBS News, February 22, 2016. https://www.pbs.org/newshour/arts/taylor-swift-donates-250000-to-kesha-after-court-denies-injunction.

Setoodeh, Ramin. "'Cats': Taylor Swift on Movie, Writing 'Beautiful Ghosts' and Hissing." Variety, December 20, 2019. https://variety.com/2019/film/news/taylor-swift-cats-movie-beautiful-ghosts-digital-fur-tom-hooper-1203449943/.

Shafer, Ellise. "Taylor Swift Reveals Meaning of 'Fortnight,' 'Clara Bow,' 'Florida!!!' and More 'Tortured Poets Department' Tracks in Amazon Music Commentary." Variety, April 22, 2024. https://variety.com/2024/music/news/taylor-swift-tor-tured-poets-department-meaning-fortnight-clara-bow-florida-1235977904/.

———. "Taylor Swift's Eras Tour: Every Surprise Song She's Played so Far." Variety, March 9, 2024. https://variety.com/2024/music/news/taylor-swift-eras-tour-surprise-songs-list-1235578714/.

Shaffer, Claire. "Taylor Swift Asks Her Cats If She Should Release a Christmas Song." Rolling Stone, December 5, 2019. https://www.rollingstone.com/music/music-news/taylor-swift-cats-christmas-song-922547/.

Shouse, Meghan. "Taylor Swift Reportedly Bought a Mansion in London for Christmas." House Beautiful, December 15, 2023. https://www.housebeautiful.com/lifestyle/entertainment/a46129272/taylor-swift-london-house-orangery/.

Simpson, Michael Lee. "Taylor Swift's Sweetest '22' Hat Moments on 'the Eras Tour.'" Us Weekly, August 20, 2024. https://www.usmagazine.com/entertainment/news/taylor-swifts-sweetest-22-hat-moments-on-the-eras-tour/.

Sisario, Ben. "With a Tap of Taylor Swift's Fingers, Apple Retreated." The New York Times, June 23, 2015, sec. Business. https://www.nytimes.com/2015/06/23/business/media/as-quick-as-a-taylor-swift-tweet-apple-had-to-change-its-tune.html.

Skinner, Paige. "We Spoke to the Swiftie Who Started 1, 2, 3, Let's Go Bitch during Taylor Swift's Delicate." BuzzFeed News, March 30, 2023. https://www.buzzfeednews.com/article/paigeskinner/taylor-swift-123-lets-go-bitch-eras-video.

Spangler, Todd. "'Taylor Swift: The Eras Tour' Breaks Disney+ Record as No. 1 Most-Streamed Music Film." Variety, March 19, 2024. https://variety.com/2024/tv/news/taylor-swift-eras-tour-disney-plus-streaming-record-1235946013/.

Spanos, Brittany. "Taylor Swift Cancels Tour amid 'Unprecedented Pandemic.'" Rolling Stone Australia, March 1, 2021. https://au.rollingstone.com/music/music-news/taylor-swift-lover-fest-can-celed-23662/.

———. "Taylor Swift Reveals Meaning behind 'Cardigan' Video for Vevo's 'Footnotes.'" Rolling Stone, August 17, 2020. https://www.rollingstone.com/music/music-news/taylor-swift-cardigan-video-vevo-footnotes-1044577/.

Specter, Emma. "Taylor Swift Gave Thousands of Dollars to Fans Affected by the Coronavirus Pandemic." Vogue, March 26, 2020. https://www.vogue.com/article/taylor-swift-gives-fans-donations-coronavirus.

St. James, Emily . "The Taylor Swift and Nicki Minaj Twitter Feud, Explained." Vox, July 22, 2015. https://www.vox.com/2015/7/21/9012179/taylor-swift-nicki-minaj-twitter.

Staff, Billboard. "Justin Bieber, Taylor Swift, Eminem Top 2011 Billboard Music Awards." Billboard, May 23, 2011. https://www.billboard.com/music/music-news/justin-bieber-taylor-swift-eminem-top-2011-billboard-music-awards-471540/.

Staff, CMT. "Brad Paisley Plans Tour with Three Opening Acts." CMT News, January 9, 2007. https://web.archive.org/web/20170811054815/http://www.cmt.com/news/1549598/brad-paisley-plans-tour-with-three-opening-acts/.

———. "CMT Insider Interview: Taylor Swift (Part 1 of 2) | CMT." web.archive.org, November 26, 2008. https://web.archive.org/wcb/20150123055134/http://www.cmt.com/news/1600309/cmt-insider-interview-taylor-swift-part-1-of-2/.

Street, Mikelle. "All the Drag Queens (and Who They Appear As) in Taylor Swift's New Video." OUT, June 17, 2019. https://www.out.com/drag/2019/6/17/taylor-swift-drag-queens-you-need-to-calm-down.

Suddath, Claire. "Taylor Swift, 'Mean' | the Best and Worst of the 2012 Grammys | TIME.com." TIME, 2025. https://entertainment.time.com/2012/02/12/the-best-and-worst-of-the-2012-grammys/slide/taylor-swift-mean/.

Sullivan, Becky. "A Taylor Swift Instagram Post Helped Drive a Surge in Voter Registration." NPR,

September 22, 2023. https://www.npr.org/2023/09/22/1201183160/taylor-swift-instagram-voter-registration.

Swift, Taylor. "30 Things I Learned before Turning 30." ELLE, March 6, 2019. https://www.elle.com/culture/celebrities/a26628467/taylor-swift-30th-birthday-lessons/.

———. "For Taylor Swift, the Future of Music Is a Love Story." The Wall Street Journal, July 7, 2014. https://www.wsj.com/articles/for-taylor-swift-the-future-of-music-is-a-love-story-1404763219?gaa_at=eafs&gaa_n=ASWzDAiV8I1bO2DOU5nvAszkydzhxeGZ-LyvQiPhK4AsTG4p0c-qJz2j0etsKP-2ol0o%3D&gaa_ts=-6841f2a5&gaa_sig=Ln5bxP-5mp-SbV2tF_2Ak2kHLYGdWu-Fi2zwH6I7g2PdeQGglMJX_z5h-Zl-LocF78oZJJbXa4oBScBYA7d-dGqnFw%3D%3D.

———. "Journey to Fearless," October 11, 2010.

———. "Taylor Swift - #VEVOCertified, Pt. 3: Taylor Talks about Her Fans." YouTube, October 29, 2012. https://www.youtube.com/watch?v=ehLp-0cjqkRk.

———. "Taylor Swift - Lover's Lounge (Live)." YouTube, August 22, 2019. https://www.youtube.com/watch?v=dDO6HnY7h24.

———. "Taylor Swift | MySpace." Myspace, July 25, 2008. http://myspace.com/taylorswift.

Taylor Swift. "Taylor Swift Tumblr." Tumblr, October 29, 2012. https://www.tumblr.com/taylorswift.

Taylor Swift VEVO. "Taylor Swift - Fearless." YouTube, February 26, 2010. https://www.youtube.com/watch?v=ptSjNWnzpjg&list=PLv2Y-BcEUwiQmvNI749At4IQ68gwjiYMy-C4&index=5.

Taylor Swift Wiki. "Cats." Fandom, Inc., 2022. https://taylorswift.fandom.com/wiki/Cats.

Taylor Swift Wiki. "Filmography." Fandom, Inc., 2019. https://taylorswift.fandom.com/wiki/Filmography.

Taylor Swift Wiki. "Karyn." Fandom, Inc., 2018. https://taylorswift.fandom.com/wiki/Karyn.

Taylor Swift Wiki. "Stella X Taylor Swift," 2020. https://taylorswift.fandom.com/wiki/Stella_x_Taylor_Swift.

Taylor ThrowbackVidz. "Taylor Swift Buying Fearless at Hendersonville Walmart." YouTube, August 18, 2013. https://www.youtube.com/watch?v=zcGQRiuhV3I.

The Ellen Show. "Taylor Swift on Her New Cat!" YouTube, October 27, 2014. https://www.youtube.com/watch?v=VFTa1KTnQ7E.

The Tonight Show Starring Jimmy Fallon. "Taylor Swift on Growing up on a Christmas Tree Farm and Her Fearless Album | Fallon Flashback." YouTube, December 13, 2024. https://www.youtube.com/watch?v=ULgGwEdlZNc.

———. "Taylor Swift on Growing up on a Christmas Tree Farm and Her Fearless Album | Fallon Flashback." YouTube, December 13, 2024. https://www.youtube.com/watch?v=ULgGwEdlZNc.

Thompson, Eliza. "A Complete History of Taylor Swift's Fourth of July Parties." Cosmopolitan, July 2, 2018. https://www.cosmopolitan.com/entertainment/celebs/a22019918/taylor-swift-fourth-of-july-party/.

Us Weekly. "Taylor Swift and Calvin Harris' Romance: The Way They Were," October 27, 2023. https://www.usmagazine.com/celebrity-news/news/taylor-swift-and-calvin-harris-romance-timeline-w200954/.

Vanderbilt University Medical Center News. "Photo: Star Power," January 8, 2010. https://news.vumc.org/reporter-archive/photo-star-power/.

Vogue. "73 Questions with Taylor Swift | Vogue." YouTube, April 19, 2016. https://www.youtube.com/watch?v=XnbCSboujF4.

Wang, Jenna. "Fans on Taylor Swift's 'Swiftmas': 'No One in the Music Industry Has as Big a Heart as She Does.'" Billboard, December 24, 2014. https://www.billboard.com/music/pop/taylor-swift-swiftmas-6415161/.

Weaver, Caity. "Kim Kardashian West Has a Few Things to Get off Her Chest." GQ, June 16, 2016. https://www.gq.com/story/kim-kardashian-west-gq-cover-story.

Weiner, Natalie. "Taylor Swift Admits She 'Cried a Little Bit' after Losing Album of the Year Grammy | Billboard." Billboard, October 9, 2015. https://www.billboard.com/music/pop/taylor-swift-cried-after-losing-album-of-the-year-grammy-interview-6722714/#.

West, Bryan. "Fans Drop Everything, Meet Taylor Swift in Pouring Rain at Hamburg Eras Tour Show." USA TODAY, July 23, 2024. https://www.usatoday.com/story/entertainment/music/2024/07/23/fans-drop-everything-meet-taylor-swift-in-pouring-rain-at-hamburg-show/74449283007/.

Whitaker, Sterling. "13 Years Ago Today, Taylor Swift Launched Her First Tour." Taste of Country, April 23, 2022. https://tasteofcountry.com/taylor-swift-first-headlining-tour-fearless-tour/.

White, Jessica. "Why Taylor Swift Sends Kelly Clarkson Flowers after Every 'Taylor's Version' Release." NBC, February 28, 2025. https://www.nbc.com/nbc-insider/why-taylor-swift-sends-kelly-clarkson-flowers-after-every-re-release.

Widdicombe, Lizzie. "You Belong with Me." The New Yorker, October 3, 2011. https://www.newyorker.com/magazine/2011/10/10/taylor-swift-profile-you-belong-with-me.

Wikipedia. "Xyloband," January 4, 2023. https://en.wikipedia.org/wiki/Xyloband.

Willman, Chris. "Getting to Know Taylor Swift." EW.com, July 25, 2007. https://ew.com/article/2007/07/25/getting-know-taylor-swift/.

———. "Taylor Swift: No Longer 'Polite at All Costs.'" Variety, January 21, 2020. https://variety.com/2020/music/features/taylor-swift-politics-sundance-documentary-miss-americana-1203471910/.

Woodward, Ellie. "Taylor Swift Reveals Exactly Why She Sends Her Fans Gifts and It's Lovely." BuzzFeed, March 2, 2015. https://www.buzzfeed.com/elliewoodward/taylor-swift-reveals-exactly-why-she-sends-her-fans-gifts-an.

Yahr, Emily. "Taylor Swift's Stunning Statement: Famously Apolitical Star Slams Tennessee Republican, Endorses Democrats." Washington Post, October 7, 2018. https://www.washingtonpost.com/arts-entertainment/2018/10/08/taylor-swifts-stunning-statement-famously-apolitical-star-slams-tennessee-republican-endorses-democrats/.

Yasharoff, Hannah. "Taylor Swift Auditioned for 'Les Mis'; Director Tom Hooper Explains Why She Wasn't Cast." USA TODAY, December 26, 2019. https://www.usatoday.com/story/entertainment/movies/2019/12/26/cats-director-taylor-swift-nearly-starred-les-miserables/2748256001/.

YouTube. "Pennsylvania Native 11-Year-Old Taylor Swift Sang during a Sixers Game (2002)." YouTube, April 12, 2002. https://www.youtube.com/watch?v=6E-63AeaHczE.

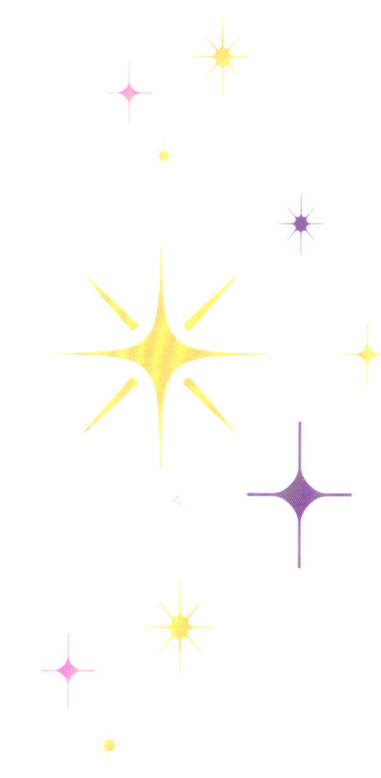

AFTERWORD

When I was first approached to write this book, I was like, "RIP ME. I'M DYING. DEAD." I have spent the better part of my young adult life poring over everything that is Taylor Swift. I watched every interview, listened to all the songs, followed every social media post, attended concerts, and watched every single movie or TV show that featured Taylor. In 2013, I even worked at Taylor's perfume booth at The Red Tour stop in Pittsburgh. If I had an honorary degree, it would be in Taylor Swift.

Having pored over everything that is Taylor, I thought to myself, "What could I possibly learn about Taylor that I didn't already know?"

The truth is, there weren't a ton of factual things I didn't know, but there was a whole new level of appreciation that I learned. I was able to really look at the exact timeline in a fresh way, especially since time feels like it's moving at lightning speed. I got to sit with old MySpace interactions with fans. I got to watch the growth of a sixteen-year-old wide-eyed young girl, so excited for the tiniest moments, transform into a thirtysomething-year-old woman standing in front of a sold-out stadium with that same amazed look. I got to read about fan interactions. I got to rewatch the oldest interviews that I'd completely forgotten about. I got to see Taylor be funny, goofy, ambitious, motivated, bold, and unwavering.

In reviewing Taylor's timeline, I also got to see a timeline of my own journey: from my own wide-eyed amazement at the successes of my writing career to the harsh realities of business deals gone wrong to navigating the complexities and emotions of a sick parent.

Red, for example, released about a month after my dad died of cancer. While *Red* is arguably a breakup album, it was my grief album when dealing with the loss of my dad. The song "Bad Blood" was my anthem of dealing with a really

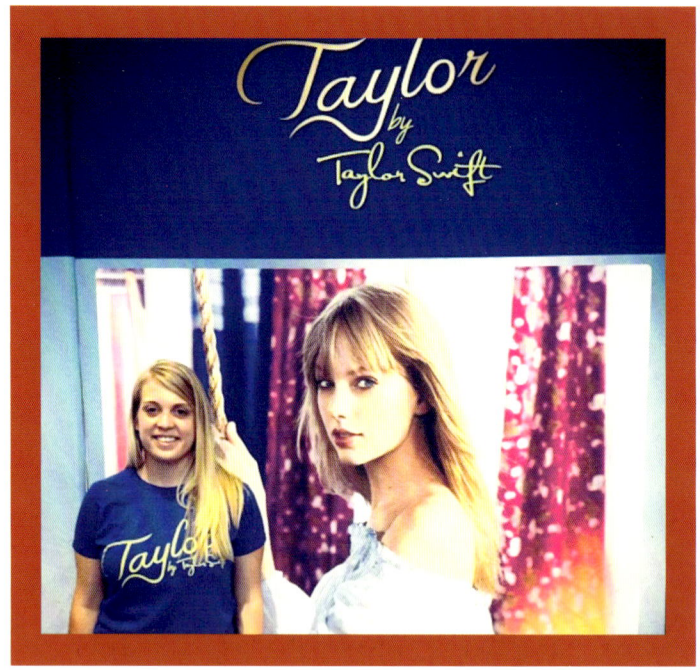

painful business relationship that left me questioning my worth. Taylor's *The Eras Tour Book* and movie release reminded me of my own journey of self-publishing my work and the importance of staying true to myself.

Taylor has always said that she hopes for us to take her music and make it our own. That we relate it to our own lives and experiences and give it the meaning we need. I feel that reviewing her timeline can do the same thing. We can remember where we were, what we were doing, and the feelings we felt as if her soundtracks were the steps we took in our own lives.

So not only did I learn a bit more about Taylor and have an absolute blast writing this book (there were a few tears, of course), but ultimately I got to know myself more. I left writing this as (dare I say) an even bigger fan of Taylor, but more importantly, with a deeper appreciation of my own journey.

ABOVE: The author working at the Taylor Swift perfume booth during the Pittsburgh stop on The Red Tour.

OPPOSITE: Kicking off the Australian leg of The Red Tour in Sydney, Australia, December 4, 2013.

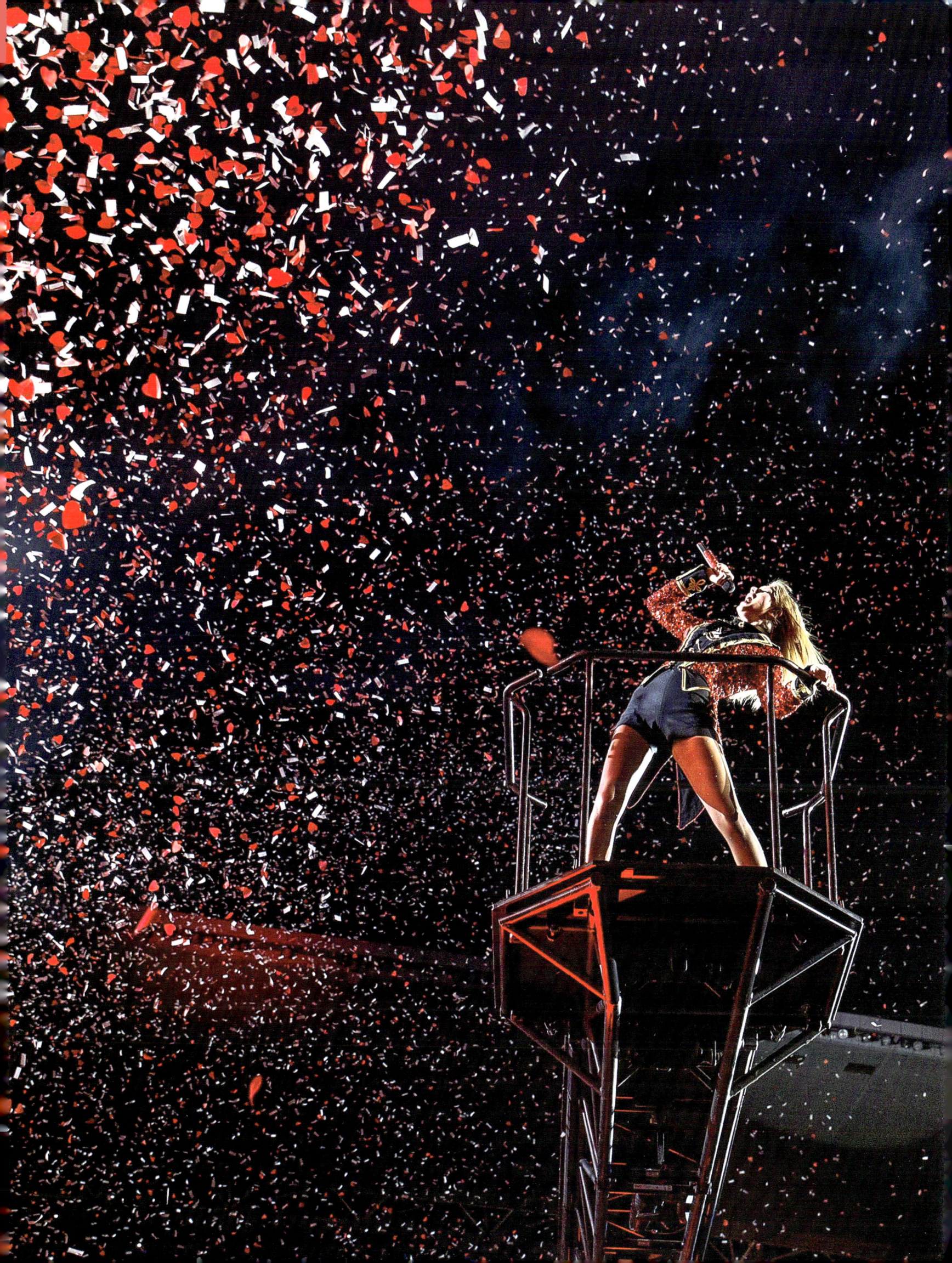

weldonowen

an imprint of Insight Editions
P.O. Box 3088
San Rafael, CA 94912
www.weldonowen.com

CEO *Raoul Goff*
SVP Group Publisher *Jeff McLaughlin*
VP Publisher *Roger Shaw*
Executive Editor *Karyn Gerhard*
Editorial Assistant *Jon Ellis*
VP Creative *Chrissy Kwasnik*
Art Director *Megan Sinead Bingham*
Managing Editor *Michelle Hope*
VP Manufacturing *Alix Nicholaeff*
Senior Production Manager *Greg Steffen*
Strategic Production Planner *Lina s Palma-Temena*

Weldon Owen would also like to thank Dominik Sklarzyk.

Case design by *Megan Sinead Bingham*

Editor: *Annika Geiger*
Photo researcher: *Nicole DiMella*
Layout design: *Ashley Prine*, *Tandem Books*

Illustrations by *Laurie-Anne Poquet*

Text © 2025 Lindsey Smith

ISBN: 979-8-88674-288-6

Manufactured in China by Insight Editions

10 9 8 7 6 5 4 3 2 1

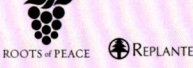

Insight Editions, in association with Roots of Peace, will plant two trees
for each tree used in the manufacturing of this book. Roots of Peace is
an internationally renowned humanitarian organization dedicated to
eradicating land mines worldwide and converting war-torn lands into
productive farms and wildlife habitats. Roots of Peace will plant two
million fruit and nut trees in Afghanistan and provide farmers there
with the skills and support necessary for sustainable land use.

ABOUT THE AUTHOR

Lindsey Smith is a publishing professional and the award-winning author of several books.
She also writes gift products and is the co-creator of *Pup Talks* and *The Bibliophile Oracle Deck*.
Her personal work has appeared in PopSugar, *Cosmopolitan*, *Parade magazine*, the *Chicago Tri-
bune*, ABC, NBC, CBS, and her parents' junk drawer. She recently opened a bookstore, One
Idea Books and Gifts, in her hometown of Leechburg, Pennsylvania. She's an OG Swiftie and
even worked at Taylor's perfume booth during The Red Tour. To learn more about Lindsey,
visit www.TheLindseySmith.com.

PHOTO CREDITS

T=Top, B=Bottom

Alamy Stock Photo: *Aflo Co. Ltd.* 113, *James Byard* 8, *Khairil Azhar Junos* 20, *Nur-Photo SRL* 159B, *Patti McConville* 197, *Storms Media Group* 74, *Thomas Jackson* 223, *WENN Rights Ltd.* 60, 64-65, *Zuma Press, Inc.* 96; **AP Photo:** *Aaron Doster* 207, *Charles Sykes/Invision* 103, *Chris Pizzello* 178, *Evan Agostini/Invision* 238 *John Davis-son/Invision* 104-5, *Lindsey Wasson* 193, *Mark Humphrey* 12, 48; **Photo by Hanna @ holdontothememories_ts13 on IG** 204-205; **Holly Armstrong:** 26T; **Everett Collec-tion:** 220, © *Disney+* 175, *John Barrett/PHOTOlink* 81, *Kristin Callahan* 79, *Mirrorpix* 130, © *Universal Pictures* 158; **Getty Images:** *Al Messerschmidt* 18, *Angela Weiss* 182, *Barry Chin/The Boston Globe* 86, *Christopher Polk/ACMA2011* 67, *Christopher Polk/TAS* 4-5, *Dave Hogan/MTV 2012* 99, *David Becker/GC Images* 169, *Dimitrios Kambouris* 166, *Doug Peters/PA Images* 192, *Emma McIntyre* 195, *Ethan Miller* 17, *Grace Smith/MediaNews Group/The Denver Post* 226-27, *Jason Kempin* 39, 42-43, *John Leyba* 84-85, *John Shearer* 15, *John Shearer/WireImage* 24-25, *Johnny Nunez* 232, *Julien De Rosa/AFP* 221, *Kevin Kane/Stringer* 82 *Kevin Mazur/TCA 2012/Wire-Image* 88, *Larry Busacca* 40T, 59, 68, *Lester Cohen/WireImage* 26B, *Mark Metcalfe* 106, *Mark Metcalfe/TAS* 255, *NBC/NBC Universal* 45, *Raymond Boyd/Michael Ochs Archives* 28, *Rick Diamond* 46, *Rick Diamond/WireImage* 54, *Robyn Beck/AFP* 121, *TAS Rights Management 2021* 174, 176-77, *Theo Wargo/WireImage* 34, *Valerie Macon* 209, *WireImage* 90; **iStock.com:** 229, *Lukman Nul Hakim* 222; **Suzy Hackbarth** 101; **Jack Kerley** 101, 148, 159T, 198, 206; **MEGA:** 214; **Shutterstock:** *ABC* 181, *Anthony Harvey* 122, *Blitz Pictures* 126, *Carla Sloke* 22, *Casey Flanigan/imageSPACE* 2, 188, *Chelsea Lauren* 151, 161, 217, *Christian Bertrand* 133, 137, *Crisler/Mediapunch* 37, *Erik Pendzich* 155, *Frank Miceloota/Fox/Picturegroup* 145, 156, *Greg Chow* 125, *Igor Vidyashev/ZUMA Wire* 118, *John Angelillo/UPI* 152-53, 191, 230, *John Salangsang* 142, *JTTucker* 87, *Map Graphic Resources* 149, *Ray Garbo* 77, *Richard Young* 108, *Richard Wainwright/EPA-EFE* 128-29, *Robertino Mobili* 200-201, *Sipa* 57, 40B.

PAGE 2: Taylor performs at Allegiant Stadium in Las Vegas during
The Eras Tour, March 24, 2023.

PAGES 4-5: Taylor takes the catwalk at the Staples Arena in Los
Angeles during The 1989 World Tour, August 25, 2015.

PAGES 238-39: Looking out at a sea of light-up bracelets during a
performance of The 1989 World Tour at the MetLife Stadium in East
Rutherford, New Jersey, July 10, 2015.